Amesbury
Merrimac
Salisbury
Haverhill
W. Newbury
Newburyport
Ashby
Pepperell
Groveland
Methuen
Georgetown
Newbury
Dunstable
Tyngsborough
Lawrence
N. Andover
Lunenburg
Dracut
95
Rowley
Groton
3
Lowell
Boxford
495
Ipswich
Westford
Andover
Shirley
Ayer
Topsfield
Littleton
Tewksbury
93
N. Reading
Middleton
Hamilton
2
Chelmsford
Billerica
Harvard
Carlisle
Wenham
Essex
Rockport
Gloucester
Wilmington
Danvers
128
Lancaster
Boxborough
Reading
Bolton
Acton
Bedford
Burlington
Lynnfield
Beverly
Manchester
Stow
Concord
Peabody
Clinton
Maynard
Woburn
Wakefield
Salem
Lexington
Stoneham
Marblehead
Berlin
Hudson
Lincoln
Winchester
Melrose
Saugus
Lynn
Sudbury
Wayland
Arlington
Swampscott
Boylston
Marlborough
Weston
Malden
Belmont
Everett
Medford
Revere
Nahant
20
Waltham
Northborough
Chelsea
Southborough
Watertown
Somerville
Winthrop
West-borough
9
Natick
Cambridge
Newton
Boston
Ashland
Framingham
Brookline
Wellesley
Hull
Grafton
Hopkinton
Needham
Sherborn
Dedham
Upton
495
Dover
Quincy
Westwood
Milton
Holliston
Medway
Northbridge
Millis
Medfield
128
Braintree
Hingham
Hopedale
Milford
Norwood
Weymouth
Cohasset
Walpole
Canton
Mendon
Randolph
Scituate
Norfolk
Uxbridge
95
Sharon
Holbrook
Franklin
Avon
3
Norwell
Bellingham
Millville
Stoughton
Rockland
Wrentham
Blackstone
Foxborough
Brockton
Abington
Hanover
Easton
Whitman
Pembroke
Marshfield
Hanson
Plainville
Mansfield
N. Attleborough
24
E. Bridgewater
W. Bridgewater
Duxbury
Norton
Bridgewater
Kingston
Provincetown
Attleboro
Halifax
Raynham
Plympton
Taunton
44
Truro
Plymouth
Berkley
Rehoboth
Middleborough
Carver
Seekonk
Lakeville
Dighton
Wellfleet
Somerset
25
Swansea
Freetown
140
Wareham
Rochester
Fall River
Eastham
Sandwich
Bourne
195
Acushnet
Fairhaven
Marion
Orleans
6
Westport
Dennis
Brewster
New Bedford
Mattapoisett
Yarmouth
Barnstable
Chatham
Mashpee
Harwich
Dartmouth
Falmouth
Gosnold
Oak Bluffs
Tisbury
W. Tisbury
Chilmark
Edgartown
Gay Head
Nantucket

MASSACHUSETTS

A Guide to the Pilgrim State

By Ray Bearse

Vermont: A Guide to the Green Mountain State
Maine: A Guide to the Vacation State
Massachusetts: A Guide to the Pilgrim State

THE NEW AMERICAN GUIDE SERIES

MASSACHUSETTS

A Guide to the Pilgrim State

SECOND EDITION

REVISED AND ENLARGED

EDITED BY RAY BEARSE

ILLUSTRATED WITH MAPS AND PHOTOGRAPHS

HOUGHTON MIFFLIN COMPANY BOSTON

1971

First Printing C

Copyright © 1971 by Houghton Mifflin Company
All rights reserved. No part of this work may be
reproduced or transmitted in any form by any
means, electronic or mechanical, including
photocopying and recording, or by any
information storage or retrieval
system, without permission
in writing from the
publisher.

ISBN: 0–395–12091–8 Hardbound
ISBN: 0–395–12762–9 Paperbound

Library of Congress
Catalog Card Number: 68–16270

Printed in the United States of America

Acknowledgments

MANY PEOPLE made this new edition possible including old friends of more than a score of years: John Aiken, artist, Boston; Harry Andrews, Boston Public Library; John Andrews, artist, Boston and Paris; Mrs. Emmeline Bearse, Boston; Miss Genevieve Bearse, Centerville; Oliver Prince Bearse, Hyannis; Mr. and Mrs. Oliver P. Bearse, Jr., Wilbraham; the late Percy F. Bearse, formerly of Osterville and Brandon, Vt. and my father; Fred Brady, Boston *Herald;* D. Angus Cameron, New York City; Lawrence Dame, former Boston newsman; Dr. Charles Haney, Charles Haney, Jr., and William Haney, Haney Associates, Concord; the late Fred Harris, Warwick; the late Albert Hickman, boat designer, Boston; Howard Isaac Hine, Yankee Folklorist, Boston; the late Captain Thomas Horgan, USNR, Associated Press colleague and master mariner, Boston; Thomas Lyman, former United Press newsman, Cambridge; Joseph Lee, friend and Boston School Committeeman; the late Elliot Paul, writer, Boston; Janet Peterson, Bolton, Vt.; Jack Saville, artist, Norwood; Dwight Sargeant, curator, Nieman Foundation, Harvard University; Arnold Silverman, Massachusetts book authority, Goodspeed's Book Shop, which spared no trouble in finding long-out-of-print books, Boston.

Special thanks are due my friends and editors at Houghton Mifflin, including Mrs. Ruth Hapgood and Jeff Smith, who checked hundreds of details in nearly 1600 pages of manuscript. Thanks are due to Mrs. Charlotte Roberts, Wellesley; Leo Roberts, Cambridge; and Albert Snow, Orleans.

There is a special note of thanks to Francis "Jeff" Wylie, my former news colleague, long Boston Bureau Chief of Time–Life and currently Director of Public Relations, Massachusetts Institute of Technology, Cambridge.

My gratitude to Frederic Pruyn, Manchester, Vt., and Vero Beach, Fla., for his financial assistance and friendship.

Directors and staffs of the following libraries, museums and societies were very helpful: American Antiquarian Society, Worcester; Boston Museum of Science; Boston Public Library; Boston Athenæum; Bostonian Society; Essex Institute, Salem; Massachusetts Historical Society, Boston; New England Historic Genealogical Society, Boston;

Massachusetts State Library, Boston; Society for the Preservation of New England Antiquities, Boston; and Widener Library, Harvard University, Cambridge.

Thanks are due to the many unnamed librarians, town boards of selectmen, town clerks, school boards and other officials who took time out to verify facts, look up a book or tell a good local story or discuss local legends.

Ray Bearse
Osterville
October, 1969

Preface to the Second Edition

TELEVISION SETS, atom and hydrogen bombs, supermarkets, moon landings, infantile paralysis prevention, guided missiles, detergents, supersonic and jet aircraft, mini- and maxi-skirts, filter cigarettes, and laundromats were in the future when the first edition of this book, originally titled *Massachusetts: A Guide to its Places and People,* was published. That was 1937.

Most of that era's Americans had never heard of Dunkirk, Guadalcanal, Belsen, Okinawa, Attu, Malmédy, Yalta, Yalu River or Dienbienphu. Tonkin was known as a ski pole and fishing rod material and not as a gulf or a congressional resolution.

Franklin D. Roosevelt was beginning his second presidential term; the bright political hope of the Kennedy-Fitzgerald clan was Harvard student Joseph P. Kennedy, Jr.; clarinetist Benny Goodman was "King of Swing." This was the year Amelia Earhart Putnam was lost on a round-the-world flight; the USS *Panay,* our gunboat on the Yangtze River, was sunk by the Japanese; Hitler repudiated Germany's World War I guilt; Britain's umbrella-toting prime minister Neville Chamberlain sold out Czechoslovakia to Germany.

In Massachusetts the first edition of this book caused a new controversy in the state's long history of literary censorship and suppression.

The WPA art projects, writers, art, theater, and music, had early become the whipping boys of anti-administration newspapers and politicians. The Massachusetts attack on the book commenced when a Boston reporter discovered that the Sacco-Vanzetti case (still on the conscience of many Bay Staters and other Americans) had more lines (about one page) than did the Boston Tea Party or the misnamed Boston Massacre. The headlines began:

> SACCO VANZETTI PERMEATE NEW GUIDE
> PURGE OF COMMUNIST WPA WRITERS DEMANDED
> REDS LINKED TO GUIDE BOOK
> GUIDE BOOK SEIZURE URGED ON GOVERNOR
> GUIDE CHANGED BY REDS ON WPA

A former Democratic governor demanded, "Take the books to Boston Common, pile them in a heap, set a match and have a bonfire."

A *Globe* writer noted, "It is impossible to escape the conclusion that certain radicals in the WPA, from outside Massachusetts, deliberately plotted to discredit the state."

Houghton Mifflin was asked to delete all references to the Sacco-Vanzetti case, plus references to every progressive act in the state's history. There was to be no mention of strikes, including the famed Boston Police and Lawrence strikes, or of child labor laws, welfare legislation, and unions. Labor Day was even to be dropped from the list of official state holidays!

Fortunately WPA administrator Harry Hopkins and the publishers did not knuckle under to the emotional pressures of the era.

Readers interested in the background of the first edition should read *Government and the Arts: The W.P.A. Experience* (*American Quarterly,* Winter, 1961) by the distinguished American historian Ray Allen Billington, who was director of the *Massachusetts Guide* at the time of its publication.

A NOTE ABOUT TECHNIQUES

We commenced work on this book in June, 1964. During the next thirty months we traveled to more than 300 Massachusetts cities and towns. We then submitted the first-draft manuscript for each community to one or more individuals or groups within that community. Later drafts were rechecked and painfully cut down to fit a single volume. At all stages from conception to birth a concerted effort was made to make necessary changes that occurred during that time. However, churches and other landmarks may have been torn down or burned without our knowledge.

A major difference in this edition is the elimination of the mile-by-mile tours and the substitution of a gazetteer section describing every city and town. All the information on one city or town can now be found in one place, whereas in the first edition it was often scattered among the tours. Each method has its advantages but we decided that under today's conditions the gazetteer would be more useful.

This edition contains more than a dozen new chapters. The remaining original chapters have been updated.

WHAT THIS BOOK IS ABOUT

This book is a regional geography with occasional historical notes. It is not a regional or state history, or a local genealogy.

The book is not a guide to accommodations or restaurants. This information can be readily found in a number of annual publications, including the *Northeastern Tour Book* of the American Automobile Association.

While checking copy, we had vehement protests from some local residents who would have us write that all Massachusetts communities — especially their own — are beautiful and that only great good men have been born or lived there. The editor's first responsibility is to the reader. It would be dishonest to say some ghastly mill town was lovely or that all the dead are listed in *The Dictionary of American Biography.*

Harvard man Dana Doten, director of an American Guide Series volume, once noted, "Some communities have a perfectly legitimate grudge against us — others should thank God we did not learn more about them." Amen.

RAY BEARSE
APRIL, 1971

Contents

Illustrations

(Unless otherwise specified, all photos are courtesy of the Massachusetts Department of Commerce and Development.)

How to Use This Guide

THE FIRST TWENTY-ONE CHAPTERS of this volume provide a guide to Massachusetts history, climate, natural resources, wildlife, transportation, education, writers, arts and other general backgrounds.

The gazetteer section describes Massachusetts' 39 cities, 312 towns and prominent geographical features. Each city, town, locality, settlement or hamlet is listed alphabetically. The information for each settlement or locality is listed under its appropriate city or town. Hyannis — a village in Barnstable Town — is listed under Hyannis where the cross-index notation reads HYANNIS (see Barnstable). Some towns have six or more settlements.

Each noteworthy settlement or village is described, though some place names shown on various maps may include no more than two or three houses.

The cross-index saves time and confusion. You will discover that while West Barnstable lies within Barnstable Town and South Boston and East Boston lie within Boston City, West Bridgewater is a town separate and distinct from Bridgewater. In each instance where there are several settlements, villages or localities within one town, the chief settlement is listed first. Remaining settlements are listed thereafter in alphabetical order.

Ski Areas: These are listed under the town in which they are located.

State Parks and Forests: These are listed under the name of the town in which they are located. Where a park or forest includes two or more towns, the forest is listed under one town and cross-indexed under the others.

Beaches: Beaches are listed under the name of the town they are located in.

Cape Cod National Seashore: This federal reservation has several beaches in several towns. Beaches are described under the names of the communities they are located in. See also CAPE COD NATIONAL SEASHORE.

Tours: Eight tour maps may be found among the descriptions of towns and cities. See pages 196–197, 264, 268, 356, 372, 387, 452, and 462.

The abbreviations TOR and SPNEA stand for Trustees of Reservations and Society for the Preservation of New England Antiquities.

*General Information**

Area: 8257 sq. mi. (total); land, 7833 sq. mi.; water, 424 sq. mi.; ranks 45th

Population: 5,630,224; ranks 10th; density: 676 per sq. mi.

Settled: 1621

Union Admission: 1788 (6th state)

Capital: Boston

Nicknames: Bay State, Old Colony State, Baked Bean State, Pilgrim State, Puritan State

Motto: Ense petit placidam sub libertate quietem (By the Sword We Seek Peace but Peace Only Under Liberty)

Song: "Hail Massachusetts" (unofficial)

State Flower: Mayflower

Tree: American Elm

Bird: Chickadee

Per Capita Income: $4138, compared to New England average of $3556; Connecticut high of $4256 and Maine low of $2857. U.S. average is $3680.

Automobile Registrations: 2,456,692

Drivers' Licenses: 2,900,773. Renewable every four years.

Drivers' Minimum Age: 17 (16½ with driver's education certificate), those under 18 have a junior license and cannot drive between the hours of 1:00 and 5:00 A.M. unless accompanied by a parent or guardian.

Gasoline Tax: $.06½ per gallon.

Speed Laws: Mass. Turnpike and Interstates, 65 m.p.h.; divided highways, 50 m.p.h.; general highways, 40 m.p.h.; residential and business zones, 30 m.p.h.; school zones, 20 m.p.h.

General Taxes: state income tax; meals 5%, sales tax 3%, inheritance and property taxes

Minimum Drinking Age: 21

Voting Age: 19 to vote in national, state, and local elections; no literacy test

* 1969 or 1970 figures.

PART ONE

Massachusetts
The General Background

I

Here's Our Bay State

IN MASSACHUSETTS secessionist town clerk Sam Adams, financed by merchant prince John Hancock and aided by fiery agitator James Otis, helped sire the American Revolution. There might have been no "Father of His Country" role for Virginia militiaman George Washington had not Sam Adams and his friends subversively and then openly promoted complete independence from England. Every Adams' move was calculated to force His Majesty's ministers to order liberty or to make profit-suppressing measures.

Every day Massachusetts residents and visitors, particularly those in the Greater Boston area, see evidences of their history: jutting skyward is the Old North Church's sturdy, slender white spire atop the belfry in which Revolutionary plotter Paul Revere saw the signal lantern; Boston Harbor, into which more than 300 chests of tea were dumped; Faneuil Hall, site of subversive meetings; Old South Church where Lobsterbacks ripped out pews so Redcoat officers could have a riding hall; Boston Massacre site; Lexington Village Green where the shooting war started; stone walls from behind which Minutemen potshot at retreating British regulars; Breed's Hill where the Battle of Bunker Hill was fought until Yankee powder horns were empty; Cambridge headquarters of General Washington; Cambridge Common cannon, captured by Ethan Allen at Fort Ticonderoga and brought by sleds to Boston to help root Britishers out.

Sometimes in our history, unfortunately, emotions and prejudices overbalance reason and sound judgment. Witches have been hung on Boston Common and books burned. Boston saw antiabolitionist mobs leading William Lloyd Garrison with a rope around his neck.

Massachusetts produced the Adams family with its presidents, diplomats, historians and yachtsmen; Lowells, Lodges, Cabots and Eliots.

The Irish gave us John Fitzgerald Kennedy, roguish and Robin Hoodish James Michael Curley, political strategist John McCormack and U.S. senators Edward and Robert Kennedy.

We have Harvard, Amherst, Williams, Radcliffe, Wellesley, Smith and Mount Holyoke and private schools such as Groton, Phillips Andover, Deerfield, Saint Mark's, Mount Hermon and many others.

Boston is the world's medical center, where come rajahs and workmen seeking further years of life. Cripples come to walk again, battered hearts are repaired and cancer is fought in surgery and laboratory.

This is the state of poets Henry Wadsworth Longfellow, William Cullen Bryant, Emily Dickinson, Amy Lowell, Robert Lowell, Dr. O. W. Holmes and James Russell Lowell.

Massachusetts Yankees not only made history but they wrote it. Nearly every 19th century American historian came from the Bay State. Most of today's top historians, including Samuel Eliot Morison and Arthur M. Schlesinger, Jr., are either Bay State natives or have studied or written here.

Many transatlantic and national airlines' jet contrails mark Bay State skies, and wide, multilane highways fan across the state from north to south and east to west; but there is a Cape-to-the-Berkshires trail for horse lovers. Hikers may enter at the Connecticut line and walk north through the Berkshires into Vermont and then continue, if they wish, to the Canadian border. Back roads, mostly paved, provide excellent cycling fare.

More than 60 state forests, parks and beaches have picnic sites, and many have campsites. There are 50 ski areas.

Art museum visitors find paintings from primitives through Picasso. Boston is a world art center, and many cities have their own museums. Andover has the famed Addison Gallery of American Art while Lincoln has the De Cordova Museum. Harvard has more museums than many major American cities or even states.

There is fare for music and dance lovers in all seasons. The Boston Symphony is at home during the winter and at Tanglewood in the Berkshires during the summer. Arthur Fiedler's "Pops" Orchestra gives summer concerts in the Hatch Shell along Boston's river-bordered Esplanade. Boston is a fine winter theater town, and summer theaters are found from the Cape to the Berkshires.

There are hundreds of miles of saltwater beaches. Nearly every coastal town has facilities for yachtsmen and small-boat owners. Fishermen have first-rate salt- and freshwater sport.

Throughout the three hundred years of the state's history an east wind blew steadily among its women, producing such champions of women's rights as Mary Lyon, Mary Livermore, Lucy Stone, Susan Anthony, Lydia Maria Child and Margaret Fuller. The first attempt of women to exercise the right of free assembly was made by Anne Hutchinson who, after being tried on a joint charge of sedition and heresy, was banished from Boston in 1638. Mary Dyer, twice banished, returned to Boston in 1660 to test the legality of the law which sentenced to death Quakers who visited the colony after being expelled and was publicly hanged. An early rebel against the discrimination suffered by women in industry was Louisa Morton Green, who refused to do man's work at a spindle in a Dedham woolen mill unless she was paid man's wages. Working 14 hours a day for two dollars a week and board, she found time to study to be a schoolteacher and later became active in the antislavery cause, industrial reform and woman suffrage. An early organizer of the Red Cross, and its first president, was Clara Barton. In medicine, religion, astronomy, physics, education and the arts, scores of Massachusetts women battled for their sex. Phillis Wheatley was but one of many Negro women of Massachusetts who contributed to our literature, art and social movements.

Nowhere has the east wind blown so vigorously in the state as through the schools. The spirit of the famous Act of 1647, which required each township of 50 families to have a primary school and each township of 100 families to establish a grammar school, remained in force for 200 years. An early governor of the state, James Sullivan, urged its citizens to throw off "the trammels they had forged for us" — *they,* of course, being the English — and called for an American system of general public education, remarking, "Where the mass of people are ignorant, poor and miserable, there is no public opinion excepting what is the offspring of fear." As late as 1834 the Association of Farmers, Mechanics, and Other Workingmen demanded at its convention a better quality of instruction in the public schools. Not until the middle of the 19th century when Horace Mann fought his bitter battle did the state acquire a decent system of graded schools, with properly qualified, trained and compensated teachers.

For more than two centuries the state has been predominantly industrial and commercial. As early as 1699 Edward Ward complained: "The Inhabitants seem very Religious, showing many outward and visible signs of an inward and Spiritual Grace: But tho' they wear in their Faces the Innocence of Doves, you will find them in their Dealings as Subtile as Serpents. Interest is their Faith, Money their God, and Large Possessions the only Heaven they covet." Although the 19th century, with its wind of liberalism, proved these strictures one-sided, it is worth recalling that the Massachusetts Bay Company was a joint stock company organized solely for profit, that the state early became a center for the accumulation of capital employed in the south and west. The first U.S. corporation as the term is understood today arose here.

The essentially urban character of the people is emphasized by the fact that every citizen literally lives "in town," as the 316 towns and 39 cities comprise the total area of the state. At the town meetings, still held in 93 percent of corporate communities in New England, qualified voters elect their selectmen, the chairman or moderator and administrative officers. Under pressure from large and mixed populations, certain towns still unwilling to adopt representative city government have devised the "limited town meeting," attended by elected delegates chosen by vote according to precinct. Although the town meeting is supposed to favor perpetuation of what has been called "a sort of untitled squirarchy," its champions maintain that this system keeps public officials under constant public scrutiny.

In spite of the "town" character of its political life, there are still farmers in the state, although their number is decreasing.

When Boston was Tory, rural Massachusetts was Whig. When Boston was Federalist, rural Massachusetts was Republican and radical. Even today a rural resident of the state when not a Republican is a different breed of Democrat. The hinterland's distrust of the political power of the metropolis was apparent in the fact that the Boston police force was, until the administration of Mayor John Collins in the early 1960's, under the control not of the mayor but of a commissioner appointed by the governor — who, although he no longer need be certified as "a Christian worth £1000," received a lower salary than the mayor of Boston. Now Boston's mayor appoints the city's police commissioner. But the farmer, with all his political difference, partakes of the racial admixture and the turn of mind of other residents of the state. He, too, is very likely to be a trader, though he may do most of his trading with Berkshire or Cape visitors.

Making a campaign speech for Lincoln at Philadelphia in 1860, Charles Francis Adams of Massachusetts, facing what he termed "the most conservative city in America," half apologized for coming from "a more excitable community." The state has always been full of stimulating crosswinds. Life within its borders has never been conditioned by the slow swing of the seasons, the easy tilling of an abundant earth. Marooned on a rocky soil, Massachusetts men had to be ingenious to survive, and they early became skilled at devising shrewd "notions," commercial and intellectual. Used to dealing with people, they learned to think in small and individual terms rather than in broad geographical concepts. The ideal supposed to be the tenet of all Americans, that because a thing is bigger it is better, was never adopted here.

Skillful of hand, sharp at a bargain, stubborn of mind, the Bay Stater possesses a character which with its mixture of shrewdness and idealism is often labeled hypocrisy. He exhibits a strong tendency to conform — provided he thinks conformity is his own idea. But let conformity be thrust upon him, and the east wind again begins to thrum! The blowing of that wind brought to the state much early social legislation: the child labor law in 1836, a law legalizing trade unions in 1842, the first state board of health, the first minimum wage law for women and children, and the first state tuberculosis sanatorium. Against wide opposition, first use was made of inoculation and of an anesthetic within the state.

Massachusetts is parochial, yet it is never long out of the main currents of American life. It is a state of tradition, but part of its tradition is its history of revolt. Its people are fiercely individualistic, yet they have fierce group loyalties. It is noted for conservatism, yet it exports not only shoes and textiles but rebels to all corners of the earth. Its sons and daughters live in small houses, worship in small churches, work in small factories, produce small things and vote in small political units, yet time and again their big spirit has burst beyond our borders.

2

Land and Water

MASSACHUSETTS' TOPOGRAPHY ranges from the Berkshire Hills through the central rolling farmlands to the granite boulders of Cape Ann and southward along the sandy beaches of the South Shore, Cape Cod and the offshore islands.

Massachusetts' land has been continually worn down and built up for millions of years. It has been eroded by wind, water and ice. It has seen the lifting of plains and seashore, the filling in of valleys and troughs, volcanic eruptions and lava intrusions and the invasions of continental glaciers.

The state has four basic physiographic provinces: coastal lowlands, interior lowlands, dissected uplands and ancient mountain residuals — the Berkshires.

Coastal Lowlands: These spread out at Narragansett Bay, cut through Rhode Island's belly and cross Massachusetts to the New Hampshire line. They include eastern Massachusetts with Cape Cod and the offshore islands. Massachusetts' coastline with its rugged mountainous shore — except the South Shore and Cape Cod — and deep indentations is obvious evidence of early submergence and later uplift. Submerged river mouths, many good harbors and the great bays of Boston, Buzzards and Narragansett, are prominent topographic features. Further inland the effect of lowering the coastal plain is found in river falls and rapids.

In the northeastern section of the lowlands, bedrock is near the surface. Rock outcrops are seen in many places. It is this outcropping along the coast that gives our North Shore its rugged picturesque character. This northeastern division has many shallow troughs and basins that eroded on softer rocks and were enclosed by the higher uplands of more erosion-resistant formations. The largest and most important depressions are Boston and Narragansett Basins.

Cape Cod peninsula, the outstanding feature, extends 65 miles as an arm bent upward at the elbow. Glacial in origin, it was reshaped by wind and waves. Nearby are islands of the same origin — Martha's Vineyard, Nantucket and the 16 Elizabeth Islands. Previously glacial outwash plains, Martha's Vineyard and Nantucket are now broad grassy heaths. Cape Cod's southward deltalike plain has been cut along high cliffs by the surf. This plain is covered with pitch pine and scrub oak. Much of the Cape's "forearm" is bleak grassy country while the outer end is a wild desolate region with long yellow beaches. Much of this is now preserved in the Cape Cod National Seashore. The Cape and Islands, lacking land fit for farming, reared a tough breed of men who "farmed" the sea for fish and whales and brought home gewgaws from far places like Canton, Ceylon and Zanzibar.

Interior Lowlands: The Connecticut River Valley and the Berkshire Valley are our two interior lowlands. Each is enclosed by uplands. The Connecticut River Valley extends southward from the New Hampshire-Vermont frontiers through Connecticut to Long Island Sound. It is drained throughout its length by the Connecticut River. Weak red sandstone gives its soil a distinctively ruddy tint. The valley's landscape is dominated by curved wooded ridges running longitudinally to the river. These ridges originated with the intrusive lava that resisted erosion after the outer and weaker layers had worn away. Some traprock elevations rise in the southern part, high above the valley, ranging from 954 feet to 1628 feet in Mounts Holyoke, Tom and Grace.

The Connecticut River Valley with its rich soil and mild climate is productive agricultural country and the seat of prosperous cities and towns. Broad open meadows, reddish soil and tobacco fields present an aspect unusual in New England.

West of the Connecticut River Valley lies Berkshire Valley, shut off by the Berkshire plateau (hills) in the east and by the Taconic Mountains in the west — an isolated world of its own. The Berkshires and the Taconics contain the state's least populous towns. The northern part of the valley is watered by streams cutting through the Taconics to the Hudson River. The southern part is watered by the source of the Housatonic River. The valley, from Pittsfield north to Vermont, is only six miles wide, but southward toward Connecticut it opens up into meadowlands largely devoted to dairying.

Uplands: Massachusetts' eastern and western uplands are divided by the Connecticut River and join north of the valley to form northern New England's great central uplands.

Western uplands and the Berkshires are a continuation of Vermont's Green Mountains. Deeply dissected, they include several ranges and small valleys. The Taconic Range, along the New York State frontier, attains its maximum elevation in Mount Greylock at 3535 feet and decreases southward to Mount Washington in the southeastern corner. The Hoosac Range, further east, varies from 1200 to 1600 feet with Spruce Hill at 2588 feet its highest point.

Farms and hamlets are found atop the elevations. These are the famous "hill towns" of the Berkshires. Many visitors are attracted to their healthy atmosphere and scenic beauty. Best known hill towns are Florida — one of the cooler towns — and Peru. The terrain east of the Taconics and Hoosac Ranges slopes southeasterly toward the Connecticut River Valley and is deeply slashed by rivers like the Deerfield, Farmington and Westfield.

The Eastern uplands — mostly Worcester County — rise gradually from the Connecticut River Valley eastward to a maximum elevation of 1100 feet in the middle of the state. They then slope downward toward the coast. This central plateau is the southern extension of New Hampshire's White Mountains, crossing Massachusetts into Connecticut. Monadnocks — solitary peaks rising high above the surrounding country — are the outstanding geomorphic landforms characteristic of this region. Monadnocks Mount Wachusett and Mount Watatic are solitary remnants of once lofty peaks.

WATER

The Bay State has more than 250 miles of coastline, much of which consists of excellent sandy beaches. The coastline, including tidal waters, is nearly 2000 miles long. Inland waters including lakes, ponds, streams and reservoirs occupy about 400 square miles.

The Charles — our longest river lying wholly within the state — meanders slightly more than 100 miles from its source near Hopkinton to its mouth on Boston Harbor.

The Connecticut bisects the state at the eastern foot of the Berkshire Hills. The river, now dammed at several places, once brought down huge logs from northern Vermont and New Hampshire forests to the Holyoke paper mills. On many occasions the Connecticut flooded and destroyed millions of dollars of property; now flooding has been largely controlled through the construction of flood control dams on Vermont tributaries like the West River.

3

Plants and Wildlife

DECIDUOUS TREES that shed their leaves at the approach of winter make up most of this state's forest cover. Some well-defined areas, however, have evergreens: Cape Cod, the sea margin from Cape Cod to New Hampshire, the central uplands, the rugged Berkshires and the peaks of the two highest mountains, Greylock and Wachusett.

Cape Cod, the state's only approach to a coastal plain, has trees and plants similar to southern New Jersey. Northward from Cape Cod there are many plants which do not stray far from the coast, like low-lying beach plants, marsh grass, sedges and rushes.

The state's largest area — uplands — is covered with a typical northern deciduous forest of maples, birches, beeches and oaks with occasional pine, hemlock and larch stands. The forest floor is covered with low-growing plants varying with the habitat.

Low marshes have early spring plants like skunk cabbage, marsh marigold, American white hellebore, white and blue violets. Higher, drier slopes have false spikenard, Solomon's seal, trailing arbutus, bloodroot and wild oats.

From early spring to late fall there is a constant parade of gorgeous color with striking plants like rhodora, azalea, mountain laurel, shad, dogwood and viburnum, augmented by herbaceous types. Ferns, from the low delicate maidenhair to large graceful osmundas, add charm to the landscape.

The Berkshires offer another scenic and floristic type, more rugged than the last, and to some much more beautiful. The forest is still of the deciduous type, but with a ground cover differing in certain respects, for here are found plants more often associated with cooler regions.

Space does not permit mention of the great variety of plants growing within the state, but there are available at least three collections of mounted plants. The New England Botanical Club has an excellent representative collection at the Gray Herbarium at Harvard University. Hadwen Botanical Club's herbarium, at Clark University, Worcester, specializes in the flora of Worcester County, which is of the general upland region; while that at Amherst College contains western region plants. These herbaria are available to the genuinely interested person. Harvard has the famous Arnold Arboretum where trees and shrubs are appropriately planted and labeled.

WILDLIFE

The effigy of a codfish hanging in the State House on Beacon Hill, and the fact that early settlers used beaver skins as currency, testify to the firmness with which the existence of early Massachusetts men was rooted in the abundance of wildlife. Fishing has maintained its economic importance through three centuries, but when in 1636 William Pynchon removed to the wilderness of Springfield to trade in beaver, he signified the beginning of a process of extinction of Massachusetts fauna halted only in recent years.

Forests today have a narrower range of wildlife. The gray wolf and the black bear have been extirpated. The lynx, once common, only accidentally finds its way into the mountainous portions of the state at long intervals. The beaver is plentiful to the point that it needs to be controlled. The whitetail deer, almost driven out during the 19th century, has appeared in larger numbers in late years. The red fox, cross fox and black fox are still commonly seen.

Of the family Leporidae, the eastern varying hare or white rabbit is occasionally seen. The northern cottontail or gray rabbit is common, except in western Massachusetts, where the varying hare is more common. The family Muridae is represented by many varieties of mice and rats and by the muskrat. The skunk is common in open woodlands and fields. There are two varieties of weasels: the little brown weasel, often seen in stony places, and the New York weasel, which is not very common and usually lives in the woods. The large brown mink is sometimes found along the coast. Shrews and moles exist in numbers, and several varieties of bat are common. Especially large is the family of Rodentia, whose members are the northern gray squirrel and the southern red squirrel, the chipmunk or ground squirrel, the woodchuck or groundhog, the rare Canadian flying squirrel and the more common southern flying squirrel. A most remarkable creature, the one member in the state of the family Zapodidae, is the Hudson Bay jumping mouse.

Whales, no longer numerous, are sometimes sighted off the coast or washed up on the beach. Many varieties of snakes are found, as are lizards, tortoises, and toads, frogs and salamanders.

BIRDS

The seacoast and secluded streams and inland ponds are the home of a large variety of water, marsh and shore birds, including the diving birds, the grebe, the puffin, guillemot, murre, razor-billed auk, little auk and loon. The great northern loon and the red-throated loon visit the state during part of the year.

Gulls and terns are the best-known members of the long-winged swimmers. In this same class are the skuas and jaegers, virtually sea hawks, with powerful wings, beaks and claws.

Tube-nosed swimmers, having tubular nostrils and exceptional flight powers, are represented by fulmars, shearwaters and petrels. The four-toed, fully webbed or totipalmate water birds include gannets, cormorants and man-o'-war birds.

River ducks include black, red-legged black, baldpate and wood. The European widgeon, the blue-winged teal and the pintail are sometimes seen. The sea ducks are the canvasback, scaup, lesser scaup, golden-eye, bufflehead, oldsquaw, eider and scoter ducks, as well as the rare ring-necked and harlequin varieties. About 10,000 Canada geese and 6000 brant visit the state during part of the year. The whistling swan is a rare visitor.

Among the wading birds are the great blue heron, little blue heron, green heron, black-crowned night heron, American bittern and the rare least bittern. A few Gruiformes still remain, chiefly the sora, Virginia rail and coot; gallinules are rare, and the crane is merely an accidental visitor.

Shore birds are waders differing from herons and marsh birds in that their breasts are plump and rounded, with a less prominent sternum. They are small in size and have short tails and long legs.

The ring-necked pheasant is widely stocked by the state Division of Fisheries and Game. Quail (bobwhite), which flourished locally and were protected when introduced, may be hunted on Cape Cod and Nantucket Island. The ruffed grouse has made a comeback, particularly in rural areas with cutover timberlands. The domestic dove or pigeon is found in larger cities where it is both a nuisance and a health hazard.

Several kinds of hawk, including red-tailed, red-shouldered, rough-legged, broad-winged and sparrow, are found in the state. Owls such as the great horned, barn, barred, saw-whet and screech are located here.

The Caprimulgidae, Apodidae, Trochilidae, with peculiar wing development and frail feet, include the whip-poor-will, chimney swift, nighthawk and ruby-throated hummingbird. There are several species of the woodpecker family. Belted kingfishers are frequenters of streams and ponds and more often seen than the yellow-billed and black-billed cuckoos of forest and brush.

Perching birds are the largest order. The songless perching kingbird is familiar. Perching songbirds include the lark, starling, blue jay, bobolink, cowbird, blackbird, meadowlark, oriole, rusty blackbird and grackle. About 30 species of the finch exist in Massachusetts.

FISH

Bay State Fish include the alewife, bass, rockbass, bluefish, bonito, butterfish, carp, catfish, cod, cunner, cusk, eel, flounder, haddock, hake, halibut, herring, kingfish, mackerel, Spanish mackerel, perch, pickerel, pollock, salmon, scup, shad, skate, smelt, sturgeon, swordfish, tautog, tomcod, trout, turbot and weakfish. The state is well known for its shellfish: clams, lobsters, oysters, scallops and shrimp.

CONSERVATION

Wildlife has declined but interest in conservation and natural history is increasing. Louis Agassiz (1807–73) laid the basis for preeminence in biology, and it has been retained by Massachusetts institutions and societies to this day. Agassiz' pioneer classification work was carried on by his son Alexander (1835–1910). His students, Jeffries Wyman (1814–74) and Nathaniel Southgate Shaler (1841–1906), became leading biologists. Harvard's biological museum was named after Agassiz, who founded Woods Hole Marine Biological Laboratory.

Massachusetts philosophers and naturalists from Thoreau through Dallas Lore Sharp (1870–1929) drew much of their inspiration from wildlife. Artists, particularly waterfowl etcher Frank W. Benson and animal painter Jack Murray, have their works in museums and private collections. Charles Heil did watercolors of waterfowl.

The Massachusetts Audubon Society with headquarters on Drumlin Farm, Lincoln, has educational programs for adults and children. The Society is a leading force for conservation.

The Boston Museum of Science is a contemporary project of the former Boston Society of Natural History (1830) which itself was the outgrowth of the Linnaean Society, founded in 1814.

The state's Department of Natural Resources has over a dozen divisions, including the Conservation Services Division. Their Conservation Commission movement has been a natural leader in encouraging local acquisition of conservation and recreation lands.

4

Our Weather

OLD FRED RICHARDSON, for more than 80 years, lived in southern Vermont a few yards north of the Massachusetts line. A minor Vermont-Massachusetts boundary readjustment placed Fred's homestead in Massachusetts.

"How does it seem, Mr. Richardson, to be a Bay Stater after having been a Vermonter all your life?" asked a *Berkshire Eagle* reporter. "Those Vermont winters were too damn cold," Fred said.

CLIMATE

Massachusetts has New England's typical weather: wait a few minutes and it changes. Its variety was noted by Mark Twain:

> Probable nor'-east to sou'-west winds, varying to the southard and westard and eastard and points between; high and low barometer, sweeping around from place to place; probable areas of rain, snow, hail, and drought, succeeded or preceded by earthquakes with thunder and lightning.

The state lies within the worldwide belt of prevailing westerlies, and most air movement in the state comes from the west.

The three typical air masses have three sources: (1) cold damp air moving inland from the Atlantic, (2) cold air moving south from the Arctic — TV weathermen usually call this "cold Canadian air," (3) moist warm air coming northward from the Gulf of Mexico through the Appalachian trough.

The state's climate for a ten-mile-wide belt along the coast and the offshore islands is maritime. The ocean is a winter radiator and summer air conditioner. Average annual temperature is about 50°F.

Beyond the coastal belt the state has a continental climate. The Western Division — about 25 percent of the state's area — includes the Taconic Mountains along the New York State frontier, Berkshire Hills and the Berkshire Valley. Average annual temperature is about 46°F.

The Central Division — about 55 percent of the state's area — lies between the eastern foothills of the Berkshires and the coastal belt. Average annual temperature is about 48°F.

The lowest Massachusetts temperature, recorded by the U.S. Weather Bureau, was −34°F., January 18, 1957, at Birch Hill dam. The highest temperature, 106°F., has been recorded several times at various places. This maximum has been equaled in only one other New England state, New Hampshire.

Cape Cod and the offshore islands, averaging less than one day per year with a temperature of 90°F. or above, have the most comfortable summer temperatures. The rest of the state averages 5–15 days annually with temperatures of 90°F. or above. An exceptionally hot summer may see 25 days with temperatures of 90°F. or higher.

The night and day temperature range of the Cape and offshore islands averages 10–15 degrees but the inland range averages 20–30 degrees.

The daily temperature variation is much greater in winter than in summer. The average daily January temperature in the Western Division is in the low 20's, in middle or upper 20's in the Central Division and in the 30's for the Coastal Division.

GROWING SEASON

The growing season — the number of days between the last killing frost in the spring and the first killing frost in late summer or fall — ranges from a minimum 120 days in the west to a maximum 200 days along the southeast coast or on the offshore islands. The average range is Western, 120–140 days, Central, 140–160 days and Eastern, 160–200 days. There are local exceptions like the coastal cranberry bogs which are low, damp and easily frosted.

RAIN AND SNOW

Much of normal rainfall comes from "nor'-easters" (northeasterly winds bringing precipitation as snow or rain). During the 1960's the state had a four-year drought in which rainfall averaged slightly more than one-half normal precipitation. There were not enough of the "nor'-easters," and it rained about the normal number of days but the total rainfall was less than average.

There is usually measurable precipitation one day out of three but rainfall is more frequent at higher elevations. The coast gets more precipitation as rainfall during the winter, but its annual total precipitation is about two inches less than in the Central and Western regions.

February 16, 1958, was a memorable day for Boston with a record 19.4 inch snowfall. On Blue Hill, 12 miles away and 600 feet higher, the snowfall was 22.3 inches. There is a wide variation in snowfall from year to year and from place to place. Cape Cod and the islands have had as little as four inches during an entire winter while the Western Division's higher altitude had 100 inches. The total amount of snowfall increases as distance from the sea increases as do the number of days snow remains on the ground. Snow cover rarely lasts more than a few days in coastal areas. Western Division snow cover lasts well into spring. Maximum depth usually occurs in mid- or late February.

FLOODS

The Connecticut River, long the raging terror of its valley, has been tamed by flood control dams on upstream tributaries like Ball Mountain and Townshend Dams on Vermont's West River and Union Village Dam near Ompompanoosuc-on-the-Pompanoosuc.

The Connecticut's first known flood was in 1683. The last disastrous floods were in August and September 1955. Other major floods occurred in November 1927, March 1936, July and September 1938 and December 1948.

STORMS

Hurricanes hit Massachusetts in 1938, 1944 and 1954, but old-timers say the November 1898 storm that sent the Portland-bound steamer *Portland* down with all hands was the worst they can remember.

Tropical storms — not necessarily hurricanes — hit Massachusetts about every other year. Such storms hit twice in one year about once in a decade. These storms originate in the tropics, and they are sometimes the tail end of a hurricane. Tornadoes are more frequent than is generally known. Most of them hit in the state's large remote or uninhabited areas. The worst tornado, June 9, 1953, is known as the Worcester Tornado from the area of its devastation. Most tornadoes occur from 2–5 P.M. between May 15 and Sept. 15.

Between 20 and 30 thunderstorms occur each year, usually in the summer but sometimes in winter. The most severe thunderstorms are usually accompanied by property- and/or crop-destroying hail.

SUNSHINE AND FOG

Massachusetts, except for the Berkshires, averages 90–120 days of sunshine annually. The Berkshires have somewhat less because of the higher precipitations. Heavy fog covers Nantucket Island one day out of four. Some areas have no more than 15 foggy days during the year while the islands and Cape Cod may have up to 90.

WEATHERMEN

Dr. Charles F. Brooks of MIT and Harvard and long-time director of the Blue Hill Observatory was the father of modern meteorology. He evolved many of the techniques for recording and forecasting weather. MIT probably offers the most comprehensive meteorological courses in the world. The American Meteorological Society — an organization of professional weathermen — has its headquarters in Boston. The New England headquarters of the U.S. Weather Bureau are in Boston's Custom House Tower. Boston television stations have their own professional meteorological staffs.

5

First Americans

EARLY BAY STATE INDIANS were nomadic hunters and fishermen. They had simple crude stone tools but no axes, pottery or tobacco.

These early people — the pre-Algonkians — were probably kin to Newfoundland's Beothuk Indians. Burying places belonging to their culture have been unearthed at Marblehead and near Fresh Pond, Cambridge. Excavations on Grassy Island, Berkley, on the Taunton River, indicate that a village was once located there. The depth of the salt peat overlay makes the site at least 1000 years old.

By the time of the first known European visitors, Massachusetts was inhabited by Indians of a stock that ranged from Canada's Maritimes to Florida and west to the Mississippi. Speaking an Algonkian language, Massachusetts' Old Algonkians came from the west. They pushed pre-Algonkian inhabitants to the coast where they either intermarried with the newcomers or were killed. The falls of the larger rivers, future damsites for white men, were favorite Indian campgrounds.

Old Algonkians from the southwest introduced agriculture to the hunting and fishing pre-Algonkians. They also brought the art of pottery making for tobacco pipes and cook pots. Many cook pots had pointed bottoms and had to be suspended over fires. Ornamentation was simple — dots and lines arranged in a few patterns.

Early Massachusetts Indians got most food from the sea. Some inland tribes visited the saltwater; others lived along the shore. Clams, quahogs, scallops and oysters were important food sources.

Early European contact with Massachusetts Indians did not begin in Plymouth. Before the Pilgrims came more than 400 ships were whaling and fishing along our coast. Many sailors traded with friendly Indians.

THE TRIBES

Seven tribes lived in Massachusetts: Nausets, Nipmucks, Pennacooks, Mohicans, Pocumtucs, Wampanoags and Massachusetts.

The Massachusetts dominated the Boston, Charlestown, Braintree, Dorchester, Hingham, Malden, Weymouth area. The 1616–1617 plague destroyed their influence. There were about 500 survivors by 1631. They were rounded up into the villages of "Praying John" Eliot's Christian Indians.

Wampanoags held sovereignty from Cape Cod to Massachusetts Bay with some control over a few petty interior tribes.

Friendly Nausets occupied Cape Cod and adjacent islands. Many became Christians before King Philip's War. Eastham's Nauset Light commemorates these gentle red men.

The Pennacooks, allies of Maine's contumacious Abnaki who frequently raided Massachusetts, lived in northern Massachusetts. After King Philip's War (1676) Pennacook survivors migrated to Canada.

Nipmucks roamed west from Boston to near Bennington, Vt., north to Concord, N.H., and south to Rhode Island and Connecticut. They headquartered around Worcester.

Mohicans, nearly wiped out by the 1616 plague, once ranged from New York into the Housatonic Valley. In 1664 their council moved from Albany, N.Y., to Stockbridge. Colonists corralled most survivors into a Stockbridge mission — a forlorn hope for survival.

All these Bay State Algonkians had smooth skins, swarthy complexions, high foreheads, broad shoulders and small hands and feet.

"WELCOME ENGLISHMEN"

Plymouth citizens were surprised when in March 1621 an Indian appeared and spoke in English, "Welcome, Englishmen!" Samoset offered aid. He had learned a few English words from Monhegan fishermen and spoke with drama, unaware his friendly words spelled doom for his people.

The Pilgrims settled on land belonging to Wampanoag Chief Massasoit. Massasoit, in 1621, ratified the first New England white man–Indian treaty. The treaty lasted the remaining 54 years of Massasoit's life. Massasoit never became a Christian, but without the generous help of this "heathen," Massachusetts settlement would have been difficult if not impossible.

Not all tribes were as friendly — notably the Pequots, who battled their way into eastern Connecticut. Bostonians in 1636, with Hartford, Windsor and Wethersfield residents, attacked the Pequots. Religious Bostonians sold surviving Pequots as slaves to Bermuda Islanders. Purchasers reported their slaves were no bargain; Indian slaves were "sullen and treacherous." They wanted freedom. Pequot slaves were poor field hands but became skilled sailors and whalers.

KING PHILIP'S WAR

Massasoit's son King Philip, who became chief of the Wampanoags in 1662, believed white men would exterminate red men. Gradual white expansion over 50 years resulted in conflict over land. Roger Williams, in a letter to Governor Bradford, hotly protested the legality of the colony's land claims. "James has no more right to give away or sell Massasoit's lands and cut and carve his country than Massasoit has to sell King James' kingdom or to send Indians to colonize Warwickshire."

Meddling colonists insisted in administering identical "justice" to white and red men. The Indians rightly considered this an unwarranted interference with their rights. It was impossible for them to obtain fair court hearings.

Philip's brother Wamsutta had been murdered by white men. He made secret, intelligent preparations for war. Shortly before war broke out Massachusetts' governor asked Philip for a peace pledge. Diplomatically proud Philip replied, "Your governor is but a subject of King Charles. I shall not treat with a subject. I shall treat of peace only with the King, my brother. When he comes I am ready."

Philip planned a simultaneous movement of seaboard tribes against all white settlements. An unexpected event precipitated the war a year before he was ready. Philip's tribesman Sassamon was a Harvard man and a Christian who taught school in the Indian village of Natick. After he became Philip's aid, Sassamon "leaked" Philip's plans to the Plymouth governor. Philip discovered the treachery. Sassamon was slain. Three of Philip's tribesmen were hung in June 1675.

Philip attacked Swansea. Town after town fell. Since the Narragansetts had not yet heartily engaged in the campaign, Philip sought their support. In December 1500 whites trapped the Narragansett nation in a South Kingstown, Rhode Island, swamp. Philip was defeated.

Philip went to Pokanoket but was driven out. He was finally killed by one of his own men. His head was cut off and displayed atop a pole in Christian Plymouth.

The power of New England's southern tribes was destroyed but the war dragged out until 1678. The Wampanoags and their lesser allies were nearly exterminated. Survivors fled to Canada or west of the Hudson.

Christian colonists paid a high price for their barbarism. One out of ten English colonists of military age was killed or captured. It was 40 years before the devastated frontier was reoccupied.

CONVERTS TO THE CROSS

"Praying John" Eliot was a sincere, industrious evangelist who mastered the Algonkian language and translated the Bible. He believed Indians would have to be civilized before they could accept Christianity.

"Praying John" and his few white helpers established 30 towns of Christian Indians. Each town had a school. Natick, the first "Praying Town," was established in 1651. Bylaws were adopted. An Indian Waban was appointed justice of the peace.

Eliot traveled, teaching, preaching and supervising his flocks. At first he was violently opposed by local chiefs and shamans who feared loss of their powers, but behind Eliot's teachings was the force of the English authorities. Soon open opposition ceased.

By 1674 there were 1100 converts in Plymouth Colony. Some conversions were genuine. Whether they were due to religious convictions, fear of English "justice" or from friendship for Eliot is problematical.

Eliot planned higher education for his protégés. Harvard's first brick structure was erected as an Indian dormitory. The building soon became a print shop because there were not enough Indian students. Caleb Cheeshahteamuck graduated from Harvard in 1665. Three other Indians studied but did not graduate.

Christian Indians were treated by Philip as allies of the English while the whites treated them as secret allies of Philip. One of the many black pages in Colonist-Indian relations was the English treatment of the Christian Naticks. There was no question of the Naticks' wartime loyalty, but they were ordered to migrate without food or shelter in mid-winter. "Praying Indian Town" Wamesit (Tewskbury) residents were ordered to Long and Deer Islands in Boston Harbor.

In the spring survivors were taken to Cambridge where Thomas Oliver gave them refuge on his Charles River lands. A few returned to their ruined homes, but they were too feeble to maintain many towns. Remoter towns were abandoned.

By 1684 only four "Praying Towns" remained. John Eliot's life work was undone by his fellow "Christians."

Natick Indians who once held all town offices were replaced by whites who stole Indian lands. Reservations were established. Restricted life was unfavorable to Indians, and they degenerated physically and mentally when forced to adopt white men's customs.

THE NEW INVASION

For some time, the Indian population has been about 1200. Between 1950 and 1960, there were over 2000 Indians in the state. The increase came as a result of the tremendous amount of construction in the state; many Indians are high steel workers who follow foot-wide paths of steel 50 stories above the streets instead of the warpaths of their tomahawk-toting ancestors. Few, if any, pureblooded Bay State native Indians survive today.

6

Historical Notes

ERIC THORVALDSSON (Eric the Red), not Columbus, discovered North America, but there is no concrete evidence that either his son Leif Ericson or fellow Norseman Thorfinn Karlsefni reached Massachusetts shores.

The first white visitor to what is now Massachusetts was Venetian navigator John Cabot (1450–98), who sailed from England in 1497–98.

The Reformation, not trade, was the reason for the first permanent Massachusetts settlement. The Reformation came to England under Henry VIII, but his daughter Bloody Mary's anti-Protestant policies gave one basis for the anti-Catholicism of Massachusetts settlers. Mary's successor Elizabeth attempted a compromise — the Church of England — which satisfied neither liberal Protestants nor Catholics.

Separatists or Pilgrims believed each local congregation should be entirely independent of any outside rule. Some Separatists driven from their native Scrooby found religious freedom in Protestant Holland, but these patriotic Englishmen, while they disagreed with the Church of England, wanted their children to grow up in an English atmosphere.

After securing support from English financiers some of them obtained in 1619 a patent to settle along the James River in Virginia. The *Mayflower* sailed in 1620. Storms drove the tiny ship off course, and she cast anchor in Provincetown Harbor on a bleak November day. Pilgrim women washed clothes and gossiped while men brewed beer and looked for more congenial surroundings. They selected Plymouth Harbor and began to erect their common house, December 26, 1620.

MAYFLOWER COMPACT

The Pilgrims settled on land which they knew had not been assigned, but it was too late in the season to move. Since they were on unassigned land they were, in a sense, beyond English law which would have governed them had they continued to Virginia.

They drew up the Mayflower Compact. This document, despite great claims by their alleged descendants, was not unusual. The compact was their church covenant modified to meet immediate circumstances. This simple covenant of the Congregational Church — more a set of principles than rules — was the basis for that purest form, in theory at least, of American government, the town meeting, in which everyone can directly participate in community decisions.

The 102 Pilgrims included 35 Separatists from Leyden and 67 Londoners. The Pilgrims soon demonstrated that a colony could be self-supporting through farming, fishing and trade and household work, such as spinning, weaving, candlemaking and soapmaking. London backers were repaid. The Pilgrims' example encouraged others to attempt colonization.

OTHER SETTLEMENTS

Several small communities dedicated to trade and fishing were established along the coast. Their grants were secured from the Council for New England which had taken over Plymouth Company's claims.

These small villages could not have expanded unaided into a united colony, but they gave Englishmen a foothold and an interest which laid the foundations for the commonwealth — and for the United States of America.

MERRY MOUNT

Plymouth's Pilgrims had little in common with the gay community of Merry Mount (at the present site of Quincy) founded by Thomas Morton, a fur trader and seller of guns to the Indians.

"They also set up a Maypole," wrote Plymouth's horrified Governor Bradford, "drinking and dancing aboute it many days togeather, inviting Indian women for their consorts, dancing and frisking togeather like so many fairies."

Capt. Myles Standish captured the post and deported Morton to England in 1628.

MASSACHUSETTS BAY COLONY

Americans frequently confuse Plymouth Pilgrims with Massachusetts Bay Puritans. Pilgrims like William Bradford (1590–1657) and

William Brewster (1567–1644) were "Separatists" advocating and then practicing complete separation from the Church of England.

Puritans like John Endecott (1589–1665) believed the Church of England should have been "purified" from within, but the church was as opposed to being purified from within as it was to the Separation movement. Endecott and his coreligionists hoped America would provide a place where they could freely practice their own religion.

Puritans were granted territory from three miles south of the Charles River's mouth north to the Merrimack's mouth. Endecott and his settlers sailed in 1628.

A 1629 royal act created the Massachusetts Bay Company. The charter failed to stipulate that the colony's legislative sessions had to be held in England. Thus the entire governing process was transferred to America.

Two legislative bodies administered the colony's affairs: (1) all stockholders or freemen meeting in quarterly sessions and (2) the governor together with his deputy and 18 assistants.

John Winthrop and his followers sailed off in March 1630 to create their theocratic commonwealth. Salem did not please Winthrop who had gotten himself elected governor. He moved to Boston.

A period of almost unprecedented growth followed, and by 1640 more than 16,000 people had joined the migration.

THEOCRATIC COMMONWEALTH

The colony leaders planned a social order in which individual freedom was subordinated to God's will as interpreted by His clergy. Winthrop and his clerical cohorts believed they alone were proper interpreters of Divine Will. They illegally vested nearly all governmental powers in themselves by providing that only church members could sit in the General Court. In 1634 discontented freemen demanded to see the charter. General Court members, realizing their rights had been infringed, hastily passed legislation which vested governmental authority in their representative hands.

These struggles speeded New England's development. As long as the governor and clergy could direct the settlement movement they approved, if only because God's word would be planted in new soil. Land was granted freely to any town proprietors who were churchmen.

Frontier towns were created as malcontents flowed westward from England through Boston. On the South Shore, Duxbury (1632), Scituate (1633), Hingham (1636), Barnstable (1638), Yarmouth

(1639), Mansfield (1640) and Eastham (1649) were founded, and on the North Shore, Saugus (later Lynn) (1631).

Bostonians meanwhile were settling other colonies. The Rev. Thomas Hooker's Cambridge congregation, dissatisfied with preacher John Cotton's rule, founded Hartford, Connecticut (1635).

PURITAN PATHS

Social, economic, political and spiritual influences which distinguished Massachusetts — and eventually other New England colonies — from other colonies and states were implanted in these small towns.

Long, harsh, cold winters with deep snows made a compact community a practical necessity. House lots and the meetinghouse which served as church and town hall, taverns and shops clustered around a village green or common. Forests surrounding the village were cleared to make room for growing crops. Open areas along rivers were reserved for hay growing. Houses were individually owned, but for many years cropland and meadows were owned in common.

"Independence" had real meaning to these Yankees. They raised their own vegetables and grains in field and garden. Milk came from their own cows while field and forest provided deer meat, wild turkeys and grouse. There were fish in the lakes and rivers. Families cut wood for their own winter heating and summer cooking fuel. Sheep provided wool for homespun clothes. Lack of factories and stores developed the classic New England jack-of-all-trades. Farmers, during the long winter nights, made their own harnesses, repaired equipment needed for spring plowing and often made their own furniture.

The minister, the town's acknowledged leader, frequently served as schoolmaster, doctor for horses and humans, and lawyer. Fortunately his ministerial rule was not absolute. Each town was governed by a town meeting in which every freeman had an equal vote.

The town meeting, the most democratic and representative of all republican forms of government, spread from Massachusetts to other Yankee commonwealths. Through this institution New Englanders were prepared to meet the challenge of creating a stable government when the colonists slashed away the mother country's yoke.

These town meetings not only managed ordinary governmental functions, but the life of each inhabitant was carefully regulated. Individual liberty was sacrificed to detailed legislation regulating habits and social conduct. These "blue laws" represented a desire for simplicity natural to a group that had rebelled against the ceremony of the Established

Church; they reflected, too, the realization that hard work was necessary to conquer a wilderness. The shiftless were "warned out" of Massachusetts towns; holidays such as Christmas were forbidden. There was work to be done, and the town fathers were determined to see that no one shirked.

The Congregational Church initiated education in America. Puritanism presupposed an intelligent clergy capable of interpreting Scripture. It also presupposed an intelligent, literate congregation who could understand the Bible and the meaning of the several hours of sermons which they were subjected to every Sunday. Schools were needed to train clergymen and a literate congregation.

In 1636 the General Court appropriated funds to start the College of Newtowne (Cambridge). When young clergyman John Harvard left his money and his books to the school, a grateful legislature named the college in his honor (see EDUCATION). Popular education dates from 1647 when all towns of 50 families or more were required to maintain an elementary school, for which parents paid a small annual fee.

BACKSLIDERS

Puritan excesses led to a declining interest in religion. In the 1650's Puritan forces focused on Quakers. Beaten and banished, they returned. Willful persecution turned people against the clergy and magistrates. Younger people, who had not suffered for their religion, together with the rising commercial class demanded a less theocratic government. They won their first victory in 1657 with the adoption of the Half-Way Covenant. This allowed baptized as well as converted church members to vote.

DOMINION OF NEW ENGLAND

The withdrawal of the colony's charter in 1684 was the result of the Stuart Restoration. The Empire after 1660 tightened imperial control to draw the colonies closer together so that they might be more useful — in time of war for example — to the mother country.

Massachusetts leaders, undisciplined by 20 years of imperial inefficiency, refused to grant liberty of conscience or citizenship to Church of England members. They pointed out they had founded a religious colony and that it was not right to expect them to admit possible subversive elements. They snubbed agents sent to investigate conditions and flagrantly violated Parliament's trade laws. The government successfully instituted court proceedings which canceled the liberal charter.

A government, known as the Dominion of New England, was provided. Massachusetts, Rhode Island, Connecticut, New Hampshire, Maine (then part of Massachusetts) and later York and Jersey Provinces were united into a single governmental unit under Royal Governor Sir Edmund Andros. Able administrator Andros immediately provoked colonial wrath by tyrannical acts.

ROYAL COLONY

Massachusetts wanted its liberal charter restored. It was liberal in that it gave the colonial government the liberty to practice illiberality on others. In 1691 William and Mary created a royal colony similar to Virginia. Massachusetts had annexed New Hampshire and Maine. The former was now made a separate royal colony. To compensate for this loss Massachusetts Bay Colony was given jurisdiction over Plymouth Colony and the offshore islands of Nantucket and Martha's Vineyard.

The royal governor was appointed by the Crown. Former assistants became the Governor's Council, elected by the Assembly. Two legislative houses were recognized.

The most important provision of the new charter was the abolition of church membership as a prerequisite for voting. Massachusetts was now a civil rather than a Bible commonwealth. The church was still powerful. Catholics were barred from the colony.

SEEDS OF SEDITION

The 1691 charter initiated forces which a century later led Massachusetts to revolt. Farmers, accustomed to relative freedom since 1630, resented the possible interference of a Crown-appointed governor. The governor had veto power over assembly laws. The assembly, however, controlled the governor's salary.

TRADE AND TROUBLE

Massachusetts people were sensitive to trade regulations because they interfered with profits. Starting with fishing ventures, their trade became increasingly profitable as Yankee skippers used the many harbors and plentiful lumber for shipbuilding. They searched the seas for profitable trade — and found it. Massachusetts bottoms became carriers for all colonies. Her ships hauled West Indian sugar and Virginia tobacco to England and returned with manufactured goods.

The market for many Colonial products was confined, by regulations, to England. Colonists were forbidden to buy manufactured goods, no matter the source, except through English channels.

Canny Yankees developed the famous Triangular Trade. Bay Colony lumber, foodstuffs, livestock and fish were taken to the West Indies and swapped for molasses which was brought back and made into rum — Medford and Newburyport were rum-making centers — which was traded in Africa for slaves. The slaves were swapped in the West Indies for gold which was welcomed by English merchants. The Indies, however, were not large enough to absorb all Massachusetts' products. Yankees developed a bootleg trade with the sugar islands.

Royal governors winked at smuggling. Many great fortunes — some are still around — were founded on this illegal but respectable trade. It was not until after the long French wars ended that England realized the full extent of her colony's illicit acts. The English-French conflict lasting for more than a century culminated in the Seven Years' War (1756–63), as the French and Indian War was known on the continent.

Into Massachusetts backcountry came French and Indian raiders, accompanied by Jesuit priests, sweeping down through the Champlain Valley. Eastern shippers, impervious to frontier barbarities, continued illegally trafficking with the French sugar islands and Canada. French armies were thus supplied with foodstuffs necessary to carry out raids on Massachusetts frontiers.

Yankee traders, enticed by war profits, carried on this trade so extensively that England's superior navy was unable to starve the French Indies into submission. Yankee foodstuffs were cheaper in the French Indies than in England.

SUGAR AND STAMPS ACTS

This scandalous conduct convinced England her Colonial administration needed reform. The needed reforms, too stringent, possibly, finally led to America's independence.

The 1765 Stamp Act provided that revenue stamps be affixed to publications and legal and commercial papers. The Crown thus hoped to raise part of the revenue needed to maintain troops for protecting colonists against Indian attacks made imminent by the outbreak of Pontiac's Rebellion.

The 1764 Sugar Act ended the foreign trade on which the colony depended. The 1765 Stamp Act drained the little money remaining away from Boston. The colony was undergoing a postwar depression, magnified by the new acts. It is easy to understand why Sam Adams and his political henchmen gathered in the Green Dragon Tavern to plot drastic measures.

THE GREAT AGITATOR

Harvard graduate Samuel Adams (1722–1803) failed as a businessman and lawyer, but he became one of the world's most successful revolutionary agitators. Adams was one of the first colonists to desire complete independence from England. Adams, the "Great Agitator," wanted England to take the strictest repressive measures possible against his neighbors and fellow colonists to fuel an increasing flame of hatred toward the Crown and ministries. Whenever England eased up on restrictions, Adams created new situations deliberately designed to provoke her into further restrictive measures.

Sitting in the Provincial Assembly for several terms during the 1760's, Adams, whose subversive activities were financed by merchant John Hancock, opposed Boston's wealthy merchant class as often as he did British misrule. Adams contended the Massachusetts legislature was "subordinate" to but not a "subject" of Parliament.

Adams foresaw great opportunities when British troops were brought to Boston. His street gang, the "Sons of Liberty," were able rabble-rousers. Adams' great propaganda opportunity came the cold blustery night of March 5, 1770.

THE RABBLE AND THEIR RIOT

About 150 Bostonians, infiltrated by Adams' agents, gathered before the Custom House. A solitary Redcoat sentry, Private Hugh White of the 29th Worcestershire Regiment, was walking his post in the prescribed military manner. Taunts and sundry solid objects were thrown at him. Mulatto Crispus Attucks — he was part Indian — threatened White with a huge stick of cordwood. A 19-year-old bookseller, Henry Knox, later chief of Washington's artillery and our first Secretary of War, futilely attempted to dissuade the mob. He also warned White that to fire now might cost him his life. The crowd increased. Verbal insults grew viler. The solid missile barrage intensified. Patient but worried, White shouted, "Turn out, Main Guard."

Officer of the Day Captain Thomas Preston responded, accompanied by Lt. James Bassett, Corporal William Wemms and Privates John Carroll, James Hartigan, Matthew Kilroy, William McCauley, Hugh Montgomery and William Warren. The nine Redcoats traipsed out to aid White. The screeching mob moved in with swinging clubs. Hugh Montgomery, after being knocked down by Attucks, panicked and fired. His comrades, thinking a "fire" order had been given — it was impossible to hear a command above the howling rioters — also fired.

When the clouds of black powder smoke slowly lifted, Samuel Gray, Michael Johnson and Attucks were dead. Samuel Maverick died a few hours later. Agitator Patrick Carr lingered a few days — too late to get his coffin silhouetted in Paul Revere's pirated print.

To Sam Adams' dismay, the British, deeply regretting the incident, withdrew the two regiments to an island in the harbor. John Adams and Josiah Quincy defended the British soldiers. Seven men were acquitted. Kilroy and Montgomery were found guilty of manslaughter and were punished by being branded on the thumb.

The misnamed "massacre" became a great American legend. Sam Adams' masterly use of the incident together with Paul Revere's distorted pictorial version reinforced by uncritical patriotic acceptance created a master myth.

Nearly four years after the passage of a tea tax — met by a Colonial boycott on tea — Adams discovered the East India Company had 342 tea chests aboard a merchantman. Adams was afraid that if the tea landed his fellow townsmen might be tempted by the discount-priced tea. He called a meeting for that night, December 16, 1773, in the Old South Church. The "Great Agitator" concluded his fiery speech to the overcrowded hall with "Gentlemen, there is nothing more this meeting can do to save the country."

This prearranged signal brought forth war whoops from Sons of Liberty thinly disguised as Indians. Followed by a huge mob, the "Indians" did a war dance to the wharf where they boarded the ship and heaved the tea into the harbor.

COERCIVE ACTS

England was outraged, and Lord North's ministry made blundering reprisals. Boston Port was closed to trade. Other penalties were inflicted to be removed only when restitution was made for the tea. The merchants would have agreed, but the mere thought that England would take such drastic reprisals for a "prank" put the Liberty Party in control. Unable to secure the merchants' cooperation in boycotting England, they attempted successfully to unite political action between Bay Colony communities and other colonies. A call for a Continental Congress was issued. Acceptances came quickly.

The Massachusetts Assembly chose its congressional delegates with the legislative chamber door locked. Irate royal governor Thomas Gage vainly shouted through the keyhole that he had dissolved the legislature and it could transact no business. The delegates, of course, were Adams' radicals and they quickly dominated the Philadelphia Congress.

SUFFOLK RESOLVES

Delegates from Suffolk County towns met in Dedham and then in Milton in September 1774 to protest the Coercive Acts. Delegates, incited by Dr. Joseph Warren (1741–75), voted to refuse payment of any taxes to England, to cut off all relationships with the mother country, to refuse to obey the Coercive Acts and to hold weekly militia musters. These acts, approved by the delegates, were the first direct steps toward independence. They were heartily approved by most Continental Congress delegates.

Congress on October 14 adopted a Declaration of Rights and less than a week later created an association which advocated nonexportation, nonimportation and nonconsumption of British goods.

"LET IT BEGIN HERE!"

Tension rose in the colony after the arrival of Gen. Thomas Gage's troops, sent to enforce the Coercive Acts. Pelting Lobsterbacks with snowballs was a favorite schoolboy sport. Bostonians resented the Quartering Act which forced them to house the hated Redcoats in their homes. The QA, as it was known, was responsible for our Third Amendment, which generally prohibits such billeting. Sam Adams arranged to purchase arms. They formed and drilled Minutemen who prepared to act against the British at a minute's notice.

Late on April 18, 1775, Gen. Gage sent 700 regulars to seize and destroy provincial military stores hidden in Concord. Sam Adams and John Hancock, the two "most wanted" men, were hiding there.

March orders were discovered by Boston subversives. Riders Dr. Prescott, William Dawes and Paul Revere went forth to arouse the countryside.

Revere reached Lexington and warned Hancock and Adams but was captured by a British patrol who seized his horse — it belonged to Deacon John Larkin of Boston and its name is unknown — and then released him. Revere and Hancock's clerk John Lovell removed Hancock's trunk, containing subversive papers, to safety. Dawes fled a British patrol. He fell off his horse and lost his watch in making his escape.

When Revere reached Lexington he met Dr. Samuel Prescott on his way home from a late courting session. Prescott volunteered to ride to Concord. He was the only rider to reach there.

Minutemen were gathering off Lexington Green in Landlord Buckman's cozy tavern for a few tots of rum to ward off the predawn chill. Word finally came, "Lobsterbacks are down the rud, apiece." Slamming down pewter tankards and grabbing smoothbore muskets, Minutemen mustered on the green. As Maj. John Pitcairn's weary equippage-laden but still snappy regulars came onto the greensward, leather-faced Cap'n John Parker, French and Indian War veteran, took a chew of tobacco, peered through the lifting mist, tinted red by the rising sun, spat and gave history a ringing phrase: "Don't fire unless fired on, but if they mean to have a war let it begin here."

RED ON THE GREEN

Pitcairn halted his men directly in front of the ranked Minutemen. "Disperse, ye rebels, ye villains, disperse, disperse in the name of the King. Lay down your arms." The sun's low, slanting rays glinted off Britishers' bright brass buttons. Pipe-clay-whitened, broad, crossed chest belts were dusty from the nightlong march. Dawn's stillness was shattered as front-rank regulars thumbed back clumsy musket hammers. Without waiting for Parker's command — what would it have been? — grumbling Minutemen broke ranks.

Then, Anglo-American history's fatal moment: a concealed sniper — was he a trigger-happy, rum-valiant Minuteman or Adams' agent? — fired.

Front-rank Redcoats squeezed triggers, a click, ponderous Brown Bess hammers fell forward and down, struck flint, directed sparks through waiting touchholes onto polished, coarse-grained black powder — and then ignition. Black powder's heavy blue smoke, mingling with mist, slowly lifted. Eight Minutemen were dead or mortally wounded; ten would recover to fight another day.

Pitcairn's men, having defended themselves, reranked and moved toward Concord. Minutemen were dispersing.

The Britishers reached Concord and destroyed remaining stores, but the smoke alarmed the countryside and 450 Minutemen led by Maj. John Butterick repulsed the regulars at North Bridge. The Britishers, retreating toward Boston, were continually harassed by snipers until they were reinforced by Lord Percy's relief column. Once the reinforced regulars resumed their march, snipers renewed their harassing tactics to the outskirts of Boston. Score: 49 Americans and 73 British killed. Total killed and wounded on both sides: 366. Sam Adams had his war.

The colonists were not then fighting for independence from England but for their rights as free Englishmen. They got more than they fought for — Independence.

BREED'S HILL

Once the Minutemen had the British in Boston they decided to keep them there. The city then lay at the tip of a narrow peninsula, so this could be easily accomplished if all avenues to the mainland were guarded. Boston Neck was carefully guarded by the 20,000-man army, authorized by the assembly. It was first commanded by Gen. Artemas Ward (1727–1800) and after July 2 by George Washington (1732–99).

Another possible escape route was narrow Charlestown Neck. Bunker and Breed's Hills gave commanding views of the neck and harbor. During the night of June 16 Colonial officer William Prescott was sent to fortify Bunker Hill but instead occupied Breed's Hill. The famous Battle of Bunker Hill was actually fought on Breed's Hill.

On the 17th, wave after wave of gallant British regulars swept in magnificent array toward the redoubt, but they were repulsed by Yankee musketry. Finally, as the decimated British ranks were about to retire, the Yankees' powder ran out. Redcoats, hampered by heavy packs, swept over the primitive breastworks, and the battle ended in a final savage burst of shooting, clubbing, bayoneting, stabbing and saber slashing. Stones — the Yankees' final weapon — were seized from the breastworks after musket stocks shattered against British bones.

Losses on this fratricidal day: Americans, 441 killed, wounded or taken prisoner; British; 1054 casualties. Dr. Joseph Warren, Sam Adams' cohort, serving as a private, and Maj. Pitcairn were killed.

New Hampshire militiaman Gen. John Stark (1728–1822), who would whip the Hessians at Bennington, turned in a superb performance.

Both sides won and lost the Battle of Bunker Hill. It was a military victory for the British though their casualties were more than twice that of the Americans. The Yankees lost the day, but for the first time colonists realized colonial troops could, under some circumstances — odds are usually with defenders of a fortification — take on the King's regulars.

SIEGE

The siege of Boston went on until the spring of 1776. Henry Knox (1750–1806) went to Fort Ticonderoga and brought back the post's spare cannon. These weapons, strategically placed by Knox, pounded the British. Gen. Howe recognized a hopeless situation. On March 17, the British Army together with local Tories — many of them merchants with "Colonial eggs" (big paunches) — sailed to New Scotland (Nova Scotia). Washington occupied Boston. Massachusetts launched the military phase of the revolution and gave Americans their second victory — the first was Ethan Allen's taking of Ticonderoga in New York. Massachusetts was free of hostile troops for the remainder of the war.

DISCONTENT

The last General Court, held under the Royal Charter, convened in 1774. Bay Colony was then governed by a Provincial Congress that had no legal basis and was not representative. Berkshire County farmers refused to let courts convene until they were given a voice in a permanent government, so a constitution, drafted by the Provincial Congress in 1777–79, was submitted to the people for ratification — the first state constitution to be tested by popular vote. It contained few provisions for separation of powers and no Bill of Rights. It was promptly rejected. In 1778, a popularly elected constitutional convention accepted a governmental framework drawn up largely by John Adams. Meanwhile Massachusetts' Provincial Congress ran the state.

The new constitution was ratified June 7, 1780. Massachusetts was the last state to adopt a written constitution, yet so wisely had its framers labored that it still exists.

The Revolutionary epoch was one of social, economic and political upheaval. Many past governmental and commercial leaders were pilloried as Tories. They migrated to Canada and England. A new aristocracy arose, which drew its wealth from the sea. The financial resources of the state were concentrated along the coast, leaving dissatisfied farmers struggling vainly with the stubborn soil. Dissatisfaction was fanned to open rebellion by the economic depression which swept over the newly created United States.

Worcester County and Berkshire hill farmers demanded legislative relief in the form of paper money and stay laws to prevent mortgage foreclosures by greedy moneylenders. These inarticulate hillmen found a voice and leader for their local uprising in Revolutionary War hero Capt. Daniel Shays (1747–1825), a Pelham farmer. The legislature repeatedly failed to help the farmers, and they rallied around the popular ex-officer. In August 1786, they prevented the Court of Common Pleas from sitting. In September, Shays and his men moved to prevent the sitting of the traveling Supreme Court in Springfield.

Shays and his men moved against the Springfield arsenal — then state-owned — in January 1787. They were defeated by Gen. Benjamin Lincoln (1733–1810) and fled. Lincoln's militia caught them at Petersham and again routed them. The rebel army was dispersed. Fifteen leaders, sentenced to death, were eventually pardoned as was Shays who had found refuge with friendly Ethan Allen (1738–89) in the independent Vermont Republic. The militia under Lincoln had been illegal, financed by Boston merchants.

Such rebellions alarmed Boston's merchant princes. They now supported the swelling movement for a national constitution to replace the Articles of Confederation which proved so useless in promoting trade, stabilizing finance and protecting the propertied classes. Massachusetts was the sixth state to ratify the Constitution, and this act was accomplished by adroit skulduggery. A majority of the ratifying convention opposed the government. Most hill farmers and those from Maine — then part of Massachusetts — opposed ratification and very plainly said so. Conservative leaders wooed and won John Hancock who was switching from revolution to reaction. As usual, he retired to his home with a gout attack until he could determine popular sentiment. He was offered the governorship.

Meanwhile, on the national scene, Virginia had failed to ratify the Constitution, which meant native son George Washington was ineligible for the presidency. Hancock, idol of the less affluent classes, supported the Constitution and thus made its ratification possible.

Massachusetts then proposed a series of national constitutional amendments. This practice was followed by other states, and from the proposals came the first ten amendments, the all-important Bill of Rights.

PEACE AND PROFITS

New trade routes were discovered, particularly that immensely profitable China trade which — except for 1812–15 — thrived unchecked until ugly steamships supplanted beautiful clippers. In every part of the world Yankee sailing masters sought cargoes and fortunes. After 1793, when England and France were locked in the first of a new series of wars, Massachusetts bottoms took over most of the carrying trade formerly monopolized by those powers. New wealth flowed into the commonwealth. The depression that sired Shays' Rebellion was now a fast-dimming memory.

Prosperity shaped politics. Massachusetts was wedded to the Federalist Party. Native John Adams was President. Many supported the anti-American Alien and Sedition Acts through which Federalists sought to solidify their party's power during France's 1798 Naval War. Jefferson's 1800 election was considered a major calamity by Federalists.

SECESSION NOW?

Jefferson's ex-Federalist supporters soon admitted their mistake, for their leader's tangled foreign policy bore harder on maritime Massachusetts than on any other state. The embargo with which Jefferson attempted to combat French and English interference in American shipping forced the commonwealth into a depression. Massachusetts' people protested interference with their trade, their livelihood and their profits. Protests swelled to mass rebellion when Jefferson's successor James Madison responded to the expansionist west and carried the United States into the needless War of 1812. For the three years the commonwealth's trade stagnated, driven from the seas by the British Navy. Massachusetts refused to allow her militia to be used outside the state, gave minimal monies to the national war effort and held celebrations to cheer English victories over Napoleon.

THE ESSEX JUNTO

Some Massachusetts Federalists, especially those from Essex County, considered themselves "wise, good and rich" and were very pro-British. They wanted war with revolutionary France, not with England. They organized the 1814 Hartford Convention which called for New England and New York to secede from the Union for nullification of the Constitution. But the war ended before the "Essex Junto" could press their campaign for secession.

THE REFORMERS

State leaders, alarmed at the exodus of western-bound Bay Staters, engaged in Puritan self-scrutiny. They agreed that one expelling force was the antiquated governmental and religious system, and that only a reform in that system could stem the exodus. Politically, this reforming spirit found expression in the release of Maine and in the constitutional convention in 1820. This convention yielded to the demand of the people for a greater voice in their own government by drafting ten amendments to the Constitution providing for the incorporation of cities, the abolition of property qualifications for voting, the removal of religious tests for officeholders and other much needed reforms. In 1833, another constitutional amendment completely separated Church and State. Congregationalism, hitherto favored by governmental support, was placed on the same plane as other religions. Aristocratic Puritanism was swept from the statute books. Democratic ideals were brought nearer reality.

The reforming spirit was not stilled by concrete gains. Unitarianism, begun in America at King's Chapel (Boston) just after Independence, swept through the commonwealth under the guidance of William Ellery Channing (1818–1901). Its liberal doctrines threatened to bury the Congregational Church under an avalanche of popular disapproval. Only the valiant efforts of the Rev. Horace Bushnell (1802–76), who sought to reconcile the old Calvinistic theology with the gentle humanitarianism of the new era, saved Congregational power and influence. In Concord, Emerson, Thoreau and their disciples preached the cult of individualism and the doctrine of the nobility of man in verse and prose. Dorothea L. Dix (1802–87) shocked the state into providing the first decent care for the insane before beginning her countrywide crusade. Horace Mann agitated valiantly and successfully in behalf of the revolutionary doctrine of universal education. His efforts elevated Massachusetts to leadership in this sphere. Total abstinence societies, formed first in Boston in 1826, spread through the state and nation, beginning that organized movement that was to end in the disastrous Eighteenth (and Twenty-First) Amendments. At Brook Farm, near West Roxbury, at Fruitlands, near Harvard, and elsewhere bewildered idealists like Hawthorne, Alcott and Margaret Fuller sought refuge from the changing world in the simple life and communism— an experiment gently but effectively satirized by Hawthorne in *The Blithedale Romance.*

From this mad, shifting world emanated the crusade against slavery, centered in Boston and New York State, where the revivalism of the Rev. Charles G. Finney (1792–1875) whipped his disciples into action against "the peculiar institution" of the south. William Lloyd Garrison (1805–79) established his Boston newspaper *The Liberator* in 1831. It was committed to the immediate emancipation of all humans held in bondage and was vitriolic in the abuse it heaped on slaveholders. The New England Anti-Slavery Society, formed in 1832, within a year became the American Anti-Slavery Society and spread over the north, stirring sentiment in favor of uncompensated emancipation. The movement that plunged the nation into civil war was launched here.

Garrison and his followers were opposed by milder men, led by William Ellery Channing, who favored legal, peaceful methods of freeing slaves. Respectable society became alarmed lest the agitation check the flow of cotton from the south, on which the Massachusetts textile industry depended. Garrison's movement attracted John Quincy Adams, Wendell Phillips, John Greenleaf Whittier, and later outstanding Massachusetts men and women. Abolitionists strongly opposed the Fugitive Slave Act and established "Underground Railroad" stations to hurry escaping slaves to freedom in Canada. They organized the New England Emigrant Aid Company, which vainly tried to win Kansas for the north by peopling it with freedom-loving individuals who would bar slavery from that territory.

MEXICAN WAR

The Mexican War (1846–48), thought many Bay Staters, was fought solely to extend slavery into new territories. The state supplied 1057 men. Thirty were casualties.

Henry Thoreau (1817–62) correctly saw the war as being fought to bring in more slave states. He was jailed for refusing to pay his poll tax which he said would be used to defray the cost of a morally unjustifiable war.

COME THE CELTS

The late 1840's and 50's saw a steady stream of Irish Catholics pour into the commonwealth. Boston would soon become predominately Celtic and Catholic. Massachusetts Protestants, alarmed by this alien invasion, gave their vote in the 1854 election to the American Party (Know-Nothings) pledged to check immigration and to combat Roman Catholicism. The newly formed Republican Party and its presidential candidate John C. Fremont with his antislavery program received the Bay State's electoral votes in 1856. Lincoln carried the state in 1860.

"WE'RE COMING, FATHER ABRAHAM."

Massachusetts citizens, despite previously overwhelming anti-Abolitionist sentiment, considered the Civil War almost as a holy war — a war to end slavery and to preserve the Union. Forgotten was the War of 1812 era when Massachusetts merchant princes supported the 1814 Hartford Convention at which it was proposed that New England secede from the Union.

Early in 1861 Gov. John A. Andrew (1818–67) evoked laughter and cries of "waste" when he ordered new overcoats for Massachusetts militiamen. Later that same year, militiamen along the cold damp Potomac were thankful for Andrew's farsightedness.

On April 15, the day after Maj. Robert Anderson hauled down the flag at Fort Sumter, S.C., Secretary of War Simon Cameron wired Gov. Andrew to mobilize three militia infantry regiments. Andrew, looking ahead, ordered up four regiments: Third (New Bedford), Fourth (Quincy), Sixth (Pepperell) and Eighth (Lynn). Three regiments were ready to leave by 6 P.M. the following day. Meanwhile Cameron ordered up the Quincy Regiment, and Andrew called a fifth regiment.

The Sixth Massachusetts arrived in Baltimore, April 19. Seven of the ten companies were transferred across town to the Washington Depot by horsecars. Meanwhile patriotic, southern sympathizers mobbed the final three companies with rocks. Four Bay Staters were killed and 36 wounded. This incident, the first blood spilled in the

Civil War, occurred 86 years from the day in April 1775 when Lobsterbacks fired on Minutemen in Lexington and Concord.

The first call was for 3736 men to serve for three months. Before Appomattox Courthouse, Massachusetts furnished 122,781 white troops, 3966 black troops and 19,983 sailors. Many Bay Staters enlisted from other states and are not included in these figures. Massachusetts exceeded her four-year quota by more than 30,000 men. Bay State casualties were 13,942.

"MINE EYES HAVE SEEN THE COMING"

The Civil War was a musical mix-up. Stirring "Dixie" — the battle song of the Confederacy — was written by a New Yorker. The music of the mighty "Battle Hymn of the Republic" was taken from a southern camp meeting song. Massachusetts militiamen stationed in Boston picked up the tune from U.S. Regulars who had learned it while on duty in the prewar south. Meanwhile, Gov. Andrew sent Dr. Samuel Gridley Howe to inspect Bay State troops stationed around Washington. His wife, Julia, first heard the tune while watching Massachusetts troops parade through the city. That night she could not sleep. Memory of the tune kept her awake. She lit the kerosene lamp in her hotel room and sat down to compose the words of this nation's greatest marching song — with the possible exception of "Dixie."

"GRAPES OF WRATH"

Massachusetts men participated in most major battles of the war. Sound the roll call for the Second Massachusetts Infantry Regiment: Winchester, Cedar Mountain, Antietam, Chancellorsville — Lee lost his good right arm, Stonewall Jackson, here — Gettysburg, Resaca, Atlanta, The March to the Sea, Savannah, Sherman's Carolina Campaign.

Look at the 20th Massachusetts: Ball's Bluff, Fair Oaks, Glendale, Malvern Hill, Antietam, Fredericksburg, Marye's Heights, Gettysburg, Bristoe Station, the Wilderness, Spotsylvania Courthouse, Cold Harbor, Petersburg, Appomattox Courthouse.

Hadley native "Fighting Joe" Hooker (1814–79), successor of inept Gen. Ambrose Burnside as commander of the Army of the Potomac, unfortunately did not live up to his "Fighting" handle. He was succeeded by able Gen. George Gordon Meade. Hooker redeemed himself at Lookout Mountain in the Battle of the Clouds.

Charles Francis Adams (1807–86), a Bay State native, helped keep England out of the Civil War during his service as U.S. Minister to England. He was the son of President John Quincy Adams, a grandson of President John Adams and the father of historians Henry (1838–1918) and Brooks (1848–1927) Adams.

INDUSTRY'S INCREASE

Appomattox closed a chapter in American life. Exports temporarily declined with monotonous regularity, but imports were of consequence. Massachusetts was not a distributor beyond the confines of New England, but its industries required a constantly increasing amount of raw materials. The great white sails which once left Salem and New Bedford were never succeeded by dirty steamer funnels. Only Boston remained a vital shipping and reshipping point. Fishing thrived but a new economy had begun. Improved steel production methods and petroleum development assured the success of the new industrialism, but it ended the great whaling days. War and whaling disasters hastened the decline. Now that whale oil was no longer in demand, a few diehard whalers pursued the bowhead whale whose bones provided corset stays — and even these were eventually doomed. The glamor of whaling ships, like that of clippers, faded into legend, but a supply of fluid capital had been created which poured into western railroads and local industries.

Massachusett's industrial evolution is the economic history of the nation in miniature. Manufacturing, like people, was drawn by the magnet of the west with its cheap or free land and greater opportunities. Massachusetts, however, remained preeminent in several fields until the century ended. More than one third of the nation's woolen production came from Bay State mills. During the eighties Fall River led the nation in cotton manufacture, while Lawrence, Lowell and New Bedford were close rivals. New Bedford, partly because of its mild climate, became famed for its cotton goods while northern New England mills developed heavier fabrics. Lawrence, by 1890, was the third largest cotton-producing city in the nation, and Lowell was a close fourth.

The shoe industry made considerable progress, and with technological advances in power production the industry's importance increased substantially. Lynn factories in 1866 produced $12,000,000 worth of shoes. Twenty-four years later the annual output was $26,000,000.

Brockton, Haverhill, Marlborough and Worcester were also among the nation's leading shoe production centers. Massachusetts resisted serious shoe competition from New York and St. Louis, until after 1900 when much of the nation's shoe output began to be produced outside the commonwealth.

SUMMER FRACAS OF '98

The summer affair with the Spanish in 1898 was short, but a reported 20,000 Massachusetts men were in the services, though few saw combat. The Second Massachusetts Infantry went to Cuba where, attached to the Second Cavalry Brigade, it fought at San Juan Hill.

The Sixth Massachusetts Infantry Regiment, remembering its four dead and 36 wounded when it was transported through the city in 1861, requested and received permission from the War Department to follow the same route through Baltimore that it had taken in '61. The volunteers were fed and flower-bedecked by Baltimoreans. The regiment saw no action during its occupation duty in Cuba and Puerto Rico. The Ninth Massachusetts Infantry, however, lost 177 men in its 18 days at the front.

The Cuban and Puerto Rican pacification campaigns, together with the Philippine Insurrection and Boxer Rebellion, were the last overseas duties performed by Massachusetts fighting units. Some Bay Staters served with General Pershing on his punitive expedition to Mexico against Pancho Villa in 1916.

"OVER THERE"

In the First World War, Massachusetts soldiers, like those of many other states, were disappointed when they could not serve in their own distinctive state organizations. The Yankee (26th) Division, however, was composed of New Englanders and was commanded by Bay State resident, Maj. Gen. Clarence Edwards (1860–1931). The first shot fired by an American outfit in France was reportedly made by Battery A, 101st Field Artillery, 26th Division. Bloodied at Apremont, the Division suffered 25 percent casualties at Château-Thierry.

Many Bay Staters served with the 82nd Division which was composed largely of southerners. The state contributed several specialist outfits, the 14th and 33rd Engineers, 317th Field Signal Battalion. The 401st Telegraph Battalion was organized by the New England Telephone and Telegraph Company. Base Hospital Unit #5, commanded by great brain surgeon Dr. Harvey Cushing, operated a 2000-bed hospital.

The Bay State sent an estimated 200,000 men to war. Only 83,220 were draftees. More than 5200 men were killed in action or died from wounds or disease.

More than 100,000 soldiers including doughboys from the other Yankee states were trained at Camp Devens near Ayer. Boston Navy Yard outfitted and repaired ships. New ships were built in the Fore River Shipyards, Quincy. Springfield manufactured several hundred thousand M1903 Springfield rifles with which many doughboys were armed. Several hundred million rounds of caliber 30 cartridges were made in the U.S. Cartridge Company's Lowell plant. Smith and Wesson, Springfield, made more than 150,000 M1917 caliber 45 revolvers. The Mills textile plant, Worcester, made several million pistol belts and rifle cartridge belts. The National Fireworks Company, Hanover, provided the ingredients for tracer and incendiary cartridges. Shoes and uniforms were made by many Bay State firms.

BOSTON POLICE STRIKE

In August, 1919, the Boston Social Club, an organization of 1290 Boston police, joined the American Federation of Labor in a body. The patrolmen complained that their wages failed to keep pace with the cost of living, that the police stations were unsanitary and that they worked overtime without compensation. Police Commissioner Edwin U. Curtis issued an order on August 11 forbidding members of the police force to "join any organization outside the department except posts of the G.A.R., Spanish War Veterans, and American Legion." Despite this order, on August 15 the Boston Social Club was chartered as the Policemen's Union under the A.F. of L., and the Boston Central Labor Union, representing 80,000 organized workers, assured the new union of its support. Commissioner Curtis preferred charges against eight policemen; as sole judge, he passed on the validity of the ruling he had issued, and, declining to hear counsel for the policemen in rebuttal, found the men guilty. The Policemen's Union thereupon called a strike, to become effective at the hour of the evening roll call on September 9. Only 30 of the 420 patrolmen due at that roll call appeared. A citizens' committee, appointed as an arbitrating body, stated that "the Boston Policemen's Union should not affiliate or be connected with any labor organization," but urged that "the present wages, hours, and working conditions require material adjustment."

Striking patrolmen placed 20 pickets at each police station. Mayor Peters called on "all citizens to do their part to assist the authorities in maintaining order." Governor Calvin Coolidge called out 100 state police. President Lowell of Harvard appealed to students "to prepare themselves for such services as the governor may call upon them to render." Dean Greenough organized an "emergency committee." Coach Fisher was reported by the press as having declared, "To hell with football if men are needed." "Come back from your vacations, young men," a press release credited Professor Hall of the Physics Department of Harvard with saying, "there is sport and diversion for you right here in Boston."

Sympathetic citizens gathered around police stations to cheer the strikers and boo patrolmen who remained on duty. Guardsmen opened fire with rifles and a machine gun on a cheering crowd of sympathizers in South Boston, killing two boys and wounding several bystanders, and in Scollay Square, cavalry charged on a crowd, shot a woman and killed a man. Metropolitan Park (state) policemen thereafter refused to go on further strike duty, were suspended and joined the union. The possibility of a sympathetic general strike neared. Hoodlums came into Boston from nearby cities and towns. President McInnis of the Policemen's Union placed responsibility for rioting and looting on Commissioner Curtis. Mayor Peters blamed Governor Coolidge for not acting. Coolidge offered an "implied rebuke" of Peters. By September 11 seven people had been killed and more than 60 wounded. Volunteer policemen — vigilantes — were called out. The press reported that E. B. McGill was shot and killed by trigger-happy guardsmen as he was walking along Howard Street. Crap-shooting Henry Grote was killed in Jamaica Plain. A striking patrolman was killed while attempting to disarm two special policemen.

Governor Coolidge wired A.F. of L. President Samuel Gompers, "There is no right to strike against the public safety by anybody, anywhere, any time." Gompers ordered the strikers back to work. Union members, deserted by their national leadership, voted to return to work. There were no jobs awaiting them. A new force was on duty and the defeated strikers sought jobs elsewhere.

"KEEP COOL WITH COOLIDGE"

Coolidge's telegram brought him into the national spotlight and in that "smoke-filled Chicago hotel room" he gained the GOP vice-presidential nomination as Harding's running mate.

In August 1923, President Harding died after a short illness. Coolidge succeeded to the presidency. He was visiting his aged father, a Justice of the Peace, at his birthplace in Plymouth, Vermont, when the news of Harding's death reached him. He was sworn into the presidency by his father that night by the light of a kerosene lamp. This scene, so homely and so typically democratic, captured the imagination of the American people as no other connected with the presidency had since the days of Abraham Lincoln. Not since Lincoln, in fact, had there been a President so essentially homespun as Coolidge was. Those commentators who have expressed the belief that Calvin Coolidge's Yankee terseness, simple ways, and oft-repeated love of both the rigors and the beauties of his native state were a part of a sustained political pose are deluded by their own sophistication. In 1924, Coolidge was elected President.

Coolidge was the most popular GOP president in American history. Let the record speak: Coolidge in his 1924 race against Democrat John Davis racked up a 2–1 popular vote margin. The popular vote was Coolidge: 15,725,016 — Davis: 8,385,586. Electoral vote, Coolidge: 382 — Davis: 136. Roosevelt's most popular vote percentage was considerably less than dour "Silent Cal's" impressive 2–1.

Coolidge was the first Massachusetts resident to attain the presidency since John Quincy Adams. Because of his economies and brief speech, he has become a greater figure in American folklore than many more able presidents.

"THE SHAME OF MASSACHUSETTS"

—ELIOT PAUL

In 1920 two Italians, Bartolomeo Vanzetti, "a poor fish peddler," and Nicola Sacco, "a good shoemaker," were arrested and charged with the murder of a paymaster and guard during the course of a $13,000 payroll robbery in South Braintree. The two men, who spoke no English, though they later learned it in prison, were tried before Judge Webster Thayer in Dedham. The prosecution relied mainly on eyewitnesses, some of whom remembered more at the trial than they did immediately after the crime. Despite good alibis the two men were convicted.

The conviction took place in an atmosphere redolent of the later-day Sen. Joseph McCarthy's "Red Scares." Attorney General Alexander Mitchell Palmer and investigator John Edgar Hoover were determined to rid the country of foreign-born radicals. Many were arrested and thrown into jail and some were deported on the "Soviet Ark." Later careful investigation by the Senate showed that many were innocent of wrongdoing. It told against Sacco and Vanzetti that they were not only foreigners but had evaded military service in WWI. They were opposed to violence and to organized government.

The two men waited in prison or jail for seven years before the death sentence was pronounced April 9, 1927. The loot was never found; and the firearms evidence was suspect. Judge Thayer, during the trial but outside the courthouse, stated he would get "those anarchist bastards." Repeated attempts to get a new trial were futile. Hundreds of thousands of people became convinced that the two men were innocent and that they were political martyrs. New England Yankees did not like them because they were foreigners and political radicals. Catholics did not like them because they had rejected the religion of their fathers. Men like future U.S. Supreme Court Justice Felix Frankfurter, then a Harvard Law School professor, argued their innocence on the basis of evidence or the lack of it.

There was considerable evidence, including a confession by a gang member, that the crime had been committed by the Morelli gang of Providence. This evidence was not accepted. There were demonstrations throughout the world in the condemned men's behalf.

Governor Alvan T. Fuller appointed a three-man panel to study the evidence. They were Harvard President A. Lawrence Lowell, Judge Robert Grant and MIT President Samuel W. Stratton. Their report criticized Judge Thayer's intemperate remarks but it adjudged the verdict a correct one. Some have thought that those able, honest men could not overcome their inbred dislike of radicals and foreigners. The two men were executed August 23, 1927. More than a hundred books, plays, movies and poems — and even a record and many paintings — have been done about Sacco and Vanzetti, and their guilt or innocence is violently argued even today.

DEPRESSION AND RECOVERY

Industrial and financial Massachusetts was hit hard by the Depression. Several hundred thousand workers were unemployed as mills and factories closed for want of purchasers for their products. Psychologically, the vast number of proud but often poorly paid and unorganized white-collar workers suffered the most. Many people lost their entire life's savings when banks closed and failed to reopen.

The state and its people began their long, slow climb to prosperity with newly elected President Franklin D. Roosevelt's "New Deal."

Federal funds poured into the commonwealth, and the long line of alphabet agencies, despite mistakes, fed hungry, jobless people, put them on the road to recovery with jobs, and, most important of all, helped hundreds of thousands to regain their self-esteem.

WORLD WAR II

Five hundred and fifty thousand Bay Staters volunteered or were drafted for service in World War II. Casualties were a reported 16,500. Fort Devens was an induction and basic training center. Camp Edwards — now Otis Air Force Base — was a training camp and later a German POW camp. Boston Naval Shipyard was a ship-outfitting and repair center. Italian POW camps were located outside Boston. Chelsea Naval Hospital treated wounded and injured sailors including Lt. (jg) John F. Kennedy. Springfield Armory together with Harrington and Richardson, Worcester, manufactured M1 (Garand) rifles. Smith and Wesson, Springfield, made revolvers for the Air Force, Navy and our British Allies. Savage Arms, Chicopee, made Thompson submachine guns. Harrington and Richardson made Reising submachine guns for the Marine Corps. Lawley's and Fore River Shipyards built PC's, LCI's and other warcraft. Electronic firms like Raytheon made radar equipment. MIT and Harvard conducted research in many fields.

THE CONTEMPORARY SCENE

V–J Day was shortly followed by a mass movement of many industries to Dixie where tax benefits, cash inducements and cheaper hired hands were available. This was particularly true in the textile industry. Fortunately — and this was largely due to the Harvard and MIT brain pool — research, development and manufacturing facilities established themselves in the area, notably along Boston's periphery — Route 128.

The missile and space programs brought further prosperity to Massachusetts though in 1970 deflation resulted in severe cutbacks and unemployment in the space, missile and electronics industries.

When she was Boston School Committee chairman, the ebullient Louise Day Hicks gained national notoriety when for several years she denied that *de facto* segregation existed in Boston schools.

Massachusetts public schools and colleges, like those elsewhere in the nation, are overcrowded. Harvard and MIT, however, despite current riots and upheavals, maintain their roles as the world's leading universities, in their respective disciplines.

In the early 1960's the National Aeronautics and Space Administration (NASA), realizing the vast brain pool of Harvard and MIT together with the concentration of electronic research and production facilities in the Cambridge area, decided to build a $61,000,000 Electronics Research Center there. After a prolonged row with property owners and local politicians over land prices and location the center was nearing completion when in late 1969 NASA announced the center would be closed for lack of funds.

One-time governor John Volpe, now Secretary of Transportation, announced that his department would use the center for transportation research and that nearly 80 percent of the 700 employees would be retained.

THE KENNEDY YEARS

The triumphs and tragedies of the Kennedy clan sparked the history of the '60's. Ambassador Joseph P. Kennedy (1888–1969) had the proud and tragic experience of having one son, John Fitzgerald Kennedy (1917–1963), who became president, and two more, Senator Robert Francis Kennedy (1925–1968) and his eldest, Joseph P. Kennedy, Jr. (1914–1944), killed before they could make the challenge. The fourth son, Edward M. Kennedy (b. 1932), became one of Massachusetts' senators in Washington in 1962.

The Kennedy years saw a host of bright young able public servants appear on the public scene. Governor Endicott Peabody, governor 1963–64; Lawrence Francis O'Brien, currently national chairman of the Democratic Party; former presidential aide Kenneth O'Donnell; historian Arthur M. Schlesinger, Jr. Liberal Republican Edward William Brooke, Massachusetts attorney general from 1962 to 1966, is the only Negro in the United States Senate. These men and their lesser known colleagues carry much of the future of the Commonwealth and country on their shoulders.

7

Government

PRESIDENTS JOHN ADAMS (1735–1826), John Quincy Adams (1767–1848), Calvin Coolidge (1872–1933) and John F. Kennedy (1917–63) went directly from Massachusetts to the White House. Three non-natives who were Harvard graduates reached the White House: Rutherford B. Hayes (1822–93) who graduated from the law school after receiving a degree from Kenyon College (Ohio), Theodore Roosevelt (1858–1919) and Franklin D. Roosevelt (1882–1945).

John Adams, Elbridge Gerry (1837–1927) and Calvin Coolidge were vice presidents. Gerry gave us the political phrase "gerrymandering," meaning to juggle election districts for the advantage of a particular party.

CABINET

George Washington had plump Maj. General Henry Knox (1750–1806), onetime Boston bookseller and wartime chief of artillery, as secretary of war from 1785 to 1794 and Samuel Osgood (1748–1813) as postmaster general from 1789 to 1791. Former postmaster general (1965–68) Lawrence Francis O'Brien (b. 1917), special assistant to President John F. Kennedy, is a Springfield native.

John Quincy Adams (1817–25), Daniel Webster (1841–43 and 1850–52), Edward Everett (1852–53), Richard Olney (1895–97) and former governor and congressman Christian Herter (1959–61) were secretaries of state.

Samuel Dexter (1801) and George Boutwell (1869–73) were secretaries of the treasury.

Maritime Massachusetts supplied secretaries of the navy: Benjamin W. Crowninshield (1814–18), David Henshaw (1843–44), historian George Bancroft (1845–46), William H. Moody (1902–04), George von L. Meyer (1909–13) and Charles Francis Adams (1929–33).

United States attorneys general from Massachusetts have ranged from Levi Lincoln (1801–04) through Robert F. Kennedy (1961–64). In between were Caleb Cushing (1853–57), Ebenezer R. Hoar (1869–70), Gen. Charles Devens (1877–81), Richard Olney (1893–

95) and William H. Moody (1904–06). Olney broke the Pullman strike at the request of the Railroad Trust.

George von L. Meyer served as postmaster general (1907–09). William F. Whiting (1928–29) and Sinclair Weeks (1953–58) were secretaries of commerce. Maurice Tobin, onetime governor and mayor of Boston, was secretary of labor (1949–53).

Onetime Boston *Herald* newsman George Cabot Lodge, great grandson of U.S. Senator Henry Cabot Lodge and son of onetime U.S. Senator and former ambassador to South Vietnam Henry Cabot Lodge, served as assistant secretary of labor for international affairs.

Henry Cabot Lodge, better known as Cabot Lodge to distinguish him from his grandfather, was defeated for reelection to his Senate seat in 1952 by Congressman John F. Kennedy. In 1962 George Cabot Lodge was defeated in his first race for the U.S. Senate by Edward M. Kennedy.

The first Republican secretary of transportation and the second such secretary in our history — the post was created by Congress October 15, 1966 — is construction magnate and former governor John Anthony Volpe (b. 1908). Former federal highway commissioner (1956–57), Volpe was a member of the Massachusetts Public Works Commission (1953–56) and GOP governor 1961–63 and 1965–69. Volpe was the first Bay state governor elected to a four-year term.

Former Massachusetts lieutenant governor (1964–68) Elliot Richardson was U.S. assistant secretary for legislation in the Department of Health, Education and Welfare. He became assistant secretary of state in 1969 and is now secretary of Health, Education and Welfare.

EARLY GOVERNMENT

On reaching Cape Cod in December of 1620, the Pilgrims established Massachusetts' earliest government at The Colony of New Plymouth. Before landing, they drew up the Mayflower Compact, which pledged allegiance to the king but established majority rule as the form of government. Valid title to the lands was secured through the patents of 1621 and 1630, issued by the Council for New England. Under the Mayflower Compact, the governor was elected annually by the people. His assistants, also elected, helped govern and acted as the judiciary. All freemen were admitted to the General Court until 1639, when, because of increased population, deputies were elected. John Carver, the first governor, died in 1621 and was succeeded by William Bradford, who, except for five years, governed until his death in 1657.

The people voted for a constitutional convention, which convened in Cambridge in September 1779. James Bowdoin presided. John Adams drew up the constitution.

Massachusetts, today, is the only state governed under its original constitution. The constitution has endured solely because of its flexible character. It was the first document to boldly establish the principle of the separation of powers, *i.e.,* executive, legislative and judicial. It assures the protection of stated inalienable rights. An important provision is the right of the governor, the council and the legislature to require opinions from the Supreme Judicial Court. Other notable provisions are the removal of judges by address and the inapplicability of martial laws to citizens except by consent of the legislature.

THE TOWN

The town was the earliest government unit. It was not for some century and a half that there was a formal statute declaring the town "a body politic and corporate," capable of suing and being sued; yet early in the history of the colony the town became a self-governing unit — a miniature republic. Travel difficulties, the dangers of leaving frontier farms open to Indian pillage, and inveterate distrust of arbitrary power favor local independence. The General Court at Boston among its first actions granted the scattered infant towns incorporation and the right to make regulations, although at first these applied only to stray swine. Towns slowly assumed local authority.

Town growth was so vigorous between the formal end of the colony and the beginning of the province (1682–94) that the town organization and privileges were recognized by the crown. Andros' efforts to tax towns, command public assemblies and interfere with the town meetings were major factors in arousing the people to depose him. Convinced of the inalienability of their right to self-rule, towns successfully demanded that the 1691 provincial charter granted by William and Mary be amended to include self-rule for towns.

In the 18th century, town growth was spasmodic because of Indian perils. Tax lists show 111 towns in 1715, 156 in 1742, 199 in 1768 and 239 in 1780. The General Court passed a law by which persons who abandoned their town forfeited their estates.

The same passion for self-rule displayed during Andros' time prompted towns to embrace the principles of the Revolution. They voted to support the Declaration of Independence and provided supplies, ammunition and bounties for volunteers. The towns, impelled by the ideals of self-government, were the backbone of the revolt.

The 1780 constitution, after 150 years of doubt, confirmed local autonomy. A 1786 act named elective officers and provided the rights to assess taxes, make bylaws and punish offenders. Voters were guaranteed the right to place a proposed article in a town meeting notice or even to compel a justice of the peace to hold a special town meeting. By 1790 there were about 300 towns with a total of about 400,000 people.

CITIES

An 1820 constitutional amendment gave the General Court the right to charter cities. Two years later Boston, which had made five attempts since 1784 to discard the town system, was incorporated. The genesis of city government was in the Colonial chartered borough. New York in 1686 had the first borough charter modeled on the English community corporation. The Mayor and council or aldermen acted as opposing checks.

At first council committees handled matters like public works and water supply, but separate departments were finally created for such purposes. Wherever a mayor secured the veto power, the council declined in importance. Inefficiency, laxity in enforcing state laws, squandering of public funds and poor policing led to increasing state interference in the years preceding the Civil War. After the Civil War, towns continued to shift to city government. In 1865 there were 14 cities and in 1875, 19, with more than 50 percent of the population. In 1885 there were 23 cities with 60 percent of the population.

As immigration rose, general optimism prevailed. With the population interested in business rather than civic pursuits, public debts, inefficiency and the spoils system flourished. By 1900 city government reform was a major issue. Many towns of increasing population sought to discover a modified town system and avoid city organization with its maze of problems.

By the Optional Charter Law of 1915, the Massachusetts Legislature, which has authority to grant or annul a city charter, made four choices possible: mayor and council elected at-large, mayor and council elected partially by wards and at-large, the commission form or city manager form. The system of providing a charter by special acts is followed, thus theoretically basing each charter on each community's particular needs.

The city form has not appealed to many large towns. In 1915 Brookline adopted the limited or representative town meeting to regulate its size. Any citizen may speak, but only elected representatives may vote. Watertown followed this example in 1919, Arlington in 1921 and about twelve others up to the present date.

THE COUNTY

The county system was first patterned after the English model familiar to first settlers. Its organization here was chiefly for judicial purposes. In the west, as in the English counties in Saxon days, the county has developed legislative powers, but in the Bay State towns and cities, some of whose officers are today county commissioners, were too strong to permit it. The first counties were organized in 1643 as Suffolk, Middlesex, Essex and Norfolk. By the Revolution, 12 of the present 14 counties were in existence. Franklin was organized in 1811 and Hampden, the last, in 1812. Early officers were appointed. After the Revolution, most of them became elective.

In Nantucket County (which is the same as Nantucket Island and Nantucket Town) selectmen serve as county commissioners. The town treasurer is the county treasurer. In Boston the mayor and city council together with the board of aldermen of Chelsea, Revere's city council and Winthrop's selectmen serve as Suffolk County commissioners.

County officers include county commissioners, judge of probate and insolvency, register of probate and insolvency, sheriff, clerk of courts, treasurer, registrar of deeds, masters in chancery and public administrators.

The county, today, is an obsolete institution. Modern transportation has made obsolete the county jail. Some government authorities advocate the replacement of county jails with regional jails each of which would serve several of the present counties. The same holds true for courts and other county institutions and offices.

THE GOVERNOR

Plymouth Colony's six governors served 72 one-year terms between 1620–1692. The first was John Carver (1620–21), and the last was Thomas Hinckley (1681–92). Governor William Bradford served 31 annual terms. Governors in this period were elected by the people, *i.e.,* members of the Congregational Church.

Laws are supposed to be administered by the governor with the aid of his council. The governor actually has a dual rôle: he heads a political party, and he originates much legislation. With this practice of inspiring legislation and with an enormous amount of patronage under his control, the governor's position is no longer one merely of dignity and honor, but of constantly increasing power.

Under the colonial charter, all governors save the first were elected by the people for a one-year term. James II, before he was deposed, broke this procedure. Thereafter, under the charter of William and Mary, the governor was subject to appointment by the Crown. He became vice-regal, a military figure with power to prorogue or dissolve the General Court. Since 1780 the governor has been elected at-large. John Hancock was elected six terms. A majority vote was required, resulting in 1855 in a change to a plurality vote after the election had several times been forced into the General Court for selection of the winner.

From 1917 to 1966 the governor's term was two years instead of one. Since 1966, as result of a 1964 referendum, governors are elected for four-year terms. The governor's present salary is $35,000. There is no executive mansion.

The governor is commander-in-chief of the state's militia and naval forces. With advice of the council he may prorogue the House and Senate and appoint all judicial officers, may appoint and remove state department heads and exercises the power of pardon for every verdict but impeachment.

GOVERNOR'S COUNCIL

Massachusetts, together with Maine and New Hampshire, retains a governor's council. The seven assistants to Plymouth Colony's governors were the ancestors of the present council which was shorn of some power after a 1964 referendum.

The council has been attacked on the grounds that it is a dispensable colonial relic, that it makes impossible a concentration of responsibility, that its pardon proceedings are secret, that its revision of sentences is prejudicial to the courts, that its work could be performed by the Senate and on the grounds of economy. It has been defended as a check on the power of the governor, and for the reason that numerous duties now performed by it would otherwise have to be delegated elsewhere.

THE GENERAL COURT

The legislature in Massachusetts is known as the General Court, although it has long since created courts for the state's judicial affairs. Today the General Court is exclusively a lawmaking body. Bicameral, it consists of a lower popular body, the House of Representatives, over which the speaker presides, and a smaller upper body, the State Senate, over which the president presides.

The first General Court under the constitution met in Boston on October 25, 1780. The number of its members varied considerably. At times it had more than 400. The establishment of Maine as a separate state reduced the number, but it was not until 1857 that a constitutional amendment fixed it at the present membership of 240 for the House and 40 for the Senate.

Most states have biennial sessions, but Massachusetts retains annual sessions. Under the right of free petition, any commonwealth citizen, by requesting either a representative or senator, may introduce a petition to alter or abolish an old law, or establish a new one.

The General Court meets annually in January. Members are paid $11,400 annually plus limited expenses. In recent years Democrats have outnumbered Republicans by a 3–1 margin in both House and Senate. In early 1971 the annual salary was still being debated.

THE JUDICIARY

Originally all malefactors were brought before the General Court at Boston. This resulted in such delays that in 1635 the General Court established courts at Ipswich, Salem, Newtowne and Boston. In 1699 county courts were set up and a Supreme Court of Judicature established. This became the Supreme Judicial Court in 1780 and still exists today as the state's highest court. It has had a continuous existence longer than any court in the U.S.

The Supreme Judicial Court has a chief justice and six associate justices. Not only is it the state's highest court of appeal; it can give advisory opinions on the constitutionality of forthcoming legislation.

Next in rank is the Superior Court, with 46 justices. This court holds civil, criminal, and equity sessions in the various counties. If a trial by jury is in order, the case will probably come before this court.

Within each county are 73 district courts, including the Municipal

Court of Boston. They have original jurisdiction in criminal and civil cases. In general, cases are decided in these courts without benefit of jury. Three appellate courts hear appeals from district courts.

In addition to these, there are the specialized Land Court and Probate Court.

Small claims cases, where the amount involved is less than $300 and no lawyer is needed, come before the district courts. Massachusetts was the first state (1920) to set up a statewide system for rendering this form of justice. Another first credited to Massachusetts: the first statewide system of public defenders to provide lawyers for persons unable to pay for them. The state also pioneered in juvenile courts. The Boston Juvenile Court was created in 1906 and Boston, Springfield and Worcester now have separate juvenile courts. In other places, district courts hold separate sessions for juvenile cases involving persons 14 to 17.

The U.S. First Circuit Court of Appeals — jurisdiction, Maine, Massachusetts, New Hampshire, Rhode Island and Puerto Rico — sits in Boston. So does the U.S. District Court for the Commonwealth of Massachusetts.

Seven Bay State jurists have served on the U.S. Supreme Court. Among them was U.S. Supreme Court Justice Oliver Wendell Holmes (1841–1935), regarded by many Americans at the time of his death as their number one citizen. He served on the Supreme Judicial Court of Massachusetts from 1882 to 1902, on the U.S. Supreme Court from 1902 to 1932. Holmes came to the bench when the country was torn between the property rights of employers and the human rights of workers.

"A constitution," Holmes noted, "is not intended to embody a particular economic theory whether of paternalism . . . or of *laissez faire.* It is made for people of fundamentally differing views, and the accident of our finding certain opinions natural and familiar or novel and even shocking ought not to conclude our judgment upon the question whether statutes embodying them conflict with the Constitution of the United States . . . Constitutional law, like other moral contrivances, has to take some chances . . . The Constitution is an experiment, as all life is an experiment."

Holmes' decisions, many of them dissents, played a major role in shaping American judicial and social-economic history.

Four jurists were natives of the state. Earliest was Scituate native William Cushing (1732–1810), the first associate justice named to the court. Cushing was president of the state convention which ratified the U.S. Constitution.

Joseph Story (1779–1845) upheld the sanctity of contracts in the famed *Charles River Bridge* vs. *Warren Bridge* case. Story founded Harvard Law School and published noted legal commentaries. He and Chancellor James Kent founded America's equity system. He served on the Supreme Court from 1811 until his death in 1845.

Horace Gray (1828–1902) served on the Supreme Judicial Court of Massachusetts (1864–81) and on the U.S. Supreme Court (1881–1902). He founded the noted law firm — it still exists — of Ropes & Gray.

William H. Moody (1853–1917) was on the U.S. Supreme Court (1906–10) after having served as a GOP congressman, secretary of the navy, and attorney-general. He was a noted "trust buster."

Native Kentuckian Louis D. Brandeis (1856–1941) was the first Jew appointed to the Supreme Court; this Wilson appointment was carried despite much opposition. He was a Zionist and noted liberal.

Austrian-born Felix Frankfurter (1882–1965) was a leading defender of Sacco and Vanzetti and a longtime personal adviser to President Franklin D. Roosevelt. He was appointed to the Supreme Court in 1939.

8

Education

FRANKLIN D. ROOSEVELT, shortly after his first inauguration (1933), visited recently retired Justice Oliver Wendell Holmes, Jr. The justice was reading Plato.

"Why do you read Plato, Mr. Justice?" Roosevelt asked.

"To improve my mind," replied the 92-year-old Holmes.

Yankees have always been great on "improving the mind," and Massachusetts Yankees pioneered American education. Boston Latin (1635) was the first public school in America. Roxbury Latin (1645) was one of the first private schools in America. Both schools are still in existence. The present public school system in America was conceived by Bay Stater Horace Mann (1796–1859).

Some Yankees left the New Canaan they had so mightily labored to create in the wilderness. They fared forth to found new beacons of learning throughout the land. In 1746 Hatfield native and Presbyterian preacher Jonathan Dickinson founded the College of New Jersey in Elizabeth Town. The school soon moved to another site and took the name of its new town—Princeton. Yale, of course, was founded (1701) by Harvard men. Horace Mann, the Bay State's first commissioner of public education, founded the state's common school educational system—which was followed by many other states—and then went on to found Antioch College (1852) in Yellow Springs, Ohio.

THE PREACHING TEACHING ELIOTS

"Praying John" Eliot (1604–90) tried to educate Massachusetts Indians. His descendant William G. Eliot (1811–87) of New Bedford founded the first Congregational Church in Catholic St. Louis. He organized the St. Louis public school system and founded Eliot Seminary (1853), now Washington University.

Charles William Eliot (1834–1926) entered Harvard in 1849 when the struggling college had 350 students. He was Harvard president for 40 years (1869–1909) and introduced the elective system and brought the college into the ranks of the world's great universities. Unfortunately, he is known to most non-Harvard Americans only as the editor of the famed "Five Foot Shelf of Harvard Classics."

HIGHER EDUCATION

Massachusetts is blessed with Harvard (see CAMBRIDGE), America's oldest (1636), wealthiest (assets: $1,000,000,000 plus) and one of the greatest of the world's universities.

Massachusetts Institute of Technology (MIT) is probably the world's foremost technological complex (see CAMBRIDGE).

Williams and Amherst are small first-rate colleges.

Northeastern University (1898), Boston, the state's largest college with 41,000 full-time, part-time and night students and 1600 faculty members, ranks eighteenth nationally in student enrollment. The university has a law school.

Boston University (1869) started out as a Methodist theological school in Newbury, Vt. The college, today, is essentially nondenominational. There are about 23,000 students and 1600 faculty members. The five graduate schools are in law, medicine, education, theology and physical education.

Tufts University in Medford, which was chartered in 1852 and became a university in 1955, has medical and dental schools. Its Fletcher School of Law and Diplomacy was the first of its kind in the country. Part of this school is the Edward R. Murrow Center of Public Affairs. Tufts has about 5100 students and 600 faculty members.

Clark University (1887), Worcester, with about 2900 students and 250 faculty members, is noted for its advanced course in geography.

Brandeis University (1947), Waltham, named after noted jurist and Justice of the Supreme Court of the United States Louis D. Brandeis (1856–1941), is noted for its fine faculty and the seriousness of its 2200 students. Faculty members number about 400.

American International College (1885), Springfield, founded by the YMCA, has 3000 students and about 125 faculty members.

Suffolk University (1906), Boston, offers a variety of courses and has a law school. There are about 4000 students and 175 faculty members.

Western New England College (1919), Springfield, has 3100 students and about 200 faculty members.

WOMEN'S COLLEGES

Several of the nation's best women's colleges are in Massachusetts. Smith (1871), Northampton, has 2500 students and nearly 260 faculty members. It is particularly noted for its school of social work.

Wellesley (1870), Wellesley, has 1800 students and about 200 faculty members. It was the first women's college to have scientific laboratories.

Radcliffe (1879), Cambridge, with 1200 students, uses Harvard faculty members for instructors. Radcliffe students now sit with Harvard students in many of the latter's classes.

Mount Holyoke (1837), South Hadley, one of the oldest women's colleges, has 1800 students and about 200 faculty members. It was originally called Mount Holyoke Female Seminary.

These colleges offer a "junior year abroad" program in which students may elect to spend their third year studying in France, Italy or another approved country.

Simmons (1899), Boston, noted for its social work, publishing and library courses, has 2200 students and 300 faculty members.

Wheaton (1834), Norton, one of the oldest women's colleges in the nation, has 1150 students and 105 faculty members.

Jackson (1910) is the woman's coordinate undergraduate college to Tufts.

CATHOLIC COLLEGES

Worcester's Holy Cross College (1843) for men is the oldest Catholic institution for higher learning in the Bay State. Boston College (1863), the largest and the only coeducational Catholic college in the state, has 10,000 students and 1000 faculty members. Assumption (1904), Worcester, has 1400 men students and 100 instructors.

Catholic women's colleges include Cardinal Cushing (1952), Brookline; Anna Maria (1946), Paxton; Emmanuel (1919), Boston; Newton College of the Sacred Heart (1946), Newton; College of Our Lady of the Elms (1928), Chicopee; and Regis, Weston.

SPECIALIZED SCHOOLS

Babson Institute (1919), Babson Park, is a four-year business college, founded by stock consultant Roger Babson (1875–1967) who gained fame by predicting the 1929 crash while the country's economy was booming. Seventy-five faculty members teach about 1200 students.

Bentley College of Accounting and Finance (1917), Boston, turns out finance technicians and future CPA's. There are about 2000 students and 115 faculty members.

Emerson (1880), Boston, trains future thespians. A 125-member faculty teaches about 1350 students.

Art students in the Boston area can attend the Art School of the Museum of Fine Arts (1876) or Massachusetts College of Art (1873).

Future druggists can attend Massachusetts College of Pharmacy (1823) with its 650 students and 50 faculty members. Massachusetts College of Optometry (1894), Boston, has 150 students and 40 faculty members. Future singers, music teachers or instrumentalists can choose Boston Conservatory of Music (1867), Boston, with 450 students and about 75 faculty members or the New England Conservatory of Music (1867), Boston, with about 550 students and 100 faculty members.

SOME STATE INSTITUTIONS

State-supported schools — other than teachers' colleges — include the University of Massachusetts, established after WWII. UMass, as it is known regionally, took over the facilities of Massachusetts State College (1863), a farmers' training school. UMass, today, has 17,000 students and 1000 faculty members. A Boston branch (1964) has 4000 students and 200 instructors. A medical school may be constructed in Worcester.

Lowell Technological Institute (1895), long known for its textile courses, expanded its curricula when the textile business began slipping out of the state. The school has 2800 students and 260 teachers.

Merchant marine officers are trained at Massachusetts Maritime Academy (1891). There are 200 cadets and 20 instructors.

TEACHERS' COLLEGES

State teachers' colleges are called state colleges in Massachusetts. Eight schools admit both men and women. Framingham is for women only. There are state colleges in Boston, Bridgewater, Fitchburg, Lowell, North Adams, Salem, Westfield and Worcester. Students wishing to study the teaching of art often attend Fitchburg. In all these colleges there are too many students and too few faculty members. The advantage of these state colleges is their relatively low tuition and lower entrance requirements. Enrollment in 1969 ranged from 7500 in Boston to 1375 in North Adams. Total enrollment for all schools is about 32,000.

Two private nonprofit women's teachers' colleges are Lesley (1909), Cambridge, with 600 students and 50 faculty members, and Wheelock (1889), Boston, with 550 students and 60 faculty members.

JUNIOR COLLEGES

There are several types of junior colleges in Massachusetts: state-supported, city-supported, private nonprofit, proprietary profit and those supported by various religious denominations. Most junior colleges offer courses similar to those offered during the first two years of four-year colleges. There are business colleges like Becker (1887) in Worcester and Northampton Commercial (1896) which are secretarial business schools. Burdett (1879) in Boston offers a similar curriculum. Boston's Franklin Institute (1908) is a technical trade school.

Massachusetts junior colleges also include Berkshire Community College (1960), Pittsfield; Bradford (1803), Bradford; Dean (1865), Franklin; Endicott (1939), Beverly; Garland (1872), Boston; Holyoke Regional Community (1946), Holyoke; and Lasell (1851), Auburndale. Bradford, Endicott and Lasell are women's colleges.

Several state and municipal community colleges are in planning stages.

PUBLIC SCHOOLS

Massachusetts has 428 school districts, most of which are elementary, junior and senior high schools in cities and towns but which also include regional, vocational, technical and agricultural schools. In the past few years, considerable progress has been made in the development of regional school districts, which have expanded programs and serve areas of the state with small populations.

Total enrollment in the public schools is approximately 1,148,000 and is increasing at a yearly rate of about 3 percent. Enrollments at the twelfth-grade level are rising because of increased attention to vocational education opportunities and efforts to decrease the number of dropouts in the upper grades. Kindergarten enrollments are increasing at the most rapid rate — 8 percent — because of recent state action stimulating the development of kindergartens in Massachusetts towns and cities. Private and church-affiliated schools have more than 350,000 pupils.

Tax receipts from Massachusetts communities contribute 77 percent of the funds applied to public school education. The state contributes

18 percent through Chapter 70 general aid to education and other programs. The federal government contributes 5 percent through various public laws.

Lowell Senior High School has more than 3000 pupils and is the largest single school in the state. The largest elementary school is the Mather School in Boston with approximately 1100 pupils. The smallest school is in Gosnold at Cuttyhunk with four pupils.

VOCATIONAL SCHOOLS

The state gives financial aid to more than 60 boys' day industrial training schools. Some of these schools are municipally operated while others are vocational regional schools. There are six girls' day industrial schools, twelve practical nursing schools, nine day household arts schools and five agricultural schools.

SCHOOLS FOR THE HANDICAPPED

The state operates four schools for mental defectives: Walter E. Fernald State School, Waverley; Wrentham State School, Wrentham; Belchertown State School, Belchertown; and the Paul A. Dever School, Taunton. The Massachusetts Hospital School, Canton, is operated for mentally normal but physically handicapped children.

The state aids the Perkins School for the Blind in Watertown.

9

Cranberries, Cows and Chrysanthemums

MASSACHUSETTS, the state which gave us the Plymouth Rock hen, is a major cranberry producer and home and birthplace of the "Plant Wizard," Luther Burbank (1849–1926).

According to a 1964 survey, the average Massachusetts' farm value is $43,492 compared to a New England low of $19,979 for Maine and high of $67,429 for Connecticut. The average New England farm value is $24,860. Arizona, with farms and ranches having an average value of $330,549, has the nation's most valuable farms. West Virginia farms at $13,882 have the lowest average value in the nation.

The value per acre of Massachusetts farmland is $484 while that of Arizona is a mere $52 per acre. Maine farms at $100 per acre have the lowest value in New England while Connecticut's at $560 have the highest per acre value in New England. New Jersey with an average acre value of $662 is the highest in the nation.

Massachusetts' agriculture produces one tenth of the state's income. The state's 8000 farmers annually spend more than $150,000,000 for goods and services needed to produce crops and livestock and for consumer goods and services. They provide 15,000 full-time farm jobs. Supplying farmers with grain, tools, machinery and other farm needs requires 425 businesses employing 3000 people with a $10,000,000 annual payroll. The assembling, wholesaling, retailing and processing of their products employs 166,000 workers with payrolls exceeding $500,000,000.

THE AGRICULTURAL REGIONS

1. *Western Dairy Region,* a highly specialized area with some poultry and fruit raising, occupies the Housatonic and Hoosic River Valleys.

2. *Berkshire Hills Dairy Region*'s potatoes are a major crop. Less than five percent of the area is cropland.

3. *Western Franklin Dairy Region* includes about eight small hill villages, which are replete with excellent soil for hay and apple production.

4. *Connecticut Valley Cash Crop-Dairy Region* occupies a narrow band on either side of the Connecticut River Valley's entire course through Massachusetts. Its level land, sandy soil and long growing season produce tobacco, onions, fresh vegetables and potatoes. There is some dairying and poultry and fruit raising.

5. *North Central Dairy Region* has a short growing season and hilly terrain.

6. *South Central Dairy Region* includes southern Worcester and eastern Hampden Counties. The Brookfield area is noted for dairying.

7. *Southern Transitional Dairy-Poultry Region* lies east and south of metropolitan Worcester. Poultry farming is important here.

8. *Northeast Dairy-Vegetable-Poultry-Fruit Region* includes Middlesex and Essex Counties' farm area and some of Norfolk County. There is mixed farming in this sizable region with poultry raising centered about Fitchburg and truck garden crops about Concord.

9. *Nashoba Fruit-Dairy-Poultry Region* (10 towns in the Stow-Hudson-Ashland area) has good soil, excellent drainage, rolling topography and fairly long growing seasons.

10. *Norfolk Dairy-Poultry Region* includes most of agricultural Norfolk County. Poultry is the major agricultural enterprise here.

11. *Bridgewater Dairy-Poultry Region* (Quincy-Brockton metropolitan areas) has the most concentrated dairy-poultry production in the state. It has more farm workers, cows and laying hens per square mile than any of the state's 13 other agricultural regions.

12. *Providence Market Dairy-Vegetable-Poultry Region* includes nine towns and cities in the Providence, Rhode Island, area.

13. *Westport-Dartmouth Dairy-Poultry Region* (Fall River, New Bedford, Acushnet, Dartmouth and Westport) is characterized by intensive dairying.

14. *Cape Cranberry Region* includes 11 Cape Cod towns plus off-Cape towns like Plymouth, Marshfield and Mattapoisett. Carver is the cranberry center of the world. Five percent of the region is cropland, and most of this area is taken up by cranberries. Cranberry picking is a seasonal occupation.

15. *Nonagricultural Areas* include part of Boston's metropolitan area; wooded Mount Washington Town; the Cape Cod towns of Eastham, Wellfleet and Provincetown; Gloucester; and the islands of Martha's Vineyard and Nantucket. The lack of agriculture results from poor soil or urbanization.

THE PRODUCTS

Dairying. Milk remains the Bay State's number one farm product despite a 30-year reduction in dairy farms from 20,000 to 1400. Though farms have decreased in number the number of cows per farm has more than doubled. Milk production increased 20 percent in the 1960–70 decade, and the trend is continuing. Massachusetts' total annual income from milk is over $55,000,000. Dairying provides employment for about 2000 full-time farm workers.

Today's dairy farms are more efficient. In 1914 one hour's work purchased 2.5 quarts of milk. In 1970 one hour's work buys about ten quarts of milk. Despite this increased efficiency, three out of every four quarts of milk consumed come from Vermont.

Poultry. Nearly thirty cents out of every Massachusetts' farm income dollar is created by Bay State poultry flocks. Four out of five poultry farms have closed or switched to other agricultural products. Since 1940, flocks have more than doubled in size. Egg production per hen has multiplied. During a recent year Massachusetts' hens produced more than 750,000,000 eggs. The eggs plus the sale of other poultry products brought farmers about $35,000,000.

Flower Crops. Every eighth dollar of Massachusetts' farm income is produced by the sale of flowers from more than 900 greenhouses. Nearly 700 commercial greenhouses each sell better than $2000 in products annually. More than 100 growers have $50,000 or more in annual sales. Nearly 330 growers take in $10,000–$50,000 yearly. Sales during a recent year totaled more than $20,000,000.

Floriculture, combined with ornamental nursery production, competes with the poultry industry, after dairying, among leading agricultural-horticultural products in the state. Middlesex County has about 40 per cent of the greenhouses and produces about the same proportion of flowers and nursery products.

Major flower crops include roses, carnations, standard chrysanthemums, pompon "mums," snapdragons, bulbs and pot plants.

Vegetables. One cent in every ten of Massachusetts' farm income is produced by vegetables, most of which are grown in the Connecticut River Valley, north central Bristol and parts of Middlesex and Essex Counties. Most of these vegetables are grown for fresh market sale. Cucumbers and tomatoes are processed by canneries.

Potatoes. A small item in Massachusetts' farm income, spuds account for about one-and-one-half cents in the farm income dollar. Most potatoes are grown in the Connecticut River Valley. Less than 200 full-time workers harvest about 6800 acres.

Fruit. About 12,000 acres of apples, peaches, pears and other fruits bring in about one thirty-third of the state's farm income.

Cranberry Production. One out of every four cranberries comes from the town of Carver. During a recent average year, 13,000 acres of cranberries brought in $5,500,000 or 3.3 percent of the total income from agricultural products. Most cranberries are sold through a grower's cooperative — Ocean Spray.

Honey, Hogs, Hay and minor products account for about five percent of the state's total farm income.

Tobacco. This product, shade-grown for cigar wrappers, has decreased in acreage and value in recent years. The crop employs 500 full-time workers and some seasonal pickers. It produces about five cents of our farm income dollar.

Young John Coolidge spent his summers as a tobacco field hand. The morning after President Harding died and his father was sworn in as President of the United States, a fellow worker remarked to John, "If my father were President of the United States you can bet that I wouldn't be working here."

"If he were my father, you would," replied Coolidge.

10

Industry's Increase

Oh! They sing of Lydia Pinkham
And of her love for the human race.
Now, Mrs. Jones had no children
Though her need for them was great,
So, she took six bottles of Pinkham's
And now she has seven or eight.
—*Folk Song*

LITTLE DID LYNN'S impoverished Lydia Estes Pinkham (1819–83) realize while struggling to support a growing brood by peddling her home-brewed "Lydia E. Pinkham's Vegetable Compound" that for more than 90 years her beverage would solace millions of women suffering from "Female Complaints or Disorders."

Women took to Pinkham's like cats to catnip. Vegetable Compound's Golden Age came between its 1875 introduction and the 1906 Pure Food and Drug Act. Many Pinkham imbibers were devout, active Anti-Saloon Leaguers and Women's Christian Temperance Union workers. These stern advocates of teetotalism were mortified when they read the post-1906 label, which, as required by law, stated in fine print that Vegetable Compound was nigh 30 percent alcohol by volume.

THE TINKERERS

In 1872 West Dennis native Luther C. Crowell (1840–1903) designed the first square-bottomed paper bag and machinery to make this standard supermarket item. In 1716 printer Ben Franklin (1706–90) and his father made the first commercial soap in America. Taunton resident Isaac Babbitt (1799–1862) created babbitt metal, the anti-friction bearing-metal, before joining his cousin, Benjamin T. Babbitt (1809–89), in making "Babbitt's Best Soap," still used a century later. Chesterfield native Ebenezer Brown (1795–1889), America's first Methodist missionary, invented the detachable collar. New Bedford's Frederick Grinnell (1836–1905) designed the first successful automatic fire-sprinkler alarm.

Spencer's Elias Howe (1819–67) designed the first successful sewing machine, so important to the Bay State's apparel and shoemaking trades. Brimfield native Thaddeus Fairbanks (1796–1886) moved to Vermont where he founded the world-renowned Fairbanks Scale Company. Sterling's Mr. and Mrs. Ebenezer Butterick invented the standardized clothes patterns (1863), still widely used by thrifty American housewives. A Charlestown Congregationalist preacher's son, Samuel F. B. Morse (1791–1872), invented the telegraph.

FISH

The ancient dusty cod hanging in the State House has been around for nearly 200 years. It is rightly called the "sacred" cod, for it represents the tradition of our oldest industry, fishing — and a much newer one, fish processing.

Dried codfish — which can still be bought — was the colony's first export. Three years after the Pilgrims landed, Gloucester's men were exporting dried cod.

Massachusetts ranks third in U.S. fish sales value and fourth in poundage caught. Fish and seafood, including lobsters, landing in Bay State ports one recent year totaled 409,000,000 pounds. Another 300,000,000 pounds were prepared fish blocks ready for processing.

Gloucester and New Bedford with 32 percent each led in total poundage. Boston followed with 25 percent, while all other Bay State ports landed 11 percent.

Gloucester leads in whiting and ocean perch landings, while Boston leads in haddock. New Bedford scallopers bring in about 50 percent of all sea scallops landed in the world. New Bedford's 500 scallopers average 16,000,000 pounds of this gourmet food.

Landlubbers often buy so-called scallops which are not sea scallops but pieces chopped out, cookie-cutter fashion, from skate wings. These are good but not as good as scallops, and it is unfair to peddle them as such.

Fish brought into Massachusetts' ports include cod, cusk, flounder, haddock, hake, halibut, mackerel, pollock, ocean perch, scrod, skate, swordfish, tuna and whiting.

FOOD PRODUCTS

Cape Codder Gustavus Swift (1839–1903) had sore feet from walking barefoot while herding hogs from Barnstable to Boston. Gustavus got up the gumption, moved to Chicago and established his meat-packing dynasty. He pioneered refrigerator car use for year-round meat shipping and made profitable utilization of animal parts, which has since been discarded. Swift, today, has 15 plants in the Boston area.

Table Talk Pastry, Worcester, makes more than 1,000,000 servings of pie daily. Cushman's Bakery, Lynn, has 350 salesmen offering 150 different eatables. Continental Baking's new $9,000,000 Natick plant may be the world's largest bakery. Educator Biscuit, Lowell, makes crackers and Girl Scout cookies.

Salada, Araban and LaTouraine are some Bay State coffee and tea processors and packagers. Sugar for these products is prepared by New England's two refineries, Paul Revere and Domino, both in Boston.

Watertown's William Underwood Company, founded in 1821, the nation's oldest canning firm, numbers deviled ham among its meat and fish products. Malden's Friend Brothers make one of the few tinned beans which are oven-baked before canning. Most "pork and bean" outfits can beans before baking them. Some companies sell oven-baked beans, but they are usually Friend's beans under the distributor's own label.

MATCHLOCKS TO MISSILES

Massachusetts and Connecticut, after two centuries, remain the center for small arms research, design development and manufacture. Two major Connecticut arms firms were founded by Bay Staters Samuel Colt (1814–62) and Oliver Winchester (1810–80). Westboro native Eli Whitney (1765–1825) devised the vital principle of making interchangeable firearms components.

Springfield Armory (1794) was for many years the major source of U.S. military rifles. It was a manufacturing and design development center. "Springfield" was synonymous with the U.S. service rifle from the War of 1812 through the Korean war. The M1 semiautomatic rifle, adopted by the U.S. Army as the shoulder weapon in 1936, was designed by Springfield employee John C. Garand. The armory was phased out in 1968.

The Colt revolver's runner-up in winning the west and today's wars was the Smith and Wesson revolver, originally designed and made by Horace Smith (1808–93) and Daniel B. Wesson (1825–1906) in 1857. Their firm, which makes some of the world's best handguns, is still active after more than a century. Savage Arms, Westfield, absorbed J. T. Stevens Company and now manufactures and imports rifles and shotguns. Savage during WWI made Lewis light machine guns. In WWII it made several million British service rifles, more than 1,000,000 Thompson submachine guns and many Browning machine guns.

Harrington Richardson, Worcester, made WWII Reising submachine guns, M1 rifles, M14 service rifles and M16 rifle barrels. Iver Johnson, Fitchburg, made cheap pocket revolvers and rimfire rifles. Boston lawyer Melvin Johnson (1909–64) designed the Johnson semiautomatic rifle and the Johnson light machine gun used by the Dutch, U.S. Marine Corps and Ranger battalions in WWII.

Hesse-Eastern, in Everett and Brockton, artillery shell and fuse makers, developed and manufactured the M72 Rocket Grenade Launcher System. This five-pound anti-tank buster is widely used in Vietnam.

Space-age weaponry, as differentiated from conventional small arms, includes Minuteman missiles by Sylvania, Polaris missile guidance systems by Raytheon, missile gyroscopes by Precision Products, advanced design antisubmarine Mk 44 torpedoes by GE, and ICBM reentry vehicles by AVCO.

NONELECTRICAL MACHINERY

Making machinery is the state's most important industry. About 70,000 workers manufacture nonelectrical machinery. Electrical machinery is a separate industry.

The first U.S. continuous steel rolling mill was devised by Charles Morgan in 1883. Morgan Construction Company, Worcester, has made mills for every steel producing country in the world.

John Norton made pottery in which abrasives were used. His kin founded the Norton Company, the world's largest abrasive maker. More than 5000 of the firm's 15,000 employees work in Worcester.

Athol's United Drill & Tool, formerly Union Twist Drill, is one of the world's largest makers of cutting tools like high-speed drills. Dies, fixtures, jigs, taps and gauges, all used in manufacturing processes, are made here.

FABRICATED METAL PRODUCTS

The Bay State is a major maker of tools for both craftsmen and home tinkerers. About 40,000 mill hands produce nearly $500,000,-

000 worth of tools and other fabricated metal products. The annual payroll is about $250,000,000.

Fitchburg's Simonds Saw & Steel Company is the world's largest saw blade producer. In 1912, Maine native Laroy S. Starrett (1836–1922) became president of the Athol company which bears his name and now leads the world in the production of precision measuring instruments such as micro-calipers and verniers.

ELECTRICAL MACHINERY

Thomas Edison's (1847–1931) bulky direct-current generators brought electricity to the home, but it was Great Barrington resident William Stanley (1858–1916) who devised a method for producing alternating current, making it possible to use electrically powered equipment in mills. He also invented the two-phase motor.

General Electric, with 30,000 workers, is the state's largest employer and its largest electrical machinery, equipment and appliance manufacturer. Major plants are in Lynn and Pittsfield. Others are in Ashland, which produces electric clocks; Fitchburg, small industrial turbines; Everett, jet engine components; Chelsea, industrial paints and lacquers; and Lowell, insulated cable. Lynn makes turbine generators, military engines and other specialized equipment and Pittsfield produces guidance and control systems for Polaris missiles, fire control equipment for guns, large utility electric transformers and other items.

Westinghouse, Boston, manufactures industrial ventilation equipment; Westinghouse, Springfield, household appliances; Sylvania, Danvers, is the world's largest fluorescent lighting manufacturer.

ELECTRONICS

Only one dollar in every eight resulting from electronics manufacture comes from Massachusetts but the state — in which few consumer electronics products are made — is a key producer of strategic components for RADAR (Radio Detection and Ranging) defenses, SAGE (Semi-Automatic Ground Control), BMEWS (Ballistic Missile Early Warning System) and TIROS (Television InfraRed Observation Satellite). Harvard, Massachusetts Institute of Technology and other Massachusetts research organizations developed these systems.

The digital computer was born in Harvard in 1944. MIT and its personnel played a major role in computer development, but today private research and development firms make the major advances in computer design and techniques. Most key personnel on the private projects are Harvard- and/or MIT-trained.

Today's electronics industry owes its basic inception to MIT's WWII Radiation Lab and Project Lincoln. Route 128, which rims Boston, has several hundred electronics plants and research organizations.

Massachusetts' largest — and one of the world's largest — electronics manufacturer is Raytheon, which produces electronic items such as sonar for antisubmarine warfare, systems for missiles and spacecraft, microwave communications equipment and electronic ovens.

Massachusetts' electronics industry employs nearly 100,000 scientists, engineers and workers. About 30,000 scientists and engineers, all with advanced degrees, work in the Boston area. Many of these people prefer living here because of the fine private schools for their children, university and laboratory facilities for advanced research, invigorating climate and recreation facilities.

INSTRUMENTS

The relatively new instruments industry in which Massachusetts is a leader has 30,000 workers with an annual payroll of nearly $200,000,000 dollars.

Boston's Edgerton, Germeshausen & Grier — MIT professor Edgerton designed stroke flash for stopping high-speed action — was a three-man firm when founded in 1934. Today its annual production exceeds $50,000,000, and there are plants in several states. EG&G conducted many of America's early developmental nuclear tests.

William Beecher founded American Optical Company, Southbridge, with four workers in 1833 to become the first American eyeglass maker. Today, one half of AO's 10,000 employees work in Southbridge, producing optical safety equipment and making glass rods used in laser devices. AO's new Photo-Coagulator uses a laser beam's hot light to "weld" or coagulate separated pieces of the human eye.

Athol's L. S. Starrett Company is one of the largest manufacturers of precision measuring instruments in the world. Surgical and medical instruments are made there.

SPACE

Newspaper readers thought Professor Robert H. Goddard was insane — and so did the newspapers. Professor Goddard toward the end of a

1918 Smithsonian Institute report predicted that man might reach the moon via rocket by the year 2000. He was off by 31 years.

Undeterred by adverse comment, Goddard fired the world's first liquid-propelled rocket to a height of 41 feet. The 1926 blast-off occurred on his aunt's Auburn farm near Worcester. This short flight, unspectacular by today's standards, confirmed the theory on which contemporary rocketry is based.

By 1936 Goddard-designed rockets had reached 7500 feet at speeds of 700 m.p.h. Neither the Washington government nor any other Americans paid significant attention to the work of the "Father of Rocketry" until World War II.

Astronauts' silvery space suits, familiar to all TV viewers, are built by Worcester's David Clark. Each astronaut has three suits: (1) practice, (2) mission and (3) spare. Suits cost $28,000 each.

When our first three-man spacecraft reached the moon, two men traversed the planet's surface in a Burlington-built LEM (Lunar Excursion Module). The "bug" was built by RCA's Aerospace Systems.

Apollo was guided to the moon and back by Raytheon's 70-pound onboard computer. Space telescopes for the first OAO (Orbiting Astronomical Observatory) were built by Sylvania. When Gemini Six and Seven made their historic orbiting rendezvous, the high intensity winking lights seen on TV were a product of Edgerton, Germeshausen & Grier. The line which hauled John Glenn's Friendship Seven aboard its carrier was made by Boston's Samson's Cordage. To detect potential spacecraft malfunctions, Canton's Instron developed devices to test stress and strain on space crafts and their components. Shipboard and land-tracking station antenna are built by GE, Pittsfield. Worcester's Norton Company is creating ceramics to withstand the heat created by reentry into the earth's atmosphere.

PAPER

All Americans are keenly interested in the paper produced since 1879 by Crane & Company, Dalton. This paper, heavily guarded during manufacture, is the stock U.S. currency is printed on. Government paper standards are as tough as the paper, which is capable of being folded 4000 times in any one place and is difficult to counterfeit.

Massachusetts' first paper mill commenced operations on the Neponset River, Milton, in 1730. Paper was made of cloth scraps until the Civil War cloth shortage. Stockbridge papermaker Albert Pagenstecher found a way to make paper from wood pulp.

America's first gum labels were made in 1901 by Dennison, Framingham, which also introduced Christmas tags and seals. It is the largest gum label and crepe paper manufacturer in the country.

The Bay State makes paper and paper matches to burn paper. One hundred and twenty million cigarettes can be lighted daily from the 6,000,000 books of paper matches produced daily by Diamond National Match, Springfield.

PRINTING

In 1638 Congregational minister Jesse Glover bought a printing press, hired locksmith Stephen Daye (1594–1668) as a printer and sailed for America. Reverend Jesse died en route. Daye and his son Matthew set up shop in Cambridge. Two years later Daye printed *The Bay Psalm Book,* the first book printed in America and the most valuable of all American books (only 11 known copies survive). Daye printed 22 publications before Samuel Green (1615–1702) took over in 1649. The press is in the Vermont Historical Society, Montpelier.

Printing 38 daily and about 100 weekly newspapers, Massachusetts employs 12,000 workers.

Novels, nonfiction, telephone directories, textbooks, law books and technical, juvenile and crossword puzzle books are printed here by hard-cover and paperback printers.

Riverside Press, located beside the Charles River in Cambridge since 1852, was founded by Vermonter Henry O. Houghton, who organized the beginnings of Houghton Mifflin Company in 1880. Riverside Press printed many books for HMCo as well as other publishers. For more than 100 years it printed Webster's Dictionary for the Merriam Company, Springfield. Now owned by Rand McNally, Riverside Press has moved to Taunton.

In 1964, New England's largest book printer, Colonial Press, Clinton, printed 500,000 copies of the Warren Commission's Report on President Kennedy's assassination in 45 hours. Their time is a record.

RUBBER

Woburn resident Charles Goodyear (1800–60), after years of experimentation, accidentally discovered vulcanization, when, legend says, he dropped a ball of crude latex atop a hot stove. Today Bay State rubber companies employ more than 20,000 workers.

Leading rubber products are rubber or rubber and canvas shoes and boots. Converse Rubber, Malden, makes footwear and wet weather wear for sportsmen. American Biltrite's Chelsea and Stoughton plants make heels and soles. New Bedford's Goodyear Tire & Rubber Company — one of the world's largest bicycle tire makers — produces more than 5,000,000 tires annually.

Leading golf ball makers are Acushnet and A. G. Spalding, Chicopee. Acushnet balls are sold through "pro" shops.

SHOES AND LEATHER

Massachusetts produces one out of every six pairs of American-made shoes, most of the nation's wet weather footwear and about all U.S. shoemaking machinery. The leather and rubber in most Bay State–made footwear is Massachusetts produced. Footwear, excepting rubber apparel, is a major industry with 36,000 workers paid $135,000,000 annually to produce nearly 85,000,000 pairs of shoes and slippers worth a factory value of nearly $375,000,000.

The leather industry has 6000 workers with a $32,000,000 annual payroll. The 162 plants ship goods exceeding $175,000,000.

United Shoe Machinery Corporation (1899) is the world's largest shoe machinery maker. The floor space in the Beverly plant equals 18 football fields. The firm has plants in 26 countries. International Shoe Machine Corporation, Brighton (1938), is the world's second largest maker of shoe machinery.

Haverhill was "The Queen Shoe City of the World," but the largest Bay State shoe plant is H. H. Brown, Worcester. Boston, Brockton, Lynn and Marlboro are shoe centers. Cowboy boots, Capezios, sandals, work shoes, dress shoes, hunting boots and baby shoes are made in Massachusetts. Quality ranges from poor to first-rate.

Peabody, the self-styled "Leather City," has the state's largest tannery, the A. C. Lawrence Company, with 1500 workers. Sixty-odd years ago Mr. and Mrs. Dana Buxton of Springfield began making wallets; today, Buxton is one of the nation's largest billfold makers.

TEXTILES

Birthplace of the textile industry in America, Massachusetts remains a leading textile center and also makes more than half of all American-made textile machinery. Colleges offer textile courses, and

Boston: New State House

Boston: Old State House

Boston: Faneuil Hall

Boston: Louisburg Square

Boston: A Beacon Street doorway

Boston: Old North Church

Boston: Paul Revere statue with the Old North Church in the background

Left—Boston: Saint-Gaudens' Colonel Robert Gould Shaw Memorial on Boston Common

Boston: Prudential Center and the War Memorial Auditorium

Boston: A gull's-eye view

the exhibits of the Merrimack Valley's Textile Museum, North Andover, show the industry's development. Boston handles imports of more than 200,000,000 pounds of fiber annually with a total value exceeding $150,000,000.

Colonists homespun fibers into cloth, but demand exceeded production. Cloth prices were regulated in 1633, subsidies for cloth manufacture were offered and skilled weavers were brought over from the British Isles. The Revolution saw New England producing all its own cloth. The first wool-processing mill was built in Rowley in 1636 and the first cotton mill in Beverly in 1787. Samuel Slater (1768–1835) developed new spinning machinery. Factories sprang up in many towns.

Lawrence and Lowell were company towns created for textile making. The huge demands for Civil War uniforms and blankets brought quick expansion. The industry generally prospered until the Depression, when many mills closed or reduced operations. When World War II ended obsolescence, increasing labor costs and competition from southern mills forced many plants to leave the state. Mill owners lured by nonunion workers and tax benefits moved south. Textile towns were hard hit, but the remaining manufacturers survived by utilizing new techniques, equipment and the synthetics. Today's 45,000 textile workers are paid about $200,000,000 annually for producing goods valued at about $350,000,000.

APPAREL

Bostonian John Simmons accidentally created the crease in men's trousers and was the first to attempt standardization of men's clothing sizes.

Boston was the Army's Civil War clothing procurement center. The Loomis Company suggested making uniforms in three standard sizes. The suggestion, approved, sired the gag about two military clothing sizes, "too big and too small."

Massachusetts, the nation's textile center until 1875, slowly turned to women's wear, previously either homemade or created by seamstresses. Thus, the contract system was slowly replaced by mills.

Women's sportswear is a $100,000,000 business. Massachusetts makes more than 60 percent of the nation's wet weather wear. Bay State Yankees gave us the first slicker and the first reversible and nylon raincoat. William Carter, Needham, has made underwear for the whole family for more than a century. Men's garters were invented by Bay Stater F. Barton Brown in 1878.

Boston, Fall River, New Bedford and Springfield-Holyoke are major apparel production centers. Nearly 60,000 workers are annually paid $200,000,000. The finished product value is about $325,000,000.

FURNITURE

Massachusetts has dropped from first to twelfth in furniture manufacture. High freight rates and different styles and tastes in living created furniture factories elsewhere.

Gardner, the "Chair City of the World," once produced 4,000,000 chairs in one year. Gardner manufacturers include Conant Ball, Heywood-Wakefield, S. Bent, Nichols & Stone and Gem Industries. Irving & Casson, Cambridge, makes custom furniture and church pews.

II

"Solidarity Forever"

INDUSTRIAL-LABOR RELATIONS during the 1950–70 period were better than in any other industrial state; Massachusetts' time lost due to strikes (in manufacturing man days) was the lowest in the country. In 1970 the state had 650,000 manufacturing workers, one third of the state's total labor force. In this period Michigan, with one half more workers than Massachusetts, lost 18 times as many work days in strikes. The Bay State has the lowest percentage of manufacturing days lost per worker, 0.33. It has not always been peaceful, however.

LABOR'S THORNY PATH

Capital's solidarity was matched by the beginning of labor solidarity. Organization was an untried weapon when a few leaders began advocating unity during the 1820's. Factory hands labored long hours for low wages — in Lowell the workday varied from 11.5 to 13.5 hours and wages ranged from $1.00 to $5.00 a week. More than 3000 Massachusetts persons were annually imprisoned for debt. Unstable currency and compulsory military service penalized workers. Young children were widely employed for long hours at wages even lower than that of their parents.

Dissatisfied workers began drifting into unions of particular skilled crafts. Boston printers organized by 1809. The "Columbian Charitable Society of Shipwrights and Calkers" was formed in 1823 after a futile 1817 Medford shipbuilders' strike. An 1825 attempt by 600 journeyman carpenters to secure a ten-hour day collapsed in the face of determined builders' opposition and the lack of support from other crafts.

During the 1830's union organization went on rapidly, inspired by Jacksonian Democracy and the rapid price increases that preceded the 1837 Panic. Wages had failed to keep pace with rising prices. Laborers, for the first time, began to realize their problems could be solved only by united action. Trade unions multiplied. The most famous was the "Female Society of Lynn and Vicinity for the Protection and Promotion of Female Industry," which had more than 1000 members. More significant were the city trade unions with representatives of all craft unions in a particular region. Boston organized such a union in 1834.

Solidarity gave labor new confidence and resulted in a series of strikes for higher wages and the ten-hour day in the mid-1830's. Eight hundred Lowell mill girls walked out when their demands for a 15 percent wage increase were denied. They soon returned to work but without the increase because the public, horrified at such blatant feminism, turned against them. Boston masons and carpenters lost their strike for a ten-hour day, but their action established a pattern soon followed by workers in other cities. Eventually ameliorative legislation was passed.

The 1837 Panic abruptly changed the Massachusetts labor movement. There was a continuous depression for workers between 1837 and the outbreak of the Civil War. Food and clothing prices began to rise in 1843 and continued upward for more than 20 years. The increase became even more noticeable after the inflationary effects of the 1849 California gold strike reached Massachusetts.

An 1851 family of five required $10.37 a week for the barest necessities of existence. Lynn shoemakers did not average more than $4.00 or $5.00 for a minimum 72-hour work week. Women shoebinders, by working 17 hours a day, could, if uninterrupted by domestic chores, earn $2.40 for a 102-hour work week. Wages were rarely paid in cash but were in company script which had to be used at a company-owned store with exorbitant prices. Houses were usually owned by the company. By 1850 Lowell power-loom operators were averaging $1.75 a week plus board, but board could not always be relied on. When a Holyoke plant manager found his hands "langerous" in the early morning he worked them without breakfast. He was pleased that elimination of breakfast increased cloth production by 3000 yards a week. "Produce cheap and sell dear" was the philosophy.

Workers were degraded while factory owners enjoyed an increasing prosperity. Textile mill dividends varied from 5 to 43 percent annually. Lawrence Company stock earnings averaged 10.26 percent annually. During this period Lowell mills averaged 5 to 14 percent annually. The gap between the reward of labor and of capital was widening. Wages fell or remained stationary, while production costs declined and prices and profits advanced.

For 25 years unions did not dare to strike. Since immediate relief was impossible, organized labor accepted the leadership of philosophical liberals who advocated ultimate relief by radical social reform. Meanwhile, more practical men tried to develop cooperatives. Massachusetts played a leading role in the cooperative movement. As early as 1831 cooperation was discussed in Boston by an "Association of Farmers, Mechanics and Other Working Men." In 1832 Lynn journeymen leather workers experimented with cooperation. The "Working Men's Protective Union," formed in 1845, expanded until in 1852 it was distributing goods to its members valued at $2,000,000 annually. An 1853 schism marked the beginning of the end.

WORKERS ORGANIZE

Post-Civil War industrial prosperity led to a burst of labor activity. Workers were not sure how to cope with problems incidental to rapidly expanding factories. Attempts were made to revive many panaceas advocated before the Civil War. Boston machinist Ira Steward developed the theory that a general 8-hour day would solve all problems of capital and labor. His "Grand Eight-Hour League of Massachusetts" became the model for similar organizations in other states and greatly influenced legislation toward shorter hours. Others believed labor should imitate capital and organize along national lines. Of the national trade unions that became prominent in this period, one of the most important, as far as Massachusetts was concerned, was the Knights of St. Crispin, a secret union of shoe workers formed at Milwaukee in 1867. A third solution was offered by the Greenbackers, who became prominent in Massachusetts during the 1870's under the leadership of Wendell Phillips and Governor Benjamin Butler. By their ambitious plans, the state would finance with fiat money cooperative associations of workmen who would eventually drive private capitalism out of existence by the competitive route.

When these schemes brought few results, labor drifted back toward a policy of unionism and tried two great experiments along national lines. The first was an attempt to organize all workers regardless of craft or skill into one body known as the Knights of Labor. After 1886, the Knights were beginning to crumble and a new organization, the American Federation of Labor (A.F. of L.), was rising. Unions affiliated with this national organization formed a Massachusetts Federation of Labor in 1887.

The first attempt at a general organization of the state's textile workers was made in 1889 when the National Cotton Spinners' Union was formed. Within a short time ring spinning had swept the trade of mule spinning from existence, and in 1901 a new union, the United Textile Workers, was organized along industrial lines. Although designed to include all textile workers, regardless of craft, its development was slow, partly because of the large numbers of women and children employed in the textile industry. More success was enjoyed by the Boot and Shoe Workers' Union, which began organizing the shoe trades in 1900.

The rise of these strong unions and employers' efforts to combat them led to many labor disputes. Between 1881 and 1900 there were 1802 recorded strikes and lockouts, Massachusetts ranking fourth among the states in strikes and third in number of lockouts.

THE LAWRENCE STRIKE

Declining Massachusetts trade and industry ushered in serious labor difficulties. Skilled workers whose abilities had erected the state's industrial empire resented employers' attempts to lower wages to match declining production. Factory owners felt that they could face new competition only by slashing labor costs and establishing wage levels comparable to those given unskilled workers in other states. This clash of interests led to a rapid organization of the industrial workers of Massachusetts and to friction along the entire labor front. Two events in this struggle gained nationwide attention: the 1912 Lawrence strike and the Boston police strike in 1919. (See HISTORICAL NOTES.)

A 1911 labor law reduced women's working hours to 54 per week. Manufacturers retaliated by slashing wages. According to a report by the U.S. Commissioner of Labor, "the average amount actually received [in Lawrence] by the 21,922 employees, during a week late in 1911, in which the mills were running full time, was $8.76." Most workers were unorganized — the United Textile Workers had 2500 members and the Industrial Workers of the World a few hundred. After three days, nearly all unskilled and semiskilled workers were out. Joseph Ettor of the General Executive Board of the I.W.W. came to Lawrence to assume leadership. On January 15, strikers picketed in mass, and the Mayor requisitioned four out-of-town troops of militia in addition to the four local companies. On January 16, the mills were reopened with the protection of police and the militia. Picketers were driven back by bayonet points. William M. Wood, president of the American Woolen Company, refused to meet with a strike committee. On January 19, skilled operatives joined the strike. The next day several sticks of dynamite were "discovered" in the strike district, seven strikers were arrested, and four additional companies of militia were brought in. Subsequently a leading businessman was tried, convicted, and fined

$500 for "planting" the dynamite; President Wood was exonerated in court after failing to explain a payment to the purchaser of the dynamite. On the day of a huge demonstration, January 29, a woman striker was killed. The city council voted to turn the town over to the commander of the militia, which was reinforced by the addition of ten more companies of infantry and two cavalry troops. Ettor and Arture Giovanitti, editor of *Il Proletario,* were accused of the murder and later acquitted. While Ettor was in jail, William "Big Bill" Haywood took command of the strike. One hundred and nineteen strikers' children were sent to New York, where they were greeted by a crowd of 5000. Later 92 more children were sent out of harm's way. When once more a new group of "refugee" children was ready to board the train, fifty police and two companies of militia clubbed their parents and dragged children and parents to jail. After the organization of the largest picket line ever seen in Massachusetts, comprising 20,000 workers, the strike was won, with wage increases, time-and-a-quarter for overtime, and guarantees of no discrimination against union members.

The relief committee during the strike raised a large sum, appealing in a circular for "bread" for the striking workers. The attorney-general contended the money should be spent only for bread, whereas portions of the fund had been used for legal expenses, transportation of children, contributions to the national organization, etc. He secured a court order compelling the strikers to turn over $15,379.85 to the court to be expended for "charitable purposes," with an accounting for monies already paid out.

THE TERRIBLE THIRTIES

Textile employees entrenched in the United Textile Workers since the beginning of the century staged spectacular strikes in 1934 but secured no great concessions from an industry crippled by the depression. The union was weakened by this loss of prestige, and in 1936–37 deserted the American Federation of Labor to cast its lot with the Committee for Industrial Organization (C.I.O.).

Attempts to organize the shoe industry led to serious internal disputes within labor organizations and to the migration of many shoe factories to other states. One bitter struggle occurred in 1929 when Lynn, Boston, Chelsea and Salem shoe workers struck, with the major demand for recognition of their union, the United Shoe Workers of America, as opposed to the Boot and Shoe Workers' Union, an A.F. of L.

affiliate. The strike lasted six months. Strike-breakers were imported from neighboring states, but the strike was finally broken by a court injunction based upon findings that it was illegal. During this strike many shops left Massachusetts and moved to nonunion centers in other states. The frequency with which these shops moved earned them the title of "factories on wheels." A 1933 attempt to unite all shoe workers into a national union, the United Shoe and Leather Workers' Union, resulted in internal dissensions and wholesale factory removals. In 1933–34 there were 21 factories in Boston employing some 7000 workers; by 1935–36 there remained only four factories, employing about 2000.

TODAY

In 1955 the national organizations of the conservative craft type unions, the American Federation of Labor and the more militant and progressive Congress of Industrial Organization amalgamated. By 1958 the Massachusetts membership of the two organizations had completed their unification.

Today, one out of every four Bay State union members is a woman. Of the 565,000 union members, including those in independent unions, 140,000 are women. There are about 2200 locals of which nearly 500 are in Boston.

Boston locals have about 215,000 members. Springfield ranks second with 35,000 members; Worcester is third with nearly 24,000 members. Fall River, Lynn and New Bedford are fourth with about 20,000 members each. Brockton, Lawrence and Waltham have about 13,000 each. Lowell and Quincy have 10,000 union members each. Membership in Cambridge, Chicopee, Fitchburg, Holyoke and Pittsfield ranges between 6000 and 8000.

12

Highways and Skyways

SAILORMEN for the past 150 years have been grateful to Salem native Nathaniel Bowditch (1773–1838), who revised John Moore's *The Practical Navigator* as *The New American Practical Navigator* (1802), still the standard work on navigation.

Many a seafarer and his passengers would have failed to reach port if Cape Codder Winslow Lewis (1770–1850) had not designed his effective lighthouse light in 1811. Shipwrecked sailormen could be thankful to Bostonian Joseph Francis (1801–93), designer of the first successful lifeboat (1845). He also designed a floating watertight wagon for the army (1855) — forerunner of the amphibious DUK.

Albert Hickman (1878–1957) created the sea sled hull, famed for its stability at high speeds. This design, now widely copied, is used in boats such as the *Boston Whaler.* Hickman-designed sea sleds were used in both world wars for high speed patrol and rescue craft. The first steam locomotive used east of the Mississippi River was built in Taunton. George Pullman's first sleeping car was built in Springfield in 1864–65. Osgood Bradley's Worcester company was the longtime second largest manufacturer of railroad passenger cars in the United States. Charles and Frank Duryea made the first successful gasoline-powered motorcar in the United States (1892) and built the first automobile factory (1895). Carlton W. Maxim's Middleborough company has been making fire engines since 1914.

HIGHWAYS

During the 1850's most turnpike companies were bankrupt. High operating costs, poor upkeep and too high or too low tolls contributed to their demise. Some communities erected "shunpikes" or roads which travelers could take to avoid turnpike tolls. Toll roads reverted to control of cities and towns in which the roads were located.

The 1893 legislature established the Massachusetts Highway Commission after an investigation which disclosed that the roads of the state were in a deplorable condition. The commission was authorized to take over, lay out and maintain roads, and to unite the more important cities by trunk lines of large traffic capacity. The first state appropriation, amounting to $300,000, was made in 1894. By 1916 a total of $11,767,000 had been spent. Obviously some portion of this gathering cost had to be turned back in some way to those who benefited. The old turnpike toll in a different form is paid by motorists of today. In 1925 the state legislature established the Highway Fund, whereby the proceeds of motor vehicle fees and fines and of the tax on gasoline are pledged to the construction and maintenance of both state and local highways. Between 1912–37 the cost of new road construction was about $105,000,000.

TODAY'S HIGHWAYS

More than 2,000,000 motor vehicles travel daily over the state's 27,000 miles of highways. Only 1700 miles are unpaved. Traffic authorities estimate that 4,000,000 vehicles will travel daily over the highways by 1985.

The federally aided Interstate program scheduled for completion by 1971 will have 453 miles of multilane divided limited access highways, which will include the 131.4 miles of the Massachusetts Turnpike (tolls), largely completed before commencement of the Interstate program. The Federal Bureau of Public Roads has requested the state to upgrade some of the already completed interstate mileage to comply with the bureau's recently adopted 1985 highway standards.

STEAMCARS TO DIESELS

The first steam railroad in America, built in 1826, was a three-mile-long road which hauled Quincy granite to Neponset River wharves. The only profitable railroad in Massachusetts today is a nine-mile line from Hoosac Tunnel Village to Monroe Bridge and Readsboro, Vermont. This is the famous "Hoot, Toot & Whistle," so called after the initials of the "Hoosac Tunnel & Wilmington" railroad.

Despite advantages obvious to the foresighted, Massachusetts was slower than other sections of the country in accepting railroads. The first coaches were severely censured and so were the first railroads. Puritanism was always suspicious of anything that made for physical comfort. Many people were sincerely convinced these iron highways would lower morality.

During the building of the Western Railroad from Worcester to Springfield in 1837, so much adverse criticism was directed against this project that the road owners sent a letter to all the churches in the state asking that *sermons be preached on the beneficial moral effect of railroads.*

New England's first three important railroads were completed in 1835. They were the Boston and Lowell, Boston and Providence and Boston and Worcester.

The reaction of the people to the new method of transportation is found in the newspapers of the day. In the July 18, 1835 issue of Worcester's *Maine Farmer,* there is the following comment concerning the trip between Boston and Worcester: "The usual passage is performed in two and a half or three hours, including stops — A few years ago, 14 miles an hour would have been considered rapid traveling. ... So great are the advantages gained, that already one of the principal dealers here has offered to lay a side track from the road to his own storehouse . . . A person in business here informed me that he left Worcester one day at 12 o'clock, arrived in Boston, had one and a quarter hours to transact his business, returned by the four o'clock car, and arrived here at seven o'clock in the evening — thus traveling 88 miles in eight and three quarter hours. . . . Some of the passenger cars on this road are very elegant, and will hold from 20 to 30 persons. The motion of the cars upon the road is so easy that I saw a little child walking from seat to seat as if in a parlor."

Passenger train service now exists only because the commonwealth pours millions of dollars annually into subsidizing the tottering Boston and Maine and the New Haven lines. The Interstate Commerce Commission has repeatedly denied requests by both railroads to eliminate passenger service.

THE MASSACHUSETTS BAY TRANSPORTATION AUTHORITY

The first street railway company in Massachusetts was organized in 1854, and a road of three miles, between Cambridge and Bowdoin Square, Boston, was completed in 1856. Soon after, cars drawn by horses over rails connected Boston with several suburbs. In 1887, consolidation of competing transportation companies resulted in the West End Street Railway.

In 1889, electric cars were seen in Boston. In 1894, the Boston Elevated Railway Company was incorporated and services and construction of tunnels were expanded. In 1922, the first motor bus appeared on the street and in 1936 the first trackless trolley was seen.

The Boston Elevated Railway became the Metropolitan Transit

Authority in 1947. The MTA was created by the Legislature as a political subdivision and came about after the purchase of all the BER's stock. It served 14 cities and towns in Metropolitan Boston.

In 1964 the MTA became the Massachusetts Bay Transportation Authority and the number of towns it served was expanded to 78. Now serving 79 cities and towns, each is assessed proportionate shares of its deficit.

The authority is governed by a five-member board of governors, with a chairman, appointed by the governor, serving a five-year term.

The MBTA has 6514 employees, 1843 vehicles, and an annual passenger load of 194 million.

CANALS

About 1800 a new — to Massachusetts — and radically different method of transportation was devised — the canal. Stagecoaches were not adapted to handling freight, and the huge freight wagons later so important in developing the west had not yet been devised. Surveys were taken but little was done. Only one large canal was built during the 19th century. This was the Middlesex, completed in 1808, which extended from the Merrimack River near Lowell to the Charles River in Boston. The development of steam railways curtailed canal construction.

The Cape Cod Canal, completed shortly before WWI, made an island of Barnstable County. This canal eliminates the dangerous bad weather trip around the shallow waters off Provincetown.

SKYWAYS

Boston's Logan International Airport lies closer to Europe than the airport of any other American metropolis. This distance factor, however, has lost some of its importance in the jet age.

By 1970 more than 5,000,000 persons were flying out of Logan annually. More than 300,000 were international passengers. (For airport facilities see BOSTON.)

Springfield is served by Bradley Field, south of the Connecticut line, north of Hartford. Worcester also has airline facilities. There is seasonal air service to Hyannis, Provincetown, Martha's Vineyard and Nantucket.

The state has more than 160 airports, 105 for private use, 27 for commercial use, 25 publicly owned and 6 seaplane bases.

U.S. AIRBASES

U.S. Air Force Bases are Hanscom (Bedford), Otis (Falmouth), Westover (near Springfield), the U.S. Naval Air Station (Hingham) and the U.S. Coast Guard Air Station (Salem). Massachusetts Air National Guard planes are based at Logan International Airport.

13

Keeping Posted

There was a young maid from Back Bay
Whose manners were very blasé.
While still in her teens,
She refused pork and beans,
And once threw her *Transcript* away.

PROPER, AND SOME IMPROPER, Bostonians were very fond of their *Transcript* which carried occasional headlines in Latin and featured genealogical data illustrated with coats of arms. Four newsmen once went to a Brahmin's Beacon Street home for an interview. The butler piously announced, "Three reporters and the gentleman from the *Transcript.*"

The *Boston Transcript* (1830–1941), founded by Harvard man Lynde Walters, was the first major American newspaper edited by a woman, Miss Cornelia Walters. A gentleman's paper, it died in the early 1940's for want of readers — and advertising. Two noted *Transcript* alumni are Charles Morton, associate editor of *Atlantic,* and Brooks Atkinson, the *New York Times* drama critic (1925–60) and 1947 winner of the Pulitzer Prize for distinguished foreign correspondence. The dean of American dramatic critics for many years was the *Transcript*'s H. T. Parker (1867–1934).

THE CHRISTIAN SCIENCE MONITOR

The *Christian Science Monitor,* established in 1908 by Mary Baker Eddy (1821–1910), the founder of Christian Science, though edited and published in Boston, is not a local paper but one with international readership and prestige. Onetime Hearst newsman Willis J. Abbot (1863–1934) started the paper on its policy of distinguished foreign and domestic news coverage during his editorship (1921–27). A four-man editorial board ran the paper from 1927 until its present editor Erwin D. Canham took the reins in 1941.

The *Monitor,* under the editorship of Canham, has built a superb staff of domestic and foreign correspondents. Longtime Moscow correspondent Edmund Stevens won the 1950 Pulitzer Prize for international reporting.

The paper has had a national edition in 1911; an international edition has been printed in Boston since 1913, and since 1960 in Los Angeles and London. In accordance with the principles of Christian Science, it carries no drug, liquor or tobacco advertising. Its circulation is about 220,000. There is no Sunday edition.

HEARST IN BOSTON

News tycoon William Randolph Hearst (1863–1951) invaded Boston with his *American* in 1904. Harvard man Hearst, who was expelled for giving his professors as Christmas presents their portraits pasted on the inside bottom of chamber pots, bought the staid hundred-year-old *Advertiser* in 1917. It is now published only on Sunday (414,000). He bought the *Record,* founded in 1884, in 1920. His heirs killed the evening *American* and merged the name with the *Record,* a paper which now has the largest circulation (410,000) of any New England morning paper.

THE BOSTON GLOBE

The *Boston Globe,* founded in 1872 by Maturin Ballou (1820–95), was about to collapse when it was taken over by Gen. Charles H. Taylor (1846–1921). He slashed the price to two cents and joined the Democratic Party. Within three weeks circulation jumped from 8000 to more than 30,000. A few years later circulation passed the 150,000 mark. Gen. Taylor and his heirs stressed features and somehow and somewhere each year carried the names of thousands of subscribers even if the story were but four lines long.

The paper — still in the Taylor family — is now under the editorship of Thomas Winship, son of able longtime editor Laurence Winship (b. 1890). The Sunday *Globe,* with a circulation of close to 581,000, is New England's largest Sunday paper. The combined circulation of the morning and evening *Globe* is nearly 456,000.

THE BOSTON HERALD TRAVELER

The *Boston Journal,* originally the *Mercantile Journal* (1833), was one of the newspapers purchased by Frank Munsey (1854–1925), who earned the description "a dealer in dailies" by selling several newspapers after running them for a short time. Munsey bled the *Journal* to such an extent that its purchaser, the *Boston Herald Traveler,* killed it in 1917.

The *Herald* (1825) became New England's first Sunday paper, the Sunday *Herald,* in 1861. The *Herald* purchased the *Traveler* (1845) in 1912. The morning *Herald* in 1966 had 160,000 readers and the evening *Traveler* had 140,000 readers.

In 1970 the *Herald Traveler* merged, publishing a morning paper with a circulation of 210,000 and a Sunday paper, circulation, 261,000.

THE BOSTON POST

The *Boston Post,* founded by Charles G. Greene, was taken over by Edwin A. Grozier (1859–1924) in 1891. Grozier had been city editor of Pulitzer's *New York World.* Using Pulitzer's "yellow journalism" techniques, Grozier, by 1900, had pushed the once-faltering *Post*'s circulation to an alleged 450,000, making it the largest morning paper in America.

Grozier's heirs sold the paper to John Fox, once the "wonder boy of Wall Street," whose manipulations gave him control of Western Union. Several years later the *Post* was dead — and Fox was broke.

Novelist Kenneth Roberts (1885–1957) was probably the *Post's* most celebrated alumnus. The *Post* won the 1921 Pulitzer Prize for exposing con man Charles Ponzi.

NIEMAN FELLOWS

Massachusetts' greatest contribution to contemporary American journalism may be Harvard's Nieman Fellowships. Agnes Wahl Nieman, widow of Lucius W. Nieman (1857–1935), founder of the *Milwaukee Journal,* left her share of the paper to Harvard "to promote and elevate the standards of journalism and to educate persons deemed especially qualified."

Other University presidents might have founded just another journalism school, but President James B. Conant created a unique institution — the Nieman Fellowships. Each year about a dozen working newsmen, on leave from their paper for a year, attend Harvard and pursue whatever studies they are interested in. They receive no credit. Their regular salaries are paid by the Nieman Foundation. Some newsmen have specialized in a particular field such as law, government, history or economics while others range widely.

PULITZER PRIZES

The *Boston Globe* (1966) and the late *Boston Post* (1921) are the only Hub newspapers to win the coveted Pulitzer Prize for meritorious public service. Four *Boston Herald* editorial writers and two *Traveler* photographers have won Pulitzer Prizes.

Editorial Prize: Frank Buxton (1924), F. Lauriston Bullard (1927), John H. Crider (1949) and Don Murray (1954).

News Photography: Frank Cushing (1948) and Harry A. Trask (1957).

The *Christian Science Monitor*'s Moscow correspondent Edmund Stevens won the 1950 Pulitzer Prize for international reporting. *Monitor* correspondent John Hughes won the 1967 Pulitzer Prize for international reporting. *Monitor* newsmen Howard James (1968) and Robert Cahn (1969) won Pulitzer Prizes for national reporting.

DAILY PAPERS

Thirty-eight of the state's 39 cities have at least one daily newspaper. Cambridge, the state's third largest city, has no daily newspaper. Cantabrigians read Boston and/or New York papers. Springfield (*Union* and *News*) and Worcester (*Telegram* and *Gazette*) are the only cities outside Boston with two dailies.

The state, including Boston, has 47 daily newspapers. Of the 41 daily newspapers published outside of Boston only two, the *Worcester Telegram* and the *Springfield Union,* are morning papers.

THE WEEKLY PRESS

Nearly 100 Massachusetts communities have about 110 weekly newspapers. Sudbury has three weeklies, while Concord, Hingham, Holden, Hull, Maynard, Natick, Needham, Newton, Provincetown, South Boston and Watertown have two weeklies. Many weekly papers are members of the Massachusetts Press Association.

The new importance of the community press is illustrated by the increasing number of awards given to weekly newspapers. Owen McNamara, editor of the Brookline *Chronicle-Citizen,* in 1966 won the Golden Quill Award, given by the International Conference of

Weekly Newspaper Editors. In 1967 and 1970 he received awards in their Golden Dozen category. Other weekly award-winning newspapers include the Danvers *Herald,* Ipswich *Chronicle,* Hamilton-Wenham *Chronicle,* and Reading *Chronicle.*

TELEVISION

Of Massachusetts' 1,700,000 families, some 1,650,000 own television sets. Boston's WMEX had experimental television in the mid-1930's. The city's first commercial TV station, WBZ-TV (channel 4), an NBC affiliate, commenced operation in 1948. WBZ-TV is noted for its fine public service editorials and news staff. Boston's ABC station is WNAC (channel 7), and the CBS station is the Herald-Traveler-owned WHDH-TV (channel 5). Channel 38, run briefly by the Roman Catholic Archdiocese, is now a commercial station, WSBK, and the church has only closed circuit educational TV. WKBG-TV (channel 56) is owned by the Boston Globe and California's Kaiser Industries Corp.

Boston has two educational TV stations under the same management, WGBH (channel 2) and WGBX (channel 44). These non-profit stations, financed by grants and contributions, originate several fine shows including "The French Chef" with Julia Child and Thalassa Cruso's "Making Things Grow," "Evening at Pops" with Arthur Fiedler and "Jean Shepherd's America," which are shown by ETV stations throughout the nation. WGBX's pioneering program "Catch 44" schedules air time for individuals or groups with something on their mind, a way of providing access to the airwaves for the voiceless public.

Other Massachusetts TV stations are in New Bedford, WETV (channel 6) and Springfield, WWLP (channel 22), WRLP (channel 32) and WHYN (channel 40). Worcester's WJZB (channel 14) is inactive. Channel 19, atop Mount Greylock, is a satellite (relay station) for an Albany, N.Y., station. Out-of-state stations picked up in some areas are WMUR (channel 9), Manchester, N.H., and WJAR (channel 10) and WPRO (channel 12) of Providence, R.I.

Boston University's School of Public Communications has excellent professional and technical courses in motion picture and TV production.

14

Writers

MASSACHUSETTS, notorious for book banning — a not entirely deserved reputation — has produced many of the nation's most influential writers.

The civil disobedience philosophy of Concord's Henry David Thoreau (1817–62) as adopted by Mohandas K. Gandhi led to India's freedom — and to the very effective civil rights disobedience campaign in the United States. Lincoln gave American Negroes legal emancipation, but Henry Thoreau gave them means to practical effective emancipation.

"Rags to Riches" through honesty, thrift and hard work, America's longtime theme song, was propounded in 119 novels by a poor parson's son, Horatio Alger (1834–99) of Revere. Alger's titles tell the tale: *Ragged Dick, Tattered Tom, Tony the Hero, Mark the Match Boy, Ben the Luggage Boy* and *Phil the Fiddler.*

STEPHEN DAYE

When the Puritans arrived, they found the Plymouth congregation, a group of democratic dissenters, before them. To their alarm the Salem church shortly fell under this radical influence. In the resulting battle of words conservatives were represented by John Cotton; Nathaniel Ward, author of *The Simple Cobler of Aggawam* (1647); apostle to the Indians, John Eliot; Samuel Sewall, diarist; Cotton Mather, harsh and dogmatic in religion, progressive in natural science and medicine; and subtle-minded Increase Mather. The democrats counted fewer but on the whole more trenchant writers: Hugh Peter, Nathaniel Morton, Edward Johnson, author of *Wonder-Working Providence* (1654), Roger Williams, John Wheelwright.

The first press to be set up in the new country was that of Stephen Daye (1594–1668) in Cambridge, under the control of clerical Harvard College. The Daye press issued *The Bay Psalm Book,* that monument to early printing and bad rhyme, in 1640. Daye was succeeded by Samuel Green (1615–1702), who printed John Eliot's Indian New Testament in 1661 and the entire Bible in 1663. In 1669 Green issued

Morton's *New England's Memorial,* noteworthy for having not only a printer but a publisher, H. Usher of Boston. John Dunton, Scots bookseller, remarked in 1686 that there were eight bookshops in Boston village. Boston's first press (1675) was established by John Foster.

Not only theological tracts and sermons by Massachusetts writers were published during the 17th century. Mary Rowlandson's account of her captivity among the Indians, written in a vivid style without literary pretense, appeared in a second edition in 1682 (no copy of the first edition has survived). The anonymous *Relation,* descriptive of Plymouth and its settlement, appeared in 1622; Edward Winslow's *Good News from New England,* written like a letter home, described the new country. William Bradford, governor from 1621 to 1657 save for five years, wrote a *History of Plimoth Plantation* in 1630–46, the manuscript of which was lost for two hundred years, finally turning up to be published by the Massachusetts Historical Society in 1856. Captain Nathaniel Morton had access to the manuscript, for he used much of it in his *New England's Memorial* (1669).

Verse flourished no less than prose: Peter Folger's satire, *A Looking Glass for the Times* (1677); Benjamin Tompson's 650-line epic on King Philip's War, *New England's Crisis* (1650); and Michael Wigglesworth's *Day of Doom* (1662), an epic of the last judgment, were widely read for a hundred years.

EARLY DAYS

For almost one hundred years, before a Massachusetts printer dared publish a book he had to secure what practically amounted to an *imprimatur;* and if an author wrote a book with an heretical taint, he published it, if at all, in England. This condition existed until 1721 when Benjamin Franklin's brother James founded the lively *New England Courant* with the aid of the Hell Fire Club, hardly a clerical organization. Benjamin Franklin contributed the satiric *Silence Dogwood* papers to the *Courant,* slipping the first of them anonymously under the door. The *Courant* was an American *Spectator,* differing in its liveliness and literary tone from the *Boston Gazette.* Two years after the *Courant* first appeared, Benjamin Franklin went to Philadelphia, and his direct connection with Massachusetts ended.

Courant editors continually jeered at the dullness of its contemporaries, their staleness, their lack of American news and political comment. In self-defense, perhaps, *The New England Weekly Journal* was founded by a more sober group. The *Journal* had something of the liveliness of the *Courant,* but it was conservative in tone, and endeavored to offset the damage to faith, morals and politics being worked by the Franklins' paper.

THOMAS AND THE SPY

During the years 1770–76 Isaiah Thomas published *The Massachusetts Spy,* which pleaded the cause of revolution. This enterprising publisher, founder of the American Antiquarian Society, later published *The Royal American Magazine* (1774–75) noted for its Paul Revere engravings, *The Worcester Magazine* (1786–88), and *The Massachusetts Magazine* (1789–96). Other early Massachusetts magazines were *The American Magazine and Historical Chronicle* (1743–46) and *The New England Magazine* (1758–60).

During this period of political pamphleteering every agitator was an author and every author an agitator. Advocate-general James Otis was the most brilliant. *The Rights of the British Colonies Asserted and Proved* (1764) and the *Letter to a Noble Lord* (1765) are his best-known writings. John Adams and Josiah Quincy produced political pamphlets, as did Noah Webster, author of the dictionary and the blue-backed speller, who was as radical in politics as he was later to be in spelling. Samuel Adams, with his Committees of Correspondence, his *Massachusetts Circular Letter* (1768), is the prototype of them all.

HISTORIC HISTORIANS

Some Massachusetts folk but not many over the past years have written novels. Bay State Yankees, along with their fellows in the other five Yankee states, thought novels a waste of time both in the writing and the reading—and some still do. History was knowledge and Yankees have always been great for history. Many Yankees have written history, but even more have lived history.

The writing of American history, commencing with William Bradford's *History of Plimoth Plantation* (published in full, 1651), was almost a Bay State invention. Many products of early presses, and priceless manuscripts, were in the library of the Reverend Thomas Prince (1687–1758) of Boston, which, stored in the tower of the Old South Church, was dispersed and partly destroyed when British troops were quartered there during the American Revolution. Among these manuscripts was Bradford's *History of Plimoth Plantation.* Prince published in 1736 the first volume of his *Chronological History of New England in the Form of Annals,* which he unsuccessfully endeavored to continue in six-penny serial parts. His careful use of sources makes him the first trustworthy American historian: "I cite my vouchers to every passage," he said — and did.

A new note among Colonial historians appeared with the publication of the first volume of the *History of the Colony of Massachusetts Bay* in 1764. Its author, Thomas Hutchinson, was a descendant of Anne, and as unpopular as she, though for different reasons. He was a merchant, with conservative leanings, and the rising revolutionary temper of the people made Bostonians actively mistrust him as a Tory. His history was the first account of the Colony to be written without theological bias, and notwithstanding its conservative tone, it displays a considerable political sense.

Massachusetts historians like Jared Sparks (1789–1866) and George Bancroft (1800–91) pioneered in research and writing American history. Nearly all the 19th century's important historians were either Bay State natives or were associated with Harvard.

The family Adams made and wrote history. Presidents John and John Quincy Adams left voluminous correspondence and journals. Charles Francis Adams (1835–1915) authored *Three Episodes of Massachusetts History* (1892) and *Massachusetts: Its Historians and Its History* (1893). Brooks Adams (1848–1927), advocate of the cyclic theory of history, wrote *The Emancipation of Massachusetts* (1887), while brother Henry (1838–1918) wrote the autobiography, *The Education of Henry Adams* (privately printed, 1906; general publication, 1918).

Editor and Harvard President (1849–53) Jared Sparks was Harvard's first professor of nonreligious history (1839–49). Sparks, one of this nation's first major historians, published *The Life of Gouverneur Morris* (3 vols., 1832), *The Writings of George Washington* (12 vols., 1832–37) and *The Works of Benjamin Franklin* (10 vols., 1836–40). His work was marred by a failing common among his contemporaries: deleted and rearranged portions of his subjects' writing, notably Washington's. Sparks' greatest contribution was his determined effort to secure and preserve the papers of Washington, Franklin and other history-making Americans.

Salem native William Hickling Prescott (1796–1859), though nearly blind during much of his writing career — a fellow Harvard student hit his eye with a crust of bread — wrote excellent historical biographies: *History of the Reign of Ferdinand and Isabella the Catholic* (3 vols., 1836), *History of the Conquest of Mexico* (3 vols.,

1843), *History of the Conquest of Peru* (1847) and *History of the Reign of Philip the Second* (incomplete). Prescott, adept at selecting salient historical points, was a vivid narrator. Though some of his work is obsolete because of new archaeological discoveries and the finding of errors in his authorities, Prescott remains highly readable.

Worcester native George Bancroft wrote the first major *History of the United States* (10 vols., 1834–74). He also authored a two-volume *History of the Formation of the Constitution of the United States of America* (2 vols., 1882). Democrat Bancroft, a rarity in Federalist Boston, was Polk's secretary of the navy (1845–46). In 1845, acting secretary of war Bancroft sent Gen. Zachary Taylor into disputed Texas territory, thus laying the foundation for the acquisition of land from Mexico. He was U.S. minister to Great Britain (1846–49) and Prussia (1867–74). Bancroft's monumental work was marred by neglecting social and economic factors — a failing common among his era's historians. Yankee George Bancroft should not be confused with western states historian Hubert Bancroft (1832–1918).

Diplomat John Lothrop Motley (1814–77), Dorchester, Massachusetts, native who died in Dorsetshire, England, wrote *The Rise of the Dutch Republic* (3 vols., 1856), *The History of the United Netherlands* (4 vols., 1860–68) and *The Life and Death of John Barneveld* (2 vols., 1874).

Boston Brahmin Francis Parkman (1823–93) was 19th-century-America's greatest historian. Parkman saw the New World conflict between England and France as a struggle between the ordered democracy of England and the military tyranny of France. His great contribution was his long study of France and England in the New World which commenced with *History of the Conspiracy of Pontiac* (2 vols., 1851) and finished with *A Half-Century of Conflict* (2 vols., 1892).

Parkman, unfortunately, is best known to the general public for his *The California and Oregon Trail* (1849) rather than for his major historic works. Written shortly after his graduation from Harvard, the book narrates a journey he and his kinsman, Quincy Adams Shaw, took over the Oregon Trail. The book, marred by his youthful Brahmin prejudices, is considered by such western historians as Bernard DeVoto as inferior to several other trail books.

Boston's Justin Winsor (1831–97) authored *The Memorial History of Boston* (4 vols., 1880–81) and edited the *Narrative and Critical History of America* (8 vols., 1884–89). The former work has not been superseded but needs updating, while the latter remains useful for geographic material up to 1787. Winsor's permanent contribution to American history is primarily his correction of many geographic and cartographic errors which existed in earlier works. He made substantial contributions to library science and was Librarian of Boston Public Library (1868–77) and Harvard College (1877–97).

Holder of a Ph.D. in American history, Henry Cabot Lodge (1850–1924), the senator noted for his opposition to American membership in the League of Nations, was a prolific if pedestrian historical biographer. His works include *Alexander Hamilton* (1882), *Daniel Webster* (1882) and *George Washington* (2 vols., 1888). *The Senate and the League of Nations* (1925) is his account of the controversy over the Peace Treaty and Covenant.

Prolific historian Alfred Bushnell Hart (1854–1943) edited or wrote nearly 100 volumes of history, government and biography. Foreign policy specialist Hart wrote *Foundations of American Foreign Policy* (1901) and *The Monroe Doctrine: An Interpretation* (1917). He was the editor of and a major contributor to the "American Nation" series (28 vols., 1904–18).

Bostonian Samuel Eliot Morison (b. 1887) has won the Pulitzer Prize for biography twice with *Admiral of the Ocean Sea* (1942) and *John Paul Jones: A Sailor's Biography* (1959). He wrote *The Oxford History of the American People* (1965) which may be the best one-volume history yet written about his native land. As U.S. Navy historian Admiral Morison authored the official 15-volume *History of United States Naval Operations in World War II* (1947–62). Harvard professor and historian Morison has written many historical works including *The Maritime History of Massachusetts, 1783–1860* (1921, new ed., 1941), *Builders of the Bay Colony* (1930) and *Tercentennial History of Harvard College and University* (1936).

While still a Harvard graduate student, Morison wrote a widely praised two-volume biography about his great-grandfather Harrison Gray Otis: *The Life and Letters of Harrison Gray Otis, Federalist* (1913). Fifty-six years, 31 books and 45 volumes later Morison rewrote and revised the book and issued it in one volume titled *Harrison Gray Otis 1765–1848: The Urbane Federalist.*

Arthur M. Schlesinger's (1888–1965) works are often confused with those of his son, former Harvard historian Arthur M. Schlesinger, Jr. Both are American historians. Ohio native Arthur, Sr., was one of the first historians to focus attention on economic and social rather than on military and political aspects as had historians of the 19th and early 20th century. Schlesinger first exposed this new focus in *New Viewpoints in American History* (1922). He was coeditor of the 13-volume *History of American Life* series (13 vols., 1927–48), and his *Rise of Modern America* has long been a standard college history text.

He was an ardent campaigner to preserve historic American landmarks. Dr. Schlesinger was one of the late Senator Joseph McCarthy's outspoken foes. He taught history at Harvard from 1924 to 1954.

Historian Arthur M. Schlesinger, Jr. (b. 1917), speech writer for Adlai Stevenson and special assistant to President John F. Kennedy, won Pulitzer Prizes for *The Age of Jackson* (1945) and *A Thousand Days* (1965). After writing *A Thousand Days,* his intimate glimpse of the Kennedy administration, Schlesinger indicated he would complete his sympathetic study of the New Deal period, *The Age of Roosevelt.* Three volumes had been published: *The Crisis of the Old Order* (1957), *The Coming of the New Deal* (1958) and *The Politics of Upheaval* (1960). His first book, *Orestes A. Brownson: A Pilgrim's Progress* (1939), was written during his Harvard undergraduate days.

Americans, a westering people, are bound together by a continental experience. Bernard DeVoto (1897–1955) ably told the story and interpreted that experience in his trilogy, *The Year of Decision: 1846* (1943), *The Course of Empire* (1952) and the Pulitzer Prize-winning *Across the Wide Missouri* (1947). He was the nation's most outspoken writer on conservation during the time he was "The Easy Chair" editor of *Harper's Magazine* (1935–55). From 1936–38, he was editor of the *Saturday Review of Literature.* DeVoto was the official editor of Mark Twain's manuscripts at Harvard and published three books on Twain.

Brooklyn, New York, native and Harvard historian Oscar Handlin, winner of the 1952 Pulitzer Prize in history for *The Uprooted,* focuses his lens on immigration's influence on American culture. Handlin's numerous works include *Boston's Immigrants 1790–1865* (1941) and *Race and Nationality in American Life* (1957). Librarian Walter Muir Whitehill and Boston Athenæum director since 1946 has written several useful works including *The East India Marine Society and the Peabody Museum of Salem, A Sesquicentennial History* (1949), *Boston Public Library, A Centenary History* (1956), *Boston: A Topographical History* (1959) and *Independent Historical Societies* (1962).

Boston native and Holmes biographer Mark De Wolfe Howe (1906–67) died after completing only two volumes of his projected biography: *Mr. Justice Holmes: The Shaping Years 1841–1870* (1957) and *Justice Holmes: The Proving Years 1870–1882* (1963).

THE MAKING OF A PRESIDENT

Contemporary historian Theodore H. White (b. 1915) went through Harvard on a newsboy's scholarship, graduated *summa cum laude* in 1938 and went on a fellowship to China. After serving as

Time-Life bureau chief in wartime Chungking and in the China-Burma-India Theatre of Operations, he wrote *Thunder Out of China* (1946) in collaboration with colleague Annalee Jacoby. He edited *The Stilwell Papers* (1948) and wrote *Fire in the Ashes* (1953), a nonfiction bestseller about postwar Europe.

His *The Making of the President, 1960* (1961) won him a Pulitzer Prize for general nonfiction. He followed this work with *The Making of the President, 1964* (1965). The 1960 book has become a political campaign bible for free world statesmen. Britain's Harold Wilson studied President Kennedy's techniques, as expounded by White, in his successful 1964 campaign. *The Making of a President, 1968* (1969) provided a fascinating and penetrating insight on the Democratic primaries and the Nixon-Humphrey presidential contest.

President John F. Kennedy (1917–63), a 1940 graduate of Harvard, won the 1957 Pulitzer Prize for biography for *Profiles in Courage,* an inspirational rather than scholarly work. He was probably the most widely read President in our history. He made history and would probably have written it if he had survived his presidency. The Kennedy Library at Harvard will be the repository of his papers and other important documents.

CONCORD

Many mid-19th-century American intellectuals and liberals orbited about Concord and its residents Ralph Waldo Emerson (1803–82) and Henry David Thoreau (1817–62). Transitory inhabitants included Nathaniel Hawthorne (1804–64) and Bronson Alcott (1799–1888), whose daughter Louisa May Alcott (1832–88) wrote sentimental tales for young people. Frequent village visitors included Dr. O. W. Holmes, William Ellery Channing, and Harvard President Charles William Eliot.

America's political independence came July 4, 1776, but its intellectual independence, according to Dr. Holmes, came in 1837 when Emerson delivered his Phi Beta Kappa Society speech, "The American Scholar," at Harvard. A former Unitarian minister, Emerson was the "first philosopher of the American spirit," but he was not a philosopher with a planned program. He believed in inspiration. He did not think that man was damned for original sin. Heaven, he said, was attained through good works. Such thinking was radical in those days.

Henry David Thoreau, though not too well thought of in his day, survives as a powerful force. Gandhi freely admitted that his civil disobedience campaign which freed India was directly taken from Thoreau's 1849 essay, "Civil Disobedience." *Walden* (1854), an account of his life at Walden Pond, is an American classic. Several of nature lover Thoreau's books were published posthumously: *Excursions* (1863), *The Maine Woods* (1864), *Cape Cod* (1865) and *A Yankee in Canada* (1866).

Salem-born novelist Nathaniel Hawthorne is one of America's great writers. His *The Scarlet Letter* (1850) is one of the few pre-Civil War novels still in print. Some of his writing was done in Concord, but he wrote much more while he was employed in various minor capacities by the federal government. In and out of office under the Whigs, he was retained by the Democrats and sent by his friend and Bowdoin classmate President Franklin Pierce (1804–69) to Liverpool as consul (1853–58). Hawthorne had earned this reward by writing a campaign biography of Pierce in 1852. Other novels and short story collections include *Twice Told Tales* (1837), *Mosses from an Old Manse* (1848), *The House of the Seven Gables* (1851), *The Blithedale Romance* (1852) and *The Marble Faun* (1860). During his Berkshire residence in the early 1850's he encouraged his friend Herman Melville to complete *Moby Dick.*

HERMAN MELVILLE

Herman Melville (1819–91) was born and died in New York, but his paternal grandfather, Maj. Thomas Melville, was a Bostonian. Melville sailed on Yankee ships and wrote *Moby Dick* (1851) in Massachusetts. He married the daughter of Massachusetts' Chief Supreme Court Justice Lemuel Shaw. His other major works include *Typee* (1864), *Omoo* (1847), *Israel Potter* (1855) and *Billy Budd, Foretopman* (c. 1889). *Moby Dick* did not sell well. It soon went out of print and was not rediscovered until about 1920, when the great Melville revival began.

POETS

Henry Wadsworth Longfellow (1807–82) was born in Portland while Maine was still part of Massachusetts. He was the average 19th-century-American's favorite poet. Bowdoin graduate (1825) Longfellow taught modern languages at Harvard (1836–54) and revealed his prose narrative skill in *Tales of a Wayside Inn* (1863). He converted the forgotten Paul Revere into a folk hero. *The Court-*

ship of Myles Standish (1858) gave us the deathless phrase, "Why not speak for yourself, John?" Longfellow spent his Cambridge years in Craigie-Longfellow House, Brattle Street, now a historic shrine.

Haverhill native John Greenleaf Whittier (1807–92), poet, politician, Quaker and abolitionist, is best known for his poem, "Snowbound" (1866). The gentle yet sometimes fierce Whittier was probably the 19th century's best balladist and produced a great amount of poetry and political writing.

Editor William Cullen Bryant (1794–1878), New Yorker by residence, Bay Stater (Cunningham) by birth and poet of the Berkshire Hills, is usually remembered for his poem, "Thanatopsis," which he wrote at 16 and published in 1817.

Amherst native Emily Dickinson (1830–86) drifted into poetry after an unhappy love affair. Only two poems (one of these, in the Springfield *Republican,* appeared with no signature) were published during her lifetime. Now regarded as one of America's greatest poets, her poems have been meticulously edited by Thomas H. Johnson.

Amy Lowell (1874–1925), a poetic and social rebel, wrote sensitive impressions or "images" of life around her. Her first poems were published by the *Atlantic Monthly* in 1910. She wrote about a dozen volumes of poems and criticism and was posthumously awarded the 1926 Pulitzer Poetry Prize for her *What's O'Clock.*

To the poetry renaissance which began in Chicago about 1912 Massachusetts contributed T. S. Eliot, S. Foster Damon, Conrad Aiken and Robert Hillyer, among others, who were at first encouraged by Amy Lowell and then satirized in *A Critical Fable,* patterned after her great-uncle James Russell Lowell's satire. Miss Lowell introduced to young American poets the French symbolists and impressionists of the 1890's along with the Imagists. Her free verse and polyphonic prose forms directly influenced many. The 1912–16 movement, so promising in its inception, was fatally cut off by WWI. Miss Lowell, sister of Harvard president A. Lawrence Lowell (1856–1943) and astronomer Percival Lowell (1855–1916) succeeded Ezra Pound as leader of the Imagist movement in poetry. Pound promptly dubbed his ex-followers, "Amygists."

Amy Lowell's distant cousin, Bostonian Robert Lowell, Jr. (1917), won the 1947 Pulitzer Prize for poetry for his second volume of verse, *Lord Weary's Castle.* His other works include *Life Studies,* 1960 National Book Award winner, *Phaedra* (1961) and *For the Union Dead* (1964).

PHILOSOPHERS

William and Henry James were native New Yorkers, but their names are intimately associated with Massachusetts and Harvard. Henry (1843–1916) attended Harvard Law School and then moved to England and became a novelist. William (1842–1910) remained in Cambridge as a pioneer psychologist. His Harvard contemporary was the remarkable scientific realist Charles S. Peirce (1839–1914). Josiah Royce (1855–1916) and George Santayana (1863–1952), a Spaniard with a Boston mother, were of a slightly later vintage.

Louis Agassiz (1807–73), nourished on idealistic philosophy, remained during 25 Harvard professorial years the storm center of opposition to Darwinism. He was accused by his European contemporaries of trading his scientific birthright for a mess of Puritan pottage. His students became evolutionists to a man.

NOVELISTS

Long a Provincetown resident, John Roderigo Dos Passos (1896–1970) was essentially a social documentarian rather than a novelist. His superb massive trilogy *U.S.A.*—*The 42nd Parallel* (1930), *Nineteen-Nineteen* (1931) and *The Big Money* (1936)—will probably never be excelled for its comprehensive sensitive coverage of American life during the century's first three decades. Dos Passos' literary devices, the Camera Eye and Newsreel, originally appeared in *Manhattan Transfer* (1925).

Novelist John P. Marquand (1894–1960), once the author of Mr. Moto thrillers, portrayed proper Bostonians in the Pulitzer-Prize-winning *The Late George Apley* (1937), *Wickford Point* (1939) and *H. M. Pulham, Esq.* (1941). Marquand was not a native of Massachusetts, having been born in Delaware, but he wrote for the *Boston Transcript* for some years during World War I.

Providence native and former Boston radio newsman Edwin O'Connor (1918–68) portrayed colorful James Curley—or so Curley said after he discovered the book's popularity—as politico Frank Skeffington in *The Last Hurrah* (1956). O'Connor's *The Edge of Sadness* (1961) was awarded the Pulitzer Prize for fiction.

Ex-Bostonian Nancy Hale (b. 1908), novelist and short story writer, authored *The Prodigal Woman* (1942), a novel about Beacon Hill residents. Boston native Henry Morton Robinson (1898–1962) wrote the best-selling *The Cardinal* (1950), based on the lives of several priests.

Novelist Esther Forbes (b. 1894), a Westborough native, won the 1943 Pulitzer Prize for history for *Paul Revere and the World He Lived In.* Her novels include *Johnny Tremain: A Novel for Young and Old* (1943), *The Running of the Tide* (1948) and *Rainbow on the Road* (1954).

Onetime Boston and Paris newsman Elliot Paul (1891–1958) of Malden wrote the moving account of his Paris between the wars in the best-selling *The Last Time I Saw Paris* (1942) and of his Majorca years in *The Life and Death of a Spanish Town* (1937). *Bon vivant* Paul, possessor of either a prodigious memory or a lively imagination, wrote many other delightful, lusty and humorous autobiographical books, *e.g., Linden on the Saugus Branch* (1947), *Ghost Town on the Yellowstone* (1948) and *My Old Kentucky Home* (1949).

Quincy native John Cheever (1912), longtime *New Yorker* magazine short story writer, won the National Book Award in 1958 for his first novel, *The Wapshot Chronicle.* This story about a New England family was followed in 1964 by the sequel *The Wapshot Scandal.*

PUBLISHERS

The North American Review was founded in 1815. The short-lived *Pioneer,* whose three issues included contributions by Poe and Hawthorne, was published in 1843 by James Russell Lowell, who became the first editor of the *Atlantic Monthly* in 1857. With the establishing of the *North American Review* and of two great publishing houses, Ticknor and Company (1833), later Ticknor and Fields, the direct predecessors of Houghton Mifflin Company (1864) and of Little and Brown (1837), literature in Massachusetts had a firm underpinning.

Authorship until the mid-19th century was not a livelihood but an avocation of amateurs and gentlemen of means. As late as 1842 William Ellery Channing remarked that Hawthorne was the only American who supported himself by writing. Channing was mistaken, although not very much so. Jedidiah Morse (1761–1826) of Charlestown, America's first geographer, had been one of the few writers in America to make writing pay, although his school geographies and gazetteers scarcely rank as literature. In 1790, Congress passed a law to protect literary property. But in the absence of substantial publishing houses or magazines that paid for contributions, and in view of the continual pirating of books by English and American authors on both sides of the Atlantic, writing was a poor trade. Even after the great Boston magazines and publishing houses were established, Bryant had to edit anthologies and a newspaper; Whittier struggled desperately until the publication of "Snow-Bound"; Mrs. Stowe made less than a living from her books until the phenomenal success of *Uncle Tom's Cabin;* and Prescott was the first historian to achieve financial success from his writings. None of these authors received any income from the European editions of their works. It was not until writers organized in the American Copyright League (1883) and publishers in the American Publishers' Copyright League (1887) that international piracy was halted by the copyright agreement of 1891.

Harvard University Press is one of the largest American university presses. The University of Massachusetts also publishes papers and books as does MIT.

Other publishing firms and their products include Addison-Wesley (text), Allyn and Bacon (text), Baker's (plays), Barre Publishers (regional nonfiction), Beacon Press (general nonfiction, juveniles), Gambit (trade), Ginn (text), D. C. Heath (text), Bruce Humphries (trade, educational), Identity Press (a few selected works available by subscription), G. & C. Merriam (Merriam-Webster dictionaries), Porter Sargent (reference, camp and school directories), Prindle, Weber and Schmidt (text), Peter Smith (reprints) and The Writer, Inc. (books for writers).

PULITZER PRIZES

Hungarian-born Joseph Pulitzer (1847–1911), founder of two great newspapers, the *St. Louis Post-Dispatch* and the late *New York World,* established a fund "for the encouragement of public service, public morals, American literature, and the advancement of education." Literary prizes are awarded annually in fiction, drama, history, poetry, autobiography or biography and, since 1962, general nonfiction.

Massachusetts writers, notably those associated with Harvard, have won Pulitzer Prizes for the works and in the years cited:

History: Charles Warren, *The Supreme Court in United States History* (1923); Paul H. Buck, *The Road to Reunion* (1938); Esther Forbes, *Paul Revere and the World He Lived In* (1943); Arthur M. Schlesinger, Jr., *The Age of Jackson* (1946); Bernard DeVoto, *Across the Wide Missouri* (1948); Oscar Handlin, *The Uprooted* (1952).

Biography or Autobiography: Laura Richards, Maude Howe Elliott, *Julia Ward Howe* (1917); Henry Adams, *The Education of Henry Adams* (1919); Henry James, *Charles W. Eliot* (1931); Ralph Barton Perry, *The Thought and Character of William James* (1936); Samuel Eliot Morison, *John Paul Jones* (1960); Arthur M. Schlesinger, Jr., *A Thousand Days* (1965).

General Nonfiction: Theodore H. White, *The Making of the President, 1960* (1962); Howard Mumford Jones, *O Strange New World* (1965).

Fiction: John Marquand, *The Late George Apley* (1938); Edwin O'Connor, *The Edge of Darkness* (1962).

Poetry: Amy Lowell, *What's O'Clock* (1926); Archibald MacLeish, *Conquistador* (1933) and *Collected Poems 1917–1952* (1953); Robert Lowell, *Lord Weary's Castle* (1947). Occasional Massachusetts resident Robert Frost (1874–1963) has been the only four-time poetry award winner.

Drama: Archibald MacLeish, *J.B.* (1959). Four-time winner Eugene O'Neill (1888–1953) began his career in Provincetown.

Pulitzer Prizes for biographies or autobiographies have been written by and/or about several other Massachusetts natives or residents. Harvard lawyer and educator M. A. DeWolfe Howe, *Barrett Wendell and his Letters* (1925); brain surgeon Harvey Cushing, *The Life of Sir William Osler* (1926); Ray Stannard Baker, *Woodrow Wilson, Life and Letters* (1940); Samuel Eliot Morison, *Admiral of the Ocean Sea* (1943); Carleton Mabee, *The American Leonardo: The Life of F. B. Morse* (1944); Russel Blaine Nye, *George Bancroft: Brahmin Rebel* (1945); Wellesley president Margaret Clapp, *Forgotten First Citizen, John Bigelow* (1948); Worcester-born historian and educator Samuel Flagg Bemis, *John Quincy Adams and the Foundations of American Foreign Policy* (1950); John F. Kennedy, *Profiles in Courage* (1957); David Donald, *Charles Sumner and the Coming of the Civil War* (1961); Ernest Samuels, *Henry Adams* (1965).

Pulitzer Prizes for history awarded to Bay Staters and/or for books about Bay State subjects include James Truslow Adams, *The Founding of New England* (1922); Harvard graduate Van Wyck Brooks, *The Flowering of New England* (1937); Arthur M. Schlesinger, Jr., *The Age of Jackson* (1946); Williams College president James Phinney Baxter III, *Scientists Against Time* (1947); and Northampton native Sumner Chilton Powell, *Puritan Village: The Formation of a New England Town* (1964).

15

Artists

MASSACHUSETTS is rich in its arts. It has a good tradition in handicraft, was once the stronghold of eminent portrait painters, and abounds with art museums and historic houses.

MUSEUMS

Museums outwit each other in acquisition of rarities and in publication of researches. While museums show increasing range of interest, each in its way has a splendid collection or a department in which it excels. The Boston Museum of Fine Arts is particularly notable for superb Far Eastern treasure, while the Worcester Art Museum draws attention by its magnificent mosaics of the Middle Ages. The Smith College Art Museum has concentrated on modern French pictures, and at the Fogg Art Museum, Harvard, there is an exceptional display of Italian primitives. The Addison Gallery of American Art at Andover is one of the most important specialized collections of American art in the land. This, together with the Germanic Museum at Harvard and the De Cordova Museum in Lincoln, shows a marked interest in living art through exhibition and purchase. Western Massachusetts has the notable Sterling and Francine Clark Art Institute in Williamstown.

PURITAN CONTRIBUTIONS

In its earliest days, Massachusetts did not provide a hospitable environment for the living artist. Restraints of economic necessity and puritanic bias prevented free expression in the arts.

Puritanism's anti-art attitude had some very positive benefits. America's most beautiful churches — with the possible exception of a few clean-lined missions in the southwest — are New England's pre-1800 white churches with clear glass windows and simple lines.

Puritan handicraft was directed toward articles of household use, furniture, utensils, pewter, silver, textiles and some solemn likenesses of early worthies. Based upon English prototypes, the articles conformed to local needs. Viewed today in historic houses or museums, they show good taste and adaptation of materials. Puritanism was opposed in principle to art. There was not the impulse of native taste or the urgency of demand to propel artists' imaginations.

PORTRAITS

The personal pride, luxurious indulgence and forgivable conceit which prompted Americans to have their portraits painted revealed unmistakably their forceful characteristics and newly acquired finery. It was a painting of form and feature, flounce and frill, with rarely a sidelong glance at nature, or critical observation of society. The early limners held forth with reserve, as artisans who had branched from the more useful calling of coach or sign painting, and some, in the well-known matter-of-fact manner, peddled their wares from house to house. They carried portraits painted completely except for the face, to be bargained for by the anxious client.

Early portraits are flat and descriptive, lacking the lifelike character and subtle handling of European portraiture of the time; possessing, on the other hand, the decorative beauty which to present-day taste is so appealing in provincial art. Interesting early portraits are in the Worcester Art Museum. "Mrs. Freake and Baby Jane" is one of the handsomest and most touching of seventeenth century portraits. "John Freake" is there too, an imposing likeness in which particular attention has been paid to ornate costume. In Worcester's American Antiquarian Society are portraits of Samuel, Increase and Cotton Mather.

Portraiture developed in the 18th century into a specialty. John Smibert (1688–1751) came from Scotland to Boston to paint, and incidentally designed Faneuil Hall in Boston. Joseph Blackburn (flourished 1753–63), Robert Feke (about 1705–50) and Ralph Earle (flourished 1751–61) were among the early exponents, and their portrayals are on exhibition at Harvard University and in the museums in Boston, Worcester and Andover.

Portraiture attained a notable height in the canvases of John Singleton Copley (1738–1815). In the opinion of many, Copley executed his finest pictures here at home, before he departed — in what was to become a too-common practice among Massachusetts artists — to England to live. There was something in the native environment, in the types of personages he portrayed, in the limited tradition out of which his style developed that proved salutary to Copley. In England he lost individuality, acquired suaver traits. Colonial personalities, humble, smug, forceful, are clearly characterized in the Copleys shown throughout Massachusetts.

Boston resident Gilbert Stuart (1755–1828) painted outstanding Americans of the early republican days. Athenæum-owned portraits of George and Martha Washington hang in the Boston Museum of Fine Arts. Stuart differs from Copley in the swift summary handling and the emphasis upon facial features and expression, with comparative indifference to costume. Portraits in smaller dimension are scattered throughout the state. Besides its 300 painted portraits, Essex Institute in Salem possesses a fine collection of silhouettes. Edward Greene Malbone (1777–1807) miniatures are in Worcester and Boston museums. Wax miniatures are displayed in several historic collections.

During the same period household arts surpassed pictorial arts. Cotton Mather had written that within a dozen years after the granting of the charter to the Massachusetts Bay Colony "artificers to the number of some thousands came to New England." Early Boston silversmiths included notables Robert Sanderson (1608–93), who instructed many in the art, Jeremiah Dummer (1645–1718), John Coney (1655–1722) and, in the 18th century, the versatile Paul Revere (1735–1818), who, in addition to tankards, punchbowls and candlesticks, made silver dental plates which he advertised as "of real Use in Speaking and Eating." The first articles of furniture of artistic significance to be made in the state were carved oak chests, which slowly evolved into highboys and writing desks. Dartmouth native John Goddard (1723–85), who produced stately pieces in Santo Domingo mahogany, practiced his craft in Rhode Island. As early as 1638 crude glass lamps and bottles were being manufactured in Peabody, but Deming Jarves (1790–1868), head of the Boston and Sandwich glass works, revolutionized the glass industry with his new methods of furnace construction, his rediscovery of the method of manufacturing red lead and his inventions in color-mixing. The Decorative Arts Wing of the Boston Museum has many interesting period rooms. The historic houses throughout the state give evidence of excellent handiwork, indicating the changes in taste from the early days of rigorous thrift to later luxury and finesse. Objects of folk-interest — samplers, coverlets, mourning pictures, painted Bible pictures — reveal imaginative qualities which painters in a more formidable craft lacked.

The art of carving found a touching expression in gravestones, which apparently deserved special attention in the solemn judgment of colonials. Such memorials are extant in burying grounds of Deerfield, Salem, Concord, Boston and towns on Cape Cod. They show an authentic talent for carving decorative borders, sacred symbols and ruminative epitaphs. This manner of commemoration was original and appropriate and showed far more vitality in design and feeling for the craft than was revealed in native plastic art of later date.

Portraiture's popularity continued in the early days of the republic. Painters went abroad for study and stimulus. Massachusetts, which had such a favorable atmosphere for the ripening of Copley's style, could not hold its painters. They wandered to London and Paris but were not shrewd enough to ally themselves with the best teachers. Benjamin West (1728–1820) took young Americans under his wing. Samuel F. B. Morse (1791–1872), seeking instruction abroad, boasted of having studied with Washington Allston (1779–1843), whose unfinished masterpiece, "Belshazzar's Feast," is in the Boston Museum. Massachusetts artists were eager but lacked taste and tenacity. Abroad they responded to the official and obvious. They seemed to favor the literary and rhetorical. Morse gave up painting, as there was no market and no recognition. He turned to inventing, where his successes never consoled him for his failure as an artist. His "Self Portrait" hangs in the Addison Gallery in Andover. Chester Harding (1792–1866) carried portraiture well into the 19th century, when changes took place with the rapid growth of the republic and there were political and industrial reverberations abroad.

THE GO-AWAYERS

James Whistler (1834–1903) and Winslow Homer (1836–1910) were Massachusetts-born, but there was little at home to foster the talents of a painter. One escaped to the solace and enhancement of European life; the other withdrew to solitude at Prout's Neck on the Maine coast. Whistler possessed skill and wit, and his pictures are an odd mixture of influences from Turner to Degas, from the Pre-Raphaelites to the Japanese. Whistler did not follow his fellow countrymen to the academy. He did not like the sleek, photographic and artificial. He had a fine decorative sense, and a taste for the diffuse and atmospheric. His etchings rank him with masters in that medium. Nevertheless, he remained a wanderer, lacked a mooring and fell short of greatness as a painter.

Winslow Homer went abroad, but he did not stay for long. He found watercolor a more responsive medium for his direct, decisive reaction to the outdoors. He painted what he saw with the impact of the first fresh impression. His straightforward, realistic portrayals mark him one of the first Massachusetts painters with a dynamic style. Homer furnishes the moral to escaping artists. He helped deliver New

England artists from a sense of inferiority, from the uncontroverted domination of foreign ideas which were not too well selected, not too thoroughly assimilated. In summer, Homer painted at his Prout's Neck studio in Maine but preferred the warm, lush climate of subtropical Florida and the Bahamas in winter. The finest Homer collection, including many of his best works, is in Boston's Museum of Fine Arts.

RYDER AND HUNT

New Bedford native Albert Pinkham Ryder (1847–1917) also painted the sea, but his portrayal was veiled in poetry, shaded with mysticism, softened with sentiment. Ryder avoided the American scene, not as Homer or Whistler, but by withdrawing into himself, painting from personal resource, inner feeling. In Deerfield dwelt another native artist who painted in a gentle sentiment, George Fuller (1822–84).

Vermonter William Morris Hunt (1824–79) exercised considerable influence upon Bostonians through his great interest in the Barbizon school in France, especially F. D. Millet. The atmosphere at home seemed unsympathetic to him, too. He longed for what was lacking: an impetus to paint. An entire gallery of his paintings is in the Boston Museum. His pupil and friend, John La Farge (1835–1910), was commissioned by architect Henry Richardson to paint murals in Trinity Church on Copley Square. On the same square stands the Boston Public Library, where murals cover the walls on the second and third floors. There is one series by the French neoclassicist, Puvis de Chavannes (1824–98), the illustrative "Quest of the Holy Grail" series by Edwin Abbey (1852–1911) and the elaborately wrought theological sequence by John Singer Sargent (1856–1925), to some his greatest performance.

SCULPTORS

Massachusetts sculptors have worked under a handicap that is more universal, for their special craft struggles to survive in a world which seems to find no urgent need of it. That native Americans enjoyed whittling and carving is apparent in their early houses, furniture, ship figureheads, gravestones, weather vanes, wild fowl decoys, scrimshaw (there is an interesting collection in the Whaling Museum in New Bedford); but when they applied their gift to the formal art of portraiture, they showed little taste and insufficient vitality. Samuel McIntire (1757–1811) had a peculiar gift for carving portals and architectural decorations with the wholesome application of craft to function. That peculiar attribute of functionalism in style is rooted in Massachusetts craft. The most classical example is that of the Shaker workshops, which provided a variety of articles for daily use, admonishing the maker to do the job as efficiently as possible, with an eye to simplicity and usefulness.

Horatio Greenough (1805–52) went to Italy to assimilate neoclassical ideas. Sculptors, like many painters, possessed enthusiasm and eagerness but no commensurate creative imagination. They lacked roots. There were sculptors like Henry Kirke Brown (1814–86), Harriet Hosmer (1830–1908) and Thomas Ball (1819–1911) who did an equestrian statue of George Washington that stands in the Public Garden in Boston. Many pieces, generally Italianate or official in character, are on view throughout the state. Most native are the diminutive groups executed by John Rogers (1829–1904) of Salem, ingenuous portrayals of everyday life of Americans and realistic scenes of the Civil War, a descriptive sculpture illustrating life in America and true-to-life aspirations in Massachusetts. At Essex Institute there is a very large collection of Rogers groups.

Outstanding Massachusetts sculptures are the "Shaw Memorial," a high relief in bronze by Augustus Saint-Gaudens opposite the State House and "Dean Chapin" by the same sculptor in Springfield. The "Minuteman" in Concord and "John Harvard" in Cambridge were executed by Daniel Chester French, who had studied sculpture under a Boston teacher. Cyrus Dallin, sympathetic portrayer of the American Indian, did "Appeal to the Great Spirit," in front of the Boston Museum of Fine Arts.

CONTEMPORARY ART

Contemporary artists began to obtain public recognition of their works through the Federal Art Project of the Works Progress Administration. This New Deal agency hired unemployed artists and used their works to decorate the walls of federal buildings. Much of the Art Projects' works were of the conventional "why it looks just like a photograph" type, partly due to the controversial nature of the project and in part to the conventional tastes of federal officials who controlled the purse strings. The project did, however, provide many capable young artists with a living so that their spare time could be devoted to more creative painting and sculpture.

Conventional Newbury Street galleries once continued to reject contemporary paintings, but many artists found Boris Mirski, a onetime painter turned creative picture framer, willing to display their paintings on the walls of his tiny cellar shop on Beacon Hill. Mirski's gallery today is but one of many contemporary galleries along Newbury Street. Its proprietor after nearly 40 years of exhibiting contemporary painters continues to seek new talent though he often exhibits many of his former protégés.

Rockport, Gloucester, and Provincetown are still pre-eminent as Bay State's art colonies after more than a half century in this role. Provincetown marine painter John Whorf (1903–59) now lies in his adopted town's burying ground. Rockport's Aldro Hibbard (b. 1886), known for his Vermont winter scenes, is still active at 84, as is his neighbor the well-known marine painter Stanley Woodward (b. 1890).

Berlin native Karl Zerbe (b. 1903), director (1937–53) of the Museum of Fine Arts' school of painting, and long a substantial influence among young Boston area painters, unfortunately has swapped Boston's climate for that of Tallahassee where since 1954 he has been associated with Florida State University's art department. Zerbe, an able exponent of the encaustic technique — hot wax mixed with oil paint — has been compelled to abandon this medium because of a physical allergy to the ingredients. Bostonian Jason Berger, a former pupil of Zerbe at the Museum School, continues to achieve international recognition for his fine oils.

The Museum School continues its substantial role in developing area artists — many come a far distance to attend — and the art departments of the state's many universities and colleges, notably Harvard's School of Fine Arts, are establishing their own painters. Like Boris Mirski, the Institute of Contemporary Art on Beacon Street exhibits both local and internationally known contemporary artists.

16

Theater

THE HEADMISTRESS of the female seminary told Harvard President Charles William Eliot she wanted a promising Harvard professor to head her English department. The candidate, she said, must have a Ph.D.

"Thank God! We can keep Kittredge," retorted Eliot.

George Lyman Kittredge (1860–1941) was one of America's foremost authorities on Shakespeare and Chaucer and taught English at Harvard for fifty years.

George Pierce Baker (1866–1935) with his Harvard Workshop 47 introduced in 1905 the first course in practical playwriting offered by an American college. Following the first performance of a student-written play, Baker had each member of the audience write a criticism. Students included future playwrights Eugene O'Neill, George Abbott and Sidney Howard and novelist and occasional playwright Thomas Wolfe (1900–38). Baker probably did more than any other American to elevate the standards of playwriting.

SLOW BEGINNINGS

While Massachusetts' early history is nearly synonymous with that of the United States, its theater history began much later than it did in cities such as New York, Philadelphia and Providence.

When Henry Vane failed to be re-elected as Massachusetts governor in 1637, he returned to England, thus ending his, John Winthrop's and the town fathers' effort toward a more liberal policy. Nearly fifty years later, in 1686, Increase Mather continued this unfortunate trend by publishing a "Testimony Against Profane and Superstitious Customs," in which he cried out against the "discourse now of beginning Stage Plays in New England."

Since our forefathers had little knowledge or interest in the arts, outside liberalizing influences had to wait for liberalizing influences from within the Puritan community.

When occasionally private plays were given at the beginning of the 18th century, fear of the building of a playhouse prompted the passage of "An Act to Prevent Stage Plays and Other Theatrical Entertainments" (1750). The General Court, supported for the most part by public sentiment, levied a fine of twenty pounds on anyone who allowed his premises to be used as a stage and a fine of five pounds on anyone who attended or acted in a performance.

In the latter half of the 18th century, however, liberal members of the community, particularly those whose business took them to New York where theater was flourishing, pressed for the repeal of the act. They failed, and, in 1778, the Continental Congress resolved that any officeholder of the United States who attended a play would immediately lose his position. In 1784, the antitheater act was reenacted in Massachusetts.

The act finally met its end in the 1790's. The New Exhibition Room opened on what is now Hawley Street, Boston, with a performance of a variety show in 1792. *Romeo and Juliet, Hamlet* and *Othello,* billed as "moral lectures," followed. With the subsequent arrest and discharge on a technicality of manager Joseph Harper, Massachusetts' theater history began. In 1794, Charles Bulfinch designed the Boston Theater, at the corner of Federal and Franklin Streets. The theater went bankrupt at the end of its first year, but a second theater, the Haymarket, was completed a year later. Until it was torn down in 1803, a fierce competition between the two theaters enlivened Boston's social life.

The Boston Theater did well for a quarter of a century with a fine stock company, and the Boston Museum, on Tremont Street, had one of the best stock companies in the country from 1860 to 1880. But the "star" system early made Boston a theatrical dependency on New York, and only such fleeting successes as that of John Craig and Mary Young at the Castle Square were singularly Boston enterprises.

THE PROVINCETOWN PLAYERS

The Provincetown Players, one of the first "little theaters" in the country, is noted for giving Eugene O'Neill's plays their first productions. Founded in 1915 by George Cram Cook, the company opened in 1916 with O'Neill's *Bound East for Cardiff* at the Wharf Theatre, Provincetown, on Cape Cod. Other O'Neill plays produced there include *The Long Voyage Home* (1917) and *The Moon of the Caribees* (1918).

THEATER NOW

Boston today is one of the top theater cities in the country. Many Bostonians are avid theatergoers with well-developed critical faculties. The city is a most important tryout city for future Broadway shows and depends on New York for its Broadway musicals and plays. On any given date, most Boston shows are either headed for or are on national tour out of New York. Boston's three "Broadway" theaters are the Colonial, Shubert and Wilbur.

The Charles Playhouse and the Theatre Company of Boston are the city's two professional "off-Broadway" houses. Both groups present approximately six plays between fall and spring and have many yearly subscribers. The Charles group was founded in 1955 by Frank Sugrue and Michael Murray in a loft on Charles Street; the Theatre Company was started by David Wheeler in 1963. Both groups have recently suffered major financial difficulties.

Boston theater groups which have sprung up in the past five years and which usually play in churches and former coffeehouses include the Atma Theatre, Caravan Theater (Cambridge), Hub Theatre Centre, People's Theatre Company, and the Rose Coffee House. The Proposition in Inman Square, Cambridge, presents evenings of improvisations. Now in its fourth year, it is one of the most popular entertainments in the area.

Harvard's Loeb Drama Center presents a spring-through-fall series of plays as well as a summer series. The center recently has hosted foreign touring companies, such as France's Le Treteau de Paris and West Germany's Die Brücke, which perform in their native language.

A Harvard tradition is the spring Hasty Pudding Show, a comedy-musical written and produced by members of the Hasty Pudding Club. All members of the cast are male and usually play the female role with astonishing veracity.

Other college and university theaters include Boston University Theater, Brandeis' Spingold Theatre, Emerson College Theater, MIT's Kresge Auditorium and Tufts' Arena Theater.

SUMMER THEATER

Massachusetts, Provincetown in particular, is the home of the summer theater. The state's three major summer vacation areas, Cape Cod and the islands, the North Shore, and the Berkshires, are summer theater centers. Communities in these areas which have no such facility are within a few minutes' driving time of a town which does. Major summer theaters usually have a name actor or actress in the lead role. Shows usually change every week.

Theaters-in-the-round such as the North Shore Music Theatre in Beverly and the South Shore Music Circus in Cohasset have become increasingly popular. These tent theaters with circular stages — no backstage — usually have musicals boasting a Hollywood, TV or Broadway star every week.

17

The Sound of Music

BOSTON'S MOST CACOPHONOUS day came during the 1872 World Peace Jubilee when 30,000 Bostonians and rural visitors jammed temporary benches near Copley Square to see and hear Patrick S. Gilmore (1829–1892) out-Barnum P. T. Barnum. Irish-born bandmaster Gilmore, author of "When Johnny Comes Marching Home Again," had drummed up a 10,000-voice chorus, a 1000-piece band-orchestra, 40 soloists, the world's biggest bass drum and 4 giant organs pumped by 12-man relays. Fifty Boston firemen in white caps, red shirts and blue pants banged lustily on real anvils the "Anvil Chorus" of *Il Trovatore*. Meanwhile, church and schools bells pealed, steamboat and mill whistles tooted, cannons roared repeated volleys, girls shrieked, little boys hollered and off-key imbibers sang "How Dry I Am."

Not all Massachusetts' music has been of such doubtful quality, however. Julia Ward Howe (1819–1910) and Katherine Lee Bates (1859–1929) will long be remembered for "The Battle Hymn of the Republic" and "America the Beautiful," while Harvard's Walter Piston (b. 1894) won the Pulitzer Prize in 1948 and 1961 for *Symphony No. 3* and *Symphony No. 7*. New Yorker Edward A. MacDowell (1861–1908), one of America's first major composers, taught, composed and conducted during his 1888–96 Boston residence. Composer-conductor Leonard Bernstein, onetime protégé of Boston Symphony conductor Dr. Serge Koussevitzky, is a Massachusetts native.

MUSICAL NOTES

Massachusetts' musical history begins in Puritan days when singing was frowned on though unaccompanied psalm singing was soon approved of. The nation's first pipe organ was installed in 1714 in King's Chapel. The first known advertisement of an American concert was in the *Boston News-Letter*, 16–23 December 1731. An early vocal and instrumental concert was held in 1744 in Faneuil Hall.

The opening of theaters during the 1790's stimulated interest in music. The program for the opening night of the Boston Theatre February 3, 1794 included a "grand symphony by Signor Haydn."

One of the earliest musical societies — still in existence — was the Stoughton Musical Society (1786), founded by America's first native composer, William Billings (1746–1800) of Boston. A tanner by day and tunesmith by night, his crude but popular collections of church music include *The New England Psalm Singer* (1770), *The Singing Master's Assistant or Key to Practical Music* (1778) and *The Suffolk Harmony* (1786). He was the first American to use the pitch pipe in churches. Billing's spirited "fuguing" style did much to free church music from the everlasting Puritan drone.

Changes began to occur after 1800. In 1808 some Harvard students founded the Pierian Sodality, which led to the formation of the Harvard Musical Association, created in 1837 by former Pierian Society members. This group retired in 1881 when Major Henry Lee Higginson (1834–1919) founded the Boston Symphony Orchestra. The Harvard society is reported to have had more profound influence on American music than any other group in the nation. About 1810 Boston music publisher and engraver Johann Christian Gottlieb Graupner (1767–1836), once first oboist under Haydn, founded the Phil-harmonic Society. This native Prussian directed the weekly Saturday concerts of what became the Boston Philharmonic Orchestra.

In 1815 Graupner, together with Bostonians Asa Peabody and Thomas Webb, founded the famed Handel and Haydn Society as a permanent choral group. Its first concert was held Christmas Day, 1815, at Stone Chapel. Now an annual event in Boston, Handel's *Messiah* was first performed by the Society in 1818.

The first major step toward professional training for musicians came in 1833 when Medfield native Lowell Mason, with G. J. Webb, established the Boston Academy of Music. This admirable institution — long since defunct — gave free vocal instruction to upwards of 1000 children and 500 adults a year and in 1837 succeeded in introducing music into the Boston public schools. Its services to the teaching of music were inestimable, but perhaps even more fraught with consequence was its 1840 decision under the leadership of Boston Mayor Samuel A. Eliot, its president, to give up teaching and "to engage the best orchestra it can afford and give classical instrumental concerts." The immediate result was the first hearing of Beethoven in Boston, the First and Fifth Symphonies being performed by the Academy of Music Orchestra in its first season of eight concerts. The orchestra was small — 25–40 — and by no means perfect, but its seven-year existence made the coming of the Boston Symphony Orchestra inevitable.

Other stages were to intervene. One of these was the 17 years of Harvard symphony concerts from 1865 onward under Carl Zerrahn

(1826–1909). The German-born Zerrahn first came to the United States as a flutist with the Germania Orchestra, which visited Boston for a series of concerts beginning in 1848. He conducted the Handel and Haydn Society for forty years and until 1898 was a teacher at Boston's New England Conservatory of Music. The Conservatory, founded in 1867 by Dr. Eben Tourjee (1834–91), is one of the nation's finest music schools.

In the field of serious music Massachusetts stands almost alone. Bay State composers, either native or resident, include Lowell's George Chadwick (1854–1931); Charles M. Loeffler (1861–1935); Newton's Frederick S. Converse (1871–1940), whose *The Pipe of Desire* (1906) was the first opera composed by an American to be played in the Metropolitan Opera House (1910); Salem's Arthur W. Foote (1835–1937); Cambridge's Edward B. Hill (1872–1960); Marion's Carl Ruggles (b. 1876); and Cape Cod resident Bainbridge Crist (b. 1883).

THE BOSTON SYMPHONY

The Boston Symphony, one of the world's finest orchestras, was established by native New Yorker Major Henry Lee Higginson, a onetime Union soldier who made and lost several fortunes in Boston's financial world. Higginson organized the Boston Symphony in 1881 and paid its annual deficit until 1918.

The first concert was held in the Boston Music Hall, October 22, 1881. Concerts continued to be held there until the present Symphony Hall opened in 1900. From its inception until 1918, when wartime hysteria prevailed, German musical influence predominated. Beethoven, Mozart and Schubert were the favorites.

Sir George Henschel, the first conductor (1881–84), was followed by Wilhelm Gericke (1884–89 and 1898–1906), Arthur Nikisch (1889–93), Emil Paur (1893–98), Karl Muck (1906–08 and 1912–18) and Max Fiedler (1908–12), no kin to Arthur Fiedler of the Pops Concerts.

In 1918 Major Higginson gave more responsibility to the Board of Trustees. The Francophiles on the board, as almost their first act, fired Karl Muck and hired Henri Rabaud (1918–19). He was followed by Pierre Monteux (1919–24), who undertook to rebuild the orchestra which had been demoralized by anti-German hysteria.

Russian-born dynamic, dramatic Dr. Serge Koussevitzky (1874–1951) led the orchestra in many new directions in the years 1924 to 1949. He increased the number of recordings, began the famous summer Tanglewood series in 1938 and organized the Berkshire Music Center in 1940. Eleven years earlier he instituted the free Esplanade concerts under the direction of Arthur Fiedler (b. 1894). Music director Koussevitzky retired in 1949 but remained as Berkshire Music Center director until his death in 1951.

Conductor in the years from 1949 to 1962, Charles Münch (b. 1891) began foreign tours under the auspices of the Washington government which wished to parade American cultural achievements abroad. In 1951 he rescued the practice, favored by Major Higginson, of holding open rehearsals for the public. Dr. Münch at his retirement in 1962 was succeeded by Austrian Erich Leinsdorf (b. 1912). In 1968 Leinsdorf left and was replaced by William Steinberg (1899), conductor of the Pittsburgh Symphony. Michael Tilson Thomas is the Boston Symphony's associate conductor and in 1971 was appointed as music director of the Buffalo Philharmonic.

The symphony is so popular that the seven series and open rehearsals are usually sold out on a season basis. When seasonal subscribers receive their tickets in the early fall they discover the identities of the season's guest artists. For each Friday matinee 261 second balcony seats are withheld from subscription and sold on a "rush basis."

BOSTON "POPS" CONCERTS

It was in 1885 that Wilhelm Gericke decided that if his musicians were to keep at top performance pitch they should play during the usually nonplaying summer months. He organized the first "Pops" concert July 11, 1885. It was directed by Adolf Neuendorff. Symphony Hall is slightly refurbished for these spring concerts of popular music. Tables are placed on the main floor, and wine and beer are served in the old German tradition. The light music is played by specially selected musicians from the symphony orchestra. The "Pops" has been conducted by Arthur Fiedler since 1930.

ESPLANADE CONCERTS

Arthur Fiedler's long fight for money to support a series of outdoor concerts played by selected musicians from the Boston Symphony finally succeeded when the free Esplanade concert season opened in 1929. The concerts, now played in the Hatch Memorial Shell at the foot of Beacon Hill along the Charles River, sometimes entertain over 20,000 persons nightly.

TANGLEWOOD

Tanglewood takes its name from Nathaniel Hawthorne's *Tanglewood Tales,* after the estate Tanglewood owned by a friend of the writer.

The Boston Symphony was invited to give a series of concerts at the Berkshire Symphonic Festival in 1936. That same year descendants of Hawthorne's friend William A. Tappan offered Tanglewood as a gift to the Orchestra, which accepted the magnificent 210 acres.

When a storm destroyed the huge tent used for concerts, over $100,000 was raised to build a 6037-capacity music shed. More than 100,000 people annually visit the festival. Several smaller theaters, chamber music halls and studios have been built around the great shed.

The Berkshire Music Center — long a dream of Koussevitzky — was established in 1940 to provide facilities for musical hopefuls to continue their professional training under leading musicians. Since 1965 the center has been divided into the *Performance Department* and the *Tanglewood Institute.* Tanglewood Institute offers musical laymen and teachers a series of specialized seminars. The *Performance Department* admits singers, instrumentalists and composers.

CHAMBER PLAYERS

Music director Leinsdorf organized the symphony's first players into the Boston Symphony Chamber Players. The public concerts of chamber music, conducted by Leinsdorf for many years, include chamber music written for brass, strings, wind and string trios and quartets and wind quintets. The chamber players during their first season gave performances in Boston, New York, Tanglewood and Washington. Their music is recorded on RCA Victor Red Seal Records.

The symphony's influence has been far-reaching. From it have come such notable institutions as the Kneisel Quartet, Long Club, Longy School of Music and Flute-Players' Club. The great orchestra continues to give Boston its creative music focus.

OPERA IN BOSTON

In 1957, Sarah Caldwell, who from birth was a musical prodigy and from her days at the New England Conservatory a lover of opera, founded the Boston Opera Group with $5000 and the interest and help of a small group of Boston citizens. The following year, after a coast-to-coast tour of the American première of Jacques Offenbach's musical fantasy *The Voyage to the Moon,* the Opera Group trustees organized "Operation Opera," a membership drive which enrolled 5000 members by the time the group had launched its first subscription season with Puccini's *La Bohème.*

Since then the company, now known as the Opera Company of Boston, has produced over 40 operas, ranging from standard repertoire to the world premieres of Luigi Nono's *Intolleranza,* Rameau's *Hippolyte and Aricie,* Arnold Schoenberg's *Moses and Aaron* and Gunther Schuller and John Updike's children's opera *The Fisherman and his Wife.*

The Opera Company of Boston also numbers many firsts in its productions. It presented Alban Berg's *Lulu* for the first time on the East Coast. Joan Sutherland has played a major role in two of the company's firsts; she appeared in the only staged performance in the United States of Bellini's *I Puritani* and in the first staged performance of Rossini's *Semiramide* in this country since 1906.

The Boston Opera Association, a completely separate group from the Opera Company, for over 35 years has brought New York's Metropolitan Opera to Boston.

THE BOSTON BALLET COMPANY

The Boston Ballet Company was permanently established in 1963 with the assistance of a Ford Foundation Grant, thus crowning the work and dedication of E. Virginia Williams, artistic director for the group. Miss Williams had formed the New England Civic Ballet Company in 1958 to furnish an appropriate base where students could perform and develop artistically and professionally.

In 1962 the company was renamed the Boston Ballet Company and now provides a full season of ballet in Boston and vicinity. In 1965, a performance of *Nutcracker* was so successful that it is now an annual Christmastime event. George Balanchine is the company's artistic advisor.

18

Architecture

MASSACHUSETTS' ARCHITECTURAL TRIUMPHS and monstrosities, spanning three-and-one-third centuries, range widely: Fairbanks House (1636), the oldest frame dwelling in America; Charles Bulfinch's many homes and public buildings, including the present State House (1793–1800); Samuel McIntire's austere, beautiful federalist Salem houses; Harvard's monstrous Memorial ("Mem") Hall; H. H. Richardson's Romanesque Trinity Church (1872); Charles McKim, W. R. Mead and Stanford White's Boston Public Library (1887); Carl Koch's clean-lined utilitarian Techbuilt dwellings; new Boston buildings largely designed by Architects' Collaborative, a firm founded by German-born and -trained Walter Gropius, an architectural genius long at Harvard, and Hugh Stubbins' new medical library combining Harvard and Boston Medical collections in the Countway Library of Medicine.

EARLY DAYS

New England's first settlers reproduced the type of homes they had left in England. They did not, contrary to myth and legend, live in log cabins. The log cabin was not an American design or invention. It came to this country from Sweden where it had long been an established residence in the woods of Jamtland and other provinces.

Wooden versions of the English country cottage could not be built at once in this new land. The need for immediate shelter forced a direct retrogression to an earlier type much more primitive than those left behind. Common folk were first housed in conical huts of slanting poles covered with brush, reeds and turf, sometimes with a low wall of branches plastered with clay. These "English wigwams" referred to in contemporary chronicles were but a transplantation of English charcoal burners' huts. Some temporary shelters were mere cellars built into the hillside, walled and roofed with brush and sod. Some of these shelters may be seen in Salem's "pioneer village," reconstructed in 1930.

Colonists dug English-type sawpits in which they produced boards for their houses. They exported surplus boards; in 1626, when the

Fortune sailed from Plymouth for England, "clapboards and wainscott" were aboard. In 1623, Gov. Bradford mentions the building "of greate houses in pleasant situations," and later wrote that "they built a greate forte with good timber." In 1627, Isaac De Rasières described the fort as "a large square house made of thick sawn planks, stayed with oak beams." When the fort was taken down in 1676, the timber was given to William Harlow, who built the Harlow House which still stands in Plymouth.

The usual house of the 17th century was a two-story structure, the second story overhanging, with two rooms upstairs and down, a small entry and a large chimney; lean-tos were often added later. The Fairbanks House, Dedham, solidly framed of oak, rejoices in an unadorned simplicity lost in later more academic houses. The Boardman House (1651), Salem, combines the overhang and original lean-to. The long unbroken slope of its roof is well designed to withstand the cold north winds.

Ornament occurs in the Parson Capen House (1683), Topsfield, where heavy carved pendrils or drops suspended from the bottom of the overhang lend an Elizabethan flavor. The overhang, however, evolved in England for the purpose of gaining additional space above the street level. In the new, spacious country it dwindled and soon disappeared. It was still used in frontier blockhouses for possibly another two centuries, since defenders could shoot directly down through holes in the floor on Indian raiders.

CHURCHES

Early New England church architecture was influenced by English medievalism. The only 17th century church still standing in the state, the Old Ship Church, Hingham, was erected by ship carpenters in 1681. Its roof, a truncated pyramid, is surmounted by a belfry and lookout station. This church, constructed to fulfill its congregation's simple needs, is devoid of frivolity or pretense.

A more studied architecture came with the 18th century when roofs were less steep, sash windows replaced casements and there was a tendency to use a uniform cornice with a hip roof. Boston printseller William Price designed Christ Church (Old North Church) in 1723, adorning its simple front with a lofty wooden steeple reminiscent of Christopher Wren. The Old South Church, a more imposing structure, erected from plans by Robert Twelve, is in the same style, which strongly influenced colonial church architecture during the entire 18th century. The builders were satisfied by the steeple, and little effort was made at further decoration beyond an occasional elaboration of the eaves into a classical cornice.

CAPE CODDERS

Fishermen along the bended elbow of the state built little "Cape Codders." These one-and-a-half story cottages with lean-tos hugged the earth for warmth over shallow, unfinished cellars. Cellar entrance was provided by a trap door inside the house or by an outside bulkhead, hidden by a flowering shrub. The first story was rarely more than seven feet high with the half story used as a storeroom and as sleeping quarters for the children. There was little second-story headroom. The typical Cape Cod cottage had a shingle roof, large central chimney, a sometimes painted clapboard front and shingled sides and rear which salt air weathered to a dull silver. The windmill, with its shingled walls and skeletonlike vanes silhouetted against the dunes, is peculiar to Cape Cod and Nantucket.

Pine floors were wide-cut, painted or "spattered." Doors ordinarily had six panels and opened with a thumb latch. First-floor windows had four "lights" each, those in the upper floor but three. Smaller windows, set irregularly in the walls, provided light for closets. The parlor, more carefully finished than the kitchen, contained a "chair rail," a narrow moulding running around the wall about two and a half feet from the floor. So simple a cottage made up for its bareness by the bright polish of its windowpanes and the gleam of its scrubbed floor.

The "half-a-cape," with a chimney at one end, derived its name from the fact that its owner hoped to add the other half and convert his cottage into a proper house with a central chimney.

The "saltbox" — the origin of the name no longer so apparent now that salt comes in cardboard containers — has a northerly lean-to roof. The "rainbow roof" rises in a convex curve to the ridgepole, with the appearance of an inverted boat's hull. The familiar roomy gambrel roof is not often seen on the Cape.

NEW ENGLAND GEORGIAN

As seacoast towns grew wealthier, builders indulged in classic Queen Anne and Georgian styles. Georgian colonial had a profound influence upon domestic American architecture. Georgian colonial buildings were harmonious, and errors were apt to be on the side of smallness and reserve. Medford's Royall House (1723) and Byfield's Dummer Mansion (1715) are fine examples of New England Georgian's first phase. The second phase (1745–80) is exemplified in Marblehead's Lee Mansion (1768). The transition from Georgian to classicism, showing a strong Robert Adam influence, was dominant in the last phase, which included Bulfinch and McIntire's best works.

THE AMATEURS AND PETER HARRISON

In the absence of professional architects in Massachusetts during the 18th century, cultivated amateurs turned to the drafting board. Royal Governor Sir Francis Bernard (1712–79) designed Harvard Hall (1765). Nearby Massachusetts Hall (1720) had been designed by presidents John Leverett (1662–1724) and Benjamin Wadsworth (1670–1737). Portrait painter John Smibert (1688–1751) drew the plans for Faneuil Hall (1724). This historic building was later enlarged and modified by Charles Bulfinch (1763–1844). British-born Peter Harrison (1716–75), though without professional training, was America's most distinguished Colonial architect. The influence of Christopher Wren and his successor James Gibbs is evident in Harrison's King's Chapel (1752). The exterior is dour and unattractive, but the interior with its rich sobriety, repose and studied suavity of proportions remains one of the finest churches in existence. In 1761 Harrison designed Christ Church in Cambridge.

HAIL BULFINCH!

Charles Bulfinch was the first professional architect in Massachusetts. At first a cultivated amateur, Harvard man Bulfinch made an architectural "grand tour" of Europe. A gentleman of means and taste, his hobby was designing houses for friends. He planned the State House on Beacon Hill, the original brick core of which stands sandwiched between two white annexes.

Bulfinch went bankrupt in 1796, and fortunately for architecture used his talent to earn his living. In his handling of detail and ornament the Adam and Chambers influence is obvious, but in the sterner matters of plan and composition Bulfinch struck out in new directions. His designs, characterized by slender proportions, a delicacy well suited to execution in wood, tall pilasters of slight projection, light cornices and balustrades, slender columns, shallow surface arches, fanlights and sidelights with tenuous tracery, were a departure in line and detail. Bulfinch studied Chambers's fine new Somerset House, in London, as is apparent from a comparison of his first State House sketches, submitted in 1787, with the façade of the Old British Navy Office. A volume Bulfinch purchased abroad, "Le Vignole Moderne" (Paris, 1785), contains some of the motifs used on the State House portico as well as a good dome. His work in directing the completion of the federal Capitol Building in Washington after 1817, when at President Monroe's invitation he replaced British-born Benjamin H. Latrobe (1764–1820) as Capitol architect, shows that his once bold, fresh approach had become subdued.

Salem's Elias Hasket Derby Mansion profited from the combined efforts of Bulfinch and Samuel McIntire (1757–1811). The affluent Derby could afford the best, so he retained Bulfinch but was dissatisfied so he called in the best local man, McIntire. The latter designed the house along his own ideas but incorporated some Bulfinch features.

Chairman of the Boston selectmen Bulfinch was influential in transforming Boston Common from a cow pasture to a park. He drew the plans for India Wharf's warehouses. Significant Bulfinch structures remaining in Massachusetts include Faneuil Hall (addition and revision, 1805), the Harrison Gray Otis House (1796), the Sears House (second Harrison Gray Otis House, 1800), Wadsworth House (third Harrison Gray Otis House, 1807), Bulfinch Building, Mass. General Hospital (1818) — all in Boston; University Hall, Harvard, in Cambridge; Lancaster Church; Taunton Meeting House; and at Phillips Academy in Andover, Pearson Hall and Bulfinch Hall.

MIGHTY MAC

As the 1780's depression was succeeded by better times, Yankee vessels poured wealth into Boston, Salem and other seafaring towns. In seacoast towns soon clustered the square white houses of shipowners and shipmasters, their roofs often crowned with roof decks, known as "captain's walks" or "widow's walks," originally lookout points for scanning the harbor for homecoming ships. Many house builders had been ship carpenters and had learned economy of line and material from the exacting demands of their craft. Thus, their houses possessed a fluidity of line. The greatest of these carpenter-architect-carvers was Bulfinch contemporary Samuel McIntire. McIntire shows the influence of European masters, notably Robert Adam, but Mighty Mac possessed too much native genius to be content with servile adaptation. He borrowed but he repaid with interest.

McIntire houses, many of which, happily, are preserved in Salem, have little exterior grace. They are big, foursquare and three stories high. Salem houses, like captains' ladies, guard themselves from the world by a prim, prudish exterior. Within, however, is amiability, charm and finely studied, eloquently executed detail, apparent in the broad staircases with carved balusters and twisted newels. Wood mantels are enriched with figured ornaments and delicate cornices. Exteriors are flanked with great pilasters surmounted with well-proportioned cornices. McIntire's houses were often enclosed by elaborate wooden fences.

McIntire's final houses (1805–11) were brick. This less pliable material combined with a growing classical influence gave these constructions an even more austere character than his wood houses. Among his best works are Pierce-Johonnot-Nichols House (1782), Samuel Cook House (1804), John Gardner House (1805), Hosmer-Townsend-Waters House (1795) and Dudley L. Pickman House (1810), all in Salem. His Peabody houses are the Elias H. Derby House (1799) and "Oak Hill" (1800). Three complete McIntire rooms from "Oak Hill" have been installed in the American Wing, Museum of Fine Arts, Boston.

McIntire's contemporary Asher Benjamin (1773–1845) designed the Old West Church (1806) and the Charles Street Church (1807), Boston. Benjamin had neither the genius of Bulfinch nor of McIntire, but he made an important contribution to American architecture through his books. *The Country Builder's Assistant* (1797) is believed to be the first book on architecture published in the United States, and he wrote *The Practical House Carpenter* (1830) and other books.

GREEK REVIVAL

Greek revival, started in the early 19th century by Benjamin Latrobe with his Bank of Pennsylvania design, did not reach New England until the second decade. Alexander Parris (1780–1852) and Solomon Willard (1783–1861) were the Bay State's major proponents of this revival. In 1819 Parris designed St. Paul's Cathedral, Tremont Street, Boston, built by Willard, the architect of Bunker Hill Monument. The two also collaborated on the design of Quincy Market (1825), Boston.

Long after the Greek influence had passed on, one of the most studied efforts in this style was the Boston Customs House (1847) by Ammi B. Young (1798–1874). This building was originally domed, but later a tall shaft was added, transforming it into Boston's first skyscraper and an apt tombstone to the Greek movement. The dome was not removed from the interior base of the shaft, but lower floors were allowed to form a shell about it, and thus hide it. It was long the common practice for commercial buildings designers to make imitation Greek porticos and entries. They attached them without discrimination to banks and market fronts.

The demise of the Greek Revival era was followed by an experimental period from which came little of lasting beauty. Dwellings took the form of Italian villas or of mansard-roofed boxes. The results were tedious mediocrity occasionally punctuated with an outstanding atrocity. French influence fared somewhat better than the English or Italian. The Athenæum, Arlington Street Church and the old MIT Building, now Rogers Hall, all in Boston, were intelligent adaptations of Renaissance motifs.

RUSKIN

In 1865 Massachusetts Institute of Technology, then located in Boston, established the first professional architectural school in America. The organized teaching methods used by the École des Beaux Arts were introduced by the school's first director, William R. Ware (1832–1915).

The post-Civil War era was infected by John Ruskin's (1819–1900) fervent advocacy of medievalism and his sweeping condemnation of Renaisance architecture as immoral. Ruskinian or Victorian Gothic, derived from Italian Gothic, is typified by Harvard's Memorial Hall (1878), a creation of William Ware. "Mem Hall," the most severely condemned of Ruskinian buildings, shows the laboring of an architect of taste and scholarship hampered by a poor style.

When Boston's Copley Square, long a swamp dear to duck hunters, was filled in, architects looked for suitable building designs. One of those they came up with resulted in the new Old South Church (1876), designed by Ruskinite Charles Cummings (1833–1905).

RICHARDSON ROMANESQUE

Just across Copley Square from the new Old South Church, Henry Hobson Richardson (1836–86) was raising Trinity Church (1872–78). This structure, long considered by Richardson Romanesque lovers to be the best of its type, took as its departure point southern France's Romanesque, with strong, vigorous, picturesque masses of rock-faced stonework. John LaFarge's (1835–1910) interior, particularly the windows, harmonizes with the richness of the exterior.

Richardson, the second American to study architecture at the École des Beaux Arts, worked for Henri Labrouste, architect of the Library of Ste. Geneviève, Paris. Richardson's Trinity Church is antedated by the First Baptist Church of Boston, formerly the Brattle Square Church (1870–74), a failure acoustically but notable for its tower with the four trumpeting angels, locally known as the Holy Beanblowers.

When Richardson designed the tower he sent for Auguste Bartholdi (1834–1904), a fellow student at Beaux Arts, to execute the heavy frieze. Bartholdi, enamored of his surroundings, was so moved that he eventually designed the "Light of Liberty," later reproduced in New York Harbor.

Richardson designed not only churches but the Auburndale (1881) and Wellesley Hills (1885) railroad stations, Harvard's Sever Hall (1878) and the Woburn (1877), North Easton (1877) and Quincy (1880) public libraries.

Richardson Romanesque was widely imitated but seldom well adapted. An excellent adaptation, however, to a commercial purpose is the Ames Building (1891), corner of Washington and Court Streets, one of Boston's first tall buildings and the last to employ all masonry instead of steel construction. It was designed by Shepley, Rutan and Coolidge, who carried on Richardson's work.

CLASSICAL REVIVAL

The 19th century's epochal achievement in Boston architecture which began a direct revival of classical forms was Charles Follen McKim's (1847–1909) Boston Public Library. Using the simple unbroken lines of Labrouste's Library of Ste. Geneviève, he fused with this influence the most robust character of Leone Battista Alberti's San Francesco (1450), Rimini, Italy. McKim's monumental building, chaste in ornamentation, has dignity, restraint and severity without coldness.

Contemporary with, but independent of, the classic revival, Ralph Adams Cram (1863–1942) began a medieval Gothic revival. Cram turned from the present to the medieval past in his All Saints Church, Ashmont; St. Stephen's, Cohasset; First Unitarian, West Newton; All Saints and the Church of Our Saviour, Brookline.

CONTEMPORARY DESIGN

Carl Koch (b. 1912) was one of the few Bay State architects to design "contemporary" homes before World War II. Imaginative Koch, together with a few friends, purchased a seemingly worthless hillside and hilltop in Belmont. Much of the acreage was straight up and down the rock-faced cliff, but Koch designed houses to fit atop the hill and some to fit against the cliffside so that the rock face became an inner wall of a house. This neighborly development of friends became the famed "Snake Hill" project.

Koch, wherever possible, used standard size precut fabricating materials as a means of reducing labor costs. After extensive experiments Koch and his associates developed the "Techbuilt" houses. These sturdy contemporary houses were probably the first well-constructed prefabricated houses in America. There was considerable opposition in some communities where either zoning laws or obsolete building codes failed to recognize the sound qualities of "prefabs" like Techbuilt.

No apartment houses were built in intown Boston between the late 1920's and 1951 when River House, at Embankment Road and Pinckney Street, was erected. This apartment house was notable for a feature used on Swedish apartment houses since the early 1920's — balconies. Similar but improved apartment houses were then constructed along Memorial Drive, Cambridge.

Universities, notably Harvard and MIT, led the way in erecting structures of contemporary design. An important influence was German-born Walter Gropius (1883–1969), who was long the chairman of the Department of Architecture in Harvard's School of Design. Harvard and MIT maintain the Joint Center for Urban Studies, founded in 1960 and numbering among its directors Martin Meyerson and Daniel Patrick Moynihan. Lawrence Bernhart Anderson has headed MIT's Department of Architecture and Planning since 1946.

Some notable university buildings include Harvard's Lamont Library for undergraduates (1949) and William James Hall (1964). MIT has the 20-story Cecil and Ida Greene Building, housing the Earth Sciences unit. Famed Finnish-born architect Eero Saarinen (1910–60) designed Tech's Chapel (1955) and Kresge Auditorium (1955). Boston University fortunately switched from its immediate post-WWII pseudo-Gothic to contemporary design in its Law and Education Building and Library. Engineer and designer R. Buckminster Fuller, a Milton native, remains a *tour de force* in radical design. Fuller is the inventor-discoverer of energetic-synergetic geometry, geodesic structures and tensegrity structures.

PART TWO

Massachusetts Recreation

19

General Recreation

CAMPERS, PICNICKERS and sun lovers will find more than 100 parks, forests and beaches in Massachusetts. Additional recreational facilities are provided by the Trustees of Reservations, a nonprofit organization. Towns, cities and some counties maintain beaches, forests, parks, picnic sites, playgrounds, swimming pools and skating rinks. The Metropolitan District Commission (MDC), a state agency, provides extensive recreational facilities, particularly in the Greater Boston area.

PUBLIC CAMPGROUNDS AND DAY USE AREAS

There are 87 sites for public camping in Massachusetts. An alphabetical list, including locations, follows:

Ames Nowell S.P.* — Abington, Rte. 123 & 18
Ashland S.P. — Ashland, Rte. 135
Bash Bish Falls S.F. — Mt. Washington, Rte. 23 & 41
Beartown S.F. — Monterey, Rte. 123 & Rte. 102 S. Lee
Bradley Palmer S.P. — Topsfield, Rte. 1
Brimfield S.F. (Dean Pd.) — Brimfield, Rte.20
Buffumville S.P. — Oxford, Rte. 12
Campbells Falls S.F. — Southfield, Rte. 272
Catamount S.F. — Colrain, Rte. 2 & 112
Charles M. Gardner S.P. — Huntington, Rte. 112
Chester S.F. — Chester, Rte. 20
Chicopee S.P. — Chicopee, Ext. No. 6 Mass. Tpk.
Clarksburg S.P. — Clarksburg, Rte. 2 & 8
Cochituate S.P. — Cochituate, Rte. 30
Cohasset S.P. — Cohasset, Rte. 228
Conway S.F. — Conway, Rte. 116
Cookson Property — New Marlborough, Rte. 183
D.A.R.S.F. (1) — Goshen, Rte. 9
Demarest Lloyd S.P. — South Dartmouth, Rte. 6
Dighton Rock S.P. — Berkley off Rte. 24

Douglas S.F. — Douglas, Rte. 16
East Mtn. S.F. (2) — Great Barrington, Rte. 23
Erving S.F. — Erving, Rte. 2
F. Gilbert Hills S.F. — Foxboro, Rte. 1 & 140
Fed. Womens Club S.F. — Petersham, Rte. 122
Fiske Property — Framingham, Millwood St.
Fort Phoenix Beach S.R. — Fairhaven, Rte. 6, 195 & 140
Freetown S.F. — Assonet off Rte. 24 & 79
Georgetown Rowley S.F. — Georgetown, Rte. 133
Granville S.F. — Granville, Rte. 57
Greylock Mtn. S.R. — Adams, Rte. 2, 7, 8
H. O. Cook S.F. — Colrain, Rte. 8A
Hampton Ponds S.P. — Westfield, Rte. 202
Harold Parker S.F. — North Reading, Rte. 125
Hawley S.F. — Hawley, Rte. 8A
Holland S.P. — Holland, Rte. 20
Hopkinton S.P. — Hopkinton, Rte. 85
Horseneck Beach S.R. — Westport, Rte. 6, 195, 24 & 88
Lake Dennison S.P. — Winchendon, Rte. 202
Leominster S.F. — Fitchburg, Rte. 2 & 31
Lowell Dracut S.F. — Lowell Mammoth Rd.
Ludlow S.P. — Ludlow via Plumbley St. & Tower Rd.
Martha's Vineyard S.F. — Martha's Vineyard Island
Massasoit S.P. — Taunton off Rte. 18–44–79–28–24
Mohawk Trail S.F. — Charlmont, Rte. No. 2
Monroe S.F. — Monroe, Rte. 2
Moore S.P. — Paxton, Rte 31
Mt. Grace S.F. — Warwick, Rte. 78
Myles Standish S.F. — South Carver, Rte. 3, 44 & 58
Nantucket S.F. — Nantucket Island
Northfield S.F. — Northfield, Rte. 2A
October Mtn. S.F. — Lee & Lenox, Rte. 20 & 7
Otis S.F. — Otis, Rte. 23
Otter River S.F. — Winchendon, Rte. 202
Pearl Hill S.P. — Townsend, Rte. 119
Peru S.F. — Peru, Rte. 143
Petersham S.F. (1) — Petersham, Rte. 32
Pittsfield S.F. — Pittsfield via West St.
Plum Island S.P. — Newburyport, Plum Island
Quinsigamond S.P. — Worcester, Rte. 9
R. C. Nickerson S.F.P. — Brewster, Rte. 6A
Robinson S.P. — Agawam, North St. Feeding Hills

Rutland S.P. — Rutland, Rte. 122
Salisbury Beach S.R. — Salisbury, Rte. 495–95–110–1–1A
Sandisfield S.F. — Sandisfield, Rte. 57
Savoy Mtn.–Florida S.F. — Florida, Rte. 2 & Rte. 116 Savoy
Scusset Beach S.R. — Bourne, Rte. 6 & 3
Shawme Crowell S.F. — Sandwich, Rte. 3–6A & 130
Skinner S.P. — South Hadley, Rte. 47
South River S.F. — Conway, Rte. 116
Spencer S.F. — Spencer, Rte. 31
Standish Monument S.P. — Duxbury, Rte. 3 to 3A
Taconic Trail S.P. — Williamstown, Rte. 2
Tolland Otis S.F. — Otis, Rte. 23 & 8
Upton S.F. — Upton, Westborough Rd.
Wachusett Mtn. S.R. (2) — Princeton, Rte. 31
Wahconah Falls S.P. — Dalton, Rte. 9 & 8A
Warren Manning S.P. — Billerica, Rte. 3
Warwick S.F. — Warwick, Athol Rd.
Watson Pond S.P. — Taunton, Rte. 138
Wells S.P. — Sturbridge, Rte. 20
Wendell S. F. — Wendell, Wendell Rd.
West Lake Recreation Area — Sandisfield, West Rd.
Whitehall S.P. — Hopkinton, Rte. 135
Willard Brook S.F. — Ashby, Rte. 119
Willowdale S.F. (1) — Ipswich, Linebrook Rd.
Windsor S.F. — W. Cummington, Rte. 9 & Rte. 116 Savoy

* *Legend*
S.F. State Forest
S.P. State Park
S.R. State Reservation

(1) Hunting in certain areas only
(2) Leased ski areas

There is a $1.00 parking charge for the use of picnic and other facilities in state parks and forests. The $1.00 fee is for a two-hour period. Individuals and families planning to make extensive use of these facilities should purchase a seasonal pass for $10.00. Pass holders have all-day use of park or forest facilities, including picnic tables, fireplaces, swimming, parking and boat-launching ramps. All parks are open from May 1 to Oct. 15, with hours from 10 A.M. to 8 P.M.

Standish Monument Reservation is an exception to the $1.00 parking fee. Here it is $0.50. A ten-cent fee is charged for climbing the observation tower.

Visitors who walk into all parks and forests pay $0.25 each.

PUBLIC CAMPSITE REGULATIONS

All campsites are on an unreserved basis and, between the last Saturday in June and the Saturday before Labor Day, the maximum camping period is limited to two weeks.

No person may camp anywhere nor may he occupy a cabin or campsite until he has registered at the headquarters and paid, in full, the required fee for the period of rental.

No camper shall vacate an area at the termination of his stay without first notifying the supervisor or attendant on duty.

Requests for refunding of an unused portion of a campsite rental fee must be initiated by the camper through the Forest and Park Supervisor or attendant on duty at the area where the camping was done.

Check-out time for campers vacating their cabin or campsite shall be not later than 1:00 P.M.

Between the last Saturday in June and the Saturday before Labor Day, campers may occupy a campsite for not more than two weeks, with the provision that the supervisor may grant an extension of the camping period for one week at a time, but with a limitation of four weeks for the maximum camping period provided that, at the time an extension is granted, all applications for a tent site from newly arrived campers have been taken care of. At all other times there will be no limit on the allowable camping period.

At the conclusion of the maximum camping period, campers will be required to remove all camping equipment from the forest or park where they are camping and will not be permitted to return to the same forest or park before Labor Day.

Unless the campsite is occupied immediately after registration, and the camper shows definite signs of occupancy until the end of his registered period, the rental will be canceled.

If a campsite remains unoccupied for a period of more than twelve hours, the rental may be canceled and the equipment removed.

Persons occupying a campsite shall be responsible for keeping it clean and neat during the period of occupancy and shall remove or deposit all garbage or refuse in containers provided for that purpose. Waste material from trailers must be deposited in dumping stations only.

All unnecessary noise shall be avoided between 10:00 P.M. and 7:00 A.M.

Occupancy of a campsite shall be restricted to the person who received it, together with his wife (her husband) and unmarried children living at home. Any deviation from this rule must be approved by the Forest and Park Supervisor.

No children shall be left unattended at campsites at any time.

Not more than *two tents* may be erected at any campsite. The ground area covered by each to be limited to not more than 260 square feet for the larger and 81 square feet for the smaller. With the exception of tent flies, no other equipment or structure shall be erected on the site.

Only one car shall be permitted to be kept at each site.

Visitors to campers will be required to park their cars in such places as the attendant on duty shall designate and pay a fee of one dollar ($1.00). No fee shall be charged if a *Seasonal Day-Use Pass* is in the car. Visitors must leave the area by 10:00 P.M.

LOG CABINS

The Mohawk Trail, Myles Standish, Savoy Mountain and Willard Brook State Forests have one- and three-room log cabins for rent. Mohawk Trail and Willard Brook cabins have electricity. Cabins will not be rented for less than one week nor more than two weeks to any one party during the regular season (last Sat. in June–Sat. before Labor Day). The required $5.00 deposit will not be returned unless written notice is received by the state forest supervisor at least one week before the first day of the requested week. Checks must be made payable to the Commonwealth of Massachusetts and should be mailed to the supervisor of the forest where the desired cabin is located several months before the opening of the season. Before and after the regular season cabins may be rented for any period of time desired. Check-out time is 1:00 P.M.

Daily rates: one-room cabin, $4.00; three-room cabin, $5.00.

BEACHES

Cape Cod National Seashore beaches, such as New Beach and Race Point Beach, both in Provincetown, have bathhouses and parking areas. The seashore contains many miles of isolated beaches which offer no organized facilities but which do have privacy — a rare commodity these days.

There are county-commissioner-operated beaches like Edgartown-Oak Bluffs Beach. Crane's and Castle Hill Beaches are owned and operated by the Trustees of Reservations.

The Metropolitan District Commission owns and/or operates amusement park-beach areas like Revere and beaches with bathhouse facilities in the metropolitan Boston area.

Many towns along the Massachusetts coast have community beaches. Some are barred to nonresidents, though the word "resident" has an elastic meaning. Rules and regulations may vary from year to year. In any case would-be bathers or sun worshipers within a whiff of saltwater can find a good beach nearby.

APPALACHIAN TRAIL

The 2050-mile-long Applachian Trail — Georgia to Maine — enters Massachusetts at the Connecticut line and leaves via Vermont's Long Trail at Williamstown. Eighty-three miles of the trail are in the Bay State. The main trail, marked by white paint blazes, serves as a major access trail to several Berkshire Country mountains. Unlike the Long Trail in Vermont and many Appalachian Mountain Club trails, this section has few shelters along the way. Carry a tent or use convenient off-trail accommodations.

Secure from your bookseller or write Appalachian Trail Conference, 1718 N. St. N.W., Washington, D.C. 20036, *The Guide to the Appalachian Trail in Massachusetts and Connecticut.* Price $2.50.

Hikers headed north from Massachusetts use the Long Trail over the Green Mountains to U.S. 4 and then swing east to New Hampshire and Maine via the Appalachian Trail. The Long Trail continues north over the Green Mountains to the U.S.–Canadian frontier.

APPALACHIAN MOUNTAIN CLUB

This organization with headquarters at 3 Joy Street, Boston, pioneered in White Mountain trailblazing and shelter erecting. The club publishes guides for several regions. Massachusetts hikers, for areas other than the Appalachian Trail, should secure the A.M.C.'s *Massachusetts, Rhode Island Trail Guide.* Price $4.50. Those wishing to join must be sponsored by two members.

TERRAIN VEHICLES

An increasing number of state and local recreation areas make provision for the popular sport of snowmobiling, and there were 22,000 registered snowmobiles in Massachusetts in 1970. Except in the case of an owner using his own machine on his own property, snowmobiles must be licensed by the Motor Boat Division of the Registry of Motor Vehicles, as must dune buggies and minibikes, even though none of them are allowed on roads.

20

Hunting

MASSACHUSETTS is not a state whose game prospects entice hunters to come there solely for hunting. It does have, however, some of the best pheasant hunting in the northeast. Duck and coot shooting, depending on varying federal regulations, is usually fair to good. Deer can also be taken. Quail shooting is limited to a few areas. Be sure to get a handbook on new hunting laws when securing license.

WILDLIFE MANAGEMENT AREAS

The Massachusetts Division of Fisheries and Game is steadily acquiring acreage to provide public hunting areas. These areas help offset the land that is lost to hunting through posting, real estate development and highway construction.

More than 20 areas had been created by the mid-1960's. Some are on land owned by the Division of Fisheries and Game, while others are on property controlled by other state agencies or the federal government, or by lease from individuals or corporations. No special fee or license is required to hunt these public areas, which are also used for fishing, camping, berry picking, bird watching, wildlife photography, horseback riding, picnics, swimming and boating. Most of the areas are subject to special game-stocking programs. Regular bag limits, seasons and regulations prevail on these public areas.

Some of the areas prohibit camping. A special free daily permit must be secured from the checking stations in the Fort Devens Wildlife Management Area.

For information on specific areas see ASHFIELD, ATHOL, AYER, BARRE, BECKET, BELCHERTOWN, BOURNE, BROOKFIELD, CHESHIRE, CHESTER, CONCORD, CONWAY, FALL RIVER, FALMOUTH, GEORGETOWN, GROVELAND, HUBBARDSTON, HUNTINGTON, LANCASTER, LEICESTER, LENOX, MENDON, MIDDLEBOROUGH, NEW BRAINTREE, NEWBURY, NORTH ANDOVER, NORTHBRIDGE, OAKHAM, OXFORD, PAXTON, PERU, PETERSHAM, PHILLIPSTON, PLYMOUTH, ROWLEY, ROYALSTON, RUTLAND, SAVOY, SHIRLEY, SPENCER, SUDBURY, TEMPLETON, UPTON, UXBRIDGE, WARE, WEST BRIDGEWATER, WEST BROOKFIELD, WEST NEWBURY, WESTBOROUGH, WILLIAMSTOWN, WINCHENDON, WORTHINGTON.

RABBIT

The cottontail rabbit is the Bay State's number one game animal. More shooters hunt the cottontail than any other game animal.

The cottontail is found throughout the state, usually in open country, except in the Berkshires and the heavily wooded central northeast.

DEER

Deer, while ranking high on some hunters' agenda, are a secondary game animal in Massachusetts. Deer were plentiful when the Pilgrims arrived in 1620 but were nearly extinct by 1698 when the first closed season was instituted. The closed season ran from January 15 through July 14. The statewide herd had its ups and downs until 1898 when deer hunting was entirely prohibited. In 1910 the season was reopened in the five western counties. Three years later hunting was permitted throughout the state except in densely populated areas where there were no deer to hunt. Since 1910 when 1282 deer were reported the top year has been 1958 when 4887 deer including 32 taken by archers were reported. Nineteen-eighteen with 832 deer and 1919 with 833 deer were the low years. The large number of hunters in the armed forces possibly accounted for these lows.

The best deer-hunting areas are northwestern Middlesex, northern Worcester, Franklin and Berkshire Counties. The Division of Fisheries and Game no longer releases a town-by-town kill report. Officials, and properly so, believe that too many hunters descending on limited areas would foul up hunter-landowner relationships. Barnstable County in Cape Cod is a fair deer-producing area.

Rifles are prohibited. Only shotguns — no larger than 10 bore magnums — can be used. Sunday hunting is of course prohibited in puritan Massachusetts. Hunting hours during the six-day season are 6 A.M.–5 P.M. All kills must be reported to checking stations within 48 hours.

A special archery stamp ($1.10) is required during the mid-November bow-and-arrow season. Archery kills, which were first counted in 1957, have ranged from a low of 23 for the first year through a high of 46 in 1959.

Few Bay State deer reach maturity (3.5 years for doe and 5.5 years for bucks). Ninety percent of the deer inspected range from fawns through 3.5 years. The sex ratio is 53 percent bucks, 47 percent doe. Live weight ranges from 100–250 lbs. Deer breed in November, though late fawns may breed in December. Fawns are usually born between May 24 and June 8. Doe usually produce one fawn the first time and two annually thereafter. About 38 percent of the statewide herd die each year. Hunters account for about 25 percent while the remainder die from accidents, dogs and illegal killings.

Deer of either sex may be taken in Massachusetts.

UPLAND GAME

There is good pheasant shooting in the Bay State. More than 50,000 game farm-reared birds are released annually. The best shooting is found wherever there is open farmland, and this includes most of the state east of the Berkshires and northern Worcester County's woodland area. The season opens in late October and lasts through November. Only cocks can be taken. Daily bag limit is two birds.

First-rate partridge shooting is found throughout most of the state in cutover forest areas, old pastures and farmland. The season opens in early October and lasts through November.

Both native and migratory woodcock are found. Good timberdoodle shooting is found along many streams among tag alders.

QUAIL NOTES

The cheery note of bobwhite is no longer heard throughout the commonwealth. Heavy winter kills in the early part of this century made severe inroads in the statewide quail population. Today, shooting is confined to Bristol, Plymouth, Barnstable, Dukes and Nantucket Counties. Daily bag limit is five birds, total possession is ten and season bag is limited to 25 birds. The highest season bag limit of any upland gamebird is for quail. Less than a 1000-bird harvest is reported annually. There are many more quail that can be taken, but few Bay State gunners are quail buffs. The state would increase its stocking program if there were a greater demand for quail.

WILDFOWL

Massachusetts, once the great scene of fall and spring brant shooting, today offers wildfowlers a fare which is restricted by the migratory wildfowl program. An estimated 35,000–50,000 black ducks winter off the coast but are protected if they arrive after the season set by the federal government for the Atlantic flyway. Black duck and mallards are the most populous birds. There is some goose shooting along Cape Ann and Cape Cod. There is some wildfowling along the Connecticut River and on inland lakes and ponds.

CHUCK SHOOTING

Woodchucks, which eat their own weight in hay, alfalfa or garden produce every 48 hours, are unprotected. There is excellent chuck shooting for the long-range rifleman with a scope-equipped varmint caliber rifle throughout the open farmlands in the commonwealth. Ask the landowner's permission before you shoot; most farmers are only too willing to grant it.

COON

Many Bay State farmers wish there were more coon hunters and less coon. There is no total season bag limit on these nightlife "critters." The daily limit — between sunset of one day and sunset of the following day — is three. No more than six coon can be taken within this time period no matter how large the hunting party. Coon are hunted at night with the aid of lights and dogs. Coon shooting is a popular rural sport, and many city hunters are now finding fun in this nighttime pastime. The season runs from late September through December.

MIXED BAG

The black bear season opens in late September and runs through December, but the few bear taken each year are usually shot by deer hunters. The Berkshires are prime bear country.

There is no limit and no closed season on bobcat, fox, porcupine or red or flying squirrels.

The gray squirrel season runs from late October through November, but not many hunters, except youngsters, shoot them. "Bay State squirrels," commented a game official, "are fast, sassy, and undershot." Many hunters are missing good shooting — and eating — when they pass up grays.

21

Fishing

BAY STATE WATERS, fresh and salt, provide sport fishermen with the fighting striper, large and smallmouth bass, trout and the eastern states' inland fish. The Division of Fisheries and Game does a splendid job of stocking inland waters. Fishing for tuna in Ipswich Bay is an exciting sport. Ponds and lakes provide ice fishing. Every coastal community can provide boats, bait, guides and local information. Most inland ponds and lakes have facilities for fishermen. Be sure to get a handbook on new fishing laws when securing license.

STATE-LEASED TROUT RIVERS

The Division of Fisheries and Game has leased miles of stream banks along the state's best trout rivers to insure public access to fine fishing.

Deerfield River. The Mohawk Trail — Mass. 2 parallels much of this river which rises in southern Vermont and flows through the Massachusetts towns of Monroe, Rowe, Florida, Charlemont, Buckland, Shelburne, Deerfield and Greenfield and into the Connecticut River. Fishing, especially early and late in the season, is excellent. Fishermen in the Deerfield should watch for a sudden rise of several feet in the stream level. This occurs when the hydroelectric plant upstream in Vermont opens its gates. Ten miles of the Deerfield River in the towns of Charlemont, Rowe and Florida are leased by the state for public fishing. Motel accommodations are available throughout the area.

Westfield River has three main branches: West, Middle and East. The West Branch paralleled by US 20 has about seven miles of leased streamside in the towns of Huntington, Chester, Becket and Middlefield.

Middle Branch has nine miles of leased streamside in the towns of Chester, Huntington, Middlefield and Worthington.

East Branch is composed of several small mountain streams including the spectacular Swift River. Mass. 9 parallels much of the 14 miles of leased stream in the towns of Chesterfield, Cummington and Huntington. The lower portion of the river is now part of the federal government's flood control scheme.

Farmington River, with 12 miles of leased stream in the towns of Otis, Sandisfield and Tolland, rises in Becket and flows through the above towns into the Connecticut River. The stream flows through the Tolland State Forest (see TOLLAND).

STOCKED TROUT WATERS

The state stocks several hundred streams, rivers, lakes and ponds annually in every county but Nantucket. There is trout fishing in Boston's Jamaica Pond (secure special permit from Boston Park Department, 33 Beacon St.). Interested trouters should write the Division of Fisheries and Game, Westborough, for the latest stocking report.

LARGEMOUTH BASS

Better than average largemouth bass fishing will usually be found in Arlington, Spy Pond; Barnstable, Lawrence Pond; Becket, Yokum Pond; Bourne, Flax Pond; Bridgewater, Robbins Pond and Lake Nippanicket; Brookfield, Quaboag Pond; Charlton, Buffamville Reservoir; Cheshire, Cheshire Reservoir; Framingham, Farm Pond; Goshen, Lower Highland Lake; Groton, Knopp's Pond; Hanson, Indian Head Pond, Maquam Pond and Monponsett Lake; Hardwick, Hardwick Pond; Harvard, Bow Hill Pond; Hopkinton, North Pond; Hudson, Lake Boon; Ipswich, Hood's Pond; Lunenburg, Massapoag Pond; Mendon, Nipmuc Pond; Millbury, Lake Singletary, 22 Northboro, Bartlett Pond and Little Chauncey Pond; Palmer, Forest Lake; Pembroke, Furnace Pond; Plymouth, Curlew and Five Mile Ponds; Randolph, Ponkapoag Pond; Sharon, Lake Massapoag; Shrewsbury, Jordan Pond; Spencer, Thompson's Pond; Stoughton, Pinewood Pond; Sturbridge, Cedar Pond, East Brimfield Pond and Walker Pond; Taunton, Sabbatia Lake; Tyngsborough, Flint's Pond; Wakefield, Lake Quannapowitt; Wayland, Dudley Pond; Webster, Webster Lake; Westfield, Hampton Pond; Worcester, Indian Lake and Lake Quinsigamond; Yarmouth, Long Pond.

SMALLMOUTH BASS

Better than average smallmouth bass fishing will usually be found in Barnstable, Garrett's Pond; Fall River, South Watuppa Reservoir; Hopkinton, North Pond; Huntington, Norwich Pond; Mashpee, Mashpee-Wakeby Pond; Methuen, Forest Lake; Millbury, Lake Singletary; Plymouth, Charge Pond and College Pond; Sterling, East Waushacum Pond; Wales, Lake George; Webster, Lake Webster; Westborough, Lake Chauncey.

CHAIN PICKEREL

Fairly good chain pickerel fishing will usually be found in Barnstable, Muddy Pond; Braintree, Sunset Lake; Brookfield, Quaboag Pond; Cheshire, Cheshire Reservoir; Framingham, Farm Pond; Hanson, Monponsett Lake; Hopkinton, North Pond; Hudson, Lake Boon; Littleton, Long Pond; Lunenburg, Massapoag Pond; Millbury, Lake Singletary; North Andover, Stearns Pond; Northborough, Bartlett's Pond; Plymouth, White's Pond; Sharon, Lake Massapoag; Stoughton, Ames Pond; Sturbridge, East Brimfield Reservoir; Tyngsborough, Flint's Pond; Wakefield, Lake Quannapowitt; Wales, Lake George; Wayland, Dudley Pond; Webster, Lake Webster; Westfield, Buck Pond and Hampton Pond.

WHITE PERCH

Above average fishing will usually be found in Becket, Center Pond; Belchertown, Quabbin Reservoir; Hanson, Indian Head Pond; Hardwick, Quabbin Reservoir; Lakeville, Long Pond; Millbury, Lake Singletary; Sturbridge, East Brimfield Reservoir; Wareham, Dick's Pond; Worcester, Indian Lake and Lake Quinsigamond.

YELLOW PERCH

Above average yellow perch fishing is usually found in Amesbury, Lake Gardner; Arlington, Spy Pond; Barnstable, Lawrence Pond; Becket, Center Pond; Belchertown, Quabbin Reservoir; Groton, Duck Pond; Hanson, Maquam Pond, Monponsett Lake; Hardwick, Quabbin Reservoir; Hudson, Lake Boon; Littleton, Long Pond; Mendon, Nipmuc Pond; Millbury, Lake Singletary; Northborough, Little Chauncey Pond; Plymouth, Curlew Pond and White Pond; Stoughton, Ames Pond and Pinewood Pond; Sturbridge, East Brimfield Reservoir; Wales, Lake George; Webster, Lake Webster; Westfield, Buck Pond and Hampton Pond; Wilmington, Silver Lake; Worcester, Lake Quinsigamond.

BROWN BULLHEAD

Fairly good brown bullhead fishing will usually be found in Amesbury, Lake Gardner; Arlington, Spy Pond; Barnstable, Muddy Pond; Belchertown, Quabbin Reservoir; Cheshire, Cheshire Reservoir; Groton, Duck Pond; Hanson, Indian Head Pond; Hardwick, Quabbin Reservoir; Hudson, Lake Boon; Mendon, Nipmuc Pond; Millbury, Lake Singletary; New Salem, Quabbin Reservoir; Stoughton, Ames Pond and Pinewood Pond; Sturbridge, East Brimfield Reservoir; Westborough, Lake Chauncey; Westfield, Hampton Pond; Worcester, Indian Lake.

CAPE COD SURF FISHING ACCESS AREAS

Town	*Location*	*Access Locations*
Bourne	Cape Cod Canal	North and South Side (unlimited)
Sandwich	Scorton Creek, East Sandwich	East End Beach Road
Barnstable	Sandy Neck	Sandy Neck Road, off Route 6A
Truro	Pamet River	Off Fisher Road
Provincetown	New Beach	State Beach, Route 6
Provincetown	Race Point	Race Point Coast Guard Station
Truro	Highland Light	Highland Road, off Route 6
Wellfleet	Newcomb's Hollow	Cross Hill Road
Eastham	Nauset Light	Cable Road
Eastham	Nauset Beach North	Doane Road at Coast Guard Station
Orleans	Nauset Beach South	Beach Road
Chatham	Morris Island	Off Morris Island Road

SALTWATER FISHING GUIDE

SPECIES	LOCATION	SEASON	BAITS AND LURES	METHODS
Striped Bass	WHOLE COAST For details on hot spots, surf-casting beaches, rivers, see special section.	May–October	Sea worms, eels, eel skins, squid, herring. Jigs of all types, plugs, spinners, spoons, flies.	Casting with light tackle, fly casting, casting from boat, surf casting, trolling, plugchumming.
Giant Tuna	Ipswich Bay, Cape Cod Bay, Provincetown.	Late July–September	Whole mackerel, other bait fish, squid. Large feathered lures.	Trolling or chumming. Heavy tackle only.
School Tuna	South of Cape Cod, off Nantucket Island, Buzzards Bay.	Late July–September	Whole mackerel, other bait fish, squid. Large feathered lures.	Trolling or chumming. Medium tackle.
White Marlin	Nantucket Sound, south of Martha's Vineyard and Nantucket.	Late July–September	Mullet, mackerel, cut baits. Feathered lures.	Trolling. Medium tackle.
Swordfish	Northeast of Cape Ann, Gloucester, Nantucket Sound, south of Martha's Vineyard, Nantucket.	July, August	Mackerel, menhaden, mullet, herring, squid, all either whole or cut.	Trolling. Heavy tackle.
Bluefish	All waters south of Cape Cod and islands, outer Cape Cod beaches. Occasionally north of Cape Cod.	August–September	All smaller fish. Jigs, spoons, small plugs, spinners, streamer flies.	Fly or bait casting tackle, boat rods, surf casting.
Snapper Bluefish	Waters south of Cape Cod. River mouths, coves, bays.	August–September	Spinners, spoons, streamer flies, small plugs.	Fly or bait casting tackle.
Bonito	South of Cape Cod, outer Cape Cod waters, Martha's Vineyard, Nantucket.	Late July to September	Any small bait fish, small mackerel, crab or clam bits, sea worms, squid, small jigs, spoons, plugs, streamer flies.	Fly or bait casting tackle, light boat rods.
Pollock	Provincetown, Manomet, Plymouth, north to New Hampshire line.	May to October. Best runs May and September.	Plugs, wet and dry flies, jigs, spinners, spoons, feather lures. Almost any bait.	Still fishing, casting from boat with surf, bait or fly rod.
Squeteague or Weakfish	Cape Cod Bay, Nantucket Sound, outer Cape Cod waters off rapidly shelving beaches,	Late June–September	Minnows, shrimp, sea worms, shedder crab, squid, plugs, spinners, spoons, small jigs. Feathered lures, flies	Still fishing, float fishing, chumming, surf casting, fly and bait casting, trolling.

SPECIES	LOCATION	SEASON	BAITS AND LURES	METHODS
Mackerel	Whole coast.	July–September	Small bait, fish, crab or clam bits, sea worms, squid strips, small jigs, spoons, spinners, streamer flies, small plugs.	Trolling, chumming, fly and bait casting.
Tautog or Blackfish	Whole coast. Rocky bottom inshore, bays, harbors, jetties, beaches, breakwaters.	May to November	Crabs, clams, all shellfish. Rarely on artificials.	Still fishing, surf casting, boat fishing.
Seabass	Cape Cod and south. Rocky shores, rocks in water less than 15 fathoms deep around wrecks.	Mid-June–September	Crabs, shrimp, clams, menhaden, sand eels.	Still fishing.
Scup or Porgy	Cape Cod Bay, outer Cape Cod waters from 2 to 20 fathoms, prefer sandy bottom.	May–October	Clams, sea worms, shrimp, crab claw, squid bits.	Still fishing from boat, pier, breakwater. Fly rod gives best sport.
Winter Flounder	Whole coast. Shoal water, usually sandy bottoms.	Year round	Clams, sea worms, squid bits, shrimp.	Still fishing from boat, pier, breakwater.
Summer Flounder or Fluke	Whole coast. Best fishing south of Boston.	Mid-June–September	Live minnows, clams, squid bits, shrimp. Small jigs, spinners, feather lures, fish deep.	Still fishing from boat, pier, breakwater, deep trolling, surf casting.
Whiting or Kingfish	South of Cape Cod. Inshore, often run into fresh water, prefer sandy or hard bottom.	May to October	Shrimp, crabs, clams, sea worms, minnows, small jigs, spoons, feathered lures, spinners.	Still fishing, surf casting, boat casting or trolling, chumming.
Cod	Whole coast. Deep water. Run inshore during late fall and winter.	Year round	Almost any bait.	Still fishing. Surf casting with fish finder rig.
Haddock	North of Cape Cod.	May to November	Almost any bait.	Still fishing from boat.
Shad	Brackish and fresh water at river mouths. Connecticut River north to Holyoke Dam.	April–June	Flies, spinners, small shiny lures. Garden hackle with spinner.	Fly and bait casting. Chumming, still fishing after spawning.
Smelt	River mouths along whole coast.	Best late fall and winter. Move offshore spring, summer.	Sea worms, shrimp, minnows, clams, small red flies.	Still fishing from boat, ice fishing, fly casting.

PART THREE

Massachusetts Town and Country

Massachusetts Town and Country

ABINGTON (Plymouth County, settled 1680, incorp. 1712, alt. 200, pop. 12,334, area 9.97 sq. mi., town meeting, route, Mass. 123) originally contained neighboring Rockland and Whitman. Half of its original territory was parceled out as land grants in payment for public service to Plymouth Colony. Hundreds of acres were purchased by men from Weymouth (in Massachusetts Bay Colony).

Abington was named for Anne Venables Bertie, Countess Abingdon (both spellings were used in early days). Andrew Ford, Jr., Old Abington's first settler, began clearing his land in 1672. About 1680, after King Philip's War, he returned to build his cottage behind the house now numbered 54. A bronze plaque is on the outcropping of stone just beyond (in the point of Adams and Washington streets).

Residential Abington has little industry but is known for its excellent school system. In 1873, the east and the south wards, which had both built their schoolhouses within the funds allotted, refused to be taxed for the center schoolhouse which had exceeded its budget. Within two years, both sections had separated from the old town.

Island Grove Pond (Mass. 123). For many years the south side of the dam, below the pond, was occupied at one time or another by a saw- and gristmill, tack factory and woolen and fulling mill. The first 12-cylinder automobile in the United States was manufactured here in 1907 by H. H. Buffum. Here is one of the two Abington factories making textile machinery.

Ford House (private), 770 Washington St. The back part is Ensign Andrew Ford III's "new house," built in 1735, the *oldest house* to retain any of its original appearance in Old Abington.

Memorial Bridge crosses *Island Grove Pond* and the historic picnic grounds in *Island Grove Park.* A *Memorial Boulder,* erected in 1909 by Capt. Moses N. Arnold of the 12th Massachusetts Volunteer Militia, commemorates stirring antislavery meetings held in the grove.

Memorial Bridge and Arch, honoring the soldiers and sailors of several wars, was dedicated June 10, 1912, the 200th anniversary of Old Abington township. President William Howard Taft was the guest of honor. The arch is surmounted by Bela Pratt's 11-foot bronze eagle, 50 feet above the water. On the supporting columns, facing the water, are life-size figures in bas-relief, representing a soldier and a sailor of the Civil War.

Dyer Memorial Building (1932), Centre Ave., houses a museum, a historical reference library, the headquarters of the Historical Society of Old Abington and the Centre Abington public library. The *Historical Museum* and *Research Library* are outstanding for a town this size. The historical section (*free*) is open Mon., Thur. and Sat. afternoons and Mon., Tues., Thurs. and Fri. evenings.

Historic *Satucket Indian Path* through Old Abington was a major trail followed by Indians in their seasonal treks between saltwater fishing at Wessagusset (Weymouth shore) and the herring weir in East Bridgewater.

AMES NOWELL STATE PARK'S facilities are boating, fishing, hiking, picnic tables, snowmobiling.

ACTON (Middlesex County, sett. *c.* 1680, incorp. 1735, alt. 268, pop. 14,770, area 20.31 sq. mi., town meeting, routes, Mass. 2, 2A, 27, 62, 111, 119) was originally a "Praying Indian" village. The town, granted in 1643 to a Mr. Wheeler and called Concord Village, was settled about 40 years later. The Fitchburg RR (1844) gave industrial impetus to South and West Acton but not to Acton Center, a fact which probably accounts for the latter's charm. Industrial development was retarded after an 1862 fire destroyed some of West Acton. Today's industries include chemicals, electrical equipment, stone, clay and glass products, electronics, auto fabric manufacturing, liquid gas and wood products.

ACTON CENTER, with its lovely tiny village green, is as charming a settlement as can be found in New England or elsewhere. The small green is dominated by a monument, about 75 feet high and topped by a flagpole. The monument honors Capt. Isaac Davis, the first victim of British musketry at Concord, and other Acton patriots in that action. Across from the green is the library of post-Civil War vintage. Further north along the street is Meeting House Hill, now a park, site of the first meetinghouse.

EAST ACTON is a series of houses and mercantile establishments strung along Mass. 2A and 119.

NORTH ACTON, north and east of East Acton, is a small community of houses and business establishments bordering Mass. 2A, 27 and 119.

SOUTH ACTON, as previously noted, has some industries and pleasant homes.

WEST ACTON, the town's industrial center, has an attractive old Baptist Church.

ACUSHNET (Bristol County, sett. *c.* 1659, incorp. 1860, alt. 46, pop. 7767, area 18.0 sq. mi., town meeting, route, Mass. 105) — "Bathing Place" in Indian — was nearly destroyed during King Philip's War. In September 1776 local minutemen swapped shots with Lobsterbacks. Immigrant influence is evident in local victuals: Yankee hasty pudding, fish cakes, pumpkin pie, French-Canadians' hard bread and salads, Portuguese spiced sausages, Polish cabbage soup. Artists Clement Nye Smith and William Bradford were Acushnet natives. "Acushnet" golf balls and wood boxes are made here.

ADAMS (Berkshire County, sett. 1762, incorp. 1778, alt. 799, pop. 11,772, area 23.01 sq. mi., representative town meeting, routes, Mass. 8, 116). One hundred years after its incorporation Adams, named in honor of Sam Adams, was divided into North Adams and Adams.

Adams contends she is the Mother Town. A legend illustrates the point: When the Mohawk Trail opened in 1920, Adams' indignation exploded when North Adams erected a sign reading "This is the City of North Adams, the Mother of the Mohawk Trail." Adams erected a sign at the joint boundary, reading "You are now leaving Adams, the Mother of North Adams and the Grandmother of the Mohawk Trail."

Industrial development began in the early 19th century when William Pollock secured capital by selling a horse won in a lottery. He built and operated the old stone Broadly Mill. Paper and textile print works have long been the leading industries.

Friends Meeting House (open) (1784), corner of Friend and Maple Sts., is a two-and-a-half-story gable-end structure. The outer doors and movable partitions, raised during regular services, provided privacy during separate meetings. No provision was made for lighting. Women were allowed to sit on the left to receive more heat from the fireplace.

Birthplace of Susan B. Anthony (1820–1906) (open by permission), East Rd., was built about 1810. Miss Anthony's favorite room has its original furnishings. Beyond the house is the little schoolhouse (private) which the pioneer woman suffrage leader attended as a girl.

RENFREW is a mill village. Its *Blue Lake,* an artificial pond, derives its deep blue tint from the waste deposits of the limeworks.

ZYLONITE (alt. 726), once a thriving settlement, received its name from a mineral deposit found here and formerly used in manufacturing. That industry is gone. South of the village *Mt. Greylock* (alt. 3505), the highest mountain in the state, is visible.

MT. GREYLOCK STATE RESERVATION'S (Mass. 2, 7, 8) facilities include fishing, hiking, picnic tables, 30 campsites, hunting, snowmobiling, scenic views.

MT. GREYLOCK SKI AREA (off Mass. 2), located on the highest peak in the state (3491), has Thunderbolt Ski Run where many eastern state and state championship races are held. Several trails. No tows. Ski lodge is always open.

AGAWAM (Hampden County, sett. 1635, incorp. 1855, alt. 88, pop. 21,717, area 23.35 sq. mi., town meeting, routes, Mass. 5A, 57, 75, 187) — Indian for "Crooked River" or "low meadows" — takes its name from the river which meanders along the northern boundary. An agricultural town until about 1920, Agawam is now a suburb of Springfield. Buxton Leather Goods Company is a major employer. Electronics equipment is made here. In the Feeding Hills section farmers engage in market gardening, dairying, poultry and some tobacco raising.

ROBINSON STATE PARK contains two large picnic areas with fireplaces and tables, a beach and recreation building.

ALANDER (see MOUNT WASHINGTON)

ALFORD (Berkshire County, sett. c. 1740, incorp. 1775, alt. 939, pop. 302), a tiny hill town, was named for John Alford, founder of the Alford professorship of Moral Philosophy at Harvard. Alford marble was used in New York's City Hall, in the State House, Market and Law Building at Albany. Quarrying has been discontinued.

Tom Ball Mountain (alt. 1930). On its western slope is the *Devil's Den* (reached by a 0.5 mi. footpath), a large cave with constantly dripping cold water and an uneven floor.

ALLSTON (see BOSTON)

AMESBURY (Essex County, sett. 1654, incorp. 1668, alt. 150, pop. 11,388, town meeting, routes, Interstate 95 & 495, Mass. 110, 150). Amesbury, situated at the foot of *Lake Gardner,* in the shadow of rounded glacial hills, has quiet elm-shaded streets lined with neat white houses and picket fences. The town was once an important shipbuilding center. The Powow River flows beneath the streets and buildings around Amesbury Square to its junction with the Merrimack River.

Many legends concerning the powers of darkness are still told in Amesbury. Town witch Goody Whitcher's loom bangs night and day even though she has been dead for nearly three centuries. People strolling the quiet streets during the late hours are often said to see a man toting his severed head beneath his arm. On *Barrow Hill* late at night favored ones can see the lights from witches' fires while shadowy forms dance about the summit.

A boulder marks the *Site of the Home of Susanna Martin,* better known as Goody Martin, an Amesbury witch, tried, convicted and sentenced to hang at Salem in 1693. The story goes that on the scaffold she uttered incantations which caused the rope to wriggle and dance about so that the hangman could not tie the knot, till a crow, flying overhead, cawed down the advice to try a noose of willow withe. When this was done, the execution was completed.

Whittier House (open Tues.–Sat. 10–5, holidays by appointment, donations), corner of Pickard and Friend Sts., was the residence of Quaker poet John Greenleaf Whittier (1807–92) from 1836 to 1892. The simple frame house contains manuscripts and possessions. His grave is in *Union Cemetery.*

Mary Baker Eddy House (open Apr. 1–Nov. 30, weekdays, except holidays, 2–5, fee), 277 Main St., was for a time the residence of the founder of The Christian Science Church. She wrote *Comments on the Scriptures* while living here.

Friends Meeting House (1851), Greenleaf St., is a plain frame structure. Whittier's pew is marked.

Captain's Well, Main St. at corner of schoolyard, is a granite reproduction of the old wooden well described in Whittier's poem, *The Captain's Well.* A three-panel relief shows Capt. Valentine Bagley, the poem's hero. On the school lawn is sculptor Leonard Craske's *Doughboy Statue.*

Victoria Park on the summit of Powow Hill has a fine panoramic view.

Rocky Hill Meetinghouse (open May–Oct., weekdays 9–5, donations) (1785), between Amesbury and Salisbury n. of Mass. 110, is an excellent example of an 18th century meeting house. Very few alterations have been made. Quaker services are held on three Sundays during the summer.

Notable residents have included lithographer Nathaniel Currier (1813–88) of Currier and Ives fame. Daniel Webster's mother Abigail Eastman was born here and so was Dr. Josiah Bartlett (1729–95), signer of the Declaration of Independence and first New Hampshire governor. George Washington visited here in 1789.

AMHERST (Hampshire County, sett. 1703, incorp. 1775, alt. 356, pop. 26,331, area 27.70 sq. mi., town meeting, routes, Mass. 9, 116) has Amherst College and the University of Massachusetts.

Quiet dwellings and elm-shaded streets make Amherst attractive and individual. It was named for Lord Jeffery Amherst (1717–97), a French and Indian War general. The town was once part of Hadley.

Two streams furnished waterpower for small industries. Shortly after the Revolution, a paper factory opened; it was followed by three others in 70 years. Palm-leaf hats, "Shaker" hoods for women, sleds, baby carriages and rifles were made here.

The inhabitants' agrarian skill and the lusty health of their cattle as shown in annual fairs attracted statewide interest which culminated, in 1863, in the founding of Massachusetts Agricultural College, which later, with a broadened curriculum, became Massachusetts State College. It became the University of Massachusetts in 1947. The college was established as a result of the Morrill Land Grant Act of 1862, which allotted to Massachusetts the sum of $208,464 realized from the sale of 360,000 acres of land granted by the federal government. From a perpetual fund set up for the promotion of education in agriculture and the "mechanic arts," one third was to be given to the Massachusetts Institute of Technology and two thirds to the Agricultural College. After WWII the university was reorganized and expanded. A Boston branch was established in temporary quarters in 1964 and in the same year the legislature approved construction of a medical school in Worcester. The student body in 1970 was about 17,000.

Amherst College was founded in 1821, to educate "promising but needy youths who wished to enter the Ministry." Amherst College had an initial enrollment of 47 pupils, two professors and the president. Emphasis was placed on missionary work.

Shortly after 1830, the slavery question nearly split its academic ranks. Financial stringency threatened to complete the ruin, but the college weathered this crisis and established itself on a firm basis. Liberal education instead of mere vocational training has always been the aim. Amherst was the first U.S. college to adopt student government.

Amherst is one of the most noted smaller colleges for men in the United States. Graduates include Henry Ward Beecher, Calvin Coolidge and Dwight Morrow. Noah Webster, Helen Hunt Jackson, Eugene Field and Ray Stannard Baker (David Grayson) lived in Amherst. Their presence fostered a literary atmosphere very congenial to the college. Robert Frost was a faculty member for several years. A campus library was named in his honor.

What to See and Do

Jones Library (open Sept.–June, Mon. and Fri. 10–5:30, Tues., Wed., Thurs. 10–9:30, Sat. 10–5:30), Amity St., a gambrel-roof fieldstone building, is one of the most luxurious small public libraries in the United States. There are 12 large rooms and 16 smaller ones. All are paneled in Philippine white mahogany or walnut. Many have Oriental rugs and comfortable chairs and divans. *Room of Amherst Authors* has representative and extensive editions of the works of Emily Dickinson, Robert Frost, Eugene Field, Helen Hunt Jackson, Noah Webster and others.

Strong House (open early July–Labor Day, Mon.–Fri. 2–5) (1744), Amity and N. Prospect Sts., is a three-and-a-half-story, gambrel-roof brownish frame dwelling, now the home of the Amherst Historical Society. The second oldest house in town, it was built by local craftsmen of hand-hewn timber and handwrought hardware.

Helen Hunt Jackson House (private), 249 S. Pleasant St., a two-and-a-half-story yellow frame dwelling, was the home of "H.H.," the pseudonym under which Mrs. Jackson (1830–85) wrote *Ramona* and other popular novels. Mrs. Jackson's classic *A Century of Dishonor* was one of the first major attacks upon the U.S. government's brutal and dishonest policy toward Indians.

The Lord Jeffery Inn (open all year), a Treadway Inn, is a charming replica of a colonial brick tavern with some 40-pane windows. It houses French and Indian War prints, maps, autographed letters and papers of Lord Jeffery Amherst, George Washington, William Pitt, General James Wolfe, George II and Louis XV. This air-conditioned inn is known for setting a fine table.

Emily Dickinson Home (open Tues. 3 P.M. by appointment), 280 Main Street, behind a high evergreen hedge, is now owned by Amherst College. The first brick house in Amherst, it was built about 1813 by her grandfather Samuel Dickinson, a founder of Amherst College. Here Emily Dickinson was born in 1830, lived her life apart and died in 1886—a poet and mystic, who, after her death, was acclaimed as one of the very few great American poets. Her withdrawal from the world, following a youthful renunciation of love, became almost complete during her later years as she devoted herself to writing hundreds of poems. As she wished, only two or three poems were published during her lifetime. After her death her sister Lavinia and her niece and heir Martha Dickinson Bianchi made her work available to the public. Nothing pertaining to the Dickinsons remains in the mansion. The *Evergreens* just across the way was the home of her sole brother William Austin Dickinson and the home of her niece and biographer Martha Bianchi.

ANDOVER (Essex County, sett. *c.* 1642, incorp. 1646, alt. 150, pop. 23,695, area 31.10 sq. mi., town meeting, routes, Mass. 28, 133, 125) is the seat of Phillips (Andover) Academy, one of the nation's finest preparatory schools. The land was purchased about 1642 by John Woodbridge for six pounds and a coat. Known as Cochichowick (Indian for "Place of the Great Cascade"), it was named Andover, the English hometown of several settlers.

Powder mills built here during the Revolution were operated by Samuel Phillips (1752–1802). Harvard man Phillips was a delegate to the Massachusetts Provincial Congress (1775) and to the state constitutional convention (1779–80). He established a paper mill. Abraham Marland made wool cloth. The first flax mills in the nation opened here.

Andover is one of the state's most attractive villages. Ancient elms shade lawns and stately homes. The hill is topped by the well-designed buildings of Andover Academy.

Andover Historical Society (open Mon., Wed., Fri. 2–4, free), 97 Main St., has its headquarters here in the Deacon Ames Blanchard House (1819).

America House (private), 124 Main St., is where 24-year-old Sam Smith (1808–95) wrote the words of *America* (1832). He was a Baptist preacher.

Abbot Academy (1829), one of the earliest incorporated girls' schools in New England, was founded by Mrs. Nehemiah Abbot, wife of a Phillips Academy steward.

John-Esther Art Gallery (open weekdays 9–5, free), Abbot Academy, has paintings, bronzes and wood carvings.

Addison Gallery of American Art (open weekdays 9–5, Sun. 2:30–5, free), Chapel Ave. at Phillips Academy. Completed in 1931, this Georgian-style building houses an excellent collection of American paintings, including works by Ryder, Sully, Copley, Sargent, Whistler, John Marin, Preston Dickinson and Abbott H. Thayer. There is a fine collection of American silver, furniture, models of famous American ships, prints and sculpture.

Benjamin Abbot Homestead (private) (1685), corner Andover St. and Argilla Rd., is said to be the oldest house in town. The walls, dark and weathered, and the lean-to roof with pilastered central chimney link it in age with the gigantic elm tree in the yard.

Phillips Andover Academy, established in 1778 by Samuel Phillips, is the oldest incorporated school in the United States. The Phillips family helped found Andover Theological Seminary, now situated in Newton. The Academy and the Seminary drew Lowells and Quincys from Massachusetts, Washingtons and Lees from Virginia. Eminent graduates have been Samuel F. B. Morse, Oliver Wendell Holmes, Josiah Quincy and George Herbert Palmer.

Phillips Academy Archaeology Museum (open weekdays 9–5, free), Phillips Academy, corner Phillips and Main Sts., has prehistoric items from all over the United States.

Bulfinch Hall (1818), named after its architect, has a beautifully proportioned cupola. The interior has been altered, but the exterior is about the same as it was when Phillips graduate Dr. Oliver Wendell Holmes described it in his poem "The Schoolboys." *Memorial Tower* with its 37-bell carillon was dedicated to Academy men who died during WWI. *The Oliver Wendell Holmes Library,* in Georgian style, has a collection of Dr. Holmes' first editions.

Andover Inn (open all year), Chapel St., harmonizes with the surrounding buildings and is furnished with colonial pieces and Currier and Ives prints. The inn, operated by Treadway Inns for the academy, has a pleasant taproom and serves excellent New England food.

HAROLD PARKER STATE FOREST is in Andover, North Andover, and North Reading.

CHARLES W. WARD RESERVATION (270 acres), owned and maintained by TOR, includes 420-foot-high Holt Hill, the highest elevation in Essex County. A fire lookout tower is located on the summit. There are several miles of nature trails and a few ski slopes. Main entrance to the reservation is at the end of Prospect St., about 0.5 mi. from the intersection of Mass. 125 and Prospect St.

SHAWSHEEN, a village in Andover, was formerly an American Woolen Company town.

ANNISQUAM (see ROCKPORT)

ARLINGTON (Middlesex County, sett. *c.* 1630, incorp. 1867, alt. 50, pop. 53,524, area 5.18 sq. mi., representative town meeting, routes, Mass. 2, 2A, 3, 60).

The story of Arlington — a Boston residential suburb — has been a quiet one since April 19, 1775 — the day of Lexington and Concord. In 1797 gunsmith Amos Whittemore invented a machine for making cotton and wool cards. This process greatly reduced manufacturing operations and vastly increased production. Arlington's industrial prosperity was blighted by the War of 1812. The Whittemore plant was sold and Arlington lost its main industry. During the 1850's the Gage, Hittinger Company cut Spy Pond ice and shipped it to many tropical countries. From 1850 to 1890 Arlington was a truck garden crop supplier for the Boston area. The pleasant countryside became popular with city dwellers whose demand for homes forced farmers to become lot salesmen. When trolleys reached Arlington just before 1900 the city became a Boston residential suburb.

Ancient Burying Ground, corner of Massachusetts Ave. and Pleasant St. (behind Unitarian Church), has a monument to the 12 Americans killed while pursuing the British to Boston, April 19, 1775.

On the *Unitarian Church* lawn a tablet reads "At this spot, April 19, 1775, the old men of Menotomy [an early name for Arlington] captured a convoy of 18 men with supplies on the way to join the British at Lexington." Arlington's brief but effective moment of glory occurred when the "old men" heard that a British supply train was coming through with only a small guard. They crouched behind a wall and rose as the Lobsterbacks approached, covered them with leveled muskets and forced a surrender.

Spy Pond. Old Mother Batherick was digging dandelions — for food or wine — on April 19,1775, when six British grenadiers fleeing from "the old men of Menotomy" passed by. She took them off guard and marched them to the local jailhouse — so says legend.

Cooper Tavern Site, corner Massachusetts Ave. and Medford St., is marked by tablet. Jason Winship and Jabez Wyman, sitting over their rum toddies, were killed April 19, when retreating Redcoats fired blindly through the tavern windows.

Black Horse Tavern Site, Massachusetts Ave. opposite Linwood St., was the meeting place for the local Committee of Safety. Provincial Congress met here April 18, 1775.

John Adams House Site (1652), identified by a marker on the village green, was Continental Army hospital during the Siege of Boston (1775–76).

ASHBURNHAM (Worcester County, sett. 1736, incorp. 1765, alt. 1028, pop. 3484, area 39.15 sq. mi., town meeting, routes, Mass. 12, 101, 119) was founded upon seven land grants: Starr Grant given to the heirs of

Pequot War surgeon Thomas Starr; Cambridge Grant (1734), to Cambridge as compensation for maintaining a bridge across the Charles between Brighton and Cambridge; Lexington Grant, sold in 1757 to seven German immigrants and known as Dutch Farms; Bluefield Grant, to three men for erecting an inn on the Northfield Rd.; Converse Grant, to heirs of Major James Converse, Woburn, for services to the Colony; the Rolfe Grant, to heirs of Rev. Benjamin Rolfe of Haverhill, slain by the Indians; and (1735), Dorchester Canada Grant of six square miles divided among descendants of 60 soldiers from Dorchester who fought in the 1690 Canadian expedition.

Cushing Academy, a boy's preparatory school, is located here.

ASHBY (Middlesex County, incorp. 1767, alt. 900, pop. 2274, area 23.66 sq. mi., town meeting, routes, Mass. 31, 119) is a typical New England farming community with fine orchards. Mountain laurel covers the wayside with pink blossoms in late spring.

First Parish Church (1809), a fine example of Federal architecture, is notable for its triple door and well-proportioned belfry.

Many Ashby residents commute to nearby cities. Micro-Tool, precision instrument makers, recently moved from Fitchburg to Ashby. The town has zoning laws. Children (grades 7–12) attend North Middlesex Regional High School. The Ashby Historical Society, Inc., recently reactivated, flourished from the late 1800's to 1940.

WILLARD BROOK STATE FOREST lies alongside Mass. 119. Beach and bathhouse on shores of Damon Pond. Log cabins available at modest rental. Facilities: fishing, hiking, hunting, fireplaces, picnic tables, campsites (21), swimming, snowmobiling.

ASHFIELD (Franklin County, sett. *c.* 1743, incorp. 1765, alt. 1244, pop. 1274, area 40.28 sq. mi., town meeting, routes, Mass. 112, 116), unlike most New England towns, has no green.

The *Town Hall* (1814), originally the Ashfield Church, has a fine spire. *Sanderson Academy* (1888), a two-story building with an octagonal belfry, was founded in 1816.

SPRUCE CORNER is a crossroads settlement. Farming is the principal occupation.

CHAPELBROOK (128 acres), owned and maintained by TOR, has a brook, waterfalls and Pony Mt. Take Williamsburg Rd. off Mass. 116 at South Ashfield or take Ashfield Rd. off US 9 in center of Williamsburg. Informal picnic sites.

POLAND BROOK WILDLIFE MANAGEMENT AREA provides public hunting in Ashfield and Conway.

ASHLAND (Middlesex County, sett. *c.* 1750, incorp. 1846, alt. 188, pop. 8882, area 12.41 sq. mi., town meeting, routes, Mass. 126, 135). Original settlers were attracted by fertile valleys. The *Sudbury River* was harnessed and by 1850 Ashland was a flourishing mill community. After 1872, when Boston obtained control of the Sudbury River and divided it for part of its water supply, only a few small factories remained.

In 1750 Sir Harry Frankland, descendant of Oliver Cromwell, friend of the Earl of Chesterfield and a Crown official in Boston, built a manor house here. While visiting Marblehead he saw beautiful Agnes Surriage scrubbing a tavern floor. He took a fancy to her and sent her to Boston to receive a polite education. They traveled a great deal. Agnes's beauty and grace aroused ardent admiration in all the gay capitals of Europe. In 1755, during a visit to Lisbon, Portugal, the pair were caught in an earthquake. This caused Sir Harry to think on his later end. He married Agnes Surriage. He died in 1768. In 1775 Lady Agnes, suspected of Tory sympathies, sailed to England, where she married another titled gentleman. Ashland's cherished story has been told in *Agnes,* a poem by Oliver Wendell Holmes; in *Brampton Sketches,* by Mary B. Claflin, a native of Hopkinton and wife of Governor Claflin; in *Old Town Folk,* by Harriet Beecher Stowe; and in *Agnes Surriage,* a novel by Edwin L. Bynner.

The *Public Library,* Front St., has a cannon used for coastal defense in the early 1800's. The *Ashland Historical Society Headquarters* (open by appointment), in the town hall, has Colonial furnishings and local history documents.

General Electric Company (clocks) is the town's largest employer.

ASHLAND STATE PARK (320 acres) includes the shoreline of Ashland Reservoir. Beach, picnic tables, fireplaces. Swimming, boating, fishing, snowmobiling. One mile off Mass. 135.

ASSINIPPI CORNER (see HANOVER)

ATHOL (Worcester County, sett. 1735, incorp. 1762, alt. 535, pop. 11,185, area 32.34 sq. mi., representative town meeting, routes, US 202, Mass. 2, 32) was named by leading proprietor John Murray, who said the scenery resembled that about the Duke of Atholl's Scottish castle. He was the duke's son. Athol, originally a farming community, in the 19th century became industrialized, with factories producing scythes, cotton and paper.

The *L. S. Starrett Co.* (visitors welcome), founded in 1868 by Maine-born Laroy S. Starrett, is one of the world's leading manufacturers of precision measuring instruments. Another large industry, now known as

Union-Card Division, UTD Corporation, had its beginning in Athol in 1894 and manufactures drills, reamers and other cutting tools. Both industries have other U.S. and foreign branches.

MILLERS RIVER WILDLIFE MANAGEMENT AREA shares public hunting with Royalston and Phillipston.

ATTLEBOROUGH (Bristol County, sett. 1634, town incorp. 1694, city incorp. 1914, alt. 130, pop. 32,907, area 27.51 sq. mi., mayor-council.)

"The Nation's Number One Jewelry Manufacturing Center" is the proud—and probably correct—boast of Attleboro's residents, many of whom work in the jewelry industry.

Attleborough Museum (open Tues.–Sun. 2–5, closed holidays, free), Capron Park, has several interesting local art collections.

Bronson Museum (open Mon., Tues., Thurs. 9:30–4:30, free), Bronson Bldg., contains Indian relics.

AUBURN (Worcester County, sett. 1714, incorp. 1837, alt. 600, pop. 15,347, area 15.70 sq. mi., representative town meeting, routes, Mass. Pike, US 20, Mass. 12) is where Robert Hutchings Goddard on March 16, 1926, fired the world's first liquid propellant rocket. The event took place on the Ward Farm, Pakachoag Hill, now the Pakachoag Golf Course.

Auburn was first named after Revolutionary War General Artemas Ward, but due to later confusion between the names of Ward and Ware, the name was changed to Auburn in 1837.

AVON (Norfolk County, sett. before 1700, incorp. 1888, alt. 250, pop. 5295, area 4.35 sq. mi., town meeting, route, Mass. 28) was part of the grant known as the "land beyond the Blue Hills," made to Dorchester in 1637. Its present name honors William Shakespeare of Stratford-on-Avon.

As East Stoughton, it was one of the earliest towns to manufacture boots and shoes, an important product by the mid-19th century. Today, however, it is a residential suburb of Brockton and Boston. Electronic gear, tools, dies, engineering products and the distribution of health aids are current major industries.

AYER (Middlesex County, sett. *c.* 1668, incorp. 1871, alt. 240, pop. 7393, area 8.82 sq. mi., town meeting, routes, Mass. 2A, 12, 110, 111) was named after James C. Ayer, a patent medicine tycoon of Lowell who extended financial aid to the town.

The *Public Library* houses shards of Nashoba Indian pottery, old paper currency, a service flag and Fort Stevens' first papers.

The town today is an agricultural center with some residents making sewing machines and cutlery. Many local people are employed as civilians at Fort Devens.

Fort Devens (1917), a U.S. Army post, was a training cantonment for American Expeditionary Force (A.E.F.) troops. It was named after Gen. Charles Devens (1820–91), a Massachusetts Civil War fighter. Between World Wars, Fort Devens, earlier known as Camp Devens, was the home post of the 13th Infantry whose motto was "Vicksburg, First Forty Rounds." The 66th Infantry (light tanks), a pioneer tank outfit, was also stationed here. It was an induction center during WWII and the Korean conflict and is used for training in the Vietnam war.

FORT DEVENS WILDLIFE MANAGEMENT AREA is a public hunting area lying in Ayer, Shirley, and Lancaster. Special free daily permit.

BACK BAY (see BOSTON)

BALDWINSVILLE (see TEMPLETON)

BARNSTABLE COUNTY (est. 1685, pop. 96,656, area 394.04 sq. mi., shire town, Barnstable) has 15 towns and no cities. Towns include Barnstable, Bourne, Brewster, Chatham, Dennis, Eastham, Falmouth, Harwich, Mashpee, Orleans, Provincetown, Sandwich, Truro, Wellfleet, Yarmouth.

Barnstable County is Cape Cod (see CAPE COD).

BARNSTABLE (Barnstable County, sett. 1636, incorp. 1638, alt. 50, pop. 19,842, area 60.16 sq. mi., town meeting, routes, US 6, Mass. 6A, 28, 149).

Barnstable, shire town of Barnstable County, and in area the largest town in the state, includes Hyannis village, summer home of the Kennedy family. It was in the Kennedy family compound — the several Kennedy houses with their common yard — that in late 1959 the president-to-be planned his forthcoming primary campaign. He returned here after his Los Angeles nomination for a few days' sailing before taking the 1960 campaign trail. He waited here for Richard Nixon's concession speech. Here his ailing father was reluctantly told of his son's tragic death.

Barnstable has more villages and localities than a wagon wheel has spokes. It was settled about 1637 by preacher Joseph Hull, surveyor Austin Bearse, Thomas Dimmock and others. Pioneers were attracted by the great marshes that yielded an abundance of salt hay for cattle. A trading settlement set up in 1700 swapped codfish caught from Grand and other banks for rum and West Indian molasses. By 1800 Barnstable was prospering from a coastal trade.

Barnstable was a prime source of the nation's master mariners and deep-water shipmasters during the great clipper ship era. Cap'n Frank Bearse in the *Flying Scud* set a longtime unofficial record of 446 miles under sail in one day. Cap'n Richard Bearse of the *Winged Arrow* sailed from Cape Horn to the Golden Gate in 31 days. Cap'n Lorenzo Dow Baker brought the first cargo of bananas to the United States.

Barnstable "boys" sailed to faraway ports like Canton, Melbourne, the fabled isle of Zanzibar, Cape Town and Valparaiso and brought home teak chests and other furniture, ivory, jade and gewgaws for the womenfolk. When clippers gave way to stinking steamers, skippers who'd made their pile retired to their neat white homes. Some, loath to leave the sea, stayed for a while in the coastal trade.

In the 1890's summer folks—those who could afford it—came to Barnstable boardinghouses or inns. The automobile brought a great influx of summer visitors. Some come for the weekend while others hire a house for a month or the season. Some own summer places.

Sturgis Library (1645), a good example of the old Cape Cod house, is one of the oldest library buildings in the United States.

On a small triangular green at the junction of US 6A and Rendezvous Lane is the *Site of the Liberty Pole,* erected in Revolutionary days. When the pole disappeared, Aunt "Nabby" Freeman, a defiant Tory who had publicly threatened "straightaway to heave that dead tree up," was tarred, feathered and ridden from town astride a rail.

Sacrament Rock, US 6A, a large boulder with bronze tablet, is inscribed: "Here the settlers received their first sacrament in 1639, and held their first town meeting."

Coach House (1640) is a good example of the saltbox house; this building, gay with Cape Cod blue trim, has never been structurally altered.

Barnstable Harbor (north side of the Cape) is overlooked by "Shoot Flyin' Hill" once famous for its wildfowlers and coot shooters.

BARNSTABLE VILLAGE (US 6A), an attractive settlement, has not been as commercialized as Hyannis. It still retains much of the charm of old Cape towns.

CENTERVILLE (s. off Mass. 28) is a small settlement with lovely homes and a fine old *Congregational Church.* Natalie Kalmus, developer of the technicolor process which gave Hollywood and America its first good color movies, had a summer home here.

COTUIT (off Mass. 28) is the name of a small summer settlement and of the world famous, delicious Cotuit clam.

CRAIGVILLE is Barnstable's beautiful long beach—one of the finest in the East—overlooking Nantucket Sound. Facilities include bathhouses.

HYANNIS (Mass. 132 off US 6 or US 6A) is the trading center of Barnstable.

HYANNISPORT, site of the Kennedy compound, has many fine summer homes.

MARSTON'S MILL is a small settlement at the junction of Mass. 28 and 149.

OSTERVILLE (head south from Marston's Mill) is a small settlement of pleasant homes.

WEST BARNSTABLE (US 6 and US 6A) has on Mass. 49 what is believed to be the oldest *Congregational Church* building (1717) in America. The burying grounds on the hill behind the church contain some of the oldest tombstones of English colonists in America.

WIANNO, a small summer settlement, has many fine homes. It is the site of the private Wianno Club.

BARRE (Worcester County, sett. *c.* 1720, incorp. 1774, alt. 886, pop. 3825, area 44.30 sq. mi., town meeting, Mass. routes 32, 62, 122) was incorporated as Hutchinson but renamed in 1776 for Col. Isaac Barre, a friend of the colonists in the English Parliament. A large, beautiful, triangular common, scene of the annual musters for the surrounding area, and the lovely old Colonial homes and white steepled churches give this small town a typical New England appearance. Once famous for its palm-leaf hat manufacturing, the town has a flourishing woolen mill founded in the early 19th century and a machine shop and foundry which help maintain local prosperity.
Ware River Intake Works, Quabbin Aqueduct connecting the Quabbin and Wachusetts Reservoirs of the Metropolitan Water System, is on Mass. Rte. 122.

COOK'S CANYON WILDLIFE SANCTUARY, South Street (35 acres), features a dramatic gorge where the stream drops nearly 200 feet within a half-mile. The Mass. Audubon Society sponsors a residential natural history camp here. The sanctuary is a society project.

Historical Society (open Sun. afternoon, May–Oct.) is an 1833 Georgian Colonial home on the common, containing the museum of local history.

ROCKINGSTONE PARK — Rte. 122 west of the village, ten-acre tract containing an unusual boulder-upon-boulder formation, result of the glacial deposit.

Barre Falls Dam — U.S. Corps of Engineers flood control dam in the midst of the Metropolitan District Commission (MDC) watershed, a haven for sportsmen.

Felton Field—Athletic field formerly the old Worcester County West Agricultural Society Fair Grounds. Covered grandstand and track.

PHILLIPSTON WILDLIFE MANAGEMENT AREA is a public hunting area lying in Phillipston, Barre, and Petersham. Barre Falls Area takes in parts of Barre, Hubbardston, Rutland, and Oakham.

BEACON HILL (see BOSTON)

BECKET (Berkshire County, sett. *c.* 1740, incorp. 1765, alt. 1574, pop. 929, area 46.92 sq. mi., town meeting, routes, US 20, Mass. 8), lacking good farmland, originally depended upon its abundance of granite and hemlock bark. Scarcity of water power and exhaustion of natural resources arrested development in the 1880's. Basketmaking, silk thread and paper manufacturing and quarrying became the only year-round nonagricultural activities. Becket village was inundated by 25 feet of water from broken Ballou Dam in 1927. The silk factory was abandoned. Becket is a quiet residential area.
Becket Falls plunges 25 feet into a grotesquely worn rock channel. At the foot of the cascade is a popular swimming hole.
The *First Congregational Church* (1758) has the only Paul Revere Bell in Berkshire County.

The gradual transformation of Becket into a residential and summer recreational area is reflected by the many homes and children's camps located around its picturesque natural and man-made lakes and ponds.
Jacob's Pillow Dance Festival and School of the Dance, founded by Ted Shawn in *West Becket* (off Mass. 20), has achieved international fame and has played a large part in helping build the reputation of the Berkshires as a summer cultural capital.

BECKET WILDLIFE MANAGEMENT AREA has public hunting.

BEDFORD (Middlesex County, sett. 1640, incorp. 1729, alt. 135, pop. 13,513, area 13.73 sq. mi., town meeting, routes, Mass. 4, 25, 62 and just off Mass. 128), once a farming area, has *L. G. Hanscom Field* (limited visiting), a major USAF electronics research center. Some farming areas have been made into middle-class residential developments and industrial areas. Massachusetts Institute of Technology, Electronics Corporation Laboratory, Howell Associates, Radio Corporation of America and Raytheon Corporation maintain research, development and/or manufacturing facilities on or near the field. The Air Force reported during the late 1960's that 3500 employees with an annual payroll approaching $25,000,000 were located on the base. The impact on Bedford's economy is considerable.
Bedford U.S. Veterans' Hospital (1500 beds) employs more than 1000 staffers. In the late 1960's the annual payroll exceeded $5,000,000.

Bedford was settled around an Indian trading post, *Shawsheen House.* In the library is the Bedford Flag, designed in England in the 1660's and carried by Nathaniel Page III, when on April 19, 1775, he left his wife and baby to join the Minutemen.
Two Brothers Boulders along the Concord River are named Dudley and Winthrop. Here Gov. Winthrop and Deputy Governor Dudley in 1639 settled the boundaries of their grants.

BELCHERTOWN (Hampshire County, sett. 1731, incorp. 1761, alt. 613, pop. 5936, area 56.7 sq. mi., town meeting, routes, US 202, Mass. 9, 21, 181) was named for Gov. Jonathan Belcher (1682–1757), a co-founder of Princeton College. *Holland Glen* honors native son Josiah G. Holland (1819–81), poet, novelist and editor of *Scribner's Monthly* magazine. *Springfield Republican* editor Holland wrote *History of Western Massachusetts* (1855). Sleigh, wagon and carriage making has been replaced by dairy farming and apple growing.
Clapp Memorial Library (1882), South Main St., was founded on a $40,000 bequest by John F. Clapp. Built in the form of a Latin cross, the building has two stained-glass memorial windows.
Stone House and Henry Ford Building (open May 15–Oct. 15, Wed. and Sat., fee), US 202, has the relic collection of the Belchertown Historical Association. *Carriage Shed Annex* donated by Henry Ford contains early farm implements and vehicles once made here.

SWIFT RIVER WILDLIFE MANAGEMENT AREA has public hunting in Belchertown and Ware.

BELLINGHAM (Norfolk County, sett. 1713, incorp. 1719, alt. 293, pop. 13,967, area 18.55 sq. mi., town meeting, routes, Interstate 495, Mass. 126, 140), when settled by Jacob Bartlett, was called No Man's Land. The town was settled around the Congregational Church, and much of its early history is identified with that institution. Leather and textile production became important after 1800.

North Bellingham was the birthplace of William T. Adams (1822–97), author of juvenile fiction under the pen name Oliver Optic. He wrote over 1000 short stories. More than 2,000,000 copies of his 126 books were sold.

BELMONT (Middlesex County, sett. 1630, incorp. 1859, alt. 74.0, pop. 28,285, area 4.67 sq. mi., representative town meeting, route, Mass. 60), a Boston suburb, derives its name from the estate of China trade merchant John P. Cushing.

Belmont's early history is identical with Watertown and West Cambridge from which the town was formed. Fertile soil lent itself to agriculture. In 1795 Holstein cattle were introduced into this country by Winthrop W. Chenery. The first annual Strawberry Festival (1859) became so popular that in 1863 about 2000 people feasted here.

Improved transportation facilities changed the town. Today meadows are occupied by homes. Belmont has many residents in education, business, science, medicine and arts. It has been said that Belmont has more people listed in *Who's Who in America* than any other town — not city — in the country. The town meeting government was modified in 1926 when Belmont was divided into precincts, each electing its representatives to the town meeting.

On Pleasant St. is the *Abraham Hill House* (private) (1693), a clapboard dwelling that was a haven for patriots April 19, 1775. This house was the birthplace of Zachariah Hill's five Minuteman sons.

Captain Stephen Frost House (private). On his way to Concord on April 19, 1775, Capt. Frost and "the old men of Menotomy" captured a British company.

Town Hall, Pleasant St. and Concord Ave., was built in 1881 on the site of Jeduthan Wellington's Tavern. In 1824 Lafayette stopped to drink cider with the proprietor, who had fought under him at Dorchester Heights. On the lawn of the town hall is a cannon, removed from the U.S. Frigate *Constitution* in 1931.

At the northwesterly corner of the junction is the present *Belmont Women's Club,* built by Winslow Homer's uncle. This region was a favorite haunt of James Russell Lowell, whose poem, "Beaver Brook," was dedicated to it.

BERKLEY (Bristol County, sett. 1638, incorp. 1735, alt. 77, pop. 2027, area 15.56 sq. mi., town meeting, routes, Fall River Expressway) is a rural town where shipbuilding flourished for about a century.

Berkley Common is described by "child poet," Nathalia Crane, in "The Janitor's Boy."

The *Congregational Church* is a two-story building with a high, peaked roof and windows with diamond-shaped panes of stained glass. The little church has two entrances, one beneath a tiny turret standing about six feet high and the other beneath the tower.

Berkley, a small town surrounded by farms, has a wood-working plant. Many residents commute to nearby cities.

DIGHTON ROCK STATE PARK includes famous Dighton Rock in Taunton River and has fireplaces and picnic tables.

BERKSHIRE COUNTY (est. 1761, formerly part of Hampshire County, pop. 149,402, area 934.18 sq. mi., shire town, Pittsfield) includes the cities of North Adams and Pittsfield and 30 towns: Adams, Alford, Becket, Cheshire, Clarksburg, Dalton, Egremont, Florida, Great Barrington, Hancock, Hinsdale, Lanesborough, Lee, Lenox, Monterey, Mount Washington, New Ashford, New Marlborough, Otis, Peru, Richmond, Sandisfield, Savoy, Sheffield, Stockbridge, Tyringham, Washington, West Stockbridge, Williamstown, Windsor.

BERLIN (Worcester County, sett. 1765, incorp. 1812, alt. 300, pop. 2099, area 13.01 sq. mi., town meeting, routes, Mass. 62, Interstate 495) is an agricultural community despite unfavorable soil conditions. There are a few orchards and dairies.

BERNARDSTON (Franklin County, sett. 1738, incorp. 1762, alt. 366, pop. 1659, town meeting, routes, Interstate 91, US 5, Mass. 10), a hill town formerly called Falls Fight after a 1676 battle between settlers and Indians, was renamed to honor provincial governor, Sir Francis Bernard. Four forts were built in this frontier settlement about 1736 when settlers were intermittently warring with the Indians. There have been several attempts at industrial development, but the chief occupation remains farming.

NORTH BERNARDSTON has a few houses and an eating place strung along US 5. At the north end a road leads west to the remote hill hamlet of Leyden.

BEVERLY (Essex County, sett. *c.* 1626, town incorp. 1688, city incorp. 1894, alt. 44, pop. 38,348, area 15.14 sq. mi., mayor-alderman, routes, US 1A, Mass. 127, 128) has the world's largest plant for manufacturing shoemaking machinery. The United Shoe Machinery Company's plant is open to visitors. Beverly was the site of one of the nation's last witchcraft trials.

It is hard to visualize the post-Revolutionary decades when Beverly merchant princes sent their vessels to sea and the fisheries aided by federal subsidies were flourishing; when rich cargoes from Africa and the Spice Islands scented the waterfront air.

The schooner *Hannah* commissioned by George Washington is said to be the first vessel to fly the Continental flag.

The original *First Church,* Cabot St., was erected in 1656. During the witchcraft hysteria of 1693, Mistress Hale, exemplary wife of the Beverly minister, was accused. Her case was dismissed, and shortly after, witch trials were abandoned.

BEVERLY FARMS, a section of estates along the waterfront, was the longtime summer home of the late Justice Oliver Wendell Holmes, Jr. Once when the justice was away, the horse pulling his wife's buggy got out of control. As horse, buggy and Mrs. Holmes careened down the dusty street, she yelled at a friend, "Tell him that I loved him." This was after nearly 40 years of marriage.

PRIDE'S CROSSING, another elite section.

MONTSERRAT, still another elegant Beverly area.

BILLERICA (Middlesex County, sett. 1637, incorp. 1671, alt. 250, pop. 31,648, area 25.48 sq. mi., town meeting, routes US 3, Mass. 3A, 4, 129), home of the Wamesit tribe and a "Praying Indian" town, was originally Shawsheen. It was later named for Billericay in Essex, England. Many settlers were massacred in the French and Indian Wars.

Billerica is a growing residential and industrial town. Most industry is in contemporary design buildings scattered throughout the surrounding country. The major industry is textiles.

Billerica Historical Society (open June–Labor Day, Sun. 2–5), 36 Concord Rd., has an interesting collection of early American furniture, Colonial portraits, pewter, glass and china.

Middlesex Canal Museum (same hours as above or by appointment), 36 Concord Rd., has maps, models, prints and original documents relating to the old Middlesex Canal.

WARREN H. MANNING STATE PARK'S facilities are picnic tables, fireplaces and a children's spray pool.

BLACKSTONE (Worcester County, sett. 1662, incorp. 1845, alt. 186, pop. 6566, area 10.97 sq. mi., town meeting, routes, Mass. 122, 126) was named for Episcopalian clergyman, William Blackstone, the first white settler on the banks of the river, also named for him. In 1809 the first cotton mill was established, and a woolen mill followed in 1814. Industry reached its height in the second decade of the 20th century when the Blackstone Cotton Manufacturing Company attained a capitalization of $1,000,000 and the Laramac Mills of the American Woolen Company approximated this amount. Popcorn, potato chips and iron products are made here. Some residents commute to Rhode Island factories.

Roosevelt Park, on St. Paul St., is well planned and equipped as a recreational center for the community.

St. Paul's (Catholic) *Church* (1852) is near the park on Saint Paul St. The Rhode Island line cuts diagonally through the building. Half the congregation sits in Rhode Island and the other half in Massachusetts. The organ plays in Massachusetts and produces its tones in Rhode Island.

BLANDFORD (Hampden County, sett. 1735, incorp. 1741, alt. 1452, pop. 863, area 52.70 sq. mi., town meeting, routes, Mass. Turnpike, 23), settled by Hopkinton Scotch-Irish, was first called Glasgow. Glasgow, Scotland, folk offered the town a bell if the name were retained. Provincial governor Shirley, who arrived from England on the ship *Blandford,* denied the name petition and gave the town its present name.

About 1807, Amos M. Collins convinced the farmers that they should turn from grain and wool cultivation to butter and cheese production. He purchased the cows, sold them to the farmers and accepted cheese as payment. Blandford became one of the richest Berkshire towns. Orchards have superseded dairy farming.

NORTH BLANDFORD (alt. 1360). The wild and rugged country surrounding Long Pond was the setting for scenes in *The Littlest Rebel* with Shirley Temple.

BLUE HILLS RESERVATION (5700 acres in Milton, Canton, Braintree, Quincy, Randolph), located off Mass. 3, 28, 128, 138, is a major Boston recreation area maintained by the MDC.

There are several bridle paths and horses can be hired at nearby stables in Braintree, Canton, Milton, Quincy and Randolph. A number of foot and nature trails lead through the area. In winter there is ice skating at Houghton's Pond. Picnic sites with tables and fireplaces are found in numerous areas in the reservation.

Observation Tower: Weather station atop Blue Hill (alt. 640).

Ski Area: WILLIAM F. ROGERS SKI SLOPE, Mass. 138, has three floodlighted slopes for novice, intermediate and expert. Double chair lift, two J-bars, three rope tows, ski shop, snack bar, ski school. Slopes have artificial snow-making equipment.

Golf: PONKAPOAG GOLF COURSE, two 18-hole courses, clubhouse, snack bar, pro shop.

Trailside Museum (open May–Sept., Tues.–Sat. 10–5, Sun. 1–5, Oct.–April, Thurs.–Sat. 10–5, Sun. 1–5, very small fee), 1904 Canton Ave.–Mass. 138 (Exit 64 n. off 128), Milton, is operated by the Boston Zoological Society. Live animals and other displays show fauna and flora of the region. Lectures and nature trails. Conducted tours for groups of 15 or more.

Freshwater Fishing: Ponkapoag Pond, Canton (outboard motors, canoes and sailboats prohibited). Blue Hill River, Milton-Canton, runs parallel with Blue Hill River Road for 3.5 miles in Milton-Canton. Houghton's Pond (Hoosickwhisick Pond), Hillside St.; Hultman's Pond, Blue Hills Parkway and Canton St.; Pine Tree Brook; and Trout Pond, near Harland St. and Unquity Road; Fisherman's Beach (two connections from MBTA Mattapan Square Sta.). Bath house, picnic area, tot lot. Band concerts are announced in Boston area papers.

Freshwater swimming is available.

BOLTON (Worcester County, sett. 1682, incorp. 1738, alt. 387, pop. 1905, area 19.93 sq. mi., town meeting, routes, Mass. 85, 117) in its early years had a lime kiln, potash and pearl ash works, a comb factory and brickyards.

The removal of industries to larger centers left fruit, milk and poultry as the major products. Former South African missionary, George T. Becker, established a profitable business making handmade ostrich feather dusters.
Godings House (private), Main St., alleged to be a remodeled blockhouse, has vertical wallboards, 18-inch wide pine floorboards, wooden latches and bolts on the heavy doors.
Spindle Hill (alt. 400) has a footpath leading to the boulder-covered summit. There is a wide view of the countryside.
Country Manor (1740), west of the village on Main St., erected by Gen. Amory Holman, has white columns and balcony, stands on a hill and is surrounded by beautiful gardens.

BOSTON (Suffolk County, sett. 1630, incorp. 1822, alt. 10, pop. 641,071, area 43.18 sq. mi., routes I–95, I–495, US 1, Mass. 2, 3, 128) is America's most legend-encrusted city. Today's "New" Boston, in the eyes of many Americans — and even some Bostonians — is obscured by the legends.

Tradition holds Boston to be the "Hub of the Universe," its intellectual center, populated by superior persons, a closed Brahmin society. Boston visitors, harboring such preconceived notions, are likely to have them confirmed for all time by the sight of a gentleman crossing Boston Common carrying a green book bag or a tweed-clad little old lady emerging from the New England Historic Genealogical Society with the *Atlantic* under her arm.

Boston has intellectuals, culture and old families; it plays its role in national and world affairs. Not all Bostonians live serenely on the river side of Beacon St. or the sunny side of Commonwealth Ave., nor do they all read the *Atlantic* or spend their summers with relatives on the North Shore and eternity with their ancestors in Mount Auburn Cemetery, Cambridge.

Few Bostonians are now buried in Boston — the cemeteries are full up with their forefathers, many of whom fought in the Revolution. Mount Auburn Cemetery, a former Cambridge cow pasture, is the proper burying ground.

Boston is a composite of Silas Lapham's Boston — southerly Beacon Hill, Charles River Embankment, Beacon Street and Commonwealth Avenue — and the Boston symbolized by what was once Ward 8, the kingdom of Boss Martin Lomasney, densely populated, scornfully ignorant of the proprieties of the prunes-and-prisms school, but vigorously alive.

It is the paradoxical city which has inspired 50 Boston novels in the past 50 years. It has wide streets overarched by spreading elms, "quaint," crooked, narrow streets, magnificent parks, fine public buildings, handsome residences and a general air of well-scrubbed propriety and gracious leisure. It is also the Boston where acres of ugly wooden tenement houses line drab streets. Fortunately, many of these tenements will be replaced by modern low-cost housing units, or so says the Boston Redevelopment Authority.

It is the Boston of the music lovers, with Symphony Hall and the New

England Conservatory of Music; the Boston of the art lovers, with the Museum of Fine Arts, the Gardner Museum and the Public Library; the Boston of the well-to-do churches and numerous universities.

And Boston is a sports city. It is the home of baseball's Red Sox, basketball's Celtics, hockey's Bruins, and until 1971 football's Patriots.

The Red Sox, last American League pennant winners in 1967 and World Series winners in 1918, play home games at Jersey Street's Fenway Park (capacity 33,375). The Celtics, world champions in 1956–1957, for eight consecutive seasons from 1958–1966, and again in 1967–1968 and 1968–1969, play home games in Boston Garden in North Station (capacity 17,500). The Bruins, winners of the Stanley Cup in 1969–1970 for the first time since 1940–1941, also play in the Garden. The Patriots, American Football League Division champions in 1963, played in Fenway Park and Harvard Stadium and will now make their home in Foxborough and be known as the New England Patriots.

The Other Bostons

Legendary Boston is bounded by North Station, South Station, on the east by Atlantic Avenue's wharves and on the west by Copley Square. This area, which visitors usually think of as "Boston," contains Boston Common, the Public Garden, Beacon Hill, both State Houses, old burying grounds, the waterfront, the old market, the business district, the main shopping area and most of Boston's — and America's — historic shrines.

The "visitors' Boston" shelters less than one sixth of the city's residents. Outside its confines, Beacon Street — once the road to the city's poorhouse — and Commonwealth Avenue parallel the Charles River to the Brighton-Allston area (annexed 1874) in whose hive of private houses and apartments live many of Boston's civil servants, professional and clerical people and small tradespeople.

East Boston, an island across the harbor, has been part of the city since 1636. South Boston, "America's Dublin," has produced able public servants like former Speaker of the House John McCormack.

Charlestown (annexed 1874), north across the inlet where the Charles River flows into Boston Harbor, has the Boston Naval shipyard, Mystic Wharves and Bunker Hill Monument. Roxbury (annexed 1868), West Roxbury, Jamaica Plain (annexed 1874) and Dorchester to the south have several hundred thousand residents. Hyde Park is another well-populated suburb that is part of Boston.

Most Boston islands have no residents. Several contain abandoned military posts or military prisons. Deer Island has a jail. Many islands — those without "No Trespassing" signs — can be visited by small craft.

Immigration

There are more Bostonians of Irish and Italian descent than of any other nationality, though no figures were kept on early immigration. The Irish started coming here en masse during the Great Potato Famine of the 1840's and the Italians about 50 years later.

In the Metropolitan Boston area — Boston and surrounding cities and towns — the largest number of foreign-born residents came from Canada (83,000). Most of these are Protestants from Newfoundland and the Maritime Provinces. Italians are second with 59,000. The Irish in third place (39,000) are closely followed by Russians with 29,000. United Kingdom immigrants — England, Scotland, Wales and Protestant Northern Ireland — are fifth with 26,000. Most Russians, many of them Jews, came from the Ukraine. Most UK immigrants are Protestants. Most of the 12,500 Poles are Jews. Germans (9000), Greeks (8000) and Swedes (6500) are next. The city has Lithuanians (6400), Turks (3700) — mostly Armenians — Norwegians (2100) and Frenchmen (2100).

First Settlers

Boston's first settler, William Blackstone (1595–1675), a gentle scholarly hermit and formerly a Church of England preacher, built a hut on Beacon Hill. He planted an orchard on what is now Boston Common.

Blackstone's realm was bounded on the west by a mud flat (now filled-in Back Bay), on the north by a deep cove (later dammed to make a millpond), on the east by a small river which made an island off the North End and on the south by another deep cove. Blackstone read his books, farmed a little and traded with friendly Indians. He was fortunate enough to breathe air uncontaminated by any other white man.

His seven year solitude was shattered in 1630 by John Winthrop and 900 colonists who settled in present Charlestown. Their settlement would be difficult to defend in event of an Indian attack. Blackstone invited them to settle on his peninsula. They eagerly accepted.

More than 200 colonists failed to survive their first winter. In the spring a long overdue provision ship arrived. Famine was averted. Later that year the freshly tilled soil yielded a good crop. The colony survived and expanded.

Fisheries were established. Fur and lumber were exported. By 1634 more than 4000 colonists — all English — had arrived. Twenty villages were established around Boston. A Puritan commonwealth was in the making.

Sunday gave colonists a brief respite from the six hard workdays that preceded. Women, with spinning, weaving, family clothes to make, children to tend, meals to prepare, had little time for social intercourse. Pioneer life was hard and drab with few comforts. Wood was the sole fuel.

"Free Liberty"

Divines were preoccupied with dismal theological abstractions, but statute books reveal there were secular souls who displayed a wholesome proclivity for life. "Tobacco drinking" (smoking), tippling, cardplaying, dancing and bowling caused the town fathers much alarm. Sunday strolls or street kissing were subject to heavy fine. Christmas, reminiscent of "popery," was banned.

Punishment was based upon the theory that ridicule was more effective than imprisonment. Market squares had stocks, pillories and ducking stools. Public floggings were common, and offenders were often forced to display on their clothing the initial letter of the crime committed.

Boston, dedicated to Calvin, neither understood nor admired toleration. Quakers and other nonconformists were ruthlessly persecuted. Roger Williams (1603–83) was banished for having "broached and divulged diverse new and dangerous opinions against the authority of the magistrates." Mistress Anne Hutchinson followed Williams into banishment. Quaker Mary Dyer was hanged on Boston Common in 1660; Mary Jones, Mary Parsons and Ann Hibbins were hanged as witches. The town fathers were content to sacrifice freedom in their attempt to achieve unity. The Reverend Nathaniel Ward, speaking for all good Puritans, remarked, "All Familists, Anabaptists, and other Enthusiasts shall have free liberty to keepe away from us."

Trade

Boston, despite a narrow religious and moral outlook, was assured future greatness by her commerce. Scarcely a year after the Puritans had invaded the splendid isolation of Mr. Blackstone, Governor Winthrop launched the *Blessing of the Bay.* The *Rebecca* sailed to Narragansett to purchase Indian corn. Vessels returned to Boston with oranges, limes and the equally exotic potato. They put in at New Amsterdam to traffic with Dutch burghers. Twelve years after the founding of Boston ships laden with pipe staves and other products tied up at English docks. Shipbuilding, fishing, whaling, industry and exchange made the colony a bustling outpost of imperial Britain.

From 1630 to 1680, Great Britain, absorbed in troubles at home, with the exception of the 1651 Navigation Act, gave little attention to regulating her infant colonies. In 1691 a royal governor was sent, and in 1733 the Molasses Act was passed, but the Colonial merchants had virtually free trade until 1764 when British prime minister George Grenville began vigorous enforcement of mercantilistic measures.

The American Revolution resulted from a series of bewildering subtleties, but many dramatic episodes, reflecting the broad issues of the controversy, took place in Boston's crooked streets. The Boston Massacre (1770) on King Street (now State) occurred in the shadow of the Old State House. News of the British advance on Lexington and Concord was signaled to Paul Revere by a lamp from the belfry of the Old North Church. Faneuil Hall rang with the impassioned oratory of the champions of liberty. It was the Boston Tea Party which confronted the British cabinet with the choice of capitulation or force, replied to by the Port Act, which marked the beginning of a policy of coercion and led swiftly to open warfare. The Battle of Bunker Hill — actually fought on nearby Breed's Hill — in Charlestown was an early major battle. The British considered Boston a major objective, and their failure to retain control dealt a serious blow to Tory confidence (for details see HISTORICAL NOTES).

Commerce suffered during postwar years, but the discovery of profitable oriental trade was quickly exploited by Yankee traders. The China trade and the exploitation of the Oregon coast, rich in sea otters, restored Boston to its former eminence. In 1780, 455 ships from every quarter of the globe docked in Boston Harbor, while 1200 vessels engaged in coastwise traffic out of Boston. During a single year (1791) 70 Yankee merchantmen cleared Boston for Europe, the Indies and Canton.

Boston's maritime prosperity was stimulated by the Napoleonic Wars. In 1807 Boston shipping totaled 310,309 tons, or more than one third of U.S. tonnage. Jefferson's Embargo and the War of 1812 crippled maritime development. Although Boston recovered, and although the era of the clipper made Massachusetts famous throughout the world (the *Sovereign of the Seas,* built by Donald McKay in East Boston (1852), was the envy of the British Admiralty), the War of 1812 really marked the beginning of the end of Boston's maritime supremacy.

In 1822, Boston became a city; railroads were being built from 1830 on and played an important part in urban development; the first horsecar line, connecting Cambridge and Boston, was built in 1853. Between 1824 and 1858, the Boston peninsula was enlarged from 783 acres to 1801 acres by cutting down the hills and filling in the Back Bay and the great coves with the excavated gravel as a basis for reclamation. The neck, which William Blackstone could not always cross on foot because of the tidewater, was raised and broadened, so that what was once the narrowest part of Boston proper is now the widest.

Capital of Culture

Between the War of Independence and the Civil War, Bostonians, stimulated by European currents of thought and the philosophy of the frontier, revolted against Calvinist theology, a revolt typical of the democratic spirit of the 19th century. Unitarianism threatened to dissolve Puritan Congregationalism. The new doctrines were embraced by Harvard and became the fashion in Boston, but hardly had the rebellion against Congregationalism subsided when new dissension broke out within Unitarian ranks. Ralph Waldo Emerson shocked his parishioners of the Second Church (1832) by tendering his resignation and retiring to Concord to ponder the mysteries of Transcendentalism.

John Lowell, Jr., bequeathed a fortune to establish Lowell Institute (1839) in order to provide the people of Boston with free lectures by "foremost scholars and thinkers of the English-speaking world." This democratization of education was supplemented by the creation of the

Boston Public Library (1852). Horace Mann (1796–1889) devoted his reforming spirit to the development of formal education. Dr. Samuel Gridley Howe (1801–76) dedicated his efforts to the emancipation of the deaf and blind. With the financial assistance of Thomas H. Perkins (1764–1854), the Perkins Institute and Massachusetts School for the Blind (first located in South Boston, later removed to Watertown) was founded, a unique institution for its day (1832). The first public surgical operation which made use of ether as an anesthetic was performed (1846) at the Massachusetts General Hospital.

Nowhere was the reforming spirit more active than in the antislavery movement. William Lloyd Garrison (1805–79) had no respect for the interests of cotton, whether expounded by planters or manufacturers. He invaded Boston and founded the *Liberator* (1831). The development of cotton manufacture in Lowell and later Lawrence affected State Street and Beacon Hill. "Respectable" elements thought it best to refrain from harsh criticism after southern statesmen began to ask pertinent questions concerning workers in Lowell and Lawrence mills. Garrison attacked the Constitution because it recognized slavery as legal. Boston patriots could hardly suffer so sacred a document to be disparaged and Garrison was manhandled by a mob in 1835. Garrison's fervor attracted Wendell Phillips (1811–84), a brilliant orator whose lineage was almost as old as Boston. He became a zealous advocate of the cause. Other converts were enlisted — Channing, Parker, Lowell, Longfellow, Dana — and under the championship of such ultrarespectable persons, the antislavery crusade gained ground rapidly.

Boston played a less important role in the Civil War than in events preceding it. Unable to meet the prescribed quota of soldiers by voluntary enlistment, the city fathers first employed the draft in 1863, precipitating the Boston Draft Riots. The poor, irritated when their neighbors purchased immunity from compulsory service for $300, objected so strenuously that the militia had to quell disorders. Among the regiments which did march south to uphold the honor of Boston, one of the most famous was commanded by Colonel Robert Gould Shaw (1837–63), an abolitionist "of gentle birth and breeding." Composed of Negroes, this regiment led the attack on Fort Wagner where Colonel Shaw and nearly half of his followers fell.

After the war, the proud, graceful clippers that sailed from Boston were replaced by smoking, belching, stinking steamers, largely of British ownership.

Money once invested in shipping now flowed into mills. Shoe and textile industries which boomed with the war now advanced under the stimulus of capital released from shipping. Factories came to Boston. The intellectual "Hub of the Universe" became the industrial hub of New England.

This new commerce maintained Boston as a leading Atlantic coastal port for many years. Raw materials like cotton, wool and leather were brought here to factories. Ships sailing out of Boston in 1901 carried goods valued at nearly $150,000,000 while imports amounted to $80,000,000.

Early 20th-century Boston had two claims to fame: John L. Sullivan, the first great heavyweight fighter, and the first American subway. The subway ran from Arlington at Boylston Street to the North Station. The horsecar was discarded in 1910. Bicycles, drays and carriages still dashed about at the reckless rate of eight m.p.h. Electric surface-car lines were built throughout the city. An elevated railroad, begun in 1909, pushed into Forest Hills suburb. Downtown Boston underwent a face-lifting with steel, marble and cut stone; National Shawmut Bank, William Filene's Sons and Jordan Marsh buildings were all erected after 1907.

Industry's growth was paralleled by that of labor. One of the labor movement's most historic strikes was the 1919 Boston Police walkout (see HISTORICAL NOTES), which made Calvin Coolidge vice president.

The tragic stock market vagaries, censorship with all its trail of Rabelaisian mirth and the police strike were temporarily forgotten in the great Tercentenary Celebration which ushered in the third decade. Even the approaching depression cast no shadow on gala preparations.

The Boston Tercentenary Committee, in conjunction with statewide subcommittees, mapped out a gigantic program. The ceremonies formally opened on Boston Common, with the chief address delivered by H. A. L. Fisher, Warden of New College, Oxford. "Little did the founders reckon," said Professor Fisher, "that a time would come when . . . in the fullness of years, their New England would be followed by a New Ireland, a New Italy, a New Germany, a New Poland, and a New Greece, all destined to be merged into a great and harmonious Commonwealth."

Boston in the '20's was the storm center of the crisis revolving around the trial of two Italian anarchists, Sacco and Vanzetti (see HISTORICAL NOTES).

Spectacular events are no exception in the city's history. The biggest robbery in America was one — the Brink's, in which $1,218,211.20 of the $2,775,395.12 was cash. The hoodlums were caught and convicted, but only about $50,000 of the loot has been recovered.

Boston, as the seat of state government and with a cross section of major state industries, has been conscious of labor efforts. There was a pitched battle in 1924 over the ratification of the Child Labor Amendment. During the Depression there were numerous strikes both for the right to organize and for better wages and modicum of job security.

During the 1920's and to a lesser extent in the '30's Boston became notorious for its so-called book banning. The principal agitator was the New England Watch and Ward Society, a private group which used agent provocateur methods against booksellers. Few books were legally banned, but timid booksellers voluntarily withdrew "questionable" titles like Hemingway's *The Sun Also Rises.* One bookseller withdrew more than 50 titles in one year. Many of these books are now American classics. Boston authorities refused to permit Eugene O'Neill's *Strange Interlude* to be produced in Boston. The producers moved the play to Quincy where it had a long run before packed houses, most of the audiences coming from Boston.

New Boston

After WWII, community-minded financial leaders like Ralph Lowell and Charles A. Coolidge, Mayor John Hynes and other forward-looking politicians and many civic-minded citizens became increasingly concerned about Boston's blight of decay that was extending destructive tentacles through the city.

Two projects were attempted during the 1950's. Neither was successful. The highly controversial West End project demolished an entire compact community. Only the long obsolete Charles Street Jail, Massachusetts General Hospital's vast complex, St. Joseph's Church, the Harrison Gray Otis House and the Old West Church along with a few minor structures escaped bulldozer blades and the wrecker's ball. People who had been neighbors since they came from the Old Countries more than a half century past were compelled to leave their homes and seek more expensive apartments elsewhere. Dozens of small shops and businesses were closed. There was no room, and sadder still, no need for them outside the West End. The problem has never been satisfactorily solved.

West End residents, forced to evacuate their modest rental tenements and apartments, became even more bitter when three high-rise, high-rental apartments replaced their former homes. Most of the expense of the clearing and construction was paid for by the federal government.

Boston by 1960 was in desperate straits. Population in ten years dropped from 801,444 to less than 600,000. Few buildings had been built in Boston since the 1920's. No hotel had been built for the past 30 years. During the Depression several hundred million dollars worth of property had been sold for a small fraction of its value, much of it for taxes. In depression years landlords did little, and indeed could do little, to maintain their properties. Then came the war. Rents were frozen, materials were scarce and apartments were in demand. After the war returning GI's married and so apartments were still in demand. However, by 1950, many GI's had completed their postwar education, and immediately moved to the much pleasanter suburbs.

Better schools than Boston had to offer were a major goal of many suburb-bound Bostonians. Nearly 50 percent of Boston students attended schools more than 50 years old. Some schools had been built shortly after the Civil War. These ancient buildings typified the troubles of the school system.

Boston for many years was the shopping center for the suburbs, but the Hub's crowded streets, poor parking facilities, jammed approach highways, together with mass population exodus, led to a sharp decline in retail trade.

High taxes discouraged property owners from undertaking necessary improvements. The city's 1969 tax rate — $144.40 — was one of the highest of major American cities. In the same year New Yorkers paid $55.40; Chicagoans, $65.82; Seattleites, $78.79; and Philadelphians a mere $44.75.

Vast sections of industry, partly because of the high tax rate, were moving out of Boston into the suburbs and countryside. No new industries replaced the outgoing textile and leather plants. Some textile plants moved south. Boston's Port business dropped sharply because of adverse freight rates and antiquated inadequate loading and unloading facilities.

State and federal government agencies, never too efficient, were sprawled throughout the city because of severe space shortages. Much of the city was becoming a vast slum.

A badly needed elevated express highway through downtown Boston not only was expensive in terms of construction but removed millions of dollars of property from the tax rolls. Property surrounding the highway decreased in value.

Mayor John Collins hired successful New Haven, Connecticut, redevelopment administrator, young Edward J. Logue. Collins and Logue wanted no more West End demolition projects. Instead they proposed a series of sectional projects where the emphasis would be on area rehabilitation. This all-Boston program was to cost an estimated $90,000,000 with $60,000,000 of the total from federal funds. A citywide area-by-area survey was made.

Residential rehabilitation was but one part of the proposed Boston Redevelopment Authority program. Major features include:

(1) The 61-acre Scollay Square honky-tonk area was demolished. It was replaced with a Government Center with several state service and office buildings, a 26-story Federal Building, a new Boston City Hall and a large private building for stores and offices.

(2) The Prudential Insurance Company erected a 52-story office building — the highest in the U.S. outside of Manhattan — together with a city auditorium, Boston's first new hotel in 30 years, several apartment houses and commercial buildings. The $150,000,000 complex was built on and over the Boston and Albany Railroad's 31-acre Back Bay yards. (These buildings were completed in 1965.)

(3) A $200,000,000 Central Business District — surrounding the Boston Common — includes stores, offices and apartment houses.

(4) A $100,000,000 Waterfront Renewal Plan is sponsored by the Greater Boston Chamber of Commerce. The chamber financed a $150,000 study of the downtown waterfront and Faneuil Hall area. The survey disclosed that more than 90 percent of the Atlantic Avenue area property was in bad shape. Atlantic Avenue properties had declined 29 percent in tax values between 1950 and 1960.

The city's tax rate will always be higher than in many cities of comparable population because about 40 percent of the property in Boston proper reportedly belongs to churches, schools and other tax exempt institutions.

Beacon Hill Tour

This famed area is today a mixture of Brahmin residences, apartments and artists' studios. Charles St. resembles the shopping section of New York's Greenwich Village.

1. *Robert Gould Shaw Memorial,* facing the State House from the edge of the Common, is a notable group in high relief by Augustus Saint-Gaudens (1848–1907). Col. Shaw, his horse and the Negro troopers are all sculptured with remarkable sensitivity to the medium and the subject. Charles F. McKim (1847–1909) designed the frame, a wide pink granite exedra with crouching eagles, Greek urns and low benches, shadowed by two enormous English elms.

Walk west on Beacon St.

2. *Women's City Club* (open by permission) (1818), 40 Beacon St., is believed to be a Bulfinch work. Beautifully preserved, it exemplifies gracious post-Colonial architecture. Its beautiful spiral stairway is as fine as any in New England.

3. *Wadsworth House* (third Harrison Gray Otis House, private) (1807), 45 Beacon St., reveals the influence of Bulfinch's sojourn in France by his use of an oval drawing room on the garden side and by his placing the entrance at ground level and the important rooms on the story above. The house is a fine example of an aristocratic city mansion of the Federal Period.

Turn right on Charles St.

4. *Charles Street Church* (cor. of Charles and Mt. Vernon Sts.) (1807). The red-brick Federal structure with a well-designed facade and low cupola was designed by Asher Benjamin, who, as author of *The Country Builder's Assistant* and other works on architecture, propagated the Bulfinch and McIntire mode.

Turn left on Mt. Vernon St. to corner of Brimmer.

5. *Samuel Eliot Morison House* (private), 44 Brimmer St. (corner of Mt. Vernon and Brimmer Sts.), is the residence of a leading U.S. historian. (See WRITERS.)

6. *Church of the Advent* (High Episcopal), across the street from Morison's house, is a steepled red-brick structure.

Turn right (north) on Brimmer St.

7. *Admiral Richard E. Byrd's Home* (private), 7–9 Brimmer St. Byrd was the first man to fly over both North and South Poles.

Right on Pinckney St., right along Charles to Chestnut. Left on Chestnut.

8. *Francis Parkman's House* (private) (1824), 50 Chestnut St., was the home of the noted historian.

9. *Edwin Booth Home* (private), 29A Chestnut St., has a few of the original purple windowpanes once favored in this district, which sun and time transformed to a lilac hue, to the despair of imitators. This house has the small, wrought-iron second-story balconies introduced by Bulfinch and

Benjamin. The entire house has a princely, brooding air suggestive of *Hamlet,* Booth's most famous role.

10. *Julia Ward Howe Home* (later *John Singer Sargent's*) (private), 13 Chestnut St., is attributed to Bulfinch. For many years this house was the meeting place of the Radical Club that succeeded the noted Transcendental Club.

Left from Chestnut St. on Walnut St.

11. *Ellery Sedgwick House* (private) (1805), 14 Walnut St., home of the late *Atlantic Monthly* editor and the most individual house on the Hill, has three stories, gray-painted brick ends and black blinds. A large tree-shaded garden, which, owing to the slope of the hill, is elevated high above the street and buttressed by a base wall.

Right from Walnut St. on Mt. Vernon St.

12. *Thomas Bailey Aldrich's House* (private), 59 Mt. Vernon St., is distinguished by its white marble portico.

13. *Home of Charles Francis Adams, Sr.* (private), 57 Mt. Vernon St., is of a conservative elegance to be expected of the Civil War Minister to England, son of John Quincy Adams and father of the author of *The Education of Henry Adams.* Its four substantial stories face a trim lawn.

Retrace Mt. Vernon St.

14. *Sears House* (Second Harrison Gray Otis House, private) (1800), 85 Mt. Vernon St., is a good example of Bulfinch's domestic design. The square house with roof balustrade is excellently proportioned and has the typical Bulfinch arched recesses surrounding the lower windows. Although somewhat altered, the architecture of this dignified Federal mansion remains impressive.

Right from Mt. Vernon St. into Louisburg Square.

15. *Louisburg Square,* looking much like some square in London's Mayfair, is the epitome of Beacon Hill style. Noted residents have included William Dean Howells, Louisa May Alcott and her father, Amos Bronson Alcott, Jenny Lind and Minnie Maddern Fiske. The houses, inhabited by "Proper Bostonian" families, are large three- or four-story brick dwellings, mostly with bowfronts and plain doorways. The central green, enclosed by an iron fence with no gate, belongs to the proprietors of the Square. The small statue of Aristides the Just, at the south end, and that of Columbus at the north have been adopted affectionately by the residents through many years of custom, but when their donor, Joseph Iasigi, a wealthy Greek living at No. 3 also included a fountain, it was hastily removed.

At Christmas each year the Square echoes with Christmas carols, sung by trained voices usually selected from musical groups with sufficient prestige to be asked to contribute carolers.

Right from Louisburg Square on Pinckney St.

Pinckney St. was named for South Carolina's Charles Cotesworth Pinckney (1746–1825), who reportedly told Talleyrand: "Millions for defense but not one cent for tribute."

Left from Pinckney St. on Joy St.; right from Joy St. on Cambridge St.

16. *Harrison Gray Otis House* (open 10–5, 25¢ fee), 141 Cambridge St., built in 1795, has been since 1916 the headquarters of the Society for the Preservation of New England Antiquities. The interior has not been altered. The Society restored the exterior to its former beauty.
17. *Old West Church* (West End Church), 131 Cambridge St., was built in 1806 from designs by architect-writer Asher Benjamin. Characteristic of his work, it is of well-studied proportions, but more solid and masculine than the work of his contemporaries, Bulfinch and McIntire. Its facade, with stepped gable and lofty tower, is capped by a square gilt-domed cupola. The church for some years was the West End branch of the Boston Public Library.

Waterfront Tour

Visitors should take the waterfront tour now because this historic area is being torn down and rebuilt.

The tour covers the old waterfront, once the port for all ships, now devoted to coastwise shipping and fishing boats. Vessels from European ports now dock in East or South Boston.

W1 *Constitution Wharf,* 409 Commercial St. at the foot of Hanover St., is occupied chiefly by a high brick warehouse which cuts off the harbor view. A bas-relief tablet on the Commercial St. wall commemorates the launching (1797) of the famous U.S. Frigate *Constitution* (*Old Ironsides*), the Queen of the Navy, which made history in the War with Tripoli and the War of 1812.

Just beyond *Lewis' Wharf,* 32 Atlantic Ave., is the first delightful glimpse of the actual waterfront, where freighters use the same slips as the humble powerboats of small fishermen. Along the quays are marine hardware shops and lunchrooms. On the hottest summer day, the air has a cool salty tang, becoming definitely fishy as one passes the brief row of fish markets.

W2 *Long Wharf* (1710), 202 Atlantic Ave., was once a great deal longer, beginning up by the present U.S. Custom House which now soars in the background. The British embarked for home here, March 17, 1776. Today hundreds of tourists embark daily for Provincetown. In March, 1968, a fire destroyed many of the buildings on the wharf. Redevelopment plans will maintain this historic extension of State St. and a historic vessel will be moored here.

W3 The *United States Custom House* (open daily 9–5) (1847), designed by Ammi B. Young (1798–1874), was among the last monuments of the Greek Revival. The dome with which it was originally crowned is concealed within the tall shaft of floors which in 1915 transformed the building into a 500-foot skyscraper. The tower resembles that of the Metropolitan Building in New York, although on a much smaller scale. A balcony near the top offers a splendid panorama of Boston.

W4 The *New England Aquarium* is located on Central Wharf. This site was acquired from the Boston Redevelopment Authority in 1965 and was opened to the public in June, 1969. In the giant ocean tank are the aquarium's largest saltwater animals, including turtles, sharks, stingrays, moray eels, stripers and species of angelfish, parrotfish aand porcupine fish. The fresh water tray has the inhabitants of semitropical swamps, including toads, frogs, various lizards and turtles, wading birds, carp, gar, Mississippi catfish and sturgeons. A children's aquarium contains plants and animals found in tide pools. Youngsters may pick up living starfish, crabs and sea urchins.

W5 *India Wharf,* once the site of ancient lofts occupied by riggers and sailmakers, is slated to become private apartments.

W6 *Rowe's Wharf,* 344 Atlantic Ave., serves a number of excursion boats. It was the scene of the deposition of Governor Andros (1689).

W7 *Boston Tea Party* (Dec. 16, 1773) took place at the northeast corner of Atlantic Ave. and Pearl St., then *Griffin's Wharf,* when a group of patriots disguised as Indians boarded British ships loaded with tea and threw the cargo overboard. A tablet on the Atlantic Ave. wall of the commercial building now occupying the site gives the Boston version of the party.

Government Center

G.C. 1. *City Hall* (Visitors' Gallery open 24 hours a day every day), the most striking of American city halls, was built for $25,000,000 to replace the city hall of 1865. The design was one of 256 submitted by American architects. A notable feature is the interior open courtyard. Architects were Gerhard Kallman, Edward Knowles and Noel McKinnell, N.Y.

G.C. 2. *John F. Kennedy Federal Building* has two connected 26-story towers with an adjacent 400′-long annex. The 25 acres of office space house 12 federal agencies formerly scattered throughout downtown Boston. The $29,000,000 building was designed by Architects Collaborative, Cambridge. Walter Gropius was one of the partners in charge.

G.C. 3. The 22-story *State Office Building* now houses 33 state agencies, many of which formerly were scattered throughout Metropolitan Boston. The $14,000,000 building and its 300-car underground garage were designed by Emery Roth and Sons, N.Y.

G.C. 4. *Commonwealth Health, Welfare and Education Service Center,* foot of Bowdoin St. between Staniford, Merrimac and New Chardon Sts., occupies an 8-acre tract. The $29,000,000 complex will include the 5-story *Mental Health Center Building* (architects, Desmond, Shepley, Bulfinch, Richardson and Abbott of Boston) and the 23-story building housing the state department of *Health, Education and Welfare.*

Freedom Trail Tour

F1 *Boston Common,* part of a tract set aside by Gov. Winthrop as a cow pasture and training field, retains as paved walks the casual paths worn by grazing cattle. Here stocks and pillory once stood, as well as a pen where those who desecrated the Sabbath were imprisoned. Several Quakers are thought to have been hanged and buried on the Common. Both British and Massachusetts regiments were mustered on it, and it is still used on occasion as a drill ground.

Free speech is a Common tradition. Group arguments on social and economic problems are in daily progress around the Grecian *Parkman Bandstand,* and orators address the public along the *Charles Street Mall.* The *Frog Pond* is patronized during hot weather by children.

During WWII several hundred thousand U.S. and Allied servicemen were entertained in the U.S.O. Clubhouse, since taken down.

F2 The *State House* (open weekdays 9–5) (1795), with its golden dome, crowns the hill. The "Bulfinch Front" is a monument to Charles Bulfinch's genius and is an expression of classicism in American design. This original front is sandwiched between huge, inappropriate wings. The "Bulfinch Front" cannot be seen merely as a unit of the structure; its quality sets it apart as a thing to be known and revered independent of its setting. Bulfinch was the first professional architect of the republic. The State House was his greatest work. He spread across its front a colossal portico; he completed it with a high and dominating dome.

Doric Hall contains portraits of some Massachusetts governors. *Hall of Flags* displays state regimental flags of the Civil, Spanish-American and World Wars. In the *House of Representatives* (third floor rear, left) hangs the Sacred Cod, the state emblem symbolizing a historic basic industry.

F3 *Park Street (Congregational) Church* (1809) (Open Mon.–Fri. 9–5 (July and August 9–4), Sat. 9–Noon; Sun. 9 A.M.–1 P-M., 4:30 P.M.–9 P.M. Services at 10:30 A.M. and 7:30 P.M.), corner of Tremont and Park Sts. This building was designed by Peter Banner. It bears little evidence of the Classic Revival felt in contemporaneous work but closely maintains the character of earlier buildings. Unusual are the semicircular porches between the tower base and the body of the main building. The church still houses a Trinitarian congregation formed to protest spreading Unitarianism. It stands on the site of the Old Granary Building where the U.S.S. *Constitution's* sails were made.

F4 The *Old Granary Burial Ground* (open), hemmed in by business blocks and Tremont St., contains the graves of three signers of the Declaration of Independence, Samuel Adams, John Hancock and Robert Treat Paine. Paul Revere, Peter Faneuil, Benjamin Franklin, Boston Massacre victims, nine early governors of the state and Mother Goose (a real person actually named Mary Goose) rest here.

F5 *King's Chapel* (Unitarian) (open Mon.–Fri. 9–4, Sat. 9–11:45 A.M. and 12:45–4, Sun. 9–4), corner of Tremont and School Sts. Services at 11 A.M. One of America's most historic churches, it was the first Episcopal Church in New England and the first Unitarian Church in America. The church was organized in 1686. The present building was begun in

1749 and completed about 1754. It was designed by Peter Harrison. The Newport gentleman-architect possessed too much native genius for his design to be a servile copy of British masters. The bold cold masonry exterior is topped by a low, squat base intended to support a tower which was never built. The interior, replete with original touches characteristic of its designer, is perhaps the finest Colonial church interior extant. The present building was erected (1754) around a wooden building which was then dismantled.

British royalty favored King's Chapel. Its communion plate, donated by George III, is still in use. Queen Anne contributed the plush red cushions and vestments.

King's Chapel Burying Ground (next to chapel) for thirty years (1630–60) was Boston's only burying ground. William Dawes, Jr., who rode with Paul Revere, and Governor John Winthrop rest here among other Colonial notables.

F6 *Site of First Public School in America* (tablet on School St. side of the Parker House) commemorates Boston Public Latin School (1635), the first public school in America. Samuel Adams, Cotton Mather, Ben Franklin, Ralph Waldo Emerson and John Hancock attended school here.

F7 *Benjamin Franklin Statue, School St.* (in front of Old City Hall), honors Boston's great native son.

F8 *Old Corner Bookstore,* corner of Washington and School Sts. This structure "built sometime after 1712" (*c.* 1718) by Dr. Thomas Crease is on the site of the house built in 1634 by William Hutchinson (1612–42), husband of "heretic" Anne Hutchinson (1591–1643). She used the house for religious meetings. The house burned in the "greatest of all Boston fires" (1711). Rebuilt, it was used as an apothecary's shop and was remodeled in 1829 by Timothy Carter, who opened the Carter & Hendee Bookstore. Eventually it was taken over by two men who were to make it famous: William D. Ticknor (1810–64) and James T. Fields (1817–81). Fields, later *Atlantic* editor, had one of the most remarkable lists of authors of any publisher, anywhere, anytime: Longfellow, Whittier, Thackeray, Hawthorne, Dickens, Louis Agassiz, John Godfrey Saxe, Emerson, the Lowells, Prescott, Parkman. It was "a busy clubhouse for literary giants."

The Old Corner Bookstore fell upon evil times after the last bookseller left in 1903. The bookstore was to be demolished, but when John Codman, chairman of the Beacon Hill Architectural Commission, came up with the proposal that funds be raised by subscription, if they could not be raised any other way, the building was purchased, restored and used by tenants whose business was in keeping with the traditions. The *Boston Globe* in-town classified advertising and subscription offices are now located there. Visitors are welcome during business hours.

F9 The *Old South Meeting House* (open Oct. 1–June 1, Mon.–Sat. 9–4, June 1–Oct. 1, Mon.–Fri. 9–5, Sat. 9–4, open holidays except Thanksgiving, Christmas and New Year's; closed Sundays, admission 25¢, children under

12 with adult free, educational groups with leaders free) (1729), corner of Milk and Washington Sts.

The Old South Church served Colonial Boston as both a church and meeting house. In the original structure (1669) Ben Franklin was christened and Judge Samuel Sewall did penance for his condemnation of witches.

This building shared with Faneuil Hall the most fervid momentous oratory of Revolutionary days. Old South meetings were always danger signals to Burke and Pitt. The church, built by Joshua Blanchard, has a simple mass with a severely plain exterior of brick laid in Flemish bond. The 180-foot wooden steeple is of conventional design, perhaps influenced by its predecessor, the Old North Church.

The interior with its gate pews was restored after the British had used it for a riding school during the Siege of Boston. In 1876, the pews were again removed when the building was used as a post office after the great fire of 1872. The parts of the original building are the walls and their framework, including the windows and doors, and the double tier of white galleries. The high, broad white pulpit only dates back to 1857 but from under the sounding board above it resounded the voices of James Otis, Samuel Adams, Josiah Quincy, Dr. Joseph Warren and John Hancock. Here began the Boston Tea Party. Here General Warren, prevented by the British from entering the pulpit by the stairs, climbed into it through a rear window. The beautiful, gilded *Gallery Clock,* surmounted by a spread eagle bearing in his beak a double string of gilded balls, is a reproduction of the original designed by Boston clockmaker Simon Willard (1753–1848). Patriotic women purchased and saved this landmark from destruction in 1876, when it was proposed to sell the building because of the great increase in value of the land. The parish, formed in 1669 (Congregational), worships at the "New Old South" in Copley Square.

F10 *Benjamin Franklin's Birthplace Site,* Milk St., is marked by a plaque.

F11 *The Old State House* (open Mon.–Sat. 9–4, April 19 (Patriot's Day), July 4 and Labor Day) (1713), corner of Washington and State Sts.

It was the state house of the new commonwealth until the present Bulfinch-designed State House was ready. Boston Massacre occurred nearby. Bostonians heard the first Boston reading of the Declaration of Independence from its balcony. Here President George Washington reviewed a 1789 parade in his honor.

Built on the site of its predecessor, the building has been restored to its original robust appearance.

In 1881, it was proposed to demolish the Old State House, because the land was valued at $1,500,000. Chicago offered to transfer the building to Lincoln Park on Lake Michigan and pay all the expense of removal, reassembly and maintenance. The offer stung Boston so sharply that the city fathers agreed to stand the loss on the land in perpetuity and never again to threaten the building with removal or destruction. The building is the headquarters of the Bostonian Society and houses intimate historical relics and a fine marine museum.

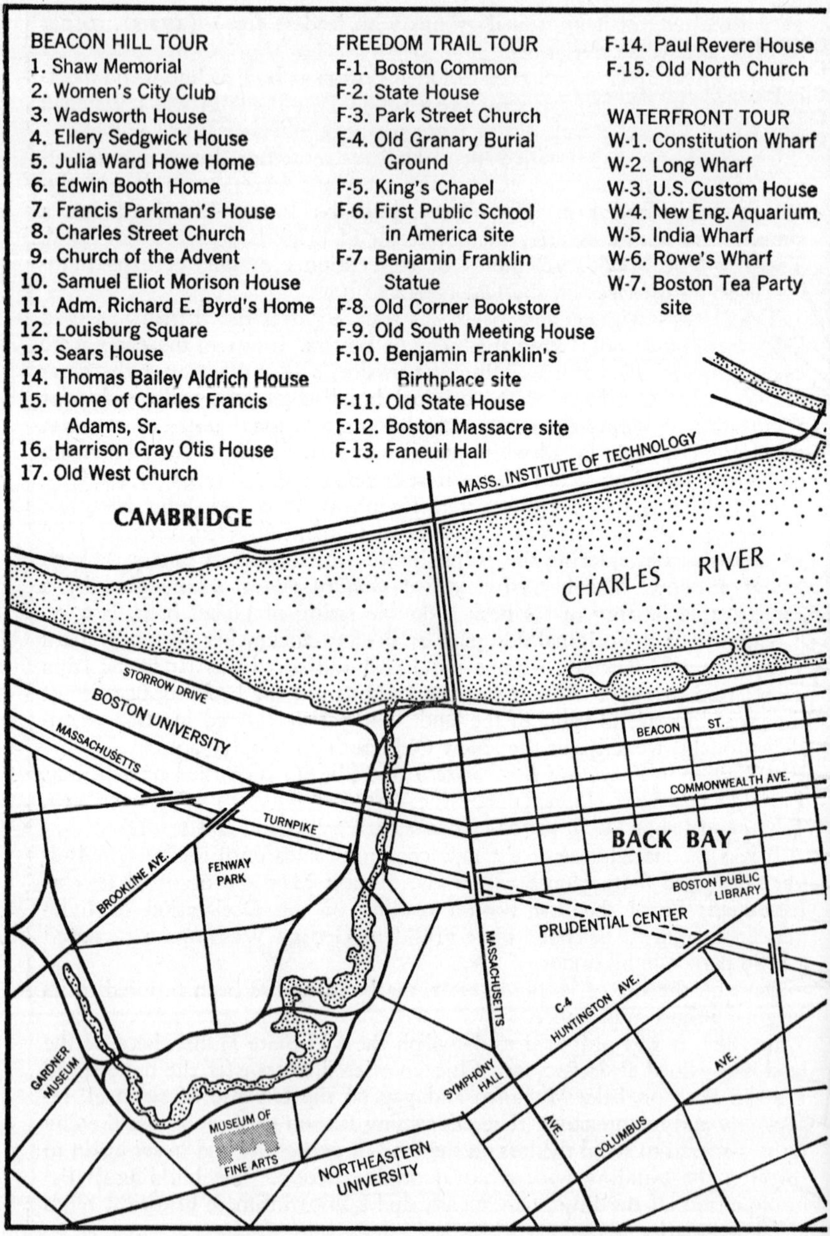

BEACON HILL TOUR
1. Shaw Memorial
2. Women's City Club
3. Wadsworth House
4. Ellery Sedgwick House
5. Julia Ward Howe Home
6. Edwin Booth Home
7. Francis Parkman's House
8. Charles Street Church
9. Church of the Advent
10. Samuel Eliot Morison House
11. Adm. Richard E. Byrd's Home
12. Louisburg Square
13. Sears House
14. Thomas Bailey Aldrich House
15. Home of Charles Francis Adams, Sr.
16. Harrison Gray Otis House
17. Old West Church
FREEDOM TRAIL TOUR
F-1. Boston Common
F-2. State House
F-3. Park Street Church
F-4. Old Granary Burial Ground
F-5. King's Chapel
F-6. First Public School in America site
F-7. Benjamin Franklin Statue
F-8. Old Corner Bookstore
F-9. Old South Meeting House
F-10. Benjamin Franklin's Birthplace site
F-11. Old State House
F-12. Boston Massacre site
F-13. Faneuil Hall
F-14. Paul Revere House
F-15. Old North Church
WATERFRONT TOUR
W-1. Constitution Wharf
W-2. Long Wharf
W-3. U.S. Custom House
W-4. New Eng. Aquarium
W-5. India Wharf
W-6. Rowe's Wharf
W-7. Boston Tea Party site
CAMBRIDGE
MASS. INSTITUTE OF TECHNOLOGY
CHARLES RIVER
STORROW DRIVE
BOSTON UNIVERSITY
MASSACHUSETTS
TURNPIKE
BEACON ST.
COMMONWEALTH AVE.
BACK BAY
BROOKLINE AVE.
FENWAY PARK
BOSTON PUBLIC LIBRARY
PRUDENTIAL CENTER
MASSACHUSETTS
C-4
HUNTINGTON AVE.
AVE.
SYMPHONY HALL
AVE.
COLUMBUS
GARDNER MUSEUM
MUSEUM OF FINE ARTS
NORTHEASTERN UNIVERSITY

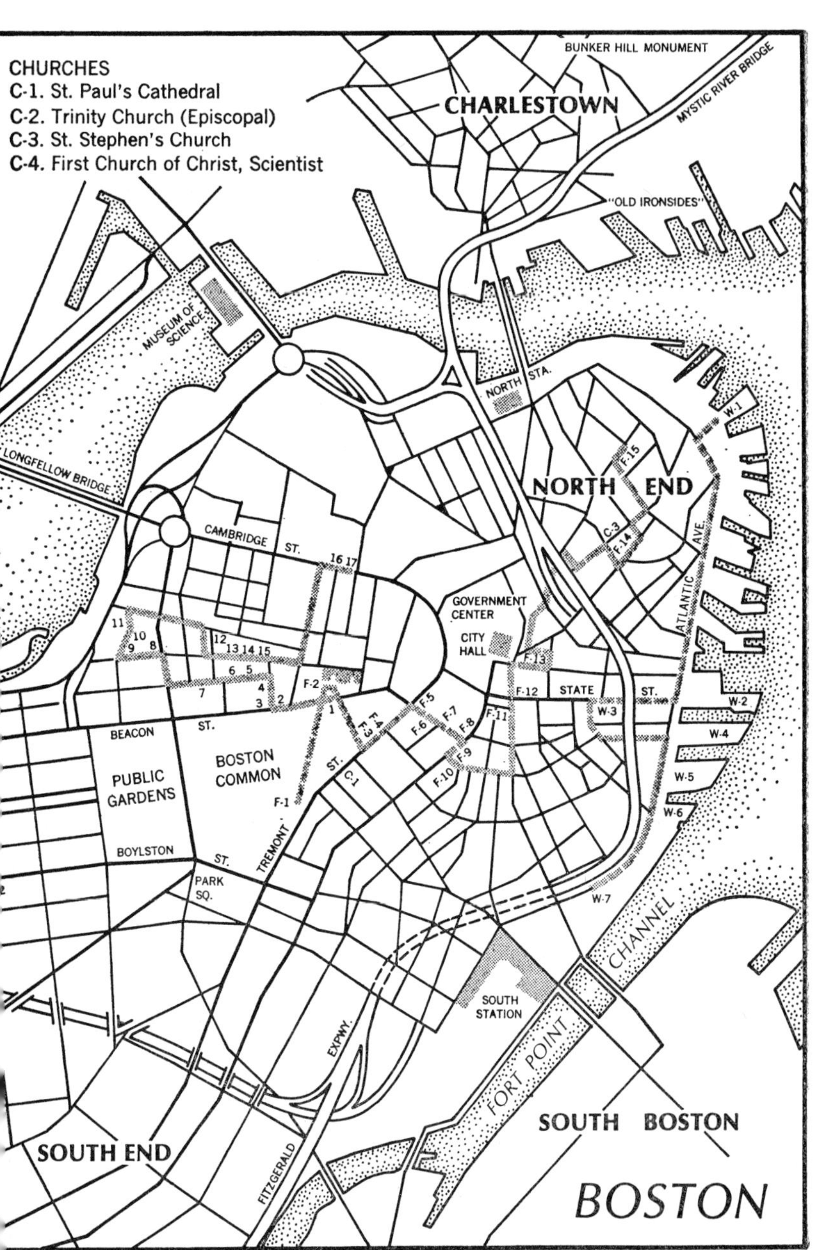
CHURCHES
C-1. St. Paul's Cathedral
C-2. Trinity Church (Episcopal)
C-3. St. Stephen's Church
C-4. First Church of Christ, Scientist
BUNKER HILL MONUMENT
CHARLESTOWN
MYSTIC RIVER BRIDGE
"OLD IRONSIDES"
MUSEUM OF SCIENCE
NORTH STA.
LONGFELLOW BRIDGE
NORTH END
CAMBRIDGE ST.
GOVERNMENT CENTER
CITY HALL
STATE ST.
ATLANTIC AVE.
BEACON ST.
BOSTON COMMON
PUBLIC GARDENS
TREMONT ST.
BOYLSTON ST.
PARK SQ.
SOUTH STATION
CHANNEL
FORT POINT
EXPWY.
FITZGERALD
SOUTH END
SOUTH BOSTON
BOSTON

F12 The *Boston Massacre Site,* 30 State St., is marked by a brass arrow pointing into the street where a cobblestone indicates the reported spot where the first of Samuel Adams' men fell mortally wounded (see HISTORICAL NOTES).

F13 *Faneuil* (Fan'l) *Hall* (Dock Square) (open Mon.–Fri. 9–5, Sat. 9 A.M.–12 noon, Sun. 1–5 P.M. Faneuil Hall Armory, open Mon.–Fri. 10–4).

Faneuil Hall is the "Cradle of Liberty," because many important meetings held here fomented the Revolution. It was the first Colonial attempt at academic design. It was completed in 1742 from the plans of Colonial portrait painter John Smibert. Boston merchant, Peter Faneuil, gave it to the town of Boston. It contained a town hall above and a public market below. When fire destroyed the building in 1762, it was rebuilt on the original plan. Charles Bulfinch added a third story (1805) and doubled the original 40-foot width, but retained the original style of the building. Its weathervane, a grasshopper, the most noted steeple adornment in Boston, was modeled by Shem Drowne of Hawthorne's story, "Drowne's Wooden Image." An American consul once tested those claiming Boston citizenship by asking them what is on top of Faneuil Hall. The Hall's chief present treasure is G. P. A. Healy's gigantic oil painting, "Webster's Reply to Hayne."

Faneuil Hall is protected by a charter against sale or leasing. It is never rented but is open to any group upon request of a required number of citizens agreeing to abide by certain regulations. The lower floor is occupied by market stalls.

Faneuil Hall Armory. Two flights upstairs from the hall are the headquarters and historic arms collection of the *Ancient and Honourable Artillery Company,* oldest military organization in America (1638), which still parades in Boston on important occasions, dressed in elaborate historical uniforms.

F14 *Paul Revere House* (open Mon.–Sat. 9–4, closed Sundays and holidays, small fee) (*c.* 1677), 19 North Square. This is the only seventeenth-century structure now standing in downtown Boston. Claimed by some to have been built in 1660, there is more proof that it stands on the plot once occupied by the Increase Mather Parsonage that burned in the great fire of 1676, so it is likely that it was built within the next year. It has undergone many changes, but in 1908 it was rescued by the Paul Revere Memorial Association and restored to its original condition. It is the only 17th-century wooden house still standing in any major U.S. city.

The house has four rooms and an attic. It contains beautiful old furniture and china (not much of it Revere's) and two enormous fireplaces with brick ovens and ancient utensils. Its 1750 wall paper depicts in block pattern the Church of Saint Mary le Bow in London. Some Revere etchings and manuscript letters are displayed.

Paul Revere, silversmith, coppersmith, bellmaker, dentist and agitator, lived here from about 1770 until 1800.

F15 *Old North Church* (1723), (open Oct. 1–May 31, 10–4, June 1–Sept. 30, 9:30–4:30, Sunday services at 11, voluntary contributions), Salem St. This church's original belfry is known to every young American because of Longfellow's poem, "One, if by land, and two, if by sea; and I on the opposite shore will be." The eight melodious bells in the tower are inscribed, "We are the first ring of bells cast for the British Empire in North America," and Paul Revere was one of the first bell ringers.

This historic Episcopal church was the work of Boston printseller and draftsman William Price, who adapted designs by Christopher Wren. The chandeliers came from England in 1724, and when they were lighted on Christmas day every member present was breaking the law, since the celebration of Christmas was still illegal. The organ, which can still be heard playing the old music appropriate to an 18th-century church, dates from 1759.

The steeple has blown down twice. An 1804 gale destroyed the original which was replaced in 1808 after a design by Charles Bulfinch. Hurricane Carol blew that steeple down in 1954 and it was replaced by popular subscription, a copy of the original.

The lovely interior is modeled after Wren's design. Pews carry small brass plates inscribed with the names of 18th-century merchant prince holders. Some pews are still held by their descendants. Eleven hundred of the early members are buried beneath the church.

Libraries

Greater Boston harbors some of the world's greatest libraries. Boston Public Library ranks high in the scale of municipal libraries. Harvard's *Widener Library* is the finest university research library in the world. Possibly only the Library of Congress has a better collection of American books while Widener's foreign book collection is magnificent. Harvard, of course, has the world's most comprehensive law and medical libraries (the Harvard Law Library in Cambridge and the Countway Library at the Harvard Medical School in Boston). The university's departmental libraries are among the world's finest. There is probably no better anthropological library than Harvard's. MIT has the world's most comprehensive science and engineering libraries. *Boston University's African Library* is first rate. Its *School of Communication Library* contains the basic books on the world press, its history and development. Each of the many colleges and universities in the area have fine libraries which are being constantly improved.

Many of the college and university libraries while not open to the general public are open to qualified students, researchers and scholars.

Boston Athenæum (open to scholars by guest card obtained at the desk) is at 10½ Beacon St. The building (1847–49) was designed by Edward C. Cabot in the Palladian style. The Athenaeum, which contains one of the most famous private libraries in the country, is a descendant of the Anthology Club, formed in 1807 by Ralph Waldo Emerson's father. Among its 450,000 volumes are rare collections of historical documents, of books published in the south during the Civil War and much of George Washington's private library.

Boston Public Library (open Mon.–Fri. 9 A.M.–9 P.M., Sat. 9 A.M.–6 P.M., Sun. 2–6 P.M., closed Sun. June–Sept.), Copley Square. Take any MBTA westbound car at Park St. Sta. to Copley Sq.

This library is unique among city-owned libraries in the scope of its large collection of rare and scholarly research volumes, particularly in the 18th and 19th centuries. Many of the central library's 2,680,000 volumes are reference works. Nearly 30 branch libraries are conveniently situated throughout the city. A $23,000,000 addition to the present central building will be completed in the early '70's.

The library's basic plan is simple. Double bronze doors with allegorical figures in low relief were designed by sculptor Daniel Chester French.

The Stair Hall walls are yellow Siena marble. Marble steps lead to the *Main Corridor.* The Stair Hall's upper walls are divided into eight arched panels. Within these panels and on one wall are symbolic murals by Puvis de Chavannes. *Bates Hall,* the main reading room, is 218 feet long. Edwin Austin Abbey's "Quest of the Holy Grail" occupies the upper portion of the *Delivery Room.* On the upper (special libraries) floor is *Sargent Hall* whose walls are covered with John S. Sargent's murals depicting "The Triumph of Religion."

Groups of dioramas by Louise Stimson of Concord represent *Dickens' London, Alice in Wonderland, The Arabian Nights,* and *Printmakers at Work,* based on the Library's print collection.

The library has a large open shelf department containing thousands of current popular fiction and nonfiction works. There are also large record and film loan libraries. The library, thanks to members of the *20th Massachusetts Infantry,* a Civil War outfit, has an outstanding collection of Civil War books. There is also a fine collection of basic books on other American wars and Indian fighting.

A changing display from the Library's Rare Book Collection is on view in Sargent Hall. Special treasures include the Sabatier collection on St. Francis of Assisi and the personal libraries of John Adams, Nathaniel Bowditch and George Ticknor. The Thomas Prince Collection includes an original copy of the *Bay Psalm Book* — the first book printed in the English Colonies in America. These are many of Benjamin Franklin's books and engravings.

The library, finished in 1895, was designed by Charles Follen McKim of McKim, Mead and White, New York. McKim was inspired by the bold lines of Labrouste's *Library of Ste. Geneviève* in Paris. He fused this influence with Alberti's *San Francesco* at Rimini. The interior court, however, is an adaption of Rome's *Palazzo della Cancelleria.*

"The Great Palace of Books" stands upon a granite platform elevated by six broad steps. The facade has 13 deeply raked arches, each separated by massive piers.

Massachusetts Historical Society Library (open Mon.–Fri. 9–4:45, open only to scholars), 1154 Boylston St., cor. Fenway. The Society was founded in 1791 (incorporated 1794) by historian and Congregational minister Jeremy Belknap (1744–98), author of the remarkably accurate, comprehensive and perceptive *History of New Hampshire* (1784–92). The Society has one of the finest private historical research libraries in the nation.

The Adams Papers — now available in 608 reels of microfilm — and the *Henry Knox Papers* are among the many manuscript collections of the Society. The annual "Proceedings and Collections of the Society" can well serve as a model for other societies.

Only those visitors with serious motives should intrude on the premises.

Massachusetts State Library (open Mon.–Fri. 9–5), State House, Room 341, founded in 1826, has more than 500,000 volumes including many priceless documents concerned with the early history of the state and nation. The library is a depository for documents of the federal government printing office. There are many rare papers, books and documents on Canadian affairs, and a complete set of the so-called Sessional Papers of the Canadian government from confederation in 1866 to 1925 when publication of the papers ceased. India, New Zealand, South Wales and other governments contribute their state documents to the library. There is material on Massachusetts, New England and American history. This excellent library, whose fine facilities are too little known, should have substantially larger appropriations for acquisition and other purposes. More space is needed. The library is intended for convenient use of legislators and public officials, but books can be used by any citizen.

New England Historic Genealogical Society (open Mon.–Fri. 9–4:45, closed holidays, free), 101 Newbury St., is one of the best, if not the best, sources for checking your ancestral background.

Art Museums and Galleries

Boston with its Museum of Fine Arts and Harvard with its Fogg, Germanic and Semitic art museums, together with many galleries, are major exhibiting centers. Newbury Street during the past few years has become the center for Boston art galleries. Formerly only such classic galleries as Doll & Richards and the Guild of Boston Artists were here. The first major exhibitor of contemporary art to move here was pioneer Boris Mirski, who came shortly after WWII.

Boston Museum of Fine Arts (closed Mondays; open Tues. 10–9, Wed.–Sun. 10–5; adult admission $1.00, members and children under 16 free; free Tues. 5–9; 50¢ Sun. 10–1), 465 Huntington Ave. Take Huntington Ave. car from Park St. Sta.

Notable exhibits include the following:

1. Largest collection of Colonial painters including portraitists John Singleton Copley and Gilbert Stuart.
2. Impressive Impressionist and post-Impressionist collection.

3. Sizable Winslow Homer collection.
4. Many European old masters, El Greco's "Fray Felix Hortensio Paravicino," Velasquez' "Don Balthasar Carlos and His Dwarf," Rogier van der Weyden's "St. Luke Painting the Virgin."
5. Comprehensive Greek, Roman, and Near Eastern Art collection, the Minoan Snake Goddess, the "Bartlett head of Aphrodite" from the 4th century B.C., the Cycladic Idol from the 3rd millennium B.C
6. Many Egyptian works including Fourth Dynasty statue of Mycerinus and His Queen Kha-merer-nebty.
7. Finest collection of Asiatic art forms in the New World.
8. The nation's most complete collection of silversmith Paul Revere's work.
9. The M. and M. Karolik Collection of American Painting, Drawing and Watercolors (1814–65).
10. The M. and M. Karolik 18th-century American Art Collection.
11. Leslie Lindsey Mason Musical Instrument Collection.
12. Fine ship model collection.

Children's Art Center (open Sept.–July, Mon.–Fri. 9–5, Sat. 9–1, small registration fee), 36 Rutland St., South End. Contemporary paintings, sculpture, etc., exhibitions changed monthly. Art and handicraft classes for children.

Institute of Contemporary Art (open Mon.–Sat. 10–4:30, closed major holidays, no admission fee), 33 Beacon Street. Changing exhibits of contemporary art forms. Members may use art library. Paintings may be rented.

Isabella Stewart Gardner Museum (open Tues., Thurs., Sat. 10–4, open to 10 P.M. every first Thurs. of month except Aug., Sun. 1–5:30, free), 280 The Fenway. Music on Thursdays and Saturdays at 3, Sunday at 4, except first Thursdays at 8:30. One-hour guided tours at 11 and 2, Mon., Wed., Fri. for first 30 people who apply, otherwise closed on these days. Take Huntington Ave. car from Park St. to Ruggles St. stop. Walk three blocks west.

This fascinating residence-museum, better known as Mrs. Jack Gardner's Venetian Palace, built in 1902, is a composite of fragments and materials from Italy. Architect Edward H. Sears drew the plans, but the edifice is obviously the work of a collector with a strong personal taste. The museum houses works of Raphael, Titian, Rembrandt, Cellini and many other old masters. Chamber-music concerts are given in the romantic setting of the *Tapestry Room.*

Mrs. John Lowell Gardner (1820–1924), known to Boston during her lifetime as "Mrs. Jack Gardner," was the most picturesque figure in the social, art and music world during Boston's Mauve Decade. The daughter of a wealthy New York merchant with an artistic and musical flair, she was witty and independent, flouting social tradition. She knew many artists and musicians. In the small portrait of her by Anders Zorn, she is shown flinging open the doors of her Palazzo Barbaro in Venice, her face a mysterious vague blur without features, but her shapely arms and hands very prominent, even reflected in the doors.

Other Museums

Museum of Science (open Mon.–Sat. 10–5, Sun. 11–5, Fri. night to 10, closed New Year's Day, July 4, Labor Day, Thanksgiving, Christmas, fee: adults $1.50, children 5–16 75¢, members free), Charles River Dam Bridge between North Station and Lechmere Square, Cambridge — Science Park MBTA stop. This museum, one of the finest of its kind in the world, is continually developing and should be on the must list of every adult or child visiting Boston.

Many exhibits such as "Hear Your Own Voice" are of the do-it-yourself type. The museum features science, natural history, astronomy, the human body, space vehicles and rockets. The *Pierce Hall of Medical Science* features "How Your Heart Works" and "How Your Life Began." There are interesting demonstrations and lectures with live animals and snakes.

Lyman Science Library has a fine collection of science and natural history volumes.

Skyline Cafeteria (lunch, dinner, snacks) is a wonderful place to take the children — and yourself — for a view of the Boston-Cambridge skyline. Prices are reasonable.

Charles Hayden Planetarium (open every day) on museum grounds. Fee adults 75¢, children 5–16 50¢ plus museum entrance fee. Children under five are welcome in the museum but not allowed in the planetarium. There is a 45-minute show with lecture and realistic views of night skies all over the globe.

Note: Museum prices are subject to change.

Children's Museum (open daily 2–5, Sat.–Sun. 10–5. Also open 10–5 Boston school holidays and vacation days. Fee: children 3–15 75¢, adults $1.25, members free), 60 Burroughs St. (US 1).

This museum, housed in a stucco building, was founded in 1913 to stimulate children's interest in nature studies and science. The museum is supported by private subscriptions.

Natural history specimens, including animal skeletons and stuffed animals and birds, are displayed, and a collection of variegated minerals illustrates the simpler stages of geologic history. There is a small but instructive industrial exhibit, as well as a collection of dolls, ancient and modern, dressed in typical costumes of various countries.

Many exhibits are devoted primarily to man-made things. There are working models of home appliances. Emphasis in recent years has shifted from exhibits to observe to participating exhibits. You can grind corn in an Algonquin wigwam, make a movie, look through a microscope, play on a giant's desktop, rummage through grandmother's attic, light the world's smallest light bulb.

Churches

Boston, with more historic churches than any other American city, is the world headquarters of the Unitarian-Universalist Church and of the Christian Science faith. Many churches such as the Congregational have regional headquarters here. Boston is the seat of the Boston Archdiocese of the Roman Catholic Church.

In the following section historic churches located on the Freedom Trail are cross-indexed.

First Baptist Church, cor. Commonwealth Ave. and Clarendon Sts. (formerly New Brattle Square Church), was designed by H. H. Richardson and built in 1870–72. The exigencies of the corner site resulted in an asymmetrical composition, with the entrance located on a side street and the tower placed on the corner. The first Richardsonian work definitely Romanesque rather than Victorian Gothic, its style is not typically "Richardsonian Romanesque." Once vacated because of bad acoustics, the church is notable for its tower, with the heavy frieze by Bartholdi, a fellow student of Richardson at the École des Beaux Arts. This frieze of trumpeting angels is responsible for the irreverent but affectionate name, "The Church of the Holy Beanblowers."

First Church in Boston (Unitarian-Universalist), cor. Berkeley and Marlborough Sts., originally Congregational, was formed by Gov. Winthrop in 1630 as the first parish. This church was almost completely destroyed by fire in March, 1968, and is now being rebuilt.

First Church in Roxbury (Unitarian), Eliot Square, erected in 1804, was designed after the First Unitarian Church, Portsmouth, N.H., and is a typical New England meeting house, simple and dignified, with a clock tower and open belfry.

Church treasures are John Eliot's chair and a Simon Willard Gallery Clock, surmounted by a spread eagle, holding in its beak two strings of gilded balls. This famous design is often copied, but the clock is one of the two or three authentic examples.

First Church of Christ, Scientist (open daily 10–5), cor. St. Paul, Norway and Falmouth Sts. This is the "Mother Church" of the Christian Science faith. Two church structures are connected by an interior passage. The smaller one with a square granite tower, erected in 1894, is the first Christian Science church building in Boston, though its congregation dates from 1879. The main church (1904), Italian Renaissance, with a 224-foot-high central dome, is of limestone, trimmed with granite below and with glazed white tiles above. Its open nave, seating 5000 people, rises 108 feet with no pillar support. Doors and pews are richly carved Domingo mahogany. Walls are limestone. The wide pulpit contains two lecterns.

Christian Science Publishing House (open daily except Sundays and holidays, tours 1:30 and 3:00), Massachusetts Ave. and Norway St. (across from church), issues the widely read and respected *Christian Science Monitor,* an international newspaper published daily except Sunday. The house also publishes Christian Science literature including Mary Baker Eddy's "Science and Health."

Mapparium located in publishing house (open Mon.–Sat. 8–4, closed Sundays and holidays) is a large global map. A bridge passes through the globe's interior at the equator. New developments at this Christian Science center will include a 28-story administration building, and a colonnade building with exhibit room, the whole to cover thirteen acres.

First Parish Church (Unitarian), Meeting House Hill, Dorchester, houses a *Roman Mosaic* from Dorchester, England, dating from Britain's conquest by Caesar. The vestry's Anglo-Chinese clock of 1770 has English works and a Chinese case. This case, larger than needed for the clock, was used before the Revolution for smuggling tea, an undertaking then considered so patriotic that it did not disturb the conscience of the church when the gift of the clock was made.

Holy Cross Cathedral (Roman Catholic), 1400 Washington St., was the first Catholic parish in Boston. The church used to be on Franklin St.

New Old North Church (see Freedom Trail F15)

Old South Church (Third), 645 Boylston St., cor. Dartmouth St., built in 1875 from the plans of Cummings and Sears, is probably one of the best examples of the Victorian Gothic style beloved in the 19th century. The campanile, which soars to a height of 248 feet, was for many years the "leaning tower of Copley Square." When, in 1932, it was in danger of toppling, it was removed, stone by stone, and rebuilt on a steel skeleton anchored to deep-sunk piles.

Old South Meeting House (see Freedom Trail F9)

Old West Church (West End Church), 131 Cambridge St., was on Tuesday, Nov. 8, 1960, the balloting place for residents of the Third Precinct, Sixth Ward. John F. Kennedy, whose official address was 122 Bowdoin St., cast his ballot in what had been a Protestant church for more than 150 years. The church was built in 1806 from architect-writer Asher Benjamin's plans.

The church for many years prior to 1959 had served thousands of West End residents, mostly immigrants, as the *West End Branch* of the *Boston Public Library.* One of the few structures to escape the wrecker's ball during the destruction of the West End, it is now a Methodist Church.

Park Street Church (see Freedom Trail F3)

Saint Paul's Cathedral (1819–20), Tremont St. opposite the Common, seat of Massachusetts' Episcopal bishops, is the city's earliest example of Greek Revival architecture. The architects were Alexander Parris, who later built the Quincy Market, and Solomon Willard. There is no stained glass. Pewholder Daniel Webster was on the building committee.

Saint Stephen's Church (Roman Catholic), 401 Hanover St., was, in 1802, designed and constructed by Charles Bulfinch as a "New North Church." The church is on the site of the wooden Meeting House of the New North Congregational Society, built in 1714.

Tremont Temple (Baptist), 82 Tremont St., stands on the site of an earlier temple in which Jenny Lind sang (1850–52). Founded in 1839 because the Charles Street Church, then Baptist, decreed that any member bringing a Negro into his pew would be expelled, it is one of the most popular evangelical congregations in Greater Boston.

Trinity Church (Episcopal) (open daily), Copley Square, was built in 1877. It was one of H. H. Richardson's first major projects. The design had to conform to the small triangular lot, bounded by three streets. Richardson adapted the dominant central tower theme from 11th-century southern France's Romanesque. The design of the tower itself was influenced by Spain's Salamanca Cathedral. Native Massachusetts material such as yellow Dedham granite and reddish-brown Longmeadow freestone were major construction materials.

Richardson selected John La Farge to direct the interior decoration and windows. The dominant interior wall color is red. The best windows, designed by Sir Edward Burne-Jones, were executed by William Morris, La Farge and several Londoners. Richardson admirers consider Trinity a masterpiece of Richardson Romanesque.

Recreation

RICHARD T. ARTESANI MEMORIAL PLAYGROUND, Soldiers Field Rd., Allston-Brighton. Picnic tables, fireplaces, boat launching, fishing and wading pools.

CONSTITUTION BEACH, East Boston. Picnic tables on beach, playground, athletic field. Route C–1. Take MBTA Rapid Transit from Government Center.

FRANKLIN PARK, Dorchester. Picnic tables and fireplaces on zoological garden grounds. MBTA Rapid Transit from Green St. or Egleston Stas.

REV. F. TAYLOR WEIL FAMILY PICNIC GROUNDS, Turtle Pond Parkway at Smithfield Rd., Hyde Park.

WOOD ISLAND PARK, East Boston. Picnic tables, fireplaces, music shell for concerts, athletic field, basketball and handball courts. Take MBTA Rapid Transit from Government Center (Scollay Sq.) to Day Square.

Parks and Walks

Charles River. The Charles River Embankment section, also known as Storrow Drive, lies on the banks of the Charles between Science Park and Boston University Bridge. This area provides footpaths, fishing sites, boat launching sites, music shell for summer concerts, five children's playgrounds and ample greensward for sun bathing. Footpaths extend beyond the

Charlestown: "Old Ironsides" with Bunker Hill Monument in the background

Provincetown: Fishing fleet

Gloucester: Drying cod

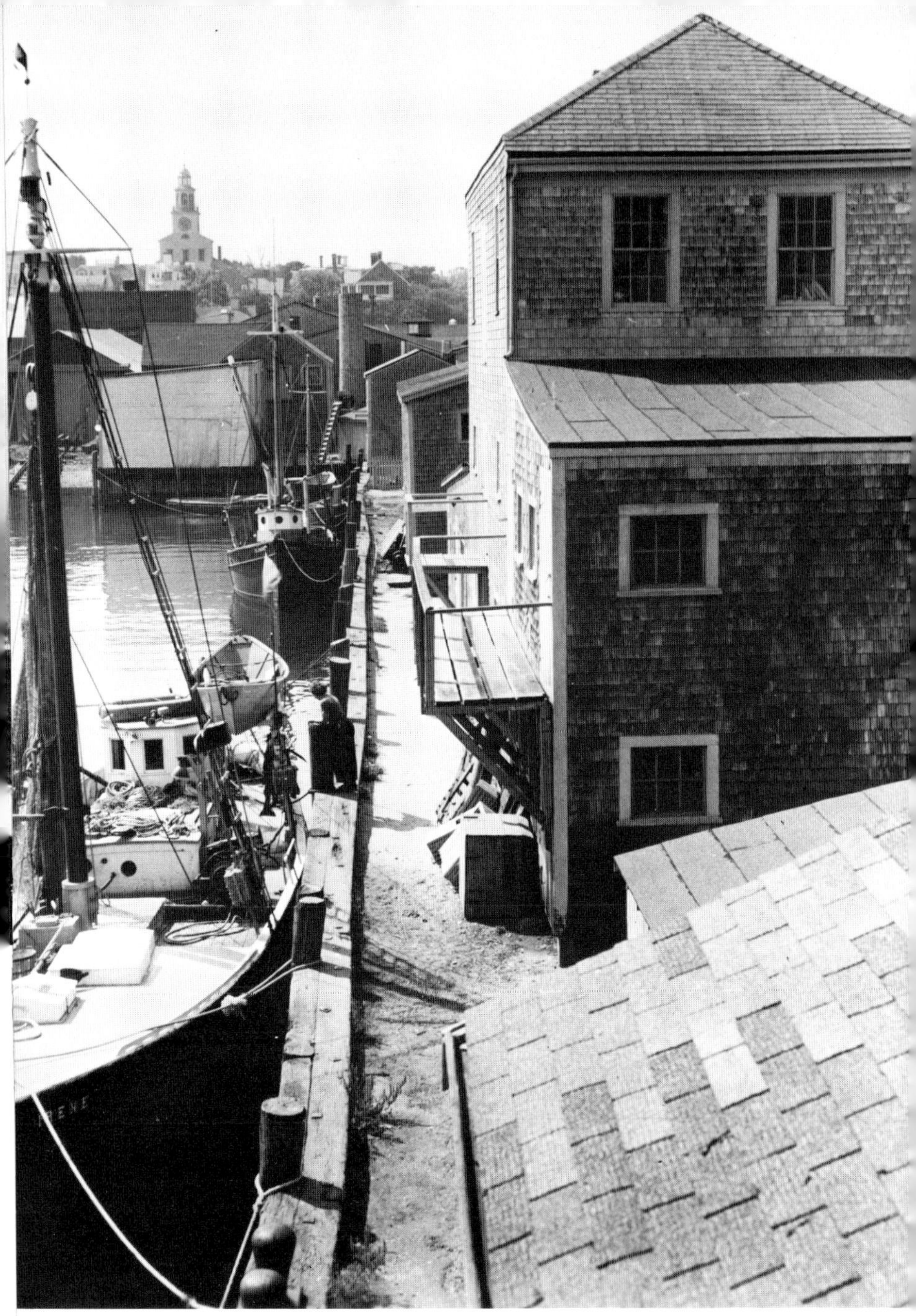

Nantucket: Commercial Wharf

Martha's Vineyard: Gay Head cliffs

Right, above—Edgartown: Old homes of former sea captains

Right, below—Cape Cod: Antique shop

Rockport: Painters' motif number one

so-called Embankment section along the river to Cambridge. It is a pleasant four-mile walk from Longfellow Bridge to Cambridge via the Eliot Bridge. Informal picnics are permitted.

Marine Park, City Point, South Boston. Route C–37 or MBTA Rapid Transit to Andrew Sq. and Dudley St. Stas.

For other parks and walks in the Greater Boston area see Cambridge, Dedham, Hull, Lynn, Nahant, Revere, Watertown, Wollaston. In Boston, see Boston Common, Public Gardens and The Fenway.

Botanical and Zoological Gardens

Arnold Arboretum (open daily, sunrise to sunset, free), off US 1, Jamaica Plain, pedestrians only (see also Middlesex Fells Zoo and Stoneham). It is the largest living tree and shrub museum — unless you include national parks — in the country. In May and early June its several hundred acres are a paradise of blooming lilacs, cherry trees, forsythias, plum trees, magnolias, rhododendrons and azaleas. Endowed (1872) by New Bedford merchant James Arnold, the Arboretum is owned by Harvard and contains the *Bussey Institute of Horticulture and Agriculture.*

Franklin Park Zoo (open daily, 10–5, no fee for general zoo, small fee for children's zoo section during summer, no fee during winter), Blue Hill Ave. and Seaver St. (Dorchester).

Franklin Park is both a botanical and zoological garden. More than 50 acres of exhibits. Includes lion house, bear den, bird house, rose garden. Zoo contains more than 300 mammals and 400 bird specimens. Picnic sites include tables and fireplaces.

Take MBTA Rapid Transit from Egleston or Green St. Stas.

Boston Area Skiing

These ski areas are within a 60-minute — or less — drive from downtown Boston.

BLUE HILL SKI AREA, Mass. 138, Canton, has double chair lift, 3 rope tows, 2 T-bar lifts, ski school, ski shop, ski rentals, restaurant, snowmaking machines, night skiing. Special student group rate. Open daily from 9:30.

BOSTON HILL, North Andover, Mass. 114, has rope tows, J-bar, ski rentals, instruction, night skiing. Open daily.

BRADFORD SKI AREA, Old Cross Road, 2 mi. from Bradford Common, has 3 rope tows, 2 open slopes, 1 trail, lodge, snack bar, ski rentals, repairs, night skiing. Open daily 10–10.

HAMILTON SKI AREA, Moulton St., 3 mi. north US 1A, has 2 rope tows, 4 slopes, 2 trails, instruction, snack bar, night skiing.

MT. HOOD SKI AREA, Melrose, 1 rope tow, night skiing. Open daily.

PRIEST'S SKI AREA, Groton, Mass. 119, has 5 rope tows, toboggan rentals. Open weekends, Wednesday and holidays.

PROSPECT HILL, Waltham, 1 rope tow.

SKYFIELD SKI AREA, Groton, Mass. 119 from Mass. 2 or 2A, has 4 rope tows, snack bar, ski rentals, instruction. Open weekends, Tues. and Fri. afternoons. Evening skiing by arrangement.

HARTWELL HILL SKI AREA, Littleton, Mass. 2 to Interstate 495 from Boston, has 4 slopes, 2 trails, instruction, snack bar, warming hut, ski repairs and rentals, cross-country ski and snowshoe trails. Open weekends and holidays, 10–5.

HEAVENLY HILL SKI AREA, Wollaston section of Quincy, rope tow, slope, instruction, snack bar. Open daily.

JERICHO HILL SKI AREA, Mass. 9 and 85, Marlborough, has 2 rope tows and instruction. Open evenings, weekends, holidays.

AMESBURY SKI TOW, Mass. 107, Amesbury, has 5 rope tows, novice and expert slopes, warming hut, snack bar, ski patrol, ski shop, ski rentals. Open 9–5 Sat., Sun. and holidays. Evening skiing Mon.–Fri. 7–10, Wed. 1–5; during school vacations, 9–5 and 7–10 daily.

Water Sports

All beaches unless otherwise noted are operated by the Metropolitan District Commission (MDC) (open June 15 through Labor Day, small fee for use of lockers and/or towels). Lifeguards on duty.

For salt water beaches outside of Boston but within the Greater Boston area see Hull, Lynn, Nahant, Quincy, Revere, Swampscott and Winthrop.

Probably the best beaches within no more than one hour's ride from downtown Boston are *Crane's* and *Castle Hill Beaches* in Ipswich.

CARSON BEACH, Day Boulevard, South Boston. Bathhouse. Mass. C–37. MBTA Rapid Transit to Columbia Station.

CITY POINT BEACH, South Boston. Bathhouse. Band concerts on Sunday afternoons. Mass. C–37. City Point bus from Broadway or Andrew and Dudley St. MBTA stations.

CONSTITUTION BEACH, East Boston. Bathhouse. Mass. C–1. MBTA Rapid Transit from Government Center (Scollay Sq.).

M STREET BEACH, Day Boulevard, South Boston.

MALIBU BEACH, Morrissey Boulevard, Dorchester. Bathhouse. Mass. C–37. MBTA Rapid Transit to Savin Hill Station.

PLEASURE BAY BEACH, South Boston. Mass. C–37. City Point bus from Broadway or Andrew Square and Dudley St. MBTA Rapid Transit stations.

SAVIN HILL BEACH, Dorchester. Mass. C–37. MBTA Rapid Transit to Savin Hill station.

TENEAN BEACH, off Morrissey Boulevard, Dorchester. Bathhouse. Mass. C–37. Neponset trackless trolley from Fields Corner Rapid Transit MBTA station.

MDC pools are open June 15–Sept. 15, 10–9. Very small admission fee. Learn-to-swim classes are held July–Aug.

Boat-Launching Sites

Brooks Street at Nonantum Rd., Brighton.
Clarendon Street at Charles River Embankment.
Community Boat House, sail boating, Charles River Embankment.
Dartmouth Street at Charles River Embankment.
Hatch Shell, Charles River Embankment.
Kelley's Landing, Day Boulevard, South Boston.
Pinckney Street (outboard boats for hire), Charles River Embankment.
Science Park, Charles River Dam.
Speedway Beach at Speedway Beach, Soldiers Field Rd., Brighton.
Summer Theatre Site, Soldiers Field Rd., Brighton.

For other public (MDC) boat-launching sites in the Greater Boston area see Brookline, Cambridge, Medford, Newton, Saugus, Watertown, Weston and Winchester.

BOSTON METROPOLITAN AREA (pop. 2,753,700, area 988.29 sq. mi.) includes the cities of Beverly, Boston, Cambridge, Chelsea, Everett, Lynn, Malden, Medford, Melrose, Newton, Peabody, Quincy, Revere, Salem, Somerville, Waltham, and Woburn and the towns of Arlington, Ashland, Bedford, Belmont, Braintree, Brookline, Burlington, Canton, Cohasset, Concord, Danvers, Dedham, Dover, Duxbury, Framingham, Hamilton, Hanover, Hingham, Holbrook, Hull, Lexington, Lincoln, Lynnfield, Manchester, Marblehead, Marshfield, Medfield, Middleton, Millis, Milton, Nahant,

Natick, Needham, Norfolk, North Reading, Norwell, Norwood, Pembroke, Randolph, Reading, Rockland, Saugus, Scituate, Sharon, Sherborn, Stoneham, Sudbury, Swampscott, Topsfield, Wakefield, Walpole, Watertown, Wayland, Wellesley, Wenham, Weston, Westwood, Weymouth, Wilmington, Winchendon, and Winthrop.

BOURNE (Barnstable County, sett. *c.* 1640, incorp. 1884, alt. 50, pop. 12,636, area 41.02 sq. mi., town meeting, routes, US 3, 6, Mass. 6A, 28), originally Monument village in Sandwich Town, was named for resident Jonathan Bourne. Freight-car manufacture was an important industry until 1928. Hundreds of "40 & 8" boxcars so familiar to doughboys were shipped to France in 1917–18. The boxcars were called "40 & 8" because they would hold 40 men or 8 horses. In 1935 the federal government purchased the abandoned plant to make way for an enlargement of the *Cape Cod Canal.* Tourism, cranberry growing and dairying are major industries.

Aptuxcet Trading Post (open till dark, April–Oct., closed Mon. except during June–Aug., small fee), off Shore Rd. The cellar walls and hearthstone of the original structure (1626) were incorporated in the new one-and-a-half story, unpainted building with its tiny diamond-shaped panes and steep roof. Colonists established the Indian trading post.

Gray Gables Inn, Shore Rd., was the summer White House during President Grover Cleveland's administrations. A newel post at the foot of the stairs has notches cut in it by the President when he marked the height of his children.

Bourne Bridge (1935), spanning the Cape Cod Canal, has a 135-foot clearance at the central span.

Buzzard's Bay (alt. 17) is Bourne's trading center. *Administration Building* (State Pier) was built in 1932 to meet the needs of increased shipping through the canal.

OTIS AIR FORCE BASE WILDLIFE MANAGEMENT AREA provides public hunting.

SAGAMORE (alt. 18). Here US 6 crosses the Cape Cod Canal.

BOXBOROUGH (Middlesex County, sett. 1680, incorp. 1783, alt. 300, pop. 1451, area 10.39 sq. mi., town meeting, routes, I–495, Mass. 2, 111) is named because of the original square form of the township. The community produces fruits and dairy products. Population has nearly doubled since 1960 because of the lovely village's proximity to Boston.

BOXFORD (Essex County, sett. 1645, incorp. 1685, alt. 100, pop. 4032, area 24.39 sq. mi., town meeting, routes, US 95, Mass. 97, 133) occupies an unspoiled stretch in an area with low, rolling hills, woods and large ponds.

The Ames murder trial attracted widespread attention. John Adams was attorney for the defense. This trial was perhaps the only one in New England at which the ordeal by touch was employed—a superstition that a corpse would bleed if the murderer touched the body.

On the green stands *Boxford Town Hall* (1893).

Left of the green, on Georgetown Rd., is the *First Church, Congregational* (erected 1838, incorporated 1702), a charming white meeting house with a row of horse sheds still standing. At the left of the church on Middleton Rd. stands "Journey's End" (1817). In this garden was built a miniature sand village which inspired G. Stanley Hall (1844–1924) to write *The Story of a Sand Pile* (1897), a book that made a distinct contribution to the modern playground movement.

Second Congregational Church (1843), West Boxford, the second building on this site, has recently been renovated and enlarged. The bell was made by an apprentice of Paul Revere.

Zoning laws (1946) indicate residents' determination, despite rapid growth and construction of more and more homes, that Boxford retain its pleasant rural atmosphere.

Boxford was part of a large tract once occupied by the Agawams. In 1638 Sachem Masconomet deeded to white settlers all his right to this land for twenty pounds. *Masconomet Regional Junior-Senior High School* (1959) serving Boxford, Topsfield and Middleton has 1600 students.

Boxford Historical Society is in the Holyoke-French House. This Georgian mansion (1760) was built for Elizur Holyoke.

BOYLSTON (Worcester County, sett. 1705, incorp. 1786, alt. 519, pop. 2774, area 15.84 sq. mi., town meeting, routes, Mass. 70, 140), a residential village once part of Lancaster and Shrewsbury, was named for Boston's Boylstons, who gave a Bible, communion cups, a bell and money to the Congregational Church.

Wachusett Reservoir covers 2700 acres of town land.

The former Home of *John B. Gough* (private) belonged to the temperance advocate who captivated audiences all over the country with his funny stories combined with serious appeals for abstinence.

BRAINTREE (Norfolk County, sett. 1634, incorp. 1640, alt. 70, pop. 35,050, area 13.70 sq. mi., representative town meeting, routes, Mass. 3, 27,128), once known as Monoticut (Indian for "abundance"), formerly included Quincy and Randolph.

In 1665, the town bought land from Chief Wampatuck for £21, 10s. Fishing and hunting rights were reserved by the sachem. Roger Williams and Anne Hutchinson followers found refuge here en route to Rhode Island.

Braintree was agricultural until the mid-19th century when the railroad fostered industrial growth. After 1910 the plants became smaller and industries more diversified.

Here in 1920 occurred the holdup and murder of a paymaster and guard for which Sacco and Vanzetti were executed. (See HISTORICAL NOTES.)
Thayer Academy, Washington St., was founded by Gen. Sylvanus Thayer, superintendent of the United States Military Academy at West Point (1817–33), a native who gave the town its public library.

BLUE HILLS RESERVATION: nature museum, freshwater fishing, freshwater beaches, bridle trails, foot trails, band concerts, playground, picnic sites, ski area, observation tower, ice skating, golf. See BLUE HILLS RESERVATION.

BREWSTER (Barnstable County, sett. 1656, incorp. 1803, alt. 39, pop. 1790, area 22.55 sq. mi., town meeting, routes, US 6, Mid-Cape Highway, Mass. 6A, 24, 39, 137) was named for William Brewster (1567–1644) of Plymouth Colony. Fortunes made at sea in the early 19th century brought wealth to the town and built luxurious homes. This is the geographic center of Cape Cod.
Captain Elijah Cobb House (1800), off US 6, west of the Center, is a two-story late Georgian house surmounted by a widow's walk. The stirring life of wealthy shipmaster Cobb is told in *The Memoirs of a Cape Cod Skipper.*
Joseph C. Lincoln Birthplace, north of the Center, is a small one-and-a-half story white clapboard house. Lincoln (1870–1944) used Brewster as a setting for many Cape Cod novels, including *Rugged Water.* His father was the last of a long line of sea captains.

RONALD C. NICKERSON STATE PARK AND FOREST has 400 campsites on and around the shores of several freshwater ponds. *Flax Pond* area has picnic tables, fireplaces, a bathhouse, snowmobiling. This is one of the most popular state parks.

Cape Cod Museum of Natural History (open mid-June thru mid-Sept., Mon.–Sat. 10–5, Sun. 2–5, small fee), with headquarters in Brewster Town Hall and a "summer" pavilion just off US 6, houses Cape Cod flora and fauna. There are several nature trails. During the winter the museum holds nature lectures. There are summer courses for children. Field trips are held for adults. Write the director for information.

Freshwater fishermen will find 25 freshwater lakes and ponds in Brewster. State Park ponds are annually stocked with trout. Smallmouth bass, yellow perch and pickerel are native to these waters.

Saltwater fishermen find excellent surf fishing for stripers. Tuna is the major boat sportsfish. Brewster has seven boat landings for fishermen who bring their own craft. Charter boats are available.

BRIDGEWATER (Plymouth County, sett. 1650, incorp. 1656, alt. 104, pop. 11,829, area 27.29 sq. mi., town meeting, routes, Fall River Expressway, Mass. 18, 28, 104) during the 18th century was a major American iron-making center. Many Revolutionary War cannons were cast here. During the Civil War some material for the U.S. Navy's first ironclad ship, the *Monitor,* was made here. Shoes, nails and bricks are current products.

In 1817 young Eleazer Carver established a mill to make cotton gins. This and other local industries attracted many Italian and Portuguese immigrants. The Italians planted vineyards for their wine. The Portuguese celebrate the Holy Ghost festival in July.

Nicola Sacco and Bartolomeo Vanzetti, after their May 5, 1920, arrest in Brockton for alleged participation in the slaying of a paymaster and a guard in South Braintree, were indicted for an attempted holdup in Bridgewater. Sacco, who had unimpeachable witnesses, was not tried, but Vanzetti, whose only alibis for the Bridgewater affair were provided by his customers — he was a fish peddler — was tried and convicted before Judge Webster Thayer in the Plymouth court during June–July 1920. A year later both men were convicted of the South Braintree affair. (See HISTORICAL NOTES.)

Facing the common, *The Washburn House* (private) was the home of a Colonel Edson, a Tory, whose property was confiscated. The *Unitarian Church of the Congregational Society* (1845) has a fine Christopher Wren type spire.

Bridgewater State College is the site of the first state normal school building in America.

BRIGGSVILLE (see CLARKSBURG)

BRIGHTON (see BOSTON)

BRIMFIELD (Hampden County, sett. *c.* 1706, incorp. 1731, alt. 660, pop. 1907, area 35.37 sq. mi., town meeting, routes, US 20, Mass. 19), with its white Colonial church overlooking the green, and street-lined with closely planted elms, is on the old stagecoach route. Its few industries did not survive the mass production era.

WEST BRIMFIELD. Here is the Captain Nicholas House (private), an old brick building used for quarters by the Hessian soldiers who marched from Saratoga to Boston in 1777.

BRIMFIELD STATE FOREST (3158 acres): Dean Pond area has fishing, hunting, fireplaces, picnic tables, snowmobiling, scenic views, swimming. Off US 20 between Springfield and Worcester.

EAST BRIMFIELD DAM — swimming — Route 20.

BRISTOL COUNTY (est. 1685, pop. 444,301, area 554.34 sq. mi., shire towns, New Bedford and Taunton) includes the cities of Attleborough, Fall River, New Bedford and Taunton. The 16 towns are Acushnet, Berkley, Dartmouth, Dighton, Easton, Fairhaven, Freetown, Mansfield, North Attleboro, Norton, Raynham, Rehoboth, Seekonk, Somerset, Swansea and Westport.

BROCKTON (Plymouth County, sett. 1700, town incorp. 1821, city incorp. 1881, alt. 100, pop. 89,040, area 21.37 sq. mi., mayor-council, routes, Mass. 24, 27, 28, 123).

Brockton, a major shoe-manufacturing center, also produces plastics, clothing and electronic equipment. The city, once a trading village for farmers, is now a metropolitan service center for over 500,000.

In 1649 Indians deeded the land to Myles Standish and John Alden for $30. Brockton was part of Bridgewater until 1821, when it became North Bridgewater. The Brockton name was adopted in 1874.

The Revolution was remote, but the postwar depression found residents vigorously opposing ruthless laws affecting small debtors. Militant townsmen snatched their hunting guns from the walls and came into the street to support Shays' Rebellion.

The McKay sewing machine, which sewed shoe uppers and soles together instead of pegging them, changed North Bridgewater from a small farm center to one of the foremost industrial cities in Massachusetts.

The Civil War brought prosperity to the shoe industry. It became America's largest shoe city as half the Union Army was shod here.

Workers streamed into town. By 1880 the population had tripled.

Before the Civil War social life consisted almost wholly of church functions characterized by a minimum of gaiety — a residue from Puritan days. With the influx of foreigners gatherings assumed a livelier cast. Swedes were the first group to sanction dancing, holding their parties in the church vestry. The Firemen's Ball became the most brilliant and colorful social event of the year. Workers organized trade unions. Foreign-language groups erected halls which later became community centers.

The first U.S. central power station from which power was distributed through three-wire underground conductors was located here. An experimental electric street railway was developed here. Thomas Edison came to see the first car run over the line. In 1893, Brockton solved the sewerage disposal problem for inland cities. Investigating committees came from foreign countries and many U.S. cities to learn the Brockton system and arrange for its adoption.

In 1929, in the neighborhood of Brockton there were thirty thousand skilled shoe workers employed in 60 factories. During the last few years the emigration of shoe industries from New England has noticeably affected Brockton. This movement has been a primary factor in the decline of the shoe industry. By 1970 the city had over 200 diversified industries.

Brockton Fair Grounds, Belmont St., site since 1874 of the annual Brockton Fair.

William Cullen Bryant House (open by appointment), 815 Belmont St., is a frame dwelling where the poet lived.

Public Library (open daily), White Ave. and Main St., houses the Walter Bryant Copeland collection of Masters of American Art.

Brockton Art Center (open daily 10–5, Thursdays to 10, Sundays 1:30–5:30, closed Mondays. Admission $1.00 to non-members, children 16 and under free. Group tours), Oak Street. This new museum and art school opened in 1969, given by geologist Myron Fuller as a memorial to his father. New exhibits every 4–5 weeks. Thursday night series of films, lectures, and concerts. Art sales department and rental service.

The museum building, designed by J. Timothy Anderson and Associates, is beautifully sited along ponds and running water. It is surrounded by 19 acres of woodland belonging to the art center, set in the 700 acres of Field Park.

D. W. FIELD PARK, Oak St., has lovely woods, ponds, gardens and artificial waterfalls. The park, named after its creator, shoe manufacturer, farmer and writer Daniel Waldo Field, has facilities for picnics, swimming, golf and fishing.

BROCKTON METROPOLITAN AREA (pop. 189,820, area 162.91 sq. mi.,) includes the city of Brockton and the towns of Abington, Avon, Bridgewater, East Bridgewater, Easton, Hanson, Stoughton, West Bridgewater and Whitman.

BROOKFIELD (Worcester County, sett. 1664, incorp. 1718, alt. 700, pop. 2063, area 15.68 sq. mi., town meeting, route, Mass. 9) was once Quabaug. Territory surrounding Brookfield was granted by the General Court to Ipswich residents in 1660. There was a large boot and shoe industry here in the 19th century. The region is known for Jersey milk cows.

Merrick Library houses the writing desk of Louis XVI and Marie Antoinette, a gift to William Draper in 1863 from the Marquis Bernard de Marigny.

QUABOAG RIVER WILDLIFE MANAGEMENT AREA has public hunting in Brookfield and West Brookfield.

BROOKLINE (Norfolk County, sett. *c.* 1638, incorp. 1705, alt. 40, pop. 58,886, area 6.63 sq. mi., representative town meeting, routes, Mass. 9, 30).

Brookline, once Muddy River Hamlet, the state's largest town and the birthplace of President John F. Kennedy (1917–1963), is a residential town. Over Fisher, Corey and Aspinwall Hills, along Beacon Street and Commonwealth Avenue, around the Reservoir and over into Chestnut Hill spread the homes of people who work in Boston.

Early in the 20th century, Brookline was the "Town of Millionaires," but by 1910 it opened its doors to residents of more modest means. Some of Brookline remains a closed citadel of wealth and leisure while the rest is a modern residential hive for the better paid of the busy workers of Boston.

History and Development

In 1630, the Company of Massachusetts Bay arrived from London. Bostonians soon found their common overcrowded with cows. Town fathers sought a bigger cow pasture.

Urbane, affable John Cotton — the foremost divine of Boston — was granted the first tract of land. Other Bostonians soon grabbed generous grants. By 1639 available acreage was running out. Later grants were smaller, more numerous and made to less-well-known applicants.

Agriculture was the first most important industry. Farms raised produce for sale in Boston. In 1705 the village was granted recognition as the separate town of Muddy River Hamlet, having been named for the estate of Judge Samuel Sewall, who owned a large tract in Muddy River.

By the mid-19th century a larger town hall was built, the first railroad ran through the town and telegraph wires appeared; the Coolidges — no known kin to Massachusetts governor Calvin Coolidge — had a store near the spot known today as Coolidge Corner. Many affluent Bostonians were attracted to this rural suburb. Taxes were low. Brookline, near Boston, could easily and quickly be reached by train or horsecar. The fare was moderate. It was an ideal commuter's town.

Boston, beginning in 1870, tried six times to annex this prize tax plum. Brookline today is almost an "island" surrounded by Boston. Brookline prefers representative town government to a city form.

Brookline's Hannah Adams (1755–1831), a Medfield native, was probably the first female professional writer in America. Noted residents have included Music Director Serge Koussevitzky (1874–1951) of the Boston Symphony Orchestra, Negro tenor Roland Hayes (b. 1887) whose work furthered acceptance of the Negro spiritual as a vocal art form, and Pulitzer-Prize-winning poet Amy Lowell (1874–1925).

What To See and Do

Brookline Public Library (1910), 361 Washington St., houses the Desmond Fitzgerald Collection of Paintings, in which such artists as Maufra, Bloos, Banderweiden and Dodge MacKnight are represented.
Corey Hill Outlook (alt. 265) is the best vantage point of Brookline. Beneath it, to the west, lie Brighton and Watertown, with the tower of *Perkins School for the Blind* quite noticeable. To the north the horseshoe of the Harvard Stadium is easily distinguished, with college buildings on its right. To the east, the Charles River widens to its greatest breadth and merges with Boston Harbor in the distance.
Brookline Trust Company (open Mon.–Fri. 9–3), 1341 Beacon St., has the Ernest B. Dane Collection of Tapestries, including four Gobelin tapestries valued at several million dollars.
Edward Devotion House (open Wed. 2–4, also by appointment, small fee), 347 Harvard St., was built in 1680 by Edward Devotion, town constable, fence viewer and tithing man. The neat cream and yellow two-and-a-half-story frame house with small-paned windows, gambrel roof and central chimney stands on the premises of the Devotion School. The house is the headquarters of the Brookline Historical Society.
Green Hill (The Goddard House, private), 235 Goddard Ave., was built as a farmhouse for Nehemiah Davis in 1732. The great drawing room with chambers above was added in 1797. Other alterations have been made. This house is one of the oldest in Brookline.

A tercentenary marker opposite Reservoir Park indicates the *Site of the Zabdiel Boylston House.* Here, in 1736, lived Dr. Zabdiel Boylston, the first American physician to inoculate for smallpox. In 1721, despite popular prejudice, he inoculated his son and two slaves. After this successful experiment, public hostility slowly subsided. Smallpox inoculations came into general use, and the disease ceased to be a scourge.
Larz Anderson Antique Auto Museum (open daily, except Mon., 1–5, small fee), off Mass. 9, shows the development of American transportation 1850–1926. Many interesting old autos and carriages.
Longyear Foundation (open weekdays, 1–5, closed holidays, free), 120 Seaver St., has historical data on Mary Baker Eddy, the founder of Christian Science.
President John F. Kennedy's birthplace (open daily 9–5, sometimes closed Mon.; adults 50¢, children under 16 and educational groups, accompanied by adults, free), 83 Beals Street. Phone: 556–7937.

BUCKLAND (Franklin County, sett. 1779, incorp. 1794, alt. 420, pop. 1892, area 20.07 sq. mi., town meeting, routes, Mass, 2, 112), once a small mill town with factories powered by the Clesson River, has long since reverted to farming.

Today's industries include the manufacturing of steel products. Buckland shares with neighboring Shelburne the famed *Bridge of Flowers.*

Buckland has two interesting houses, but neither is open to the public. They are the Baron Rudick House (1796), a fine example of period architecture, and the home of Holyoke College founder Mary Lyon (1797–1849).

The *Buckland Historical Society* has taken over an abandoned schoolhouse and has converted it into an excellent local museum.

BUCKLAND RECREATION AREA has picnic sites and a swimming pool.

BURLINGTON (Middlesex County, sett. 1641, incorp. 1799, alt. 220, pop. 21,980, area 11.88 sq. mi., town meeting, routes US 3, Mass. 3A, 128). Burlington is an agricultural community with a growing industrial belt along Mass. 128. The *Marion Tavern* (open), on Center St., a low rambling house, was known in coaching days as the Half-Way House. *Old Burying Ground,* Bedford St., a peaceful spot where goldenrod and lazy creeping vines mask the weather-beaten slabs in summer. The *Old Meeting House* (1732), now the Church of Christ, has been remodeled, but the oaken interior remains.

CAMBRIDGE (Middlesex County seat, sett. 1630, town incorp. 1636, city incorp. 1846, alt. 10, pop. 100,361, area 6.25 sq. mi., city manager-council (Plan E), routes, US 3, Mass. 2, 3, 16). Cambridge is the site of Harvard and Massachusetts Institute of Technology.

Cambridge, on the north bank of the Charles River, occupies a level plain broken only by Mt. Auburn, both a cemetery and a hill. The city is bisected by busy Massachusetts Avenue and bordered by the leisurely sweep of Memorial Drive. Four cities occupy Cambridge's confines: elm-shaded streets, fenced dooryards and landmarks still represent Old Cambridge, and the Cambridge that succeeded it—the Home of the Literati. Visible in lusty existence are the other Cambridges: University City and Industrial Cambridge.

University City houses nearly 25,000 people within and around the walls of Harvard. Harvard Yard is a hive of scholarship. University City houses 1215 female Radcliffe students. University City can also claim Massachusetts Institute of Technology with its 7500 students and thousands of scientists. Its libraries, laboratories, museums, art galleries, historic shrines, scholars, scientists, students, illustrious authors, poets, philosophers and historians are world renowned.

A hundred thousand residents throng Industrial Cambridge's subways, stores and crowd its buses. Hundreds of plants produce scores of nationally known products. Its second mercantile section, Central Square, is lined with department stores and small retail shops.

Early Days

Old Cambridge dates back three centuries. In 1630, Gov. John Winthrop needed a fortified place for a capital, protected against the enemy most to be feared — not the Indians, but King Charles' warships. "Wherefore they rather made choice to enter further among the Indians, than hazzard the fury of malignant adversaries that might pursue them . . . and erected a town called New Towne, now named Cambridge."

An early episode had much to do with determining New Towne's destiny. In October, 1636, the General Court of the Massachusetts Bay Colony agreed to give £400 toward a school or college — a sum equal to the whole colony tax. It remained to select the place.

In Charlestown lived a young minister, John Harvard, and as the friends of higher education "were thinking annd consulting, how to effect this great work . . . it pleased God that he died, and it was then found he had bequeathed his library to the proposed college, and one-half his estate — in all some £1,700." It was decreed the new college should bear John Harvard's name. The Court ordered that "New Towne shall henceforth be called Cambridge," after the English university town.

Less than a decade later, the synod stated all known opposites to the Church of England. This was the famous "Cambridge Platform," wherein the powers of the clergy were minutely defined. The duty of commoners was stated to be "obeying their elders and submitting themselves unto the Lord." Church and State were now united by law. The clergy's rule was absolute.

At Harvard, Bible study was most important. The student was expected to live under a monastic code. The main aim of his life was "to know God and Jesus Christ." He was to read the Scriptures twice a day, and not to "intrude or inter-meddle on other men's affairs." He couldn't use tobacco without permission of the president or prescription of a physician, and then only "in a sober and private manner."

The infant college, however, was not free from the taint of "willfulle heresie." Obstinate President Dunster would not renounce nor conceal his opposition to infant baptism. A grand jury removed him from office for "poisoning the minds of his students and thus unfitting them to become preachers of the truth." By the 18th century the college had fallen into decay. Buildings were dilapidated, the student body reduced. Available funds did not amount to £1000.

Cambridge was primitive. The forest was nearby. There was good wildfowling along the Charles. The town had less than 250 taxable residents. "A great many bears are killed at Cambridge and the neighboring towns about this time," wrote Harvard man and historian Jeremy Belknap (1744–98).

Revolutionary Cambridge

Wealthy aristocratic families gave social strength to the Congregational Church. Phippses, Inmans, Vassals, Sewalls, Lees, Ruggles, Olivers and Lechmeres were in "comfortable circumstances." Luxurious town houses lined Brattle Street way into Watertown. The street became known as Tory Row.

Tories were unpopular in Cambridge. In 1768 delegates from the provinces' 95 organized towns met in protest in Faneuil Hall—among them two Cambridge delegates. On March 8, 1770, the Meeting House bell tolled while Boston Massacre victims were carried through the Hub's streets to their final resting places. Cambridge, despite efforts by Tory moderator William Brattle to prevent it, elected a Revolutionary Committee of Ten. The night following Boston's Tea Party, thousands of Cambridge revolutionists assembled outside the courthouse. They forced the Crown officials including the High Sheriff, judges and councillors to resign.

It was a chillish April night when hoofbeats echoed through the stillness—rider William Dawes Jr. (1745–99) was on his mission to warn outlaws John Hancock and Samuel Adams, both hiding in Lexington, that the British were coming. Paul Revere clattered through on his way to becoming a temporary prisoner. Minutemen hastened to Cambridge.

Before the week's end a rude 20,000-man "rag, tag and bobtail" army gathered in Cambridge, now Continental Army headquarters.

Shortly after the Battle of Breed's Hill—misnamed the Battle of Bunker Hill—Cambridge citizens and a light horse troop gathered by the Watertown road. They were met by Gen. George Washington, newly commissioned by the Continental Congress as commander-in-chief. A sign there now reads:

Near this Spot
on July 3, 1775
George Washington
took command of the American Army

On January 1, 1776, a new flag of thirteen stars was unfurled over the camp. On March 2 cannon fire announced that the bombardment of Boston had begun. The Continentals expected a British counterattack, but on the 17th British troops accompanied by the despised Tories left the city. Gen. Washington moved his GHQ to New York. Cambridge's military days were over.

College life flowed quietly along. The church gave impulse to the college, the college gave impulse to the town. A major scandal occurred when the Rev. Abiel Holmes, who wrote the *Annals of America* (1805) and was the father of Dr. O. W. Holmes and grandfather of Justice O. W. Holmes, Jr., was turned out of his pulpit in the First Church when his parishioners switched from Congregationalism to Unitarianism.

Dr. Oliver Wendell Holmes, the kindly, talkative, cocky "Autocrat of the Breakfast Table," was a disarming wit, too sensitive to continue practicing medicine — he was a Harvard Medical School professor — despite his discovery of the cause of childbirth fever. He entered upon a new career — literature. Associated with him was Henry Wadsworth Longfellow (1807–82). Longfellow was a Harvard oddity — a Bowdoin graduate. No poems of the era entered more deeply into the lives of the people than his. Before 1900 his *Psalm of Life* would be translated into 15 languages. Cambridge schoolchildren took up a subscription to give him a chair made from the wood of the "spreading chestnut tree."

Now appeared the literary journal, the *North American Review* (1815–1939), which was an outgrowth of the *Monthly Anthology and Boston Review* (1803–11) and was close to Harvard and the spreading Unitarianism. The magazine, soon to be eclipsed by Boston's *Atlantic Monthly*, moved to New York City in 1878. Next came *The Dial* (1840–44) edited by Margaret Fuller, the short-lived journal of the Transcendental Club. Two famous presses, the *Riverside* and *Harvard University*, were practical factors in Cambridge's literary domination.

Cambridge's history is peppered with names of scholars, historians and scientists like Henry Adams, John Gorham Palfrey (1796–1881), George Ticknor (1791–1871) and many others.

Radcliffe was created, unofficially, in 1879, as a mere association of Harvard instructors, who agreed that in response to popular demand they would give women "some opportunity for systematic study in courses parallel to those of the University." There was no official connection with Harvard until 1894. In that year the college was named after Ann Radcliffe of England, donor of the first Harvard scholarship fund. The school was long known among the irreverent as Harvard Annex. Serious qualms were felt by respectable citizenry at the idea of "hosts of young women walking unescorted through the town."

MIT

Massachusetts Institute of Technology, possibly the world's foremost technical and engineering school, commenced life in 1865 as a small Boston school "for practical science." Its founder, geologist William Barton Rogers, in proposing the formation of the school, wrote in 1846:

> I doubt not that such a nucleus school would, with the growth of this active and knowledge-seeking community, finally expand into a great institution comprehending the whole field of physical sciences and the arts with the auxiliary branches of the mathematics and modern languages, and would soon overtop the universities of the land in the accuracy and the extent of its teachings in all branches of positive knowledge.

Though chartered in 1861 the Civil War delayed the opening until 1865 when 6 professors and 15 students met for the first classes. The school, located about Boston's Copley Square, was known as "Boston Tech" until its move to Cambridge in 1916.

Three days of pageantry attended the move across the Charles River. Notables Franklin D. Roosevelt and Senator Henry Cabot Lodge, both Harvard men, together with telephone inventor Alexander Graham Bell and plane inventor Orville Wright, were spectators. The MIT seal and charter were carried across the Charles River in the *Bucentaur,* a replica of the Venetian state barge. A professor clad as Christopher Columbus paced the quarterdeck. The landing party was greeted by a professor dressed as Merlin the Magician. Five hundred singers accompanied by a 100-member orchestra competed with fireworks for the attention of the spectators.

MIT has five schools: Engineering, Science, Humanities and Social Science, the Alfred P. Sloan School of Management and the School of Architecture and City Planning. More than 7000 students — and the faculty of 1500 — have access to nearly 1,000,000 volumes in the Institute's libraries. About 300 women attend MIT.

MIT, in addition to its classic role of education, is making substantial contributions through research in fields like electronics, high voltage engineering, naval architecture, computer technology, solar energy, spectroscopy, biology, nuclear science, aeronautics, astronautics and servomechanisms. More than 70 laboratories are continually involved in basic and practical research. Notable facilities include the Computation Center, Laboratory for Nuclear Science and the Research Laboratory for Electronics. MIT and Harvard jointly operate the 6,000,000,000 electron volt Cambridge Electron Generator. This, of course, is the largest generator in the world.

Major teaching and research facilities include Van de Graaf electrostatic generators, ship model towing tank and the National Magnet Laboratory which can produce the world's largest magnetic field. MIT, together with eight other universities, operates Brookhaven National Laboratories on Long Island, N.Y., and the Radio Astronomy Observatory, Green Bank, West Va.

Cambridge, the Industrial City — the site of many major research organizations and industries — began when Washington was President. Far-sighted men erected buildings on the edge of a marsh in the far corner of the town and reclaimed the then useless mud flats along the river where great industrial plants stand today.

A minor but exciting incident occurred in the last century when town dignitaries were hoisted to a temporary platform on the just completed 124-foot high chimney of the New England Glass Company. There the dignitaries were dined and entertained.

Harvard Tour

Harvard University began a lustrous history in 1636 with half of John Harvard's estate (£ 780) and all 320 volumes of his library. It is the United States' oldest university. Originally a school for the education of Puritan ministers, it now contains Harvard College and graduate schools of divinity, law, arts and sciences, education, engineering, public administration, business administration, medicine, public health, and dental health. As the '70s opened it had a total enrollment of over 15,000 students.

Wadsworth House (semiprivate, housing the Alumni Association), edge of Harvard Yard opposite Holyoke St., built in 1726, is a typical yellow clapboard two-and-a-half-story Colonial house of considerable dignity with a brick ell. Harvard presidents from Wadsworth to Leverett lived here. George Washington stayed here for a time in 1775.

Harvard Yard, the university campus and original center of the college, has retained most of its Old World charm. It is similar to Lincoln's, Fields and Gray's Inn, in London, and is contemporary with them. It shares their characteristic blending of Georgian stateliness and mellowed red brick. Contemporary additions are adapted to their surroundings. It is one of the most beautiful, if indeed not the most beautiful, college campuses in America.

Widener Memorial Library (open to scholars and qualified researchers by special permission) is a memorial by the family of former Harvard man Harry Elkins Widener (1885–1912) who went down with the *Titanic.* The world's largest university library, it is one of the finest research libraries in existence.

Lamont Library (1949) is for undergraduate use.

New Yard, which Widener Library faces, is bounded on the east by *Sever Hall,* on the north by *Memorial Church* and on the west by *University Hall* and was the scene of the 1939 Tercentenary exercises.

University Hall (1813–15), designed by Charles Bulfinch, is one of the most beautiful buildings in the Yard. Its gray Chelmsford granite body, white wood pilasters and white chimneys provide an excellent foil for the Georgian red brick which surrounds it. The *Faculty Room,* with its tall windows, white wainscoting and attractive walls, is considered by many to be the handsomest room in the university.

John Harvard Statue (in front of University Hall), done by Daniel Chester French (1850–1931), is an imaginary likeness. No known portrait of John Harvard is known to exist.

Massachusetts Hall, erected in 1720 with funds granted by the Province of Massachusetts, was designed by President John Leverett. The oldest Harvard building, it is the archetype of later buildings. Standing opposite University Hall, but endlong to it, Massachusetts Hall plays a lesser part in the general impression of the Yard than the houses which face directly on the Yard. Simple in line, it has an air of great solidity.

Harvard Hall (north of Massachusetts Hall and parallel with it), built in 1766 from the design of Sir Francis Barnard, has been largely spoiled by 1842 and 1870 additions.

Hollis and *Stoughton Halls,* to the north — almost identical twins — built from the designs of Colonel Thomas Dawes.

Holworthy Hall (1812), which closes the north end of the Yard, does the most, along with University, Hollis and Stoughton Halls, to give the Yard its character. It was named for Sir Matthew Holworthy, an English benefactor of the college. Its architect was Loammi Baldwin (1780–1838).

Holden Chapel (between Hollis and Stoughton) is a tiny building of which the most conspicuous feature is the huge coat of arms (much imitated in the new college houses) which adorns the bright blue gable of the eastern end. It is also the best small example of pure Georgian Colonial architecture to be seen in the Yard and one of the finest in America. Built in 1744, its plans were probably drawn in London.

Appleton Chapel or *Memorial Church* (open daily), built in 1932 as a War Memorial for Harvard men, was designed by Coolidge, Shepley, Bulfinch and Abbott. *Memorial Room* commemorates the 373 Harvard men who died in WWI. Low-relief figures on the north wall are by Joseph Coletti. The sculptured group is by Malvina Hoffman.

Robinson Hall (1901) was designed by McKim, Mead and White. The entrance is properly from the south, the side which faces Emerson Hall, which, together with Sever Hall and the Fogg Museum (across Quincy St.), forms *Sever Quadrangle,* one of the pleasantest quadrangles in the Yard and the scene of Harvard commencements.

Sever Hall (1880) was designed by H. H. Richardson.

Emerson Hall (1905), designed by Coolidge, Shepley, Bulfinch and Abbott for the philosophy department, is a somewhat heavy building whose massive brick columns and pilasters, of Doric design, dominate Sever Quadrangle from the south. Beyond this, in the southeast corner of the Yard, are the *President's House* (private) (1912), a brick Colonial home designed by Coolidge, Shepley, Bulfinch and Abbott, and the *Dana-Palmer House* (private) (1820), built by Thomas Foster. To the west of this, behind Widener, and somewhat cramped for room, is *Wigglesworth Hall* (1931), which together with *Straus Hall* in the southwest corner of the Yard and *Lionel* and *Mower Halls* in the northwest (1926–31) are modern additions to the Yard, showing on the whole a very skillful adaptation of Massachusetts Hall.

Memorial Hall (open), the one true monstrosity in all the Harvard group, is an immense pile of red brick in Victorian Gothic style, with a gargoyled tower that partly burned in 1956. Dedicated as a memorial to Harvard men who died in the Civil War and built between 1870 and 1878 from the designs of Ware and Van Brunt, this remarkable building is fascinating if only as a monument in a style now wholly discredited.

Busch-Reisinger Museum (open weekdays 9–5, closed Sundays and holidays, closed Sat. and Sun. in summer), formerly known as the Germanic Museum or Adolph Busch Hall, cor. Kirkland St. and Divinity Ave. This museum, built with funds largely contributed by genial St. Louis brewer of Busch Bavarian Beer, Adolph Busch, is a curious limestone building with red tile roof. It was done from designs by Professor Germain Bestelmeyer of Munich, in pre-WWI Munich "kunstlerisch" style, the designs then being adapted for the local environment by Dean H. Langford Warren, Harvard School of Architecture. The low clock tower is impressive.

Exhibits include Middle Ages, Renaissance and contemporary examples of Germanic art. There are excellent reproductions of great Germanic medieval sculpture which are found nowhere else in America.

Fogg Art Museum (open weekdays 9–5, closed holidays and Sun. except open the last Sun. of every month from Nov. through May, closed Sat. during July and Aug., free), Quincy St., across from Harvard Yard. For current information phone 495–2387. Exhibits include permanent collections of ancient, Oriental, Romanesque and Gothic sculpture and paintings. Many special exhibitions of painting and sculpture. Free lectures and concerts. Guided tours by appointment.

Peabody Museum of Archaeology and Ethnology (open weekdays 9–4:30, Sun. 1–4, closed July 4 and Christmas, free), Divinity Ave. off Kirkland St. This superb Harvard University Museum has an excellent collection of mid-19th century Navajo woven blankets and Eskimo and North American Indian artifacts, including totem poles. Sizable collection of material both primitive and contemporary from primitive — and some not so primitive — people from the Americas, Africa, Asia and Oceania. Model villages of American Indians, old South American Indian temples and Southwestern cliff dwellings.

Semitic Museum houses collections relating to the history and arts of Arabs, Aramaeans, Assyrians, Babylonians, Hebrews and Phoenicians. Assyrian reproductions include bas-reliefs from the palace of Ashurnazirpal II, King of Assyria (884–860 B.C.), and the Black Obelisk of Shalmaneser III (860–825 B.C.). In the Babylonian collection is the oldest known map, dating from 2500 B.C. and discovered by a Harvard expedition.

University Museum (open weekdays and holidays, 9–4:30, Sun. 1–4:30, closed July 4 and Christmas, free except Glass Flowers which has small fee, children under 16 admitted free when accompanied by an adult), Oxford St., is a six-story rambling brick structure. Its most celebrated and popular exhibit is that of the *Glass Flowers.* Glass models of the humbler flowers of field and wood are realistically reproduced with an astonishing delicacy of detail and complete botanic accuracy. The secret of this art was discovered in the 19th century by a German family named Blaschka, and it remains with them.

North American Birds form one of the most complete collections. *Harvard Forest Models* depict the history of land clearing and reforestation.

The building also houses Botanical, Mineralogical, Comparative Zoology, Geological and Peabody Museums.

Harvard Law School's headquarters is *Langdell Hall,* a two-story limestone building with an Ionic colonnade. This is the oldest law school in the United States. O. W. Holmes, Jr., and President Rutherford B. Hayes are but two of the many distinguished graduates. The school has the world's most complete law library.

Across the Charles River is *Harvard Business School* (graduate).

Harvard Stadium, 60 feet high and two city blocks long, is not the largest in the country but was the first, and, with its ivy-clad arches and classic colonnade, one of the most beautiful. It seats 22,000 on the concrete and with temporary seats can accommodate nearly 60,000.

Radcliffe Campus architecture derives from the Georgian, but the more modern buildings are tempered with a strain of refinement — especially in interior work — which distinguishes and feminizes them.

Fay House, the Administration Building, is the oldest structure. It was built in 1807 by Nathaniel Ireland as a private home from, according to tradition, designs by Charles Bulfinch. *Agassiz House* and *Bertram Hall* were designed by Henry Wadsworth Longfellow.

Cambridge Observatory of Harvard University (open weekdays 9–5, closed Sun. and holidays), 60 Garden St.

There is a public exhibit of *Astronomical Pictures* on glass plates lighted from behind. These are magnified examples of some 400,000 glass plates made in studying variations of celestial objects. This collection is studied by astronomers from all over the world. The beehive-like houses in the Cambridge grounds are shelters for powerful photographic telescopes and sky-patrol cameras, which on every clear night swing the circuit of the universe, noting everything that happens for billions of miles.

Harvard has made some equally remarkable contributions to modern architecture, including the *Harkness Commons and Graduate Center* (1950) (just north of the Law School's Langdell Hall) by Harvard's Walter Gropius and Architects Collaborative; the *Carpenter Center for the Visual Arts* (1963) (Quincy St. next to the Fogg Art Museum), the only building by Le Corbusier on the North American continent; the *William James Hall* (1964) (Divinity Ave. and Kirkland St.) by Minoru Yamasaki.

Historic Cambridge

Brattle Mansion (open) is a three-story clapboard, gambrel-roof house. For many years after its erection (1727) it was a Cambridge showplace. Margaret Fuller lived here for a time (see CONCORD).

Village Smithy Site, immortalized by Longfellow's poem, is marked by a tablet on the corner of Story Street.

The Window Shop (open), 56 Brattle St., was built in 1811 as the home of Dexter Pratt, the village blacksmith ("The smith, a mighty man is he").

Read House (private), 55 Brattle St., was built in 1725. It is a two-and-a-half-story frame dwelling with a white doorway.

Samuel Longfellow's Home (private), 76 Brattle St., is a two-and-a-half-story brown frame dwelling with a flat-roofed ell. Its onetime owner, brother of the famous poet, wrote several fine hymns still in general use.

John Fiske House (private), corner of Ash St., is a Victorian dwelling with a tower, which the eminent historian (1842–1901) was building at the time of his sudden death. An early champion of the then heretical theory of evolution, Fiske was not invited to teach at Harvard. After the university embraced the theory it still thought Fiske a little too "popular" to adorn its faculty but awarded him an honorary degree.

Belcher House (private), 94 Brattle St., is an impressive yellow frame mansion, with a mansard roof and white roof rail. Having both east and west main entrances, it could easily be mistaken for a double house. The west end was constructed first — some experts say as early as 1635 because of the use of shell plaster in its chimney. The east end dates from 1700. The house has been altered, but it is still a dignified example of large Colonial homes.

Craigie-Longfellow House (open Mon.–Fri. 10–5, Sat. and Sun. 1–5, Nov.–Apr.; Mon–Fri., 10–4, Sat. and Sun. 2–4, May–Oct.; small fee), 105 Brattle St., built in 1759 by future Tory Major John Vassall, was Gen. Washington's Cambridge headquarters (July 1775–April 1776). Poet Longfellow lived here for many years. The house is a three-story square yellow clapboard mansion with white Ionic pilasters, a white roof rail and yellow brick chimneys capped with ornamental hoods. Side piazzas on the east and west overlook wide lawns. A small park runs almost to the Charles River.

This was one of the seven famous houses that made up Tory Row. When Major Vassall fled to Boston in 1774, Gen. Washington made the house his headquarters. Martha Washington joined him in December, and on January 6 they celebrated their wedding anniversary here. Later the house was occupied by Dr. Andrew Craigie, who added the banquet hall behind the study and entertained lavishly.

Longfellow came here in 1837, in his second year of teaching at Harvard. His study at that time had once been Washington's private chamber. Here the poet wrote "Hyperion," "The Wreck of the Hesperus" and other early poems. Here he brought his second bride, Frances Appleton, whose father gave them the house as a wedding present. In 1845 the poet's study was transferred to the right-hand front room on the lower floor. In the hall outside the room stands *The Old Clock on the Stairs.*

Until his death some years ago the house was occupied by Longfellow's grandson Henry Wadsworth Longfellow Dana. Controversial Dana, a descendant of lawyer and novelist Richard Henry Dana (1815–82), was a leading authority on the Soviet Union's theater and films.

Longfellow Park, opposite Craigie-Longfellow House, was given to the city by his family and friends. At the lower end of the park stands a *Memorial Monument* by Daniel Chester French, embellished in bas-relief with figures of some of the poet's best-known characters, including "The Village Blacksmith," "Myles Standish," "Evangeline" and "Hiawatha."

Old Burying Ground (open daily) dates from 1636. Dexter Pratt, Longfellow's "village smith," is buried here.

Site of the House of Stephen Daye. He was the first printer in British America. He arrived in 1638 and set up his press under the auspices of Harvard. His press is now in the Vermont Historical Society's museum.

The *"Bishop's Palace"* (Apthorp House) (private), half hidden in a courtyard and reached by a footpath, is a three-story mansion built in 1760 by the first minister of Christ Church (Episcopal) and named irreverently by provincial dissenters. It is now the residence of the Master of Adams House, the nearest to the Yard of the "New Houses."

Cambridge Historical Society (open Thurs. 3–5, small fee) (1660), 159 Brattle St., is in the Nichols-Lee House. The house was once occupied by Joseph Lee, a mild, kindly Tory who thought best to flee during the Revolution, but who was such a general favorite as a citizen that he was allowed to return at its end without confiscation of his property. When he died at over 90 years of age the entire city mourned.

An excavation shows the massive 12-foot square chimney. Interesting exhibit of French wallpapers.

American Thomas Lee's House (private) (1685), 153 Brattle St., is one of several sumptuous and beautiful old mansions to be seen hereabout.

Baroness Riedesel's House (private), 149 Brattle St., was the home of Baron and Baroness Riedesel, prisoners in the Revolutionary War. The baron was Burgoyne's chief staff officer at Saratoga, and the redheaded baroness' gay and vivid letters about her social life in Cambridge show that the city treated her well, despite its Revolutionary sympathies. After the baroness left, Washington gave the house to "English Thomas Lee," a Tory who changed over to the American cause. English Thomas was so named to distinguish him from his neighbor "American Thomas Lee."

Oliver Wendell Holmes' Birthplace is marked by a granite tablet within the triangular green opposite the common (Massachusetts Ave.). Here as a young physician he first displayed his shingle, on which he considered inscribing: "The smallest fevers thankfully received."

Shady Hill (private), 136 Irving St., is a broad two-story mansion (1790) with a long front piazza. Charles Eliot Norton (1827–1908), Harvard professor of art, lived here.

CANTON (Norfolk County, sett. 1630, incorp. 1797, alt. 100, pop. 17,100, area 19.01 sq. mi., town meeting, routes, I-95, Fall River Expressway, Mass. 128, 138) received its name because of the whim of a prominent citizen who estimated that the town was exactly antipodal to Canton, China. In the late 18th and early 19th centuries, the town was a manufacturing center. Muskets for the War of 1812 were made here.

Plymouth Rubber Mill (open), Revere St., on the site of a foundry Paul Revere set up in 1808, was the first copper-rolling mill in the country. It supplied the rolled copper for the State House dome and the boilers for Fulton's first steamboat. Revere operated a powder mill here during the Revolution and the War of 1812.

Canton industries include Draper Bros. Co., Instron Corp., Emerson & Cuming, Groveton Papers Company, Duval Corp. and Nexus Corp.

BLUE HILLS RESERVATION: Golf, nature museums, freshwater fishing, beaches, foot and bridle trails, band concerts, playgrounds, picnic sites, ice skating, skiing, observation tower. See BLUE HILLS RESERVATION.

CARLISLE (Middlesex County, sett. *c.* 1650, incorp. 1805, alt. 200, pop. 2871, area 15.37 sq. mi., town meeting, route, Mass. 225) was named for the Scottish birthplace of James Adams, who, banished by Oliver Cromwell for political offenses, became the first settler. About 1850 the farmers successfully objected to vegetation-killing fumes from a local copper smelter.

Residential Carlisle has many commuting scientists.

Old Wheat Tavern (private), Westford St. (Mass. 225) facing the town green, was originally a station on the Boston and Vermont post road.

CARVER (Plymouth County, sett. 1660, incorp. 1790, alt. 96, pop. 2420, area 38.41 sq. mi., town meeting, routes, US 44, Mass. 58), cranberry-producing center of the United States, has more than 3000 acres of cranberries within the town's corporate limits.

Rural Carver's principal tourist attraction, the *Edaville Railroad and Railroad Museum,* is located in South Carver off Mass. 58.

The Edaville RR is a 5.5-mile-long strip of narrow gauge (24-inch wide) track which takes travelers through cranberry bogs. The original purpose of the railroad was to haul cranberries from selected pickup sites in the extensive bogs to a central location. The railroad and bog owner, however, decided to attract additional dollars by establishing sightseeing trips through the bogs. He created tiny villages along the way. The engines, all steam cars, and the coaches, freight cars, are all scaled to the narrow gauge roadbed. Rolling stock was secured from many sources including narrow gauge passenger lines, freight lines and lumber camps.

Train schedule: May 30–Sept. 9, 10 A.M.–4 P.M., Sept. 9–Sept. 16, 12 noon–4 P.M., Sundays throughout the year, 12 noon–4 P.M. During the Christmas season (Thanksgiving–Jan. 1) trains run all day, including evening, to view special Christmas lighting arrangements. Small fee.

Railroad Museum (open same hours as railroad operates, small fee) contains the Locomotive Historical Society's collection of rolling stock. There are antique fire engines and guns.

NORTH CARVER, a peaceful farming community, was named for John Carver, first governor of Plymouth Colony.

CENTERVILLE (see BARNSTABLE)

CENTRAL VILLAGE (see WESTPORT)

CHARLEMONT (Franklin County, sett. *c.* 1742, incorp. 1765, alt. 584, pop. 897, town meeting, routes, Mass. 2, 8A), once known as Charley Mount, is a farming town. Dairying, fruit and vegetable growing and beekeeping are the main sources of income. Some seasonal income is derived from maple sugar groves.

Charlemont, now a popular winter sports center, is a Mohawk Trail town, readily accessible from Boston and other Massachusetts metropolitan areas.

One of the state's four covered bridges still in use is located north of Mass. 2. A sign at the junction of the Mass. 8A road and Mass. 2 directs the visitor to *Bissell Covered Bridge.*

CHICKLEY ALPS SKI AREA (Mass. 8A off Mass. 2) has 10 trails for novice, intermediate and expert, 4 open slopes, 4 rope tows, warming hut, canteen. Open weekends and holidays.

MOHAWK TRAIL STATE FOREST, Mass. 2, offers cabins, fishing, hiking, hunting, fireplaces, picnic tables, campsites, snowmobiles, and swimming.

SAWMILL HILL SKI AREA has a J-bar lift, 10-acre open slope, two 1600′ trails, base lodge with snack bar, night skiing.

THUNDER MOUNTAIN SKI AREA (off Mass. 2) has 2 double chair lifts, 2 T-bar lifts, rope tows, 6 trails, 2 open slopes, novice area, summit house, base lodge, cafeteria, ski shop, ski rentals, dancing, entertainment, day and night ice skating, nursery, snow-making equipment, rooms, meals.

ZOAR (unnumbered route north of Mass. 2), a locality in Charlemont, has about six houses, several barns and a chicken house.

CHARLESTOWN (see BOSTON)

CHARLTON (Worcester County, sett. *c.* 1735, incorp. 1754, alt. 895, pop. 4654, area 42.86 sq. mi., town meeting, routes US 20, Mass. 31), named for Sir Francis Charlton, a privy councilor of England. Agriculture is the chief means of livelihood. The lack of waterpower hinders industrial development.

On the common is a *Memorial to William Thomas Green Morton* (1819–68) (see BOSTON), given by the dentists of America to honor the man whose experiments with ether first made anesthesia possible during surgical operations. He started experiments to enable him to extract deep roots of teeth, working with Dr. Charles T. Jackson, a dentist. Dr. Morton did his first tooth extraction with ether on September 30, 1846, and a month later gave a public demonstration at the Massachusetts General Hospital for a major operation. Dr. Morton was born in Charlton.

The *Masonic Home,* north of the center on a broad hill, is one of the finest of fraternal homes for the aged in New England.

The old *Burying Ground* (1750), Main St., now called Bay Path Cemetery, contains three *Photograph Stones*—headstones provided with small glass-covered niches in which were placed daguerreotypes of the deceased. Once the vogue, few of these curious stones now remain.

Also buried here was *James Capen Adams* (1807–60), better known as "Grizzly" Adams, one of the last of that wonderful breed, "the Mountain

Men." When he headed West in 1852, Adams was a discontented 45-year-old cobbler. During his eight remaining years he became a friend and slayer of grizzly bears. He survived several hand-to-claw-and-fang encounters. Showman Phineas T. Barnum signed Grizzly for a successful tour. Adams died with his boots on in bed in Neponset, Massachusetts, "a fur piece" from his beloved Rockies.

Adams, like many another wandering Yankee, was buried in his native state. A carved bas-relief of buckskin-clad Grizzly—ordered by PT himself—decorates his headstone.

CHATHAM (Barnstable County, sett. 1656, incorp. 1712, alt. 59, pop. 4554, town meeting, route, Mass. 28) named for William Pitt, the first Earl of Chatham.

Chatham Village, on the Cape's south shore outside of the elbow, passed resolutions forbidding tea usage but citizens voted against the Declaration of Independence. Chatham industries have been fishing, whaling, shipbuilding, saltworks and shoe factories. Today, tourism is the major business.

At the center, on the corner of Main St., is the *Congregational Church* (open daily) (1830), a fine example of early architecture, containing two unusual modern murals by Alice Stallknecht Wight. One represents a Chatham fisherman preaching from a beached dory. The other depicts a church supper, at which all the participants are Chatham people, neighbors of the artist.

Chatham Shore Drive, bordered by stately homes, provides a marvelous view of the harbor, the shoals and the ocean beyond. The former *Summer Home of Joseph C. Lincoln* (private) is a gambrel-roofed house behind a well-kept privet hedge.

Chatham Light (open) and *Mack Memorial Shaft.* The monument was erected in memory of a life-saving crew, commanded by Captain Mack, that set off in heavy seas to rescue the crew of a wrecked fishing vessel. All but one were drowned, and old-timers say that he was so ashamed of being rescued that he would neither discuss the tragedy nor accept commendation. A sunrise service is held Easter mornings on the bluffs by the lighthouse.

Atwood House (open late June–early Sept., Mon., Wed., Fri., Sat. 2–5 P.M.) (1752), 1 mi. s. of Mass. 28, is the town's oldest surviving house. It contains an interesting model saltworks.

Chatham RR Museum, open June 15–wk after Labor Day, Mon., Wed., Fri. 2–5 P.M., donations), in former RR station on Depot St. Model trains, photographs of old trains, old railway telegraphic equipment.

Fish Pier. Sport fishermen (stripers, snappers, bluefish) headquarters. Commercial fishermen return daily with their catch.

Famous summer residents have included U.S. Supreme Court Justice Louis D. Brandeis (1856–1941), Cape Cod novelist Joseph C. Lincoln (1870–1944) and Professor Arthur M. Schlesinger (1888–1965). Summer homes of actress Shirley Booth and General Lucius Clay.

MONOMOY POINT NATIONAL WILDLIFE REFUGE. Once the greatest gunning spot on the eastern seaboard for fall and spring brant shooting. Now that the eel grass has disappeared, brant rarely come. No shooting now. Excellent surf casting for bass.

CHELMSFORD (Middlesex County, sett. 1633, incorp. 1655, alt. 150, pop. 31,432, area 22.54 sq. mi., town meeting, routes, US 3, Mass. 4, 27, 110) named for Chelmsford in Essex, England. At the Battle of Bunker Hill, resident Joseph Spalding described firing the first shot. "I fired the shot ahead of time and General Putnam rushed up and struck me for violating orders. I suppose I deserved it, but I was anxious to get another shot at Gage's men ever since our affair at Concord. The blow from Old Put hit me on the head, made a hole in my hat, and left me a scar."

Early 19th-century mills produced lumber, corn, powder and cotton cloth; the textile factory later produced woolen cloth. An iron foundry processed bog ore, mined as early as 1656. Ice harvesting and granite quarrying have also been important to the town's prosperity.

Fiske House (private) (1790), at the corner of Littleton and Billerica Sts., is a clapboard structure with brick ends, and four end chimneys. Originally a tavern, its bar and early furnishings have been preserved.

Unitarian Church (1840) of the First Congregational Society (organized 1644), the fourth church on the site, has a red-brick base, white wood front, clapboard sides and a steeple with an open belfry and a four-faced clock. The first pastor, Rev. John Fiske, came from Wenham in 1655, bringing most of his flock. He was the author of the "Chelmsford Catechism," the only known copy of which is in the New York Public Library.

Adjacent to a school is the *Deacon Otis Adams House* (private) where in 1866 a school for the deaf, using the purely oral method, was established. Pupil Mabel Hubbard married Alexander Graham Bell.

Spaulding House (private), corner of North and Dalton Rds., was the home of Col. Simeon Spaulding, a member of the 1775 Provincial Congress. This two-and-a-half-story white frame house with its large central chimney has been subjected to mid-Victorian renovations; garish ornaments and oddly cut decorations in wood have been attached to its gables and slopes at every possible point.

SOUTH CHELMSFORD (alt. 220). Here in 1835 Ezekial Byam manufactured lucifer matches that had to be scratched on sandpaper and were sold at 25¢ a hundred. The business moved to Boston in 1848.

CHELSEA (Suffolk County, sett. 1624, town incorp. 1739, city incorp. 1857, alt. 10, pop. 30,625, area 1.86 sq. mi., mayor-council, routes US 1, Mass. 1A, 28, 107, Mystic River Toll Bridge).

Historic Chelsea, once a city of lovely homes and noted for Chelsea clocks, is a major junkyard center.

The city, now undergoing an extensive urban renewal program, has large "salvage yards," heel-making and printing plants.

Many of the city's lovely homes and fine mercantile establishments were destroyed in a fire during the mid-1890's.

A century's upbuilding vanished in smoke. Because of a heavy gale, the flames spread with remarkable rapidity. Within ten hours all buildings burned were in ruins. The city was a devastated waste. Seventeen thousand four hundred and fifty people were homeless. It is said that in the entire burned area there was not enough combustible material left to start a kitchen fire.

In the reconstruction of the city, the business section was considerably enlarged and the population took on a decidedly cosmopolitan cast. Today Irish Catholics, Jews, Italians, Poles and Armenians represent over 90 percent of the population.

Two of the city's three hills are topped by hospitals, *U.S. Naval Hospital* and *Chelsea Memorial Hospital.* The third hill, Powderhorn, has a *Soldiers Home.* Gen. George Washington viewed the British occupation of Breed's Hill — the mount where the Battle of Bunker Hill was actually fought.

Local legend says rags-to-riches writer Horatio Alger (1834–99) was born here, but records including the Bureau of Vital Statistics in the State House give Revere as his birthplace.

USAF Major-General William H. Blanchard (1916) is said to have been born in Chelsea.

Abraham Lincoln personally campaigned here.

City Hall, Broadway, in Bellingham Square, is in the Georgian Colonial style, its design having been based on that of Independence Hall in Philadelphia.

The *Thomas Pratt House* (occasional visitors welcome), (*c.* 1662), 481 Washington Ave., occupied by a descendant of the original owner, sits back from the road, its steep, sloping roof and huge chimneys distinguishing it from the modern dwellings which surround it.

The *Bellingham-Cary House* (open Thur. 2–5 and 7–9), 34 Parker St., is a square hip-roofed frame house with interior chimneys. The original portion was built in 1629 and was at one time the home of Governor Bellingham. It was remodeled by Samuel Cary in 1791–92 and was purchased by the Cary House Association in 1912. In it Washington quartered the last outpost of the left wing of the Continental Army besieging Boston.

Samuel Cabot Company, 229 Marginal St., pioneer in chemical experimentation. It is famous for its shingle stain and paint researches.

CHESHIRE (Berkshire County, sett. 1766, incorp. 1793, alt. 963, pop. 3006, area 27.06 sq. mi., town meeting, Mass. 8, 116) has always depended on dairying. In 1801 a local cheese weighing 1235 pounds was laboriously carted down to President Jefferson by admirers. The town has had small saw-, grist- and iron mills — and for about 100 years local calcium carbonate has been mined and made into lime.

The *Cole House* (open), opposite the Baptist Church, was built about 1804. The two-and-a-half-story structure with central chimney has a "Christian" door with eight panels forming a double cross — supposed to protect the house against witchcraft. In 1809 the house was a meeting place for the Franklin Masonic Lodge. Some years ago, under five layers of wallpaper, Masonic emblems were found — the royal arch, beehive, Bible-balance, square and compass — painted on the walls.

HORN'S BEACH RECREATIONAL AREA (Hoosac Lake) has an excellent beach house, swimming and a fine picnic area.

STAFFORD HILL WILDLIFE MANAGEMENT AREA has public hunting.

CHESTER (Hampden County, sett. 1760, incorp. 1783, alt. 1200, pop. 1025, area 36.76 sq. mi., town meeting, routes, US 20, Mass. 112) was incorporated as Murrayfield after the proprietors' treasurer John Murray. Some years later citizens voted to change the name to Chester.

Farming, including maple sugar production, the mining of mica, emery and corundum and granite quarrying have been major occupations. *Hamilton Memorial Library* has a large collection of minerals.

CHESTER STATE FOREST (2328 acres), Mass. 20, has scenic Sanderson Brook. Facilities: hiking trails, hunting, trout fishing, fireplaces, picnic tables. The *Boulder Park* section, on the south side of US 20 between Huntington and Chester, has a swimming pool and bathhouse.

CANADA HILL WILDLIFE MANAGEMENT AREA includes parts of Worthington, Chester, and Huntington for public hunting.

CHESTERFIELD (Hampshire County, sett. *c.* 1760, incorp. 1762, alt. 1427, pop. 704, route, Mass. 143), originally New Hingham, possibly was named for the polished Earl of Chesterfield. Farming and cattle raising have always been prominent activities. The forests encourage lumbering.

WEST CHESTERFIELD is on the East Branch of the Westfield River. Families — an average of ten children per family — were a prime crop in the early days. Today, potato and dog raising are the area's industries.

CHESTERFIELD GORGE (61 acres) is owned and maintained by TOR. The rugged scenery is created by the passage of the Westfield River through a narrow chasm. Picnic tables and fireplaces. Small fee.

CHICOPEE (Hampden County, sett. 1638, town incorp. 1848, city incorp. 1890, alt. 93, pop. 66,676, area 20.10 sq. mi., mayor-board of aldermen, routes, Mass. Turnpike, US 5, I–91 and I–391).

Chicopee, one of the oldest communities in western Massachusetts, produces tires, sporting goods, electronic components, machinery, surgical dressings and electrical equipment. Chicopee's more than 100 diversified industries include printing the *Wall Street Journal.*

During the Civil and western Indian Wars, Chicopee was famed for its cavalry sabres made by the Ames Manufacturing Co. Troopers often talked of giving their opponent "Chicopee Steel," the equivalent of slashing him — fatally if possible — with an Ames sabre.

Chicopee derived its name from the river named by local Indians. Chicopee River Indians were known as "Nipmucks," or "Fresh Water Indians." New England Indian authority John C. Huden gives the derivation as meaning "violent water," after the Chicopee River Falls. The suffix "pee" is an Algonkian word meaning "water." Mashpee, another Bay State town, has the meaning "water near the great cover" or "standing water."

The Chicopee River slashes through the city into the Connecticut River.

In 1641, Nippumsuit deeded land now included in Chicopee to William Pynchon for 90 feet of wampum and "one yard and three quarters of double shagg bags, one bow, seaven knifes, seaven payer of sessars and seaven owles with certaine fish hooks and other small things given at their request."

Farming was the major occupation until 1786 when several men including Benjamin Belcher, who was later to own the iron foundry, began to utilize the river's waterpower. Bog iron ore mining with blast furnaces to process the ore was the first major industry. In 1806 a paper mill was built. David Ames introduced machinery and is alleged to have invented the first rotary paper-making machinery. In 1822 Edmund Dwight, industrialist, philanthropist and coauthor of the Massachusetts School Law (1837), established large cotton mills here.

In 1829 Nathan Peabody Ames and his brother James established a plant for making table cutlery, swords and sabres. U.S. military swords and sabres had been previously purchased abroad. In 1853 the Ames Company established the first American factory for making bronze statuary. The famous bronze doors at the east and west wings of the Capitol building in Washington, D.C., were cast here.

The first friction "kitchen" matches, first known as "lucifers," were made in Chicopee in 1834 by the Chapin and Phillips Company.

On April 29, 1848, Chicopee, then Cabotville, separated from Springfield and was incorporated as a town.

Shoe manufacturer Albert G. Parker hid slaves and helped raise funds to purchase freedom for some slaves.

In 1864 inventor-gunsmith Joshua Stevens, who pioneered the manufacture of breech-loading shotguns, established the J. Stevens Arms Company. The firm was purchased in 1920 by the Savage Arms Corporation, Utica, N.Y., which moved its Utica, N.Y. plant to Chicopee in 1947. Savage and Stevens were major arms manufacturers for the United States and its allies during both World Wars. More than 1,500,000 Thompson submachine guns, 1,000,000 British S.M.L.E. rifles and 300,000 Browning machine guns were made by Savage during WWII. During WWI the firm made thousands of Lewis light machine guns. Savage moved to Westfield in 1959.

In 1887 Albert H. Overman, designer of the "Victor" bicycle, established the Overman Wheel Company. In 1894, about 75 percent of all U.S. bicycles were Chicopee-produced.

In 1895 the Spaulding & Pepper Company was formed to make rubber goods, specializing in pneumatic tires for bicycles. With the advent of the automobile this company pioneered and grew in stature by manufacturing automobile tires. This concern was purchased by Noyes W. Fisk in 1898. In 1939 the Fisk plant was acquired by the United States Rubber Company, presently known as UniRoyal, Inc. Some 30,000 tires daily are produced currently at the Chicopee plant.

The first gasoline automobile engine and subsequently the first gas-driven "buggy" was built in Chicopee. Charles E. Duryea designed and originated the gasoline car (1892) and operated it on experimental runs over Chicopee roads. More than 2200 Duryea cars were built here.

A. G. Spalding & Bros. Company was established (1901) for the manufacture of sporting goods by Albert Goodwill Spalding and James Spalding. The two brothers won fame as professional baseball players. The Spalding firm is the largest U.S. sporting goods manufacturer.

Nationally known Chicopee products include surgical dressings by Chicopee Manufacturing Company, a subsidiary of Johnson & Johnson, television electronic parts by F. W. Sickles, Division of General Instrument Corporation, and magneto and automotive parts by the American Bosch Arms Corporation.

Chicopee has been the home of *Westover Air Force Base* since 1939 when 6½ square miles of Chicopee land were acquired by the federal government for an air base. Westover was a WWII heavy bomber crews training base. It is now the largest Strategic Air Command base in the eastern United States.

Edward Bellamy (1850–98), author of *Looking Backward* (1888), was born in Chicopee Falls.

CHICOPEE MEMORIAL STATE PARK (1964), Burnett Road, has 115 fireplaces and picnic tables plus swimming facilities offering 300 yards of beach area and a large bathhouse in the old Cooley Brook Reservoir.

CHILMARK (Dukes County, Martha's Vineyard, sett. 1671, incorp. 1714, alt. 140, pop. 340, town meeting, located off Beetle Bung Rd.).

Chilmark, Tisbury and Elizabeth Island were granted in 1671 by patent, under the name of Tisbury Manor, to Thomas Mayhew, Sr., with the privileges of feudal lordship. Settlers were considered tenants and were required to pay quitrents. Mayhew, Jr., sold his privileges in 1685.

Menemsha, the village in Chilmark, is a small fishing village where the smell of bait ripening in the sun permeates the air. *Menemsha Pond* was connected with Menemsha Bight by the federal government to provide a harbor for the fishermen. Along the shores of this artificial saltwater pond are numerous fishermen's houses.

CLARKSBURG (Berkshire County, incorp. 1798, alt. 1051, pop. 1987, area 12.7 sq. mi., town meeting, routes, Mass. 2, 8).

BRIGGSVILLE, the trading center of Clarksburg, has many residents of Scottish descent who came here to work in the small textile mills.

CLARKSBURG STATE PARK (364 acres), 2 mi. north of North Adams on Mass. 8, has picnic tables, fireplaces, 48 campsites, boating, fishing and swimming (*Mausert's Pond*). Scenic views of Mt. Greylock and the Hoosac Range.

CLINTON (Worcester County, sett. 1654, incorp. 1850, alt. 325, pop. 13,383, town meeting, routes, Mass. 60, 70, 110).

Clinton is a residential industrial community on the periphery of metropolitan Worcester. An early profitable industry was the manufacture of coach lace. Bigelow carpets were made here (1848–1933). Lancaster Cotton Mills (1844–1930) were once the largest gingham makers in the world. Basic industries today include printing, metalwork and electrical machinery.

COHASSET (Norfolk County, sett. 1765, incorp. 1770, alt. 50, pop. 6954, area 9.86 sq. mi., town meeting, route, Mass. 3A), formerly part of Hingham, is one of New England's loveliest villages. Its history began with the landing of Capt. John Smith in 1614. At first, the town was just the summer pasture for Hingham's livestock. Fishing and farming were major trades (1737–1885), and the town was long a leading fishing port. Small vessels were built here from 1708–1889. Many inhabitants commute to Boston. The village is popular with summer residents.

The First Parish (Unitarian) Meetinghouse (1745), in the center of beautiful Cohasset Common, was originally the Second Parish Meetinghouse of Hingham (first built 1716). It is the fourth oldest Unitarian church in the U.S. *St. Stephen's Episcopal Church* (1900), with its famed carillon, contrasts oddly with the Colonial architecture. Nearby are three Cohasset Historical Society Museums: *Independence Gown Museum* (1850), originally the town's first fire station and later the police station, *Historic House* (*c.* 1800), and *Maritime Museum* (*c.* 1800), formerly a ship chandlery; all are open summers only.

MOORE'S ROCKS RESERVATION (owned and maintained by the Cohasset Historical Society), Jerusalem Road, commands a grand view of the

Atlantic Ocean and the many rocky ledges offshore, scene of several shipwrecks including that of the Danish ship *Maria* in 1793. On *Grampus Rocks,* 1.5 mi. offshore, the brig *St. John* of Galway foundered in 1849 and many Irish immigrants lost their lives. Tragedies brought about the *first U.S. lifeboat station* (1807) on Pleasant Beach and later the erection of *Minot's Light,* 2.5 mi. offshore. The original iron structure (1850) was destroyed and lost its two keepers in a gale in 1851. The present (1860) 114-foot-high granite tower was an engineering marvel in its time. Its 1–4–3 flash is a familiar Massachusetts Bay sight. This lighthouse was planned and assembled at *Government Island,* Cohasset.

John Smith Tablet commemorates the discoverer of Cohasset and bears excerpts from Smith's *Generall Historie* describing his Indian fight. *Elm Street,* between the common and the cove, was called "Captains' Row"; its mansions were the homes of Cohasset's sea captains and shipbuilders.

At the south end of Cohasset is the site of the first established home of the *Abraham Lincoln Family* (1685). Nearby is the famous Old Colony Boundary Line (1640), dividing the Massachusetts Bay and Plymouth Bay Colonies, the second oldest boundary in the U.S.

COLRAIN (Franklin County, sett. 1735, incorp. 1761, alt. 981, pop. 1420, town meeting, route, Mass. 112).

Colrain, settled by Scotch-Irish from northern Ireland, was presumably named for the Irish peer Lord Coleraine. About 1818 new mills brought French-Canadians who erected a Roman Catholic church, conducting services in French.

Sheep raising was an important pre-Civil War industry. Two absorbent gauze mills are the present industries. *Harp Elm,* formed like a gigantic lyre, stands at the entrance of the North River Cemetery.

A stone marks the *Site of Fort Morris* (1754–63).

The COLRAIN STATE FOREST (1244 acres) has some of the oldest surviving trees in the state.

COLRAIN VILLAGE has a pleasant aspect with a small triangular green, white inn, town hall, church, two stores and several houses.

EAST COLRAIN is a few houses and a church along the Green River.

GRISWALDVILLE (alt. 600) has surgical gauze plants.

LYONSVILLE (alt. 570) has the second of Colrain's two Kendall plants. The two plants employ about 500 workers. Many residents commute to nearby Vermont towns. In the village cemetery a *Boulder* commemorates Amasa and Rhoda Shippee, who in 1812 raised the first United States flag to fly over an American schoolhouse.

ADAMSVILLE no longer has any stores. There are a few houses and a sawmill along the banks of the West Branch of North River.

Chandler Hill, first village in Colrain, had 30 dwellings, but only one old house remains: the Apte family homestead. The site of the first church (1740) is designated by a stone marker. Just east of the church site is the first burying ground with markers back to 1736. Ancestors of Robert Fulton, builder of the first steamboat, are buried here.

CONCORD (Middlesex County, sett. *c.* 1635, incorp. 1635, alt. 130, pop. 16,148, area 25.77 sq. mi., town meeting, routes, Mass. 2, 2A, 62, 117, 119).

Concord, the town of Thoreau and Emerson, revolution and the Concord grape, is pleasantly situated where the Sudbury and Assabet Rivers become Concord River. The village, rich in historical and literary associations, is the site of the first day of the American Revolution — April 19, 1775. It was a haven for poets, novelists, essayists, naturalists and philosophers during the "Golden Age" of American literature.

This residential village retains a quiet Colonial atmosphere. The green is surrounded by red-brick and white clapboard shops. Along the slow-moving river stand fine houses with spacious grounds and broad green lawns that slope to the river's edge. Tall elms shade other homes distinguished by beautifully proportioned doorways and panelled interiors, a heritage of 18th- and 19th-century craftsmanship. Outlying fields, once used for farming, are being subdivided and sold as house lots.

In 1635, five years after Boston was settled, fur trader and Indian fighter Simon Willard and two ministers, John Jones and Peter Bulkeley, brought 30 or 40 families here. What is now Concord was then the Indian village Musketaquid (place of the rushes). Concord was the first settlement on Massachusetts' western frontier, away from saltwater and easy transportation.

Toward the end of the 18th century Concord became the country's shire town. The first county convention held in the colonies to protest arbitrary parliamentary acts met here in August 1774. The First Massachusetts Provincial Congress met here in October 1774. From March 22, 1775 until four days before the Lexington and Concord engagements, the Second Provincial Congress met here. Concord, a military stores depot, was the object of the British raid.

On April 19, 1775, after Dr. Samuel Prescott (1751–77) brought the captured Paul Revere's warning of the pending British raid, Lobsterbacks — the Yankee name for Redcoats — appeared near North Bridge. They were opposed by several hundred Minutemen who after a brief fight put the surprised British to flight.

The shots, when put into poetry by Ralph Waldo Emerson, some 61 years after the affray, were the famous "shot heard round the world."

It was here that the first organized attack on the British troops was made, but the command "fire" was given only after the British had fired first. The devastating sniper attack on the British during their retreat to Boston began at Meriam's Corner in Concord.

During the siege of Boston so many Boston revolutionists took refuge here that a Boston town meeting was held. When Harvard's dormitories were taken over as Continental Army barracks, classes were held in Concord.

In the early 19th century Concord became an American cultural center. Ralph Waldo Emerson wrote essays, poems and journals and revived the Transcendentalist philosophy (see WRITERS). Closely associated with the revival were Thoreau, Nathaniel Hawthorne, journalist Franklin B. Sanborn (1831–1917) and poet William Ellery Channing (1818–1901). While neither *Dial* editor Margaret Fuller (1810–50) nor Elizabeth Palmer Peabody (1804–94) were Concord residents, they were closely associated with the Transcendentalist revival.

Individualist Henry David Thoreau retreated from society and built his cabin on the shore of Walden Pond where he tried to reduce life to its simplest terms in preparation for writing his classic *Walden.*

In the *Hillside Chapel,* Amos Bronson Alcott (1799–1888) opened his School of Philosophy. His more practical wife and daughters tried to make ends meet. Daughter Louisa May (1832–88) wrote her largely autobiographical books including *Little Women,* at *Orchard House* (1868).

New Hampshire-born sculptor Daniel Chester French (1850–1931) lived and worked in Concord for many years. The town has several notable examples of his art: "Minuteman," "Melvin Memorial" and "Emerson."

It is said that Concord resident William Munroe made the first lead pencils in America. Henry Thoreau was also a pencil maker and developed an improved process for mixing graphite. In 1853 Boston native Ephraim W. Bull (1806–95) developed the Concord grape. This development began the commercial production of table grapes in America.

Concord, despite its many memories and old New England charm, is nevertheless a contemporary village. Its small, neat factories, mostly located in West Concord, supplement income from truck farms and commuters. Many Boston families have in recent years moved to Concord which is within easy commuting distance of the Hub.

What to See and Do

Monument Square has war memorials. A granite shaft is the Civil War Memorial; the boulder at the north end of the green commemorates Spanish-American War veterans, and there are two World War Memorials. *Sleepy Hollow Burying Ground* is the final resting place of the Alcotts, Channing, Emerson, Hawthorne, Elizabeth Peabody and Frank Sanborn. Here lie Daniel French and members of the political Hoar family including U.S. senator, George Frisbie Hoar (1826–1904). On the tombstone of Ephraim Bull, who lacked the shrewdness to profit from his Concord grape, the epitaph reads "He sowed, others reaped."

Bullet-Hole House (private), 36 Monument St. The original portion, built in the 17th century, is probably Concord's oldest surviving house. It is a two-and-a-half-story home with a plain board front and sloping roof. Legend says—and the hole is there to prove it—that Minuteman Elisha Jones was guarding Colonial military supplies when he rashly appeared in the front doorway. He was fired upon. The bullet hole is enclosed in a glass case.

Daniel Chester French's "Minuteman" guards the *Battleground* site. Lacking a model for his first major work, the sculptor created a statue of Apollo Belvedere dressed like a Minuteman. The Minuteman—probably America's best-known statue—has been widely used as a symbol on War Savings Bonds and Stamps.

Nearby is a reproduction of the original wooden Concord Bridge over which the Americans pursued the British attacking force. A tablet with an inscription by James Russell Lowell marks the graves of two British soldiers.

Old Manse (open April 19–May 31 Sats., Sundays and holidays, June 1–Oct. 15 daily except Mon., Oct. 16–Nov. 11 Sats., Sundays and holidays, small admission fee, enlisted personnel free, student group rate), next to Old North Bridge, was built by the Rev. William Emerson, grandfather of Ralph Waldo Emerson. Hawthorne lived here and made it the setting for *Mosses from an Old Manse.*

Colonial Inn (open), 11 Monument Square, faces the Concord Green at its northern end. The inn is a long, rambling gray structure formed by joining together three adjacent houses. The original unit was built in 1770.

Public Library, cor. Sudbury Rd., has French's Emerson statue, Thoreau's surveys, original manuscripts and period literary criticism.

Thoreau-Alcott House (private), 75 Main St. Thoreau died here in 1862. The Alcotts then lived here.

Wright Tavern (1747), 2 Lexington Rd., with a hip roof and two large chimneys, retains architectural charm. Here were Maj. Pitcairn's headquarters on April 19, 1775.

First Parish Church (Unitarian) is on the site of the building in which sat the First and Second Provincial Congresses. John Hancock presided.

Concord Art Association (open April–Oct. 15), 15 Lexington Rd., has permanent exhibits of historical interest. Resident artists hold summer exhibitions.

Emerson House (open April 19–Dec. 1, 10–11:30 and 1:30–5:30, weekdays, except closed Mon., and Sun., 2:30–5:30, small fee), Lexington Rd. and Cambridge Turnpike, is a square white house set among trees. Emerson lived here, 1835–82. During his European tour he asked Thoreau to live here. The Victorian interior shows furnishings, portraits and hangings of Emerson's era.

Concord Antiquarian Museum (open Feb. 1–Nov. 30, 10–5, Sun. 2–5, small fee), Lexington Rd. at Cambridge Turnpike, is a two-and-a-half-story brick structure. It has New England period rooms with furniture, glass, china and metalware. *Emerson Room* contains the furniture from the writer's study. Thoreau's books, flute and articles from the Walden Pond cabin are here.

School of Philosophy, Lexington Rd., was once the Hillside summer school. Bronson Alcott taught here for nearly ten years.

Orchard House (open April 19–Nov. 11, 10–5, Sun. 2–6, fee), Lexington Rd. This two-and-a-half story house was the Alcott's Concord home for 20 years. The interior and the Alcott's books, furnishings and pictures are preserved. In "Apple Slump" as she called it, Louisa May Alcott wrote most of *Little Women,* and this was its setting.

Grapevine Cottage (private), a gambrel roof house, was the home of Concord grape developer Ephraim Bull.

MINUTEMAN NATIONAL HISTORICAL PARK, partially developed, will reconstruct the scene of the April 19, 1776, battle in Concord, Lincoln and Lexington.

PANTRY BROOK WILDLIFE MANAGEMENT AREA provides public hunting in Concord and Sudbury.

WALDEN POND STATE RESERVATION (150 acres) commemorates the famed residence of philosopher-naturalist Henry Thoreau who lived here in his cabin during the mid-1840s. The site is marked by a cairn and plaque. Facilities: picnic sites, fishing, boating, nature trails.

WEST CONCORD (routes, Mass. 2, 2A, 119), now largely developed, has the Concord Reformatory, State Police outpost, and factories.

CONWAY (Franklin County, sett. 1762, incorp. 1767, alt. 558, pop. 998, town meeting, route, Mass. 116), formerly part of Deerfield, was named for Gen. Henry Conway, a British minister popular in the colonies after he secured the repeal of the Stamp Act. Indian attacks retarded early settlement. Agricultural Conway in the early 19th century reached its industrial peak, with woolen, cotton, grist and oil mills and factories making broadcloth, cutlery, combs and tinware. Marshall Field (1845–1906), the Chicago merchant, was born here. Poet and playwright Archibald MacLeish has a summer home here.

Marshall Field Memorial Library (1901), given by Marshall Field, contains historical collections.

POLAND BROOK WILDLIFE MANAGEMENT AREA has public hunting in Conway and Ashfield.

COTUIT (see BARNSTABLE)

CRAIGVILLE (see BARNSTABLE)

CUMMINGTON (Hampshire County, sett. 1762, incorp. 1779, alt. 1000, pop. 562, area 23.3 sq. mi., town meeting, routes, Mass. 9, 112) was named for Col. Cummings, purchaser of the land. Cotton, woolen and paper mills, tanneries and other factories flourished here in the early 19th century.
Cummington School of the Arts, formerly *The Playhouse in the Hills,* teaches music, sculpture, painting, writing and dancing as creative expression rather than professions. Founded in 1922 by Katherine Frazier, it includes the parsonage of the first Cummington church. A monument marks the *Site of the Birthplace of William Cullen Bryant.*
William Cullen Bryant Homestead (open June 15–Labor Day 2–5 daily except Mon., Labor Day–Oct. 15 2–5 on weekends weather permitting, small fee). Eighteen-year-old poet Bryant (1794–1878) wrote "Thanatopsis" here. The house is a lovely two-and-a-half-story Dutch Colonial with white clapboards and a wing on each side. Originally a one-and-a-half-story house, the main structure was elevated to its present height in 1856 when a new lower floor was added. Bryant used the smaller wing for a study. The interior is furnished just as it was during Bryant's residence.

The homestead is now a registered National Historic Landmark. The 189-acre site is maintained by TOR. The house is located on Mass. 112 off US 9 at the reservation sign.

WINDSOR STATE FOREST, on a branch of the Westfield River, has bridle trails, fishing, hunting, hiking, fireplaces, picnic tables, campsites (24), swimming and winter sports. See scenic Windsor Jambs, a deep flume cut through by a rushing mountain stream.

BERKSHIRE SNOW BASIN SKI AREA, on US 9, has 3 T-bar lifts, 1 rope tow, 5 trails, 3 slopes, 1 novice trail, lodge, ski school, snow-making equipment, ski rentals, snack bar, ski patrol. Open daily.

Cummington Historical Society Museum (open May 30–Oct. 15, on holidays and Saturdays, 1–5), Main St., has interesting local historical items.

DALTON (Berkshire County, sett. 1755, incorp. 1784, alt. 1150, pop. 7505, area 21.79 sq. mi., town meeting, routes, Mass. 8, 8A, 9), originally granted to Colonel Oliver Partridge and others, was first known as the Ashuelot Equivalent.
Crane Paper Mills (1801), the principal industry, have manufactured the paper on which all United States currency is printed since 1846. Notable native son U.S. Senator Winthrop Murray Crane led a gallant but futile fight to have the 1920 Republican National Convention endorse the League of Nations. He was governor 1900–02.
Crane Museum (open Mon.–Fri. 2–5, June 1–Sept. 30, free) has exhibits showing the development of Crane Mills and the paper industry.

WAHCONAH FALLS STATE PARK is a scenic area with picnic tables and fireplaces. Fair fishing. Snowmobiling. A delightful place.

DANA (Worcester County town inundated by Quabbin Reservoir)

DANVERS (Essex County, sett. 1628, incorp. 1757, alt. 39, pop. 26,151, area 13.64 sq. mi., representative town meeting, routes, US 1, Mass. 62, 114, 128).

Settlers came here from Salem in search of farmlands. The place was first called Salem Village. In 1688, Cotton Mather attended a witchcraft trial and preached a sermon which so inflamed the villagers that in 1692, when ten young girls accused a Negro nurse, Danvers became the center of witchcraft hysteria that caused 200 arrests and 20 deaths before public sanity was restored.

Seventeen Danvers emigrants joined the covered wagon caravan to Marietta, Ohio, in 1787. About this time Zerubbabel Porter, a tanner wishing to dispose of surplus leather, developed a commercial shoe factory. In 1833 Samuel N. Reed made a machine for cutting nails. In 1843 Gilbert Tapley started the manufacture of carpets. Two panics, a severe fire in 1845 and the Civil War caused an industrial decline.

Today Danvers, a pleasant residential community, has leather, shoe, electronic, lamp and chemical factories.

Town Hall has *Murals,* done as part of a federal project under the Emergency Relief Administration, depicting episodes in the town's history.

A boulder on the lawn of the Danvers Saving Bank at the edge of Danvers Square marks the *Site of the Encampment of Arnold's Forces* on their march to Quebec in 1775.

Page House (open Wed., July and Aug. 2–4, free) (1754), 11 Page St., is an attractive dwelling with gambrel roof and dormer windows. This house was the scene of the amusing incident related in Lucy Larcom's poem "The Gambrel Roof," concerning a rebellious wife who replied to her patriotic husband's edict that British-taxed tea should not be served beneath his roof by staging a tea party on the roof.

Historical Society Headquarters (open same hours as Page House), adjacent to the Page House, has eighteenth-century portraits, old china, pottery and pewter, including the baptismal bowl and communion tankard of the First Church.

Samuel Fowler House (open mid-April through mid-Sept., Mon., Wed., Fri. 2–5, small admission fee), built in 1809, is owned by the Society for the Preservation of New England Antiquities. The exterior is little changed; within is imported scenic wallpaper designed by Jean Zuber of France, the first artist (1829) to print continuous rolls in color.

Judge Samuel Holten House (open), 171 Holden St., owned by the D.A.R. This dwelling with steep-pitched roof and central chimney has two oddly placed ells, but later additions are in harmony with the original structure, which was built in 1670; it stands on a pleasant, tree-shaded, sloping lawn.

On Centre St., a sign indicates the *Site of the Church of Salem Village,* whose pastor's children, overexcited by the tales of their West Indian nurse, old Tituba, started the witchcraft epidemic.

Rebecca Nurse House (open mid-June through mid-Oct., Mon., Tues., Thurs. afternoons, small admission fee), 149 Pine St., dates from 1636. Aged Rebecca Nurse was executed as a witch. Her grave in the family burial ground is marked by a tablet bearing the names of the courageous friends who testified in her behalf.

Glen Magna (open daily in June, July and Aug.), Ingersoll Street. The main dwelling was transformed from a late seventeenth-century farmhouse into a country mansion around 1890. Formal gardens give the estate richness. In 1901 a two-story summer house, created by Samuel McIntire, was moved here. *Glen Magna* is now owned by the Danvers Historical Society which holds cultural events here.

DARTMOUTH (Bristol County, sett. 1650, incorp. 1664, alt. 43, pop. 18,800, area 61.82 sq. mi., representative town meeting, route, US 6).

Dartmouth was named for Dartmouth, England, where the *Mayflower* went for repairs after sailing from Southampton. During King Philip's War the town was annihilated, but when it was rebuilt and when whaling developed in nearby New Bedford, tradesmen and mechanics came. Portuguese arriving about 1870 on a whaleship were the nucleus of a Portuguese colony. The town, a summer resort since about 1900, also depends on farming.

PADANARAM is a section of Dartmouth village, has a lovely harbor, yachts and sailing craft.

RUSSELL'S MILLS had the first American puppet theatre.

Friends' Meeting House, on the Paskamansett River bank, a large, square, unpainted two-and-a-half story building, erected 1790, has records back to 1699. Meetings are held here in the summer.

DEMAREST LLOYD MEMORIAL STATE PARK has beach, bathhouse, boat-launching facilities on the saltwater Slocum River. Varied birdlife in area.

DAVIS (see ROWE)

DEDHAM (Norfolk County seat, sett. 1635, incorp. 1636, alt. 200, pop. 26,938, area 10.5 sq. mi., representative town meeting, routes, US 1, Mass. 128, 135), a quiet residential community with lovely homes, was an unlikely setting for America's most famous murder trial. Sacco and Vanzetti were tried and convicted here (see HISTORICAL NOTES).

Pioneer Dedham was a sober, solid community with well-recognized virtues. This reputation still endures in the substantial architecture and comfortable residences. Dedham's early settlers were neither religious enthusiasts nor sentimental visionaries.

New and cheap land, bought from the Indians, promised social and economic advancement. So settlers chose a place on a pleasant river, well watered by subsidiary streams and blessed with a fruitful soil. It is significant that in their petition to the General Court, the settlers requested that their town should be named "Contentment."

Other Massachusetts settlements might have been more conspicuous, self-assertive and finally revolutionary leaders of Colonial development; the Dedhamites went sanely and solidly on their way, laying the foundations of a prosperous industrial and residential town.

What to See and Do

Fairbanks House (open Apr. 19–Nov. 1, daily 9–6, contribution expected), at the corner of Eastern Ave. and East St., is the oldest known wooden frame house in the United States. Set on a mound lawn and shaded by giant elm trees, this long, low, faded brown house stretches along in three sections, its lower story massed by flowering shrubs. The roof sags in two deep curves on each side of the great central chimney. The central block was built in 1636, and two wings of different architecture were added later. Like Dedham itself in 1936, the house celebrated its 300th anniversary. Furnished with family heirlooms, it is a shrine for 6000 Fairbanks families incorporated as descendants of the builder, Jonathan Fairbanks. Five doors lead from a small entrance hall to other parts of the dwelling. The step down into the kitchen is a simple log, worn concave by the feet of many generations of Fairbanks.

In 1964 a careening car smashed through the ancient outer wall and ended up inside the house. Furniture was destroyed and the house badly damaged. Restoration was undertaken at considerable cost.

Dedham Historical Society (open 2–5, closed Sat. during July–Aug., free), 612 High St., erected in 1887, contains a collection which includes among many notable items an exquisitely carved mother-of-pearl tea chest, brought from China before 1775 and donated by the Quincy family, and a Simon Willard clock (made about 1780) with an unusual astronomical base.

Thayer House (private), 618 High St., a two-story yellow-painted clapboard structure with two chimneys, brick ends and a small ell, has grown shabby with the passing years, during which four generations of Thayers have lived and died within it, but on the door gleams a brightly polished brass Masonic emblem placed there in 1831 by Dr. Elisha Thayer at the time of a national attack on the Masonic Order, when Dedham Masons were being stoned in the streets.

Norfolk County Courthouse (1827) is an imposing edifice of gray stone with a dome and frontal columns. Within its walls have been pleaded many interesting cases. First of these was the controversy between the Natick Indians and the town over certain lands occupied by the Indians. The latter won, but Dedham was allotted 8000 acres in the west (now Deerfield) in compensation.

Of prime importance was the litigation culminating in 1818 with an historic decision of the Supreme Court of Massachusetts. The decision gave to the Dedham Parish, rather than to the church fellowship, the right to elect ministers, thus paving the way for the rise of Unitarianism in Massachusetts.

The most notorious Dedham trial was that of Sacco and Vanzetti before Judge Webster Thayer in 1921. The injection into the trial of political considerations, the quality of the testimony, the attitude of the judge and the prolonging of the trial over six long years aroused a worldwide storm of denunciation from pulpit and press, resulting in the appointment of a commission headed by ex-president Lowell of Harvard. The commission reported that it believed the trial had been fairly conducted and had reached a proper conclusion. Sacco and Vanzetti were executed following the publication of this report. But ten years after the case, Maxwell Anderson's *Winterset,* based on it, won the Pulitzer Prize and a brochure on the report of the Lowell Commission was circulated at the Harvard Tercentenary Celebration in 1936. "Though the tomb is sealed, the dry bones still rattle," said Heywood Broun. (See HISTORICAL NOTES.)

A tablet on the Norfolk County Registry, across from the courthouse, commemorates the *Site of Woodward (Fisher) Tavern,* where the Suffolk Convention for the drawing-up of the Suffolk Resolves was held. Another tablet marks this site as the *Birthplace of Fisher Ames* (1758–1808), a member of the Massachusetts Constitutional Convention and a distinguished Federalist, author of the "Lucius Junius Brutus" papers written in denunciation of Shays' Rebellion.

On the Church Green at the southeast corner of High and Court Sts. is the stone *Base* of the Pillar of Liberty, erected in 1766 by the Sons of Liberty to glorify William Pitt for his vigorous opposition to the Stamp Act.

First Church in Dedham (Unitarian) fronts on the Church Green. It is a dignified and simple example of American Georgian architecture built about 1768.

A tablet in front of the church marks the *Site of the First Free Public School in America* (1649) supported by general taxation.

Haven House (open as *Dedham Community House*), 669 High St., was built by Judge Samuel Haven in 1795.

Dexter House (private), 699 High St., was built about 1762 by Samuel Dexter, member of the Provincial Congress, 1774–75. The interior retains its eighteenth-century features, including the beautiful staircase with elaborate balusters, high paneled wainscoting and ample fireplaces.

Horace Mann's Law Office (private), 74 Church St., diagonally opposite St. Paul's Church across Village Square, is now a two-and-a-half-story, broad-gabled dwelling; its original character has been lost by remodeling. Horace Mann occupied it while he was a town representative (1828–35). *Powder House* (1766) opposite 162 Ames St., is a tiny cube, hardly bigger than a large closet and surmounted by a (restored) conical roof.

Granite gateposts mark the entrance to the campus of the *Noble and Greenough School* for boys, a nonsectarian institution originally established (1886) in Boston as a preparatory school for Harvard. In 1922 it moved to Dedham.

DEERFIELD (Franklin County, sett. 1669, incorp. 1673, alt. 150, pop. 3850, town meeting, routes, I–91, US 5, Mass. 116) is a Connecticut River Valley farming community with several private schools. It was settled on Pocumtuck tribal lands.

The village suffered several French and Indian attacks, including the 1675 Bloody Brook and 1704 Deerfield raids.

Deerfield was "laid out" in the Pocumtuck Valley in 1665. In 1669 Samuel Hinsdell of Dedham, a squatter, began farming where the Pocumtucks had successfully raised corn, pumpkins and tobacco. Samson Frary and others had joined him by 1672, when Hinsdell secured the General Court's assent to organize a town.

Peace and prosperity were an illusion. King Philip's War was followed by 30 years of French-Indian attacks. The 1675 Bloody Brook attack (site in South Deerfield marked by obelisk) emptied the town. Deerfield houses were vacant for seven years.

The town was again inhabited in 1682. Parson John Williams (1664–1729), destined to become the town's most famous citizen, was ordained minister in 1688. He was given the handsome offer of "sixteen cow-commons of meadow land," a "homelott," and a house "forty-two foot long, twenty foot wide, with a lentoo."

The Great Deerfield Raid

The winter of 1704 was one of the coldest experienced along the northern Massachusetts frontier. Neither cold nor deep snow kept Maj. Hertel de Rouville with 200 French soldiers and 140 Catholic Indians from raiding Deerfield. This raid was the most successful ever made by Indians against an American frontier village.

Most of Deerfield was burned. Forty-nine residents including two of Rev. Williams' children were killed. One hundred and eleven captives were taken. Not all prisoners reached Montreal. Preacher Williams' wife was tomahawked on the second day's travel from Deerfield.

Williams, his young sons, Stephen — the *Boy Captive of Old Deerfield* — and Samuel, were exchanged and returned home. His daughter, Eunice, aged seven or eight at the time of her capture, was converted to Catholicism, married an Indian and remained in Canada. Parson Williams had his tribulations, but out of this Harvard man's captivity and sorrow came *The Redeemed Captive Returned to Zion* (1707), one of the best accounts written by a former Indian captive.

Later History

A 1735 Indian treaty signed in Deerfield by Provincial Governor Jonathan Belcher finally allowed residents to harvest crops without fear. Most houses on the mile-long street survive from this period or from the Revolutionary era.

Deerfield during this time was the largest and richest town in the region. Early travelers noted the fine houses (most of which survive today). Deerfield was the center of agricultural production in the 18th century, much as the Midwest is today. Deerfieldites of the late 18th century founded cultural and literary organizations. *Deerfield Academy*'s museum, one of the earliest in America, is a fine private school museum. Williams and Amherst Colleges were founded by onetime Deerfield residents.

Nineteenth-century Deerfield was bypassed by new modes of transportation and commerce and outwardly changed very little. The town became summer host to distinguished personages from the world of arts, letters and science. Today, these traditions are carried on year-round in this still rural community by three schools, *Deerfield Academy, Eaglebrook School* and *Bement School,* and the *Heritage Foundation, Pocumtuck Valley Memorial Association* and the *Indian House Memorial.* Today, 12 historic buildings are open to visitors. Facades of the others may be viewed in a walk or ride along the street.

This is Deerfield

Old Deerfield Street, a mile long, has old houses, most of them Colonial, a church, schools and a post office. Shops are elsewhere. This long street gives an effect of being the entire village, with glimpses of open country, fields and far hills beyond. Spreading elms, 200 years old, form an arch, a setting once frequent in New England, but now rare. Some houses are handsome and still prosperous; others are plain but well tended; still others are on the verge of romantic decay. Two-leaf front doors, characteristic of the Connecticut Valley and rare elsewhere in New England, are seen on many dwellings.

The preservation of this street has been going on for over 100 years. Some houses were saved in the last century, while others have been recently preserved by the Heritage Foundation which since 1947 has opened to visitors ten buildings containing a large collection of American furnishings illustrating Deerfield life from the early eighteenth-century settler to the well-to-do late 18th-century landowner.

What To See and Do

The following houses are maintained by the nonprofit Heritage Foundation:

Wright House (1814), one of two brick houses in Deerfield, was built by Asa Stebbins for his son Asa, Jr. Presently on loan is the George Alfred Cluett Federal Period Furniture Collection with pieces by Samuel McIntire, Duncan Phyfe, John Seymour and Thomas Sheraton.

Ashley House was the 1732–80 residence of Tory preacher, Jonathan Ashley. The house, once removed from its foundations to serve as a tobacco barn, has been returned to its original site. The house contains notable 17th- and 18th-century furnishings.

Parker & Russell Silver Shop (1814) is the shop of an early American silversmith. First-rate collection of early American silver. Isaac Parker and John Russell were Revolutionary era Deerfield silversmiths.

Sheldon-Hawks House (1743) was the longtime residence of Deerfield historian George Sheldon. Original paneling is still intact. Many pieces of family china are displayed.

Hall Tavern was a famed eighteenth-century eating and drinking place on the Boston-Albany highway. The building was removed from Charlemont to Deerfield. The original bar has many period drinking containers. The tavern contains the tools used by pewterer Samuel Pierce.

Dwight-Barnard House (1754) was moved here from Springfield where a wrecking crew was about to destroy it. The beautifully proportioned rooms contain period pieces. One room is furnished as a doctor's office.

Wells-Thorn House (c. 1717) was the home of eighteenth-century settler Ebenezer Wells who later added the front section. Some rooms have the original paneling and are furnished with period pieces.

Wilson Printing House (1816) was moved five times before it was returned to its original site. It has been a printer's shop, grocery store and cabinet shop. It is now a print shop. Books and pamphlets of the last 200 years are displayed here.

Helen Geier Flynt Fabric Hall has a fine collection of old costumes and bedspreads made from fine American and European fabrics.

Asa Stebbins House (c. 1790's) was the village showpiece when it was built for the wealthiest man in town. It now contains late eighteenth- and early nineteenth-century pieces by Sheraton and Hepplewhite. Fine portraits by Gilbert Stuart and other period painters are exhibited. In the hallway early nineteenth-century French wallpaper shows Capt. Cook's South Sea voyages.

The Pocumtuck Valley Memorial Association, an historical society established in 1870 as a memorial to the 1704 Massacre victims, maintains *Memorial Hall* and the *Frary House.*

Memorial Hall (1799), built for Deerfield Academy, has been altered. It contains Colonial and Indian history exhibits. There are several rare Early New England chests.

Frary House (1689), facing the town common, was changed and enlarged in the 18th century. It is a long, massive, L-shaped, two-and-a-half-story house. Simon Frary was slain by Indians. It became a Revolutionary era tavern where Gen. Benedict Arnold closed a contract which gave his army much-needed supplies.

Indian House Reproduction (open May 1–Nov. 1, daily except Tues. 9:30–12, 1–5, Sun. and holidays 1:30–5, small admission fee) (1929), with its dark, weathered timbers and second- and third-story overhangs, illustrates a special Colonial architectural type. It takes its name from the 1704 Indian raid. The original house was torn down in 1848 after the first organized effort at historic preservation in New England failed to raise enough money to save it. But its door, with a hole made by an Indian tomahawk which killed one of the residents, may be seen at Memorial Hall. Rooms are furnished in Colonial style. One room contains an exhibit of handicraft and other work by local artists.

Old Bloody Brook Tavern (open same as Indian House), in the rear yard of the Indian House, is a long one-and-one-half-story frame building with a giant central chimney. It was probably built prior to 1700 and was moved here from South Deerfield. The building contains a pottery shop, demonstrating the craft tradition in Deerfield.

Meeting House (1824), designed by Winthrop Clapp and Isaac Damon, is the fifth meetinghouse constructed for the First Church of Deerfield. The brick structure has a gilded cock weathervane (1729).

Manse (private) (1768), one of Deerfield's loveliest houses, is a square Georgian Colonial mansion. The curious gambrel-roofed red ell in the rear was originally a separate building, one of the oldest in Deerfield. The *Manse* was the home of Dr. Samuel Willard, a First Church minister and regional Unitarian leader.

Joseph Stebbins House (private) (*c.* 1772), marked by a granite tablet, is a massive three-and-a-half-story white Georgian Colonial house.

South Deerfield, site of the *Bloody Brook Massacre* (1765), marked by an obelisk, has plastic and pickle factories. Tobacco is grown here in considerable quantity.

There is a handsome *Congregational Church* (early 19th century).

MT. SUGARLOAF STATE RESERVATION lies atop an evergreen-clad mountain. Facilities: motor road and foot trails to summit for splendid view of Connecticut River Valley. Road open during day from May through Oct.

DENNIS (Barnstable County, sett. 1639, incorp. 1793, alt. 24, pop. 6454, area 20.66 sq. mi., town meeting, routes, Mass. 6A, 28, 134).

Dennis, originally in Yarmouth, was named for the Rev. Josiah Dennis, pastor of the first meetinghouse. Dennis in 1837 had 150 skippers sailing from American ports.

Cranberry culture was started in North Dennis about 1816 by a native who noticed wild cranberries grew best when a light sand covering had been blown over them. Sand overlay is now an essential part of the cultivation of these berries.

Cape Playhouse and *Cape Cinema.* The playhouse was once a Colonial meetinghouse in Barnstable, and the cinema, one of the smallest in America, has Rockwell Kent murals and a facade copied from Centerville's Congregational Church. Many celebrated actors appear in this noted theater in tryouts of plays that become Broadway hits. The two buildings, located on a 27-acre farm, are surrounded by flower gardens and landscaped woodlands.

Scargo Hill, topped by *Tobey Tower,* affords an expansive view of Cape Cod Bay and the Atlantic, with Cape Cod a narrow arm between them.

DIGHTON (Bristol County, sett. 1678, incorp. 1712, alt. 48, pop. 4667, area 21.81 sq. mi., town meeting, route, Mass. 138) is a market-garden community of Yankees and Portuguese. Shipbuilding along the Taunton River and netting herring were once profitable.

At Mass. 138 and Elm St. was the *Council Oak,* where King Philip met with the local Pocassets.

Dighton Rock is an 11-foot-long granite boulder pockmarked with incisions, many of them alphabetic or pictorial. Some alphabetic writings are apparently meaningless scribbles done by the Indians in imitation of the white man's writings. Some were made by the Taunton haymakers of 1640, who cut hay for their stock at various points along the Taunton River and transported it on rafts. The remainder are believed to be a record of Miguel Cortereal, a Portuguese explorer whose vessel was wrecked in 1502. He made his way to Assonet Neck, became a sachem of the local Indians and left a record of his adventures with his name and the date carved on the rock.

DOUGLAS (Worcester County, incorp. 1775, alt. 580, pop. 2947, area 36.93 sq. mi., town meeting, routes, Mass. 16, 146) is the political and industrial center of Douglas Town. Settled as New Sherburn, it was renamed (1776) in honor of Boston physician William Douglas, who, in acknowledgment, gave the town $500 and 30 acres of land. Industrial Douglas depends on textiles.

DOUGLAS STATE FOREST has extensive shoreline on 286-acre Wallum Lake. Facilities: boating, picnic tables, swimming, snowmobiling.

DOVER (Norfolk County, sett. *c.* 1635, incorp. 1784, alt. 149, pop. 4529, area 15.16 sq. mi., town meeting, routes, off Mass. 109, 128, 135).

Quiet, residential Dover was formerly the site of wealthy Bostonians' summer homes. There are still a few estates. Retired U.S. senator Leverett Saltonstall has a home here. Despite the current construction of a few new houses Dover retains the charm of a small English country village. Most working Dover residents commute to Boston or other communities. In the mid-1960's Dover's industries were a small company making apparatus for teaching psychology and a prefabricated home outfit.

In the center is the brick *Town House,* topped by a graceful spire. The *Dover Church* (1839) on Springdale Ave. contains a Paul Revere bell.

Southwest of the center, Springfield Ave. passes over *Trout Brook,* which rises in Great Spring, the north source of the Neponset River.

The *Sawin Memorial Building* (open year round, Sat. 1–5, free), right from the center on Dedham St., is the headquarters of the Dover Historical Society, a two-story red brick structure erected in 1905. The *Benjamin Caryl House* (open year round, Sat. 10–5, free) (1777), also on Dedham St. near Park Ave., was once a parsonage.

DRACUT (Middlesex County, sett. 1664, incorp. 1702, alt. 160, pop. 18,214, area 20.84 sq. mi., town meeting, routes, Mass. 38, 110, 113) is a pleasant farming and manufacturing town. This region was once the capital of the Pawtucket Indians whose chief, Passaconaway, was friendly to the white men. First settler Samuel Varnum named the town after his English hometown. Dracut suffered attacks during King Philip's War.

The son of a marquis, Louis Ansart, cast cannon. In 1825 Lafayette visited Ansart. The general's presence is said to have drawn a large French population to Dracut.

The *Congregational Church* (corner of Bridge and Arlington Sts.) is a clapboard structure with an open belfry and unique steeple. Its bizarre appearance is due to 1895 additions.

DUDLEY (Worcester County, sett. 1714, incorp. 1732, alt. 650, pop. 8087, area 21.07 sq. mi., town meeting, routes, Mass. 31, 131, 197).

Resident Indians gave four acres of land for the church, and in return special pews were reserved for them. Manufacturing, begun in 1812, has been an important factor in town development.

Black Tavern (open) (1803–04), at the center, was a Hartford–Boston stagecoach stop. It was the home of the Rev. Charles L. Goodell, author of *Black Tavern Tales,* a collection of stories and legends of Dudley. This building is now owned by Nichols College of Business Administration.

Durfee Farm (open). This excellent Colonial farmhouse (*c.* 1738) has a massive central chimney with fireplaces on both sides, old hand-hewn oak timbers fastened together by hand-hewn wooden pins, handwrought door hinges and latches and wide white pine paneling. A pink *Granite Monument* (1650) marks the boundary between the territory of the whites and Indians.

Manufactories include camera lenses, optical lens blanks, periscopes, rope, woolens, cardboard, linen towels and upholstery fabrics.

DUKES COUNTY (est. 1685, pop. 6117, area 105.83 sq. mi., shire town, Edgartown) includes the seven towns of Chilmark, Edgartown, Gay Head, Gosnold, Oak Bluffs, Tisbury, West Tisbury. Dukes County is the island of Martha's Vineyard and the Elizabeth Islands in the Town of Gosnold.

DUNSTABLE (Middlesex County, sett. 1656, incorp. 1673, alt. 225, pop. 1292, area 17.02 sq. mi., town meeting, routes, US 3, Mass. 113). This farming hamlet was named for the English birthplace of Mary Tyng, mother of Jonathan Tyng, settler of Tyngsborough. (Dunstable is derived from "dun," a *hilly place,* and "staple," a *mart.*)

Fur trade, timber and fertile soil in the Merrimack and Nashua River Valleys attracted settlers from around Boston. Dunstable's development was retarded by 50 years of Indian wars. Families lived in garrisons.

The Ballad of Captain John Lovewell's Fight at Pequawket relates incidents of two expeditions from the town.

Farming, Dunstable's way of life for more than three centuries, is giving way to commuting. Farmers are taking jobs in nearby cities and towns. Dwellers in these same communities are moving to Dunstable and similar towns.

DUXBURY (Plymouth County, sett. 1628, incorp. 1637, alt. 36, pop. 7636, area 23.50 sq. mi., town meeting, routes, US 3, Mass. 3A, 53) is a pleasant summer resort and residential town. Its population increased nearly 50 percent between 1960 and 1965.

Duxbury's first known visitors were Myles Standish, Elder William Brewster, John Alden and friends, who came here about 1628. By 1632 Plymouth residents with lands in the Duxbury section of Plymouth Town were granted permission to establish a separate parish. Duxbury was granted its own town charter (1637) and became the second town in Plymouth Colony. Most early settlers were granted 20 acres along the shoreline of the Bay. When farming became the most important occupation, inland grants were made.

After the Revolution farming, fishing and trading were replaced by shipbuilding. Fishing later assumed increased importance. Shipping was an important economic factor 1812–65.

The replacement of sail by steam doomed Duxbury's shipyards. Czar of Duxbury's sailing ships was Ezra Weston. "Weston ships," reported a *Short History of Duxbury,* "were built in Weston yards, while blacksmith shops, a sail loft and a rope walk were part of the Weston buildings. Ships were stocked with produce grown on Weston farms and sailed from Weston wharf." Skippers and crew were often Duxbury men.

Home industry or "slop work" replaced shipping. Men made shoes and women made garments in the home. About 1870 nearby city residents "discovered" Duxbury was a small pleasant village. That is the Duxbury of today. There is no industry, just local mercantile establishments. That is the way residents want it.

What to See and Do

Old Burying Ground (Chestnut St. out of Hall's Corner, South Duxbury), the first Duxbury burying ground and the second in Plymouth Colony, has the graves of Capt. Myles Standish, John and Priscilla Alden. The oldest headstone is that of John Alden's son, Colonel John.
Alexander Standish House (1666) — not open to the public — at the end of Standish St., is a plain, two-story, gambrel roof frame building with a large central chimney. Alex was Capt. Myles' son.
Myles Standish Homestead Site (open), (Standish Shore), marked by granite boulder and marker has a lovely view of Massachusetts Bay.

STANDISH MONUMENT STATE PARK (small fee for parking and picnic table use). Superb view of the Bay, Plymouth, The Gurnet and Clark's Island.

Jonathan Alden House (open during summer, small fee), built by John's son, the final home of John and Priscilla. The house is owned and operated by Alden Kindred in America.
First Parish (Unitarian) Church (1840) is the fourth church in town and the second one on this site. The parish was organized in 1632 by Elder William Brewster as a Congregational Church.
Elder William Brewster Homestead Site, Standish Shore, has a marker indicating the lilac bushes which mark the Brewster homesite.
Museum (open July–Aug., 2–6, free), Washington St., contains records and relics.

EAST BOSTON (see BOSTON)

EAST BRIDGEWATER (Plymouth County, sett. 1649, incorp. 1823, alt. 40, pop. 8347, area 17.28 sq. mi., town meeting, routes, Mass. 18, 106).

One of ten communities in the Brockton Metropolitan Area, East Bridgewater is a residential town with a few small industries. Bog iron pits and water rights were responsible for early development. Samuel Rogers invented a machine for cutting and heading a nail in one operation. Eleazer Carver's cotton gin improvements led to his decoration by the Viceroy of India. Many workers now commute to Brockton and Boston.
Unitarian Church (1723), Central St., was altered in 1794 and 1849. A bell cast by Paul Revere in 1804 is displayed in the church gardens. On

display are early oil paintings of ministers, the pew used by Edward Everett while he taught school in East Bridgewater and rare maps of old Plymouth Colony.

Old Common (1721), Central St. Revolutionary War soldiers trained here. An obelisk commemorates Civil War dead.

Sachem's Rock, Myles Standish met here with Ousamequin in 1649 and purchased from him "all land running seven miles in each direction from weir." This land is now Brockton, Bridgewater, West Bridgewater, East Bridgewater, Whitman and Abington.

EAST BRIMFIELD (see BRIMFIELD)

EAST BROOKFIELD (Worcester County, sett. 1664, incorp. 1920, alt. 620, pop. 1800, area 9.89 sq. mi., town meeting, routes, Mass. 9, 67) is the youngest town in the state. The vicinity was inhabited by the Quabaug Indians, who were visited in 1655 by preacher John Eliot.

Lake Lashaway (fishing, boating, swimming, picnicking; skating, hockey, ice-boating in winter) stretches north from the main highway in the village into North Brookfield; its wooded shores, once inhabited by Indians, are a popular resort.

On Mass. 67 is the longest unbroken line of milestones known; these were set out when Benjamin Franklin was Deputy Postmaster-General of the colonies.

EAST FREETOWN (see FREETOWN)

EAST HOLLISTON (see HOLLISTON)

EAST LONGMEADOW (Hampden County, sett. *c.* 1740, incorp. 1894, alt. 226, pop. 13,029, town meeting, routes, Mass. 83, 186).

East Longmeadow, long a farming region, is now a residential area. Many residents commute to Springfield. Local industries, employing one out of five residents, produce a variety of items ranging from coffins to castings. Sandstone and Indiana limestone were once quarried here.

EAST PRINCETON (see PRINCETON)

EAST VILLAGE (see WEBSTER)

EAST WINDSOR (see WINDSOR)

EASTHAM (Barnstable County, sett. 1644, incorp. 1651, alt. 48, pop. 2043, area 14.25 sq. mi., town meeting, route US 6).

Eastham, explored by Samuel de Champlain in 1606, is today, like other Cape villages, a popular summer resort.

In 1644, forty-nine Plymouth persons formed Nauset village.

Crows and blackbirds caused so much damage to crops that a 1667 ordinance demanded that each householder kill 12 blackbirds or 3 crows a year, and one of 1695 ordered that no bachelor who had failed to kill his quota be allowed to marry.

After the Revolution fishing and coastal trading flourished. Whales and blackfish — whale family members — were sometimes driven ashore by storms and captured. In 1662 the town agreed part of the proceeds of each whale sale should be used to support the clergy. Thoreau, remarking that the support of the clergy was thus left to Providence, added, "For my part, if I were a minister, I would rather trust to the bowels of billows on the back side of the Cape, to cast up a whale for me, than the generosity of many a country parish I know."

After the 1850's fishing and shipping became secondary to farming. Eastham turnips and asparagus were famous. Methodist camp meetings were popular. On Millennium Grove, a ten-acre tract set aside for this purpose, more than 5000 listeners once congregated, some coming down from Boston.

Old Windmill, Samoset Rd. (open late June–Sept. 15, daily 10–12 and 1–5, free), was restored by the Works Progress Administration (WPA) in 1936. The mill is an octagonal, gray-shingled tower.

Crosby Tavern (private) (1750), Bridge Road. More than 20 British jack tars from the frigate *Spencer* were taken prisoner in the taproom during the War of 1812.

The former *Nauset Coast Guard Station* will become a Coast Guard Museum in the *Cape Cod National Seashore.* From the nearby dunes there is a beautiful view of the ocean and long stretches of isolated beaches. Excellent surf fishing for stripers here.

Freeman Hatch Grave (1820–89), Evergreen Cemetery, has an epitaph reading "In 1852 he became famous making the astonishing passage in the clipper ship *Northern Light* from Frisco to Boston in 76 days, 6 hours, an achievement won by no other mortal before or since."

Schoolhouse Museum. Eastham Historical Society, Inc., restored the 1869 one-room Central School and made it a museum. It is located opposite the Visitors Center, *Cape Cod National Seashore* (open June and Sept., Saturday afternoons 2–5, July and August, Mon., Wed., Fri. afternoons 2–5).

Visitors Center. The Visitors Center of the *Cape Cod National Seashore* (US 6) overlooks Salt Pond, Nauset Marsh and the Atlantic Ocean. The Center (open all year) contains a 400-plus-seat auditorium, an historical and natural history museum and public facilities. Adjoining the building is an outdoor amphitheater seating 750 for summer lectures. *Coast Guard Beach* and *Nauset Light Beach* are now in the *Cape Cod National Seashore* (lifeguards and bathhouse). Improvements and changes are constantly being made. A bicycle path runs between Visitors Center and the beach.

Old Cove Burial Ground. This was the site of Eastham's first two Congregational churches and is on US 6 in South Eastham. Many early settlers were buried here, including *Mayflower* passengers, Constance Hopkins Snow, Giles Hopkins and Lt. Joseph Rogers.
First Encounter Site. At the end of Samoset Road on Cape Cod Bay is the site where the Pilgrims, before sailing to Plymouth, first encountered the Indians. A memorial stone is on top of the dune adjoining *First Encounter Beach.*

EASTHAMPTON (Hampshire County, sett. 1664, incorp. 1809, alt. 188, pop. 13,012, area 13.29 sq. mi., town meeting, route, Mass. 10) began its industrial development in 1780, but the real foundation was created in 1822 by Samuel Williston (1795–1874). He and his wife began covering wooden buttonmolds with cloth. Ten years later he hired over 1000 families to work for him and began distributing his products throughout the nation. He financed a button-making machine. Philanthropist Williston founded Williston Seminary in 1841. He was a large contributor to Amherst and Mount Holyoke Colleges.

The first elastic webbing mill in America made shoe goring here. Looms were imported from England and skilled workmen were brought over to operate them. Textiles, today, is the town's major industry.
Old East Burying Ground, with a beautiful memorial fence and gates, is a fine site for viewing Mt. Tom.
Pascommuck Boulder, off East St., marks the site of an Indian massacre (1704).

ARCADIA WILDLIFE SANCTUARY (300 acres), Clapp St., borders the Connecticut River. Berry-bearing trees, shrubs, hummingbird garden. Natural history day camp. Presented by Professor and Mrs. Zachariah Chaffee, Jr., in memory of their son Robert S. Chaffee. Massachusetts Audubon Society project.

EASTON (Bristol County, sett. 1694, incorp. 1725, alt. 145, pop. 12,151, area 29.04 sq. mi., town meeting, routes, Mass. 106, 123, 138).

Easton Center's population is largely Swedish, Irish and Portuguese. Many inhabitants work in Easton, Brockton and Taunton mills. In the early days peat and bog iron were extracted. Iron products are still made here, but local iron is not used.

Opposite the town hall is *Rankin Farm,* where a footpath leads to a *Rock with Hoofprints.* The impressions may have been made by the Indians or by the elements. The *Leonard Home,* on Highland St., contains Indian relics, discovered along nearby Mulberry Brook.
The *Josiah Keith House* (private), Bay Rd., is a shingled house with window casements and two interior chimneys. The lower floor was cut

away and the second story rests upon the original foundation.
North Easton's *Unity Church* has stained-glass windows by John La Farge.
North Easton Library (1877) displays the individuality of architect H. H. Richardson — his adaptation of plan to function and his vigorous use of simple mass.

EDGARTOWN, on Martha's Vineyard island (Dukes County, sett. 1642, incorp. 1671, alt. 10, pop. 1481, town meeting), was first called Nunnepog (Indian for "Fresh Pond"), and, when incorporated, was named for Edgar, son of James II.

In early island elections corn and beans were used as ballots. "Freeman shall use Indian corn and Beans, the corn to manifest Election, the Beanes Contrary" — which explains the phrase "to corn a man."

In the 18th century Edgartown was the prosperous home port of Arctic whaling vessels, and in a typical year of the 19th century men were busy refining whale oil and making candles, while the women turned out 15,000 pairs of socks, 3000 pairs of mittens and 600 wigs.

Edgartown Cemetery has headstones dating from 1670 and inscribed with curious epitaphs. Also on Cooke Street are some of the oldest houses in Martha's Vineyard, including Thomas Cooke House (open) (1766), now the headquarters of the Dukes County Historical Society.
Public Library, North St., houses paintings and etchings done by famous artists and an exhibit of bronze statuary.

North Water St. continues to *Edgartown Harbor Light,* where the route turns into Pease's Point Way, which crosses Main St., passing through Edgartown Plains.

The town has excellent beaches, yacht facilities and accommodations for visitors.

The Edgartown Chamber of Commerce reported in 1968 that the town has "no overnight cabins, motor courts, trailer parks, motor camps or campgrounds." There are several summer hotels, some of which have cocktail lounges, swimming pools and patio eating places. Most Edgartown overnight visitors find accommodations in chamber-of-commerce-recommended lodging houses. Off-islanders will discover that Edgartown houses have no numbers. The chamber of commerce issues this recommendation: "Upon your arrival, simply ask the Edgartown bus driver, the policeman at Four Corners, or any permanent resident . . . Mail address does not need to include the street name; merely address envelope with name of person or house, Edgartown, Massachusetts, 02539." It is advisable to make reservations.

CAPE POGE WILDLIFE RESERVATION (347 acres), owned and maintained by TOR, is located on Chappaquiddick Island. The reservation can be reached by boat or by taking Chappaquiddick Island Ferry and driving over dunes in a 4-wheel-drive vehicle. This reservation includes sand dunes, muddy tidal flats and a two-mile-long beach. A fine place to study shore bird migration which reaches its peak in August.

EGREMONT (Berkshire County, sett. 1730, incorp. 1775, alt. 740, pop. 1138, town meeting, routes, Mass. 23, 41, 71).

SOUTH EGREMONT, a pleasant summer resort with lovely homes, was named after Charles Windham, Earl of Egremont, a friend of America in the Revolution. Early plants utilizing abundant waterpower included a chair factory, cheese factories, sawmills and axle works.

Olde Egremont Tavern (1730, restored 1931). Its Blue Grill overlooks an old swimming hole in the mountain brook at the foot of the shady lawns. Cedar Grill has a large ancient fireplace. *Egremont Inn* (1780) was a stagecoach station. *Old Blacksmith Shop* (open in summer) (1730), now sells old furniture.

NORTH EGREMONT is a small lovely settlement along Mass. 71.

CATAMOUNT SKI AREA (Mass. 23), has double chair lift, 7 rope tows, 3 T-bar lifts for novice, intermediate, expert, 2 tot tows. Meals and snacks. Ski school, ski rentals, ski shop, snow-making equipment.

JUG END SKI AREA (South Egremont off Mass. 23 and 41) has T-bar lift, 2 rope tows, 1500-foot T-bar lift, 5 trails, snow-making equipment, social evenings, cocktail lounge, snacks, meals, rooms. Phone: Great Barrington 443-1534.

EGYPT (see SCITUATE)

ELIZABETH ISLANDS (see GOSNOLD)

ENFIELD (Hampshire County town inundated by Quabbin Reservoir)

ERVING (Franklin County, sett. 1801, incorp. 1838, alt. 744, pop. 1260, area 14.01 sq. mi., town meeting, routes, Mass. 2, 63).

Land was sold to John Erving of Boston in 1752. The first settler was Col. Asaph White in 1801. Most inhabitants work in nearby towns or in local paper mills.

Left from Farley village, is *Barndoor Cave,* which cuts through 50 feet of rock and emerges on top of the cliff.

ERVING STATE FOREST surrounding Laurel Lake provides boating, fishing, hunting, fireplaces, picnic tables, campsites (28), swimming.

ESSEX (Essex County, sett. 1634, incorp. 1819, alt. 26, pop. 2670, area 14.18 sq. mi., town meeting, routes, Mass. 22, 121, 128).

Tidewater divides Essex, spinning out from the village in a web of creeks and channels woven through miles of salt marsh. Clammers' flat-bottomed dories slide along the stream, bringing their catches to sell to tourists on the causeway joining the two halves of the town. The brook is stocked with trout. Alewives (herring) run upstream to spawn.

The *First Congregational Church* (1792–93, remodeled 1842) has one of the last bells cast by Paul Revere.

The new Universalist Meeting House (1948) overlooks marinas which replaced the famous Essex shipyards. The yards launched many vessels, from small Chebacco boats of the old-time Cape Ann fishermen to modern schooners, trawlers, yachts and freighters. Tradition says the first boat was built in a garret of an ancient house and that it was necessary to cut away the windows in order to launch her.

ESSEX COUNTY (est. 1643, pop. 637,887, area 498.84 sq. mi., shire town, Salem) includes the cities of Beverly, Gloucester, Haverhill, Lawrence, Lynn, Newburyport, Peabody, Salem. The 26 towns include Amesbury, Andover, Boxford, Danvers, Essex, Georgetown, Groveland, Hamilton, Ipswich, Lynnfield, Manchester, Marblehead, Merrimac, Methuen, Middleton, Nahant, Newbury, North Andover, Rockport, Rowley, Salisbury, Saugus, Swampscott, Topsfield, Wenham, West Newbury.

EVERETT (Middlesex County, sett. 1649, town incorp. 1870, city incorp. 1892, alt. 10, pop. 42,485, area 3.36 sq. mi., mayor-council, routes, US 1, 1A) is an industrial city adjacent to Boston, employing 12,000 workers in 660 establishments. Major products are paint, turbo-engine parts, petroleum by-products and chemicals. Research and development of several products is an increasing factor in Everett's economy, as the town is located but 15 minutes from research-oriented Massachusetts Institute of Technology and Harvard. A recent R&D project by Hesse-Eastern is LAW (Light Antitank Weapon), a disposable packing case launcher that both totes and fires the rocket. By the late 1960's H-E had produced more than one million launchers, many of which are being used in Vietnam and by some NATO countries.

In 1629 Ralph Sprague and his two brothers explored the wilderness now Everett. Everett's history is entangled with Malden and it was long known as South Malden. From 1800 to 1850 South Malden had a commanding position in overland travel to Boston. From the back country one of New England's oldest roads led to the ferry and then to Boston. In 1798 a road three rods wide was laid to Malden Bridge. South Malden was the southern terminus for the Newburyport Turnpike — a privately operated highway. This step was important in making Everett a future key point in the state's transportation system. Despite a favorable location, Everett's industrial development was slow. Farming was the principal occupation until the Civil War. Toll charges on Malden Bridge were eliminated in 1859. This single act attracted many businesses and residents. South Malden became incorporated in 1870 and was named after statesman-orator Edward Everett (1794–1865).

Everett, the city's most noted native, gave a two-hour address at the dedication of the Gettysburg Battlefield. His speech, widely acclaimed at the time, all but obscured President Lincoln's "Gettysburg Address."

Everett was a U.S. congressman (1825–35), governor of Massachusetts (1835–39), minister to Great Britain (1841–45), Harvard president (1846–49), U.S. secretary of state (1852–53), U.S. senator (1852–54), candidate for vice president, Constitutional Union Party, 1860.

Monsanto Company (tours), Chemical Lane off Broadway, has been picturesquely marked for commuters for many years by high piles of bright yellow sulphur in the yards. Monsanto was a major producer of TNT during WWI.

FAIRHAVEN (Bristol County, sett. 1652, incorp. 1812, alt. 11, pop. 16,332, area 12.15 sq. mi., representative town meeting, route, US 6). First known as Sconticut, Fairhaven was settled by John Cooke as part of Dartmouth Town. The first Revolutionary War naval engagement was fought off Fort Phoenix in 1775. From 1850–60, some 50 whaling ships were owned by local residents. Shipbuilding and commercial fishing are still important. Today, boatyards build pleasure craft. Commercial fishing equipment is made here.

Artist William Bradford (1823–92), direct descendant of Plymouth's governor, was born here. His paintings were hung in the private quarters of Queen Victoria. He accompanied several Arctic expeditions.

Herman Melville (1819–91) sailed on the *Acushnet* out of Fairhaven on a voyage (1841) that helped him write *Moby Dick.*

Joshua Slocum (1844–1910) rebuilt the sloop *Spray* in Fairhaven and was the first man to sail alone around the world and write a famous book about it.

Some Civil War ships in the Great Stone Fleet blockading southern ports were from Fairhaven.

Coggeshall Memorial Building (open), 6 Cherry St., the Colonial Club's Museum, contains Colonial furnishings and paintings.

Points of interest include:

Cushman Park.

Fairhaven Academy (1798), Main St., has a beautiful fanlight over the front door. The first floor rooms have old, wide pine floorboards.

Fairhaven High School, Elizabethan, 1904.

Masonic Building.

Millicent Library (1893), Italian Renaissance, designed by Boston's Charles Brigham, was influenced by the design of the Boston Public Library.

Unitarian Memorial Church (open July and Aug., daily except Tues., free), (1904), Green and Center Sts., is an adaptation of the then prevalent Early English Gothic. The parish house and the parsonage are imitations of a later phase of the style.

FALL RIVER (Bristol County, sett. 1656, town incorp. 1803, city incorp. 1854, alt. 140, pop. 96,898, area 32.39 sq. mi., mayor-council, routes, US 6, Mass. 103, 138).

Fall River has been long noted for its Sunday School teacher, Miss Lizzie Borden (1860–1927), memorialized in these lines:

Lizzie Borden took an axe
and gave her mother forty whacks.
When she saw what she had done
she gave her father forty-one.

The jury refused to believe that prim and proper Lizzie could have so ruthlessly disposed of her doting parents. Years after her trial evidence was discovered which convinced some authorities that Lizzie could have done the "foul deed." She lived very well on her inheritance for nearly 40 years after the crime.

Fall River, outlined against the sky on a long, steep hillcrest across Mount Hope Bay, looks larger than it is. In the bay the Fall River Line boat to New York, one of an abandoned line long known through the once popular song "The Old Fall River Line," once added a picturesque accent as it lay moored awaiting its late sailing hour.

The uphill approach to the city's heart, past warehouses and mills, while architecturally unimaginative, nevertheless stimulates one sensitive to industrial drama. The business center has large stores, banks and public buildings of granite, brownstone and limestone. Moving northward one finds open areas with pleasant residential districts and some new homes.

Fall River was first called Pocasset. From 1804–34 it was named Troy. Fall River was taken from the Quequechen (Narragansett) Indian for "Falling" or "Swift water."

Farming predominated until the Revolution. Fall River had three natural cotton manufacturing advantages: waterpower, a mild, moist climate and a splendid harbor for shipping. Its boom lasted from 1871 until the Great Depression.

The city, one of the hardest-hit New England textile towns during the Depression, also suffered by the removal of cotton mills to the south and from the increased use of synthetic fabrics.

During the mid-1960's slightly more than one half or 50,722 Fall River residents were of foreign stock: Portuguese, 39 percent; French-Canadian, 26.1 percent; United Kingdom, 11.1 percent; Polish, 6.7 percent; Irish, 5.2 percent.

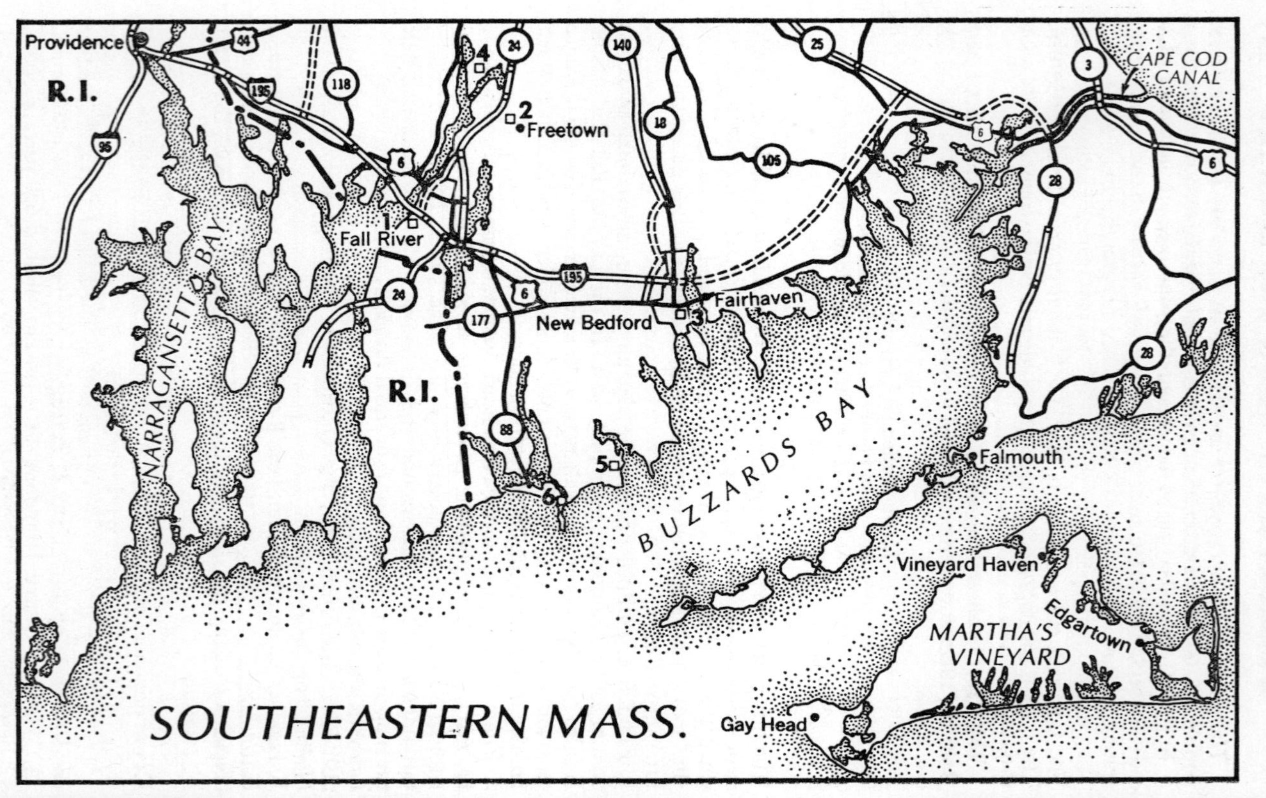
SOUTHEASTERN MASS.
Providence
R.I.
CAPE COD
CANAL
Fall River
Freetown
New Bedford
Fairhaven
R.I.
NARRAGANSETT BAY
BUZZARDS BAY
Falmouth
Vineyard Haven
Edgartown
MARTHA'S
VINEYARD
Gay Head
1
2
3
4
5
6
44
195
118
24
140
25
3
6
18
105
28
95
177
88

The city during the 1950–60 decade lost 10.7 percent (12,021) of its population. Actually almost 20,000 residents left Fall River.

In 1778, boats were discovered approaching the town. Challenged, they did not reply and were fired upon by guard Samuel Reed. Neighbors sprang to arms. Col. Joseph Durfee stationed his men behind a stone wall. They maintained a constant fire until the British brought cannon to bear. The Colonials retreated slowly to Main Street, where a stand was made. The enemy was repulsed, leaving two soldiers dead, and several wounded. Col. Durfee later started the first cotton mill here.

The 150 British set fire to Thomas Borden's home and to his saw- and gristmills. As the boats retreated the Colonials kept up musket fire, killing one soldier.

The *Sand Bank* where the skeleton in armor was found (1831) is indicated by a tablet on the gas plant at the corner of Fifth and Hartwell Streets. This discovery inspired Longfellow to write the poem, "The Skeleton in Armor." Some of the remains are at the Fall River Historical Society.

Old Church House (private), corner of June St., the oldest house in Fall River, is a vine-covered, gambrel-roofed, one-and-a-half-story red frame structure. It was occupied by a Tory, who during the Revolutionary War aided the British by using the house as one of many connecting stations which sent messages to Taunton by means of flags and beacon lights.

Fall River Historical Society Museum (open Mon.–Fri. 9–4:30, Sat. except July and Aug. 9–12, closed Sun. and holidays, free), 451 Rock St. The picture gallery has paintings by Bryant Chapin, Robert Dunning and others. A false-fronted bookcase in the parlor hides a door to the wine cellar where escaping slaves were hidden on their way to Canada. Many interesting photographs of the Old Fall River Line are displayed.

Rolling Rock, a huge rock balanced on a ledge, faces Lafayette Park on Eastern Ave. Indians discovered the rock could be rolled around on its edge without losing its balance. Legend says they used this discovery as a unique torture technique by placing their captives' arms under a raised portion of the rock and then rolled it onto them, crushing flesh and bone.

Lafayette Monument, Lafayette Park, was presented to the city in 1916 by resident Franco-Americans. Arnold Zocchi was the sculptor.

Notre Dame Church, Eastern Ave. at St. Joseph's St., contains "The Last Judgment," painted by Italian artist Cremonini.

Battleship U.S.S. Massachusetts (open daily, small fee), State Pier, an official war memorial of the commonwealth, was rescued from the scrap

---

Key to Southeastern Massachusetts

1. Battleship USS *Massachusetts*
2. Freetown–Fall River State Park
3. Whaling Museum, Ferry to Nantucket and Martha's Vineyard
4. Dighton Rock State Park
5. Demarest Lloyd State Park
6. Horseneck Beach State Reservation

heap by devoted former shipmates and historic-minded Bay Staters. The ship, now one of New England's leading tourist attractions, saw her first engagement off North Africa in 1942 and later saw active service from the Gilberts through Okinawa. She won 11 battle stars.
Fall River Battle Site is indicated by a tablet on the city hall, North Main St.

FALL RIVER WILDLIFE MANAGEMENT AREA has public hunting.

FALL RIVER METROPOLITAN AREA (pop. 137,417, area 115.14 sq. mi.) includes Fall River and the towns of Somerset, Swansea, Westport and Tiverton, R.I. Area and population figures exclude Tiverton.

FARLEY (see ERVING)

FISKDALE (see STURBRIDGE)

FALMOUTH (Barnstable County, sett. 1661, incorp. 1694, alt. 18, pop. 15,942, area 44.52 sq. mi., representative town meeting, routes, Mass. 28, 151) includes Falmouth village, East Falmouth, Falmouth Heights, Hatchville, Menauhant, North Falmouth, Quissett, Silver Beach, Teaticket, Waquoit, West Falmouth and Woods Hole.

Falmouth village, called Succanessett by the Indians, was settled in 1661 by a group of Quakers led by Isaac Robinson. The town was incorporated in 1686, and in 1694 the name was changed to Falmouth. In 1779 the townspeople repelled attacks by British ships. During the War of 1812 the British again attacked this section, and one of their ships was captured. Agriculture, shipbuilding, fishing, whaling and the manufacture of salt and glass were important industries during periods of prosperity. Falmouth with its many small settlements, harbors and beaches has become a major summer resort.
Falmouth Historical Society (open early June–mid Sept., daily 2–5 and by appointment), Palmer Ave. across from Village Green. This old house (*c.* 1790) has a widow's walk. The wallpaper was brought from France in the early 1800's. Exhibits: whaling items, Sandwich glass, period furniture, local historical relics. Genealogical library. The Thrift Shop in an old barn (back of house) is open June–Aug., Saturdays 10–12.
Katherine Lee Bates Birthplace, 15 Main St. Professor Bates wrote "America the Beautiful" when she was teaching English at Wellesley College.
Congregational Church, facing the green, has a Paul Revere Foundry bell.
Webster Rose Garden (toward Woods Hole), Quissett Ave., is open to the public during the summer. No charge.

CRANE POND WILDLIFE MANAGEMENT AREA has public hunting.

EAST FALMOUTH (Mass. 28), a small village, lies at the head of an inlet.

FALMOUTH HEIGHTS (off Mass. 28) is a summer resort. From Great Hill the shores of Martha's Vineyard are clearly visible.

HATCHVILLE (s. off Mass. 151) is a small settlement with a post office.

MENAUHANT (e. off Falmouth Heights) is a hamlet with fine views of Nantucket Sound.

NORTH FALMOUTH (Mass. 28) is a few houses along and off the highway. P.O. and beach.

QUISSETT (just outside Falmouth Village) is a hamlet overlooking Buzzard's Bay.

SILVER BEACH (w. off Mass. 28 and 28A). Good beach. P.O. (summer only).

TEATICKET (Mass. 28). Small settlement with P.O.

WAQUOIT (Mass. 28) is a village noted for strawberries.

WEST FALMOUTH (w. of Mass. 28 and 28A) is a summer colony with a fine beach surrounding an excellent harbor.

WOODS HOLE (Woods Hole Rd. from Falmouth Village) is one of the world's great marine biological and oceanographic research centers and Cape Cod's major port. Boats for Martha's Vineyard and Nantucket leave and arrive from here.

Woods Hole Oceanographic Institution (not usually open to visitors) commenced operations in 1930 with a $2,000,000-grant from the Rockefeller Foundation. Since then the institution has received many times that sum in both general grants and sums for specific research, including Office of Naval Research and National Science Foundation funds.

Staffed by leading oceanographers, it utilizes deep ocean waters, the continental abyss and inshore waters to study winds, ocean currents, temperature changes and their effects. The institution has four oceangoing research vessels, two airplanes and the deep-diving submarine *Alvin.*

Marine Biological Laboratories, Main St., supplies facilities to qualified marine biologists. Summer courses are conducted for graduate students.

Coast Guard Base, Woods Hole, is the headquarters for the command of all Cape Cod, Narragansett Bay, Martha's Vineyard and Nantucket area Coast Guard units. Facilities which support the various Coast Guard aids to navigation are here.

Nobska Light (side road from Woods Hole Rd.), with fog signals and radio beacon, has been flashing since 1829.

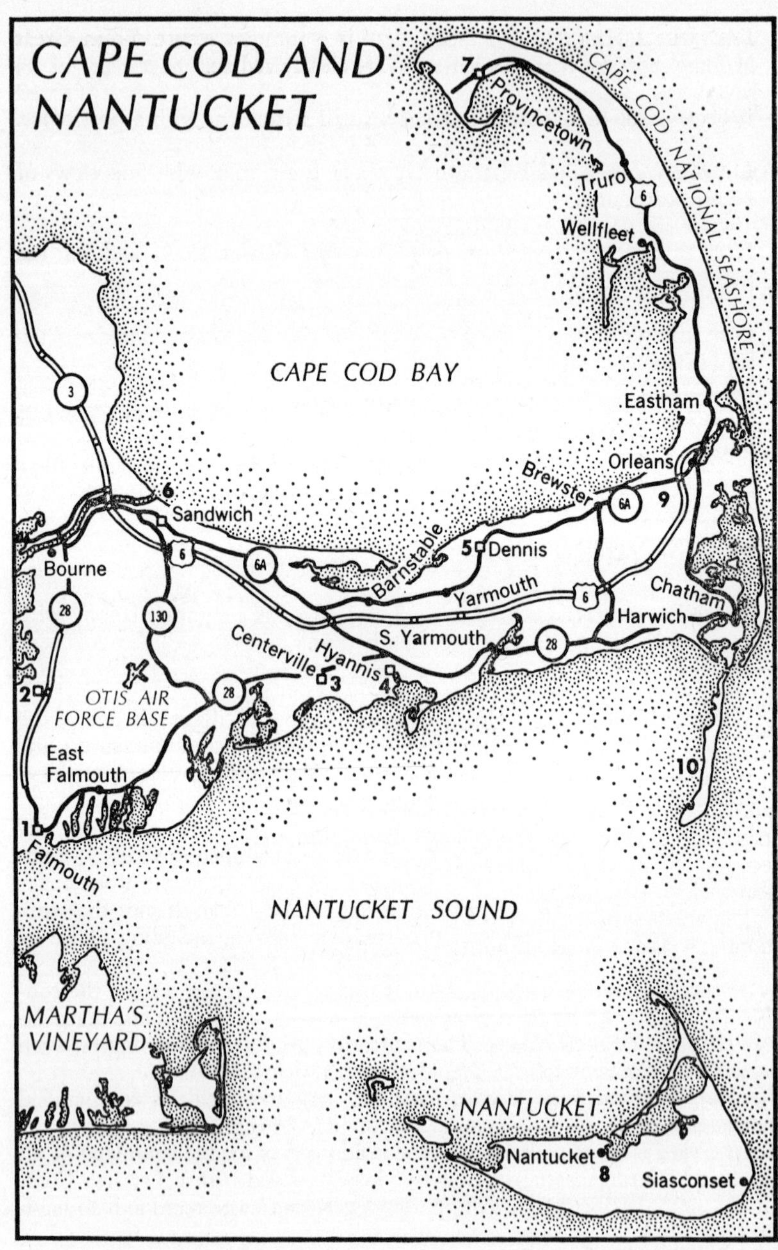
CAPE COD AND NANTUCKET
CAPE COD NATIONAL SEASHORE
Provincetown
Truro
Wellfleet
CAPE COD BAY
Eastham
Orleans
Brewster
Sandwich
Barnstable
Dennis
Bourne
Yarmouth
Chatham
Harwich
S. Yarmouth
Centerville
Hyannis
OTIS AIR FORCE BASE
East Falmouth
Falmouth
NANTUCKET SOUND
MARTHA'S VINEYARD
NANTUCKET
Nantucket
Siasconset
1
2
3
4
5
6
7
8
9
10
3
6
6A
28
130

ASHUMET HOLLY RESERVATION AND WILDLIFE SANCTUARY, northside of Mass. 151, East Falmouth (45 acres), is noted for the variety of its holly trees. Winter-hardy trees were developed here by the late Wilfred Wheeler. Massachusetts Audubon Society project.

FOLLY COVE (see ROCKPORT)

FOUNDRY VILLAGE (see COLRAIN)

FITCHBURG (Worcester County, sett. *c.* 1730, town incorp. 1764, city incorp. 1872, alt. 458, pop. 43,343, area 27.47 sq. mi., mayor-council, routes, Mass. 2, 2A, 12, 31).

Fitchburg, one of the nation's papermaking centers, nestles among rolling hills along a branch of the Nashua River. The city illustrates the trend of many Massachusetts communities, which, after more than a century as small agricultural hamlets, were transformed within a few years to industrial cities. Fitchburg is notable in its segregation of industrial and residential sections.

Fitchburg appears to be a man's town, but the census reports women lead in numbers. A Yankee twang is detected in some voices, but there are also Irish, some descended from early railroad hands, dark French-Canadians, who came as mill workers about 1860, lean, blue-eyed Swedes, brought by Iver Johnson interests in 1890, serious-faced Finns, introduced in the great immigration of 1880 to 1912, and Poles and Italians. Cooperatives, notably the Finnish Co-operative Society, the Farmers Co-operatives and the German enterprise, promote orderly living not usually found in "factory towns."

Fitchburg for 50 years after its incorporation was primarily a self-contained dairying and agricultural community. In 1793 a Boston-Fitchburg stage line opened, and the Nashua River's industrial potentialities were recognized. In 1805 General Leonard Burbank established a paper mill near the 250-foot falls.

The opening of the Boston and Fitchburg Railroad in 1845 and the Vermont and Massachusetts Railroad in 1848 insured rapid transportation fa-

---

Key to Cape Cod and Nantucket

1. Summer resort and summer theater
2. Oldest Congregational church in United States
3. Lovely old houses
4. Ferry to Nantucket and Martha's Vineyard
5. Summer theater
6. Sandwich glass exhibits
7. Pilgrim Monument, Chrysler Art Museum, Donald MacMillan Arctic Exhibits, Race Point Lighthouse
8. Beaches, sea food, old houses, whaling relics
9. Nickerson State Park
10. Monomoy National Wildlife Refuge

cilities and attracted new industries. Rollstone Hill granite-quarrying is still an important industry.

Current major products: paper and allied products, superchargers, saws, men's and boys' breeches, women's handbags, firearms, toys and hardware.

Fitchburg Teachers' College has an art school.

Simonds Saw and Steel Co. (open to special visitors), 5 North St., makes the largest saws in America, those used by the lumber trade. This was the first windowless plant in the country.

Iver Johnson Cycle Works, founded by Scandinavian Iver Johnson, manufactures a variety of goods including inexpensive firearms.

Rollstone Rock, Main St., near Caldwell Place, is a huge glacial boulder which geologists classify as "erratic," since the nearest similar rock is more than 100 miles north. The rock was moved, but its 100-ton weight prohibited its removal in a single piece. It was split into sections and reassembled.

Fitchburg Art Museum (open Sept.–June, daily except Mon. 9–5, Tues. eve. 6–9, Sun, 2–5, free), 25 Merriam Parkway, houses eighteenth-century French Provincial furniture, pottery and glass. Monthly traveling exhibits are shown, with emphasis on textiles and color prints.

Fitchburg Historical Society (open Sept. 15–June 15, Thurs. and Sun. 2–4, during summer by appointment, free), 50 Grove St. Rare exhibits include *Vinegar Bible* (London, 1777) ("vinegar" is erroneously used in the margin instead of "vineyard"), a Haitian high priest's voodoo drum and a 300-year-old English hurdy-gurdy.

Fitchburg Free Public Library (1967) has a fine book collection and a special youth section.

COGGESHALL PARK — MIRROR LAKE has winter skating, summer picnic facilities, weekly band concerts, children's playground, laurel trail in late June.

FITCHBURG-LEOMINSTER METROPOLITAN AREA (pop. 97,164, area 98.72 sq. mi.) includes Fitchburg and Leominster cities and Lunenberg and Shirley towns.

FLORIDA (Berkshire County, sett. 1783, incorp. 1805, alt. 1895 at town hall along Mass. 2, pop. 672, area 24.55 sq. mi., town meeting, route, Mass. 2), once a stage station and mentioned in Nathaniel Hawthorne's "Ride Toward Charlemont," has catered to tourists since the Mohawk Trail (Mass. 2) opened in 1915.

Elks' Monument (Drury village on Mass. 2) is a chunk of blue-gray granite surmounted by a large bronze elk, erected by Massachusetts Elks in 1923 to honor WWI lodge members.

Whitcomb Summit (alt. 2110) has a 65-foot observation tower. East is *Mt. Monadnock* (N.H.), north are Vermont's Green Mountains, south are the rounded Berkshires and west is Mt. Greylock, topped by a beacon. *Hoosac Tunnel Village* (alt. 745) on unnumbered road n. of Mass. 2 w. of Charlemont Village and e. of Florida Village. The Boston and Maine Railroad tracks pass through the village before entering the *Hoosac Tunnel,* about 0.5 mi. west. This 25,000-foot tunnel was completed in 1875, after 24 years of work; it cost 195 lives and $20,000,000. Right of the east entrance to the tunnel is a footpath leading a short distance to the *Twin Cascades,* 40 and 90 feet high; these are among the most beautiful of Berkshire waterfalls.

Hoosac Village is the southern terminal of the *Hoosac Tunnel & Wilmington Railroad.* This road which once ran about 25 miles from Hoosac Tunnel Village to Wilmington, Vermont, now runs only freight from Hoosac Tunnel Village to Readsboro, Vermont (10 mi.). During the late 1960's it was the only Massachusetts railroad making a profit (about $12,000 annually). It is affectionately known to thousands of railroad buffs as "The Hoot, Toot & Whistle."

Spectacular scenery is seen on the 10-mile drive from Mass. 2 through Zoar Village, Hoosac Tunnel Village and Monroe Bridge Village into Readsboro, Vermont. The drive winds along the bottom of beautiful Deerfield River Gorge. It is one of the finest foliage tours (mid-October) in New England.

SAVOY MT. FLORIDA STATE FOREST (10,000 acres) has bridle trails, cabins, fishing, hiking, hunting, fireplaces, picnic tables, tent and trailer sites (45), swimming, scenic views, snowmobiling.

FOXBOROUGH (Norfolk County, sett. 1704, incorp. 1778, alt. 300, pop. 14,218, area 19.79 sq. mi., town meeting, routes, I–95, I–495, US 1, Mass. 140) was named for Charles James Fox (1749–1806), British champion of the colonies. Foxborough Foundry was established to cast cannon and balls for the Continental Army. The town in 1798 passed a pioneer 8-hour-day law for heavy industry, providing "66 cents for eight hours" work and $1.33 for "eight hours work of a man and a team able to carry a ton."

Straw bonnets built up the town. Women and children braided and wove straw to help finances. Mrs. Cornelius Metcalf adopted orphans and put them to work preparing straw — a profitable combination of baby farm, child labor and sweatshop.

After the decline of the straw bonnet industry, the production of indicating, recording and controlling instruments gained importance.

The New England (formerly Boston) Patriots, New England's only member of the American Football Conference, will play their home games in Schaefer Stadium. When completed the $6,000,000 construction will seat approximately 60,000.

FRAMINGHAM (Middlesex County, sett. 1650, incorp. 1700, alt. 163, pop. 64,048, area 25.65 sq. mi., representative town meeting, routes, Mass. Turnpike, Mass. 9).

Framingham nearly doubled its population between 1930 and 1960 because of the growth of suburbanization and expanding local industries.

For 35 years after its boundaries had been settled the town was known as Danforth's Farms. Indians farmed and had their own churches and civil government. By 1700 Framingham had 70 families, including refugees from the witchcraft persecution in Salem Village (now Danvers).

Crispus Attucks, resident of the town, was a member—some historians say a leader—of the mob that attacked the King's soldiers in Boston on March 5, 1770, in the Boston Massacre. He was one of the five who were killed.

After 1800 the waterpower of the Sudbury River, which flows through the town, was used for manufacturing. In 1837 the New England Worsted Company moved its machinery here from Lowell. Other industrial enterprises were started. Many original factories folded, but shoes, paper, rubber products and carpets are still produced. The Dennison Paper Manufacturing Company (1879), the town's dominant industry, makes specialties like crepe paper, labels, gift wrapping paper. General Motors assembles Chevrolet automobiles here.

One of New England's first major shopping centers, *The Shoppers' World,* is located off US 9 in Framingham.

FRANKLIN (Norfolk County, sett. 1660, incorp. 1778, alt. 303, pop. 17,830, area 26.8 sq. mi., town meeting, route, Mass. 140).

In 1660 ten men left Dedham to break ground in Wollomonopoag. They encountered serious financial difficulties in bargaining with the Wampanoags. Finally, Captain Thomas Willett secured a purchase price of about £35.

Franklin was named after the statesman, scholar and humanist. Franklin, not insensible of the honor, wavered between presenting a church bell or books to his municipal namesake and decided in favor of the latter, because he "considered sense more essential than sound."

Industrial history began in 1713 when *Mine Brook Falls* were utilized for a sawmill. Franklin, however, remained a farming town until Asa and Davis Thayer, 99 years later, started the town's first factory. By 1865 factories were turning out more than one million bonnets yearly.

Textile and related mills have made up most of the town's payroll for more than a century.

Franklin, due to its nearness to Boston—about 26 miles—is undergoing a population boom. The town's population increased only 2100 in the 75 years preceding 1950, but in the last 17 years the population has jumped from 5000 to nearly 15,000.

FRANKLIN COUNTY (est. 1811, pop. 59,210, area 702.95 sq. mi., shire town, Greenfield) includes 26 towns: Ashfield, Bernardston, Buckland,

Charlemont, Colrain, Conway, Deerfield, Erving, Gill, Greenfield, Hawley, Heath, Leverett, Leyden, Monroe, Montague, New Salem, Northfield, Orange, Rowe, Shelburne, Shutesbury, Sunderland, Warwick, Wendell, Whately.

FREETOWN (Bristol County, incorp. 1785, alt. 32, pop. 4270, area 34.57 sq. mi., town meeting, routes, Mass. 18, 79, 140).

Freetown, a residential suburb between Fall River and New Bedford Metropolitan Area, makes mattresses, screws and boxes.

EAST FREETOWN, the principal village, was called "ye freeman's land on Taunton River." King Philip is alleged to have spent his last night in *Rocky Woods.*

FREETOWN STATE FOREST facilities: hunting, fireplaces, picnic tables, children's spray pool, snowmobiling.

FURNACE VILLAGE (see EASTON)

GARDNER (Worcester County, sett. 1764, town incorp. 1785, city incorp. 1923, alt. 1190, pop. 19,748, area 22.02 sq. mi., mayor-council, routes, Mass. 2, 68, 140).

Hospital: *Henry Heywood Memorial*

Newspaper: *Gardner* (daily) *News*

Gardner has long been known as the "Chair City of the World." Manufacturing displaced agriculture after 1805, when James M. Comee established the first Gardner chair factory in his home. Comee introduced the use of flags for chair seats; Elijah Putnam, a graduate apprentice, in 1832 began to manufacture chairs with cane seats, following a sample brought from the Connecticut State Prison by one of his workmen. Levi Heywood revolutionized the industry. Philander Derby in 1844 made a fortune by designing the Boston rocker, known to comfort-lovers throughout America and démodé only when cramped living quarters made it impracticable. Gardner chair makers received a needed boost when President John F. Kennedy focused world attention on the benefits of rocking.

On Park St. is *Greenwood Memorial Pool* (swimming). *Gardner State Hospital* is a mental institution.

GAY HEAD (Dukes County, sett. 1669, incorp. 1870, alt. 185, pop. 118, town meeting, route, off Beetle Bung Rd.), one of two Massachusetts towns still occupied mainly by people of Indian descent, has the most complete voter registration in Massachusetts. Eighty-three of the 103 residents — the rest are children — are registered voters. There are summer homes here. A paradoxical situation occurred in 1711, when the Society for Propagating the Gospel purchased the lands at Gay Head for the sole use of the Indians, their original proprietors. In the early days fishing, whaling and agriculture were the chief source of revenue which, at its best, was scanty. Labor in the cranberry bogs and the sale of bowls and jars fashioned from the colored clays of the cliffs now are the chief sources of livelihood.

A road continues to *Gay Head Light,* built in 1799, rebuilt in 1859. It contains 1003 prisms of cut and polished crystal glass and flashes every ten seconds, three white beams and one red.

Below the lighthouse a 60-foot *Cliff* drops straight down to the waters of Vineyard Sound. Composed of variegated vertical strata of clay ranging from white, blue, orange and red to tan, the precipice, in the rays of the late afternoon sun, presents a gorgeous reflection, best appreciated from offshore. Small boats make special trips for the sunset hours.

GEORGETOWN (Essex County, sett. 1639, incorp. 1838, alt. 100, pop. 5290, area 13.1 sq. mi., town meeting, routes, I–95, Mass. 97, 133) is an offspring of Rowley and one of Essex County's last settlements. Grants were held in abeyance by Ezekiel Rogers, head of the Rowley Company, so his friend Oliver Cromwell might find refuge if his efforts to dethrone Charles I failed.

The *Brocklebank House* (open, free) (1670), about .4 mi. from the common on Mass. 133, was the attractive gambrel-roof home of Capt. Samuel Brocklebank, killed in King Philip's War. The old *White Horse Tavern* sign, 1773, swings in front of it.

A road leads through an attractive wood to *Baldpate Hill* (alt. 312), one of the highest points in Essex County.

Baldpate Inn, a rambling old structure, with its seven outside doors, once the setting of Earl Derr Biggers' novel, *Seven Keys to Baldpate,* is now a private psychiatric hospital (1938).

CRANE POND WILDLIFE MANAGEMENT AREA has public hunting. It lies in Groveland, Georgetown, Newbury and West Newbury.

GILL (Franklin County, sett. 1776, incorp. 1793, alt. 269, pop. 1100, town meeting, route, Mass. 10) is a small valley community of neat homes with well-kept grounds.

RIVERSIDE. In 1676 about 200 colonists under Capt. Turner surprised 300 savages camped here. Farming is the chief occupation.

Gill is the seat of *Mount Hermon School for Boys,* founded by the late evangelist Dwight L. Moody (see NORTHFIELD). This fine school requires that every student devote some time to chores about the school and its farm.

GLOUCESTER (Essex County, sett. 1623, town incorp. 1642, city incorp. 1873, alt. 50, pop. 27,941, area 26.18 sq. mi., council-manager, routes, Mass. 127, 128, 133).

Gloucester, a leading fishing port on Cape Ann, is fringed by summer resorts ranging from fashionable *Eastern Point, Bass Rocks* and *Magnolia* to quiet *Annisquam.* Three centuries of seafaring have weathered its wharves, narrow streets and skyline of roofs and spires, over which blows the never-to-be-forgotten smell of Gloucester: a wonderful compound of tar, salt air and strong, fresh aroma of fish.

Kipling's classic *Captains Courageous* (written in Vermont) and the salty yarns of James B. Connolly spread picturesque Gloucester's fame far beyond America.

Since 1623, when the Dorchester Adventurers' colony was established, Cape Ann men have drawn their livelihood from the sea. Time brings change to Gloucester. Fast schooners sailing past the breakwater gave way to Diesel trawlers and gill-netters. Anglo-Saxon for more than 300 years, the city has been given vitality and color by Portuguese, Italians and Scandinavians.

Seafarers all, they bring their traditions to the fisheries and allied industries: spar- and sailmaking, rigging and ironworking and to manufacturers dependent on fishing — glue, isinglass and fertilizer. Gloucestermen seek their living upon the world's most dangerous waters: the fog-shrouded, berg-haunted *Grand Banks,* with swift currents and steep, short seas, and the treacherous shoals nearer home — *Georges Bank, Stellwagen Bank* and the picturesquely named coastal ledges. Ten thousand Gloucestermen have been lost at sea, but fishermen still pursue their calling without heroics but with skill and undiminished daring.

Universalist Church (1868), Middle and Church Sts., has an octagonal steeple. In an earlier church were held (1774) the first American Universalist services.

Sargent-Murray-Gilman House (open June 27–Sept. 15, 11–5 weekdays, small fee) (1768), 49 Middle St., was built for shipowner Winthrop Sargent who loaned it to preacher John Murray (1741–1815), founder of American Universalism. Murray lived here after 1788, before he became pastor of the Universalist Church, Boston, in 1793.

Cape Ann Scientific, Literary and Historical Association (open June 15–Sept. 15, Tues.–Sat. 11–4, closed Sun. and Mon., small fee), Federal and Pleasant Sts. Exhibits: ship models, period rooms, old household utensils, silver, glass, antiques, paintings.

Church of Our Lady of Good Voyage (open), Prospect St. This lovely, white, clean-lined Portuguese Catholic Church, dominating the city from its hilltop perch above the harbor, has a 32-bell carillon. Above the door is a sensitively conceived figure of *Our Lady of Good Voyage,* with a schooner in one hand while the other is blessing the waters. *Fiesta of Pentecost* is celebrated on three successive Sundays. Brilliant-eyed children march with their parents to the church where the priest places crowns on the heads of those chosen to express the community's gratitude for the intervention of the Lord on their behalf during the past twelve months. A colorful annual event is the blessing of the fishing fleet by the Boston Cardinal during the *Feast of St. Peter,* held always on the weekend nearest June 29.

Below the *Waterfront* are wharves where for nearly 350 years fishing boats have discharged cargoes. Vessels with great catches were once sailing ships with Yankee crews.

Gloucester Fisherman (Western Ave.), in bronze, executed by Leonard Craske, looks across the harbor to the open sea. Here on every Memorial Day (May 30), flowers are placed at the Fisherman's feet. Near Blynman's Bridge, the roll of those lost at sea during the past year is slowly read. Armfuls of blossoms are strewn upon the water, to be carried out by the ebb tide to unknown graves.

Ten Pound Island, purchased from the Indians for ten pounds, has a *Coast Guard station.* Farther east stretches *Eastern Point,* from the tip of which juts *Dog Bar Breakwater. Five Pound Island* has been the Fish Pier since 1937.

East Gloucester

North Shore Arts Association Exhibitions (open June–Sept., Mon.–Sat. 10–5:30, Sun. 2:30–5:30), 197 E. Main St., East Gloucester.

Rocky Neck Art Colony (turn right off E. Main St. onto Rocky Neck Ave). This is the heart of the summer writers and artists colony. Fishing shacks and sail lofts have become attractive studios. Some good seafood restaurants, informal night clubs and bars.

Eastern Point Yacht Club (members only), Eastern Point Rd.

Beauport, Eastern Point Blvd. (open June–Sept., every afternoon except Sat., Sun. and holidays, guided tours: 2:30, 3:30, 4:30, small fee, SPNEA). Each of the 20-plus rooms is decorated in a different period and style. Interesting antiques, wallpaper and paintings.

EASTERN POINT WILDLIFE SANCTUARY, Eastern Point Blvd. (26 acres), features saltwater marshes and ocean headlands. Goldenrod attracts fall visitors. Massachusetts Audubon Society project.

West Gloucester

Hammond Museum (open June 28–Sept. 4, weekdays guided tours at 11, 12, 2 and 3, Sun. tours at 2, 3, 4, special tours arranged for groups), Hesperus Ave. Medieval style stone castle has picture gallery with Gothic, Renaissance, Romantic art. Most furniture and woodwork was taken from European castles. The organ was built by former castle owner, inventor and engineer, John Hays Hammond, Jr. (1888–1965).

Rafe's Chasm and *Norman's Woe Reef* (no longer publicly owned). The chasm is a narrow cleft in the granite coast at sea level in which tides surge back and forth with a hollow boom, Boom, BOOM! Offshore is the small Norman's Woe Reef, familiar to readers of H. W. Longfellow's *The Wreck of the Hesperus.*

GOSHEN (Hampshire County, sett. 1761, incorp. 1781, alt. 1450, pop. 483, area 17.31 sq. mi., town meeting, routes, Mass. 9, 112) is in a dairying, poultry-raising, lumbering and maple-sugaring community.
Highland Lake offers boating, fishing, swimming.

LITHIA is a tiny village. *Mountain Rest* is a summer resort with a community hall and facilities for outdoor sports. The general public is accommodated, but preference is given to missionaries of all denominations, home on leave.

D.A.R. STATE FOREST provides boating, picnic tables, fireplaces, campsites (50), swimming.

GOSNOLD (Dukes County, includes all Elizabeth Islands, alt. 10, pop. 83, sett. 1641, incorp. 1864) reached only by mail boat, charter aircraft or private boat, was named for British navigator Bartholomew Gosnold (d. 1607) who settled temporarily on Cuttyhunk Island in 1602.

Cuttyhunk is an island, a village and the name of a type of fishing line, said to have originated here. The only scheduled service between Cuttyhunk and the mainland — New Bedford — is the mail boat which runs daily in the summer and twice a week in the off-seasons. The village has about two miles of roads and two boarding houses.

The island, fortunately, has not been despoiled by commercialization. To see the primitive loveliness of this archipelago and the beauty of its isolated summer estates, it is necessary to follow lanes and bypaths afoot.

ELIZABETH ISLANDS, except Cuttyhunk and state-owned Penikese Island, are privately owned.

PENIKESE ISLAND, a state game refuge, was given in 1873 to Professor Louis Agassiz with an endowment fund of $50,000 to establish a game sanctuary and a school of natural history. In 1907, the state acquired the island and established a leper colony, which was later abandoned.

Tarpaulin Cove, on the east shore of Naushon Island (private), has been a haven for pilots and pirates and was the last port of call for Captain Kidd. The *French Watering Place,* southeast of Tarpaulin Cove, was named after French privateers who swarmed in Vineyard Sound. The British cleared the island of livestock. During the War of 1812, Naushon was a British naval base. Geologists find Naushon one of the best places to study the great terminal moraine features.

GRAFTON (Worcester County, sett. 1718, incorp. 1735, alt. 380, pop. 11,659, town meeting, routes, Mass. 20, 30, 140, Mass. Pike) was originally Hassanisco (Place of the Falling Stones), "Praying Indian" town. Grafton underwent a period of industrial development, but today it is largely a Worcester suburb, with many Colonial buildings.

Grafton Common, selected as typical of New England, was used in filming the motion-picture version of Eugene O'Neill's play, *Ah, Wilderness.*

GRANBY (Hampshire County, sett. 1727, incorp. 1768, alt. 334, pop. 5473, area 28.01 sq. mi., town meeting, routes, US 202, Mass. 116) is an attractive residential village, named for the Marquis of Granby, a popular English military leader of pre-Revolutionary days. Today there is no trace of distilleries, wool and satinet factories that flourished briefly in the 19th century.

Granby's population has grown a lot but all attempts to industrialize or zone for future increase have not materialized. It is a quiet "bedroom" town.

Cold Hill (alt. 380) provides a fine view across the Connecticut Valley. Straight ahead is majestic *Mt. Tom* (with observatory); the buildings of Mount Holyoke College, looking as though they were at the foot of the mountain, are separated from it by the Connecticut River. The Holyoke Range is far to the rear (r.). To the left of Mt. Tom is the city of Holyoke with hills in the background. The river cannot be seen, but the stacks of manufacturing plants along its banks trace its course between the clustered roofs of residential sections. The old Smith College hymn gives very well the feeling of the scene:

"And where the hills with purple shadows
Eternal vigil keep,
Above the happy river meadows
In golden haze asleep . . ."

GRANVILLE (Hampden County, sett. 1736, incorp. 1774, alt. 1040, pop. 1008, area 43.2 sq. mi., town meeting, routes, Mass. 57, 179, 189).

GRANVILLE CENTER, situated on the old Massasoit Indian Trail, which followed the Little River Gorge, was settled by Springfield folk. On Liberty Hill stands the Liberty Pole, symbol of the town's Revolutionary enthusiasm. Shays' Rebellion found many sympathizers here. The town is famous for its superior blueberries and apples. Famed Granville cheese is aged here. Toy drums have been manufactured in Granville continuously since 1854 and, during the Civil War, military drums for northern regiments were made by the same company.

The *Granville Community Building* is a recent structure in neoclassic style. Ancient maple trees line the roadside at the bottom of the sloping lawn.

Mass. 57 winds through hill country to WEST GRANVILLE (alt. 1200). A fine, two-story, square brick Colonial house with a low roof and four chimneys is between the church and new schoolhouse.

GRANVILLE STATE FOREST facilities include fishing, hiking, hunting, fireplace, picnic tables, campsites (39), trailer sites, swimming, scenic views.

GREAT BARRINGTON (Berkshire County, sett. 1726, incorp. 1761, alt. 721, pop. 7537, area 45.86 sq. mi., town meeting, routes, US 7, Mass. 23, 41, 71, 183). Dutch and English names are on the deeds here, given in 1724 by Chief Konkapot. The *Great Road,* through the town, was the route of French and Indian War expeditions.

The first telegraph line with a local station was run through the town in 1848 by Ezra Cornell (1807–74) financier and founder of Cornell University. Anson Jones (1798–1858), last President of the Republic of Texas, was born here. Great Barrington, a winter–summer resort, is the summer home of many New Yorkers.

Near the Housatonic River (Bridge St.) is the site of an old *Indian Ford.* In 1676, fleeing Narragansetts were overtaken by Maj. Talcott — the area's last Indian engagement.

William Cullen Bryant House is on the main street in front of what used to be the Berkshire Inn. The house (1739) is a two-and-a-half-story dwelling with a two-leaf door of the early Connecticut Valley type and two interior chimneys. The interior is handsomely paneled. Bryant married here when he was practicing law and was town clerk (1815–25).

MT. EVERETT STATE RESERVATION (1000 acres), sw. of Great Barrington. Picnic sites atop Mt. Everett (alt. 2624) which are reached by road. Guilder Pond lies near summit. Road closed from late fall through early spring.

BUTTERNUT BASIN (Mass. 23, 2 mi. e. of Great Barrington), 4100-foot double chair lift, three electric rope tows, trails, beginners' slopes. Lodge, ski shop, ski school, ski patrol.

GREENFIELD (Franklin County seat, sett. 1686, incorp. 1753, alt. 270, pop. 18,116, area 21.47 sq. mi., representative town meeting, routes, I–91, US 5, Mass. 2), with its wide, elm-shaded streets, is one of the most beautiful western Massachusetts towns. Greenfield took its name from the fertile Green River valley. Still a prosperous agricultural town, specializing in poultry, tobacco and dairy products, it is an industrial center. Early in the 19th century the first U.S. cutlery factory was established here, but it moved to Turner's Falls. Today more than 40 factories employ 3000 workers. Major products: tap and dies — it is the world's largest producer — cutlery, hand tools, general hardware, jewelry, silverware.

Green River knives, made by J. Russell and Company, were famous throughout the era of the Mountain Men in the Old West. Stamped across the blade just below the hilt were the words "Green River Works." When a mountain man stuck his knife into an enemy the phrase was "Up to Green River." The term eventually was the mountain man's supreme accolade. If he were up to Green River he were up to snuff.

Greenfield is the eastern terminus of the Mohawk Trail — that portion of Mass. 2 which leads over the Berkshires down into Williamstown, some 40 miles away.

Potter House (private), corner Main and High Sts., shows the extent to which Greek Revival influence was carried in American architecture.

St. James' Church (1847) (Episcopal), corner of Federal and Church Sts., reproduces the Church of St. Mary the Virgin, in South Milford, England.

Greenfield Historical Society (open 10–6) has its headquarters in the brick Devlin House at the corner of Church and Union Sts.

Rocky Mountain Park, a rugged area of high ridges, wooded copses and glens, occupies the high land west of the Connecticut River.

Covered Bridge (Leyden Rd.) is one of the few covered bridges in Massachusetts.

MOHAWK TRAIL SKIWAY AREA has 3 trails, 3 slopes, 3 tows for all classes. Open weekends and holidays.

GREENWICH (Hampshire County town inundated by Quabbin Reservoir).

GROTON (Middlesex County, sett. and incorp. 1655, alt. 300, pop. 5109, area 32.54 sq. mi., town meeting, routes, Mass. 40, 111, 119, 225).

In 1884 a young preacher returned from Tombstone, Arizona, where he won the respect of frontier gunfighters like Wyatt Earp and of saloonkeepers and prostitutes who contributed to his Episcopal Church. Rev. Endicott Peabody, a likable fellow adept with his fists, was quite different from the typical uneducated frontier preachers who spent more time ranting about the evils of rum than performing good works.

Rev. Peabody founded what is in some ways America's most famous private school — Groton — and fashioned it in the great tradition of English public schools which are not public but private. Peabody rode herd on his students to such an extent that old Grotonian Ambassador Averell Harriman remarked to his father, "You know he could be an awful bully if he weren't such a terrible Christian."

Grotonians, despite their families' great wealth, live in tiny rooms, wash in basins and lead a spartan existence. Boys who survive Groton usually make out well in the world. Grotonian Franklin D. Roosevelt — he and Anna Eleanor Roosevelt were married by the rector — brought other Grotonians into the New Deal: Dean Acheson, Sumner Welles, Averell Harriman, Francis and George Biddle and Joseph C. Grew. The school's alumni wield a mighty influence in world affairs.

Groton, the town, was probably named for the ancestral home of John Winthrop's family. Destroyed by Indians during King Philip's War, it was abandoned by settlers. Later rebuilt, it was successfully defended against Indians in 1694. In 1707 several residents were killed and children were carried off.

In the *Old Burying Ground* (1678), Hollis St., lies Revolutionary War veteran *Captain Job Shattuck,* who participated in Shays' Rebellion. Tried for treason, he was convicted, sentenced to be hanged, but was twice reprieved and finally pardoned.

Opposite the town hall is *Governor Boutwell House* (owned by the Groton Historical Society), built 1851 and visited by President U. S. Grant in 1869. It is a well-preserved frame mansion. George Sewall Boutwell (1818–1905) was an organizer of the Republican Party, governor and Secretary of the Treasury under Grant. Not far from the Boutwell House is the former *Home of Dr. Samuel Abbot Green* (1830–1918), physician, antiquarian, librarian and author.

The *First Parish Meeting House* (Unitarian) southeast of the center on Mass. 119, erected in 1755, was remodeled and partially turned around in 1839, and remodeled again in 1877 and in 1916. It is a white wooden church typical of its period, with two massive columns supporting the pediment front. Its delicate, slender spire, capped by a gilded ball and cock weathervane, rests on an inverted cone atop a belfry shuttered by wooden blinds. Its bell was cast by Paul Revere's foundry in 1819. Minutemen assembled on the common April 19, 1775.

Col. William Prescott, commander of the American forces at Bunker Hill, was born here.

GROVELAND (Essex County, sett. 1649, incorp. 1850, alt. 50, pop. 5382, area 8.9 sq. mi., town meeting, routes, Mass. 97, 113) is a quiet suburban village. The town once depended on waterpower supplied by Johnson's Creek for operating its mills. Eventually woolen mills disbanded. The *Congregational Church* (1727) has a Paul Revere bell inscribed with the popular somber reminder "The living to church I call, and to the grave I summon all."

In the East Parish section, grist-, saw- and fulling mills and tanyards were located soon after the Revolutionary War. A brass foundry was succeeded by a thread mill. These mills and farming were the town's early industries. Groveland was briefly the principal productive area lying within 35 miles of Boston. Poultry, dairy and market gardening, along with many semiagricultural farms, indicate good soil and effective use of it.,

CRANE POND WILDLIFE MANAGEMENT AREA (see GEORGETOWN).

HADLEY (Hampshire County, sett. 1659, incorp. 1661, alt. 129, pop. 3750, area 23.16 sq. mi., town meeting, routes, I–91, Mass. 9, 47, 116), named for Hadley or Hadleigh, England, former home of its founders, was settled by John Webster and Rev. John Russell. They left Connecticut because of religious dissension.

In 1683 Mary Webster, accused of bewitching and murdering Deacon Philip Smith, was "hung till nearly dead," taken down and buried in the snow. A hardy Yankee, she survived, and died several years later from natural causes.

The *Hadley Farm Museum* (open May 1–Oct. 12, 10–5, closed Mondays, free) is an old barn (1782) which has a Colonial doorway with a pediment resembling the bonnet tops of highboys or secretaries. The museum contains farm implements that trace the evolution of farming in the Connecticut Valley.

Adjacent to the town hall (Middle St.) is the *First Congregational Church* (1808), with a Wren-type spire surmounted by a weathercock brought from England in 1752. Over the double door is a semicircular fanlight, the whole framed by beautifully carved trim. The church has a silver communion service and cups of odd design, presented to the parish in 1724. Several original pews are still used.

The *Benjamin Smith Tavern* (open) (18th century), on Middle St., contains old relics and furniture. This house is notable for its windows on the main facade and its gable end, with two windows and a door. A rear ell connects with an old-fashioned carriage house.

Site of the House of the Reverend John Russell. Edmund Whalley and William Goffe, of the High Court of Justice established by the Commons which condemned Charles I to death, fled to America when the monarchy was restored. They came in 1664 to Hadley, where they were hidden and protected by Rev. Russell for 15 years. Tradition says Goffe, whose identity was not known locally, gave the alarm before a surprise attack by King Philip's warriors and led the confused townsmen in a successful defense.

Porter House (1713), the oldest dwelling in Hadley, is a white two-and-a-half-story house with gable roof and large central chimney.

A large white quartz boulder opposite the Porter House indicates the *Site of the Birthplace of Major General "Fighting Joe" Hooker* of Civil War fame. Hooker replaced cocky, incompetent Gen. Ambrose Burnside as commanding general of the Army of the Potomac and was in turn replaced by Gen. George Gordon Meade.

Porter-Phelps-Huntington House (open May 12–Oct. 1, daily 1–4:30 and mornings by appointment, small fee) (1753), jct. of Mass. 9 and 47. This house was the summer home of Hadley native Frederick Dan Huntington (1819–1904), first bishop of the Episcopal Diocese of Central New York. Surrounded by a split-rail fence, this large three-story gambrel-roof structure has a kitchen ell, woodshed and carriage house.

NORTH HADLEY. Opposite the church a farm road leads through fields to the *Site of an Indian Fort* on a bluff overlooking the banks of the Connecticut River. Indian skeletons have been discovered here.

HALIFAX (Plymouth County's geographical center, sett. *c.* 1670, incorp. 1734, alt. 103, pop. 3537, area 16.15 sq. mi., town meeting, routes, Mass. 36, 58, 106). Route 58 bisects the twin *Monponsett Lakes* via the century-old causeway crossing White Island where in July 1662, Wampanoag Sachem Wamsutta, son of Chief Massasoit, was arrested in his lodge by Plymouth vigilantes on conspiracy charges. This proud sachem died during his captivity. Modern historians view the episode as a tactical error which precipitated King Philip's War (see HISTORICAL NOTES). The Halifax Militia Company, chartered by Gov. John Hancock in 1792 and the oldest in the state, was the first militia unit to respond to President Lincoln's call to arms. The state's first monument in memory of Civil War dead was erected opposite the steepled meetinghouse. This church, dedicated in 1734, claims the creation of the original Sunday School. Halifax is noted for hothouse roses. Cranberry growing is the major industry.

HALL'S CORNER (see DUXBURY)

HAMILTON (Essex County, sett. 1638, incorp. 1793, alt. 55, pop. 6373, area 14.99 sq. mi., town meeting, routes, Mass. 1A, 22).

Hamilton's most noted resident, General George Patton, Jr. (1885–1945), the fast-moving, hard-hitting, cussing, colorful, controversial cavalryman, was a study in contrast to middle-class commuters who now comprise much of Hamilton's citizenry. Few large estates remain in Hamilton. One of the largest was that of the Ayer family. General Patton married a textile magnate's daughter, Beatrice Ayer.

First Congregational Church (remodeled in 1843), with a congregation formed in 1714, has a square tower surmounted by a steeple.

Town Hall is a white frame building with a well-proportioned cupola.

Beside the church is the *Covered Wagon House* (private), from which in December 1787 departed the first covered wagon for Northwest Territory. Yale man Manasseh Cutler (1742–1823), Hamilton's second pastor, was the moving force in this emigration.

On Bridge St., 0.2 mi. e. of the center, the *Oldest House* (private) (1680) in the town has an overhanging second story with carved pendrils. Wings added in later years show three distinct periods of architecture.

The polo field belongs to the *Myopia Hunt Club* (1882), so named because all the founders were nearsighted. An annual event is a combined horse show, polo match and steeplechase.

HAMPDEN (Hampden County, sett. *c.* 1741, incorp. 1878, alt. 300, pop. 4572, area 19.66 sq. mi., routes, unnumbered route).

Hampden, a residential village on the periphery of Springfield, was isolated for many years because of its lack of connecting roads.

Many former summer homes are becoming year-round residences. Hampden is now a bedroom community for Springfield area commuters.

American pianist and composer Anice Terhune, wife of the late writer Albert Payson Terhune, was a daughter of Hampden. Her novels, *The Boarder Up at Em's* and *Eyes of the Village,* contain characters said to be local townspeople. Thornton Burgess (1874–1965), author of stories for children, owned an estate here. The estate has been purchased by the Massachusetts Audubon Society.

A delightful little book, *Early Hampden—Its Settlers and the Homes They Built* (1959) by local historian Carl C. Howlett, should be read by all Hampden newcomers or visitors.

HAMPDEN COUNTY (est. 1812, pop. 459,050, area 622.46 sq. mi., shire town, Springfield) includes the 4 cities of Chicopee, Holyoke, Springfield and Westfield and the towns of Agawam, Blandford, Brimfield, Chester, East Longmeadow, Granville, Hampden, Holland, Longmeadow, Ludlow, Monson, Montgomery, Palmer, Russell, Southwick, Tolland, Wales, West Springfield and Wilbraham.

HAMPSHIRE COUNTY (est. 1662, pop. 123,981, area 529.20 sq. mi., shire town, Northampton) includes the city of Northampton and the 18 towns of Amherst, Belchertown, Chesterfield, Cummington, Easthampton, Goshen, Granby, Hadley, Huntington, Middlefield, Pelham, Plainfield, South Hadley, Southampton, Ware, Westhampton, Williamsburg and Worthington.

HANCOCK (Berkshire County, sett. 1767, incorp. 1776, alt. 1058, pop. 675, area 35.55 sq. mi., routes, Mass.–N.Y. 43) was named after John Hancock. It is a dairying community and a winter resort town.

JIMINY PEAK SKI AREA (between US 7 and Mass. 43) has novice, intermediate and expert slopes, 2 lifts, 2 tows, snack bar, instruction. Open weekends, holidays, Christmas week. Phone: 4–4663.

HANOVER (Plymouth County, sett. 1649, incorp. 1727, alt. 60, pop. 10,107, area 15.47 sq. mi., town meeting, routes, Mass. 3, 53, 123, 139).

Hanover Center was named by the early settlers in honor of King George I, the former Elector of Hanover. Early products: anchors, fittings for ships, cannonballs, hollowware and other articles from bog iron ore.

On the green are pre-Civil War *Two Ship's Howitzers.* East of the town hall on Hanover St. is the *Samuel Stetson House* (open June–Oct.,

Mon., Wed., Fri., 10–5 and by appointment, small fee) (1694), a shingled, two-and-a-half-story frame dwelling, owned by the Society for the Preservation of New England Antiquities. The house contains Colonial and Indian relics.

HANSON (Plymouth County, sett. 1632, incorp. 1820, alt. 100, pop. 7148, area 15.17 sq. mi., town meeting, routes, Mass. 27, 58), once Pembroke West Parish, was named after Alexander Contee Hanson (1786–1819), Baltimore editor whose *Federal Republican* newspaper, hostile to Madison, was destroyed by an 1812 mob.

Hanson Center has the *Town Hall* (1871) and overlooks lovely *Wampatuck Pond.* Many ponds provide substantial recreational facilities. Hanson has many lovely old homes.

The *Cushing House* (1724), corner of Liberty and Washington Sts. Here Mary Cushing married Gen. Benjamin Lincoln (1733–1810), who received Lord Cornwallis' sword at Yorktown. From this house Lucy Cushing presented a silk flag to the Pembroke Light Infantry at the outbreak of the War of 1812.

Lt. Commander Albert Cushing Read, whose forebears had lived for generations in the town, was the first to make a successful flight across the Atlantic, arriving May 27, 1919, in Lisbon, Portugal.

HARDWICK (Worcester County, sett. 1727, incorp. 1739, alt. 880, pop. 2379, area 38.40 sq. mi., town meeting, route, Mass. 32) is an agricultural community with inhabitants of English, Polish, French and Lettish stock. The land was purchased in 1686 from Nipmucks by eight Roxbury residents. No settlement was made then because the owners were afraid Royal Governor Andros would expropriate the land. First called Lambstown, the district was incorporated as Hardwick, probably for Philip York, first Earl of Hardwicke. The town is one of the largest milk-producing communities in the state.

Hardwick has four villages. HARDWICK VILLAGE and OLD FURNACE are farming communities. In GILBERTVILLE there is a foundry and several small industries. WHEELWRIGHT has a paper mill. Hardwick is noted for its lovely old common and public buildings.

HARTSVILLE (see NEW MARLBOROUGH)
(see also OAK BLUFFS)

HARVARD (Worcester County, sett. 1704, incorp. 1732, alt. 421, pop. 13,426, area 26.35 sq. mi., town meeting, routes, I–495, Mass. 2, 110, 111), named after Harvard University's first patron John Harvard, has always been a farming community despite spasmodic industrial attempts. A mine (1783) failed to produce silver. Fruit is now a major product.

The library (1793) contains the books of William Emerson, father of Ralph Waldo Emerson.

Harvard Astronomical Observatory (open), one of the best Eastern observatories, has radar and cameras for tracking and photographing. Films made here are filed at Harvard University.

Fruitlands Museum (open May 30–Sept. 30, daily except Mon. 1–5, small fee). Buildings include *Fruitlands* of Bronson Alcott's *New Eden.* This community (1843) was established as the nucleus of a new social order in which neither man nor beast should be exploited. The consociate family adopted vegetarianism and eschewed wool, cotton and leather. Mulberry trees were planted before it was learned that silk is obtained by exploiting silkworms. Consociates attempted to pull their plows, compromising on this point only when the planting season was far advanced with little ground ready for seed. Practical difficulties were so great that the experiment ended before there was an opportunity to demonstrate its high principles.

The museum has pictures and relics of leaders of this significant movement. The house, old and dilapidated at the time of the experiment, has been carefully restored. Visitors may see the fireplaces where the Alcott "little women" hung their Christmas stockings and Louisa's attic bedroom. The square, prim *Shaker House* nearby was moved here from the old Shaker community several miles away. Here in 1781 came "Mother Ann" Lee, founder of the American branch of the United Society of Believers in Christ's Second Appearing, known as the Shakers because of the rhythmic movement that was an essential part of the sect's ceremonies. The community, communistic and celibate, manifested itself in agricultural and industrial activity that was very successful and in the contrivance of ingenious laborsaving devices. Furniture, homemade costumes, implements and documents are displayed.

Indian Museum contains relics. The main part of this museum has been veneered with bricks from the former town hall of Lancaster.

Picture Gallery contains many Hudson River School paintings and portraits by old itinerant portraitists.

HARWICH (Barnstable County, sett. *c.* 1670, incorp. 1694, alt. 55, pop. 5892, area 20.93 sq. mi., town meeting, routes, Mass. 24, 28, 39).

Queen Elizabeth called the English village for which it was named "Happy-go-lucky Harwich," a term that can be applied to this charming namesake. Embedded in the pavement at the entrance to *Exchange Hall* is an inscribed flagstone, the gift of the borough of Harwich, England. Harwich was the "Harniss" of Joseph C. Lincoln's novels.

Harwich was a whaling and shipbuilding center. In the 19th century cod fishing largely supplanted whaling. Cranberries and catering to summer visitors are major industries.

The *Old Powder House* (private) (1770), at the center, a small, square stone building, served as a storehouse during the Revolutionary War. Adjoining is the *Brooks Library* (open June–Sept., Tues. 10–12, 7–9 P.M., Fri. 6:30–7:30 P.M., Sat. 1:30–4:30), which contains a permanent exhibit of American figurines by John Rogers, comprising 46 subjects.

HARWICHPORT is a summer resort. *Wychmere Harbor* provides a scenic anchorage for pleasure craft. Along the shore are *Remnants of the Horse Race Track,* once the sporting center of Cape Cod, but inundated by a terrific storm in 1884.

SOUTH HARWICH is a large summer colony with a good beach.

WEST HARWICH is a village with beautiful homes.

HATFIELD (Hampshire County, sett. 1661, incorp. 1670, alt. 129, pop. 2825, area 16.21 sq. mi., town meeting, routes, I–91, US 5, Mass. 10).

In 1675 800 Indians were repulsed after great slaughter. A captive squaw alleged to have divulged the Indians' plans was thrown by her tribe to savage dogs who tore her limb from limb. In 1677 12 inhabitants were killed and many were taken captive; in 1677–78 Stephen Jennings and Benjamin Waite of Hadley went to Quebec, where, with the aid of Gov. Frontenac and a ransom of £200, they secured the release of their wives and children.

Sophia Smith Homestead (open) (1700), 75 Main St., was the birthplace (1796) and home of the founder of Smith College (see NORTHAMPTON). In 1915 the Alumnae Association purchased the two-story frame dwelling, and the class of 1896 restored and refurnished it.

Other educators from Hatfield were Ephraim Williams (1714–55), founder of Williams College (see WILLIAMSTOWN), the Rev. Jonathan Dickinson (1688–1747), first president of the institution that later became Princeton University, and Elisha Williams, rector of Yale (1726–39).

Chief crops are onions and tobacco.

HAVERHILL (Essex County, sett. 1640, town incorp. 1641, city incorp. 1869, alt. 50, pop. 46,120, area 33.11 sq. mi., routes, I–495, Mass. 97, 113). Haverhill, onetime residence of merchant prince R. H. Macy and motion picture mogul Louis B. Mayer, (1885–1957), is noted for hats, shoes, a housewife who killed and scalped ten Indians, and the birthplace of abolitionist poet John Greenleaf Whittier (1807–92).

Haverhill developed in 300 years from a hardscrabble frontier village to an industrial city.

Its variegated past gives the city a flavor quite different from neighboring Lawrence. New houses shoulder weathered ones along wide streets. From the Haverhill bridge one can see upstream factories, office buildings and spires. Downstream lies the long, lovely perspective of rounded hills, neat farms and broad river of an unchanged New England.

Reverend John Ward and 12 followers could never have previsioned a town larger than the quiet market town of Haverhill, England, when they landed on the muddy Merrimack shore in 1640. Swift, wide waters were too powerful for them to harness, but they soon saw modest possibilities in the small, rapid streams rushing down from the hills. They offered land grants and other inducements to such applicants as would put them to use.

Haverhill for 100 years was a frontier town cut off by the Merrimack from secure coastal settlements. Settlers had no Indian trouble until King Philip's War (1675). Their position had many advantages. Glacial hillside soil was fertile, forests provided oak and pine timber and wilderness trails were avenues for a profitable fur trade. Oak and pine provided frames and planking for the ships built along the Merrimack. The first vessel was launched from a Haverhill yard in 1697. For 150 years town merchants sent their goods adventuring in their own ships. Pelts obtained from Indians were cured in tanneries which had flourished from 1643 and which are still a feature of the town's industrial life.

Hat making, recorded as early as 1747, was an important 19th-century industry and continues on a smaller scale.

The mercantile boom that swept Massachusetts' Federal period coastal cities aided Haverhill shipyards. Four yards in 1800 were turning out ships and schooners. South and West Indies trade flourished. Haverhill's position gradually surrendered to other coastal cities. Larger vessels which gained favor after the Revolution were not suited to river navigation. Trade was even more difficult after Newburyport merchants built the Chain Bridge across the Merrimack in 1811. Haverhill merchants turned manufacturers and invested profits in shoe, hat and comb factories and tanneries. In 1836 there were 28 Haverhill shoe factories.

The Goodyear turn shoe-stitching machine (1875) assured Haverhill's position as a manufacturing center of high-grade shoes. Later manufacturers specialized in fashionable female shoes.

Haverhill was one of the first eastern cities with commission government. Such a system was built on the theory that the modern city is essentially a great business enterprise and should be administered by methods regarded as efficient by successful commercial corporations.

Thomas Sanders (1839–1911) married Nathan Saltonstall Howe's daughter. Their first child was a deaf mute. Sanders hired teacher Alexander Graham Bell (1847–1922) and loaned him $110,000 for his telephone experiments. Sanders made a million and became president of the National Telephone Company and a top executive in the Bell System.

Minsk, Russia, native Louis B. Mayer, co-founder of Hollywood's MGM Studio, began the long trail to Hollywood as a Haverhill movie house projectionist. Future magnate Mayer soon controlled all movie houses in town.

Haverhill, despite a population loss of 4000 between 1960–70, has been named, according to the chamber of commerce, as one of New England's four growth areas.

In 1968 Haverhill built a new $1,000,000 library and a new $1,000,000 courthouse along with a 220-unit apartment for senior citizens. A new junior college — *Northern Essex Community College* — with 21 buildings for 2200 students has a 110-acre campus.

An industrial renewal program and two urban renewal projects were under way the same year.

Nearly 70 percent of the workers are engaged in shoe and leather production. Other important industries are apparel, paper, nonelectrical machinery and plastics. The total number of Haverhill workers engaged in all industry, business and services in 1967 was 12,800 with a total payroll of more than $57,000,000.

What To See and Do

Hannah Dustin Statue (1879) occupies a small triangular green near the junction of Main and Summer Sts. Abducted by Indians, Hannah escaped with the scalps of ten of her captors dangling from her belt.

Haverhill Public Library, Summer St., rich in Whittier souvenirs, contains a complete valuable collection of his first editions. This library is being replaced by a $1,000,000 building.

Reverend John Ward House (open Tues., Thurs., Sat. 2–5, free), Water St., the first frame house in Haverhill, was built (1645) for the first minister. The Haverhill Historical Society, present owners, restored the rooms and furnished them in seventeenth-century style.

Buttonwoods (open Tues., Thurs., Sat. 2–5, and by appointment, small fee includes John Ward House, Buttonwoods and Tenney Hall) (1814), headquarters of the Haverhill Historical Society, is adjacent to the Ward House and terraced high above the Merrimack.

Tenney Hall, a modern wing added to the brick-end clapboard building, contains Indian relics and area antiquities.

Spiller House or *Hazen Garrison House* (private) (1680–90), corner of Groveland and Water Sts., contains unusually large fireplaces with two huge beehive-shaped ovens. The window arrangement is unusual. The hardware, which includes oak latches and strap and butterfly hinges, is mostly original.

Winnikenni Reservation has tennis courts, bridle paths and hiking trails. In the background loom the massive gray walls of *Winnikenni Castle* (1873), in imitation of a Bath, England, medieval castle.

Kenoza Lake (Indian, "Lake of the Pickerel") lies nearby.

Birthplace of John Greenleaf Whittier (open Tues.–Sat. 10–6, Sun. 1–6, small fee) (1688), on State 110, 3 mi. from city, a fine example of a New England early American farmhouse, contains the desk on which the poet's earliest rhymes and last poem were written. The gentle Quaker poet, insensitive to the industrial city, preferred to sing of country ways and of the old stock from which he sprang.

First Church of Christ (organized 1682, erected 1848), across the common, is an adaptation of the late Colonial style, adorned with columns, cornice and a graceful steeple. The tower was used as a model for that of Henry Ford's Chapel of Mary and Martha, Dearborn, Mich.

A *Boulder* on the church green claims the birth here in 1810 of the foreign missionary movement in the United States, through the organization of the American Board of Commissioners for Foreign Missions. In 1812, missionaries Adoniram Judson and his wife and Mr. and Mrs. Samuel Newell sailed for Calcutta.

Bradford Junior College, South Main St. Founded in 1803 as an academy, it is believed to be the oldest upper school for girls in New England. No original buildings now stand.

HAWLEY (Franklin County, sett. 1771, incorp. 1792, alt. 1752, pop. 224, route, Mass. 8A) is a hilly rural town named after liberal Joseph Hawley (1723–88), who led the opposition to preacher Jonathan Edwards' revivalist theology. Hawley was an active revolutionist during the war. Hawley is a tiny settlement along an unnumbered road.

WEST HAWLEY, also a small settlement, is strung along Mass. 8A.

HAYDENVILLE (see WILLIAMSBURG)

HEATH (Franklin County, sett. 1765, incorp. 1785, alt. 1667, pop. 383, routes, Mass. 8A, unnumbered route) is a delightful hill village. An unused one-room schoolhouse, church, town hall, public library, Grange hall and several houses are about the well-kept village green. There is also a community hall which was the Methodist Church. The town was named after William Heath, a major general in the Continental Army. Staves and barrels were once made here, but Heath is a farming community. The restored *Old Town House* (1835) is maintained by the Heath Historical Society.

DELL is several houses — one with a dammed pool — at the junction of Mass. 8A and unnumbered hill road leading up to Heath village.

HINGHAM (Plymouth County, sett. *c.* 1633, incorp. 1635, alt. 50, pop. 18,845, area 22.46 sq. mi., town meeting, routes, Mass. 3A, 128).

Hingham, a lovely old South Shore village with winding tree-shaded streets, is a middle-class Boston suburb. The town was named for the English home of early settlers. Inhabited by Algonkians, the territory was conveyed to the English in 1665.

In the early 19th century fishing developed. In 1831, over 55,000 barrels of mackerel landed on Hingham wharves. Industry and agriculture are almost nonexistent today.

The *Site of Captain Benjamin Church's Home,* now occupied by the Norton House, is at 102 North St. Church's company defeated King Philip.
Old Garrison House (open), 123 North St., has been occupied by nine generations of the Perez Lincoln family, who settled in Hingham, 1633–35.
Samuel Lincoln House (open year round by appointment, free), at the fork of North and Lincoln Sts., is a two-and-a-half-story wooden structure, parts of which were built in 1667.
New North Church (open by arrangement with pastor), nearly opposite the Samuel Lincoln House, erected in 1807, is the work of Charles Bulfinch.
A part of the *Old Ordinary* (open mid-June–Labor Day, Tues.–Sat. 11:30–4:30, small fee), 19 Lincoln St., was built in 1650. This two-and-a-half-story unpainted structure houses the *Hingham Historical Society Collection* of old furniture. The front door and the two windows to the right mark the original length; the two windows to the left identify the addition (1740).
The *Old Ship Church* (Unitarian) (open mid-June–Sept. 1, Wed.–Sat. 10–12, 1–4, free), Main St., was built in 1681 by ship's carpenters and is the only 17th-century church now standing in Massachusetts. The roof is in the form of a truncated pyramid surmounted by a belfry and a lookout that gives the building its name.
In *Hingham Cemetery* at the rear of the church is the grave of General Benjamin Lincoln (1733–1810). Marked by an obelisk are (l.) the *Remains of the Old Fort* that protected the early inhabitants from Indian attack.

HINSDALE (Berkshire County, sett. 1763, incorp. 1804, alt. 1440, pop. 1588, area 21.16 sq. mi., town meeting, routes, Mass. 8, 143) soon after its settlement became an industrial town, utilizing the plentiful waterpower of the Housatonic River. Raising sheep to supply wool for local mills had some importance between 1800 and 1840. About 1895 there was brief excitement over an apparent discovery of gold. With the decline of textile industries, catering to tourists is now a profitable occupation. Most Hinsdalers commute elsewhere to work. Only two working farms remain.

Wyoming cattle baron, politician, frontiersman and father-in-law of Gen. John "Black Jack" Pershing, Hinsdale's most noted native son, Francis Warren (1844–1929) was twice GOP governor of Wyoming Territory. Elected in 1890 as the state's first governor, he resigned to run for the U.S. Senate in which he served 37 years. Fort D. A. Russell, outside Cheyenne, Wyo., is now Warren Air Force Base.

HOLBROOK (Norfolk County, sett. 1710, incorp. 1872, alt. 150, pop. 11,775, area 7.30 sq. mi., town meeting, routes, Mass. 37, 139). Though one of the earliest towns to manufacture boots and shoes, it is now without a single shoe factory.
Union Cemetery on Union St. has pioneers' graves.
Thayer House (private), 56 Union St., contains Colonial relics including a Boston newspaper with details of the Boston Massacre.

Nathaniel Belcher House (1754), 324 North Franklin St., a broad-gabled, two-story clapboard dwelling with a small central chimney, sits back from the road on a knoll.

STATE FOREST FIRE TOWER on Turkey Hill (alt. 280) has tables for picnicking and an enclosed observatory offering a broad view of the countryside.

HOLDEN (Worcester County, sett. 1723, incorp. 1741, alt. 818, pop. 12,564, area 35.50 sq. mi., town meeting, routes, Mass. 31, 122A) was once known as the "North Half" of Worcester; at its incorporation it was named for Samuel Holden, a philanthropic London merchant. Truck gardening, fruit growing and poultry raising are the principal agricultural pursuits.

Holden was the home of Capt. Webb in whose company a descendant of Gov. Bradford, Deborah Sampson, disguised as a young man, served during the Revolution.

MIDDLESEX FELLS RESERVATION RECREATION AREA: zoo, foot and bridle trails, freshwater fishing, picnic sites, observation tower, swimming pool, natural and artificial ice skating, 2630 acres of woodlands and meadows patrolled by MDC mounted police (for details see MIDDLESEX FELLS RESERVATION).

HOLLAND (Hampden County, sett. 1725, incorp. 1835, alt. 743, pop. 931, area 12.35 sq. mi., town meeting, route, Mass. 15) was settled by Joseph Blodgett and named after Lord Holland, father of Charles James Fox. Destruction of a textile mill by lightning in 1851 ended a brief period of manufacture. Agriculture resumed its importance. Holland in the mid-1960's had one restaurant but no stores.

HOLLAND POND RECREATION AREA was built within the East Brimfield Flood Control Area by the U.S. Army Corps of Engineers. Facilities: fireplaces, picnic tables, swimming.

HOLLISTON (Middlesex County, sett. *c.* 1659, incorp. 1724, alt. 188, pop. 12,069, area 18.89 sq. mi., town meeting, routes, 16, 126) was named for Thomas Hollis, an early benefactor of Harvard College. An agricultural community, it is surrounded by wooded upland and open meadows.

Holliston was visited by a strange plague between 1752 and 1754 and lost more than an eighth of its population. The disease, never identified, did not spread beyond Holliston.

Winthrop Pond (off Winthrop St.), a delightful body of water enclosed by wooded banks, is stocked with perch. On the east side of the pond rises *Mt. Goulding.* Two town parks provide good swimming and boating.

HOLYOKE (Hampden County, sett. 1745, town incorp. 1850, city incorp. 1873, alt. 152, pop. 50,112, area 21.16 sq. mi., mayor-council, routes, I–91, US 5, 202, Mass. 116, 141).

Holyoke, one of the world's great manufacturing centers of fine writing paper and a leading Pioneer Valley city, owes much of its industrial importance to its location on the Connecticut River. In past years Holyoke was the end of the line for the long log drives which commenced way up river in the forests of Vermont and New Hampshire. The now placid city was then the scene of many a logger's spree after the long, dangerous drive down river. Holyoke tavern floors were pock-marked by steel-calked loggers' boots.

Volleyball was originated here in 1895 by YMCA instructor W. G. Morgan.

Entered from the north, Holyoke is modern, well-groomed and prosperous. To the south are a number of imposing Catholic institutions, educational and charitable. The manufacturing center lies along the power canals. The domestic waterworks and gas and electric plants are municipally owned. The city hall, a striking building with a great granite tower, is an object of civic pride. Cultural pursuits are evidenced by the excellent natural history museum and art gallery, both at the public library, by the Holyoke League of Arts and Crafts and by a number of musical organizations.

The first foreigners were the Irish, whose descendants constitute one third of the present population. These people, with the French-Canadians, make the city an outstanding Catholic center. Poles number about ten percent of the inhabitants. The rest are of English, Scotch, German, Italian, Greek, Scandinavian or Jewish origin. This foreign growth has come in the past 120 years, but it is the very essence of Holyoke. Indian arrowheads in the public library are the only reminder that there was a settlement here in 1725.

During the Revolution the village was a farming community centered about a tavern that was halfway between Springfield and Northampton. Hadley Falls' waterpower attracted pioneer manufacturers. After the construction of a dam in 1828, small textile, grain and metal mills were established. In 1848 Boston and New York developers secured water rights from the old Hadley Falls Company. A $75,000 dam was built but on the day of its completion, it collapsed because designers miscalculated the tremendous pressures that would be exerted on its base.

A $150,000 dam, completed the following year, lasted until 1900. The present dam and its great waterfall are visible from the uppermost bridge. The dam withstood the great 1936 flood.

Skinner Memorial Chapel (Congregational), Appleton and Maple Sts., is typical Gothic style. An interior panel representing the conversion of the Ethiopian eunuch by St. Philip is surrounded by stained-glass windows.

Church of the Blessed Sacrament (Roman Catholic), 1951 Northampton St. (US 5) and Westfield Rd., is an interesting "in the round" church of

contemporary design. Sixteen aisles spread out from the center altar. There are banks of well-executed stained-glass windows.
Holyoke Museum of Natural History and Art (open Mon.–Sat. 10–12, 1–5, free), Cabot and Beech Sts.

DINOSAUR FOOTPRINTS (7.5 acres), west bank of Connecticut River off US 5, a reservation designed to protect dinosaur footprints made 150,000,000 years ago, is owned and maintained by TOR.

MT. TOM STATE RESERVATION (1800 acres) is reached from US 5 in Holyoke or Mass. 141 from Easthampton. Facilities: fishing, skating, campsites, scenic views. It is open Apr.–Oct. 8 A.M.–9:30 P.M., Nov.–Mar. 8 A.M.–6 P.M.

MT. TOM SKI AREA (off US 5 and 5 mi. from Exit 4 of Mass. Turnpike) has chair-lift, 2 T-bar lifts, 2 rope tows. Slopes and trails for all classes. Skiing every night until 10 P.M. Ski shop, ski rentals, ski patrol, snow-making equipment, base lodge, restaurants. Certified Swiss and USEASA instructors. Open every day and night.

HOOSAC TUNNEL VILLAGE (see FLORIDA)

HOPEDALE (Worcester County, sett. 1660, incorp. 1886, alt. 300, pop. 4292, area 5.12 sq. mi., town meeting, routes, Mass. 16, 140). Originally in Mendon, the land was purchased in 1841 for the establishment of a communistic religious community by a joint-stock company under Universalist minister Adin Ballou. Hopedale Fraternal Community paid for educating its children and made its own streets, though taxes were paid to Milford. E. D. Draper succeeded Ballou as community president. Owning three fourths of the joint stock, he dissolved the experiment. Draper made textile machinery. In the small park is the *Adin Ballou* statue.

HOPKINTON (Middlesex County, sett. *c.* 1715, incorp. 1744, alt. 450, pop. 5981, area 26.40 sq. mi., town meeting, routes, Mass. 85, 135) was named for Gov. Edward Hopkins (Conn.). The highest town in Middlesex County, first settlers from surrounding villages leased the land from Harvard College, executor of Hopkins's estate. This town is the birthplace of Daniel Shays (1747–1825), leader of Shays' Rebellion, and of Lee Claflin (1791–1871), a founder of Boston University and of Claflin University in South Carolina. Pegged shoes were first made by Joseph Walker in 1818. Walker's invention changed shoemaking.
Facing the common is the *Valentine Tavern* (private) (1750), a rambling structure of cut stone and gray clapboards with a modern shingled roof; Washington, Lafayette and Daniel Webster are reported to have slept here.
In *Mt. Auburn Cemetery* (Mayhew St.), in the northeast corner adjacent

to the town vault, is the *Grave of the Unknown Indian.* For many years residents were surprised to find this grave decorated on Memorial Day. One citizen secreted himself to watch for the donor, but though he came earlier each succeeding year, the grave was always decorated before he arrived. After the death of an elderly lady, the floral tribute ceased.

Every April 19th — Patriot's Day — Hopkinton makes the sports pages, and sometimes the front page, of daily papers throughout the world. The Boston Athletic Association starts its 26-mile-long Marathon here. In recent years, the winners — mostly foreigners — have made the long grind to Boston in slightly over two hours.

HOPKINTON STATE PARK includes the shoreline of Hopkinton Reservoir. Facilities: fishing, swimming, picnicking, hiking, snowmobiling.

WHITEHALL STATE PARK (600 acres). Facilities: fishing, snowmobiling, views.

HUBBARDSTON (Worcester County, sett. 1737, incorp. 1767, alt. 993, pop. 1437, area 40.34 sq. mi., town meeting, routes, Mass. 62, 68) is named for Thomas Hubbard, a proprietor who promised to provide window glass for the first meeting house if the district were named for him.

Many residents of this rural community are Finnish. Farms produce poultry and milk. Industries include horse blanket and boot factories. The chief industries now are Wain-Roy Corporation, makers of tractors and back-hoes, and the Curtis Lumber Company.

The first settlers were Eleazer Brown and his wife, whose 60-acre farm was granted on the condition that "he or his heirs keep a house thereon for the entertainment of travelers, for a space of seven years."

About 1790 an apple tree was found in a pasture bearing apples of unusually fine flavor; this, the parent tree of the popular Hubbardston Nonesuch apple, blew down in 1895.

The town attracted notice through native rascal, Ephraim Grimes, a convicted counterfeiter, as his cropped ear indicated. He once went into a store and asked the price of enough ribbon to reach "from ear to ear." When told "a few cents," he cried, "Begin to measure off! I have one here and they have the other in Worcester."

Hubbardston Free Public Library (Main St.) was once the Jonas G. Clark Library — against the donor's wishes. He founded Clark University (see WORCESTER).

There are several recreation areas here including camp grounds and attractive spring-fed *Asnacomet Pond.* Public hunting in *Barre Falls* and *Hubbardston Wildlife Management Areas.*

HUDSON (Middlesex County, sett. 1699, incorp. 1866, alt. 250, pop. 16,084, area 11,084 sq. mi., town meeting, routes, Interstate 495, Mass. 62,

85). First known as the Mills, then as Feltonville, Hudson received its present name when Charles Hudson agreed to give $500 as the foundation for a library if the change were made. In 1816 Daniel Stratton began manufacturing shoes. Francis Brigham, introducing machinery in 1835 and utilizing Assabet River water power, made this industry the most important in the town. Dye factories, tanneries, machine shops, box factories and cloth mills appeared. Industries drew Portuguese, French, Greek, Russian, Jewish and Italian workers. On July 4, 1894, firecrackers started a fire that destroyed about 40 buildings, chiefly factories. The area was rebuilt. Hudson's principal products are textiles, machinery and leather goods.

HULL (Plymouth County, sett. 1624, incorp. 1647, alt. 50, pop. 9961, area 2.43 sq. mi., town meeting, route, eastern terminus of Mass. 128) is notable for its major playground, Nantasket Beach. Hull Beach is lined with summer cottages and hills covered with homes. The first building in this region was a trading post erected by traders from Plymouth. The first settlers were John Oldham, John Lyford and Roger Conant. Oldham and Lyford had been expelled from Plymouth Colony for sedition and alleged profanation of the church. Oldham was killed by the Indians after his companions had moved to Cape Ann and then Salem. Other settlers developed the fishing industry to such an extent that the colony was taxed one eleventh of the Boston total in 1630.

Public Library is on the site of Hunt House (1644), the first rectory in Hull. Parishioners were once so far behind in his wages that Rev. Veazie was forced to sue them; in the meantime he was in such desperate straits that, hearing the carcass of a horse was on the beach, he hurried there to get the skin, only to find a parishioner had arrived ahead of him. In desperation, the clergyman removed the horse's shoes, which he sold to the village blacksmith for 25¢.

The original rectory was torn down in 1888 by its owner John Boyle O'Reilly (1844–90), poet, professional Irish patriot and editor of the Boston Catholic weekly *The Pilot*. His wife designed the present structure. The town purchased the house and converted it to its present use.

Cushing House (private), northeast of the center on Spring St., was built in 1725. This two-and-a-half-story house, once owned by Royal Navy captain Daniel Souther, a Cushing relative, was visited by Revolutionary firebrand James Otis.

Nantasket Beach (open during summer), a three-mile-long Yankee version of Coney Island, is one of the most popular places for surf bathing on the Atlantic seaboard. Opposite it and extending half its length, *Paragon Park* offers a variety of amusements. There is a state-maintained bathhouse. *Strawberry Hill* affords a view of the Atlantic Ocean and the bay. Tradition says that many of the hundreds of vessels wrecked in early days on the rocks off Point Allerton were drawn from their courses by false lights hung by wreckers who wished to salvage the cargoes.

HUNTINGTON (Hampshire County, sett. 1769, incorp. 1775, alt. 328, pop. 1593, area 26.24 sq. mi., town meeting, routes, US 20, Mass. 60, 112), was first called Norwich and later named for Charles F. Huntington. The town was barely a year old when it organized a military company and began to store ammunition. The conservative townsfolk displayed little sympathy with Shays' Rebellion, so rebels stormed the town and captured Capt. John Kirkland, local militiaman.

This residential town has a substantial summer population.

Public hunting in *Canada Hill* and *Knightville Wildlife Management Areas.*

HYANNIS (see BARNSTABLE)

HYANNISPORT (see BARNSTABLE)

HYDE PARK (see BOSTON)

IPSWICH (Essex County, sett. 1633, incorp. 1634, alt. 50, pop. 10,750, area 32.21 sq. mi., town meeting, routes, US 1, 1A, Mass. 133), first known as Agawam, was settled by 12 pioneers, among whom were three or more "gentlemen" who set the tone for this remote 17th-century cultural center. Poet Anne Bradstreet lived here.

Rebellion Tablet marks the spot where in 1687 the townsfolk, led by John Wise, protested Governor Andros' tyranny.

On the North Green stood the *First Parish Church* (1635). Deep in the rock beside the present Congregational building (1847) is a cloven hoof-print left, legend says, by the Devil. The lovely church was completely destroyed by a lightning-caused fire in 1965. Plans are under way to build a replica.

Lacemaking, the first industry here, was supplanted by tanning, shoe-making and machine knitting. Small parts of the knitting machines were secreted in Yorkshire butter pots and brought to Ipswich in defiance of English export laws.

The *Choate Bridge* (1764) is a Mass. historic landmark of rough granite blocks spanning Ipswich River. Digging and marketing clams and tourism support many residents.

The *South Church* (1748), with white-columned portico and classic simple exterior, overlooks the South Green.

John Whipple House (open April–Oct., Tues.–Sat. 10–5, Sun. 1–5, small fee) (*c.* 1640) has an overhanging gable end, massive central chimney and a long lean-to roof. The well-preserved, age-darkened timbers are exposed in the low-ceilinged rooms — one of the very few existing with hand-carved shadow mouldings in every room. This is one of the oldest wooden houses in the United States. The house now contains the Ipswich Historical Society's collection of 17th- and 18th-century furnishings.

The garden, maintained by the Ipswich Garden Club, contains 17th-century herb types.
Thomas F. Waters Memorial (open May 1–Oct. 15, Tues.–Sat. 10–5, Sun. 1–5, small fee), was built in the 18th century by the father of Capt. Augustine Heard, noted China trade skipper. Contains Chinese and early American furnishings.
Lakeman-Johnson House (open: mid-June–Sept. 30, Tues., Thurs., Sat. 10–5, contribution), 16 East St. Furnishings and contents are said to be typical of sea captains' homes.
Emerson-Howard House (open mid-June–Sept. 30, Mon.–Thurs. 2–5 and by appointment, contribution) (1648), Turkey Shore Rd., is one of the oldest wooden houses in the United States.

RICHARD T. CRANE, JR. MEMORIAL RESERVATION (1315 acres), 6 mi. from Ipswich on Argilla Rd., includes an ocean beach several miles long — one of the finest beaches in the northeastern U.S. — magnificent sand dunes, Castle, Middle and Steep Hills. The *Great House,* a castlelike structure, once the Crane residence, is a center for summer concerts and art lectures.

CRANE'S BEACH has bathhouses, showers, refreshment stand and a parking lot for at least 1000 cars. Life guards are on duty. Charcoal grills and fires are permitted on the beach, which is open daily 9 A.M.–10 P.M., May 30–post-Labor Day weekend. Open weekends, May 1–29.

JAMAICA PLAIN (see BOSTON)

JOHNSON JUNCTION (see HARWICH)

KINGSTON (Plymouth County, sett. 1620, incorp. 1726, alt. 50, pop. 5999, area 18.55 sq. mi., town meeting, routes, Mass. 3, 27, 106). Passengers of the *Mayflower,* the *Fortune* and the *Ann* settled here. It was Plymouth Town until 1726. Shipbuilding, a thriving industry, ceased in 1887.
First Congregational Parish Church (Unitarian) (1717), Main St., is a gray frame building with an open belfry, round-headed windows and blinds.
Squire William Sever House (seen by appointment) (1760), Linden St., is a frame structure with three large, black-capped chimneys and a roof surrounded by a white railing.
Bradford House (open) (1674), with weatherbeaten, unstained shingles, retains its original appearance and contains some of the early furnishings. Windows with diamond-shaped panes, a huge fireplace with a Dutch oven, looms and an old rack for hooking rugs are well preserved.

LAKEVILLE (Plymouth County, sett. 1717, incorp. 1853, alt. 94, pop. 4376, area 36.16 sq. mi., town meeting, routes, Mass. 18, 79, 105), was once an Indian village. King Philip's brother-in-law deeded the area to Sassamon. In 1674 Sassamon revealed Philip's war plans to the colonists. Branded a traitor, he was executed by three fellow braves who were then executed by the whites.

Indians lived about Lakeville's picturesque lakes and ponds. Half-breed Charlotte Mitchell, the last of a once powerful tribe, died about 1930. Lakeville's population increased about 50 percent in the 1950–60 decade, largely because of the influx of Boston commuters.

Pond Burying Ground, along the shores of Assawampsett Pond, contains Indian graves. This pond is the largest natural freshwater body in the state (2220 acres).

LANCASTER (Worcester County, sett. 1643, incorp. 1653, alt. 300, pop. 6095, area 27.65 sq. mi., town meeting, routes, Mass. 2, 62, 117), whose greatest native son was plant wizard Luther Burbank (1849–1926), was almost named Prescott after a local blacksmith. The General Court ruled against the request of the town fathers: "Whereas no town of the Colonies had as yet been named for any Governor: and whereas it were unseemly that a blacksmith be honored ahead of his betters, the name Prescott could not be permitted."

Disappointed would-be Prescottites who knew that a blacksmith is more important than a governor, to farmers, anyway, named their town after Lancaster, England.

The settlement, destroyed in King Philip's War, was burnt by Indian raiders in 1696 and 1704. Lancaster has always primarily been a residential and farming town.

Old Meeting House (Lancaster Church) of brick laid in Flemish bond may well be Charles Bulfinch's finest church design. The building (1816) reflects the beginning of Greek influence in American architecture. The church is usually open during services only.

In the days of *Bridge Cake Plain* (origin of name unknown) two men who held adjacent pews feuded. One erected a "spite fence" between the two pews so that his devotion would not be disturbed by the sight of his hated neighbor. Church authorities ruled the high screen "un-Christian" and had it removed.

Luther Burbank's Birthplace was purchased by his friend Henry Ford and removed to Dearborn Village, Michigan.

Thayer Bird Museum (open May 15–Oct. 15, Mon., Wed., Sat. 1–5, free) was willed to Harvard University's Museum of Comparative Zoology by Col. John E. Thayer. Some birds have been moved to Cambridge, but most of them are still here.

Rowlandson Rock (George Hill) is where Mary Rowlandson and her Indian captors camped.

FORT DEVENS WILDLIFE MANAGEMENT AREA has public hunting. Special free daily permit needed.

LANESBOROUGH (Berkshire County, sett. *c.* 1753, incorp. 1765, alt. 1160, pop. 2972, area 21.16 sq. mi., town meeting, routes, US 7, Mass. 8), originally New Framingham, was incorporated as Lanesborough in honor of the beautiful Countess of Lanesborough, a "friend" of the governor of Massachusetts. Except for some white marble quarrying, farming has always been the source of livelihood.

Constitution Hill was named in memory of Jonathan Smith, who in a well-timed speech swung the state for the ratification of the federal Constitution.

LAWRENCE (Essex County, sett. 1655, town incorp. 1847, city incorp. 1853, alt. 50, pop. 66,915, area 6.75 sq. mi., mayor-aldermen, routes I–95, Mass. 28, 110).

Lawrence, a child of the Industrial Revolution, carved from the flanks of Andover on the South and Methuen on the North, is divided by the Merrimack River. Its waterpower once made it possible for residents to boast that they lived in the Worsted Capital of the World. That day has passed and as the city looks ahead it is faced with problems common to many core cities: a sagging industrial base, much substandard housing and a shrinking population.

In 1845 Boston financiers founded the Essex Company to utilize Bodwell Falls' waterpower. A 6.75-square-mile area, including present Lawrence and parts of Andover and Methuen towns, was purchased. Principal stockholder and first president Abbott Lawrence (1792–1855) and his brothers Amos (1786–1852) and William (1783–1848) had the foresight and courage to envision an industrial city where but 20 families lived.

In three years, a great dam, the heart of the enterprise, was completed. Hills were leveled, valleys filled in, factories built and equipped and long rows of dreary look-alike workers' houses erected. Two canals were dug, and a shop for constructing steam locomotives had been built along with the Prospect Hill Reservoir, a gasworks, 50 brick buildings, a large boardinghouse and several mills.

Immigrants included English and Irish mechanics, weavers, printers and engravers. French Canadians, Poles, Syrians and Armenians who came later were mostly unskilled laborers.

Boomtown Lawrence, despite the enormous construction program, lacked many community necessities. There was no store until 1846. Railroad passenger service was established by the Boston & Maine in 1847. The *Merrimack Courier* was issued in 1846. The first established church in this now predominantly Roman Catholic city was the Free Will Baptist in 1846.

Rapid growth coupled with the builders' focus upon industrial production rather than on social progress resulted in unfortunate living and working conditions. Sanitation, proper heating and ventilation were lacking. Overcrowding, long working hours and low pay prevailed. Little or no consideration was given in factory design to health or safety.

In 1860 the Pemberton Factory's flimsy roof crashed in. The debris caught fire and 525 workers were killed, burned or injured.

Strike

In 1912 workers struck in protest against intolerable conditions and low pay. Management was represented by a priest, Father James T. Reilly. The strike led by the "wobblies" of the Industrial Workers of the World and directed by onetime cowboy and miner "Big Bill" Haywood (1869–1928) and Elizabeth Gurley Flynn was successful. The strikers gained a one cent an hour increase and the privilege of returning to work without ostensible discrimination for union activity. These gains seem small judged by today's standards, but they were substantial for the time when labor's right to organize had yet to acquire a legal basis. Lawrence labor since 1912 has led a comparatively peaceful existence.

The Depression

The Depression plight of the great industries posed problems. Thousands of workers were jobless. Leading businessmen created the Lawrence Industrial Bureau, which, from 1929 into 1936, reclaimed more than 2,500,000 square feet of vacated textile manufacturing space for industrial purposes. Twenty-nine new industries employing more than 3000 workers were brought to Lawrence.

The Depression was hard on Lawrence, but its national character disguised for a time an ugly fact: mills were moving South with an alarming degree of regularity.

After WWII, Lawrence continued to lose industry and population. Ten thousand residents departed in the 1950–60 decade. The textile firms which had been the lifeblood of the urban economy completed their southward migration while the city's middle and upper classes moved into the suburbs.

Lawrence Fights Back

In the late 1950's the city's plight had become desperate enough to convince both the politicians and the businessmen that large-scale urban renewal would be necessary if the city were to survive. Accordingly, the Lawrence Redevelopment Authority was organized and a renewal program was planned. The first projects included an industrial park, a residential development and a portion of the downtown commercial area.

Lawrence's most important industries today are (1) leather products, (2) paper products, (3) wearing apparel, (4) textiles, (5) fabricated metal products. Four out of ten workers are women.

What To See and Do

Wool Mill, Merrimack and South Union St. The American Woolen Company's building (1905) was once the largest worsted mill building in the world.

Everett Mill, 15 Union Street. This building (1910) was the largest cotton mill under one roof at the time of its completion.

Mill Boarding House, 401–403 Canal St., is typical of the dozens like it which housed mill hands. Atlantic Cotton Mills workers lived in this particular building, one of the few remaining of its type.

Rowhouses, 6–38 Orchard and 111–137 Garden St., were built by the Essex Company in 1847.

Rowhouses, Wood, Washington and Prospect Ways, built by the American Woolen Company (1907), include six blocks of seven houses each, fashioned after early Philadelphia rowhouses.

The *Common,* between Haverhill and Common Sts., is surrounded by public buildings, schools and churches. Near the pond stands a large wooden flagpole which commemorates the Flag Day celebration held by vigilantes protesting the strike of 1912.

The *Bodwell House* (private), 33 East Haverhill St., erected about 1708 (ells added later), is the only early surviving landmark.

Lawrence General Hospital (Prospect St.) grounds provide an unparalleled *View of Industrial Lawrence,* with its red-brick chimneys emitting smoke periodically, miles of red-brick factories with clock towers and small-paned windows and the canal with its dull look of cooling metal.

North Canal, Union St., is about 5330 feet long. This and the South Canal across the Merrimack were startling engineering feats in their day. The North Canal, built in connection with the Great Lawrence Dam in 1845, diverts Merrimack waters to supply the mills along Canal St.

South Canal, built in 1866, is about 2000 feet long.

Great Stone Dam, above O'Leary Bridge, built in 1845 to furnish waterpower from the falls, was a notable engineering achievement.

LAWRENCE-HAVERHILL METROPOLITAN AREA (pop. 205,641, area 128.90 sq. mi.) includes the cities of Haverhill and Lawrence and the towns of Andover, Groveland, Methuen and North Andover, Massachusetts, and Plaistow, Newton, and Salem, New Hampshire. The two latter towns are excluded from population and area data.

LEE (Berkshire County, sett. 1760, incorp. 1777, alt. 888, pop. 6426, area 26.51 sq. mi., town meeting, routes, Mass. Turnpike Interchange 2, US 20, Mass. 102). Named for Revolutionary war traitor Gen. Charles Lee, Lee is a prosperous paper manufacturing town. Because of its abundant waterpower, three mills had been built by 1821; the Smith Paper Company, one of the first to use wood pulp, greatly reduced the price of newsprint. This company in 1913 began manufacturing India Bible paper, up to that time exclusively a British product. It is said that one half of the cigarette paper used in WWI was made in Lee.

Pelham: Town Hall

Lexington Green

Otis is a tiny hill town

Skiing at Thunder Mountain on the Mohawk Trail

A view of Sunderland from Mount Sugarloaf

"Fences make good neighbors" in Berkshire farm country

Only a few oxen left in Massachusetts

The slender-spired *Congregational Church* (1857) has walls and ceilings decorated by an itinerant German painter in fresco. The white marble *Public Library* occupies the site of the log house where settlers held their first town meetings.

On Orchard St. is the entrance to *Ferncliff,* an evergreen-crowned eminence, on the northwest slope of which is *Peter's Cave,* the hiding place of Peter Wilcox, Jr., condemned to die for his participation in Shays' Rebellion. He was captured but eventually pardoned.

The *Lime and Marble Quarries* supplied marble for the Capitol at Washington, D.C., and for Philadelphia City Hall. The small mill nearby has cut thousands of headstones for the graves of soldiers buried in Arlington Cemetery.

OAK 'N' SPRUCE SKI AREA (off Mass. 102 in South Lee) is a resort lodge with rope tow, 2 slopes, night skiing under lights, toboggan run, sleighing, ice skating. Dining room, cocktails, meals, rooms, dancing, ski rentals, instruction. Phone: 243–3500.

OCTOBER MT. STATE FOREST (14,000 acres), the state's largest state forest, includes a section of the Appalachian Trail (overnight shelter for hikers). Facilities: bridle trails, fishing, hiking, hunting, campsites (50), fireplaces, very scenic views, snowmobiling.

LEICESTER (Worcester County, sett. 1713, incorp. 1722, alt. 1009, pop. 9140, area 22.70 sq. mi., town meeting, routes, Mass. 9, 56), now a manufacturing and residential community, offered hospitality to Quakers and Anabaptists when they were persecuted elsewhere.

Since 1786 the town has been identified with woolen trades. By 1890 one fourth of wool cards used in the United States were produced here. Ten woolen mills were established. Present manufactures include cards and shuttles, children's games, advertising literature and flannel.

Site of the Shack of Peter Salem, a Negro who killed British Major Pitcairn at Bunker Hill. After the war Salem came to Leicester where he built a crude hut and lived in poverty until, in his old age, he was taken to the Framingham poorhouse, where he died.

MOOSE HILL WILDLIFE MANAGEMENT AREA has public hunting in Paxton, Leicester, and Spencer.

LENOX (Berkshire County, sett. *c.* 1750, incorp. 1775, alt. 1250, pop. 5804, area 21.48 sq. mi., town meeting, routes, US 7, 20).

Lovely Lenox, one of the oldest Berkshire summer resorts, was an early writers' colony; Nathaniel Hawthorne, Fanny Kemble, Catharine Sedgwick and Henry Ward Beecher were residents or visitors.

Lenox is the site of *Tanglewood,* summer home of Boston's famed Symphony Orchestra on a 200-acre estate (Hawthorne Rd.). The Music Shed seats 6000 people, but during the six-week-long Berkshire Music Festival (early July–mid-August) twice that number are accommodated on the broad Tanglewood lawns.

Hawthorne Cottage (closed to public) is on the Tanglewood grounds. Here Hawthorne wrote *Tanglewood Tales.* The original cottage was destroyed by fire in 1891 and rebuilt in 1948.

The town was named for Charles Lenox, Duke of Richmond, a defender of Colonial rights. Town industries once included an iron foundry, marble works, hearthstone mill and glass factory, but today the town is a summer resort with fine hotels and magnificent homes. Lenox has eight private schools, mostly located on former private estates.

The *Lenox Library,* at the town center, in the former County Courthouse (1816), exhibits rare books and manuscripts. A side door opens into a shaded garden with seats for readers.

The *Lenox Boys' School,* a group of fine, yellow-painted clapboard buildings with extensive grounds, was formerly Mrs. Charles Sedgwick's School for Girls. Catharine Maria Sedgwick (1798–1867), the first person to write of the natural beauties of the Berkshires, lived here.

Edith Wharton's home, *The Mount,* on the north shore of Laurel Lake, was often visited by Henry James.

PLEASANT VALLEY WILDLIFE SANCTUARY, Dugway Road off US 7 and 20 (660 acres). Turn off by Holiday Inn. This area preserves a small but representative section of the Berkshires. See active beaver pond. Visit trailside museum. Try hiking trails. Natural history day camp. Massachusetts Audubon Society project.

AVALOCH SKI AREA (West St.), 3 trails, rope tow, snack bar, ski rentals, ski school. Open daily. Phone: 637–9706.

EASTOVER SKI AREA (off US 7) has 2 rope tows, 2 slopes, 1500-foot toboggan run with cable car. Glass-enclosed, heated swimming pool. Finnish steam baths, dancing, hayrides, meals, dorms, rooms. Open year-round. Phone: 637–0625.

HOUSATONIC VALLEY WILDLIFE MANAGEMENT AREA has public hunting.

LEOMINSTER (Worcester County, sett. 1635, town incorp. 1740, city incorp. 1915, alt. 400, pop. 32,939, area 28.81 sq. mi., mayor-council, routes, Mass. 2, 12, 31), should be pronounced Lem′ inster.

The territory that is now Leominster, once part of adjacent Lancaster, was bought from Nashua Chief Sholan in 1701. The town was called Leominster after the English town. In recent years ties between the two cities have been renewed by their respective chambers of commerce and service clubs.

Farming Leominster began its industrial era — there are now more than 100 plants, most of them plastics producers — when Obadia Hills began making horn combs about 1770. By 1845 twenty-four comb factories were operating. Until the Depression the city made more than 70 percent of the nation's piano cases.

Leominster today advertises itself as the pioneer plastic city. Local products include rubber goods, apparel, paper products, nonelectrical machinery and chemical products.

Leominster's most noted native son was John Chapman (1775–1847), known as "Johnny Appleseed," who carried Pennsylvania seeds to Ohio's frontier. His plantings made him a legend in his own time. Indians considered him "heap big medicine man." On Sept. 24, 1966, the U.S. Post Office Dept. issued its first stamp in the American Folklore and Folk Hero Series. Johnny Appleseed was depicted on the stamp, which was first issued from the Leominster post office.

Other notable natives: U.S. Senator David I. Walsh, chairman of the Senate Naval Affairs Committee. His brother Jim was Leominster postmaster for many years. Railroad promoter, politician and papermaker Alvah Crocker founded the parent companies of the now nearly deceased Boston and Maine RR. His last job was U.S. congressman (1872–74).

On the common is an old *Indian Mortar,* a block of stone rudely hollowed out, about 18 inches in diameter and 8 inches in depth.

The *Public Library Museum* contains a facsimile of a hornbook used by the Pilgrim Fathers, tools made by early settlers, a hand reel for winding yarn from a spinning wheel and a wool card, shutters and bobbins from hand looms.

LEVERETT (Franklin County, sett. *c.* 1713, incorp. 1774, alt. 438, pop. 1005, area 22.90 sq. mi., town meeting, route, Mass. 63) has a box factory (1875). The town also produces charcoal, maple sugar and syrup. Early industries were shingle and textile mills, tanneries and a shoe factory.

The *Field Tavern* (1790) or Bradford Field House (open by permission), west of the center, has a sharply gabled, many-windowed ell. The old barroom upstairs and old relics are interesting.

Rattle Snake Gutter is a ravine with steep stones, crags and ledges.

LEXINGTON (Middlesex County, sett. 1640, incorp. 1713, alt. 200, pop. 31,886, area 16.48 sq. mi., representative town meeting, routes, Mass. 2, 2A, 4, 25, 128).

Lexington today presents some of its heroic past, little of its ancient rustic calm and less of its industrial fever. Its quiet streets and comfortable homes are free of industrial ugliness and urban squalor. For 364 days of the year Lexington runs along in the placid groove of a suburb of Boston, but each April 19th the town relives its part in ushering in the American Revolution.

There was no permanent settlement at Cambridge Farms, as Lexington was first called, until about 1642. Settlers supplied Cambridge with hay and wood, raised food, wove coarse fabrics for clothing and erected rude houses. In 1691 the General Court recognized the community as a separate town.

Lexington furnished at least 145 men for the French-Indian wars (1756–1763). Survivors formed the nucleus of the militia that gathered when the threat to Boston by the British in April 1775 roused Lexington to a quick response. The Rev. Jonas Clarke led his fellow townsmen to join with Boston in resistance. He formed a Committee of Correspondence to keep in touch with developments. So lively was the resentment of Lexington's patriots that in 1773 resolutions were sent to the legislature affirming that their people "would be ready to sacrifice our estates and everything dear in life, yes, and life itself, in support of the common cause."

On April 19, 1775, farmers gathered on Lexington Green to resist Gen. Gage's troops. Gage wanted to seize muskets and ammunition in nearby Concord. He planned to capture Sam Adams and John Hancock, who had fled to Lexington after Parliament ordered their arrest for trial in England (see HISTORICAL NOTES).

The famous confrontation on the green is celebrated each April 19th at the same spot it first took place. The historic houses near the green—the Buckman Tavern, the Monroe Tavern, and the Hancock-Clarke House—open their doors, and costumed citizens give visitors a glimpse of 1775. Festivities open with a sunrise parade, and Paul Revere, William Dawes and Samuel Prescott gallop again (though nearer noon than midnight).

Exhaustion and unrest were the post-Revolutionary lot of Lexington, as of most communities in Massachusetts. Debts mounted as business stagnated. Despite their passion for liberty, Lexington farmers did not join the insurrection of embittered debtors led by Daniel Shays; on the contrary, the town sent militia to aid in putting it down.

By the end of the 18th century the town had recovered its peaceful existence.

What To See and Do

1. *Lexington Battleground,* "Birthplace of American Liberty," a triangular level green, is marked by H. H. Kitson's *Minuteman Statue.* R. from Massachusetts Ave. on Harrington Rd. along n. edge of green.
2. *Old Burying Ground* (behind white-steepled church). Some slate stones with bas-relief skulls date to 1690. Here are graves of Revolutionary patriots and their "agreeable consorts." The Rev. John Hancock and the Rev. Jonas Clarke, whose successive local pastorates covered the entire 18th century, rest beneath the same stone.
3. *The Jonathan Harrington, Jr., House* (private), corner of Harrington Rd. and Bedford Sts., a white, two-story frame dwelling with green shutters, has a Georgian Colonial doorway. During the battle Jonathan Harrington was wounded by the British. He dragged himself to the door of his home, where he died at his wife's feet.

4. The *First State Normal School* in the United States, opposite corner of Bedford St., was founded in 1839, with three pupils and the Rev. Cyrus Pierce as principal. It is a two-story white building, now a Masonic Temple, at the northeast corner of the green.

5. *Buckman Tavern* (open April 19–Nov. 1, weekdays and holidays 10–5, Sun. 1–5, small fee), built probably in 1709–10, 17th-century features, but a hip roof with dormer windows has been added to make a third story. Here the Minutemen drank rum the morning of April 19, 1775, while they awaited the Redcoats' arrival. There is an excellent collection of Revolutionary era household furnishings.

6. *Belfry Reproduction,* sw. of the village green, stands where the original bell sounded the alarm that the British were coming. The bell disappeared but the timbers remain.

7. *Hancock-Clarke House,* 35 Hancock St. (open April 19–Nov. 1, weekdays and holidays 10–5, Sun. 1–5, small fee). The one-story gambrel roof ell is believed to be the original dwelling built in 1698 by Parson John Hancock, whose son John, father of Gov. John Hancock, was born here. The hand-hewn oak shows but little decay. The house was enlarged in 1734. In April 1775 it was the home of the Rev. Mr. Jonas Clarke. John Hancock and fellow conspirator Samuel Adams were hiding here the night before April 19 when Dawes and Revere warned the countryside. Hancock's future wife Dorothy Quincy brought the fugitives "a fine salmon for their dinner." The ell contains clothing — they didn't have uniforms — worn at the Battle of Lexington. The large, low-ceilinged kitchen, then the real center of family life, has period utensils and furnishings. The Lexington Historical Society has had its headquarters here since the society purchased the house in 1896.

8. *Cary Memorial Building,* 1605 Massachusetts Ave., the town hall, has Henry Sandham's painting of the Battle of Lexington, and "The Dawn of Liberty," a portrait of Lady Lexington.

9. *Monroe Tavern,* 1332 Massachusetts Ave. (open April 19–Nov. 1, weekdays and holidays 10–5, Sun. 1–5, small fee), houses beneath its hip roof a museum of period utensils, china and furniture. Washington was entertained here in 1789. The chair, table, dishes and hat rack which he used are on view.

10. *Mason House* [private], almost opposite 1303 Massachusetts Ave., was built in 1680.

11. Another *Jonathan Harrington Home* (private), 995 Massachusetts Ave. near Joseph Rd., was built by another Jonathan Harrington, a relative of the one killed in battle. He was a Minuteman fifer and the last survivor of the affair on the green. Sixteen years old on April 19, 1775, he lived to be 95 and occupied a front seat at the 25th, 50th and 75th anniversaries of the day. He always shook hands with the dignitaries present and referred to himself as the Minute Boy.

12. *Benjamin Wellington Tablet,* Massachusetts Ave. and Follen Rd., commemorates "the first armed man taken in the Revolution."

13. *Minuteman National Historical Park* (see CONCORD).

LEYDEN (Franklin County, sett. 1738, incorp. 1784, alt. 940, pop. 376, town meeting, routes, unnumbered roads from US 5 in Bernardston and via Meadows Road from Greenfield) was named for Leiden, Holland, where the Pilgrims lived for several years after leaving England and before migrating to Plymouth. The name is pronounced LIE-den.

Leyden village, built along a narrow ridge, has a church, library, town hall and a dozen homes. The town lies on 27 hills. Dairy farming is the principal industry though some residents commute. There are excellent views of the valleys below and the hills beyond. Stone was once quarried in Leyden; copper was also mined.

Leyden's most famous native was Henry Kirke Brown (1814–86), American sculptor and artist. Today, Brown's huge statues of George Washington and Abraham Lincoln stand in the public parks of New York, West Point and in Washington, D.C. John L. Riddell (1807–65), inventor, botanist and physician, also was a Leyden native.

During the last decade of the 18th century, Leyden achieved notoriety as the home of Leydenite William Dorrell (1752–1846), who expounded free love and the sanctity of all life, animal and human. His followers, the Dorrellites, held "religious" demonstrations which so shocked the community and state that the sect was vigorously suppressed. Dorrell lived in Leyden till the age of 94 when he starved himself to death, declaring he had lived long enough.

Leyden is the home of Mary Sloane, a nonobjective painter, and Masha Arms, portrait photographer of Robert Frost and other prominent Americans. William T. Arms, the author of *Leyden History* (1959) and of the Leyden historical novel, *Salute to Courage* (1966), lives here.

WEST LEYDEN is a small settlement along the banks of the Green River across from East Colrain.

LINCOLN (Middlesex County, sett. *c.* 1650, incorp. 1754, alt. 250, pop. 7567, area 14.56 sq. mi., town meeting, routes, Mass. 2, 2A, 117, 126), a beautiful residential and dairying town, was named for Lincoln, England.

De Cordova and Dana Museum and Park (open Tues.–Fri. 9–5, Sat. 9–1, Sun. 1:30–5, free) (Sandy Pond Rd.). Exhibits of contemporary art change monthly. The museum and adjacent 25-acre park were given to the town by the late Julian De Cordova.

Drumlin Farm (open daily), Mass. 117, once a working dairy farm, has, since the death in 1956 of its longtime owner Louise Ayer Hatheway, become a unique educational institution — an educational farm where visitors are offered the opportunity to see and learn about the basic animal resources which sustain us all. The farm has 220 acres and is the headquarters of the Massachusetts Audubon Society — the largest state Audubon Society in America. The farm is supported by endowments, grants, gifts, fees and membership dues.

Exhibits and the educational programs show adults and children our dependence on the soil, water, plants and animals and how human intelligence can help utilize these sources, not destroy them.

Fascinating tours and programs are available for folk of all ages. There are hayrides for children.

From 9:30–4:00 weekdays, farm programs are conducted for scheduled groups only. Late afternoons and weekends general visitors are welcome. All buildings close at 5:00. Unless special arrangements are made farm tours commence at 9:30, 11:00, 1:30 and 3:30. Programs are conducted throughout the year, rain or shine, snow or blow. Buildings are heated during the winter. Picnicking is not allowed, but visitors can bring sack lunches provided they tote off their trash and garbage. For full details and reservations write or phone Farm Program Secretary, Drumlin Farm, Lincoln, Mass. Phone: 259–9500.

Codman House (open Tues.–Thurs., Sat. 1–5, admission fee), Codman Road. First built in the early 18th century, this was remodeled as a handsome Federal mansion about 1800. Now owned by the Society for the Preservation of New England Antiquities, the house was opened to the public in 1971.

LITHIA (see GOSHEN)

LITTLE NAHANT (see NAHANT)

LITTLETON (Middlesex County, sett. 1654, incorp. 1714, alt. 498 at highest point on Oak Hill, 230 at center, pop. 6380, area 16.46 sq. mi., town meeting, routes, I–495, Mass. 2, 2A, 110, 119) was incorporated in 1654 as Nashobah Plantation for Christian Indians converted by John Eliot. Indian settlers were removed to Deer Island during King Philip's War (1675–76) and few returned. Incorporated as an English town in 1714, it was named Littleton in 1715; residential, with few farms remaining, it has several industries and many business enterprises.

The *Reuben Hoar Library,* Mass. 110 and 2A at the center, is housed in the *Houghton Memorial Building,* constructed of yellow brick in Georgian architecture. It was dedicated in 1895, the gift of the Houghton family.

Littleton has several Revolutionary War sites. *Liberty Square,* drilling ground for Minutemen, is marked with monuments. The *Tory House,* 110 and 2A, a short distance below the library, was the home of Rev. Daniel Rogers. He was a Tory, and prior to the Revolution, when patriotic sentiment was running high, an armed squad approached the house and demanded that he declare his principles. When he hesitated, a volley was fired, and the bullet holes are still in the staircase of the house and in the original door, which is in the Historical Society collection at the library. *Porter Road Bridge,* restored by the Historical Society at the time of the town's 250th anniversary celebration (1954), marks an old mill site and the crossing of the Acton-Groton stagecoach route. It is named for Col. John Porter, French-and-Indian and Revolutionary War veteran.

Tophet Swamp and Chasm was gouged out of the lower end of Oak Hill, thought by some experts to have been created by an ancient waterfall from a glacial lake. Other geologists believe its formation predates the last Ice Age. It is a half mile long with a finger-shaped, swampy floor and steep, parallel walls 75 feet apart and 80 feet high at the inner end.

The town has three principal districts: the "depot," stop for B&M Buddliner service, location of Harwood Station Branch Post Office, two important industries and many small business enterprises; the "center," the *Town House,* housing town offices, police and fire departments and a small meeting hall and the library; the "common," named for its common or village green.

It is an attractive community in a setting of natural beauty, from its rolling lowlands to its wooded hills.

LONGMEADOW (Hampden County, sett. 1644, incorp. 1783, alt. 170, pop. 15,630, area 9.03 sq. mi., town meeting, route, US 5). The "long meddowe" purchased from the Indians in 1636 rapidly became a substantial settlement. During King Philip's War, a party ventured to attend worship in Springfield. They were attacked by Indians, who killed some, wounded others and took a few captives.

In 1709 there was a general move to the more elevated section of the town owing to frequent flooding by the Connecticut River. Longmeadow was the first town in the state incorporated after the recognition of American independence. The town's natural beauty has been enhanced by skillful landscaping. The once quiet farming community is a delightful residential and social center.

Local genealogical records are unusually complete because, it is said, Jabez Colton carried a notebook and inkhorn with him wherever he went.

The late Aaron Burt, a hermit, made trips to the village, dressed in sheepskin like a prophet of old, and followed by a bullock, heifer, cow and pig — with ribbons. He was a pious fellow, and, when attending worship, frequently broke out into song to the congregation's confusion; the "Indian Philosopher," far from a hymn, appears to have been his favorite. At other times he rose and, taking the service out of the mouth of the flustered minister, delivered a stentorian harangue denouncing sin.

Storrs Parsonage (open), 697 Longmeadow St., of the Longmeadow Historical Society, has a fine collection of Colonial furniture.

At 674 Longmeadow St. is the house where *Eleazar Williams* (1789–1858), who called himself the "Lost Prince," received his education. Williams's strong resemblance to the Bourbons of France strengthened the supposition he was the missing Louis XVII, a rumor to which Eleazar felt little aversion. His story formed the basis of several once popular novels.

Colton House (open mid-June–mid-Oct., Mon., Tues., Wed. 3–5, also by appointment), 787 Longmeadow St., contains furnishings typical of 18th-century Connecticut River Valley homes. The house was built in 1734.

LOWELL (Middlesex County, sett. 1653, town incorp. 1826, city incorp. 1836, alt. 100, pop. 94,239, area 13.38 sq. mi., manager-council (Plan E), routes, I–495, US 3, Mass. 3A, 38, 110, 113).

Lowell, a leading New England manufacturing center, lies 100 feet above the confluence of the fast-flowing Merrimack and the sluggish Concord Rivers. Canals and grassy plots crisscross the business district. Mansions and tenements cling to the hills beyond the center.

Lowell's early days are identified with Chelmsford Town, of which it was for many years an insignificant part. About 1800 Francis Cabot Lowell (1775–1817), "The Father of American Cotton Manufacturing," came here. He had studied British textile mill operations and then devised a practical power loom for American use. Cabot investigated the power and navigation facilities of the Merrimack River and the Pawtucket Canal. He was enthusiastic but his untimely death came before the city commenced its development program. Five years after he died his associates formed the Merrimack Manufacturing Company. The firm's founders, mostly substantial Bostonians, became the town fathers.

Lowell became a huge company town. Single men and women lived in company-owned lodging houses, ate in company-owned dining rooms, shopped in company stores and were laid to rest in company-owned burying ground lots. Employees worked from 5 A.M. to 7 P.M., six days a week. Men were paid $5.00 or less for a 72-hour week — there was no time for carousing, but Sunday school and church attendance were required; women received about one half of men's wages for the same working schedule.

This Chelmsford section became an incorporated town in its own right on March 1, 1826. Europe watched Lowell with amazement. Its rapid rise to industrial eminence astounded economists, historians and writers. Many skilled workers were English and Irish; later came the less skilled, non-English-speaking groups who settled in their own little communities, building their churches, schools and convents and preserving their native cultures. French-Canadians, Poles and Greeks today have their own clubs and newspapers. The Greeks dominate so large a section of the city that Lowell has been called a modern American Athens.

The city's peak industrial development came during the artificial prosperity preceding 1924. There was a general decrease, ending in the devastating debacle of 1929. Many mills moved south. Other industries were liquidated. The textile industry was reduced by 50 percent. Thousands of workers were left jobless and homeless. Lowell lost its position as the most important textile center in the world. Despite losses, it began slowly to make gains. It broadened its scope to include many kinds of manufactures.

Fort Hill Park, beautifully planted in open vistas framed by birches, maples, beeches, poplars, oaks, pines, spruces, cedars and tamaracks, has from its crest a magnificent view.

Wannalancit Park, a grassy embankment shaded by trees, traversed by footpaths and dotted with benches, extends for several miles along the river.

The *Spalding House* (private), 275 Pawtucket St., originally a tavern (1760), presents a carefully restored exterior of two-and-a-half stories with hip roof and twin chimneys.

Lowell Technological Institute (coeducational) (1897) is probably the largest school in the world offering instruction in textile processes. It is now, however, the principal state-supported scientific and technical school. It offers comprehensive programs in engineering, electronics, paper chemistry, plastics and business administration. In 1968 it embarked on a program in the atomic sciences with the completion of its nuclear reactor and cyclotron. The institute has the only known building with both devices housed under one roof.

Lowell State Teachers' College (1894), 850 Broadway, is notable for its beautiful location in a broad-landscaped campus on a spacious hilltop.

Lucy Larcom Park, adjacent to St. Anne's Church, a long, narrow strip of greensward extending along the Pawtucket Canal, was named in honor of Lucy Larcom. She was a 19th-century New England poet who wrote the prose *New England Girlhood,* about her early days as a mill hand.

Birthplace of Whistler (open weekdays 10–5 except Mon., Sun. 12–5), 243 Worthen St., is a shrine for artists who often know nothing of Lowell except that it is the birthplace of James Abbott McNeill Whistler (1834–1903), painter, dandy and wit. The house (1824) stands directly on the sidewalk in what is now a quiet byway.

The *Greek Orthodox Church* (1907), corner of Jefferson St., the first of its denomination in America, is a Byzantine structure in yellow brick. It is in the Little Greece section, a center of frame dwellings and small variety shops bearing signs in modern Greek.

LOWELL DRACUT STATE FOREST, located in a pine grove overlooking Merrimack River Valley, has fireplaces and picnic tables. Snowmobiling.

LOWELL METROPOLITAN AREA (pop. 212,860, area 119.78 sq. mi.) includes the city of Lowell and the towns of Billerica, Chelmsford, Dracut, Tewksbury, Tyngsborough.

LUDLOW (Hampden County, sett. *c.* 1751, incorp. 1775, alt. 230, pop. 17,580, area 28.48 sq. mi., representative town meeting, route, Mass. 21).

Ludlow, once an independent mill town, still relies on manufacturing, but it is also a Springfield residential suburb. In its earliest years it was known as Stony Hill. A district of Springfield, it was separately incorporated

because of the difficulty of crossing the Chicopee River, dividing the two communities. Waterpower encouraged the establishment of sawmills.
The *Hubbard Memorial Library* (open) has local relics.
Indian Leap is a high, rocky cliff on the bank of the Chicopee River. During King Philip's War, Roaring Thunder and a band of his warriors leaped from the cliff to escape pursuit. Roaring Thunder waited until the last of his men had plunged into the river to escape or perish; then he followed.
Haviland Pond has bathing and fishing.

LUDLOW CENTER is the geographical center of a town that once included a prosperous glassworks and chair factory. The town for many years has been one of the world's largest jute manufacturing centers.

LUDLOW STATE PARK is atop Minechoag Mt. Excellent views from fire tower. Facilities: fireplaces, picnic tables, parking area, snowmobiling. Drinking water and sanitary facilities located in woods below tower.

LUNENBURG (Worcester County, sett. 1718, incorp. 1728, alt. 570, pop. 7419, area 26.63 sq. mi., town meeting, routes, Mass. 2A, 13, 25).
Residential Lunenburg has a library and shopping center in keeping with the town's Colonial tradition. The Historical Society has a new building to display historical relics and records. Included are a fine collection of Lunenburg Bibles, a Bible donated by John Hancock in 1772 and several objects resembling carved ivories made by Lunenburger George Gilchrest, from meat bones, when he was in Libby Prison during the Civil War.

Lunenburg's three lakes provide many summer homes and sites. An amusement park serves the area.

Lunenburg counts among its former residents, Luther Burbank (1849–1926), a well-known horticulturist, who was living here when he perfected the Red Rose Potato (see LANCASTER).

The town is noted for the superb design of its annual town reports.

LYNN (Essex County, sett. 1629, town incorp. 1631, city incorp. 1850, alt. 34, pop. 90,294, area 10.48 sq. mi., mayor-council, routes, US 1A, Mass. 107, 129).

Industrial Lynn sprawls across a plain flanked by rocky hills to the north and west and by the sea and miles of tidal flats to the east and south. General Electric's vast River Works stretches beyond the Saugus River toward the dreary shoe factories. From the congested heart of the industrial district tenement roofs, spires and brick walls rise in a chaotic jumble to the distant city heights, in great contrast with great woods and the several quiet lakes which lie, surprisingly, within the limits of this noisy machine city.

Lynn, once Saugus, was named for King's Lynn in Norfolk County,

England. *Lynn* to ancient Britons signified "Place of the Spreading Waters."

Lynn was first settled in 1629 by five Salemites. Visitor William Wood returned to England where he wrote *New England's Prospect*—possibly the first American promotional piece. Many settlers came here after reading the book.

Skilled ironworker Joseph Jenks (1602–83) helped establish the first American ironworks in Saugus. He later received the first British patent issued to an American Colonial for his patent scythe blade. He also made the dies for the Pine Tree Shilling and invented a fire engine. His son Josephs Jenckes (*sic*) (1632–1717), also a pioneer ironworker, was a founder of Pawtucket, R.I.

By 1726 Lynn yards were building brigs and schooners.

Four of the 168 Lynn Revolutionary War soldiers were slain in Lexington. The city furnished several complete companies during the Civil War. For many years the General Lander Post 5, G.A.R. (Grand Army of the Republic), was the largest local veterans organization in the country.

The shoe industry traces back to an early settler who was a tanner. He laid the foundation of a related industry that was to make Lynn famous throughout the world. Skilled shoemakers Philip Kirtland and Edmund Bridges settled near the tannery in 1635. By the 18th century almost every house had its "back-yard" shop. Soon Lynn was supplying most of the footgear for Boston. John Adam Dagyr, a Welsh shoemaker, set a high standard of workmanship which lasted for many years after his death.

The 19th century brought new life, resulting in part from the activities of Ebenezer Breed, who helped persuade Congress to protect the industry with a tariff. In 1800 the state legislature passed an act to encourage the manufacture of shoes, boots and "arctics" (galoshes). Craftsmen in 1810 manufactured about 1,000,000 pairs of shoes in their shops.

With the introduction of the shoe sewing machine in 1848, the factory system began to take over. Domestic production units of craftsmen were liquidated. Workers were absorbed into huge plants. With bewilderment and resentment, they saw their craftsmen's status fade into insignificance when they took their places at the alien machines. The ensuing friction brought about the 1867 shoe strike. All shoe factories closed for seven weeks.

The new system attracted thousands of foreigners and altered the city's ethnic complexion. French-Canadians, the largest group, dispersed throughout the city. The Irish, second in number, were forced to settle in a compact group. Italians, Greeks, Poles and Armenians formed their own distinct bilingual communities.

Czechoslovakian Thomas Bata came here to learn the trade and then returned home where he built one of the world's largest shoe plants. His plant, capable of producing many shoes at very low cost, was bitterly resented by his alma mater—Lynn.

Lynn, until 1890, was the leading shoe city in the country. A November 1889 fire destroyed 35 acres of the business and manufacturing districts.

The property loss was about $5,000,000. By 1915, Lynn had dropped to third place in U.S. shoe production. Modern machinery, which some Lynn factory owners seemed loath to purchase, decreased the reliance on skilled craftsmen. Many manufacturers moved to areas of cheaper, less-skilled labor.

Lynn today has General Electric's huge River Works plant which is the largest single nongovernment employer in Massachusetts. Jet engines are a major product. Much of the work on the development of jet engines was done — and is being done — in this plant.

Bakery goods are another major Lynn product.

What to See and Do

Lynn Historical Society (open Mon.–Fri. except holidays 9–4, free), 125 Green St., exhibits in its house and museum a collection of early furniture, household utensils, pewter, glassware and historical records.

Mary Baker Eddy Historical Home (open Mon.–Sat. Oct. 16–May 14 10–3, May 15–Oct. 15 10–5, closed major holidays, free), 12 Broad St., is the house where it is alleged the Founder of Christian Science (see Swampscott) wrote the major part of *Science and Health.* Operated by the Mother Church of Boston.

Lynn Beach (restaurants, amusements, municipal bathhouse) on Nahant Bay is a vast playground crowded in summer with throngs almost as brown as were the Indians who gathered here for contests of strength and skill.

High Rock is a bold promontory, from the summit of which an observation tower 275 feet above sea level affords a magnificent view of Lynn, the ocean and the rocky rim of the Massachusetts Bay.

Lynn Woods (entrance off Mass. 129), a 2000-acre park of wild natural beauty, begins at Lynnfield St. and Great Woods Rd. by the *Happy Valley Golf Course* (public). This park, one of the largest municipal parks in America, contains three ponds.

Burrill Hill *Observation Tower* provides an excellent view of Blue Hills, Bunker Hill Monument and the golden dome of the State House. Great Woods Rd. leads to a lovely ravine framing the long, slender mirror of Walden Pond with overhanging branches of birches and elms.

Dungeon Rock. According to tradition a group of buccaneers hid vast treasures here in a huge cave whose entrance was closed by the earthquake of 1658.

A trail passes *Lantern Rock,* where pirates once hung signal lights for small boats stealing up the Saugus River under cover of night. Near Lantern Rock is *Circle Trail,* with signs designating the unusual minerals and glacial deposits and the varieties of flora indigenous to Lynn Woods. The *Botanical Garden* has a multitude of rare blooms.

The *River Works Plant* of the *General Electric Co.* (tours). Here Elihu Thomson, one of the founders of the General Electric Company and world famous as an inventor and electrical engineer, carried on most of his experiments.

The *Lydia E. Pinkham Medicine Company* (open by permission), on Western Ave., manufactures a famous medicinal compound first made by Lydia E. Pinkham in her kitchen. Financial losses in the panic of 1873 led her to capitalize on her remedy. Once started, the fame of the cure spread rapidly through the world, and as a favorite ballad stated, "the papers printed her face." Current advertising says, "although dead, she still sends her messages of hope to millions of women."

LYNNFIELD (Essex County, sett. *c.* 1638, incorp. 1814, alt. 98, pop. 10,826, area 10.22 sq. mi., town meeting, routes, US 1, Mass. 128), an attractive north-of-Boston residential town, was for many years part of Lynn. Until the town became a Boston residential suburb, farming was the principal way of life for about three centuries. Early industries include sash and blind, saw, woolen and tool factories or mills. Present industries include beverages, instruments and publishing.

LYNNFIELD CENTER is the beauty spot of the town.

SOUTH LYNNFIELD is a crossroads settlement at the junction of US 1 and Mass. 128.

LYONSVILLE (see COLRAIN)

MALDEN (Middlesex County, sett. 1640, town incorp. 1649, city incorp. 1881, alt. 30, pop. 56,127, area 4.8 sq. mi., mayor-council, routes, US 1, Mass. 60).

Malden is a residential manufacturing city, tree-shaded and bordered on the north and northwest by the rugged, wooded cliffs of Middlesex Fells. (Manufacturing is largely confined to a limited area near the Everett border.) The main impression gained by a drive through the city is of frame houses, schools, churches, community centers and small pleasant parks. Malden's proximity to Boston is an advantage and drawback to its residential appeal. Its identity tends to be swallowed up by the greater city. There are no pretentiously wealthy districts and no shabby poverty. Malden is a comfortable middle-class residential city.

Malden settlers, mainly Puritans, landed at Charlestown, situated in a part of the grant made in 1622 to Robert Gorges by the Northern Virginia Company. In 1628 the Plymouth Council disregarded this grant and lease and sold the land to Massachusetts Bay Colony.

After the arrival of Gov. Winthrop in 1630, Charlestown extended its boundaries. Settlers crossed to the north side of the Mystic River, built homes and founded a new town. The General Court granted the charter in 1649.

Difficulty was experienced in securing competent teachers. The town was at court sessions once charged for not maintaining a school. The first schoolhouse (1712) saw only 18 years in the service of education; in 1730 it was sold to the town bellman and gravedigger. Private homes were requisitioned for use as schoolhouses.

On September 23, 1774, the townsmen voted to instruct their representative in General Court that it was their "firm and deliberate resolution rather to rule our lives and fortunes than submit to those unrighteous acts of the British Parliament which pretends to regulate the government of this Province."

Malden was regulated by five selectmen. Since 1881 city affairs have been administered by a mayor, board of aldermen and city council. Since 1958 there has been a mayor and city council with 11 councillors, one from each of the 8 wards and 3 at large.

Malden is within 24-hour rail delivery of three quarters of the nation's markets and has easy access to the major trans-Atlantic and coastwise passenger and freight lines. Its firms, of which there are approximately 600, are widely representative of varied industries.

Malden in the 1970's remains a suburban residential community. Local industry employs over 8000 workers. Several major shopping centers make Malden a trading center for smaller north of Boston communities.

Malden Public Library (1883–85), Malden Sq., was designed by H. H. Richardson. Characteristic of his work, it is an excellent example of his later and more mature designs known as "Richardsonian Romanesque."

The library contains a small distinguished art gallery, with works of French, Dutch, Italian and American artists from Claude Lorrain to the present day. Of historic interest is Albion H. Bicknell's large group portrait, "The Gettysburg Address."

The *Parsonage House* (private), 145 Main St., is a two-and-a-half-story white structure (1724). In this house in 1788 was born Adoniram Judson, the famous missionary to Burma.

Bell Rock Memorial Park is opposite the parsonage, near which stood the house where the congregation of the Church of Mystic Side gathered and where Marmaduke Matthews, the first pastor in Malden, preached. In the park is a replica of a small fortress, accessible from the street by a stairway, and at its summit stands a modern Civil War *Soldiers' and Sailors' Monument* by Bela Pratt.

MANCHESTER (Essex County, sett. *c.* 1626, incorp. 1645, alt. 57, pop. 5151, area 7.72 sq. mi., town meeting, routes, Mass. 127, 128), once a sleepy fishing village, has become a fashionable summer residence — and in some instances the year-round home — of Boston commuters.

First settlers were two fishermen who established themselves at Kettle Cove when the Cape Ann Colony broke up in 1626. The little Salem community was known as Jeffrey's Creek. It throve as a fishing village, but by the middle of the 19th century Boston merchants began to transform it into a fashionable resort. *Singing Beach,* 1.5 miles long, is one of the finest North Shore beaches.

The frame church (1809) is surmounted by an unusual tower.
Trask House (open July and Aug., Wed. only 2–5, free), 12 Union St., built about 1830, restored in 1933 and headquarters of the local historical society, contains relics.

AGASSIZ ROCK (open all year, free) (97 acres), at Essex-Manchester town line on School St., is owned and maintained by TOR. *Agassiz Rock* atop Beaverdam Hill and *Big Agassiz Rock* in a wooded swamp are huge glacial boulders discovered by Louis Agassiz.

MANSFIELD (Bristol County, sett. 1659, incorp. 1775, alt. 150, pop. 9939, area 20.22 sq. mi., town meeting, routes, Mass. 106, 140), named for Lord Mansfield, occupies an Indian winter campsite. The town has been predominantly industrial since 1800 when a tack factory opened.

Commercial gladioli cultivation was started in 1917 by a Hollander.

Principal local products include plastic eyeglass frames, bleaches and dyes, candy, baseball shoe cleats and hardware. Factories employ about 100 workers.
Fisher-Richardson House (open June 15–Oct. 1, Sat. and Sun. 2–5, free) was built in 1704, enlarged in 1800 and restored in 1930. Exhibits of early American home furnishings.

MARBLEHEAD (Essex County, sett. 1629, incorp. 1649, alt. 50, pop. 21,295, area 4.40 sq. mi., town meeting, routes, Mass. 129), in whose narrow, twisted streets traditions linger, is built upon a rock, and everywhere through the thin garment of turf protrude granite knobs and cliffs. Along the steep, winding ways weatherbeaten houses shoulder each other, with intermittent glimpses of the harbor and the sea between their grayed walls. A mass of tumbled rocks chiseled by the sea forms the grim profile of the "neck."

Reckless, hard-bitten fishermen from Cornwall and the Channel Islands settled Marblehead (Marble Harbor) in 1629 as a plantation of Salem. Rude huts clung to rocks like seabirds' nests. Said a Marbleheader of a later day — "Our ancestors came not here for religion. Their main end was to catch fish." Early Marblehead was a favorite with the powers of darkness. Many a citizen met Satan riding in a coach-and-four or was chased through the streets by a corpse in a coffin. Puritan Salem hanged old "Mammy Red" of Marblehead who knew how to turn enemies' butter to blue wool.

As war approached, His Majesty's frigates lay threateningly in the harbor. The Old Town House thundered to revolutionary speeches. Marblehead blazed with sedition. Her merchants extended shipping privileges to Boston merchants when Marblehead took Boston's place as the port of entry after the passage of the Boston Port Bill (1774). Tory merchants fled. Sailors turned to privateering with its promise of prize money and adventure and joined Gen. John Glover's famous "Amphibious Regiment" which later rowed Washington across the Delaware. The Marblehead schooner *Lee,* manned by a captain and crew of this regiment, flew the Pine Tree flag and took the *Nancy,* the first British prize.

Privateering became unprofitable when the British blockade tightened. Peace found Marblehead with its merchant fleet captured or sunk and the fishing fleet rotting at the wharves.

Lotteries were organized. The fishing fleet was reconditioned with the proceeds. As prosperity again seemed assured, the War of 1812 tied up the fleet once more and embargo closed the ports of trade. After the war the fishing fleet gallantly put to sea, but the town could not compete with Boston and Gloucester. The great gale of 1846, which took a frightful toll of men and ships, hastened the end.

Marblehead turned to industry. Backyard shoe shops, a feature of every fisherman's cottage, were amalgamated into factories. By 1850, trained hands and mass production methods were turning out a million pairs of shoes a year. Other factories produced glue, rope, twine, barrels, paint and cigars. But the spider web of railroads that spun out across the country, tapping the resources of the West and concentrating manufacturing in the larger cities, spelled doom to Marblehead as an industrial center, a doom hastened by two disastrous fires.

Ultimately it was the sea that once more brought prosperity. The harbor, where long ago the high-sterned fishing boats rode to tree root moorings, is now the yachting center of the northeastern seaboard. Summer estates line the once bleak shore of the neck and overlook the harbor where hundreds of sleek-hulled craft ride at anchor. In the yachting season more sails slant out past *Halfway Rock,* where once the fishermen tossed pennies to buy good luck and safe return than ever did in the days of Marblehead's maritime glory.

Barnegat is a district long ago named for the town on the New Jersey coast where "mooncussers" lured vessels to destruction by false lights from shore, with the purpose of plundering their cargoes. (A mooncusser is one who curses the moon for its hindrance to his nefarious designs.)

What to See and Do

Abbot Hall (open Mon.–Fri. 8 A.M.–9 P.M., Sat. to 12 Noon. June–Sept., Sundays and holidays, 1–5, free), the Victorian Town Hall in the center of the square, houses Willard's "The Spirit of '76," the familiar historical painting.

Colonel William Dee House (private), 185 Washington St., is one of the network of old houses, nearly all of them pre-Revolutionary, which form the heart of Marblehead. Col. Lee was an early merchant prince of the town, and a Revolutionary army officer. The house dates from the mid-18th century and has the wood-block front popular in Marblehead's fashionable dwellings. An Ionic portico and octagonal cupola add distinction.

Jeremiah Lee Mansion (open May–mid-Oct., Mon.–Sat. 9:30 A.M.–4:30 P.M., small fee), 161 Washington St., built in 1768, is one of the finest examples of the second phase of New England Georgian architecture. The three-story building is surmounted by a cupola with a simple portico of two fluted Ionic columns. The elaborate paneling of the "mahogany room," the magnificent staircase and the rich variety of detail in wood finish give the interior exceptional interest.

King Hooper Mansion (open May 15–Oct. 30, daily 10–5, closed Mondays, Oct. 30–May 14, small fee), 8 Hooper St., is headquarters and museum of the Marblehead Art Association. Members have restored the interior and old-fashioned flower garden. Art exhibits are held throughout the year. The house (1745) is the third of three houses built by early merchant princes. The three-story wood front gives the effect of stone coursing. Builder Robert Hooper was nicknamed "King" because of his great wealth and royal manner of life.

St. Michael's Church (Episcopal) (open daily 9–5) (1714), corner of Summer St., is probably the oldest New England Episcopal church, has gate pews and typical Colonial raised pulpit, reached by a winding staircase and surmounted by an overhanging sounding board.

The *Old Town House* (not open) (1727) is a pleasing example of early New England Georgian design — a two-story clapboard building set high upon a granite walled basement, with a low gable roof and a simple cornice.

Major Pedrick House (1756), 52 Washington St., almost as fine architecturally as the Lee and Hooper mansions, is a square, three-story house, with wood front and huge, square chimneys.

Elbridge Gerry House (private), 44 Washington St., is marked by a tablet as the birthplace of Elbridge Gerry (1744–1814), a member of the Continental Congress, governor of Massachusetts, vice president of the United States during the War of 1812 and the originator of "gerrymandering."

The *Old North Church* (Congregational) (1824), opposite the Gerry House, was the first parish in the town.

Azor Orne House (private), 18 Orne St., was the home of Colonel Azor Orne, a member of the Revolutionary Committee of Safety which included Elbridge Gerry, John Hancock and Samuel and John Adams.

Agnes Surriage Well (see Ashland) is at the end of a lane leading from Orne St. just beyond the Orne House.

The *Old Brig* (about 1720), known also as the *Moll Pitcher House,* on Orne St. opposite the lane leading to the Agnes Surriage Well, is the unnumbered, low Colonial house with the big central chimney. It was the home of the famous psychic fortune-teller, Moll Pitcher, born here about 1743, and of her ancestor the wizard Dimond. Above this house, on the rocky summit of *Old Burial Hill* among gravestones outlined against the sky, awed townsfolk often saw Old Dimond's shadowy form swaying in a wild northeaster, as with brandished arms he defied the gale and shouted to invisible satanic thralls his orders for the safe guidance of Marblehead's fleet.

Old Burial Hill contains the graves of 600 Revolutionary fighters. The low white *Obelisk* on the crest honors 65 Marblehead fishermen who lost their lives in a great gale in 1846. From the hill is obtained a panoramic view of *Marblehead Harbor,* the summer yachting center of the eastern seaboard.

Parson Barnard House (open by arrangement), 7 Franklin St., was the home of Marblehead's second and most famous pastor during his 54-year ministry from 1716 to 1770. It was Parson John Barnard who schooled the rude fishermen in the foreign commerce which brought such great prosperity to the town before the Revolution. He declined the presidency of Harvard University, referring the Committee of Invitation to his rival pastor in the town, the Rev. Edward Holyoke, who accepted. When Marblehead objected strenuously to losing either clergyman, Parson Barnard appeared in his colleague's pulpit and told Holyoke's flock in no uncertain terms how great the honor was. A visitor afterward inquired for Mr. Holyoke, and was told, "Old Barnard prayed him away."

Fort Sewall (end of Front St.), erected in 1742, kept the British at bay but has long been abandoned to the pacific uses of a small seaside park.

The *Old Tavern* (open), 82 Front St., corner of Glover St., was built in 1680. Its clapboards long held British shot fired at it from the harbor after a Marblehead patriot had disarmed several British officers in its bar by fencing with a mere stick against their rapiers.

Gen. John Glover's House (private), 11 Glover St., built in 1762, bears a tablet recording the general's crossing of the Delaware and other military services. Glover was actually a sailor rather than a soldier, and his privateer vessel, *Hannah,* manned by Marbleheaders, was the first ship of what came to be the American Navy.

CAUSEWAY and BATHING BEACH (bathhouses) continue Ocean Ave. from Marblehead to *Marblehead Neck.* On the left is *Marblehead Harbor,* gay in summer with yachts. On the right is the long, sandy, shelving beach, facing Massachusetts Bay.

Outstanding Marblehead Neck residence is the *Gove House,* Ocean Avenue, designed after the ancient Castle of Carcassonne in Southern France. It was built (1934) for Lydia Pinkham's daughter.

The *Churn,* on Ocean Ave., reached by an unmarked path leading through a field (r.) where the latter makes a short turn west, is a fissure in the rocks at tide level from which under an east or northeast wind great billows of spray rise to a height sometimes of 50 feet.

Castle Rock, adjoining the Churn (r.), a rugged granite bluff rising sheer from the sea, offers a beautiful ocean view with a long line of shore breakers.

The *Lighthouse* (open by arrangement) is a circular iron tower at the tip of the neck. From the rocks at its base is obtained the best view of the yacht races.

CROWNINSHIELD ISLAND (5 acres) in Marblehead Harbor, reached by small boat, is owned and maintained by TOR. Popular picnic spot for small-boat owners.

MARBLEHEAD NECK WILDLIFE SANCTUARY, Bonad Rd., Marblehead Neck (15 acres), is a heavily wooded area adjacent to the harbor. The water-covered marshland attracts many migratory waterfowl during their northward flight. Massachusetts Audubon Society project.

MARION (Plymouth County, sett. 1679, incorp. 1852, alt. 20, pop. 3466, area 14.28 sq. mi., town meeting, routes, US 6, Mass. 105) was set off from Rochester and named to honor "The Swamp Fox," Gen. Francis Marion, Revolutionary War hero. Small industries developed here, replacing agriculture. These were overshadowed by marine activities. Ships were built for 150 years, the last vessel leaving the ways in 1878.

Tabor Academy (1877), Front St., ranks high among the smaller private preparatory schools that contribute to Massachusetts' educational prestige.

The town has a few small industries but is essentially a residential town within the New Bedford Metropolitan Area. There are some summer resorts and activities.

MARLBOROUGH (Middlesex County, sett. 1657, incorp. 1660 as a town and 1890 as a city, alt. 596, pop. 27,936, mayor-council, routes US 20, I-495, Mass. 9, 85) was an Indian plantation site called Okammakamefit. The English knew this area as Whipsufferage. Later it was part of Sudbury Town.

Marlborough was one of John Eliot's "Praying Indian" towns. It was attacked during King Philip's War.

Marlborough once ranked fifth in national shoe production. Today its manufactures include paper boxes, wire goods, shoe machinery, plastics, electronic and missile components, metal products and sporting equipment. Marlborough's ethnic groups have been attracted by the opportunities offered in various trades.

The *Dennison Factory* (open by permission), manufactures paper boxes, paper novelties and office accessories. This is a branch (1925) of the Dennison Manufacturing Company of Framingham.

John Brown Bell, 277 Main St., taken by Marlborough soldiers from Harper's Ferry in 1861, was hidden in Williamsport, Md., until 1892, when it was brought to Marlborough.

MARSHFIELD (Plymouth County, sett. 1632, incorp. 1640, alt. 16, pop. 15,223, area 28.35 sq. mi., town meeting, routes, Mass. 3A, 139) is a coastal summer resort.

After 19th-century marsh drainage, strawberries and cranberries became important crops.

Marshfield was the scene of *In a Dike Shanty,* by Maria Louise Pool, *The Children of Old Park's Tavern,* by Frances A. Humphrey, *Into the Wind* and *Leave the Salt Earth,* by Richard Warren Hatch, and *The Autobiography of a Pilgrim Town,* by Joseph C. Hagar.

Marshfield Agricultural and Horticultural Society Fairgrounds, South St. (fair held in late August).

Peregrine White's Homestead Site. Peregrine, born on the *Mayflower* on Nov. 20, 1620, lived here after his marriage.

Winslow Burying Ground with *Daniel Webster's Grave* (1852) is on a knoll about 200 yards from the road. Peregrine White is buried here.

Daniel Webster House Site, Webster St. (on former Winslow estate). The present two-and-a-half-story building was erected by the orator's daughter-in-law after his house burned in 1890.

On Webster St. stands the *Adelaide Phillips House.* She was a contralto singer in the 19th century.

The *Winslow House* (open July 1–Labor Day, daily 10–5, small fee), corner of Caswell St., was built in 1699. It is a large hip-roofed house with central chimney, wide fireplaces and a secret chamber.

Tea Rock Hill is where Marshfield patriots staged a tea party after seizing and burning tea from a local store. A small wooden marker identifies the hill.

MARSTONS MILLS (see BARNSTABLE)

MASHPEE (Barnstable County, sett. 1660, incorp. 1871, alt. 75, pop. 1288, area 23.86 sq. mi., town meeting, routes, Mass. 28, 130, 151). This town has picturesque ponds, groves, streams and stretches of woodland. It was originally inhabited by the Wampanoag tribe, which gave allegiance to Massasoit, and was later in the township of Sandwich.

Mashpee Indians lived in rude shelters of matting hung over bent saplings. Missionary Richard Bourne converted many and taught them self-government, managing in 1660 to have 10,500 acres set apart for them. In 1834 the area was incorporated under the supervision of a commissioner appointed by the state; in 1932, owing to the economic crisis, it was placed under a state advisory commission. Hunting and fishing were superseded by employment in cranberry bogs. By 1800, full-blooded Indians had died out. Present population is a mixture of native Indian, African Negro, Cape Verdean and Portuguese.

A significant tale narrates how during an argument with the Rev. Richard Bourne the Indian medicine man lost his temper and, chanting a bog rhyme, mired Bourne's feet in quicksand. They agreed to a contest of wits which lasted 15 days. Bourne was kept from thirst and starvation by a white dove which placed a succulent "cherry" in his mouth from time to time. Unable to cast a spell upon the dove, and exhausted from his own lack of food, the medicine man fell to the ground and Bourne was free. In the meantime one "cherry" brought by the dove had fallen into the bog and grown and multiplied. Thus the cranberry came to Cape Cod.

Mashpee is a Cape Cod summer resort. There is some cranberry culture. Otis Air Force Base, formerly Camp Edwards, contributes to the town's economy.

CATAUMET: LOWELL HOLLY RESERVATION (130 acres) is owned and operated by TOR. Mass. 130 to Mashpee Center, pass firehouse, turn left on South Sandwich Rd., watch for reservation sign at dirt road entrance on left. This reservation, a peninsula, bordered by Mashpee Pond and Wakeby Pond, has a large holly grove and a splendid stand of beech trees. Facilities: fireplaces, picnic tables. ($1.00 per car on weekends.)

MASHPEE RIVER RESERVATION (375 acres) lies adjacent to the river south of Mass. 28. The Mashpee is one of the state's few rivers which still attracts "salters" as sea trout are known locally. Wetlands along the river are favored by many waterfowl. The reservation is owned and maintained by TOR.

MATTAPAN (see BOSTON)

MATTAPOISETT (Barnstable County, sett. *c.* 1750, incorp. 1857, alt. 15, pop. 4500, area 17.46 sq. mi., routes, US 6, Mass. 28), once a noted shipbuilding town (1775–1865), is now an attractive Cape Cod resort town. Salt processing and whaling were early industries.

Mattapoisett Harbor, south of the center, is a deep harbor attracting larger craft, including those of the New York and Eastern Yacht Clubs. There are four public wharves and a launching ramp. In summer, out-of-door square dances are held on the wharves each Saturday night. These colorful dances attract visitors from the southeastern New England area. In *Shipyard Park,* adjacent to the wharves, open-air band concerts are held during July and August. There is a public bathing beach with bathhouse, pavilion, raft and life guards. Swimming lessons for youngsters of town residents are held there. The *Mattapoisett Yacht Club,* off picturesque *Ned's Point Road,* conducts sailing lessons. The lovely *Ned's Point Light House* is in the *Veteran's Memorial Park* where there are cookout, pavilion, comfort station, swimming and fishing facilities available.

Mattapoisett's *Free Public Library* (12,000 volumes) was incorporated in 1881; the present building has been occupied since 1904.

The *Mattapoisett Historical Museum,* corner of Church and Baptist Sts., occupies the *Meeting House of the Mattapoisett Christian Church* (1821). The Mattapoisett Historical Society (incorp. 1958) operates the museum. The dwelling on the corner of Cannon and Main Sts. (formerly the post office) bears a plaque inscribed: "Francis Davis Millet, born Mattapoisett– Nov. 3, 1846. Drummer Boy — War Correspondent — Author — Illustrator. Went down on the *Titanic* April 15, 1912." The building was Millet's birthplace.

Shipyard Park is the site of Jonathan Holmes' shipyard, where, in 1878, the last Mattapoisett whaler, the *Wanderer,* was built. Her mizzenmast is a flagpole in the park. Many New Bedford whalers were built here.

MAYNARD (Middlesex County, sett. 1638, incorp. 1871, alt. 176, pop. 9710, area 5.24 sq. mi., town meeting, routes, Mass. 27, 62, 117) is a hill town of unusual beauty through which flows the glimmering Assabet River. Previously known as Assabet Village, it was made up of parts of Stow (1300 acres on the north side of the river) and Sudbury (1900 acres on the opposite side of the river).

Its early history dates to 1638 when Sudbury was settled. The town was named after leading employer Amory Maynard, who with William Knight began a textile mill operation in 1847. The mill became the vast American Woolen Company. The American Woolen Company is gone but its former mills are now host to twenty-one diversified businesses: computers, paper products, machinery, Teflon, patterns, woodworking, publishers, plastics and storage. Hi-fi and stereo equipment is made here. The Washington government owns about 800 acres in the town's southwest for ammunition storage and testing purposes. The town is a trading center for the surrounding towns.

MEDFIELD (Norfolk County, sett. and incorp. 1651, alt. 180, pop. 9821, area 14.43 sq. mi., town meeting, routes, Mass. 27, 109). More than half the village burned during King Philip's War. When Norfolk County was formed in 1793, Medfieldites successfully objected to their town's becoming the county seat, on the ground that visiting the courtroom would be detrimental to the townspeople's industrious habits. Many original farms are now estates. Opposite the town hall is the public library, *Medfield Historical Society* headquarters.

The *Unitarian Church,* North St., is an excellent example of Georgian Colonial architecture with its square clock tower, belfry and tall, slender spire.

Medfield today is a residential town with only about 100 workers in small local plants.

Medfield State Hospital, a mental institution with about 1300 patients, employs about 500 people, many local residents.

Medfield Rhododendrons (109 acres), southwest side of Mass. 27 opposite Kingsbury Pond, 1 mi. south of Medfield, is one of the few large fields of rhododendrons in New England. The field is owned and maintained by TOR.

MEDFORD (Middlesex County, sett. *c.* 1630, town incorp. 1684, city incorp. 1892, alt. 10, pop. 64,397, area 8.22 sq. mi., manager-council, routes, US 1, Mass. 28, 38, 60).

Medford rum and Medford-built ships, once staples of worldwide repute, today are only a legend. Still Medford thrives, a paradox accounted for by its proximity to Boston, its residential attractiveness and a fine educational system reaching its climax in Tufts College. Its hustle and bustle over, Medford has settled back to its destiny as a community of homes.

Rich loam near the river banks beckoned farmers, and the surging tides of the Mystic River offered thriving fisheries. Shipbuilding was soon under way. John Winthrop, a year before settling on Ten Hills Farm at Somerville, had launched the *Blessing of the Bay* at Medford. Then followed a century of depression, until the New England rum and slave trade sprang up.

Medford rum had its start when the Hall family set up a wooden still on the site of a spring, to which the special flavor of the rum was attributed. The Hall formula, used for 2000 years, was finally destroyed by General Samuel C. Lawrence, when Medford distilling came to an end.

Navigable Mystic River was the direct cause of the other very substantial economic activity of Medford. Freighting produce to the state capital by boat became a bustling enterprise.

Medford supplied New Hampshire and Vermont with iron, steel, lead, salt, molasses, sugar, tea, codfish, chocolate, gunpowder and rum at lower than Boston prices. Medford merchants traded with foreign and domestic ports. Barrel making and slaughtering thrived.

In the year 1802, Thatcher Magoun, a youth on a holiday from a Charlestown shipyard, was rambling about Winter Hill. In a vision he saw a thriving shipyard on the riverbanks below him, himself its master. Excitedly he clattered down the hill and boarded a two-masted schooner lying alongside a distilling-house wharf. Breathlessly he plied the amazed captain with all sorts of questions. A year later he returned and laid the keel of his first ship.

Thatcher Magoun's project came at a critical moment. The English navigation laws, after the Revolution, ended American trade with the British West Indies, and New England merchants were frantically seeking new markets.

Yankee ingenuity found a way out, in a new trade with China. Because their 200- to 300-ton capacity made possible the navigation of the shallow bays of the northwest coast, many Medford vessels were dispatched to the Pacific. "Medford-built" found its way into the idiom of the sea.

Medford builders J. O. Curtis, Hayden and Cudworth and S. Lapham had more fast California passages to their credit in proportion to the number of clipper ships built than those of any other town.

Sailing vessels became definitely unprofitable with the Civil War and the introduction of steamships. In 1873 the last Medford-built ship was launched. By 1905 the distilleries too had ceased.

Medford today is a Boston suburb, with about 10,000 workers employed in local industries including paper products, furniture and printing. The city is a trading center for area communities.

What to See and Do

Hall House (private), home of early Medford merchants and patriots, 44 High St., offers an unusual chance to compare details of Colonial architecture.

Pine Hill is approached by a wooded lane (vehicles excluded) which skirts a small pond. A number of footpaths wind to the summit, from which there is an excellent view of the Mystic Valley.

Lawrence Observatory (marked footpath), an iron tower whose summit is 310 feet above sea level, offers a beautiful panorama of pond-studded woodland and fields, with Medford and the Mystic River waterfront in the foreground.

Medford Public Library (1960), 11 High St., has several autographed letters of George Washington written to Medford patriots.

Paul Revere's Lexington route is indicated by a board on a tree at the corner of Grove and High Sts.

Royall House (open May 1–Oct. 15, daily 2–5, except Mon. and Fri., small fee), 15 George St., was once part of Ten Hills Farm. The house is the only relic of slave days in the commonwealth. Col. Isaac Royall got the property in 1732 and rebuilt it as it now stands, adding a building to house his 27 slaves. Royall's heart was with the Colonials, but his family persuaded him to join the Loyalists and leave for Halifax. His estate was confiscated. Gen. John Stark made it his headquarters before the evacuation of Boston on March 17, 1776. The government returned the estate to the Royall heirs in 1806. Money from the sale of part of the land and also from sales of land at Royalston near Worcester helped to found Harvard Law School. Royall House was once owned by pioneer cotton maker Francis Cabot Lowell, after whom Lowell is named. In 1908, it was purchased and restored by the Royall House Association.

Tufts University, coeducational, was founded in 1852 by Hosea Ballou II, nephew of the famous Universalist divine of the same name, with endowment funds and land given by Charles Tufts. The Goddard Chapel (1882–83), early Gothic style, is built of fieldstone.

Barnum Museum (open) contains the famous showman's extensive zoological collection, including the stuffed hide of Jumbo, an elephant beloved by the circus crowds of a past generation.

Tufts College had its origin primarily in the fact that dogmatic proselytizing was an approved function of the 19th-century American college. When someone asked Charles Tufts of Somerville, a man of open mind in sympathy with liberal religion, what he intended to do with the windswept heights of Walnut Hill, in a prophetic flash he answered, "I will put a light on it."

Courses are given in liberal arts, theology, engineering and law. Fletcher School of Law and Diplomacy, administered in cooperation with Harvard University, offers training for government foreign service, international business and international relations research.

The total enrollment of students is about 5000, including those attending Tufts Medical and Dental Schools in Boston. There are 1650 faculty members.

MIDDLESEX FELLS RESERVATION RECREATION AREA: 2630 acres of woodland and meadows patrolled by MDC mounted police, zoo, foot and bridle trails, freshwater fishing, picnic sites, observation tower, swimming pool, natural and artificial ice skating. For details see Middlesex Fells Reservation, under MIDDLESEX COUNTY.

MEDWAY (Norfolk County, sett. 1657, incorp. 1713, alt. 200, pop. 7938, area 11.60 sq. mi., town meeting, routes, Mass. 109, 126) is a quiet manufacturing center along the Charles River, surrounded by meadows and wooded hills. Town lands were set off in 1713, but their seclusion from the rest of the commonwealth is revealed by Medway's reluctance to send representatives to the General Court for 13 years. In 1763, the first known census in Massachusetts was taken here. The town boycotted British goods.

A residential town, Medway's industries employ less than 500 workers who produce hats and cleaning compounds.

MELROSE (Middlesex County, sett. *c.* 1629, incorp. 1850 as a town and 1900 as a city, alt. 50, pop. 33,180, area 4.73 sq. mi., mayor-alderman, route, US 1). Melrose was once known locally as North Malden.

The Boston and Maine RR (1845) helped increase the population and developed Melrose as a residential center. Melrose has a high percentage of owner-occupied homes. Residents produce electronics equipment.

Melrose native Geraldine Farrar (1882–1967) was a famous dramatic soprano and member of the Metropolitan Opera Company.

Sewall Woods Park was the gift of the heirs of Judge Samuel Sewall (1652–1730), the abolitionist. It was a condition of the gift that the park remain wooded with uncut trees.

Mt. Hood Park has an *Observatory* with a view ranging from New Hampshire's hills to the ocean horizon. Wampanoag Indians lighted signal fires by which they communicated with other tribes as far away as *Mt. Wachusett.*

MT. HOOD RESERVATION (municipal golf course, bathhouse, beach).

MENDON (Worcester County, sett. 1660, incorp. 1667, alt. 387, pop. 2524, area 17.73 sq. mi., town meeting, route, Mass. 16), originally Quinshepauge, later named for Mendham, England, was the second town formed in the county. During King Philip's War inhabitants disregarded General Court orders not to abandon the settlement. The town was burned by Indians. Conservative Mendonites, unsympathetic with Shays' Rebellion, helped quell the uprising. The town has remained essentially agricultural in its economy. Its one dairy products plant, small textile mill and boat distributor employ about 100 workers.

In the park stands the *Founders Memorial* on the *Site of Mendon's first Meeting House.* Here are also two milestones, the larger reading "37 miles from Boston T.H. 1785," the other "38 miles to Boston 1772."

The small, one-story, brick *Mendon Historical Museum* (open by appointment), nearby, served as a bank from 1825 to 1831. In it are Indian relics, numerous household utensils and furnishings of early days, files of historical data and the Kate Chapin collection of pitchers.

Old Mendon Tavern (private), Main St., a two-story house where Washington did *not* spend the night (see NORTH UXBRIDGE).

First Parish Church (Unitarian) (1820), Maple St., is a classic example of New England church architecture.

WEST HILL WILDLIFE MANAGEMENT AREA has public hunting in Northbridge, Upton, Uxbridge, and Mendon.

MENEMSHA (see CHILMARK)

MERRIMAC (Essex County, sett. 1638, incorp. 1876, alt. 107, pop. 4245, area 8.66 sq. mi., town meeting, routes, I–495, Mass. 110).

Merrimac (Indian, "Swift Waters") lies in a region where the Ice Age left traces of its passage. With the exception of two level plains, the region is sharply rolling, with a series of drumlins, many too steep for cultivation.

Mills (150 workers) produce brass products and metal castings.

The *Sawyer Home* (open by arrangement) (1750), 0.1 mi., e. on Mass. 110, a two-and-a-half-story frame structure, contains mid-19th-century furniture and utensils.

The *Pilgrim Congregational Church,* Church St., organized 1726, has a Corinthian arched portico.

Vessels for West Indian trade were built here before 1700. Trade with Newburyport was carried on "gundalows" — long, square-ended barges — which were poled up and down the winding Merrimack, carrying hogshead staves and local produce in exchange for molasses.

METHUEN (Essex County sett. *c.* 1642, incorp. 1725, alt. 100, pop. 35,456, area 22.41 sq. mi., representative town meeting, routes I–213, 495, Mass. 28, 110, 113), formerly in Haverhill, was named for Lord Paul Methuen, an English official of pre-Revolutionary days. Industrial development began after the Civil War. Today's local products are diversified.

A noted native son was Major Robert Rogers (1731–95), one of New England's first native playwrights — he authored *Ponteach: or the Savage of America* — and commander of the famed Rogers' Rangers who destroyed the St. Francis Indian village in 1759. He turned Tory during the Revolution and organized the Queen's Rangers. The best account of his life is in Kenneth Robert's *Northwest Passage* (1937).

About 0.4 mi. e. of the center, off East St., is *Daddy Frye's Hill,* topped by the gray stone towers of *Tenney Castle* and the battlemented walls of the Searles Castle and estate. During the 19th century, Mark and Nathaniel Gorrill, brothers, courted and were rejected by the same girl. They became hermits, never speaking to each other, though they continued to live in their homestead on Daddy Frye's Hill near the castle. Some years ago a townsman said he had dreamed of treasure hidden in a wall. The place was searched, and in the cellar of one of the castle's towers was found $20,000 in bonds, presumably hidden by the brothers.

The *Nevins Memorial Hall and Library,* n. of the center, built in 1888 of yellow brick, with cloistered portico and stained-glass windows, was designed by Samuel J. F. Thayer.

Vacation Farm for Horses was given to the Massachusetts Society for the Prevention of Cruelty to Animals by Harriet F. Nevins. Racehorses recuperate here between seasons, and dray horses rest from years of labor.

About 1000 workers produced leather goods, textiles and food products.

Methuen Memorial Music Hall (s. of Methuen Sq. on Mass. 28) was originally built (1857) in Germany for the Boston Music Hall. It was purchased and installed in Methuen by multimillionaire Edward F. Searles. Some of the world's great musicians perform here annually.

MIDDLEBOROUGH (Plymouth County, sett. 1660, incorp. 1669, alt. 83, pop. 13,607, area 68.1 sq. mi., town meeting, routes, US 44, Mass. 25, 105) was known to the Indians as Nemasket. The first white men were three shipwrecked Frenchmen, who were taken by the Indians as slaves. Children and grandchildren of the Pilgrims settled here. Middleborough was spared early in King Philip's War because of the friendly relations with the Indians, but eventually it was destroyed. Settlers rebuilt it.

Nineteenth-century products included straw hats and fire engines. Today, industries include ice bags, heating pads, hospital supplies, fire apparatus, metal products, shoes and cranberry processing.

ROCKY GUTTER WILDLIFE MANAGEMENT AREA has public hunting.

MIDDLEFIELD (Hampshire County, sett. *c.* 1780, incorp. 1783, alt. 1677, pop. 288, town meeting, route, unnumbered). Many settlers migrated from Connecticut and Pennsylvania after the Revolution, impoverished by their

losses at the hands of British and Indians. After 1794 woolen goods were made in homes. Later mills were established. The demand for wool encouraged the raising of Saxony sheep. In 1874 and 1901, great floods caused considerable loss. The town declined in prosperity, and its factories removed to other sites. Dairying, which replaced beef-cattle raising, is giving way to summer tourists as a major income source. Many Middlefielders commute to neighboring communities.
Middlefield Fair Grounds are located in the village on a high plateau. Here the Highland Agricultural Society (1857) holds its annual fair and cattle show early in August.

MIDDLESEX COUNTY (est. 1643, pop. 1,397,268, area 821.02 sq. mi., shire town, Cambridge) includes the cities of Cambridge, Everett, Lowell, Malden, Marlborough, Medford, Melrose, Newton, Somerville, Waltham, Woburn. The 43 towns include Acton, Arlington, Ashby, Ashland, Ayer, Bedford, Belmont, Billerica, Boxborough, Burlington, Carlisle, Chelmsford, Concord, Dracut, Dunstable, Framingham, Groton, Holliston, Hopkinton, Hudson, Lexington, Lincoln, Littleton, Maynard, Natick, North Reading, Pepperell, Reading, Sherborn, Shirley, Stoneham, Stow, Sudbury, Tewksbury, Townsend, Tyngsborough, Wakefield, Watertown, Wayland, Westford, Weston, Wilmington, Winchester.

MIDDLESEX FELLS RESERVATION (Malden, Medford, Melrose, Stoneham, Winchester, routes, off Mass. 28 and 93). Phone 396–0100 for current hours — open throughout the year. Foot and bridle trails (horses for hire), freshwater fishing, picnic sites, observation tower, swimming pool, natural and artificial ice skating, 2630 acres of woodlands and meadows patrolled by MDC mounted police.

MIDDLESEX FELLS ZOO, Pond St., off Mass. 28. Phone 438–3662 for current hours, open year round. 25 acres of zoological displays and exhibits, featuring hooved animals and exotic birds. Walk through aviary amid tropical plants.

MIDDLETON (Essex County, sett. 1659, incorp. 1728, alt. 95, pop. 4044, area 14.28 sq. mi., town meeting, route, Mass. 114) is surrounded by pine-covered hills, divided by the winding Ipswich River.
Middleton Congregational Church, Mass 62, is a white building with a tall, slender spire.

Middleton's Minutemen arrived too late to join in the Battle of Lexington, but old Tom Fuller rode after the retreating British, blazing away at their backs. The British, in grim compliment to his marksmanship, nicknamed him "Death on the White Horse."

MILFORD (Worcester County, sett. 1662, incorp. 1780, alt. 312, pop. 19,352, area 14.79 sq. mi., representative town meeting, routes, Mass. 16, 85, 109, 140) is a modern mill town. Early in its history it became economically independent. By 1819 small boot shops, employing from two to ten men and boys, were marketing their product. By 1870 the town had two of the largest boot factories in the United States. The Milford Branch of the Boston and Albany Railroad, built in 1845, accelerated industrial expansion. Local footwear production declined after 1900.

In the mid-19th century, Reverend Patrick Cuddahy discovered pink granite here and opened the first quarry. Local stone was used in the Boston Public Library, Corcoran Art Gallery in Washington and Grand Central and Pennsylvania Stations, New York.

MILL RIVER (see NEW MARLBOROUGH)

MILLBURY (Worcester County, sett. 1716, incorp. 1813, alt. 415, pop. 11,987, area 15.84 sq. mi., town meeting, routes, US 20, Mass. 122A, 146). Before English settlement this section was an important Indian center. More than 1000 handicraft items have been found near Ramshorn Pond.

The Blackstone Canal (1828) gave impetus to growth. Within a few years the town's manufacturing capacity doubled. When the canal closed in 1848 because of trouble between mill owners and waterway operators, the Providence and Worcester RR was an accomplished fact so that the progress was not hampered.

The industrial peak was reached about 1910. Textiles have declined. Today, Millbury is still an industrial community producing textiles, spindles, thread, felt and tools.

The second *Asa Waters Mansion,* Elm St., is a two-and-one-half-story structure, said to have been the finest residence in the county at the time of its erection (1826–29). It is late Georgian Colonial style. Hard pine was brought from the south, mahogany from Central America, marble from Italy and bricks from Baltimore. The finishing timber was "pumpkin pine" from Maine. As woodworking machinery had not yet been invented, the work was done by hand.

MILLIS (Norfolk County, sett. 1657, incorp. 1885, alt. 163, pop. 5686, area 12.17 sq. mi., town meeting, routes, Mass. 109, 115), on the west bank of the winding Charles, was named in honor of Lansing Millis.

On the common is the *Church of Christ,* Congregational, founded in 1714, a white clapboard building with a large green central door and a squat tower surmounted by an unpainted shingled steeple with a clock. Nearby is the St. Thomas Roman Catholic Church and St. Paul's Episcopal Church. There are two synagogues on the village street.

Dinglehole, Union St., is a pit formerly filled with water, where Puritans heard the ringing of the bell that summoned witches to their evil rites and saw on moonlight nights a headless man keeping vigil.

Millis, a residential community, has small shoe and floor tile mills.

MILLVILLE (Worcester County, sett. 1662, incorp. 1916, alt. 250, pop. 1764, area 4.92 sq. mi., town meeting, route, Mass. 122), once part of Mendon, has a history belonging with Blackstone's, which separated from Mendon in 1845, including Millville. In 1729, Daniel Darling erected a gristmill. A woolen mill was established in 1814. Industry developed rapidly. Lawrence Felting Company had mills by 1877. During WWI subsidiary plants of large rubber and knitting companies were established in Millville.

Millville, as a separate community, is one of the youngest towns in the state, having been incorporated in 1916. During the Depression, when rubber products and textiles closed, the town was in such a financial morass that a state-appointed commission conducted its affairs (1933–34).

About 200 residents work in local textile and metal products plants, while others commute to Woonsocket, R.I.

Chestnut Hill Meeting House (1769), now used by the Congregationalists, is almost square in plan, and is devoid of spire or ornament. The severe interior has been carefully preserved.

MILTON (Norfolk County, sett. 1636, incorp. 1662, alt. 110, pop. 27,190, area 13.20 sq. mi., representative town meeting, routes, Mass. 28, 37, 128), originally Uncataquisset (Indian, "Head of Tidewater"), was formerly in Dorchester town. Factories utilizing Neponset River power were early established here, making powder, chocolate, bass viols, artificial legs, pianos, medicines and dyestuffs.

Milton Library (open), Canton Ave. and Mass. 28, houses etchings by Millet, Rembrandt and Whistler and exhibits paintings by local artists. It is the headquarters of the Milton Historical Society.

Gulliver Elm, junction of Elm St. and Canton Ave., was deeded in 1823 by the First Congregational Parish in Milton to Isaac Gulliver, who gave bond for its perpetual protection.

Milton Academy (1807) Centre St., closed in 1866 when the town high school was built, but reopened in 1885 as a private coeducational institution.

About 500 feet east of the academy on Centre St. is Milton Cemetery containing the *Grave of Wendell Phillips.*

Governor Hutchinson's Field (10 acres), atop Milton Hill off Adams St., is owned and maintained by TOR. There is a sweeping view across Neponset marshes to Boston Harbor.

Pierce House, 224 Adams St., is the headquarters of the Trustees of Reservations (TOR). The Reading Room has an excellent library of nature books for use by members. The Trustees of Reservations was incorporated in 1891 as a nonprofit foundation "for the purpose of acquiring, holding, arranging, maintaining, and opening to the public under suitable regulations, beautiful and historic places and tracts of land within the Commonwealth."

Many public-spirited citizens have supported TOR's laudable programs. Persons interested in membership should write for information to 224 Adams St., Milton.

Rocky Knoll Nature Center, 74 Maple St (2 acres), is a natural history school in an urban center. For details visit center or contact Massachusetts Audubon Society, South Great Road, Lincoln, Mass.

BLUE HILLS RESERVATION (see p. 179).

MONROE (Franklin County, sett. *c.* 1800, incorp. 1822, alt. 1106, pop. 216, area 10.85 sq. mi., town meeting, route, off Mass. 2 and Vt. 8) was named in honor of the then President of the United States. Agriculture remained the town's chief occupation until 1886, when a paper mill, utilizing the surrounding spruce and poplar forest, was erected. About 1915 the mill was purchased by the New England Power Co., and subsequent development of power led to the formation of the Deerfield Glassine Company, which manufactures a material similar to cellophane.

West of the junction with Monroe Rd., the main route crosses *Dunbar Brook,* at a point where the water drops over large boulders and flows through a deep gorge.

Monroe Bridge (alt. 1040) is a few houses from the power station.

Monroe Town's eastern boundary is the Deerfield River. The Yankee Atomic Electric Plant (see Rowe) can be seen from the road above Monroe Bridge village. An observation post from which visitors can view — at a distance — the atomic power plant is located on the east side of the highway. The short drive from Monroe Bridge — a continuation of the drive from Mass. 2 and the villages of Zoar and Hoosac Tunnel — provides a spectacular view of the *Deerfield River Gorge.*

MONSON (Hampden County, sett. 1715, incorp. 1775, alt. 407, pop. 7355, area 44.84 sq. mi., town meeting, routes, US 20, Mass. 32) was originally a district of Brimfield. Provincial Governor Thomas Pownall named the town for his friend, Sir John Monson, president of the British Board of Trade.

Toilet seats are major Monson products.

Monson State Hospital, an institution for epileptics (1500 patients), employs 600 area residents.

Monson Academy (1804), is an endowed preparatory school for boys. Three Chinese students, brought to America by missionary Robbins Brown and enrolled at the academy in 1847, were among the first Chinese to study in America.

At the *Tufts House* in 1865–66, poet Eugene Field and his brother Roswell studied under James Tufts, the "grand old man" of Monson.

MONTAGUE (Franklin County, sett. 1715, incorp. 1754, alt. 235, pop. 8451, area 31.02 sq. mi., town meeting, route, Mass. 63). *Turner's Falls,* the principal settlement, is on terraces above the Connecticut River. Capt. Elisha Mack built the first dam on the Connecticut River.

The ice jam preceding the 1936 flood swept away three bridges. One of these, on top of which ran the tracks of the Boston and Main RR, was the longest covered wooden bridge in the state.

Carnegie Library (open 2–9) has a collection of Indian relics. Montague's large hydroelectric generating station (1918) once generated two thirds of the electricity sold by western Massachusetts companies.

Mayo's Point offers a splendid view of the river and hills.

MILLER'S FALLS (alt. 292), a manufacturing settlement, lies in both Erving and Montague towns. South from Miller's Falls on a road paralleling railroad tracks is *Green Pond,* r. 1.9 mi., and *Lake Pleasant,* l. 2 mi., the town reservoir.

MONTEREY (Berkshire County, sett. 1739, incorp. 1847, alt. 1244, pop. 600, area 26.55 sq. mi., town meeting, routes, Mass. 23, 57). Monterey, once part of adjacent Tyringham, was named for the American victory at Monterey during the Mexican War. It has always been a farming community. Maple sugar and stove wood are major products. There is no manufacturing. The town has two grocery stores. There are many summer residents due to Monterey's two large lakes and six children's camps.

BEARTOWN STATE FOREST includes a section of the Appalachian Trail (overnight shelter for hikers). Facilities: boating, fishing, hiking, hunting, fireplaces, picnic tables, campsites (12), swimming.

MONTGOMERY (Hampden County, sett. *c.* 1767, incorp. 1780, alt. 1050, pop. 446, area 15.01 sq. mi., town meeting, routes, US 20, 202, Mass. 112, Mass. Pike) was named in honor of Dublin, Ireland, native, Gen. Richard Montgomery (1738–75). Ephraim Avery brought his family here in 1767. During the Revolution Richard Falley made guns here. The guns, serviceable, and well finished, were much sought after by the Continental Army.

The Reverend Seth Noble, first pastor of the *Congregational Church* (1797), was excessively fond of the old hymn "Bangor" and called for it so frequently that his congregation dismissed him in 1806. He went to preach in a Massachusetts settlement that later became the State of Maine and "was sent to Boston by the officers of the town to present to the General Court a petition for the incorporation of the territory as a town under the name of Sunfield. Rev. Noble erased the word "Sunfield" and substituted "Bangor" and obtained passage of the act.

After almost 25 years of nonuse, the Congregational Church was reopened in 1958 and has been active ever since. An Historical Society was formed and is using the *Town House,* built in 1849, to house its gifts of memorabilia.

Montgomery, formerly an agricultural town, has no industries so its residents commute to business centers.

MONTVILLE (see SANDISFIELD)

MOUNT WASHINGTON (Berkshire County, sett. 1692, incorp. 1779, pop. 52, route, reached by unnumbered road from Mass. 23 and 41 or from N.Y. 22 — most direct route and best road is from Mass. 23 in Egremont).

The tiny town, located in the extreme southwestern corner of the state — N.Y. on the west and Connecticut on the south — has the smallest population of any Bay State town. It is usually the first town in the United States — or tries to be — in reporting its presidential election vote. Mount Washington voters cast their votes immediately after sunrise. They are counted, and the result is phoned to the wire services in Boston.

UNION CHURCH is the principal village of the town. The chief industry has always been farming, although considerable income is now derived from tourists. The community is without a post office or store.

MOUNT EVERETT RESERVATION is a state park of 1200 acres. *Guilder Pond* (alt. 1975) is surrounded by dense evergreens and almost covered in summer with pink and white water lilies. A foot trail circles the pond. Picnic ground and parking area is called *First Level.* From this point a foot trail leads 0.5 mi. to the *Dome* (alt. 2624). Here a steel tower with a sheltered observation platform provides a view extending to the dim outlines of the Green Mountains of Vermont and the Berkshires of Connecticut.

ALANDER (alt. 1647) was once the central village of Mount Washington. The road passes through thick woods to the Connecticut Line.

BASH BISH FALLS STATE FOREST offers the state's most majestic and spectacular waterfalls. Park can be reached from Massachusetts by following markers beginning at junction of Mass. 23 and 41 in South Egremont. Also can be reached by foot trail from Taconic Trail State Park in Copake, N.Y. (N.Y. 22).

NAHANT (Essex County, sett. 1630, incorp. 1853, alt. 45, pop. 4119, area 1.04 sq. mi., town meeting, routes, US 1A, Mass. 129), is a high rocky isle — connected by causeway to the mainland — once covered with trees, where the lonely haywards of early days guarded hedges and fences against damage by stray cattle. Nahant and Little Nahant were sold in 1730 by Chief Poquanum to Lynn farmer Thomas Dexter, for a suit of clothes, two stone pestles and a Jew's harp.

Joseph Johnson erected *The Castle Tavern* (1802). This venture and the establishment of steamboat service to Boston (1817) caused Nahant to develop rapidly as a fashionable watering place.

Off Nahant Rd., south of the center, is a public footpath winding down to the sea, along which are views of the coastline and some odd rock formations. The *estate of the late Senator Henry Cabot Lodge* (private) is on Cliff St.

During King Philip's War, fugitive Indians fled on Swallow's Cave Rd. to *Swallow's Cave* (private property), a natural recess in the rocky shore. Victims of the witchcraft persecution also took refuge here.

Fort Ruckman, once a Boston Harbor defense post, has reverted to the town. It contains a par three golf course. At *East Point* is the marine research project of Northeastern University.

NAHANT THICKET WILDLIFE SANCTUARY (4 acres) is bounded by Wharf St., Furbush Lane and Willow Boulevard. This area is a resting-place for migratory birds during spring and fall flights. Massachusetts Audubon Society project.

NANTUCKET (Nantucket County seat, sett. 1641, incorp. 1671, alt. 10, pop. 3774, area 49.53 sq. mi., town meeting, no numbered highways).

NANTUCKET ISLAND is also Nantucket town and Nantucket County.

NANTUCKET VILLAGE is in Nantucket town.

Nantucket (Island) (Indian *Nanticut,* meaning "The Far Away Land") is 14 miles long and averages 3.5 miles in width. Nantucket is an experience. The steamer rounds *Brant Point Light* and comes suddenly on "the little gray town in the sea," a town full of visitors all summer long; its cobbled lanes and bypaths are bright with holiday clothes; its beaches are covered with brown throngs and dots of color; yet the town has not lost its sense of the past, the days when it was the great whaling port of the world and only simple folk in homespun or oilskins trod its crooked paths from house and warehouse, cooper shops and rigger shops, to the quays and back again. The old cobblestone streets, the comfortable homes and well-kept estates, the open moors swept by the salt breezes of the ocean and the stately trees still entitle the island to its Indian name *Canopache* (The Place of Peace).

Nantucket was included in the 1621 Plymouth Company grant. The island was purchased (1641) by Thomas Mayhew, who in 1659 sold nine tenths of it to nine other people. Because of the Puritan severity in Amesbury and Salisbury, people from those towns, accompanied by Peter Folger of Martha's Vineyard, emigrated to Nantucket in June 1661. From 1660 to 1692, when it was ceded to Massachusetts, the island belonged to York Province.

Farming, fishing and sheep raising provided a livelihood. Farms were soon exhausted and the people turned to whaling. In 1768 the town possessed 125 whaling ships. Whale oil was exported directly to England in Nantucket vessels. The pioneer whaling town was eventually displaced by New Bedford with which it shares honors in Herman Melville's *Moby Dick.*

During the Revolution, caught between the British warships and Continental privateers, the people suffered severely. Over 1600 men were lost, and very few ships survived the blockade. The fleet was rebuilt, and Nantucket again became a thriving port.

Between 1797 and 1812 shipbuilding and nail and wool manufacturing developed. In the War of 1812, 11 Nantucket vessels were captured by the British. By 1830 Nantucket rated third among Massachusetts commercial towns in spite of the fact that the whaling fleet had by 1812 dwindled to 40 ships.

The Nantucket town village of SIASCONSET'S ('Sconset) charm lies in its grassy lanes and low, picturesque cottages, hemmed in by little white fences and gay with bright-hued flower gardens. Many have blue shutters that, tradition says, were reserved by unwritten law in the past for captains' and first mates' houses.

Just left of the bus stop, near the bluffs, a sign points out over the ocean: "To Spain and Portugal, 3000 miles." The waters below are dotted with smacks bobbing up and down in quest of shimmering cargo; in the distance the great black hulls of merchantmen and the sharp prows of ocean liners plow through the furrows of the open sea.

Sankaty Head Light (1850). A climb of 75 steps to the light's walk is rewarded by a view of the neighboring moors and the ocean.

East of 'Sconset a road runs through Polpis. It leads through undulating moors with enchanting vistas of the harbor and of small ponds. *Altar Rock* (alt. 102), the highest point on the island, provides a grand panorama of moor and blinding-white beaches.

Woods Hole Nantucket Steamship Authority — a state agency — operates ships daily between Woods Hole and New Bedford, Martha's Vineyard and Nantucket. Trips are frequent during the summer. Automobiles can be carried on board. Schedules may vary from year to year, so check with your travel agent, automobile association or write the authority, Woods Hole, for current schedule.

Northeast Airlines provides daily flights from Boston — summer flights direct from New York City — to the island.

A ferry operates out of Hyannis during July and August.

What to See and Do

Whaling Museum (open May 29–Oct. 12, daily 10–5, small fee), Broad St. Interesting collection of whaling ship logbooks, harpoons, portraits of whaling ship masters.

Historical Society Museum (open June 15–Sept. 15, daily 10–5, small fee), 9 Fair St., is the wing of the Quakers' Meeting House (1838). Excellent primitive portrait collection. Period furnishings.

Old Mill (open June 15–Sept. 15, weekdays 10–5, small fee), cor. Mill and Prospect Sts., was built in 1746 from wood salvaged from shipwrecks.

1800 House (open June 15–Sept. 15, Mon.–Sat. 10–5, closed holidays, small fee, children free), Mill St., is a restoration of a Nantucket house of the great whaling era.

Hawden House (open June 15–Sept. 15, daily 10–5, small fee), Satler Memorial, Main St., is an elegant residence built in 1845 by wealthy whale oil merchant William Hawden.

Jethro Coffin House (open June 15–Sept. 15, daily 10–5) (1686), Sunset Hill, is Nantucket's oldest house. China and period furniture.

Maria Mitchell House (open June 15–Sept. 15, daily 10–5, small fee), 1 Vestal St., is the birthplace (1818) of the famous astronomer and discoverer of the comet named in her honor. The long wooden latch on the front door is made from a bit of mahogany from a wrecked ship.

Memorial Observatory (open Mon. evenings in summer) (1908), adjacent to Memorial House.

Mitchell Memorial Library (open June 15–Sept. 15, Mon.–Fri. 10–12, 2–5, Sat. 10–12 noon, Sept. 16–June 14, Thurs. only, 10–12, 2–5, astronomy lectures, Mon. evenings) (across from observatory).

Old Gaol (open June 15–Sept. 15, Mon.–Sat. 10–5, closed Sun., holidays, small fee) (1805), Vestal St., contains pillories and stocks.

NANTUCKET COUNTY is the same as Nantucket Town which includes Nantucket, Tuckernuck and Muskeget Islands (see Nantucket). Nantucket County commissioners are the town's board of selectmen. The town treasurer serves as county treasurer. Nantucket town pays the cost of county operation. The population is 3774.

NATICK (Middlesex County, sett. 1718, incorp. 1781, alt. 100, pop. 31,057, area 14.88 sq. mi., representative town meeting, routes, Mass. 9, 16, 27, 135) was granted to John Eliot in 1650 as a plantation for his "Praying Indians." It was a self-governing community for more than half a century, but when white settlers appeared they crowded the Indians out. It was a farming settlement until the 19th century. Present industries are shoe baseball, paper box and tool manufacturing plants. There is a large brewery and a big commercial bakery. Natick has two large shopping centers, one of which has more than 40 establishments and is completely enclosed.

On the Park St. side of the common a boulder memorial marks the

Henry Wilson Tree, planted by him in 1857. Henry Wilson (1812–75), "the Natick cobbler," was born in New Hampshire in 1812. He was known as Jeremiah Jones Colbaith until he was 21 when he had his name changed by an act of the legislature. He came to Natick in 1833 as a cobbler's apprentice. Wilson entered politics and gained considerable attention with his antislavery oratory. He was U.S. senator (1855–73) and U.S. vice president (1873–75).

SOUTH NATICK has a boulder on the *Site of the Indian Meeting House* (1651) used by John Eliot. Across the street is the *Natick Historical Society Headquarters* (open). The building has many articles of historic value.

Here is the *Site of an Indian Burying Ground* and a *Monument to Eliot.*

Charles River (swimming and canoeing) is spanned at Pleasant St. by a stone bridge.

NEEDHAM (Norfolk County, sett. *c.* 1680, incorp. 1711, alt. 160, pop. 29,748, area 12.50 sq. mi., representative town meeting, routes, Mass. 128, 135).

On April 16, 1680, the Dedham Company of Watertown purchased land from an Indian, part of which, with some of Dedham, was incorporated as Needham. Before 1720 a few saw- and corn mills were operated, but farming was the chief occupation. The town is now a quiet, residential Boston suburb with its industries concentrated in the industrial park.

Needham's population has nearly tripled since WWII. The increase can properly be attributed to the substantial migration from Boston or near Boston suburbs to outer belt towns. White-collar Needham has about three Republicans to one Democrat.

Many parents move to Needham whose school system is among the finest in the state.

Fuller House (private), 200 Nehoiden St., is a trim attractive white clapboard dwelling (1754).

The *Townsend House* (private), corner of Nehoiden St. and Central Ave., a three-story, square clapboard dwelling was the home of town pastors for a century.

Gay House (private), 1196 Central Ave., is a simple little two-story white house, built in the early 1700's. The rear chimney is that of the first kitchen. Living room floor planks are over 20 inches wide.

William Carter Company, Highland Ave., is one of the largest knitted goods makers in the nation. Needham is now the national home office, as most manufacturing facilities have moved south. Goods are shipped to Needham and redistributed. The Carter Company pioneered in producing rayon and other synthetics.

NEW ASHFORD (Berkshire County, sett. 1762, incorp. 1835, alt. 1256, pop. 183, town meeting, route, US 7) was settled by Rhode Island and Connecticut emigrants. The region contains valuable quarries of blue and white marble, which were worked for some 20 years, but the transportation cost became too great to allow a profit, and New Ashford relapsed into the peace of a farming community. Humorist Josh Billings spent many summers here.

Red Bat Cave (open) was named for tiny, redheaded bats found on its walls. The cave, made up of four chambers, is 100 feet long and 150 feet deep.

NEW BEDFORD (Bristol County, sett. 1640, town incorp. 1787, city incorp. 1847, alt. 50, pop. 101,777, area 18.99 sq. mi., routes, I–195, US 6, Mass. 24, Fall River Expressway), once a famous whaling port and now a textile center at the mouth of the Acushnet River, has interesting contradictions. Gone are the whalers, but the harbor is busy with deep-sea fishing vessels and coastwise freighters. New Bedford, once the fourth largest port in the United States, is still a busy secondary port.

Mills employing many English and French-Canadian workers have not destroyed this nautical flavor, perpetuated by a whaling museum, a seaman's bethel and substantial old homes of captains and wealthy traders. Twelve thousand Portuguese live here. "The Crowning," a Portuguese religious festival the sixth Sunday after Easter and any summer Sunday thereafter, takes its name from the custom of an early Portuguese queen. Legend reports she performed miraculous cures of the sick by placing her crown on their heads. A replica of the queen's silver crown is kept for repetitions of these crownings. A Portuguese folk dance, "Chamarita," is enjoyed at their carnivals.

Bedford village was once a part of Dartmouth town. Up to 1760 there were no more than a dozen scattered farms in the village, homes of Quakers from Rhode Island and Cape Cod. Joseph Russell, the "Father of New Bedford" because he named the town after the Duke of Bedford, engaged in small-scale whaling. This attracted shipbuilders including George Claghorn, later to build the U.S. Frigate *Constitution* at Boston. New Bedford's first ship, the *Dartmouth,* was launched in 1767. In 1773 "Indians" dumped her tea cargo into Boston Harbor.

New Bedford saw the first maritime clash between the British and the Colonials. Gen. Gage, isolated in Boston since April 19, 1775, sent ships scouting for food. The *Falcon* seized two Vineyard Sound sloops for use as decoys and advanced slowly toward New Bedford. An unknown messenger made a gallant ride from Wareham with the news. Twenty-five men in a small vessel set out to intercept the British. On May 14 they captured both sloops, thereby discouraging the *Falcon.* New Bedford Harbor was a rendezvous for American privateers preying upon British shipping. This fact prompted a British invasion September 5, 1778. The 5000 soldiers met little resistance. They burned all patriot homes, vessels and business houses but spared Tories' property.

Nantucket was the leading whaling port until after the War of 1812. By 1820, New Bedford, with a population of 3847, outstripped it. New Bedford thereafter led the industry, gradually absorbing almost all Atlantic seaboard whaling. The year 1845 saw New Bedford's greatest receipts from its fleet — 158,000 barrels of sperm oil, 272,000 barrels of whale oil and 3,000,000 pounds of whalebone. Ten thousand seamen manned ships.

This industry brought wealth to certain sections, but to the waterfront it brought rough living and exploited vice. A notorious district known as "Hard Dig" was burned in 1826 by over zealous citizens.

The 1857 discovery of oil in Pennsylvania doomed the whaling industry. Today almost the entire product of blackfish oil (derived from a species of small whale and by sailors called porpoise jaw oil), a lubricant for clocks and watches, is refined here.

New Bedford was an Underground Railway station which smuggled runaway slaves into Canada. Abolitionism was fostered by Quakers. New Bedford had ships in the Stone Fleet which blockaded southern ports by sinking vessels laden with granite at southern harbor entrances.

The first important textile plant, Wamsutta Mills, was chartered in 1846. The industry grew slowly, because whaling was still dominant. New Bedford shared in New England's 1881–83 textile boom. Thereafter the city was a top manufacturer of fine cotton fabrics. Its mild, damp climate is favorable to cotton handling.

Even before the Depression, low-cost Southern production began to cut into New Bedford's business. Some mills liquidated, and others operated on curtailed schedules, creating a major unemployment problem.

Matters were precipitated, April 9, 1928, by a ten percent cut in all textile workers' wages, Dartmouth and Beacon Mills excepted. A six-months' strike involved 27,000 workers.

National press comment showed countrywide sympathy with the workers. Settlement was made on the basis of a five percent reduction in wages, to be restored as soon as conditions warranted; agreement by manufacturers to give 30 days' notice of future reductions and agreement by the workers to cooperate in an efficiency study. Several plants failed to reopen and liquidated. New Bedford's textile history is not closed. During readjustment a number of new businesses have been attracted to the city, including needle industries.

New Bedford is a modern fish-shipping center. Many Cape Cod fishing boats which formerly unloaded their cargoes directly in Boston or New York now transship their haul at New Bedford.

Public Library (open Mon.–Fri. 9–9, Sat. 9–6, closed holidays) (1856), Pleasant and Williams Sts., established in 1852, is one of the oldest free public libraries in America. Melville Whaling Room contains the finest collection of whaling books, pamphlets and manuscripts in America. Exhibits include whaling ship models and whaling implements. Notable is Audubon's elephant-size *Folios: Quadrupeds of America and Birds of America.* There are paintings by noted local artists.

Whaleman Statue (in front of library), by Bela Pratt (1867–1917) was dedicated in 1913 to the whaler's motto, "A dead whale or a stove boat."
Bourne Office Building Site, end of School St., was the headquarters of whaling merchant Jonathan Bourne who opened shop in 1848. His son Jonathan (1855–1940), U.S. senator (Oregon) (1907–13), was the first senator elected in the direct primary. Bourne Senior's furniture is in the Dartmouth Historical Society.
Waterfront. You can see from here the 3.5-mile-long breakwater completed in 1966 at a cost of $18,000,000.

What to See and Do

Old Dartmouth Historical Society and *Bourne Whaling Museum* (open June 1–Sept. 30, Mon.–Sat. 9–5, Sun. 12–5, October 1–May 31, Tues.–Sat. 10–5, Sun. 1–5, closed some holidays, small fee), 18 Johnny Cake Hill. This is a wonderful place to recapture the romance and courage of the whalers who made America great. Whaling was filthy, dangerous and uncomfortable work, but it was exciting. Exhibits: whaling prints, whaling tools, scrimshaw — whaling term for carved ivory gadgets and knicknacks — and ship models including a one-half scale model of the whaler *Lagoda.*
Seamen's Bethel (open) (1832), facing the museum, was supposed to give moral inspiration to the thousands of sailors, native and foreign-born, who frequented the city. It was immortalized by Herman Melville in *Moby Dick* and has but little changed since Melville's time. Adorning the walls are the black-bordered, marble cenotaphs inscribed in terms of bitter and hopeless grief.
Customhouse, corner of North Second St., is more than a century old. It has two stories, a portico in classic style and a winding stone stairway.
Liberty Bell Tablet, on the eastern wall of the Merchants' National Bank at the corner, reads in part: "News of the passage of the Fugitive Slave Law was brought from Boston in 1851 by an express messenger who rode all night, and the bell on the old Hall was rung to give warning to fugitive slaves that U.S. Marshals were coming."

BRIDGE PARK, head of the state bridge, is a beautifully landscaped area.

ACUSHNET PARK (privately owned, open in summer) has an open-air dance hall, public bathing beach and clambake pavilion.

Fort Rodman (open, visitors restricted), at the tip of Clark's Point, was once a key defense of the North Atlantic coast. The fort antedates the Civil War.
Rodney French Memorial Tablet, entrance to Hazelwood Park (public — tennis, baseball), was erected by city Negroes to honor an abolitionist mayor in 1853–54.

MUNICIPAL BATHING BEACH was created by Works Progress Administration (WPA) projects.

Mark Duff Home (private), between Madison and Cherry Sts., was designed by Russell Warren, early nineteenth-century Providence architect. *Perry House* (private), southeast corner of School St., a whaling mansion, is an excellent example of New England Georgian architecture.

BUTTONWOOD PARK, west end of the city, is the city's largest park.

Barnard Monument is a tribute to the whalers and to textile industry promoters.

NEW BEDFORD METROPOLITAN AREA (pop. 152,642, area 141.79 sq. mi.) includes the city of New Bedford and towns of Acushnet, Dartmouth, Fairhaven, Marion, Mattapoisett.

NEW BOSTON (see SANDISFIELD)

NEW BRAINTREE (Worcester County, sett. 1709, incorp. 1751, alt. 945, pop. 631, area 20.76 sq. mi., town meeting, route, Mass. 67), a small farming-residential community on the periphery of the Worcester Metropolitan Area, has some dairy and egg farms. Indians were active during King Philip's War. Manufacturing was unsuccessfully attempted during the 19th century.

Today's principal — and only — industry is a wood products firm. Most residents are either self-employed or commute to work in nearby communities.

WINIMUSSET MEADOWS WILDLIFE MANAGEMENT AREA has public hunting.

NEW LENOX (see LENOX)

NEW MARLBOROUGH (Berkshire County, sett. 1738, incorp. 1775, alt. 1351, pop. 1031, area 47.85 sq. mi., town meeting, route, Mass. 57).

MILL RIVER is the principal village of New Marlborough. Gunpowder and paper were once important industries. A Konkapot River mill was the second mill in the United States; here paper was made from straw. Newsprint was made in Carroll Paper Mill, during the Civil War for the *New York Tribune.*

New Marlborough was formerly a station on the famed Red Bird Stagecoach Line.

SOUTHFIELD is a small hamlet.

ROCK LEDGE, sometimes called Cook's Ledge (accessible by car), 0.2 mi., se. of Southfield, affords a sweeping view. *Tipping Rock,* 0.4 mi. sw. of Southfield, is a 40-ton boulder so delicately balanced that a pressure of the hand will sway but not dislodge it.

CAMPBELL FALLS STATE FOREST is reached by a road running from Mass. 57 in New Marlborough to Norfolk, Conn. This beautiful area offers fishing, fireplaces, picnic tables and very scenic views.

Campbell's Falls is one of the most impressive, picturesque cataracts in the Berkshires. The Whiting River pours over a split-rock ledge, drops nearly 100 feet and then rushes forward through a deep gulch.

COOKSON PROPERTY. Facilities: fishing, hiking, picnic tables, hunting, snowmobiling.

Marlborough Academy is located here.

NEW SALEM (Franklin County, sett. 1737, incorp. 1753, alt. 1048, pop. 474, area 45.04 sq. mi., town meeting, routes, US 202, Mass. 122) was named for Salem, where the original proprietors came from. After the Revolution, agriculture and lumbering flourished. By 1820 New Salem had a population of 2146. Stagecoaches running between Brattleboro and Worcester made the town a trade center. With the building of railroads, however, it was gradually isolated, and its population decreased rapidly. The town today is principally a bedroom community with residents commuting to Athol, Amherst and Orange.

New Salem natives, the Misses Sophia B. Packard and Harriet E. Giles, organized the Spelman Seminary for Negro girls in Atlanta, Ga.

NORTH NEW SALEM. Adjacent to the green is the *Curtis House* (private) (1775), once a tavern on an old stage road. The house has two-and-a-half stories, a gable roof and nine windows in front. Fugitive slaves were secreted in the second floor until they could be taken to the next station on the Underground Railway.

NEWBURY (Essex County, sett. and incorp. 1635, alt. 37, pop. 3804, area 23.97 sq. mi., town meeting, routes, US 1, Mass. 1A).

NEWBURY OLD TOWN (alt. 40). Here on the lower green townsfolk gathered when vessels arrived from trading along the coast or with the West Indies. For many years limestone provided a valuable export. Newbury Old Town's industries surrendered to Newburyport. Life here has leisurely tranquil air.

Oldtown Hill's (alt. 180) summit allows a sweeping view of the Atlantic coastline and rolling hills.
Upper Green lies almost opposite the entrance to the Plum Island Rd. As the townsfolk gradually moved back from the Parker River side, they centered their homes in the vicinity of this strip of grassy land.
Tristram Coffin House (open June 15–Sept. 15, Mon., Wed., Fri. 2–5, and by appointment, small fee) 16 High Rd., was built about 1653 and later enlarged. It is a well-preserved example of 17th-century architecture. Coffin's role in Newbury's development was traced by Joshua Coffin in his *History of Newbury, Newburyport, and West Newbury from 1635 to 1845.*
Swett-Ilsley House (closed Jan., Feb., Mar. and all Mondays), 4 and 6 High Rd., has fine old woodwork and fireplaces.
Short House (open mid-June–mid-Sept., 10–12, 2–5, and by appointment, closed Sun. and Mon., small fee), 39 High Rd., has a fine doorway and brick gable ends. It was built sometime between 1717 and 1733.

Public hunting in *Mill Creek, Northeast,* and *Crane Pond Wildlife Management Areas.*

NEWBURYPORT (Essex County, sett. 1635 town incorp. 1764, city incorp. 1831, alt. 37, pop. 15,807, area 8.3 sq. mi., mayor-council, routes, I–95, 495, US 1, 1A, Mass. 113).

Seagoing vessels once huddled so close in the Merrimack they almost bridged the river from Newburyport to the Salisbury shore. The great river now runs placidly by the city. The harbor is clogged with sand. Along the shore are a few factories. A dignified, charming city rises from the river level, bisected by the gleaming turnpike — a modern note in a setting which is otherwise almost a monument to the glorious days of Newburyport's maritime supremacy. Shipowners and captains built the stately houses which border High Street for several miles: square three-story dwellings with hip roofs, skillfully executed by men who had learned their craft as shipwrights in the famous Newburyport yards. The street is nationally known as a distinguished survival of the best in Federal architecture.

Newburyport's business district is like any busy modern city's, although in Market Square space is given to a tablet which tells the tale of old Goody Morse, victim of the witchcraft delusion. The aroma of molasses still floats from the rum factory. Fine silver is made today in a plant whose antecedents go back to Colonial days. Newer manufactures, shoes and electrical machinery, have been established, and the city strives to adjust itself to the modern tempo. It is in the upper reaches of the city, where the old jail used for British prisoners frowns over Bartlett Mall and St. Paul's Church rears its bishop's mitre high over the roofs of the old houses, that Newburyport reveals its inner character.

Early traders tapped the rich Indian country so much that Gov. John Winthrop feared outsiders might secure too firm a foothold within Massachusetts Bay Colony. In 1635, colonists set up an outpost of virtue and commerce. They futilely attempted to farm the forest at Old Newbury.

In 1642 many moved to Newburyport. Industry sprang up. Trapping and fishing were followed by whaling and international trade. The deep-channeled river and supply of lumber made shipbuilding an inevitable development. Between 1681 and 1741, 107 ships were launched from Newburyport shipyards. Along the waterfront appeared ironworks, sail lofts and rope walks. Boston's preeminence was seriously threatened, but heavy duties imposed by the Crown and exclusion of American ships from the West Indian trade and the Newfoundland fishing banks after the Revolution left the town economically prostrate. By 1790 Newburyport recovered some prosperity. The ninth shipowning community in the country, it never recovered from the disastrous Jefferson Embargo Act. The town's plight was thus mourned by a Newbury poet in 1808:

> Our ships all in motion once whitened the ocean,
> They sailed and returned with a cargo;
> Now doomed to decay, they have fallen a prey
> To Jefferson — worms — and embargo.

In 1811 15 acres in the heart of the city were burned to the ground. The Industrial Revolution was Newburyport's commercial undoing. After the War of 1812, textile mills sprang up on every natural water site in Essex County, and Newburyport's farseeing mercantile families like the Lowells and the Jacksons turned from trade to manufacture. Tariffs protected infant industries. Imports like India cottons, English woolens, Russian duck and canvas and Baltic iron — backbone of Newburyport's seaborne commerce — were practically wiped out.

Shipbuilding knew glory in the clipper ship era. The demand for packets to carry adventurers to the California goldfields in '49 gave the industry new impetus. Noted clipper ship designer Donald McKay came to Newburyport. Between 1841 and 1843, in partnership with John Currier, Jr., he turned out three packets of such perfection that his reputation was made. The record-breaking clipper *Dreadnought* was built by Currier and Townsend.

A geographical position far from the mercantile centers, the ever-increasing sandbars and dangerous shoals at the harbor mouth and the advent of steam brought to a close this last glorious era in Newburyport's history. Glamor and vitality seemed to leave the city, and Newburyport turned to manufacturing, but without enthusiasm.

PLUM ISLAND STATE PARK. Facilities: fishing, hiking, hunting, scenic views.

NEWTON (Middlesex County, sett. 1639, town incorp. 1691, city incorp. 1873, alt. 15 to 320, pop. 91,066, area 18 sq. mi., routes, Mass. Turnpike, 9, 16, 30).

Newton, "The Garden City," is noted for its public school system and for its fourteen villages.

This sprawling community has: Boston College, Andover-Newton Theological School, Newton College of the Sacred Heart. Junior colleges include Lasell, Mount Ida and Newton.

New England Industrial Park was a forerunner of the modern industrial and research plants along Mass. 128. The Massachusetts Turnpike (I-90) bisects the city on a depressed roadbed which follows the old Boston and Albany railroad tracks.

AUBURNDALE is a pleasant residential village.

CHESTNUT HILL, skirted by Commonwealth Ave., is the most opulent of the Newtons, where large estates are attached to names well known in national finance, trade or upper-bracket politics.

Chestnut Hill Shopping Center is relatively small but has local branches of several smart New York women's shops.

Boston College (9000 students) spreads its fine campus on a hill slope overlooking the beautiful Chestnut Hill Reservoir. Imposing gray stone buildings in English Collegiate Gothic accommodate the student body. Its library contains illuminated manuscripts, breviaries, missals of the medieval era and a very famous collection of Negro folklore of Africa and the West Indies. The College is operated by the Society of Jesus (Jesuits).

ELIOT is another attractive residential area.

NEWTON CENTER has several civic buildings, a shopping center and good homes.

NEWTON CORNER is the core, with several blocks of stores and offices, giving the effect of a busy small town. On turning into Centre St., the visitor enters typical residential Newton. This is one of the older sections, characterized by large comfortable Victorian dwellings or by smaller modern houses, popularly of Tudor brick and timber, which have replaced their more substantial predecessors. Handsome churches and prosperous city buildings rise as appropriate civic accents on the residential scene.

NEWTON HIGHLANDS has dignified homes clustered about a small business district.

NEWTON LOWER FALLS is a small manufacturing center. The *Baury House* (private), 2349 Washington St., a three-story Colonial house of the massive square type, has a recessed doorway with carved panels and ceilings, an architectural detail common in the Connecticut River Valley and rarely found in this section. The fleur-de-lis carving on the door lends a French touch.

NEWTONVILLE increases the conviction that there actually is a place in Newton where its citizens can shop without journeying to Boston, but in the outlying districts a pond or two, a wooded slope, here and there an open field remind the visitor of the days not so long ago when Newton was a scattering of villages.

NEWTON UPPER FALLS, a small manufacturing center, lacks the crowded look of a typical mill settlement. Workers' houses, many 100 years old or more, have an appearance of space.

Echo Bridge (1876), over the Charles River, carries the Sudbury River conduit of Newton's water system. Foundations are sunk in solid rock, and the triple stone arch is one of the largest of this type in the world.

NONANTUM bears the original Indian name of the settlement. It is a fair-sized manufacturing and commercial center.

OAK HILL is an attractive cluster of roofs and trees half encircled by the Charles River Country Club.

RIVERSIDE is a pleasant settlement along the Charles River.

WABAN is a residential section with expensive homes and a few stores.

WEST NEWTON is a large business center, surrounded by a handsome residential area. *First Unitarian Church* (1905–06), designed by Cram and Ferguson, forms a quadrangle around a central open courtyard.

NORFOLK (Norfolk County, sett. 1795, incorp. 1870, alt. 208, pop. 4656, area 15.0 sq. mi., town meeting, routes, I-495, US 1, Mass. 1A, 115).

Once the domain of the Neponset Indians, this area was claimed by King Philip. The General Court, however, ignored the title in its expansion of the Dedham settlement in 1635–36. Norfolk was created from parts of adjacent Franklin, Medway, Walpole and Wrentham. Most of today's residents commute to nearby communities.

Massachusetts' new medium security prison, *Norfolk Correctional Institution,* is located here. Part of the new maximum security correctional institution headquarters at Walpole is in Norfolk. The institution provides many local people with jobs. About 150 workers are employed in the machinery and textile mills.

Stony Brook Nature Center, adjacent to Bristol-Blake State Reservation off Mass. 115 at North St. (200 acres). Natural history day camp. Nature tours through Bristol-Blake Reservation. Audubon Society project.

NORFOLK COUNTY (est. 1793, pop. 605,051, area 398.9 sq. mi., shire town, Dedham) includes the city of Quincy and the 27 towns of Avon, Bellingham, Braintree, Brookline, Canton, Cohasset, Dedham, Dover, Foxborough, Franklin, Holbrook, Medfield, Medway, Millis, Milton, Needham, Norfolk, Norwood, Plainville, Randolph, Sharon, Stoughton, Walpole, Wellesley, Westwood, Weymouth, Wrentham.

NORTH ADAMS (Berkshire County, sett. *c.* 1737, town incorp. 1878, city incorp. 1895, alt. 1000, pop. 19,195, area 20.59 sq. mi., mayor-council, routes, Mass. 2, 8).

Visitors coming to North Adams from the east via the Mohawk Trail and its famous Horse Shoe Curve see the most spectacular vista in Massachusetts — the Berkshire Valley rimmed on the west by the Taconic Range. As visitors roll down the trail, Mt. Greylock (alt. 3505), the state's highest peak, looms ahead while eastward lies Hoosac Mountain.

North Adams, once the site of Fort Massachusetts, was attacked several times by French-led Indians. Nearly 1000 of them burned the post and settlement in 1746. The rebuilt fort repelled later attacks. In 1765 Connecticut Congregationalists failed to establish a permanent settlement. Rhode Island Quakers then settled here. The settlement, first known as East Hoosac, was incorporated in 1778 as Adams. A century later North Adams was split off from Adams and became a town itself. Hoosac Tunnel construction was a determining factor in the city's development. French-Canadians and Italians attracted by textile jobs began moving here about 1840.

MT. GREYLOCK STATE RESERVATION (8660 acres) includes the summit of the state's highest peak. A 100-foot-high Massachusetts War Memorial, lighted at night, is atop the summit. Restaurant just below summit serves meals from mid-May through mid-October. Facilities: bridle trails, campsites (30), picnic facilities, hunting.

NORTH ANDOVER (Essex County, sett. *c.* 1644, incorp. 1855, alt. 100, pop. 16,284, area 29 sq. mi., town meeting, routes, Interstate 495, Mass. 114, 125, 133).

North Andover Center is the oldest section of historic Andover. *Kittredge Memorial* commemorates Thomas Kittredge, surgeon of the 1st Regiment in the Revolution. *Kittredge Mansion* (private) (1784), north of the green at 114 Academy Rd., is a three-story dwelling with two large chimneys.

At 148 Osgood St., off Massachusetts Ave. at the end of the green, is the gambrel-roof *Phillips Mansion* (private), built in 1752 by Samuel Phillips, one of the founders of Phillips Academy, Andover. Opposite is the *Bradstreet House* (1667) with a central chimney and lean-to roof. The house was built by Gov. Bradstreet, whose poetess wife was Anne Bradstreet. As an 18-year-old girl she had come over in the *Arbella*, leaving a life of ease for pioneer hardships.

On Great Pond Rd., within sound of the Paul Revere Bell in the *North Parish Church*, is beautiful *Cochichewick Lake* (7 mi. shoreline), half hidden among the rolling hills. It supplies town water.

Parson Barnard House (open May 1–Oct. 1, Wed., Fri., Sat. 1–4, and by appointment, small fee), 179 Osgood St., was built about 1715 by the Rev. Thomas Barnard of the First Church of Christ. The dwelling was restored by the North Andover Historical Society. The house is furnished with period furniture based upon inventory of original owners.

North Andover Historical Society and Museum (open May 1–Oct. 1, Wed., Fri., Sat. 1–4, free), 153 Academy Rd., has interesting exhibits.

North Andover has several good schools. *Merrimack College*, operated by the Augustinian Fathers, had in 1968 about 1700 day and 700 night students. *Brooks School* (boys) is an Episcopalian school (ages 14–18). *Campion Hall*, a Jesuit Retreat, conducts retreats for New England laymen, boys and priests. *Rolling Ridge Methodist Conference Center* conducts weekend instruction and mixed summer retreats. *Osgood Hill* is a Boston University Conference Center.

HAROLD PARKER STATE FOREST includes *Stearns* and *Berry Ponds*. Three stocked ponds maintained by the Division of Fisheries and Game are used for pond fish propagation. Facilities: bridle trails, fishing, boating, hiking, hunting, fireplaces, picnic tables, tent and trailer sites (120), swimming.

NORTH ATTLEBOROUGH (Bristol County, sett. 1669, incorp. 1887, alt. 185, pop. 18,665, area 19.05 sq. mi., town meeting, routes, US 1, 1A, Mass. 106, 152) was once part of Attleborough. Industrial development started in 1780 with the establishment of a jewelry shop. It was not until 1807, however, that the first jewelry manufacturing company was organized.

North Attleborough Historical Society Headquarters (open 3rd Tues. of each month 2–5), 224 Washington St., is a two-and-one-half-story clapboard house with slate roof. The adjacent barn contains historical relics.

NORTH BROOKFIELD (Worcester County, sett. 1644, incorp. 1812, alt. 915, pop. 3967, area 21.11 sq. mi., town meeting, routes, Mass. 9, 67) was a farming community until about 1812 when tanning and shoemaking plants opened. Rubber goods are current major products. Dairying, poultry raising and orchardry are prime farming pursuits. The setting for George M. Cohan's play, *Fifty Miles from Boston,* is said to have been this tiny town (see WEST BROOKFIELD).

NORTH CARVER (see CARVER)

NORTH EASTON (see EASTON)

NORTH EGREMONT (see EGREMONT)

NORTH HADLEY (see HADLEY)

NORTH HANSON (see HANSON)

NORTH NEW SALEM (see NEW SALEM)

NORTH PEMBROKE (see PEMBROKE)

NORTH READING (Middlesex County, sett. 1651, incorp. 1853, alt. 100, pop. 11,264, area 13.26 sq. mi., town meeting, routes, Mass. 28, 62), after a brief era of shoe manufacturing, is now a residential and agricultural town. Facing the town square is the *Stagecoach Tavern* (1812), built by Ebenezer Damon. This was a halfway stop between Salem and Lowell and between Boston and Haverhill. The tavern had 21 rooms, 7 fireplaces, 51 windows, 7 stairways and 7 main doorways.

Willow Lane Farm, Haverhill St., is a two-story, clapboard, hip roof house, formerly the home of Sheffield native George F. Root (1820–95), author of Civil War songs, among them "Tramp, Tramp, Tramp, the Boys Are Marching." Here he composed "The Battle Cry of Freedom" and "Just Before the Battle, Mother."

HAROLD PARKER STATE FOREST is in North Reading, North Andover, and Andover.

NORTH TRURO (see TRURO)

NORTH UXBRIDGE (see UXBRIDGE)

NORTH WEYMOUTH (see WEYMOUTH)

NORTH WILBRAHAM (see WILBRAHAM)

NORTHAMPTON (Hampshire County, sett. 1654, town incorp. 1656, city incorp. 1883, alt. 130, pop. 29,664, 34.63 sq. mi., mayor-council, routes, I-91, US 5, Mass. 9, 19, 66).

Northampton, longtime home of Vermont-born U.S. President Calvin Coolidge and the home of Smith College, has wide elm-shaded streets. The many parks, Smith College campus and Round Hills are pleasant places for strolls. Residents produce cutlery, ink and coffins.

Connecticut men (*c.* 1653) petitioned Massachusetts Bay Colony for permission to settle a "plantation" north of Hartford. Crude shelters were built along a rough dirt road, now Pleasant Street. Four acres were presented to each householder, together with a generous portion of fair meadow. Fertile soil attracted other pioneers, and Hawley, Market and King Streets were quickly settled.

Early in the 18th century, Puritan divine Jonathan Edwards (1703–1758), Congregational Church pastor, was recognized as New England's mightiest preacher. He was a leader of the "Great Awakening" (1740), America's first great revival movement. Soon in a frenzy of religious hysteria townsfolk were falling into trances and seeing visions; even little children swooned in the streets from their "conviction of sin." All New England was convulsed with terror of hellfire. Edwards' Northampton career abruptly ended with his forced removal to Stockbridge as a missionary. There he wrote his great philosophical treatise, *Of the Freedom of the Will.*

After the Revolution, deprived of the independence for which they had fought, Northampton inhabitants rebelled with many of their neighbors. Led by their preacher, Sam Ely, they stormed the courthouse in 1782 to prevent the foreclosure of their farms. In 1786, near the tragic end of Shays' Rebellion, angry citizens again descended on the court to keep it from holding session. William Butler, founded the *Hampshire Gazette* (still published) to combat the discontent.

Impetus was given to town development with the establishment of *Smith College* by Hatfield native Sophia Smith (1796–1870), at a period when the intellectual standards of women's colleges were but slightly superior to secondary schools. Her phrase "the intelligent gentlewoman" expressed the ideal of the college body; the spirit of Christianity was to pervade the teachings and life of the college, but it was to be absolutely nonsectarian. Mrs. Smith left her fortune to establish the college which opened (1875) five years after her death.

Smith, which had 14 students in 1875, is among the best and largest resident women's colleges in the world (enrollment approximately 2500). During the first two years at the college, a broad general foundation is laid. An opportunity is given for specialization during the last two years. Many students study abroad for their junior year.

Wiggins Tavern (1786) is noted for Currier and Ives prints, Rogers groups, glass, pewter, brass, kitchen and table utensil collections and good food. In the courtyard is a reproduction of a late nineteenth-century *Country Store,* crammed with period products.

People's Institute was founded by popular writer George W. Cable as a reading group. In 1905, Andrew Carnegie made it possible to erect the present community center.

Smith College's original campus, bounded by Elm St., West St. and Paradise Pond, with spacious lawns, driveways and attractive quadrangles, is expanding. In order to retain the founder's "cottage idea," dormitories are small and homelike.

Smith College Museum of Art (open weekdays 9:30–5, Sun. and summertime 2–5, free), Elm St., has a fine collection of contemporary French paintings and works by Leonard Baskin.
Northampton Historical Society (open Tues., Thurs. 2–5, Sat. 10–12, free), Memorial Hall, 240 Main St. Furniture and local relics.

Coolidge Places

Calvin Coolidge's Law Office, Masonic Temple, is still marked with his name on a second-story window. Onetime mayor of the city and in 1920 governor of the state, Coolidge became vice president in 1921, and at President Harding's death in 1923 he became President of the United States.
Clarke School for the Deaf (open by permission) is a small, coeducational, well-equipped institution. It houses kindergarten through high school pupils. Massachusetts pupils are paid for by the state. Coolidge married Clarke teacher and fellow Vermonter Grace Goodhue. Mrs. Coolidge later became president of the board of trustees and was very active in school affairs after her husband's 1933 demise.
Calvin Coolidge's First Northampton Home (private), 21 Massasoit St., a square, two-family frame house with two porches, is on a modest, tree-shaded residential street. Coolidge moved here with his bride in 1905. They lived in the house through his years as city solicitor, clerk of the courts, mayor, city councilman, state representative, senator, lieutenant governor and governor and kept it through their eight Washington years. Two years after their return from Washington they moved to the greater privacy of "The Beeches." Coolidge was then paying $40 a month rent for the Massasoit St. house.

After his return from the White House, Coolidge frequently spent warm evenings on his front porch, much to the delight of numerous tourists. Once a tourist was heard to remark, "Doesn't look like much of a house for a President." Coolidge, without turning his head, said to his wife, "Huh. Must be a Democrat."
Calvin Coolidge Memorial Room (open Mon.–Sat. 9–8:30, Sun. and holidays 2–6, closed May 30, July 4, Thanksgiving and Dec. 25), Forbes Library, 20 West St. on Mass. 66, contains President Coolidge's 5000-volume personal library. He especially enjoyed reading giftbooks. There is a portrait of President and Mrs. Coolidge by Howard Chandler Christie. The non-Coolidge section of the library contains the Judd manuscript, source of data on Connecticut Valley Colonial customs.
The Beeches (private). President Coolidge moved into this $40,000 home from his two-family Massasoit Street residence. It is a large multigable residence set in a fine grove with a view of the Holyoke Range.

NORTHBOROUGH (Northboro) (Worcester County, sett. *c.* 1672, incorp. 1766, alt. 300, pop. 9218, area 18.72 sq. mi., town meeting, routes,

US 20, Mass. 35) was once part of Marlborough. Truck garden crops are raised here. In 1884 the teeth and bones of a mastadon were uncovered here. They may be seen in the Worcester Museum. About 300 workers are employed by local manufacturers. Many residents work in nearby Worcester, Framingham and Boston.

West of the town hall, Church St., is the green with its *Old Congregational (Unitarian) Church* (1808). The bell was cast by Paul Revere's foundry in 1809.

NORTHBRIDGE (Worcester County, sett. *c.* 1700, incorp. 1772, alt. 300, pop. 11,795, area 17.33 sq. mi., town meeting, routes, Mass. 122, 146).

Industrial Northbridge, once part of neighboring Uxbridge, has produced metal products since 1729 when wrought iron products were made from pig and scrap iron. A foundry was established in 1790. Cotton mills were located here in the early 1800's. Today's machine shops and machinery-producing mills originated when John Whitin established a large machine shop in 1847. The town was long noted for its cooperage shops. Barrels and casks were shipped to major cities throughout New England. John Whitin's Machine Works is still the town's largest industry and largest employer. Paper and plastics are also produced here.

WHITINSVILLE is the principal industrial section of Northbridge.

WEST HILL WILDLIFE MANAGEMENT AREA (see MENDON).

NORTHFIELD (Franklin County, sett. 1673, alt. 310, pop. 2631, area 34.8 sq. mi., town meeting, routes, Mass. 10, 63) was once called Squakheag (spearing place for salmon). Charming rural Northfield, built along the Connecticut River, is crossed by the Ashuelot River and is watered by a score of woodland and meadow streams.

Dwight L. Moody (1837–99), noted evangelist, was a Northfield native. Together with his singer and organist Ira D. Sankey (1840–1908) he preached to millions of Americans and Britishers. In 1879 he founded the Northfield Seminary — now the Northfield School for Girls — for the daughters of local farmers. Two years later in neighboring Gill he established Mt. Hermon School for Boys — now one of the nation's finest preparatory schools.

Northfield's first settlers were 14 Northampton and Hadley families who came here in 1673. After two years of incessant Indian raids they departed. The first permanent settlement was made in 1714. Farming flourished. When the Merino sheep craze swept New England in the mid-19th century, Northfield became one of the leading Bay State sheep towns. The town's major industrial venture (1853–55) was a cornbroom plant. The broomcorn was locally grown.

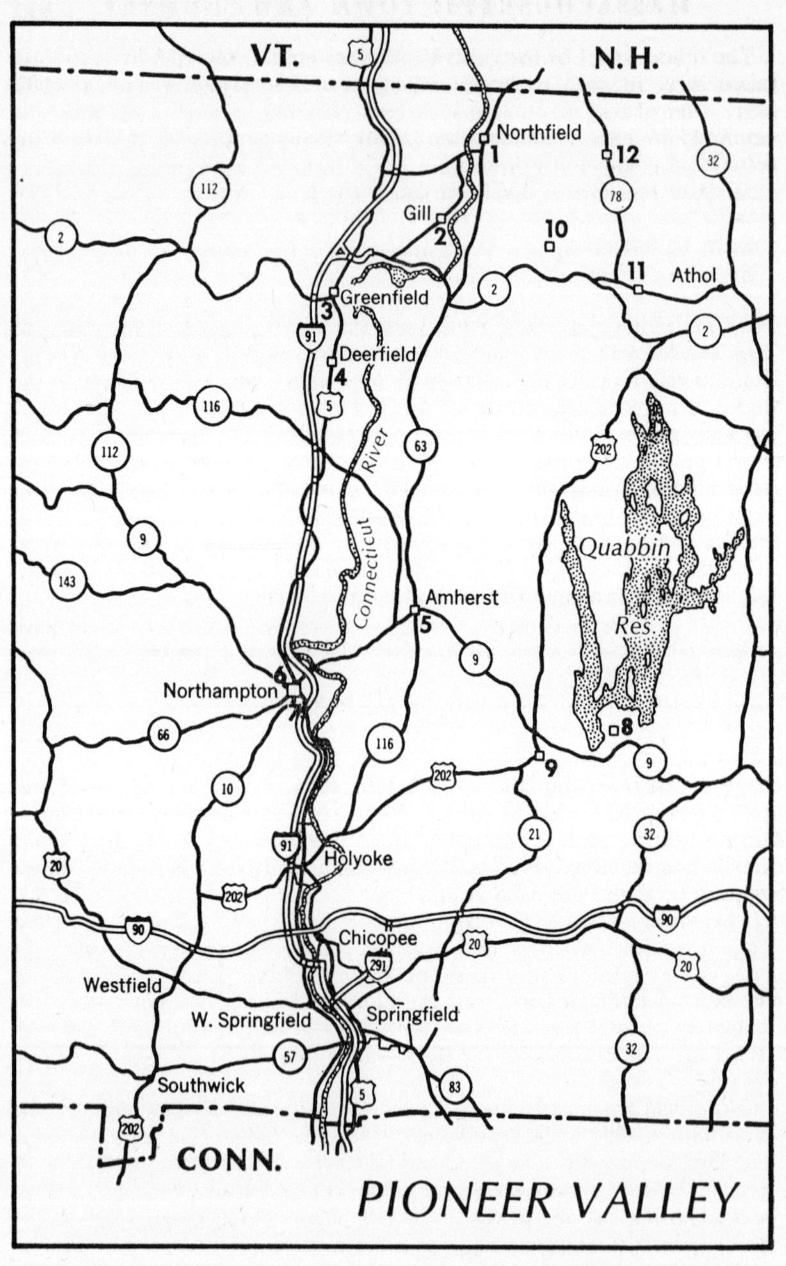

PIONEER VALLEY

The headquarters of the American Youth Hostel, founded in 1934, was located here for some years. Members who were provided with a AYH pass (original cost, $1.00 annually) could sleep at various places throughout the United States, and later in Europe. Separate accommodations were provided for boys and girls. There was a common kitchen and recreation room. Members carried their own sleeping bags.

EAST NORTHFIELD is a small settlement lying across the Connecticut River from Northfield village.

Old Janes House (private) is still occupied by descendants of the builders. Tradition has it that an underground tunnel connected it with the Young House, a white Colonial dwelling across the street, and that it served as an Underground Railway station.

Captain Samuel Field House (open by permission), opposite a marker indicating the first settlement, was built in 1784. The house has five enormous fireplaces and a large brick oven in the ell. The wainscoting is of virgin pine boards and the fine old doors have iron strap hinges.

Old Dollard House (open by permission) is a restoration but shows an arch under the massive chimney in the cellar. The carving around the front door was taken from an old house in Factory Hollow near Greenfield.

Old Pomeroy Place (private), owned by Northfield Schools, was restored by Elliot Speer, late principal of Mount Hermon, and presents a fine example of Colonial architecture.

Schell Château (open July–Aug., daylight hours, small fee), an annex of the Northfield Inn, built in 1890 by Robert Schell, who originally intended it for an English country house.

Home of the Reverend Dwight L. Moody (open) is at the corner of the first road n. of West Northfield Rd. Moody lacked educational opportunities, but his driving ambition brought him financial success. In 1855, however, he was converted, renounced the world and preached his way to fame. Sympathetic with those who yearned for an education, he founded Northfield Seminary and Mount Hermon School.

Key to the Pioneer Valley

1. Northfield School for Girls, old houses
2. Mt. Hermon
3. Attractive trading and tourist center
4. Old Deerfield historic village
5. Amherst College and UMass.
6. Smith College, Emily Dickinson home, Calvin Coolidge home
7. Benton Small Arms Museum, parks, recreational facilities
8. Quabbin Reservoir recreational facilities
9. State fish hatchery
10. Erving State Forest
11. Free fall parachuting center at airport
12. Mt. Grace State Forest

Northfield School for Girls, established in 1879, occupies 1200 acres, with buildings accommodating over 500 students. Moody had been impressed with the hopelessness of girls from poorer homes after driving past a mountain cottage where a mother and two daughters were braiding palmetto straw hats in an effort to support a family whose father was a paralytic. All students help with the housework and receive an education at low cost. Northfield Summer Conferences (religious, open to public) are held during the summer.

Birthplace of D. L. Moody, his house, his *Grave* and that of his wife are on the campus grounds. Make arrangements at *Kernarden Hall,* the administration building.

Lookout, high on the river terrace, offers an excellent view of the Connecticut River country with the towers of the *Mount Hermon Boys' School* (see Gill) in the foreground.

NORTHFIELD SKI AREA (Mass. 10 and 63 in East Northfield) has slopes for beginners, rope tows, toboggan slides, ski shop, ski rentals, instruction, snacks, meals. Phone: 498–5341.

NORTON (Bristol County, sett. 1669, incorp. 1711, alt. 100, pop. 9487, area 27.91 sq. mi., town meeting, routes, Mass. 123, 140) is a pleasant well wooded and watered town that is the home of *Wheaton College.* Despite its rural aspect nearly 800 workers make jewelry, textiles, bleaches and lenses in local mills. Much of the surrounding countryside is open pasture and meadowland.

Norton had its troubles with the powers of darkness. Dora Leonard and Naomi Burt were the town witches. Maj. George Leonard sold his soul and body to the Devil for gold. In 1716 His Satanic Majesty cashed in on his bargain by whistling the Major's soul out of his body and then carrying his body off through the roof. You can see with your own eyes the Devil's footprints on a rock below the eaves where he landed when he jumped off with his heavy burden. No one saw the corpse at the funeral, there being nothing but a log in the box, to avert the townsfolks' suspicions.

Wheaton College (1834), attractively placed on a 100-acre-plus campus, has more than 50 buildings, mostly brick and imitation Georgian Colonial architecture. The extensive campus includes the woods known as *College Pines* and a small pond. The grounds are divided between gardens, lawns, woods and meadows.

NORWELL (Plymouth County, sett. 1634, incorp. 1888, alt. 81, pop. 7796, area 20.98 sq. mi., town meeting, routes, Mass. 3, 123).

Indians were friendly until May 20, 1676, when, following an attack on Hingham, they killed several persons and burned buildings.

In its early days shipbuilding yards occupied the banks of the North River. In the 19th century trunk and box manufacture was important.

Shoes and tacks were produced on a small scale; today the chief means of livelihood is truck gardening.

First Parish Unitarian Church (1742) has three green doors with Colonial locks and hinges.

Kent Memorial Building (open), River St., built before 1680, has historical relics.

THOMAS GARFIELD PARK is a wooded recreation center for children.

NORWOOD (Norfolk County, sett. 1678, incorp. 1872, alt. 100, pop. 30,815, representative town meeting, routes, US 1, 1A) is a residential and manufacturing town — and regional shopping center. Canadian, Irish and Scandinavian immigrants and their descendants work in bookmaking plants or roofing mills.

Norwood's land was purchased from Chicataubot about 1630. The town's development was peaceful. Revolutionary War chaplain Manasseh Cutler (1742–1823), a doctor of medicine and compiler of the first scientific account of New England's flora, is best known for his promotion of the Ohio Land Company and its subsequent removal to that area. He taught school here and married a local woman.

Norwood Memorial Municipal Building has a 170-foot tower with a 52-bell carillon.

Day House (usually open Sunday afternoons and other times by appointment), 93 Day St., houses the Norwood Historical Society's collection of regional relics.

Morrill Memorial Library (open daily), corner of Beacon and Walpole Sts., was built of gray stone in the Romanesque style.

Plimpton Press (tours), Lenox St., is one of the nation's largest book printing establishments.

OAK BLUFFS (Dukes County, sett. 1642, incorp. 1880, alt. 10, pop. 1385, town meeting).

Oak Bluffs, an attractive village on Martha's Vineyard Island, has a large summer population. Its Algonquin name was Ogkeshkuppe (Damp Thicket). The earliest English name, given in 1646 by first proprietor Thomas Mayhew was "Easternmost Chop of Holmes' Hole." Mayhew granted it to John Dagget. Legend says Dagget's son Joseph married an Indian sachem's daughter. His dowry was all the land in the present town.

At the center is the *Methodist Tabernacle* surrounded by tiny, ornate cottages. Summer camp meetings have been held in the village since 1835.

East Chop Lighthouse (1869), on the north tip of Oak Bluffs, stands on a cliff 75 feet above the sea.

Broad, tarred Edgartown Rd. runs south from Oak Bluffs through HARTSVILLE, a hamlet named for a family that has for generations maintained summer homes here.

The road continues between white sand dunes, covered with coarse grass in summer, on a narrow strip of land bounded for many miles by *Sengekontacket Pond* ("Salty Waters") and by the Nantucket Sound, with the open Atlantic beyond it. The pond has several inlets permitting the tidal ebb and flow that keep it stocked with shellfish. The island affords delightful swimming.

State Lobster Hatchery (open to public), a popular worthwhile attraction, is operated by the Commonwealth's Dept. of Marine Fisheries. The lobster's life cycle is one of the many major research projects carried on here.

OAKHAM (Worcester County, sett. 1749, incorp. 1762, alt. 1050, pop. 730, area 20.99 sq. mi., town meeting, route, Mass. 122), relying on farming and lumbering, made attempts in the 1800's at industrial development. Residential Oakham now has only a few farms. Many residents commute to Worcester.

Forbes Memorial Library (1908) has an historical room with documents and relics.

Congregational Church (1814) was renovated and a Greek revival front added in 1846.

Memorial Hall (1874), built in memory of Civil War soldiers, has a town hall and a town office.

BARRE FALLS WILDLIFE MANAGEMENT AREA has public hunting in Barre, Hubbardston, Rutland, and Oakham.

OLD FURNACE (see HARDWICK)

ORANGE (Franklin County, sett. *c.* 1746, incorp. 1810, alt. 512, pop. 6104, area 35.03 sq. mi., town meeting, routes, US 202, Mass. 2, 78) was named in honor of William, Prince of Orange. Industries include Rodney Hunt Machine Company (1840), Leavitt Machine Co., Orange Shoe Co., Union Tool Co., Slencil Co., Torrington Co. and Orange Foundry.

Orange is known today for skydiving meets held almost weekly at the Orange Airport.

Lake Matawa is noted for its rainbow and brown trout.

ORLEANS (Barnstable County, sett. 1693, incorp. 1797, alt. 60, pop. 3055, area 13.94 sq. mi., town meeting, routes, Mid-Cape Highway, Mass. 28, 39).

Orleans was named for the Duke of Orleans, who visited New England in 1797. Settlers were engaged in shipping, shell fisheries and saltworks. Windmills pumped seawater for the latter into short vats.

Orleans suffered during the War of 1812 but prosperity returned. The saltworks increased to 50, cod fisheries developed and the fields, fertilized by crabs and seaweed, were cultivated. Tourism is a profitable occupation.

Orleans was the setting for Joseph C. Lincoln's novel *Mr. Pratt.* Thoreau gave excellent descriptions of it in *Cape Cod,* Elizabeth Reynard preserved local folklore in *The Narrow Land.*

In Orleans on US 6 is the *Site of Jeremiah's Gutter,* the first Cape Cod Canal. In 1717, the water had a free sweep through this cut, enabling a whaleboat to pass from the bay to the ocean.

Linnell House (1855), Rock Harbor Rd., was built by Capt. Eben Linnell, who made a record trip from the Thames to Hong Kong in 83 days.

Town Landing is the *Site of the Battle of Orleans,* in which, in December 1814, Orleans militia repulsed a British landing party.

Higgins Tavern (private), a gray two-and-a-half-story inn with red trim, was a stagecoach station. Thoreau once spent a night here before hiking 30 miles to Provincetown.

OSTERVILLE (see BARNSTABLE)

OTIS (Berkshire County, sett. 1735, incorp. 1778, alt. 1220, pop. 820, area 35.77 sq. mi., town meeting, routes, Mass. 8, 23) was named for Harrison Gray Otis (1765–1848), then speaker of the House of Representatives.

Nineteenth-century Otis had gristmills, though until recently the chief industry was poultry raising. Today, many Otis residents work in nearby Lee or in Pittsfield's giant General Electric plant.

St. Paul's Episcopal Church (1828) has windows containing old, wavy glass. Adjoining is the *Squire Filley House* (1800). Imported wallpaper depicts the Coliseum at Rome, Italian olive groves, pastorals and a marine sunset.

In 1933, the Burgoyne Trail Association opened the first *Nudist Colony* in the Berkshires. The property is now used as a camp by the Connecticut Trails Council, Girls Scouts of America, in Hamden, Conn.

WEST OTIS (alt. 1390) is a hamlet.

A trail follows *Morley Brook* to *Gilder Pond,* once owned by poet Richard Watson Gilder, a fishing companion of President Grover Cleveland. Cleveland was approached by a game warden who demanded to see his fish; he had one short bass. He was fined $10.00 at the Great Barrington District Court.

Piedmont Pond is famous in summer for pink, white and gold water lilies which with their dark green pads almost cover its placid surface.

Lake Garfield offers boating, fishing, camping.

OTIS RIDGE SKI AREA (intersection of Mass. 8 and 23) has T-bar, J-bar and Poma-lifts, rope tow, ski shop, ski rentals, 3 slopes, 3 trails, lodge, canteen, ski school, snow-making equipment. Phone 239–5443.

OTIS STATE FOREST'S facilities include boating, fishing, hiking, hunting, snowmobiling, scenic views.

OXFORD (Worcester County, sett. 1687, incorp. 1693, alt. 510, pop. 10,345, area 26.7 sq. mi., town meeting, routes, US 20, Mass. 12, 56), the birthplace of American Red Cross organizer *Clara Barton* (1821–1912). She directed the ARC from its founding in 1882 until she resigned after an investigation into her policies and handling of the organization's finances.

The town, named for Oxford, England, is on land purchased from the Nipmucks in 1681. The first attempted settlements made by French Huguenots were abandoned owing to Indian depredations. Permanent settlement was made by the English in 1713.

Manufacturing began to supplant agriculture in 1811 when Samuel Slater opened a spinning mill. Scythes, nails, hoes, chaises, harnesses, chain and bricks have been made here, but the textile industry alone has persisted.

Larned Memorial Library (1904) has a stained-glass window depicting the Pilgrims embarking at Delft Haven.

The *Church* (1792), just beyond the town hall, remodeled in 1840 to accommodate first floor stores, was the first Universalist house of worship erected in America. The society still treasures the pulpit from which Hosea Ballou preached.

Clara Barton Birthplace (open Tues.–Sat. 10–12, 1–4, contributions expected), North Oxford.

BUFFUMVILLE RECREATION AREA is operated by the U.S. Corps of Engineers in connection with a flood control program. Facilities: picnic sites, swimming.

HODGES VILLAGE WILDLIFE MANAGEMENT AREA has public hunting.

PALMER (Hampden County, sett. 1716, incorp. 1775, alt. 332, pop. 11,680, area 31.37 sq. mi., town meeting, routes, US 20, Mass. Pike, Mass. 32), a mill town, makes: pinion rods, tampax, rugs, boxboard, paper boxes, metal cutting tools and molded pulp egg cartons.

The "Elbows" was settled by John King in 1716. The name was changed to Palmer in 1752. Farming was the principal occupation until after the War of 1812. Whiskey and tanned hides were early products. Many mills were attracted by Quaboag and Swift Rivers' waterpower.

Metal polish made by the Converse Company under the direction of Capt. Franklin Bearse (1844–1925) spread Palmer's name throughout the world. Bearse was one of the last seafaring Cape Codders who successfully, though regretfully, made the transition from quarterdeck to industry.

Palmer Fish Hatchery (3 mi. n. on Mass. 32) is usually open to visitors during the day. Several varieties of trout are raised here.

PAXTON (Worcester County, sett. *c.* 1749, incorp. 1765, alt. 1134, pop. 3731, area 14.87 sq. mi., town meeting, routes, Mass. 31, 56, 122) was named for Boston Customs Commissioner Charles Paxton. Later he infuriated colonists by his participation in drafting the notorious tea tax. He was driven out of Boston. Paxtonites supporting the Colonial cause tried futilely to rid themselves of the name.

MOOSE HILL WILDLIFE MANAGEMENT AREA (see LEICESTER).

PEABODY (Essex County, sett. 1752, town incorp. 1855, city incorp. 1916, alt. 50, pop. 48,080 area 16.45 sq. mi., mayor-council, routes, US 1, Mass. 114, 128).

Peabody, self-styled "largest leather-processing city in the world," had tanning plants before the Revolution. By 1855 tanning was carried on in 27 plants. The town had also 24 currying shops. As early as 1638 glassmaking was started by Ananias Conklin, who manufactured coarse lamps and squat, heavy bottles.

Seven out of every ten Peabody workers are employed in the leather trade. *Peabody Library and Institute,* Main St., containing general and reference libraries and an auditorium, was founded in 1852 by philanthropist and multimillionaire George Peabody (1795–1869), in whose honor the city changed its name in 1868. He had poor parents, and his formal education was limited to public schools. Moving to London, he became an international banker. He declined a baronetcy offered by Queen Victoria but accepted the Queen's gift of a miniature of herself, now on exhibition in the auditorium. When Peabody died in London, a funeral service was held for him in Westminster Abbey. The man-of-war HMS *Monarch,* convoyed by French and English warships, bore his remains back to the United States for burial.

PELHAM (Hampshire County, sett. 1738, incorp. 1743, alt. 1146, pop. 937, area 24.82 sq. mi., town meeting, routes, US 202, Mass. 9) is a small agricultural community set high between ranges of forest-crowned hills. Settled by Col. Stoddard of Northampton, the grant was purchased by Scotch Presbyterians from Worcester, which called the settlement Lisburn. At its incorporation it was named for Lord Pelham, then traveling in the colony. Agriculture has never flourished here owing to the hilly country and rocky soil. Cleared land is used for pasturage and blueberry raising. The chief source of income is lumbering and stone quarrying.

Pelham was the home of Capt. Daniel Shays, Revolutionary War hero.

Shays' Rebellion resulted from currency deflation and high taxes which caused an epidemic of mortgage foreclosures. Sporadic attempts were made by armed and irate citizens in various parts of the state to prevent the courts from meeting to give foreclosure orders. Discontent was particularly strong here. Shays organized an army of 1900 men. After preventing the sitting of the Supreme Court in Springfield in 1786, he attempted to capture the arsenal but failed and was forced to retreat to Pelham. His *Encampment Site* is in the southern part of the village. He was pursued to Petersham by a large force from Boston under Gen. Benjamin Lincoln. The rebels, outnumbered and poorly armed, were dispersed. Contumacious Ethan Allen gave Shays refuge in Vermont. He was pardoned in 1788 and died in 1825 at Sparta, N.Y.

Pelham has become more populated as newcomers to the area's educational institutions have chosen it as a place to build their new homes.

PEMBROKE (Plymouth County, sett. 1650, incorp. 1712, alt. 50, pop. 11,193, area 21.53 sq. mi., town meeting, routes, Mass. 3, 16, 36) was founded as an Indian outpost by Dolor Davis and Robert Barker. Barker acquired land from the Indians in Herring Brook district in exchange for a quart of sack. Shipbuilding on the North River was the major early industry. This is the setting for "Leave the Salt Earth," by Richard Warren Hatch, and Whittier's "Songs of Three Centuries."

A stump surrounded by water lilies in nearby Hobomac Pond rose three feet above the surface regardless of the rise and fall of the water. The stump was Hobomoc, an evil spirit. The lilies were his pale-faced children, brought over the Great Water in a canoe. Indians, unable to destroy the spirit, offered tribute, throwing choice food into the pond. The gifts did little good — sicknesses came and the palefaces triumphed.

Pembroke is a residential and resort town. There is some dairying and cranberrying. Musical instruments, boxes and scales are principal manufactured products. Many Pembroke residents commute elsewhere — including Boston — to work. It is a popular residence for civil servants.

PENIKESE ISLAND (see GOSNOLD)

PEPPERELL (Middlesex County, sett. 1720, incorp. 1753, alt. 244, pop. 5887, area 22.79 sq. mi., town meeting, routes, Mass. 111, 113, 119), a rural town, was named for Sir William Pepperell, hero of the Battle of Louisburg.

On the Main St. side of the burying ground is the *Grave of Prudence Wright.* Mrs. Wright, while patrolling the road in North Pepperell to prevent Tories from reaching Boston, captured Leonard Whiting of Hollis, N.H., with a dispatch concealed in his boots. They guarded their prisoner until the authorities arrived and sent the dispatches to the Committee of Safety in Cambridge.

Pepperell's paper products are internationally known, though the largest paper plants are no longer locally owned. In 1970 they employed 98 percent of the local workers. Bemis Bag and St. Regis Paper are the largest plants.

PERU (Berkshire County, sett. 1767, incorp. 1770, alt. 2250, pop. 256, area 26.0 sq. mi., town meeting, route, Mass. 143), the highest inhabited village in the state, perches on the summit of the Green Mt. Range. First called Partridgefield, it was incorporated in 1770 under its present name.

Peru's poor were once sold at auction. In 1807 "Abagail Thayer was bid off by Shadrach Pierce at 90 cents a week for victualizing"; she was auctioned for nearly 30 successive years. The last of the oldtime "Pooh-Bahs" of the Berkshire hill towns was Frank Creamer, a shrewd, entertaining auctioneer. He held all important town offices while his wife held the minor ones.

Self-sufficiency and the ability to solve their own problems are characteristics held in high esteem. Back in 1799, Charles Ford moved to Peru with a horse, cart, yoke of oxen and one hog. Since the hog had to walk it became footsore and caused much delay. Shoemaker Ford sat down by the roadside and made boots of sole leather for the hog. He had no further difficulty.

There is excellent trout fishing and deer hunting in the area. There is a Wildlife Management Area here.

The water from the roof of Peru's hillside Congregational Church flows into the Housatonic River on the west side, and water from the east side drains off into the Connecticut.

PERU STATE FOREST'S facilities include fishing, hiking, hunting, snowmobiling, scenic views.

PETERSHAM (Worcester County, sett. 1733, incorp. 1754, alt. 1014, pop. 990, area 54.27 sq. mi., town meeting, routes, Mass. 32, 32A, 101, 122) was first called Nichewaug and then Volunteers Town and, finally, Petersham for its namesake in Surrey, England. The *Town Hall* in this delightful hill settlement burned to the ground several years ago but was meticulously restored. An old American custom, summertime band concerts by the local band on the village green, may be dying out in many places, but the custom is still observed here every Sunday evening in July and August.

It was here that General Benjamin Lincoln, representing the oppressive state government, suppressed the tiny forces of rebel Daniel Shays.

HARVARD FOREST, a 2100-acre tract, including a bird refuge, was acquired by Harvard University in 1908. It is an experimental station for the school's Forestry Department. Fine fall foliage here.

Fisher Museum (open daily 2–5), Harvard Forest, has interesting dioramas of varying land use in New England.

FEDERATED WOMEN'S CLUB'S STATE FOREST is one of the state's best picnic areas. Facilities: fishing, hunting, picnic tables, walking trails, scenic views, snowmobiling. The forest was presented to the commonwealth about 1933 by the FWC. About one sixth of the area is a bird sanctuary.

PHILLIPSTON WILDLIFE MANAGEMENT AREA (see PHILLIPSTON)

PHILLIPSTON (Worcester County, sett. 1751, incorp. 1814, alt. 1166, pop. 872, area 23.7 sq. mi., town meeting, routes, US 202, Mass. 2, 101) is part of the grant known as Narragansett Number Six, organized as the town of Templeton. When Templeton was subdivided this part was named Gerry, in honor of Elbridge Gerry, governor of Massachusetts, 1810–11, and vice president of the United States during the administration of James Madison. Gerry's political actions caused the town to change to its present name, which honors William Phillips, for 12 successive terms lieutenant governor of the state. Sawmills were of early importance. In 1837 Phillipston produced large quantities of cotton and woolen goods and palm-leaf hats. Farming, dairying, market gardening, poultry raising and fruit growing are the chief occupations.

Alongside the small common is the *Congregational Church* (1785).

PHILLIPSTON WILDLIFE MANAGEMENT AREA has public hunting in Phillipston, Barre, and Petersham.

ELLIOTT LAUREL RESERVATION (25 acres), a hillside covered with mountain laurel, off the Petersham-Templeton road at the south end of Queen Lake, is owned and maintained by TOR.

Public hunting in *Phillipston* and *Millers River Wildlife Management Areas.*

PITTSFIELD (Berkshire County seat, sett. 1752, town incorp. 1761, city incorp. 1889, alt. 1000, pop. 57,020, area 40.7 sq. mi., mayor-council, routes, US 7, 20, Mass. 9).

In the shadow of Mount Greylock, high in the rolling Berkshires, Pittsfield is the commercial gateway to western Massachusetts. Situated between upper branches of the Housatonic River, the city is traversed by streams which for more than a century have furnished power to factories producing such varied products as silk thread, mohair braid, tacks, metal goods, textiles, paper and electrical machinery.

Today the city has a prosperous, tranquil look of general comfort and cultivation which makes it one of the most attractive industrial cities in the state. Homes line elm-shaded streets with substantial residences and smooth lawns. From almost any point within the city there is a broad view of the rolling Berkshires across wide meadows, small lakes and elm-bordered streams of the plateau. Altitude provides a salubrious climate which makes it a favorite winter-summer playground.

In the late 19th century Pittsfield attracted a wealthy leisure class which resided on spacious estates.

Great estates have been subdivided for small residences or business property. The "automobile car" changed everything in Pittsfield. Sedate hotels were replaced by "tourist accommodated" homes, then by tourist cabins and now by motels. The Berkshires are a motorist's paradise, and Pittsfield is the hub of the hill country.

Indian troubles and boundary disputes with York Province delayed settlement until 1752. Pontoosuck Plantation, as Pittsfield was then known, rapidly achieved agricultural prosperity and became a trading center for Berkshire farmers.

Pittsfield joined eastern settlements in protesting English misrule. The town had some wealthy Tories, but most citizens followed the leadership of Major John Brown and Rev. Thomas Allen, the "Fighting Parson" who helped his Vermont cousin Ethan take Fort Ticonderoga. This militant pastor organized the Berkshire Militia and led it to the Battle of Bennington. More than three months before the signing of the Declaration of Independence, Pittsfield renounced royal authority.

Industry

The little community, still predominantly agricultural, shared in post-Revolution depression; but while the farmers elsewhere were crushed by poverty, Pittsfield turned to industry. Although it seems certain that a majority of the townsfolk were in sympathy with the desperate rebellion of their neighbors under Daniel Shays in 1786 and although they treated their 40 fellow citizens implicated in the rebellion with lenience, the hope of imminent prosperity deterred them from participating. In 1861 Arthur Schofield, who had invented a wool-carding machine, opened a shop to manufacture his invention and a few years later undertook the production of looms. The War of 1812 brought an abnormal demand for clothing and military supplies which definitely established the town as a manufacturing center. The consequent need for raw materials made sheep raising an important affiliated industry. Later penetration by railroads connecting the town with New York and Boston made it the shipping distribution point for the whole district. Throughout the 19th century paper and shoes were among the most important products of its busy factories.

Pittsfield now began to change from a quiet, self-insulated community to a unit integrated with the outer world. Its population grew faster between 1900–10 than that of any other Massachusetts city except New Bedford. This 47 percent increase created a serious housing problem which in turn attracted other outside capital, which was directed to housing construction and realty developments.

The Tillotson Textile Plant; Eaton, Crane and Pike Company, famous manufacturers of stationery; foundries producing machinery for the textile and paper factories — all these and others contributed to make the development of Pittsfield a microcosm of what was going on in the entire country.

City Hall Park, the old village green. The first cattle show in America was held here in 1810. The event was promoted by Plymouth native Elkanah Watson (1758–1842), a friend of Benjamin Franklin, longtime Nantes France merchant, Albany, New York, banker and an early advocate of the Erie Canal. The 1810 show resulted in the formation of the Berkshire Agricultural Society which sponsored the first American county fair.

What to See and Do

A sundial marks the *Site of the Old Elm* beneath whose lofty branches stood Holmes, Longfellow, Hawthorne, Melville and Lafayette. On this spot soldiers of all wars were mustered and honored; old taverns and stores and historic houses faced it on all sides. Here were held the Fourth of July celebrations, the cattle shows and all the country gala days.

In 1790, when the destruction of the elm was planned to make way for a new meetinghouse, Lucretia Williams, a lawyer's wife, placed herself in front of the tree when the woodchopper came. John Chandler Williams, whose former homestead, the Peace Party House, stands nearby, gave land to the town so that the park might remain an open space forever and the old elm be saved.

Such was the veneration in which the tree was held by some Pittsfield citizens that when at the age of 265 years, after being struck by lightning several times, it was so damaged that the ax had to be applied, some witnesses wept.

Berkshire Athenaeum (open weekdays 9–9), 44 Bank Row, a Victorian Gothic structure of gray granite, has been noted as a public library and art repository for many years.

Berkshire Museum (open weekdays 10–5, Sun. and Holidays 2–5), 39 South St. The mineral room is one of the most beautiful in the country; ultraviolet rays bring out the collection's beauty. Outstanding exhibits are one of the two sledges used by Admiral Robert E. Peary on this trip to the North Pole and Nathaniel Hawthorne's desk. The art collection includes old masters and Greek and Roman sculptures.

South Mountain (alt. 1870), Pittsfield's highest point of land, is at the south end of the city, w. of US 7 and US 20, just beyond the Pittsfield Country Club. The mountain offers a view of the entire city. Here are the South Mountain Chamber Music Concerts.

Holmesdale (private), Holmes Rd., is the former residence of Dr. Oliver Wendell Holmes, who spent seven seasons here and wrote "The Deacon's Masterpiece," "The New Eden" and "The Ploughman" on local themes.

Arrowhead (private), a mile farther on Holmes Rd. at the top of the hill, was the home of Herman Melville, and where he wrote *Moby Dick,* "My Chimney and I," *The Piazza Tales* and "October Mountain."

General Electric Plant (open to visitors scientifically interested, guide) is fascinating to visit. The alternating current transformer invented by the late William Stanley was developed at the Pittsfield Works of the General Electric Company. Huge transformers for Boulder Dam were made here.

Important electrical research is done here, requiring the services of internationally distinguished technicians and scientists.

In 1890 about 1500 alternating power stations in the country were operating on the alternating current system. The Stanley Electrical Manufacturing Company of Pittsfield supplied them with equipment. This corporation, employing one sixth of Pittsfield's population, became a strain on the city's limited supply of capital. Threats of its withdrawal from Pittsfield were a constant source of apprehension.

PITTSFIELD STATE FOREST is a year-round recreation area. Facilities: bridle trails, fishing, hiking, hunting, fireplaces, picnic tables, swimming, campsites (17), snowmobiling.

PITTSFIELD STATE FOREST SKI AREA has trails, open slope, lodge.

BOUSQUET'S SKI AREA (off US 7 and US 20) has 10 slopes, 10 novice trails, intermediate and expert class. Ski shop, ski rentals, canteen. Double chair lift, T-bar, 2 Poma-lifts, 6 rope tows. Snow-making equipment. Open daily. Night skiing, Wed.–Sat. Phone: HI2–2436.

OSCEOLA PLAYGROUND SKI AREA (off US 20) is for children and beginners. Easy slope and rope tow. Open daily.

PITTSFIELD METROPOLITAN AREA (pop. 79,727, area 110.48 sq. mi.) includes the city of Pittsfield and the towns of Dalton, Lee, Lenox.

PLAINFIELD (Hampshire County, sett. 1770, incorp. 1807, alt. 1600, pop. 287, area 21.29 sq. mi., town meeting, routes, Mass. 8, 116) reached its industrial peak between 1850 and 1860. Manufacturing then dwindled.

The Ruins of the Mill of Joseph Beals, hero of Charles Dudley Warner's poem "The Mountain Miller," are located in the small village.

PLAINVILLE (Norfolk County, sett. 1661, incorp. 1905, alt. 250, pop. 4953, area 10.98 sq. mi., town meeting, routes, US 1, Mass. 1A, 106) is a small manufacturing town that long ago lost its once vaunted title "world's largest specialty jewelry manufacturing center." Farming is a major occupation and crops include dairy products, hay, potatoes and berries.

Benjamin Slack House (1726) is alleged to be the oldest public library building in New England. *Whitfield Cheever House* (1807), West and Bacon Sts., has an ell with a fireplace oven large enough to hold a large iron kettle used for hog scalding and soapmaking. East of the house a path leads to the *Angle Tree Monument.* This seven-foot-high slate shaft was erected about 1740 near the North Attleborough line and reads "Massachusetts Colony" on the north side and "Plymouth Colony" on the south side.

PLEASANT POINT (see WELLFLEET)

PLYMOUTH (Plymouth County seat, sett. and incorp. 1620, alt. 50, pop. 18,606, area 97.57 sq. mi., representative town meeting, routes, US 44, Mass. 3, 13A). Plymouth — where the Pilgrims settled after first stopping at the present site of Provincetown to brew beer and to wash clothes — is one of America's most historic landmarks.

Its white beaches, stretching for 18 miles along the inside of Massachusetts Bay, are also a famed vacation site. Plymouth, contrary to popular belief, is not on Cape Cod. It is near the southern end of the South Shore. Inland hummocky hills of pines are interlaced with ponds and brooks running into Plymouth Harbor or Buzzard's Bay. Here, too, is Myles Standish State Forest with its many campsites and good bird shooting. Coastal hill and outer slope erosion left the boulders and bluffs of Manomet and lagoons and beaches of glistening white sand set against the sparkling blue sea.

Plymouth's main street, now a thoroughfare, bustles with shops and commerce as befits a shire town, but in some ways the town remains a delightful bit of old New England. Even as late as 1840, Christmas was banned by the Pilgrims — they considered it a Popish holiday.

Newcomers who put wreaths in their windows were called "piscopals." Ancient houses, few of them remodeled or modernized, line the ancient streets of the center, setting a tone which still triumphs over the outlying modern residential areas. Pilgrim stock, though now in the minority, still is conspicuous in the community.

In 1620, the *Mayflower,* bound for the Hudson River Mouth, then part of Virginia, was blown far north of her course and cast among the roaring breakers and dangerous shoals of Cape Cod. She anchored in what today is Provincetown Harbor. Finding that terrain unfriendly, about a month later the Pilgrims sailed for the mainland. They were tossed about by a storm and nearly wrecked, but at nightfall they landed on an island in Plymouth Harbor.

On December 21, 1620, 17 men made the "Landing of the Pilgrims" at their first settlement. Legends surrounding the landing are picturesque but have little basis in substantiated fact.

Most Pilgrims remained aboard ship for a month until shelters could be erected ashore. Snow covered the decks. Exposure and insanitation increased. Sickness grew apace. Scurvy and ship fever raged. Juniper was burned aboard to dispel the smell of death. Sometimes two or three died in a single day. By March nearly half the company was dead.

There was never actual starvation, for berries, wildfowl and shellfish abounded, but great disaster befell the little community in its second year when the ship *Fortune,* carrying the entire yield of furs and produce, was captured by the French.

Thomas Morton, a companion of Capt. Wollaston, set up a rival colony near by, at what is now Wollaston, in Quincy. Pilgrims were duly horrified by "Merry Mount" revels, but Morton flourished in his wickedness like the green bay tree. He swapped rum and guns for furs, and the Indians refused to take any Plymouth wampum. Myles Standish deported Morton to England.

Despite such zeal, by 1642 piety among the "Pure, Unspottyd Lambs of the Lord" of Plymouth seemed at a low ebb. Severe measures were taken to combat the powers of evil. For nearly 50 years there were but 48 freemen. They controlled town affairs. It would have been hardly human if occasionally piety had not been the handmaid of profit.

At the end of the first century, Plymouth comfortably supported 2000 people by agriculture and commerce. Settlers from the town had founded or were founding other prosperous communities, extending as far as Eastham on Cape Cod and Fall River near the Rhode Island line. Whale fishing, begun about 1690 and abandoned about 1840, occupied many daughter towns, notably Wareham and Cape towns.

By 1800 stagecoaches ran from Boston to Plymouth and thence in various directions. Alongside the wharves were 76 ships, brigs and schooners. By 1830 the population was about 5000. One hundred ships engaged in coastal trade and fishing, especially for cod and mackerel. Four vessels went whaling. The town had 40 ships, 5 iron mills, 2 cotton mills and 3 ropeworks. Among these was the Plymouth Cordage Company, which today is one of the largest rope manufacturers in the world.

Honor was brought to the town by Dr. Charles Jackson, who was awarded 2500 francs by the French Academy of Science as the co-discover of etherization.

After the Civil War, manufacturing brought German, French, Italian and Portuguese. Today the town has small factories and rope works. Poultry raising, dairy farming, stock breeding and cranberry culture are primary agricultural pursuits. Plymouth residents cater to tourists.

What To See and Do

Pilgrim Hall (open year round, weekdays 10–5, Sun., 1:15–5, small fee) (1824) is a granite building in the Greek revival style, dedicated to the memory of the Pilgrims. The hall has the famous painting "The Landing of the Pilgrims" by Henry Sargent and Robert W. Weir's "Embarkation of the Pilgrims from Delft-Haven." From this study, Weir produced the larger

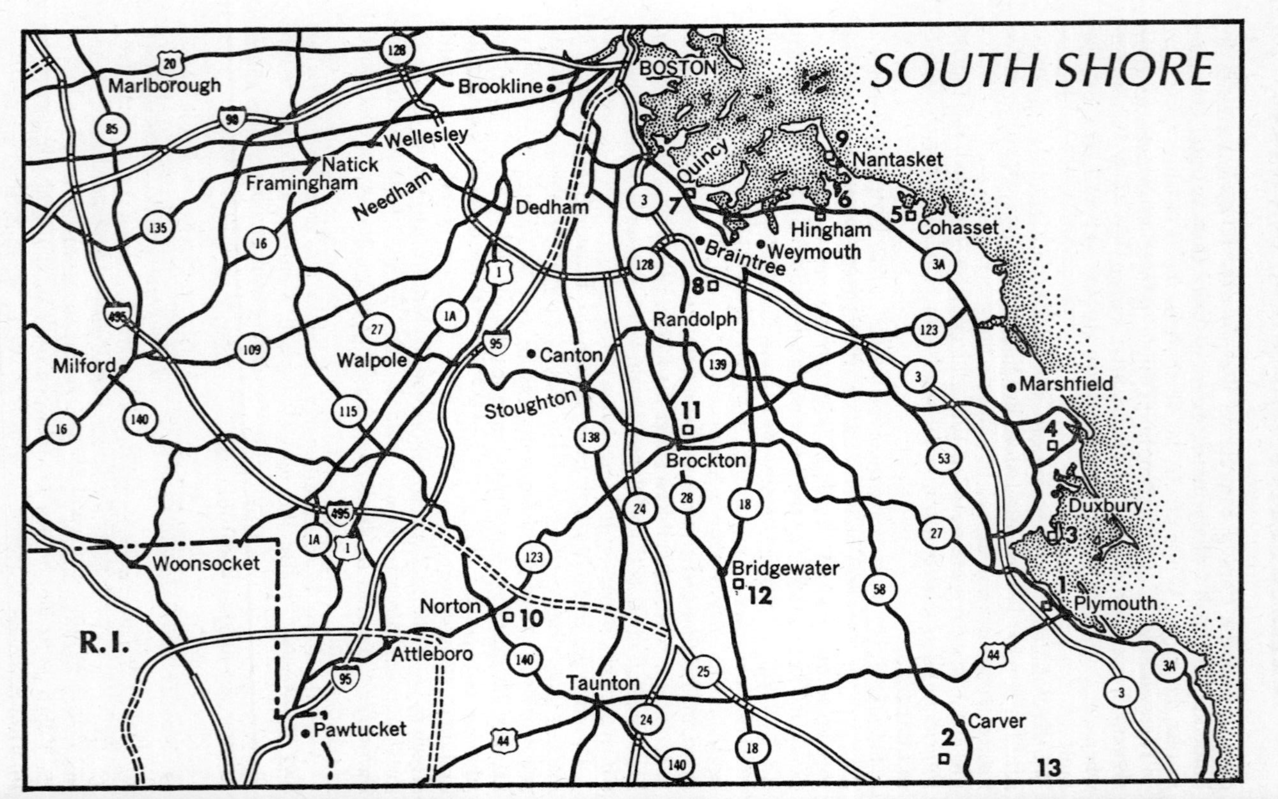
SOUTH SHORE
BOSTON
Brookline
Marlborough
Wellesley
Natick
Framingham
Needham
Dedham
Quincy
Nantasket
Hingham
Cohasset
Braintree
Weymouth
Randolph
Canton
Walpole
Milford
Stoughton
Brockton
Marshfield
Duxbury
Plymouth
Bridgewater
Norton
Attleboro
Woonsocket
Taunton
Carver
Pawtucket
R.I.
1
2
3
4
5
6
7
8
9
10
11
12
13

painting for the Capitol rotunda in Washington. Historical articles include the Plymouth Colony patent, chairs of Elder Brewster and Governor Carver, Peregrine White cradle, in which slept the first white child born in Massachusetts, Governor Bradford's Bible, printed in Geneva in 1592.

General Society of Mayflower Descendants (open May–Oct., Tues.–Sun. 10–1, 2–5, small fee), Edward Winslow House, cor. Winslow St., was built in 1754 by Edward Winslow, great-grandson of Gov. Edward Winslow of the *Mayflower* company and brother of Gen. John Winslow. Little is left of the original house, which in the 1890's was enlarged to manorial proportions.

Pilgrim Mother Fountain, cor. of Water St., was erected as a tribute to the Pilgrim mothers, historically much less vocal than the fathers, but deserving of admiration.

Plymouth Rock, with the date 1620 carved upon it, reposes under a grandiose granite portico. Two thirds of the rock is underground. An iron fence protects the remainder from souvenir chippers.

Coles Hill was the scene of the secret night burials of those who died during the first year of the settlement. Corn was planted over their graves so Indians should not know how many had perished. A sculptured sarcophagus contains many of the exhumed bones. An imposing *Statue of Massasoit,* the Pilgrim's friend, crowns the hill, now a national landmark.

The first houses of the Pilgrims stood on "First St." — now Leyden Street. "The Meersteads and Garden Plots" allotted to the early settlers and on which the houses were built sloped to the Town Brook.

Opposite the end of Carver St. is the *Site of the First "Common House,"* marked by a tablet. It was used as a shelter by Pilgrims on their trips to and from the *Mayflower* before it returned to England, April 15, 1621. Later it was used as a storehouse. In that house on February 27, 1621, the right of popular suffrage was exercised and Myles Standish was chosen captain by popular vote.

House of the Reverend Nathaniel Leonard (private) (1734), across from the Common House site, is an early house with a rainbow roof.

Burial Hill (at head of Town Sq.) was a place of defense and worship.

Key to the South Shore

1. Plymouth Rock, Old Plymouth Village, Pilgrim Hall, Plimoth Plantation
2. Edaville Railroad, cranberry bogs
3. Standish Monument reservation
4. Daniel Webster's home and grave
5. Village green and houses
6. Historic houses
7. Home of Presidents John Adams and John Quincy Adams
8. Sacco-Vanzetti case began here
9. Nantasket Beach and amusement park
10. Wheaton College
11. Ames Nowell State Park
12. Bridgewater State College
13. Myles Standish State Forest

On its summit are the sites of the *Watch-Tower* and *Old Fort. The Old Powder House* site on Burial Hill is marked by a small, round, brick house claimed to be a replica of the original.

Sites of Some First Houses (1621) are along the south side of the square. Houses were started as common property but were finished by the people who were to occupy them: Allertons, Winslows, Cookes and others.

Richard Sparrow House (open June–Oct. 1, Mon.–Sat. 10–5, by appointment during winter, small fee) (1640), 42 Summer St., has been restored and is now occupied by Plymouth Pottery Makers.

Brewster Gardens is a pleasant setting for the *Statue of the Pilgrim Maid,* dedicated to "those intrepid English women whose courage and fortitude brought a new nation into being." In Brewster Gardens are also the *Ship Anne Memorial* and *Pilgrim Spring,* the latter a delightful spot to visit.

Plymouth Antiquarian Society House (open June 15–Sept. 15, daily 10–5, small fee) (*c.* 1800), 126 Water St., is completely furnished in its period. Kitchen has century-old cookbooks, period dolls, china, glass and costumes.

Jabez Howland House (open May 15–Oct. 15, daily, small fee), Sandwich St. opposite southwesterly end of Water St. This two-and-a-half-story house was restored in 1913 and 1941.

William Harlow-Old Fort House (open May 30–Sept. 15, daily 10–5, small fee) 119 Sandwich St., was built in 1677 of timber taken from the Old Fort on Burial Hill. It is solidly constructed and clings to the crest of a knoll. Smooth, low, gambrel roof lines melt into the slope of the ground. Overshadowing it is an ancient tree that was only a seedling when the house was already old. This house has been acquired and authentically furnished by the Plymouth Antiquarian Society, which during the summer months keeps open house here and reenacts the early domestic life of the Pilgrims. Flax grown in the garden is prepared for spinning. Corn is planted by the school children, who, following the old custom, place a herring in each hill.

Pilgrim Monument is an immense, impressive memorial. The principal figure represents Faith, with a hand pointing to Heaven. At the base, four wings represent Morality, Law, Education and Liberty. On the face of each wing are marble slabs carved in bold relief which depict *Departure from Delft Haven, Signing of the Compact, Landing of the Pilgrims, Treaty with Massasoit.*

Plimoth Plantation (open mid-April–Nov. 30, daily 9–5, fee), off 3A, contains replica Pilgrim dwellings. Of special interest are *First House* (1623) and the *1627 House* along the waterfront.

Mayflower II (state pier) is the reproduction of the *Mayflower* which was built in England during the 1950's and sailed by a costumed crew to its present site (maintained by Plimouth Plantation).

HOLMES RESERVATION (26 acres), Revolutionary and Indian War mustering ground for Plymouth militiamen, has an excellent view of Plymouth Harbor. This reservation is owned and maintained by TOR.

MYLES STANDISH STATE FOREST is one of the largest and most popular campsites in Massachusetts. There are camping facilities on five ponds. Area includes log cabins and one-room sleeping cabins available for a modest daily rental. Facilities: boating, bridle trails, fishing, hiking, hunting, fireplaces, picnic tables, tent sites, trailer sites, swimming.

PLYMOUTH COUNTY (est. 1685, pop. 333,314, area 663.03 sq. mi., shire town, Plymouth) includes the city of Brockton and the 26 towns of Abington, Bridgewater, Carver, Duxbury, East Bridgewater, Halifax, Hanover, Hanson, Hingham, Hull, Kingston, Lakeville, Marion, Marshfield, Mattapoisett, Middleborough, Norwell, Pembroke, Plymouth, Plympton, Rochester, Rockland, Scituate, Wareham, West Bridgewater and Whitman.

PLYMPTON (Plymouth County, sett. 1662, incorp. 1790, alt. 105, pop. 1224, area 14.92 sq. mi., town meeting, routes, Mass. 58, 106).

Because of its nearness to Plymouth, it was named for Plympton, a borough near Plymouth, England. Industries were born and died, but a casting factory turned out cannon and balls for the Revolution.

Deborah Sampson House, Elm St., is a Cape Cod cottage once occupied by Deborah Sampson, who as "Robert Shurtleff" served in the Revolution. Deborah was born in Plympton in 1760. She fell in love with David Potter. Deborah disguised herself and enlisted in order to fight shoulder to shoulder with her young man. She served in two major campaigns under Capt. Webb of Holden. Wounded at Tarrytown, New York, she treated herself to avoid detection and carried the bullet the rest of her life. During the Yorktown campaign she contracted a fever, and her disguise was discovered. The doctor did not reveal her secret but sent her with a letter to General Washington, who gave her an honorable discharge and a personal letter of appreciation. She was married in 1784 to Benjamin Gannett of Sharon. During Washington's presidency she was invited to the capital. She received lands and a pension from Congress.

POLPIS (see NANTUCKET)

PRATTVILLE (see RAYNHAM)

PRESCOTT (Hampshire County, sett. 1742, incorp. 1822, alt. 1120) had 18 residents shortly before it was incorporated in Quabbin Reservoir.

PRINCETON (Worcester County, sett. 1743, incorp. 1771, alt. 1175, pop. 1681, area 35.39 sq. mi., town meeting, routes, Mass. 31, 62, 140), an agricultural community, was named for Thomas Prince, associate pastor of

Boston's Old South Church. In 1793 the town had grist-, saw-, fulling, and cloth mills.

Princeton was the home of Lucy Keyes, the Lost Child of Wachusett. In 1755 the five-year-old Lucy followed her sisters to Wachusett Pond. The older girls sent her home but Lucy never arrived. Frantic searching parties found nothing. Years later fur trappers from northern Vermont reported they found a "white squaw" whose only English was an unintelligible phrase containing the word "Wachusett." Happily married, she refused to leave the tribe. The mystery was revived by the dying statement of John (Tilly) Littlejohn, who had led two search parties and confessed quarreling with Robert Keyes and killing his daughter for revenge. Tilly's mind was unsound and little credence was given to this explanation.

Goodnow Memorial Building (open), an historical museum, has Lucy Keyes' cradle.

MT. WACHUSETT STATE RESERVATION (1600 acres), like Mt. Monadnock, is an isolated peak rising above surrounding low country. Scenic auto drive to summit (alt. 2006). Facilities: picnic sites, campsites, snack stand.

MT. WACHUSETT SKI AREA (off Mass. 140 south of Mass. 2) has 2 T-bar lifts, ski trails, ski shop, ski rentals, snack bar, ski patrol, ski lodge. Open Dec. 1–March. Area operated by Wachusett Mountain State Commission. Phone: 464–5547.

WACHUSETT MEADOWS WILDLIFE SANCTUARY, Goodnow off Mass. 62 (750 acres), contains Crocker Maple, one of the largest known maple trees in the U.S. This mountain upland of forest and meadow has a maple swamp which can be visited via a boardwalk. Natural history day camp. Massachusetts Audubon Society project.

PROVINCETOWN (Barnstable County, sett. *c.* 1700, incorp. 1727, alt. 13, pop. 2911, area 8.35 sq. mi., town meeting, route, US 6 [Mid-Cape Highway]).

"Plymouth Rock? That's the name of a chicken," the proud old Cape Cod Yankee snorts. "The spot where the *Mayflower* people first stepped on American soil is right here in Provincetown, and you ought to freeze on to that fact in your guide book, for it's been rising three hundred years now, and most off-Cape folks don't seem to know it yet!" After falling "amongst deangerous shoulds and roring breakers" off what is now Chatham, the *Mayflower* did indeed drop anchor in "ye Capeharbor (Provincetown) wher they ridd in saftie," November 2, 1620. That same day the first Pilgrims came ashore in America. The ship anchored five weeks before moving across to Plymouth.

Provincetown has placed a stone marker where those men climbed out of their shallop. It has scattered other markers around, too, to remind the nation that the Pilgrims came here — first. There is even a great stone tower for that purpose.

Before the Pilgrims, Basques and other daring fishermen visited these shores. Bartholomew Gosnold, who sailed around the Cape in 1602, named the tip end Cape Cod. Other explorers named it, but "Cape Cod" remained.

For nearly a century after the Pilgrims, Provincetown drew a strange assortment of transients. The Pamet Indians — Wampanoag tribe — came here often but had no permanent settlement.

In 1714 "the Province Town" was put under the jurisdiction of Truro. But pious, respectable Truro wanted no part of it. After a long campaign, the horrified goodmen of that town succeeded in getting rid of the "Poker Flats of Cape Cod," as historian Shebnah Rich terms it.

Deepwater whaling began at about that time, and the fleet grew rapidly. Provincetown and Truro took the lead. The whalemen and the Banks fishermen gave the lower Cape a fair start toward prosperity in the latter half of the 18th century. At the same time the business of "wrecking" was pursued with uncommon diligence.

Mooncussing and beachcombing — now synonyms meaning recovery of goods from the beach, chiefly cargoes drifting ashore from wrecked ships — were wreckers' work. This was a recognized means of livelihood — certainly recognized by the good citizens of "Helltown," as part of Provincetown came to be called, if not by the law. The legend of false lights hung out on moonless nights to lure unwary mariners of those days persists in the Cape's oral traditions. Rumrunning and smuggling were facilitated by long, deserted beaches, hidden from the village by the dunes.

About 1800 the Cape began making salt by evaporating seawater. Fishing expanded, reaching a peak in the last quarter of the 19th century. A *Chicago Tribune* reporter visited the town in 1900 and wrote, "Fish is bartered at the grocery stores, shoe shops and bread stores for all the commodities of life . . . The main business street is paved with rock cod. The women use the hind fin of the great halibut for brooms. Awnings shading the store fronts are made from the skin of the sportive porpoise. The bellrope in the church is made of eels, cunningly knotted by some old sailor. Over the altar was the picture of a whale. The collection plate was the top shell of a turtle. After the choir had sung "Pull for the Shore," the crew passed down the port aisle. Provincetown ladies trim their hats with red gills of the mackerel. Dog-fish often lie around the shore at low tide and bark and howl in a frightful manner."

However, in the yellowed scrapbook in which this clipping was found in Provincetown is a notation by its onetime owner, "A damned liar."

Provincetown is still essentially a fishing village, and the majority of its people are fishermen and their families. They fish aboard the trawlers, the draggers, seiners and trap boats, and they work in the five "freezers" — fish-packing plants.

The industry, however, is long past its heyday, and many an old skipper who once hung out his side lights and stood out for the Banks now hangs out a sign on his porch — "Tourists Accommodated" — and sits down to wait for the summer people.

Beyond the first of June, they do not keep him waiting long. Artists at their easels begin to dot the wayside; clicking typewriters join the nightly chorus of the crickets; poets chirp from studio attics at all hours. These are Provincetown's trusty perennials — the yearly "art colony," which, for all the confusion, has nevertheless produced many of the nation's foremost painters, playwrights, novelists and poets.

The founding of the Cape Cod School of Art here in 1901 by Charles W. Hawthorne was the real beginning of the art colony, though a few painters had visited the town before that. Hawthorne's own pictures of the Portuguese fisherfolk did much to build up the colony's prestige. Since his death in 1930, other schools have carried on, and the Provincetown Art Association's annual exhibit is an event of widespread interest.

Prominent painters who have been associated with the colony include, besides Hawthorne, Heinrich Pfeiffer, Edwin W. Dickinson, Frederick Waugh, Richard Miller, John Frazier, Hans Hoffman, Karl Knaths, Tod Lindenmuth, John Whorf, Jerry Farnsworth and Charles J. Martin.

In 1915 the Provincetown Players gathered under the leadership of George Cram Cook. They took a theater in New York City, where they carried on until 1922. Drama on Broadway, at the time they set themselves up, was stilted and heavily encrusted with outgrown traditions. The players offered plays with a fresh outlook, a new simplicity of method. The pioneer work done had a lasting influence and made the organization long remembered.

Writers and dramatists associated with Provincetown are John Dos Passos, Susan Glaspell, Mary Heaton Vorse, Edmund Wilson, Frank Shay, Wilbur Daniel Steele, Max Eastman and future winners of the Nobel Prize for literature, Eugene O'Neill and Sinclair Lewis.

Many "name" artists and writers return each summer. With them come large numbers of young unknowns. But to the old skipper of Provincetown who has retired from the sea and hung out his tourist sign, these are merely the forerunners of an even greater throng — the summer vacationers. By July all is in full swing — the painters painting, the writers writing, tourists buying and the traffic policemen swearing.

The season ends on Labor Day. Boston boats whistle a last farewell, the dealer in "Antiques" turns his sign around and Provincetown settles down again to a "nice quiet winter."

"Summer people" are estimated at about 8000. Of the 3300 year-rounders, three fourths are Portuguese — "Azoreans" (from the Azores), "Lisbons" (from the mother country) and a scattering of "Bravas" (descendants of Cape Verde islanders who came over in the whaling days). The others are "old Yankee stock," who have lost the town, politically, to the Portuguese, who deplore "off-Cape furriners" and to whom a volume of genealogy is a piece of escape literature.

Provincetown seafood is famous. The world knows many ways to cook a fish, and Provincetown claims to know an improvement on every one. To conventional recipes are added many methods of the Portuguese. Sea cooks have contributed their best inspiration.

Provincetown favorites are baked haddock, cooked Portuguese style with a sauce of tomatoes and spices; fresh mackerel, fried or baked in milk; tuna (horse mackerel) or sea catfish served *vinha d'alhos,* which involves a pickling process before frying; "tinker" mackerel, which are baby fish pickled with a variety of spices, to be served cold or fried; and stuffed fish, baked. Favorites cooked English style include all manner of chowders and such delicacies as sea-clam pie, broiled live lobster and saltwater scallops, sliced and fried or made into a creamy stew.

Portuguese are fond of *linquiça,* a form of pork sausage, and of *toitas,* small pastries served at Christmas and other feast days. *Toitas* are stuffed with a sweet potato preparation, fried in deep olive oil and coated with honey.

Beach plums grow in profusion at this end of the Cape, and housewives make the famous beach plum jelly.

Much of the ancient flavor of Provincetown has been saved by the old houses, the prim white cottages and staid Colonials that line its narrow streets and in the bright gardens, the wharves, fish sheds and vessels that still carry on with net and trawl.

The village is "only two streets wide," but for nearly four miles it skirts the inner shore of the Cape, and from there out, Long Point extends like a sandy finger crooked around the harbor. Here, at Long Point, is the tip of Cape Cod, punctuated with a lighthouse. The remainder of the township — broad dune lands reaching "up-back" to the outer or Atlantic shore — is called the Province Lands and is owned by the commonwealth.

The visitor who drives down the 122 miles from Boston, including the 65 miles on US 6 from the Cape Cod Canal, is well out to sea when he reaches Provincetown — 55 miles from "the mainland" on a sandspit where bedrock has never been found. Geologists say Provincetown owes its very underpinnings to the sea, having been left here as Father Neptune's own personal sandpile 30,000 years ago.

The town has been acknowledging its debt ever since. Provincetowners say their village covers the waterfront — when the waterfront is not covering it. "The good God," wrote Cotton Mather, after a visit here, "gives this people to suck of the abundance of the seas." But the seas, one might add, have been playing the town for a sucker from the start — invading it, battering its stone breakwaters, sneaking up on it to deliver a smashing southeaster against the bulkheads along its waterfront, in a hundred ways plotting to collect that 30,000-year debt. Sand, wind and tide are accessories before the fact, ever conspiring to fold the dunes over upon the little village, to drive it into its own harbor.

Town Wharf, a long, wide-timbered pier, is the heart of Provincetown's summer life, the landing stage of the daily Boston steamer in summer and is used by fishermen in all seasons.

The harbor view is a gay scene. Trawlers, seiners and draggers mingle with slim white yachts, low-lying cruisers and gray battleships. The short wharf on the left is littered with nets stretched to dry, lobster pots, kegs and coils of tarry rope. On the beach, artists are often at work. Gulls wheel overhead, ever on watch for tidbits from the fishing boats.

Mayflower Memorial Tablet near the town hall contains the Mayflower Compact, which was drawn up and signed in the cabin of that vessel while she lay at anchor in Provincetown Harbor. Signers names are appended.

Compact Memorial, a large bas-relief by Cyrus F. Dallin, depicts the signing of the covenant. Fifteen by nine feet, it is set in a broad granite wall flanked by stone benches.

What to See and Do

Mayflower Memorial, at the junction of Bradford St., with the steep, unmarked road leading to Pilgrim Monument, is in memory of "the five" *Mayflower* passengers who died while the ship lay in *Cape Cod Harbor.* One of the names is Dorothy Bradford, the governor's wife.

Pilgrim Memorial Monument (open Apr. 17–Nov. 18, 9–5, except July–Aug., 9–6, small fee), Town Hill. This granite tower, 252 feet high and 352 feet above sea level, is visible from many miles at sea. The monument commemorates the Pilgrims' landing at Provincetown, November 11, 1620, and the Compact signing. The view from the top is spectacular; to the north and east lie the open Atlantic; to the west, across Cape Cod Bay, are Duxbury and Plymouth; to the south, the Cape, in bold relief, curves away in a tawny half circle. The town below appears like a toy hamlet.

Town Hall is a Victorian frame building housing art treasures, seafaring trophies and local items. In the entrance hall are murals of Provincetown industries by Ross Moffett. Ground floor offices contain Charles W. Hawthorne's painting, *"Provincetown Fishermen."* In the same suite is Sir Thomas Lipton's $5000 gold and silver "Fisherman's Cup," won in 1907 by the schooner *Rose Dorothea* of Provincetown.

Historical Museum (open Apr. 15–Nov. 15, Mon.–Sat. 9–5, Sun. 10–5, except July–Aug., Mon.–Sat. 9–6, small fee), Town Hill, houses an *Arctic Exhibit* contributed by Arctic traveler Donald B. MacMillan. It contains Indian relics, old glassware, ship models and whaling implements.

Wharf Theater is a remodeled gray-shingled fish shed on a harbor pier. A summer stock company plays here.

Seth Nickerson House, 72 Commercial St., is estimated to be about 200 years old and has a white clapboard front, shingled siding, hip roof, broad central chimney and small-paned windows, around which climb rambler roses.

Church of St. Mary of the Harbor (Episcopal) has a small Mission bell. The simple and pleasing interior, with its alternating dark timbers and white plaster and its white painted uncushioned pews, is adorned with a small statue of Christ in cream-colored, glazed terra cotta, standing upon a wooden cross beam.

Chrysler Art Museum (open June 15–Sept. 15, daily except Mon. 10–10, Sept. 16–June 14, 10–5, small fee), 354 Commercial St., contains contemporary Provincetown and New England art, pre-Columbian, Greek, Egyptian and Roman sculpture, sandwich glass. A fine museum.
Provincetown Marine Aquarium (open June–Oct. 30, daily 10–10, small fee), 201 Commercial St., has Atlantic fish species well displayed. Relief map of ocean floor about Cape Cod.
The Site of the Pilgrims' First Landing, at the junction of Commercial St. and Beach Highway, is marked by a bronze tablet on a low granite slab.

To the left at a bend in the sandy isthmus are *Wood End Light* and *Wood End Coast Guard Station* and at the tip end, *Long Point Light.* Just outside, off Wood End, occurred the sinking of the submarine *S-4* Dec. 17, 1927, when she breached under the bow of the coast guard destroyer *Paulding* and went to the bottom with 40 men. Rescue operations were headed by Captain Ernest J. King (1878–1956), former commanding officer of the U.S. Navy's Submarine School, New London (as Fleet Admiral King during WWII he was commander-in-chief, United States Fleet, and chief of naval operations). Navy diver Tom Eadie was awarded the Congressional Medal of Honor — he was later commissioned — for rescuing diver Fred G. Michels. Six men, including diver Michels and Lt. Henry Hartley, skipper of the submarine rescue vessel *Falcon* were awarded the Navy Cross for heroism. Efforts to raise the craft continued through the wild winter months until she was raised and towed to Boston, March 18, 1928.
Race Point Coast Guard Station (open to visitors at any daylight hour), visible from a long distance, is a two-story, square, white frame building with a red roof and a skeleton observation tower, standing upon a sandy bluff above the open waters of the Atlantic at one of the most dangerous spots to shipping on the eastern seaboard.
Race Point Beach has magnificent sand dunes and is now part of the *Cape Cod National Seashore.* Facilities: ocean beach, bathhouses, picnic sites, surf fishing, observation tower.

QUINCY (Norfolk County, sett. 1625, town incorp. 1792, city incorp. 1888, alt. 44, pop. 87,966, area 16.51 sq. mi., mayor-council, routes, Mass. 3A, 37, 135).

Quincy owes much to the Irish, Italians, Jews, Finns, Scots, Greeks and Syrians who came to work the quarries and shipyards and contributed generously toward the city's artistic, intellectual and civic development. Thirty-two churches may be credited in part to a fund left to Quincy churches by the King family to "aid the breaking down of religious prejudice [in the belief] that a better understanding of the religious faith of one another is one of the most important movements in the world."

In 1625 Thomas Morton, the "pettifogger of Furnival's Inn," as Gov. Bradford contemptuously called him, arrived in what is now Quincy to establish Mount Wollaston, later named Ma-re Mount or Merry Mount.

Morton traded with Indians, taught them the use of firearms and swapped rum for furs. This cut into Plymouth's trade. Bradford, irked at Morton's celebration of May Day as a pagan feast, and fearing Merry Mount would become a refuge for lawbreakers, dispatched Myles Standish and eight men from Plymouth. A council pressed for his execution. Instead, he was sent to England. Eighteen months later he returned to Merry Mount and was rearrested. His house was burned, and he was again sent to England. His *Newe English Canaan* (1637), with excellent descriptions of New England scenery, bird and animal life, scathingly exposed the alleged moral hypocrisy of the Pilgrims and Puritans.

In 1789, while Quincy was still the north precinct of Braintree, local consciousness was brought to a high pitch by the election of native son, John Adams, as U.S. vice president. Eight years later, he became President. His son, John Quincy Adams, regarded as the finest diplomat in the foreign service, also became President. Quincy's inhabitants felt they should assert their right to an individual existence. The town was called Quincy in honor of Col. John Quincy, an eminent, able citizen who had occupied Mount Wollaston.

After 1830 agriculture gave precedence to industry, a transition brought about by the shoe trade, an outgrowth of the tanneries on the town brook and improved facilities for quarrying granite. Men had learned how to use iron instead of wooden wedges in splitting the rock.

In 1752 King's Chapel in Boston was built with Quincy granite. The sudden demand frightened town fathers. Fearing the supply would give out, they passed an ordinance prohibiting the sale of granite outside the town. In spite of this, Quincy's granite trade expanded until it was known the world over.

In 1883 a little shop in Braintree Fore River experimented in marine engines. The business grew so fast that in 1884 it was forced to remove to Quincy Fore River. In 1913 it came into the possession of the Bethlehem Steel Corporation. During WWI 36 destroyers were built here. Before WWII ships ranging from the seven-masted schooner *Thomas W. Lawson* to the airplane carrier *Lexington* were built here.

John Adams Birthplace (open Apr. 19–Sept. 30 10–5, daily except Mon., small fee), 133 Franklin St., is a small, red, clapboard, saltbox farmhouse (1681) enclosed by an ancient pole fence with a turnstile, small steep winding stairway, huge central chimney and mammoth fireplace. One chamber has a false front at its fireplace. The entire panel from floor to ceiling swings to reveal a space by the chimney large enough to conceal a man. Central ceiling beams are hand-hewn. The inverted gunstock post used in the house frame distributes its weight equally.

John Quincy Adams Birthplace (open Apr. 19–Sept. 30, 10–5, daily except Mon., small fee), 141 Franklin St., adjacent, built in 1716, is a red, clapboard, saltbox farmhouse with huge central chimney.

Adams National Historic Shrine (open Apr. 19–Oct. 31, daily 9–5, small fee), 135 Adams St. This house (1731) was the Adams family home from 1787 to 1927. Furnishings were used by several generations of Adams' including the twc presidents, diplomat Charles Francis (1807–86) and historians Henry Brooks (1838–1918) and Brooks (1844–1927).

Abigail Adams Stone Cairn, opposite 353 Franklin St., marks the spot on the summit of the hill where, during the Battle of Bunker Hill, Mrs. John Adams (1744–1818), with her little son, John Quincy Adams (1767–1848), prayed for the Revolutionists at Bunker Hill.

Adams and Son, by sculptor Bruce Wilder Saville, is a granite monument with a bronze bas-relief of John Adams and John Quincy Adams. Now at site of birthplace.

Church of the Presidents, 1306 Hancock St., of Quincy granite, was designed by Alexander Parris in Greek revival style. Its white colonnaded portico and open cupola soften the severe mass. The name is derived from the fact that John Adams and John Quincy Adams are buried here (crypt open upon application to sexton).

Old Cemetery (1666) is the burial place of many members of the Quincy and Adams families.

Colonel Josiah Quincy House (open May–mid-Oct., Tues., Thurs., Fri. 1–5, and by appointment, small fee), 20 Muirhead St., was erected in 1770. This square yellow house with pillared portico was, until 1850, a gentleman's farmhouse, surrounded by rolling pasture. At 40, Colonel Josiah Quincy (1709–1784) exchanged the career of successful shipbuilder for that of country gentleman. He was the father of Josiah Quincy, Jr., (1744–75), who horrified his parent by defending the British soldiers involved in the Boston Massacre. The house was inherited by Josiah Quincy III (1772–1864), who was successively mayor of Boston, congressman and President of Harvard College. Two other Josiah Quincy's were also mayors of Boston.

Dorothy Quincy Mansion (Quincy Homestead) (open daily, April 19–Oct. 31, small fee), 34 Butler Rd. corner of Hancock St., a spacious mansion built in 1706–09, was the home of the spirited Bostonian who became the wife of John Hancock. A secret chamber in the house repeatedly afforded asylum to pursued Revolutionaries.

Crane Memorial Public Library, Washington St., commissioned in 1882, is considered the best of H. H. Richardson's work in this field.

BLUE HILLS RESERVATION: golf, nature museum, freshwater beaches and fishing, foot and bridle trails, ski area, ice skating, picnic sites, band concerts, playgrounds, observation tower. See Blue Hills Reservation.

RANDOLPH (Norfolk County, sett. *c.* 1710, incorp. 1793, alt. 190, pop. 27,035, area 10.08 sq. mi., town meeting, routes, Mass. 24, 28, 128, 139, Fall River Expressway), originally called Cochato, and formerly the South Precinct of Braintree, was named Randolph after Peyton Randolph (1721–75), first president of the Continental Congress.

Nineteenth-century Randolph abandoned agriculture to pioneer in shoe manufacturing. Its factories attracted Irish, Italian and Canadians. From 1860 to 1895 shoe production and population decreased. The town is chiefly a Boston suburb.

Mary Wilkins Freeman (1852–1930) lived here and in *A New England Nun* and other works told the stories of her neighbors.

The Ladies' Library Association (1855) is one of the oldest women's clubs in the state.

BLUE HILLS RESERVATION: golf courses, nature museum, freshwater beaches and fishing, foot and bridle trails, ski areas, ice skating, picnic sites, observation tower, band concerts. See BLUE HILLS RESERVATION.

RAYNHAM (Bristol County, sett. 1652, incorp. 1731, alt. 82, pop. 6705, area 20.30 sq. mi., town meeting, routes, US 44, Fall River Expressway, Mass. 104, 138), a farming and poultry raising community, originally the east precinct of Taunton, was named in honor of Lord Townshend of Rainham, England. The settlement was left unharmed during the Indian War inasmuch as the local forge had provided King Philip with tools and repaired his weapons. Earlier settlers, however, had suffered much at the hands of Indians. Victims were interred at Squawbetty, a burial ground on the west bank of the Taunton River.

Site of an Iron Forge (Mass. 104) is locally claimed to be the first in America, established by the Leonard family in 1652 and operated by them for more than a century. Early industries were shipbuilding, shoe manufacturing, lumbering and flour milling. Current industries include a bleachery and box mill.

The Massasoit Greyhound Association holds races (nighttime) from mid-April to mid-June. This activity provides seasonal employment.

READING (Middlesex County, sett. 1636, incorp. 1644, alt. 133, pop. 22,539, area 9.85 sq. mi., representative town meeting, routes, I–93, Mass. 28, 129).

Clock, furniture and shoemaking prospered until the Civil War, when the loss of southern markets and mass production ruined business. The manufacture of organ pipes and photo mounting corners continues, but plastic-coated fabrics and printing with allied products are the principal industries. Today the town is chiefly residential.

Old South Church, on the common, is a stately 1913 reproduction of the original church built on this site in 1817–1818.

At 103 Washington St., west of Mass. 28, is the *Parker Tavern* (open May 1–Nov. 1, Sun. 2–5, and by appointment, contribution expected), built in 1694. British officers taken as prisoners of war in the Revolution were quartered here.

REHOBOTH (Bristol County, sett. 1636, incorp. 1645, alt. 50, pop. 6512, area 47.25 sq. mi., town meeting, routes, US 44, Mass. 118). The first settlers were Plymouth Congregationalists, but peaceful Baptists were permitted to reside here. A Baptist Church, the fourth in America, was founded in 1663, but owing to a violent disagreement with the Congregational brethren, it moved to Swansea.

During King Philip's War all garrison houses were destroyed. The iron industry began early in the 18th century and included the production of cast-iron plows. Early cotton mills were located along Palmer River.

The town today is a fast-growing farming and residential community. Its eight golf courses gave rise to the nickname "Golf Town, U.S.A." *Goff Memorial Hall,* Bay State Rd., a brick structure given to the town by Darius and Lyman Goff, is an auditorium, public library and museum.

RENFREW (see ADAMS)

REVERE (Suffolk County, sett. 1630, town incorp. 1871, city incorp. 1914, alt. 20, pop. 43,159, area 5.95 sq. mi., routes, I–95, US 1).

Revere is a beach bordered by a city. Blocks of crowded homes house or feed or amuse summer visitors. The three-mile-long beach is one of the best in Massachusetts. Amusement palaces line the promenade. Barkers cater to the carnival spirit. And everywhere there is music — the swaying rhythm of the dance hall, blaring loudspeakers and raucous jukebox recordings.

Revere was once aristocratic. In 1636 Boston parceled out undistributed land, part of which is now Revere. The first landowner, Sir Henry Vane, Massachusetts Bay Colony governor, received 200 acres of Rumney Marsh, as Revere was then called. His tenure was brief. Handsome Vane was an idealist. His openly stated conviction that all creeds should have equal rights appalled the Puritan clergy. Sir Henry returned to England. Rumney Marsh became the property of a dozen absentee landowners.

The necessity for reclaiming large areas of marsh discouraged settlers. Until 1710, when the first church was erected, community life progressed slowly.

For about one hundred years after 1739, when Chelsea separated from Boston, Rumney Marsh was the northern part of Chelsea. In 1846 Revere, or the territory known as "northern Chelsea," and Pullen Point became the town of North Chelsea. In 1852, Pullen Point broke away from North Chelsea as the town of Winthrop. For the next 25 years North Chelsea

(1846) was at a complete standstill; then in 1871, changing its name to Revere for the patriot, it experienced a rebirth. The now deceased Narrow Gage Railroad running out to its white, sandy shore lifted Revere out of oblivion and gave it its place in the sun.

Wonderland Park is the site of greyhound racing. Pari-mutuel betting.

REVERE BEACH (state bathhouse, moderate fee), Revere Beach Boulevard, is one of Boston's two Coney Islands.

The *Masonic Temple,* southeast corner of Eustis and Beach Sts., was originally *The Church of Christ* in Rumney Marsh, built in 1710. Its first pastor, the Rev. Thomas Cheever, was suspended from his ministry in a neighboring parish for breaking two of the Ten Commandments. At Rumney Marsh, however, he was greatly beloved for his championship of other sinners and lived to be 91.

Slade Spice Mill (tours), Revere Beach Parkway near Broadway, a small, red, wooden building, was until 1934 a tidewater mill. One of the old millstones is preserved within and can still be turned. Spice has been ground here for over a century, and the visitor is greeted by the pungent smell of mingled nutmeg, cinnamon, clove, pepper (red, white and black), thyme, marjoram and anise, much of which comes from the far-off Spice Isles of Java.

Granite Tablet, corner of Revere Beach Parkway and Railroad St., commemorates the Battle of Chelsea Creek (now Mystic River), May 27, 1775. The British, in need of meat and forage, overawed the farmers into selling them supplies. The Committee of Safety ordered Chelsea Revolutionaries

---

Key to the North Shore and Cape Ann

1. Revere Beach and amusement park
2. Essex Marine Institute, McIntyre houses, House of the Seven Gables
3. Old houses, race week
4. General George Patton's tank
5. Beauport, fishing boats, Our Lady of Good Voyage Church, Fisherman's Statue
6. Bearskin Neck Art Colony, beaches
7. Whipple House, Crane's Beach, Castle Hill
8. Plum Island, Parker River National Wildlife Refuge
9. Old houses
10. Old Iron Works (first in U.S.)
11. Beaches at Nahant, Lynn, Swampscott, Salisbury
12. Concord Antiquarian Museum, North Bridge, homes of Concord authors
13. Lexington Battle Green, historical houses
14. Minuteman National Historical Park
15. Walden Pond

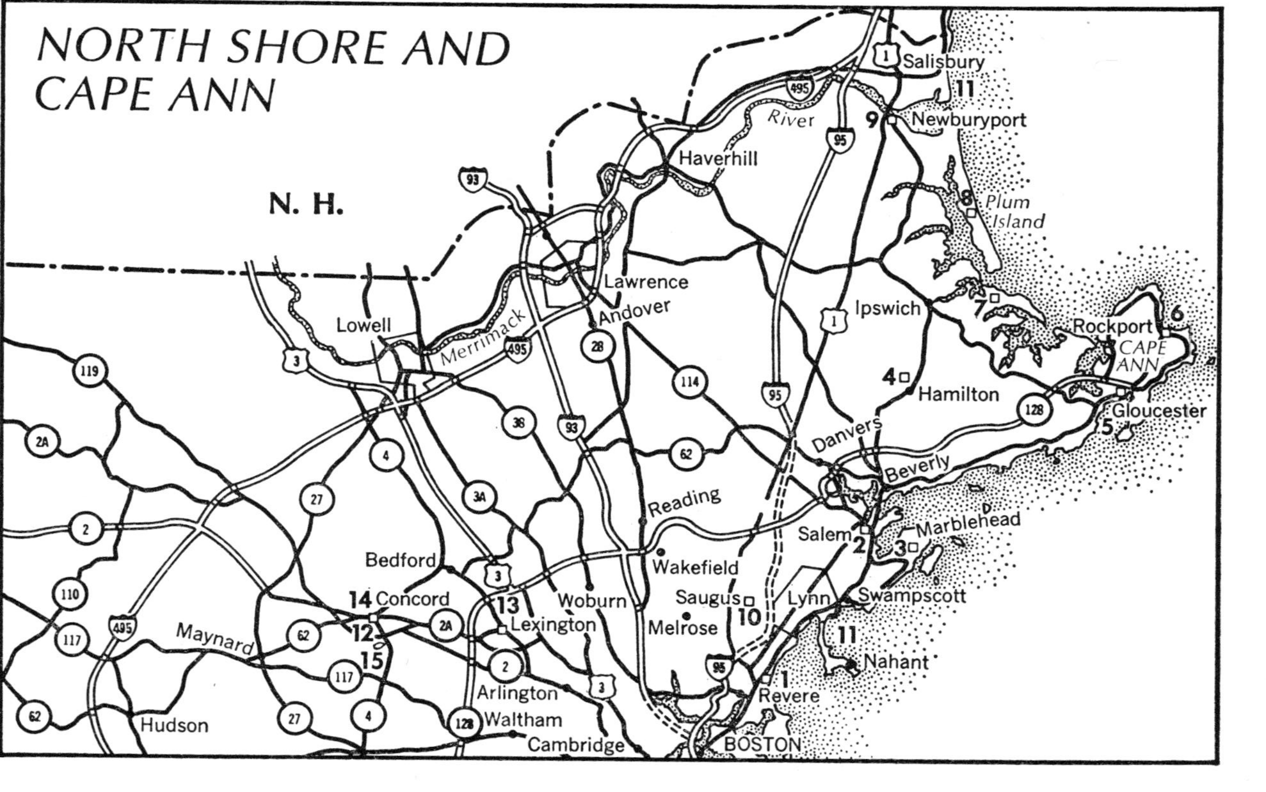
NORTH SHORE AND
CAPE ANN
N. H.
Salisbury
11
Newburyport
9
River
Haverhill
Plum
Island
8
Lawrence
Andover
Lowell
Merrimack
Ipswich
7
Rockport
6
CAPE
ANN
4
Hamilton
Gloucester
5
Danvers
Beverly
Reading
Marblehead
Salem
2
3
Bedford
Wakefield
Saugus
10
Lynn
Swampscott
14
Concord
13
Lexington
Woburn
Melrose
12
15
Maynard
11
Nahant
1
Revere
Arlington
Waltham
Cambridge
BOSTON
Hudson
1
495
95
93
3
28
114
119
2A
36
62
4
3A
27
2
110
117
128

to move their cattle, sheep and horses back from the coast. The patriots had just cleared off Hog Island and were preparing to do likewise at Noddle Island when up Chelsea Creek to the east came the British schooner *Diana* and opened fire upon the very damp "embattled farmers." Reinforcements headed by Israel Putnam waded into waist-deep water and returned the attack vigorously. The British abandoned ship and rowed home in small boats. The *Diana* was stripped and burned by the Continentals.

RICHMOND (Berkshire County, sett. 1760, incorp. 1765, alt. 1057, pop. 1461, town meeting, route, Mass. 41) was originally called Yokumtown. Richmond was incorporated as Richmont but in 1785 became Richmond in honor of Charles Lennox, Duke of Richmond, defender of Colonial rights. From 1827 to 1923 Richmond was active in the production of iron ore; Richmond iron was used for the *Monitor's* cannon. Competition ruined the mines and smelters here. Residents now commute to work elsewhere.

Steven's Glen (picnicking) is a deep ravine through which a brook winds. *Richmond Furnace* (alt. 1003) was named for the large iron smelters operating here until 1915.

Crane Pond is a breeding place for several species of fish. *Shaker Mill Pond* has speckled trout.

ROCHESTER (Plymouth County, sett. *c.* 1638, incorp. 1686, alt. 125, pop. 1770, area 33.76 sq. mi., 39.05 sq. mi. including ponds, town meeting, routes, Mass. 24, 28, 105), a farming community first known as Sippician, was named Rochester for the English home of some of its settlers. It once included the harbors on Buzzards Bay now belonging to Mattapoisett, Marion and part of Wareham, and it had a thriving coastal trade.

The *Congregational Church* (1837) has a graceful spire.

ROCKLAND (Plymouth County, sett. 1730, incorp. 1874, alt. 160, pop. 15,674, area 10.02 sq. mi., town meeting, routes, Mass. 123, 139) was part of Abington until a schoolhouse row resulted in the creation of the separate towns of Abington, Rockland and Whitman.

Two thirds of Rockland originated as the *Hatherly Grant,* the largest (9 sq. mi.) of Old Abington's 18 land grants. Because land titles were unavailable at first, this was the last section of Old Abington to become settled. Forging ahead in industrial development, however, and led by Washington Reed, the old East Ward soon outgrew the central section of the mother town.

The town excelled in shoemaking and subsidiary industries, even before power machinery, when various steps of handwork were accomplished in small, side-yard family-type shops scattered throughout the town.

Stephen Payn patented a machine for skiving (splitting) leather. Lyman Blake developed a shoe sewing machine which is still basic in the industry.

Rockland supports a fine weekly newspaper, Rockland *Standard* (1853).

At the southwest end of the dam at Studley Pond—off Mass. 123 (near 13 Centre Avenue)—stood the ancient cottage of miller Samuel Reed, first white man to live in Rockland.

The *Cottage* (94 Market St.), considered to be the oldest house in Rockland, was built as early at 1745 by Samuel Green.

On Mass. 123 is the main entrance to *Rockland Shopping Plaza,* carved largely from the farm of Mr. Gideon Studley who ran a sawmill at the dam on Studley Pond. An Indian mortar for grinding corn, dug up on this farm, shows that an Indian encampment once occupied this land.

Timothy Thayer came from South Weymouth and built where 979 North Union Street now stands as early as 1737. Peleg Stetson came from Hanover to build at 808 Market Street (1738). A frame house was built (1739) for seasonal use by the logging crews for Thaxter's sawmill on East Water Street, but the house was not used on a year-round basis until 1749. It was moved to South Weymouth before 1830.

The *Congregational Church,* Union St., is where the first meetinghouse (1812) was erected in this section.

E. T. Wright & Co. (1876), Webster and Liberty Sts., specializes in "Wright Arch Preserver" shoes. Rockland companies manufacture shoe welting, sandpaper, webbing and sport clothes.

Maria Poole House, 306 Liberty Street, a charming Cape Cod cottage built before the Revolution, was the birthplace of Victorian novelist, Maria Louise Poole.

ROCKPORT (Essex County, sett. 1690, incorp. 1840, alt. 171, pop. 5636, area 7.02 sq. mi., town meeting, route, Mass. 127).

Information: Dock Square Information Booth

Rockport, a major Bay State tourist attraction, is a small fishing village with a noted artists' colony. Major American Marine artist Stanley Woodward (1890) has a home and barn studio here, as does Aldro Hibbard (1886), known for his photographic-type paintings of Vermont landscapes.

Rockport's first settler was a sailor appropriately named Tarr. Richard Tarr of Marblehead was the first of a long line of seafaring Rockporters. The town's longtime traditional but now deceased industries were largely associated with the sea and fishing: rope, sail and spar making. Fertilizer, glue and isinglass industries depended on the fishing trade. Granite has been a major export since the mid-19th century. Many Finns came to work the granite quarries, and their descendants live here today. Tourism is the major industry. Many Rockporters commute to Boston or cities closer by.

Bearskin Neck, off Main St., is a narrow neck of land onto which are jammed art galleries, restaurants, gift shops and studio apartments. Many buildings are converted shacks. This is one of the post popular tourist spots in the state. *Bearskin Neck* takes its name, as indicated by a marker at the turn from South St., from the capture there in early days of a bear which had been caught by the tide.

At the end of the neck is the *Site of an Old Fort* which served the town in the War of 1812, when Rockport was attacked by the British.

First Congregational Church (1803), known as the "Old Sloop," has a steeple which was rebuilt in 1814 after being demolished by a shot from the British man-of-war *Nymph.*

Rockport Art Association (open June–Sept., 10–5:30, Oct.–May, 2–5, free), 12 Main St., occupies the Old Tavern. Local artists — mostly summer visitors — exhibit here. The town's great annual social affair for many years was the Artists Ball. This was an expurgated version of artists' balls held in Paris.

Motif Number One, off Bearskin Neck, is an old fishing shed which has probably been painted or photographed by every tourist.

Ebenezer Pool Mansion (private), 25 Main St., is a square dwelling erected in 1805, with four great chimneys rising from a hip roof.

Sandy Bay Historical Society and Museum (open July–Aug., daily 2–5, or by appointment, free), Sewall-Scripture House, 40 King St., contains local history items, Marine Room, Victorian furnishings, library.

Old Granite Quarries, off Granite St. (Mass. 127), are reminders of Rockport's great granite days.

Old Castle (open July–Aug., Sat., Sun. 2–5, free), junction Curtis and Granite Sts., built in 1678, has a lean-to roof (1792) and is set well back from the road in a grassy, tree-shaded yard.

Paper House (open Apr. 19–Oct. 15, 9–6, small fee) (1922), Granite St. (Mass. 127), is a house built entirely of newspapers. The walls have 215 thicknesses of paper. The furniture is also made of newspapers.

Dogtown Commons, Mass. 127 along Rockport-Gloucester Line (*fearless visitors welcome to wander*), is truly a "blasted heath," a vast, open, rolling moor, thickly strewn with glacial boulders and rendered yet more desolate by a sparse growth of stunted cedars. It contains the cellar holes of more than 40 dwellings, the homes of fishermen and their families in 1650. Through war, wrecks at sea and the removal of remaining settlers closer to the harbor, the village came to be inhabited solely by poverty-stricken widows and children, protected by ferocious watchdogs from which the settlement took its name. The majority of the cellar holes have been numbered on adjoining boulders to identify their owners. Here lived old Luce George, a wild-eyed hag, and her niece, Tammy Younger, who so bewitched the oxen hauling grain past their cabin that the animals stood with lolling tongues and would not move until part of their load had been donated to the Devil, as represented by Goody George. Old Peg Wesson, disguised as a black crow, followed soldiers to Louisburg in 1745 and annoyed them until the crow was shot by a silver bullet made from the buttons of a soldier's coat, at which very moment, back in Gloucester, Old Peg fell down and broke her leg. She soon died — some say with a silver bullet in her. *Halibut Point* (12.25 acres), a promontory, is Cape Ann's outermost tip and offers a superb vista of coast and sea. It lies off the road between *Folly Cove* and *Andrew's Point.* Picnic tables are available, but it is more fun to picnic on the rocks. Small parking fee.

ROWE (Franklin County, sett. 1762, incorp. 1785, alt. 1364, pop. 277, route, unnumbered route north from Mass. 2 in Charlemont and off Mass. Vt. 8A).

Rowe is the site of New England's first atomic power plant. The Yankee Atomic Electric Company plant, generating about 150,000 kilowatts, cost more than $50,000,000. It is open mid-May through Columbus Day, noon–5.

The town was named for wealthy Boston merchant John Rowe. Earlier, it was the site of many industries whose owners were attracted by the waterpower. In 1850 wooden bowls, designed for washing gold, were made here and shipped to California. Today residents engage in agriculture.

Sibley Road runs to the base of *Adams Mountain* (alt. 2140). A *Summit Tower* (reached by footpath) provides a splendid panorama of New Hampshire, Vermont and New York.

Pretty *Pelham Lake* is the site of summer cottages. The drive along Whitingham Rd. which follows the Deerfield River into Vermont is one of the most spectacular drives in New England.

ROWLEY (Essex County, sett. 1638, incorp. 1639, alt. 50, pop. 3040, area 19.01 sq. mi., town meeting, routes, US 1, Mass. 1A, 133).

Rowley is an agricultural center. On *Rowley Common* in 1813 the *Country's Wonder,* a 90-ton vessel, was built and afterward hauled to the river by 100 yoke of oxen. Bystanders refreshed themselves from a well into which had been poured a full barrel of Jamaica rum. Shipbuilding began here in 1780 and continued for nearly a century.

Jewell Mill (off US 1 at Glen Mills) is open to visitors.

Chaplin-Clark-Williams House (open by appointment only, contribution expected), Haverhill St. (Mass. 133), was built about 1671. Period furnishings.

MILL CREEK WILDLIFE MANAGEMENT AREA has public hunting in Newbury and Rowley.

ROXBURY (see BOSTON)

ROYALSTON (Worcester County, sett. 1762, incorp. 1765, pop. 809, alt. 1000, area 41.99 sq. mi., town meeting, routes, Mass. 32, 68) has devoted itself to agriculture except when toy manufacturing was attempted.

In 1769 when 15-year-old Katurah Babcock was struck dead by lightning, her fate was held up as an example of divine punishment for nonattendance at church. In 1845 two other children met the same fate on the same spot, an event that made the village unpopular.

The town of Royalston — last Worcester County town to be granted — once included patriots John Hancock, James Otis and Governor James Bowdoin along with Sir John Temple among its early proprietors. Early proprietors' meetings were held in Boston's famed "Bunch of Grapes" Tavern. About 4000 of the town's original 30,577 acres have been parceled out among Orange and Winchendon. Royalston added a few hundred acres from Orange and Phillipston.

Royalston was one of the few Massachusetts towns which did not vote to have its name changed when Colonel Isaac Royall remained steadfast to his King instead of joining the Boston rebels. He moved to England in 1776 and died there in 1781.

Farming was long the mainstay of life in this hill town but today only a few working farms remain. Life here is pleasant and placid except when tempers fray in town meetings or a resident on a back road "raises all git out" because of poor road conditions.

Doane Falls is located at the junction of Mill Rd. and Main Rd. from Athol. This unusual scenic area has a high falls, and fast-flowing Lawrence Brook cuts through Granite Gorge.

ROYALSTON CENTER (Mass. 68), one of the most attractive villages in the state, is essentially one street of lovely houses straddling a ridge with fine views in all directions. Royalston, unlike many New England towns, has many fine houses, some of them former estates.

SOUTH ROYALSTON (Mass. 68) consists of a small group of houses, a garage, a store and a restaurant.

Forbes Falls, sometimes known as Royal Falls (turn n. on Falls Road, off Mass. 68 e. of Royalston Center by sign reading "Country Cooper"). There may or may not be a sign reading "To Falls," depending on whether vandals or sign erectors were there last. The falls, maintained by TOR, are a lovely spectacle. Picnicking.

Country Cooper, Falls Road (second house and buildings on the left — usually open). Former mechanical engineer and designer Warren Williams is one of the few individual coopers remaining in America today. Cooper Williams, a jovial transplanted Vermont Yankee, makes buckshots, firkins and other items — all by hand.

Public hunting in *Birch Hill* and *Millers Wildlife Management Areas.*

RUSSELL (Hampden County, sett. 1782, incorp. 1792, alt. 399, pop. 1382, area 17.71 sq. mi., town meeting, routes, Mass. Pike, 20).

Here in 1858 the Chapin and Gould Paper Mills were established. Russell's Westfield River Paper Co., maker of glowing paper, and WORONOCO's *Strathmore Paper Company Plant* (open by permission), across the river, are the area's chief support.

RUTLAND (Worcester County, sett. 1716, incorp. 1722, alt. 1205, pop. 3198, area 35.42 sq. mi., town meeting, routes, Mass. 56, 68, 122, 122a).

After the Revolution, Rutland's bankrupt citizens joined Daniel Shays' insurgents. The town was headquarters of Shays' forces that marched to Worcester.

Because of the altitude, several tuberculosis sanitariums were established here. These institutions contribute to the town's stability and prosperity, providing jobs and a market for dairy and garden products and poultry.

On Central Tree Ave., a marker identifies a spot as the exact geographic center of the state.

RUTLAND STATE PARK'S facilities include swimming, boating, fishing, picnic tables, snowmobiling, scenic views.

BARRE FALLS WILDLIFE MANAGEMENT AREA has public hunting in Barre, Hubbardston, Rutland, and Oakham.

SAGAMORE (see BOURNE)

SALEM (Essex County seat, sett. *c.* 1626, town incorp. 1630, city incorp. 1836, alt. 13, pop. 40,556, area 7.99 sq. mi., mayor-council, routes, US 1A, Mass. 28, 107, 114, 128).

Salem, the city of witchcraft, merchant princes and shipmasters, home of novelist Nathaniel Hawthorne, birthplace of the great carpenter-architect Samuel McIntire and site of his creations, is one of the treasure-houses of America. Here are the haunting shades, not only of Hawthorne, but also of every character he created, of his old houses impregnated with supernatural influences and of the eerie atmosphere that still lingers in the narrow streets. Here are the more robust memories of docks and wharves from which poured crude wealth in fish and ships' supplies and into which, after many turnovers of cargo, flowed all the exotic treasure of the Indies and China. Here stored in old landmarks is the romance of swift ships, of bellying sails, of masts stripped for the gale, of sailors' oaths and roaring chanteys, of ambition and avarice, of mansions built by merchant princes and delicate women nurtured in them.

Salem has architectural treasures so numerous and varied as to recreate the development of Colonial architecture of New England. Though chiefly concentrated about Washington Square and on Essex, Federal and Chestnut Streets, houses by Samuel McIntire (1757–1811) occur throughout the old districts of Salem. He labored here all his life. Many of his houses retain their original beauty. Dwellings of the great maritime period after his death partake of his work's dignity and delicacy of detail. Salem cannot be neglected either by the student of the American tradition in architecture or by the lover of beautiful houses.

Salem's name is the Hebrew *Sholom,* meaning Peace, but never did a city have less of this spirit. It was founded by intellectual revolt and nurtured in dissension.

In 1626 Roger Conant and emigrants from Cape Ann chose this sheltered site to fish and farm, think their own thoughts and hold their own religious opinions. Trouble began when Gov. Endecott and his followers arrived two years later. Conant and his friends smarted under their assumption of superiority. There were wranglings about property rights and community regulations. Differences were adjusted, and in 1630 the name Salem was adopted to celebrate peace. This peace was brief. New quarrels broke out. Conant and followers abandoned their homes and gardens and moved across the North River.

The town grew, and as man became more confident in his dealings with nature and less conscious of physical dependence on God, religion declined. Calvinism made a desperate effort to retain what was left by preaching hellfire with redoubled energy. This was followed by a persecution of Quakers. Roger Williams fled the colony. Too many people, however, knew their Quaker neighbors were harmless, peaceable and industrious. Witchcraft persecutions, already popular in Europe, became far more fruitful in suppressing dissent.

In 1692 Salem preacher and slaveholder Samuel Parris (1653–1720) had a West Indian slave girl Tibuta, who had a talent for voodoo tales which she related well, if not wisely, to young white girls. Her grisly tales often scared them. When bedtime came after a secret session with Tibuta's tales, they shuddered, screamed and saw "things" in dark corners. The village physician said they were bewitched. The little wretches accused Tibuta and two unpopular old crones of bewitching them. The accused were questioned by churchmen with deep gravity. The little girls embroidered their original tales. Tibuta and the crones were charged with consorting with the Devil. They were sentenced and hung.

Witchcraft raged in Salem and neighboring villages. Nineteen persons were hung on Gallows Hill while several died in jail. No one was safe. In Beverly, Preacher Hale's wife, Beryl, was accused. Gov. Sir William Phips' attractive wife was accused of sympathizing with a prisoner accused of witchcraft. This was going too far. The governor, who had done nothing to stop the persecutions until his wife became involved, took steps to end the pestilence. People soon regained their reason.

Farming dominated early Salem but in the 17th century, commerce and industry gained a foothold. By 1700 the protected harbor was busy. Shipyards made new craft which would carry Salem skippers to the far ends of the earth. There was extensive trade with the West Indies and Europe.

During the Revolution, Salem skippers turned to privateering, another name for buccaneering except the piracy was confined to enemy merchantmen. Privateering was profitable at first, but a strict British blockade ruined Salem's trade. When the war ended, Salem vessels were forced to rely on a meager coastal trade.

The pendulum swung. The great Chinese market was discovered. Salem entered on its brief glorious and profitable maritime career. The *Grand Turk,* a merchantman, sailed from Salem for China in 1785. Immediately after her return from an extremely profitable voyage, 34 Salem skippers sailed for the Far East.

Instead of sailing directly for China they frequently sailed along our North Pacific Coast to pick up furs for trading. The Hawaiian Islands — then the Sandwich Isles — provided fresh fruit and sandalwood. After profitable trading transactions in China they sailed around Cape Hope for Salem. Yankee skippers were hard bargainers. They often turned over their entire cargo a dozen times before reaching home — and realized a substantial profit on each sale or swap. Huge wealth piled up. Promotion was rapid. Sometimes skippers retired while still in their thirties. Many Oriental merchants believed that Salem was a separate and wealthy country.

Rapid commercial development resulted in the cultural expansion of Salem and the growth of a romantic background. From Canton, Dutch East Indies, Philippines and Mauritius came tea, china, silks, fans, feathers, embroidered shawls, coffee, spices and teakwood chests and furniture along with glamorous tales of life in a truly fabulous country. Esther Forbes' novel *The Running of the Tide* portrays this profitable romantic period of Salem history.

The War of 1812 raised hob with Salem's maritime industry. A depression followed. Before the city could recover the recently opened Erie Canal became a serious competitor in foreign and inland trade. Salem Harbor was not deep enough for many of the deep-draft new vessels. Salem was thus denied a major role in the great clipper ship era of the mid-19th century.

Salem's commercial position faded. Prosperity returned with the advent of profitable but less colorful industry. In 1848 the Naumkeag Steam Cotton Mills were established. After the Civil War numerous tanneries, paint and shoe factories were founded. The Great 1914 fire destroyed most of the decrepit industrial zone. Many concerns preferred to move elsewhere. Most of the textile plants moved south after WWII. Today the production of electronic equipment is important.

What to See and Do

Gardner-White-Pingree House (open Tues.–Sat. 10–4:30, Sun., June–Sept. 2–4.30 P.M., small fee), 128 Essex St., built in 1810, was among the last works of Samuel McIntire and is conceded to be his finest brick work. The house is square, with a low third story capped by a cornice and balustraded parapet.

Essex Institute (open Tues.–Sat. 9–4:30, Sun. and holidays 2–5, free), 132–134 Essex St., is a library and museum. The former contains the Ward China Library — probably the finest library on China and the Chinese in the United States — logbooks and sea journals and county and town histories. Exhibits in the museum consist of Colonial portraits and paintings, miniatures and silhouettes and three period rooms, a kitchen typical of 1750 and a bedroom and a parlor of 1800.

John Ward House (open June–Oct., Tues.–Sat., small fee), behind Essex Institute, built in 1684, stands in the shady grounds to the rear of the main buildings of the institute. It has wide clapboards, a lean-to roof and an overhanging second story. In the garden are reconstructions of an *Old Cobbler's Shop,* a *Cent Shop* and *Weaving Room.*

Peabody Museum (open Mar. 1–Oct. 31, 9–5, Sun. and holidays 2–5; Nov. 1–Feb. 28, 9–4, Sun. and holidays, 2–4, closed Thanksgiving, Christmas, New Year's, free), Essex St., was endowed by George Peabody as the permanent repository of a marine collection, including a circle of reflection presented by Napoleon to his navigation instructor, a sextant which served Livingstone in the mazes of the Congo, ship models, nautical instruments and whaling implements.

The Old Town Hall (open 9–5), opposite the Salem Five Cent Savings Bank, was built in 1816, and its ground floor was used as a market for more than one hundred years. Architecturally the hall is simple and dignified.

Witch House (open June 1–Oct. 31, 10–6, small fee), 310½ Essex St., once the residence of Judge Corwin of the notorious witchcraft trials, has, unfortunately, been altered, but the interior remains very much as it was in 1692.

Ropes Mansion (open May–Nov., Mon.–Sat. 10–12, 1–5, closed Sun. and holidays, small fee), 318 Essex St., is a stately gambrel roof building (1719) enclosed by a graceful wooden fence with carved posts. The upper slope of the roof is outlined by a railing. The house was owned and occupied by Judge Nathaniel Ropes (1726–74) and his descendants for four generations. It contains a rare and valuable collection of Canton, Nanking and Fitzhue china and Irish glass.

Salem Athenaeum (adm. by invitation of a member), 339 Essex St., contains rare editions and the Kirwin Library, taken by a privateer from an English vessel and used as the basis for studies by Nathaniel Bowditch, the famous mathematician and navigator, a native of Salem.

Behind a graceful wooden fence decorated with carved urns at 393 Essex St. is the *Reverend Thomas Barnard House,* a large and delightful gambrel roof dwelling with a pedimented doorway and two great chimneys.

Chestnut Street, laid out in 1796, is one of the finest streets, architecturally speaking, in America. Most of these Federal houses, some designed by McIntire, are three-story, yellow brick and have beautiful exterior detail of porches, columns and Palladian windows. In the rear are charming gardens and picturesque buildings which form an appropriate background. Almost every house deserves study. Among them, and selected almost at random, are the *Pickman-Shreve-Little House,* No. 27 (1816), with a classic porch below a Palladian window; the similar *Dodge-Shreve House,* No. 29 (1817), with balustraded hip roof, cornice set with modillions and classic porch; the *Mack* and *Stone Houses,* No. 21 and 23 (1814–15), simple in detail but with elliptical colonnaded porches and keyed marble lintels.

Hamilton Hall, on the corner of Cambridge St., was designed by McIntire in 1805. Although somewhat altered, it retains some characteristic detail such as the five Palladian windows on the side. The famous McIntire eagle is preserved in the center panel.

Pickering House (open by appointment anytime, fee), 18 Broad St. Ten generations of Pickerings lived here. Built in 1660 this is reportedly the oldest house in Salem proper. The house has unfortunately been altered, and its fine old core is veiled by excessive "carpenter Gothic" work.

Cook-Oliver House (private), 142 Federal St., benefited greatly by that architectural tragedy, the destruction of the Elias Hasket Derby Mansion. After Derby's death, McIntire, who began this dwelling for Captain Samuel Cook in 1804, persuaded the captain to buy the gateposts and much of the beautiful wood finish of the unoccupied Derby mansion. The fence, with its elaborate gateposts decorated with urns surmounted by the flame motif, is probably the best of McIntire's many fences.

Assembly Hall (not open), 138 Federal St., an historic 1782 McIntire building, has been remodeled for private use, but the elaborate matchboarded facade, Ionic pilasters on the second story and fanlight are unchanged. The porch, added later, is elaborately decorated with scrolls, festoons and a heavy grapevine frieze.

Pierce-Nichols House (open Tues.–Sat. 2–5, small fee), 80 Federal St. This Essex Institute-owned building is one of Salem's most architecturally interesting residences. Built in 1782, it was the first flower of McIntire's genius and has, with its outbuildings, been called one of the finest wood architectural groups in the United States.

The stately houses of Washington Square, surrounding Salem Common, perpetuate the charm and dignity of Salem's past. Architectural gems: *Hosmer-Townsend-Waters House,* No. 80 (1795), by McIntire, known for its lovely, enclosed side porch and its hip roof rising to a massive central chimney; the *Boardman House,* No. 82 (1785), of beautiful proportion and detail, with an enclosed porch; the *Baldwin-Lyman House,* No. 92 (1818), with its symmetrical arrangement of great chimneys joined in pairs; and the distinguished hip roof *Andrew-Safford House* (1818), which uses roof balustrades, heavy cornice and fluted columns on a side portico for decoration but centers its emphasis on an elaborate Corinthian entrance porch below a Palladian window.

The *Roger Conant Statue,* Washington Square and Brown St., was executed by Henry Hudson Kitson.

Hawthorne Monument by Bela Pratt, at the head of Hawthorne Boulevard, is near the scenes chiefly associated with Salem's great literary figure.

Retrace Hawthorne Blvd., r. from Hawthorne Blvd. onto Essex St.
The Narbonne House (private), 71 Essex St., stands almost opposite Washington Sq. e. Built before 1671, its steep pitched roof and great central chimney proclaim its period. The Dutch door of the lean-to was formerly the entrance to a "Cent Shop" described by Hawthorne.
House of Seven Gables (open July 1–Labor Day, 9:30–7, rest of year, 10–5, small fee, proceeds to charity), 54 Turner St., the supposed setting of Hawthorne's novel by that name, is perhaps the most celebrated spot in all historic Salem. There is grave doubt whether this house is the one described by Hawthorne. There is even more doubt as to how much of the building is authentic. A good deal of imagination went into the restoration. Its present appearance is weather-beaten and rambling, with seven gables, huge chimneys, a lean-to and a second-story overhang adorned with pendrils; it shows strong medieval influence. It was probably built in about 1668.
Hathaway Guest House, behind House of Seven Gables, was built in 1682 and restored in 1911. Guest rooms available. Several rooms of exhibits and counting house open to public.
J. C. B. Smith Swimming Pool is a large and inviting saltwater cove made by damming the head of Cat Cove.
U.S. Coast Guard Air Station (open 3 to sundown on weekdays, 1 until sundown on Sat. and Sun., guide) is a modern, completely equipped depot, which includes airplane hangars.
Salem National Historic Shrine includes (1) Richard Derby House, (2) Old Custom House and (3) Derby Wharf.
Richard Derby House (open daily 10–5, small fee), 168 Derby St., built in 1762 and now owned by the Society for the Preservation of New England Antiquities, is the oldest brick house in Salem. Except for its gambrel roof, it is American Georgian in style. From its small-paned windows, the first of the line of merchant princes could watch his vessels unloading almost in his dooryard or follow with his glass their topsails receding beyond the horizon.
Old Custom House (open daily 9–5 in summer, closed Sun. rest of year, free), 178 Derby St., built in 1819, where Nathaniel Hawthorne once dreamed over his ledgers, looks down along the granite finger of *Derby Wharf.* In architecture it is akin to the Federal dwellings of Salem. Surmounting the parapet is a carved eagle.
Derby Wharf was built about 1763 and added to over the years. Salem privateers used it as a war base in the Revolution and War of 1812.
Hawthorne's Birthplace (private), 27 Union St., is a gambrel roof house built before the witchcraft year, 1692. In the shadows of the old house he spent a shy, solitary boyhood. He was a mystic and a recluse by nature and unfitted by an abnormal sensitiveness for his duties at the Custom House. His genius reached its full fruition in romantic fiction. Three volumes of short stories, *The Scarlet Letter, The House of Seven Gables, The Blithedale Romance* and *The Marble Faun* are works of major significance.
Pioneer's Village in *Forest Park* (open June–Oct. 10–dusk, small fee),

Clifton Ave. *Forest River Park* overlooks the harbor and sea, almost at the city limits. Three acres of this park are devoted to *Pioneers' Village,* a reproduction of typical units of a Puritan community of about 1630, ranging from dugouts and primitive cabins to the "Governor's Fayre House" with its huge central chimney and vast fireplace. Here can be seen true village life: a blacksmith's forge, a saw pit, a brick kiln, as well as the grim whipping post and stocks; in the garden are the same flowers and herbs that grew in the dooryards of the pioneers.

City Hall, 93 Washington St., contains the Indian deed to Salem, many fine portraits and interesting furnishings.

Essex County Courthouse, Washington and Federal Sts. Witches were tried here. Legal documents give details and testimony of trials. Pins on exhibition were said to have been used by witches to torment their victims.

Charter Street Burying Ground. Mayflower passenger Richard More, Gov. Simon Bradstreet and many other Salem notables sleep here.

Mall Street House (private), 14 Mall St. Hawthorne wrote *The Scarlet Letter* here.

Other Salem buildings worth a visit for their architectural significance:

Mansfield-Bolles House	1810	8 Chestnut St.
Hodges-Peele-West	1804	12 Chestnut St.
Goss-Osgood House	1810	15 Chestnut St.
Hawthorne's Residence	1846–1847	18 Chestnut St.
Peabody-Rantoul House	1810	19 Chestnut St.
Mack and Stone Houses	*c.* 1814	21 and 23 Chestnut St.
Hoffman-Simpson House	*c.* 1827	26 Chestnut St.
Hodges-Webb-Meek House	before 1802	81 Essex St.
Col. Benjamin Pickman House	1743	165 Essex St. *Rear*
Lindall-Gibbs-Osgood House	1773	314 Essex St.
Cabot-Endicott-Low House	1748	365 Essex St.
Wheatland House	1773	374 Essex St.
Peabody-Silsbee House	1797	380 Essex St.
Stearns House (East India Inn)	1776	384 Essex St.
Captain Edward Allen House	1780	125 Derby St.
Silsbee-Mott House	1818	35 Washington St.

SALISBURY (Essex County, sett. 1638, incorp. 1640, alt. 20, pop. 4179, town meeting, routes, US 1, US 1A, I-95).

The Quaker Whipping Stone in the tiny triangular green marks the site of Major Robert Pike's championship of three Quaker women whipped at the tail of an oxcart, a story told in Whittier's poem "How the Women Went from Dover." The stone originally served as the steppingstone of the Quaker Meeting House (1752) in Salisbury.

A marker at the north end of the square indicates the *Site of the Betsy Gerrish House,* within whose narrow walls a session of the General Court squeezed itself in 1757, when the community was a "shire town" and the only settlement north of the Merrimack River.

Two hundred yards to the right of the square is *Potlid Square,* where women of Salisbury melted their pewter pots to make bullets in the cause of liberty. Settlers from Newbury, Massachusetts, and from Salisbury, England, fought the Indians, trying at the same time to build up the fishing industry, oak stave manufacture and shipbuilding. The woolen industry, introduced in 1812, was soon transferred to neighboring towns.

Old Burying Ground is at the junction of Mass. 1A and Beach Rd. In this cemetery, laid out in 1639, are flat stones known as "wolf slabs," placed on the graves to protect fresh corpses from hungry wolves.

SALISBURY BEACH STATE RESERVATION is a 3.5-mi-long beach. Many Pentucket Indian shell mounds have been found along the beach. Facilities: ocean beach, bathhouses, saltwater fishing, picnic sites, campsites (500).

SANDISFIELD (Berkshire County, sett. 1750, incorp. 1762, alt. 250, pop. 547, area 52.51 sq. mi., town meeting, routes, Mass. 8, 57).

NEW BOSTON, the principal village in Sandisfield town, has had tanneries, woolen and silk mills, shoe and hat factories and cooperages. Today agriculture and dairying are the chief occupations.

Unitarian clergyman, Edmund H. Sears (1810–76), editor of the *Religious Magazine and Monthly Review* and a native of this town, in 1849 wrote the Christmas hymn, "It Came Upon a Midnight Clear."

SANDISFIELD STATE FOREST. Facilities: boating, bridle trails, hunting, fireplaces, picnic tables, swimming, scenic views.

WEST LAKE RECREATION AREA'S facilities include boating, fishing, hiking, hunting, snowmobiling, scenic views.

SANDWICH (Barnstable County, sett. 1637, incorp. 1639, alt. 50, pop. 5239, area 42.61 sq. mi., town meeting, routes, US 6, Mass. 6A, 130), renowned for its glass, was named for Sandwich, England. It was the first Cape Cod town to be settled. Sandwich, England, was the seat of the Earl of Sandwich, reportedly the first known individual to have used two slices of bread as a vehicle for other foodstuffs.

From 1825 to 1888, Sandwich was famous for its beautiful colored glass made from a secret formula, now lost. The first pressed and the first lace glass in America were made here. Cranberry culture and tourism are now the chief occupations.

The Sandwich Historical Museum (open May–Nov., daily 10–5, small fee), corner of Grove and Canal Sts., houses a notable collection of Sandwich glass.

Congregational Church, corner of Grove and Main Sts., with its beautiful spire, is a favorite subject for painters.
Hoxie House (open May 28–Oct. 16, daily except Sun. 10–5, Sun. and holidays, 1–5, small fee), in a lane near Shawme Lake at the head of School St., is of the saltbox type, with thick, hand-hewn timbers and recessed windows. A brick in the original chimney was dated 1637.
Dexter's Grist Mill (open May 30–Oct. 14, daily 10–5, small fee), Main St., was built in 1654 and has been restored to working condition.
Yesteryear's Doll Museum (open May 30–Oct. 15, Mon.–Sat. 10–5, Sun. and holidays 1–5, small fee), River and Main Sts., exhibits old and rare dolls and dollhouses.
Dexter Estate (open during daylight hours, fee with guide, no fee without guide), Grove St. The original landscaping is being restored to this 75-acre estate. Laurel is at its peak between mid-June and mid-July. Rhododendrons are at peak between mid-May and mid-June.

SCUSSET STATE BEACH (380 acres) is off Mass. 3 and US 6 at northern end of Cape Cod Canal. Facilities: beach, bathhouse, picnic sites, sea fishing, pier fishing.

SHAWME-CROWELL STATE FOREST lies 2 mi. from Sagamore Bridge. Campsites lie on high land overlooking Cape Cod Bay. Facilities: picnic areas, bathhouses, showers, campsites (280), snowmobiling. Saltwater beaches are nearby.

SAUGUS (Essex County, sett. 1629, incorp. 1815, alt. 27, pop. 25,110, area 10.57 sq. mi., town meeting, routes, US 1, Mass. 107), a residential town and site of the Saugus Iron Works, the world's first continuous production of cast and wrought iron. The ancient forge launched the mighty American steel industry.
Ironworks Restoration (open May 15–Oct. 15, daily except Mon. and July 4, 9–4), Central St. The forge hammer, water wheels and bellows operate on this schedule: Sat., Sun. and holidays, except July 4: 11 A.M., 1:30 P.M., 2:30 P.M., 4 P. M. Weekdays, except Mon.: 11 A.M., 3 P.M. Fee includes Ironworks Restoration, museum and ironmaster's house.
Ironworks Museum contains artifacts excavated at site of original forge.
Ironmaster's House, a restored example of seventeenth-century American architecture, was built in 1643 by farmer Thomas Dexter, one of the original owners of the ironworks. The house, one of the most delightful in the county, has diamond-paned casements, steep gables, batten doors and an immense central chimney with a buttress-like extension about 12 feet down the lean-to roof. The house has been greatly altered, many additions having been made in recent years. Among these distortions of the original structure are the odd-shaped carved ornaments attached to the peak of the gables.

The interior shows the original exposed timbers of English oak, some of them at least two feet square and ornamentally carved. It is said that the builder, never dreaming of the vast forests in this country, brought these timbers with him from England for the frame of his house. The 12-foot-wide kitchen and living room fireplaces contain pothooks and cranes supposed to have been made at the nearby forge.

Restoration costs, an estimated $1,500,000, were paid by the American Iron and Steel Institute.

SAVOY (Berkshire County, sett. 1777, incorp. 1797, alt. 1720, pop. 322, area 36.03 sq. mi., town meeting, routes, Mass. 2, 8A, 116) is often called Savoy Hollow. The town's chief export is Christmas trees.

SAVOY WILDLIFE MANAGEMENT AREA has public hunting.

SAVOY MT.-FLORIDA STATE FOREST (see FLORIDA)

SCITUATE (Plymouth County, sett. *c.* 1630, incorp. 1636, alt. 50, pop. 16,973, area 16.90 sq. mi., town meeting, routes, Mass. 3A, 123). The village suffered during the Indian wars and, in a decisive battle near the Stockbridge Mansion, was barely saved from total destruction.

The War of 1812 injured business. Legend says when an English man-of-war burned vessels in the harbor, two little girls, Rebecca and Abigail Bates, scared off a landing party at Lighthouse Point by beating on dish-pans, firing guns and otherwise simulating a lively defense force.

Scituate engaged in shipbuilding, fishing, brickmaking and later had saw-, grist-, fulling and clothing mills. Today it is one of two communities in the United States preparing Irish moss, a marine alga growing on rocks and used in brewing and dyeing and in making a delicate blanc mange particularly suitable for the diet of invalids.

Cudworth House, near the town hall, has a collection of historical relics. The community is both a popular summer resort and a commuter's haven. There is an excellent beach.

SCONSET (see NANTUCKET)

SEEKONK (Bristol County, sett. 1636, incorp. 1812, alt. 50, pop. 11,116, area 18.63 sq. mi., town meeting, routes, US 6, 44).

Seekonk (Indian, "Black Goose") indicates an abundance of these birds prior to the coming of white men. In 1862 a part of the town was set aside as East Providence, reducing the area and leaving a population of but 800.

Many Seekonk residents commute to nearby cities like Providence, Pawtucket and Attleboro, but about 350 work in local plants producing dyes, religious jewelry and metal products. For a small community, it has many fine restaurants and motel accommodations.

SHARON (Norfolk County, sett. *c.* 1650, incorp. *c.* 1775, alt. 302, pop. 12,367, area 23.58 sq. mi., town meeting, routes, US 1, Mass. 27) lies in the territory once known as Massapoag "Great Waters." Sharon is a delightful residential center.

MOOSE HILL WILDLIFE SANCTUARY, off Mass. 27 into Moosehill Parkway onto Moosehill St. (250 acres), the Massachusetts Audubon Society's oldest sanctuary, was acquired in 1916 as a gift. The top of *Firetower Trail* provides one of the finest vistas in southeastern Massachusetts.

SHAWSHEEN VILLAGE (see ANDOVER)

SHEFFIELD (Berkshire County, sett. 1726, incorp. 1733, alt. 675, pop. 2374, area 48.67 sq. mi., town meeting, routes, US 7, Mass. 41).

Sheffield, the only Massachusetts town with two covered bridges, was the first town chartered in Berkshire County. It is the site of *Berkshire School* for boys and *Winchester School.*

The town once depended on lime and marble for revenue, but today there are two plastics and one pottery plant. Its wide, tree-lined thoroughfare is one of the most beautiful in the commonwealth.

Colonel John Ashley House (open June 1–Oct. 15, 1–5, small fee), 0.75 mi. east of Ashley Falls Center, was built in 1735 and is said to be the oldest complete house in Berkshire County. French and Indian War veteran Ashley came here from Westfield to help found the town. He was active during the American Revolution. The house is a fine example of period architecture.

Bartholomew's Cobble (open Apr. 15–Oct. 15, small fee) (44 acres), at Ashley Falls on Housatonic River, west of US 7, is owned and maintained by TOR. The "Cobble" is a natural wild rock garden containing unusual specimens of plant life in the area's limestone ledges. Since 1966 over 600 types of plants and more than 200 species of birds have been identified. In 1963 TOR voted to build a museum here as a memorial to the late S. Waldo Bailey, Cobble warden for nearly 18 years.

SHELBURNE (Franklin County, sett. *c.* 1756, incorp. 1768, alt. 420, pop. 1836, area 21 sq. mi., town meeting, routes, Mass. 2, 112) was once known as Deerfield Pasture or Deerfield Northwest. About 1756 several families settled near Shelburne Falls but left during the French and Indian Wars. About 1760 a permanent settlement was made. The town was named for the second Earl of Shelburne. In 1849 cutlery manufacturing was started and remains the important local industry. The first Yale locks were made here by Linus Yale in 1851.

West of Shelburne, the Deerfield River parallels Mass. 2, 200 feet below, and the precipitous bank of the stream rises several hundred feet.

SHELBURNE FALLS, alt. 252 (towns of Shelburne and Buckland), is unusual in that it is bisected by the Deerfield River, which is the town line between Shelburne and Buckland. Shelburne Falls is actually the governmental center of two towns.

Salmon Falls, on the Deerfield River, named for the quantities of salmon formerly caught here, has three distinct cataracts with potholes at the foot.
On *Shelburne Summit* (Mass. 2), alt. 1170, is a tower (picnic grounds) that overlooks Greenfield. New Hampshire and Vermont peaks are visible from this point.
The Bridge of Flowers is an imaginative use of a former trolley line bridge. The bridge over the Deerfield River between Shelburne Falls and Buckland has been converted into two 400-foot-long flower beds with a path between the beds. The five-arch bridge is floodlighted nightly until 10:30 during the summer. Contributions expected.

MT. MOHAWK SKI AREA (Mass. 2 west of Greenfield) has 2 T-bar lifts, instruction, ski shop, ski rentals, snack bar, ski patrol. Phone MA5–9061.

SHERBORN (Middlesex County, sett. 1652, incorp. 1674, alt. 175, pop. 3309, area 17.12 sq. mi., town meeting, routes, Mass. 16, 27, 115) was an Indian settlement. Many Indian artifacts have been found here. The hand-manufacturing of shoes, the willow-weaving and the whip-making of the 19th century are gone.
Buttonballs House (private), a two-story frame structure, was named for the large sycamore trees surrounding it. The building itself is of uncertain age, though the ell is known to have been built in 1722. The main part of the structure remains as it was in 1778, with brick fireplace, brick ovens, a smoke closet, hand-hewn oak timbers and handwrought nails.

LITTLE POND WILDLIFE SANCTUARY (273 acres) lies between Lake and South Sts. and Farm Road. A variety of trees and marshes. Massachusetts Audubon Society project.

SHIRLEY (Middlesex County, sett. *c.* 1720, incorp. 1753, alt. 300, pop. 4909, area 15.81 sq. mi., town meeting, routes, Mass. 2A, 225). On the north side of the common is the *Home of the Rev. Seth Chandler* (private), where Ralph Waldo Emerson visited. It is a broad, two-and-a-half-story house with a pitch roof, ell and central chimney. The philosopher's room and its furnishings are intact.

The buildings around *Shirley Center Common* are a fine example of Colonial architecture. *The Meeting House* (1775), built on the common, was removed by oxen to the side of the training field in 1851; it houses a rare Stevens organ. Bronze plaques honor the Rev. Phineas Whitney and Rev. Seth Chandler, both of whom served 50 years in the church.

Near the common on Parker Road is the home of the MacKayes, Percy (1875–1956), poet and playwright, and conservationist Benton (1879), author of *The New Exploration,* pioneer in regional planning, a past president of The Wilderness Society and one of its founders. Benton is an honorary member of the conservation commission for the town of Shirley. *Bull Run Tavern* (Mass. 2A), a stagecoach inn where as many as 20 teams awaited a stage's arrival to catch up on the news, is now an attractive eating place.

Shirley was named for Provincial Governor William Shirley (1694–1771). A Shaker community (1871) continued until 1905 when the state took over its land and brick buildings as a reform school for boys. Some original buildings remain. *Hazen Memorial Library* has Shaker books and handmade articles.

Carpenter and minister Oliver Holden (1765–1844), author of many hymns, was born in Shirley in 1763. His "Coronation" was a Civil War battle hymn. Opposite 14 Leominster Rd. is the *Site of the Birthplace of Sarah (Edgarton) Mayo* (1819–48), poet, author and editor of the *Ladies' Repository* and the *Rose of Sharon.*

Many Shirley residents are employed at nearby Fort Devens. Local factories produce garters, sporting goods, protective accessories, marine rope, and soft drinks.

FORT DEVENS WILDLIFE MANAGEMENT AREA has public hunting. Special free daily permit needed.

BENJAMIN HILL SKI AREA (off Mass. 2) has T-bar lift, seven rope tows, novice slope, free single rope tow, instruction, cafeteria, ski shop, ski patrol, baby sitting facilities, snow-making equipment, night skiing. In the summer its large lodge, pool and two tennis courts are used as a private club for residents of area towns.

SHREWSBURY (Worcester County, sett. 1722, incorp. 1727, alt. 668, pop. 19,196, area 20.78 sq. mi., representative town meeting, routes, I–290, US 20, Mass. 9, 140) was named for Charles Talbot, Duke of Shrewsbury. Its lack of waterpower and inaccessibility to outside markets precluded the development of industries. Agriculture was once the chief occupation; today the town has rapidly growing and diversified industries. Luther Goddard, a Baptist preacher born in the town, is said to have been the first watchmaker in America. He followed watchmaking purely as an avocation, and on Sundays after his sermon he collected faulty timepieces among his parishioners and returned them the following Sunday in good repair.

Shrewsbury was established as a town in 1727. It then included all land between Lancaster, Marlborough, Sutton and Grafton. Later, parts of Shrewsbury were annexed to Grafton, Westborough and Lancaster, with the north precinct established as the town of Boylston in 1786.

The terrain is hilly with general elevations about 400-500 feet above sea level. *Lake Quinsigamond* lies along its western edge. Within its borders is located the world-famous Worcester Foundation for Experimental Biology which has expanded research facilities so that it now employs 355 service personnel and technicians. Working at the laboratory are 79 Ph.D's, and 44 M.D.'s.

When the Lexington alarm was sounded, Shrewsbury responded with 65 men under Capt. Job Cushing, 16 men in Capt. Ross Wyman's Artillery Company and 47 men in Capt. Robert Andrews' Company.

Howe Memorial Library on Main St. contains books and papers of the Artemas Ward family.

At the junction of Route 140 and Main St. is the common where in Colonial days were the stocks and whipping post required by law. The first person sent to these stocks was their manufacturer. His only payment for making them was the remittance of a fine for some previous misconduct.

Artemas Ward Homestead (open free). Ward (1727–1800), first Commander-in-Chief of the Continental Army, later became Chief Justice of the Court of Common Pleas. The estate is owned by Harvard University. The house, largely unaltered, contains the general's desk. It is a two-and-a-half story, gray-shingled building with two front entrances and two red-brick chimneys. Across the street is *Dean Park,* site of the birthplace of Artemas Ward. The park was a gift from Charles A. Dean to the town.

Shrewsbury is a residential suburb of adjacent Worcester.

SHUTESBURY, Franklin County (sett. 1735, incorp. 1761, alt. 1225, pop. 489, area 26.68 sq. mi., routes, US 202, Mass. 9, 122), originally part of a grant called Roadtown, was named for Samuel Shute, onetime Bay Colony governor. Sawmills and agriculture furnished the chief means of livelihood for many years. Basketmaking, one of the earliest industries, still survives and is carried on as a monopoly by the Pratt family.

At the center is the old burying ground in which repose the remains of "Granther Pratt" (1686–1800), a Shutesbury Methuselah who, if tombstones do not lie, actually saw the turning points of three centuries! He is buried in the west cemetery under a white marble shaft bearing the following tribute:

> He was remarkable, cheerful in his disposition and temperate in his habits. He swung a scythe 101 consecutive years and mounted a horse without assistance at the age of 110.

The general store adjoins the *Site of the Birthplace of Ithamar Conkey* (born 1815), who wrote the music for the hymn, "In the Cross of Christ I Glory."

Lake Wyola has excellent fishing, picnicking, boating, swimming.

The village with general store and an inn is becoming popular in the summer. Some old homes are being bought by retired people and commuters.

SIASCONSET (see NANTUCKET)

SNAPPY (see NANTUCKET)

SOMERSET (Bristol County, sett. 1677, incorp. 1790, alt. 60, pop. 18,088, area 7.12 sq. mi., town meeting, routes, US 6, Mass. 103, 138) is known for Rhode Island Jonny Cake (sic), a delectable white cornmeal fritter of soft batter, served with butter or maple syrup.

Jarathmeal Bowers House (1770), South St., is a spacious structure with a hip roof and central chimney.

Henry Bowers, son of the founder of Somerset, purchased and brought home as a slave the son of an African chief. All efforts to tame his free wild spirit failed, and he was shipped to sea. He escaped at Haiti and participated in a successful slave uprising. He became emperor under the name of Toussaint L'Ouverture. In 1802, Napoleon's army overthrew his empire and he died in 1803 in an Alpine dungeon.

Many Somerset residents commute to work in nearby Fall River. Local mills producing apparel, varnish and casting employ less than 200 workers.

SOMERVILLE (Middlesex County, sett. 1630, town incorp. 1842, city incorp. 1871, alt. 50, pop. 88,779, area 3.93 sq. mi., mayor-council, routes, US 1, US 3, Mass. 2A, 16, 138).

Somerville is like the many industrial-residential communities that press upon Boston's borders and which, proud of their own identity, have stood their ground against annexation to Boston. The city is the center of a network of highways reaching all New England.

Part of Charlestown until 1842, Somerville has its own distinct past. Trade traditions dominated early settlers. For the early Somervilleite, there was little concern about his neighbor's conduct and beliefs.

Cambridge and Charlestown bridges to Boston had established the city as an important outpost on the direct route from Boston to the north. The Middlesex Canal (1803) gave impetus to its industrial development. By 1822 the canal was outmoded by turnpikes. By 1835 Somerville was a regular stop on the new Boston and Lowell Railroad.

Somerville, a major Boston suburb, is an important distribution center. Meat packing and food processing are major industries. Paper products, fabricated metal products and machinery are manufactured here.

St. Catherine's Church, 183 Summer St., designed by Maginnis and Walsh and executed in 1892 in gray brick with white marble trim, shows Byzantine and Gothic influences. It has been termed by authorities as one of the most beautiful churches in America.

James Miller Tablet stands at the spot where James Miller, aged 65, was slain by the British retreating from Concord and Lexington, April 19, 1775. "I am too old to run," he said.

Prospect Hill Tablet. The Continental Great Union Flag with 13 stripes and the crosses of Sts. George and Andrew, sometimes referred to as the Grand Union Flag, was raised for the first time on Prospect Hill January 1, 1776. According to some flag historians, this was the first real national flag.

Memorial Tower crowns the fortress site. At the tower base are five small tablets. One reads: "The flower of the British army, prisoners of war who surrendered at Saratoga, were quartered on this hill from November 7, 1777, to October 15, 1778." They numbered about 4000 men, half of whom were Hessians. The winter was very cold, firewood was scarce and hardship was extreme.

Old Powder House. One of the first hostile British acts occurred September 1, 1774. Lobsterbacks raided the local powder stores, taking about 250 kegs. The powder belonged to several area towns. The raid so alarmed local citizens that they organized a watch on all land and water routes to and from Boston. The towns organized a company of 30 men. Paul Revere is said to have been a member.

At Central Hill Park is Augustus Lukeman's *Civil War Monument,* depicting an angel as bodyguard for a marching soldier. Adjoining it, directly in front of the public library, is a simpler *Spanish War Monument,* by Raymond Porter, in which the treatment of both soldier and sailor are markedly realistic. This monument is also one of the few to honor Americans in the Boxer Revolt in China in 1900.

Ploughed Hill is the site of the burning of the Ursuline Convent by an anti-Catholic mob in 1834. Below the hill was a narrow neck of land enclosed on two sides by water in 1775. It was the last hostile territory crossed by the British on their retreat from Concord and Lexington, before they plunged into present-day Charlestown, then held by them.

SOUTH BOSTON (see BOSTON)

SOUTH DEERFIELD (see DEERFIELD)

SOUTH END (see BOSTON)

SOUTH GARDNER (see GARDNER)

SOUTH HADLEY (Hampshire County, sett. *c.* 1659, incorp. *c.* 1753, alt. 257, pop. 17,033, area 17.76 sq. mi., representative town meeting, routes, US 202, Mass. 47, 116) is a farming and college town spread along the Connecticut River. Tree-shaded streets, broad front lawn and well-kept homes mark South Hadley.

The first meetinghouse (1737) took five years to complete. Several times during its construction opposing factions removed the timbers and hid them. The first minister took no notice of his prompt dismissal but kept on praying and preaching. Finally, he was forcibly removed from the pulpit. The deacons stuffed his handkerchief in his mouth so that he could not pray aloud en route to the front door.

Local Indians were peaceful, but memories of French and Catholic Indian raids, like the one which destroyed Deerfield, were never far from mind.

Residents supported the Revolution. In 1774 voters "chuse four men to inspect the District about drinking East India tee."

The post-Revolutionary era found citizens interested in utilizing the river's waterpower. By 1831 South Hadley Falls had a sawmill, gristmill, two paper plants, a tannery and a popular tavern. Today the leading industry is papermaking.

Irish immigration in the 1840's revived farming as newcomers increased food consumption. French-Canadians, Poles and Germans came to work alongside the Irish in the mills.

South Hadley is best known for Mount Holyoke College (1837), one of the country's finest female seminaries and the oldest of seven leading New England women's colleges. Mount Holyoke graduates have founded at least ten colleges. The most notable are Mills College in California founded by Susan Mills (1826–1912) and Madrid's International Institute. In 1969 Mount Holyoke had more than 1600 students. This liberal arts college offers excellent science courses.

Buckland native Mary Lyon (1797–1849), believing higher education was the best way for her sex to improve their station, organized Wheaton Seminary (see Norton) in 1834. She opened Mount Holyoke with 80 students. Cooperative dormitory management undertaken then exists today.

What to See and Do

Skinner Museum (open daily 2–5, free) occupies a small former church across the road from the beautiful Skinner estate (private). An *Historical Museum* is housed in the church, which, without its present spire, was the Congregational meetinghouse of Prescott village. It was purchased and moved to its present site during preparations for flooding Prescott by the waters of the Quabbin Reservoir.

Mount Holyoke College Campus, spreading over a naturally beautiful terrain, includes *Prospect Hill,* an athletic field, tennis courts, ample lawns and farmlands and two small lakes for canoeing, swimming and skating. At the *Pageant Field,* an open-air auditorium, is held the annual May Day Festival.

The lecture halls and dormitories are widely spaced on vivid greensward under fine trees. Outstanding are *Mary Lyon Hall,* which contains the administrative offices, and *Dwight Memorial Art Building* (open), housing a complete collection of the noted engravings of Elbridge Kingsley (1842–1918). *Talcott Arboretum* consists of plant houses, a palm house, a horticultural economics house and a house for aquatics. *Playshop Laboratory* is a small, completely equipped modern experimental theater.

Pass of Thermopylae is a narrow, rock-bound passage through the foot of Mt. Holyoke near the Connecticut River. Early settlers laboriously constructed it by pouring water on the rock in winter and raking away the frozen gravel that split off.

Titan's Piazza, a volcanic bluff of columnar formation, has been classified as one of the world's major natural phenomena. A short distance from this bluff fossil footprints have been found.

Devil's Football is a 300-ton magnetic boulder. Geologists agree that it was carried here from Sunderland or Deerfield during the glacial period. Legend says that Satan kicked it from the Devil's Garden at Amherst Notch several miles away.

JOSEPH ALLEN SKINNER PARK is on the summit of Mt. Holyoke (alt. 995). Superb scenic views. Old hotel on the summit was visited by Swedish singer Jenny Lind, Charles Dickens, Sen. Charles Sumner and Nathaniel Hawthorne. This hotel is the third to stand there. In the first one, the town planned to entertain Lafayette in 1825 with a choice of Jamaica rum, St. Croix rum, Holland gin, brandy, cognac or cherry cordial. Unluckily the marquis was late in his schedule and had to pass directly through the town without pausing for these refreshments. Facilities: hiking, fireplaces, picnic tables, snowmobiling.

SOUTH HARWICH (see HARWICH)

SOUTH LEE (see LEE)

SOUTH LYNNFIELD (see LYNNFIELD)

SOUTH NATICK (see NATICK)

SOUTH TRURO (see TRURO)

SOUTH WELLFLEET (see WELLFLEET)

SOUTH WILLIAMSTOWN (see WILLIAMSTOWN)

SOUTH YARMOUTH (see YARMOUTH)

SOUTHAMPTON (Hampshire County, sett. 1732, incorp. 1775, alt. 230, pop. 3069, area 28.58, town meeting, routes, US 202, Mass. Pike, Mass. 10) was named for Southampton, England. Tanneries, grist- and cider mills, whip factories and blacksmith shops were once important to the town. In the 19th century sawmills and woodworking enterprises used up the timber supply, and today agriculture is the main support of the community.

On a hill behind the *Old Southampton Church* is the *Old Edwards House* (private) where townspeople took refuge during the French and Indian War raids.

A *Monument* to the 104th Infantry of the 26th (Yankee) Division, recruited here in 1917, bears a bas-relief showing the presentation of the regiment's citation in France, April 26, 1918, for bravery.

SOUTHBOROUGH (Worcester County, sett. 1660, incorp. 1727, alt. 550, pop. 5798, area 13.78 sq. mi., town meeting, routes, Mass. 9, 30, 85). Richard Newton and his family formed the nucleus of the community. When there were about 50 families here, the area was separated from Marlborough and incorporated.

The town was concerned with farming, but 19th-century mills produced boots, shoes, and cotton and woolen goods. Factories disappeared. When the Metropolitan Water Commission took over 1200 acres of land and Stony Brook became a metropolitan aqueduct, the last mill was abandoned. Remaining acreage is devoted to milk or fruit production. Thousands of pine trees planted on the watershed add beauty as well as revenue to the district.

St. Mark's Episcopal Church is a beautiful edifice of multicolored stone with a slate roof.

SOUTHBRIDGE (Worcester County, sett. 1730, incorp. 1816, alt. 500, pop. 17,057, area 20.38 sq. mi., town meeting, routes, Mass. 93, 131) is a manufacturing community lying in a valley where many inhabitants are French-Canadians. Some maintain their native customs and language. The first factory was built to make cotton yarns but changed to wool.

American Optical Company (open by permission) is the most important business in the town. In the building is a *Museum* (open) in connection with the laboratories where Dr. Edgar Tillyer, an outstanding optical expert in the country, carried on his experiments.

SOUTHFIELD (see NEW MARLBOROUGH)

SOUTHWICK (Hampden County, sett. 1770, incorp. 1775, pop. 6330, town meeting, routes, Mass. 10, 57) was named after an English village. Chief products are tobacco and potatoes. During the winter ice was once harvested in large quantities in the Congamond Lakes. Near *Sodom Mountain* (alt. 1126) a rocky ledge rises abruptly from the roadside. This beautiful gorge is worth visiting.

SPENCER (Worcester County, sett. 1721, incorp. 1775, alt. 925, pop. 8779, area 33.15 sq. mi., town meeting, route, Mass. 9), named for Lieutenant Governor Spencer Phipps, instrumental in securing the town's district status, has been a manufacturing town since 1810. Josiah and Nathaniel Green began making shoes sewed with thread. Specialized hardware and brooms are current industries.

Richard Sugden Public Library, Pleasant St., houses the *Spencer Museum* (1874) of Indian relics and historical objects.

Elias Howe (1819–67), who first patented the lockstitch sewing machine, was a Spencer native.

SPENCER STATE FOREST. Facilities: fishing, hunting, fireplaces, picnic tables, swimming, snowmobiling, scenic views.

Public hunting in *Moose Hill* and *Four Chimneys Wildlife Management Areas.*

SPRUCE CORNER (see ASHFIELD)

SPRINGFIELD (Hampden County, sett. 1636, town incorp. 1641, city incorp. 1852, alt. 100, pop. 163,905, area 31.70 sq. mi., mayor-council, routes, I–91, US 5, 20, Mass. 21, 116).

Springfield, for nearly two centuries synonymous with the standard U.S. Army service rifle, is a western Massachusetts city along the Connecticut River. Strategically located for New England's western trade, the city is situated on terraces and gently-rolling slopes. Tree-shaded lawns, parks and boulevards produce an air of substance, dignity and comfort. Diversified industries, excellent highways, rail and plane facilities, large stores and fine residential areas make it an important industrial and commercial center. Fine museums, libraries and musical activities make it a major Connecticut Valley cultural center.

History

In 1636 a dozen families came to the inviting valley where the Agawam River joins the Connecticut River. Indians forced them to move across the river after livestock seriously damaged the Indians' cornfields.

Settlers led by William Pynchon vigorously built up the new colony. Pynchon's leadership was not questioned until he published a theological tract, *The Meritorious Price of our Redemption,* in 1650. The Puritan leaders felt the book contained germs of heresy. His notable services were forgotten as he was badgered by all groups. He returned to England and his son John administered the settlement.

Springfield now switched to witch hunting. Hugh Parsons' choleric temperament did not endear him to his neighbors. His wife had periodic fits, but these explanations of their eccentricities were too simple. They must be bewitched. Local savants charged them with witchcraft. Many people were disappointed when they were acquitted.

Twenty peaceful, constructive years followed. In 1675 King Philip declared war on all New England whites. Springfield was almost destroyed by fire. Townspeople rebuilt the town on a larger scale.

During the 1700's Springfield residents took their first step away from an agricultural economy by building grist- and sawmills along the river. Large clay deposits were used to make bricks.

The Revolutionary War created an acute depression. Farmers and mill owners were bogged in debt. After the war thousands joined Daniel Shays in his rebellion against the highhanded fiscal policies of eastern Bay State politicians and legislators. Shays and his men tramped western Massachusetts for six months in an attempt to prevent courts from convening where unfair judges would enter biased judgments against debtors. Their cause won numerous sympathizers, but it failed.

Metal goods manufacture was given an impetus in 1794 when Congress established the U.S. Armory at Springfield. The advent of the railroad, about 1835, stimulated business. The town then had 73 mechanic shops, 6 cotton mills, 4 printing offices, 13 warehouses, 2 card factories, 2 forges, 1 rifle factory, 1 powder mill, 6 sawmills, 4 gristmills, 3 tanneries, 2 jewelers' tool factories, 1 sword factory and 1 spool factory.

Textile manufacture brought French-Canadians, English and Scots. Irish, Italian, Swedish and German labor was plentiful. Long hours and meager wages were the lot of those whose work enriched the town. But aside from the general agitation that accompanied the crisis of 1830, there was no effective labor organization until after the Civil War.

In 1824 the *Springfield Republican* was founded by Samuel Bowles. This journal, under the liberal editorship of Dr. J. G. Holland, became almost a national institution. The first Springfield newspaper, the *Massachusetts Gazette and General Advertiser,* published in 1782, failed to survive. *Hampshire Chronicle, Hampshire Herald* and the *Federal* and *Spy* were published in this era.

In 1847 John Brown (1800–1859) opened Brown and Perkins, wool merchants. Business prospered, but Brown was often absent on "Kansas business."

Industry

An expanding postwar market aided Springfield's prosperity. Factories were enlarged. The population swelled. Labor took its first organized steps toward improving working conditions. In 1861 horsecar drivers established a benevolent association, which was forced by a threatened wage reduction to transform itself into a trade union. Workers began a united battle for the eight-hour day. Cigar makers, stonecutters, blacksmiths, carpenters and tailors organized to secure higher wages and shorter hours. The legislature investigated. Eventually the eight-hour day became a reality. In the later 1880's all city trade unions formed the Central Labor Union.

Since 1890, such large industries have been established as the Van

Norman Tool and Machine Company, the United States Envelope Company, the Fiberloid Company, the Westinghouse Electric and Manufacturing Company and the Milton Bradley Company, makers of toys, games and school supplies. On the West Springfield side of the river numerous industries have located. Radios and hot-water and air-conditioning equipment are made here.

Between 1910 and 1920 the population increased 117 percent. The largest racial group is the Irish. There are Italians, Russians, French-Canadians and Poles. Scotland, England, Sweden and Germany contribute to the foreign-born population.

The high percentage of skilled workers has been a strong influence in the social and political life of the city. The general housing situation is better in Springfield than in most industrial cities of its size. Civic life is heightened by the social clubs, singing societies and physical culture centers of the various racial groups.

The 1927 flood caused considerable loss, but it can hardly be compared to the catastrophe of 1936, when New England's worst flood inflicted untold suffering on Springfield and caused property losses amounting to millions of dollars. Efficient organization, prompt action and heroism prevented a larger loss of life.

What to See and Do

Benton Small Arms Museum (open Tues.–Sat. 1–4), Springfield Armory. One of the world's finest martial arms collections. Weapons, many developed and made in the Springfield Armory, show evolution from the Revolutionary War flintlock musket through the current U.S. service rifle — M14. The fate of this fine museum has not yet been determined. Springfield Armory was "phased out" in 1968.

Museum Center is a very sensible arrangement in which the city's major art and science museums are located around a quadrangle at Chestnut and State Streets.

George Walter Vincent Smith Art Museum (open Tues.–Sat. 1–5, Sun. except July 2–5, closed Aug., free) has a magnificent collection of bronzes, jade, porcelain and tapestries.

Museum of Fine Arts (open as above) has one of this country's finest collections of American, European and Far Eastern paintings and sculpture.

Connecticut Valley Historical Society Museum (open as above), William Pynchon Memorial Building, has several period rooms including a 1690–1720 kitchen and a 1750 bedroom. Many regional historical items.

Springfield Science Museum (open as above) includes Kirkham Aquarium. Excellent plant, animal and geological exhibits.

Planetarium (open Tues., Thurs. 3, Sat. 2–3, Tues. 8:30 P.M., special programs are held Sun. at 2:30 and 4, closed Aug.), Science Museum bldg.

Old First Church (open daily) Court Sq., congregation was organized in 1637. Present church, built in 1819, has one of three weathercocks made in England. Isaac Damon was the architect.

FOREST PARK (open daily 8 A.M.–9 P.M.), off US 5 along southern perimeter, is a 750-acre city park of unusual beauty. Facilities: picnicking, boating, bowling, baseball, tennis.

FOREST PARK ZOO (open daily 11–4:30).

City Library (open weekdays 9 A.M.–9 P.M., Sun. 2–6) was built in 1912 from Vermont marble in Italian Renaissance style. Architect Edward L. Tilton (1861–1933) was a leading U.S. library designer.

Hampden County Courthouse (1871) was designed after H. H. Richardson, but 1906 and subsequent remodeling destroyed most Richardsonian elements.

Springfield Cemetery has Augustus Saint-Gaudens' bronze relief of the *Springfield Republican's* first editor, Josiah G. Holland (1819–81).

SPRINGFIELD-CHICOPEE-HOLYOKE METROPOLITAN AREA (pop. 523,029, area 426.75 sq. mi.) includes the cities of Chicopee, Holyoke, Northampton, Springfield, Westfield. Towns include Agawam, East Longmeadow, Ludlow, Monson, Palmer, South Hadley, Warren, West Springfield, Wilbraham and Somers, Ct. Area and population figures exclude Somers.

STERLING (Worcester County, sett. 1720 (as Chicksett), incorp. 1781, alt. 505, pop. 4247, area 30.52 sq. mi., town meeting, routes, Mass. 12, 62, 110, 140) was named for Lord Stirling (William Alexander), Scottish Peer and American Revolutionary War hero. The chief industry in former years was chair making. Chairs were shipped to the West Indies and to southern states. Clocks, hats, shirts, patterns, pottery, cider, vinegar, textiles, tannery products and emery wheels were made here. In 1828 Silas Lamson patented crooked scythe snaths and started a business still carried on in Shelburne Falls. During the Civil War, natives Silas and Lucian Stuart invented a machine to make sewing-machine needles. The first standardized paper patterns for dressmaking were designed in 1863 by tailor Ebenezer Butterick. Shirt patterns met with such instant success that patterns for children's and women's clothes were added. Butterick Patterns and *The Delineator,* a woman's magazine, developed from this invention.

The town is agricultural, and fruit growing predominates, but new residential areas are being developed.

Mary Sawyer House is said to be the home of Mary's Little Lamb. Mary and her father found two newborn lambs in the barn. One was so weak that Mary took it into the house and cared for it. The pet lamb followed Mary about the farm. One day she followed Mary to school and hid beneath her desk. When Mary was called to the front for spelling class, the lamb followed her sedately down the aisle, to the amusement of the pupils, if not the teacher. The poem about Mary and her lamb was the first rhyme recorded by a phonograph. When the first record was made, Edison was asked to "say something" into the machine. The first words that came to him were the verses of "Mary Had a Little Lamb," written by John Roulstone, a young man residing in the home of his uncle, Rev. Lemuel Capen, at the time Mary was attending the old Redstone Hill School. Although there have been other claimants for the now famous lamb, and for writing the verses, research from reliable sources has substantiated Sterling's claim for this honor.

The schoolhouse was dismantled in 1856, and the lumber sold as well as the desks and chairs. Many years later, Henry Ford obtained the original lumber and reconstructed the schoolhouse at South Sudbury.

Noted native sons and/or Sterling residents include Prentice Mellen (1764–1840), U.S. Senator and first Chief Justice of the Supreme Court of Maine. Robert Bailey Thomas (1766–1846) moved early to that part of the "old Shrewsbury Leg" which later became Sterling and which is now a part of West Boylston. While in Sterling he was a teacher, Justice of the Peace, operated a book bindery and printed the first "Old Farmer's Almanac" in his father's home. Fred Herbert Colvin (1867–1965), born in Sterling, was an engineer, inventor, poet and author of more than 60 other works including *American Machinists Handbook, Aircraft Handbook* and an autobiography, *Sixty Years with Men and Machines.* Editor of the *American Machinist* for 30 years. Chief Justice Arthur Prentice Rugg (1862–1938) was the fifteenth Chief Justice of the Mass. Supreme Court and served in that capacity for about 27 years. Rugg was a dedicated researcher of historical items pertaining to the town. The Sterling Historical Society is privileged to own his personal scrapbooks containing valuable records of the town's history.

STOCKBRIDGE (Berkshire County, sett. 1734, incorp. 1739, alt. 840, pop. 2312, area 22.84 sq. mi., town meeting, routes, US 7, Mass. 102, 183), named after an English village, occupies a grant made by the General Court in 1734 to establish an Indian mission. Land was set apart for four white families. Stockbridge was the home of the Mukhekanews ("People of the Ever Flowing Waters") of the Algonkin family.

In 1745 a gristmill was established to grind the Indians' corn. White-Indian relations were disturbed in 1755, and 20 years later the Indians moved to less settled western New York State.

Grouped about the village green are the *First Congregational Church,* the *Old Town Hall* and the impressive *Field Chime Tower.* The latter is a memorial to preacher David Dudley Field (1781–1867), father of lawyer David Dudley Field, Jr., noted for his work to secure legal reforms, and of United States Supreme Court Associate Justice Stephen Field. Cyrus Field, promoter of the first Atlantic cable, was another son. Near the green stands the *Jonathan Edwards Monument,* dedicated to the noted parson who once taught in the Stockbridge Mission School.

The Berkshire Playhouse (open in summer) has a fine apprentice program and offers some of the best summer theatre in the country.

Stockbridge Mission House (open May 15–Nov. 1, weekdays 10–6, Sun. 2–6, small fee) is 0.3 mi. w. of the center on Mass. 102. This house (1739) was built by the Rev. John Sergeant, first missionary to the Indians. Parson Jonathan Edwards (1703–54), the noted Calvinist clergyman whose Northampton sermons and writings touched off the "Great Awakening" that swept northeastern America, came here as a missionary in 1751 after he had been forced out of his Northampton pulpit.

The *Mission House* with the adjacent buildings constitutes a restoration of an early Colonial village.

Ice Glen is a wild, lovely gorge containing ice in its deeper crevices the year round. A trail to this point and to *Laurel Hill,* a knoll, branches from the high school grounds.

Naumkeag Gardens (open May 1–Sept. 4, daily except Mon. 10–5:30, Sept. 5–Oct. 1, Sat. and Sun. 10–4, separate fee for house and garden tours), Prospect St., 1 mi. north of US 7 and Mass. 102 junction. The house and grounds were the estate of the late Joseph Choate (1832–1917), U.S. ambassador to England. House furnishings are Victorian. The gardens are formal.

Indian Burial Ground, off Main St., has an interesting obelisk.

Stockbridge Library (open 10–5, closed Thurs., Sun.), US 7, has Indian relics, Jonathan Edwards table and Cyrus W. Field relics.

STONEHAM (Middlesex County, sett. 1645, incorp. 1725, alt. 109, pop. 20,725, area 6.04 sq. mi., town meeting, routes, I–93, Mass. 28, 128), settled as part of Charlestown, developed small industries like shoemaking in private homes. Stoneham is a residential Boston suburb. Local industries employ less than 1000 workers. Products include shoes, artificial leather, electronic equipment, jet engine parts, plastics and computers.

On the corner of Central and Pleasant Sts. stands the first *Town House* (1826). In 1833 it was moved by 40 yoke of oxen to its present site. In the late 1960's the house, which has been in the possession of the Bryant-McCarthy families for more than a century, was occupied by Mrs. Edith McCarthy, mother of longtime town clerk Winthrop A. McCarthy.

Bear Hill (alt. 280) was visited in 1632 by Gov. Winthrop and an exploring party, who ate a meal on a rock near its base. They dubbed it *Cheese Rock* because they discovered that the governor's aide had supplied them with cheese but no bread. From the *Observatory Tower* on a clear day there is a wide view, including the Atlantic.

MIDDLESEX FELLS RESERVATION RECREATION AREA: 2036 acres of meadows and woodland patrolled by MDC mounted police, zoo, foot and bridle trails, freshwater fishing, picnic sites, observation tower, swimming pool, natural and artificial ice skating. For details see Middlesex Fells Reservation.

MIDDLESEX FELLS ZOO (open year-round, daytime), Pond St., off Mass. 28. More than 25 acres of zoological displays including moated and glass fronted exhibits of live animals like bears, elephants, lions, monkeys, penguins, seals, tigers and waterfowl. Superb walk through the aviary, with rare and colorful tropical birds among tropical plants. Phone: 438–3662.

STOUGHTON (Norfolk County, sett. *c.* 1713, incorp. 1726, alt. 232, pop. 23,459, area 16.25 sq. mi., representative town meeting, routes, Mass. 24, 27, 138, 139) was named for Lieutenant Governor William Stoughton (1630–1701), whose father, Col. Israel Stoughton, led Colonial forces during the 1636 Pequot War. William was a large landholder in Dorchester, of which Stoughton was originally a part. During the Revolution, Stoughton supplied Colonial forces in the area. By 1830, shoe manufacturing had begun, but the Civil War, depriving the town of its large southern markets, threatened prosperity.

Principal Stoughton products made by 40 firms with 1900 workers include rubber goods, textiles and leather products.

STOW (Middlesex County, sett. 1669, incorp. 1683, alt. 231, pop. 3984, area 17.68 sq. mi., town meeting, routes, Mass. 62, 117), named for John Stow, friend of Gov. Simon Bradstreet, was raided during King Philip's War. Raising hops, silkworm culture, milling and minor manufacturing have been engaged in temporarily.

Stow was on the main Boston-Albany highway. Several taverns were located here. It was the first night's stop for freight teams bound west out of Boston.

Henry Gardner, the state's first treasurer, lived here. Paul Revere's midnight ride partner Dr. Samuel Prescott (1751–77) ended his less famous ride here.

STURBRIDGE (Worcester County, sett. *c.* 1729, incorp. 1738, alt. 620, pop. 4878, area 37.39 sq. mi., town meeting, routes, US 20, Mass. Pike, 15, 131) is best known as the site of Sturbridge Village.

The town was visited by Englishmen as early as 1633 but not settled for nearly a century. Dairying, sheep raising and orchard culture were the main occupations until the waterpower attracted tanneries, shoe, cotton and auger and bit mills.

On the edge of the common is the *Hyde Library* with a copper dome and semicircular entrance. Here are Indian relics collected by Levi B. Chase. Opposite is the *Old Cemetery,* enclosed by a stone wall that was built by four companies of Revolutionary soldiers from Sturbridge — each company building one side.

Old Sturbridge Village is at the junction of Mass. 15 and 20 with the Mass. Pike I–90. Summer schedule: April–Nov. 9:30–5:30 every day. Winter schedule: Dec.–March, guided tours at 10 and 2. No guides needed Sat. and Sun. when open all day. Fee. This is a museum of living history. Here is a reconstruction of an early 19th-century New England village complete with houses, tavern, blacksmith shop, gun shop, meetinghouse, pillory and stocks. Native craftsmen recreate and demonstrate printing, pottery making, weaving, tinsmithing, cooking, herb gardening, candle dipping and other nearly lost household arts and crafts. The houses and public buildings are originals which were bought in New England, carefully numbered piece by piece, taken down, moved here and carefully re-erected. The covered bridge came from Vermont. Animals found in the New England of 150 years ago are here, too. Horses hauling a carryall tote passengers. Photographers can shoot the wandering oxcart. There are geese in the millpond. Bring your camera and stay all day.

Publick House, a Treadway-operated inn, is noted for its superb Yankee "vittles." It's best to make reservations, even for meals, in advance. Try the Indian Pudding.

Many Old Sturbridge Village visitors bring a picnic lunch and eat at one of the village's many picnic sites or they lunch in the *Old Tavern* on the green. They dine in the evening at the *Governor Lincoln House* near the Old Village entrance.

WELLS STATE PARK'S facilities include swimming, fishing, hiking, snowmobiling, scenic views, campsites (50).

SUDBURY (Middlesex County, sett. 1638, incorp. 1639, alt. 200, pop. 13,506, area 24.37 sq. mi., town meeting, routes, US 20, Mass. 20, 27, 117).

Sudbury, a pleasant country town, was granted in 1637 to Watertown residents, but most early settlers came direct from England. Their names appear on the ship *Confidence*'s list. She sailed from Southampton, April 24, 1638.

Sudbury is the only town in history to win a Pulitzer Prize for history; the 1964 prize was awarded to Sumner Chilton Powell for his *Puritan Village: The Formation of a New England Town.* Small Sudbury is the only Massachusetts town with three weekly newspapers.

Sudbury, at the outbreak of the Revolution, had 2160 inhabitants. About 500 saw war service. Sudbury officers included a brigadier general, colonels, majors, adjutants, surgeons, 24 captains and 29 lieutenants. In the 19th century, Sudbury lost territory to new towns. Industries died and were not replaced until recently. Many commuters live here.

Wayside Inn, Wayside Rd. (0.3 mi. north of US 20 and a short distance from Mass. Pike — Exit 12 or 13), gained fame from Longfellow's *Tales of a Wayside Inn* (1863). The inn, now a museum and inn-restaurant, was purchased by Henry Ford, who added a two-story wing on the north end.

He furnished it with simple authentic furniture and added historical items. Two serious fires, the last in 1965, damaged but did not destroy the original building.

Noted guests have been entertained here: Generals Washington, Lafayette and Henry Knox, Presidents Coolidge and Kennedy, Thomas Edison and Harvey Firestone. Longfellow visited here only twice. The friends he represents as swapping stories were never all here at once.

Museum (open 8 A.M.–midnight, small fee). *Restaurant* (open 7:30 A.M.–midnight). Excellent food. Small number of rooms available.

Redstone Schoolhouse (*Wayside Inn Grounds*), a small, red frame building set in a grove of pines. A tablet on a huge boulder says the schoolhouse was immortalized in "Mary Had a Little Lamb" (see Sterling). *Gristmill* (open) is a three-story, native fieldstone structure with a gable roof. The great water wheel daily grinds corn and other grains sold to visitors.

Goodnow Library (1863), Concord Rd., has books, old manuscripts and diaries.

Israel Brown House (private), Concord Rd., was built in 1725. Prior to the Civil War, it was an Underground Railroad station for slaves escaping to Canada. Brown used a stake wagon with a false bottom to carry refugees to Lancaster; though suspected and often stopped, he was never held. The house is a three-story hip roof building. Slaves were secreted in a portion of the cellar reached from a trap door near the fireplace.

Wadsworth Monument (0.5 mi. off Concord Rd.) is a granite shaft (1852). When Marlborough was fired by the Indians in March 1676, Lieutenant Curtis of Sudbury led a surprise night attack. Indian leader Metus was killed. A month later Capt. Wadsworth of Milton, marching to Sudbury, was ambushed near Green Hill. King Philip routed the Colonials by setting fire to the woods. Only 14 Americans escaped. Capt. Wadsworth and 28 men were killed. They are buried beneath this monument.

Goulding House (private), Concord Rd., is a restored two-story, center chimney dwelling built about 1690. Massive exposed beams display the fine flooring above. Wrought iron hardware and large brick fireplaces indicate the age of the house.

PANTRY BROOK WILDLIFE MANAGEMENT AREA (see CONCORD).

SUFFOLK COUNTY (estab. 1643, pop. 735,190, area 52.50 sq. mi., shire town, Boston) includes the cities of Boston, Chelsea and Revere and the town of Winthrop.

SUNDERLAND (Franklin County, sett. *c.* 1713, incorp. 1718, alt. 142, pop. 2236, area 14.36 sq. mi., town meeting, routes, Mass. 47, 116), granted to Hadley inhabitants in 1673, was abandoned during King Philip's War. Forty years later, the land, known as Swampfield, was granted anew to 40 proprietors.

Early industries included potash, hat, saddle and brickmaking and the home manufacture of covered buttons and braided palm-leaf hats. Tobacco, potatoes, cucumbers and carrots are current crops.

SUTTON (Worcester County, sett. 1716, incorp. 1718, alt. 706, pop. 4590, area 32.48 sq. mi., town meeting, routes, Mass. 122A, 146). Land was purchased from the Indians in 1704 by Boston residents. Because of the rich soil, settlement progressed rapidly. Textile factories and a paper mill were established about 1800. Industrial activity declined when railroads ignored the town. Small factories now produce chemicals and textiles. Fruit growing, dairying and market gardening are profitable enterprises.

First Congregational Church (organized in 1719), on the village green, has a beautiful Wren-type spire and a graceful green-shuttered fan window over the entrance. The building was erected in 1813.

On the *Site of the Birthplace* (1738) *of Gen. Rufus Putnam* stands the present house of brick with marble trim, built in 1818. Gen. Putnam planned the fortification of Dorchester Heights and was made chief engineer of the new army. In 1779 he assisted Israel Putnam in completing the defenses of West Point. His crowning achievement, however, was one of peace: he was a founder of the Ohio Company and superintended the settlement of Marietta, Ohio.

PURGATORY CHASM STATE RESERVATION (188 acres) is a quarter-mile-long chasm averaging 50–70 ft. deep and about 40 ft. wide. Picnic sites.

SWAMPSCOTT (Essex County, sett. 1629, incorp. 1852, alt. 50, pop. 13,578, area 3.07 sq. mi., representative town meeting, routes, US 1A, Mass. 129).

Swampscott, a summer resort and Boston suburb, was settled as an outpost of Saugus. The first white settler was Francis Ingalls, who erected a tannery in 1632.

The spot was noted for its fine fishing; lobsters were picked up at low tide, and the sunken ledges offshore teemed with cod. Beaches offered a convenient place to land catches. Frozen cod used to be stacked like cordwood near where the Swampscott Club now stands. Although there was a ready sale for fish and farmers from inland drove their wagons to Swampscott to trade geese, eggs, butter and cheese for the yield of the sea, the fishermen were poor.

By the time Mary Baker Eddy, founder of Christian Science, began her demonstrations of healing in 1866, the metamorphosis from poverty-stricken fishing village to luxurious resort was well under way. In 1815 "Farmer" Phillips had taken in the first summer boarders. A few years later "Aunt Betsey" Blaney got the scandalous price of $3 a week for room and board. The first summer hotel was built in 1835. When the farmer owning the land adjoining was offered $400 an acre for it, he ran to get the deed before the "city man" should come to his senses.

Mary Baker Eddy Historical House (open weekdays 10–5, small fee), 23 Paradise Road. Operated by the Longyear Foundation, Brookline.

SWANSEA (Bristol County, sett. 1667, incorp. 1785, alt. 42, pop. 12,640, area 22.12 sq. mi., town meeting, routes, I–95, US 6, Mass. 103, 118) was part of Old Rehoboth until the Baptists in 1667 under Obadiah Holmes, who had settled in Rehoboth in 1649, created a separate town. First blood was shed here (1675) in King Philip's War. The town was a rallying place for troops. Shipbuilding played an important part in Swansea's growth. The town is essentially agricultural. Small mills produce castings, dyes and window shades.

The *Cape Codder,* a house near Gray's corner, is about 250 years old. Although modernized, it still retains its original mammoth central chimney and traces of its early architectural lines. It was once the town hall.

SWIFT RIVER (see CUMMINGTON)

TAUNTON (Bristol County, sett. 1638, town incorp. 1639, city incorp. 1864, alt. 43, pop. 43,756, area 47.29 sq. mi., mayor-council, routes, US 44, Mass. 138, 140).

About the elm-fringed green is concentrated Taunton's business and civic life; but the city stretches out in fertile acres, broken by rocky outcrops and dotted by quiet residential sections and factories. Areawise, Taunton is the largest Bay State city. Its manufactures include textile machinery and products (curtains, dresses, uniforms), machine drills and tools, marine engines, plastics, electrical specialties, minor hardware, Britannia metalware and pewter ware, ceramic products and leather products. But it has plenty of elbow room, and that is why despite its busy manufactures the city has an air of tranquil leisure.

The fabulous annual April herring runs, when the fish swarm up the Cohannet and Taunton Rivers to spawn, attracted many colonists. When mills polluted the river the herring runs diminished—a cause of bitter controversy between fishermen and mill operators.

In 1652 Taunton built an ironworks. Quincy and Braintree works had failed. Bar iron and ironware manufacture was a longtime principal industry. During King Philip's War, when there were few Bank of England notes in circulation and no paper money had been issued by Massachusetts, Taunton bar iron was an accepted medium of exchange.

In 1684 townsfolk answered Gov. Andros' demand for poll and property taxes, saying they did not "feel free to raise money on the inhabitants without their own assent in assembly." For transmitting this message the town clerk was fined twenty marks and jailed three months. Townsmen presented him with 100 acres.

In October 1774, a Liberty Pole, 112 feet tall, was erected on the green. It bore a Union Jack lettered with the words "Liberty and Union; Union and Liberty"; and nailed to the pole was a bold declaration of the rights of the colonists as free and independent people.

In 1699 the building of the first shipyard on the Taunton River launched the city on its way to fame as an inland port. A lively coastal trade was soon built up. Small sloops and shallops of ten and twenty tons, laden with brick, hollowware and iron, sailed along the river to Providence, Newport and New York. In 1799 16 coastal vessels freighted out 3,000,000 bricks, 800 tons of ironware and 700 tons of nails. By the first decade of the 19th century the name *Taunton* was painted on the sterns of more coastal ships than that of any other New England town. The first multimasted schooners along the coast were Taunton-built and owned.

Industries established between 1800–50 include iron, bricks, cotton, paper and boxboards. The Taunton Manufacturing Company, organized in 1823, rolled copper and iron and produced cotton and wool. Reed and Barton founded a silver plate factory in 1824. Isaac Babbitt, the inventor of Babbitt metal, together with John Crossman, first produced the pewter-like Britannia ware in 1824. The Taunton Locomotive Company was one of the first, if not the first, firm to make steamcar engines in New England. The Glenwood Range Company, one of the largest stove makers in the country, began operations in 1879. The Rogers Silverware Company was incorporated in 1883.

General Cobb Boulder, Taunton Green. In September 1786, armed men sympathizing with Shays' Rebellion demanded that the court session not be held. Reactionary Cobb appeared on the courthouse steps shouting, "I will hold this court if I hold it in blood; I will sit as a judge or die as a general." The crowd dispersed but reassembled to prevent the October court session from opening. Cobb met them with a cannon-armed squad and declared, "If you want those papers, come and take them; but pass that line and I fire. The blood will be on your head." This was the last instance of armed resistance in Bristol County.

Old Colony Historical Society Museum (open Mon.–Fri. 10–12, 2–4, Sat. 10–12, closed Sun. and holidays, small fee), 66 Church Green, occupies the Old Bristol Academy Building (1852) designed by New York architect Richard Upjohn. The academy was known throughout the country for its high standards. The cannon used by Cobb's counterrevolutionists to disperse Shays' supporters is here. There is a good collection of local historical items: swords, firearms, uniforms, portraits, military equipage.

Robert Treat Paine Statue, Summer St. Bostonian Paine signed the Declaration of Independence. He moved to Taunton and married Sally Cobb of Attleboro. He was a member of the Massachusetts General Court (1773–78) and a delegate to the Continental Congress in Philadelphia.

MASSASOIT STATE PARK (off Mass. 18, 44, 79, 28, 24). Facilities: swimming, fishing, campsites (130), hunting, snowmobiling.

WATSON POND STATE PARK lies close to Taunton. Facilities: fireplaces, picnic tables, swimming.

TEMPLETON (Worcester County, sett. 1751, incorp. 1762, alt. 1141, pop. 5863, area 31.49 sq. mi., town meeting, routes, US 202, Mass. 2, 68, 101). Abundant waterpower enabled early settlers to start a sawmill, then a corn mill and finally factories producing lumber, chairs, furniture and other products.

BALDWINSVILLE, Templeton's main village, was named for Deacon Jonathan Baldwin, who was responsible for early manufacturing.

When the *First Baptist Church* was moved to its present site, the removal process lasted several days. On Saturday night the structure straddled the railroad tracks. Because the congregation banned Sabbath labor, the railroad schedule had to be canceled for that day.

Baldwinsville Cottages (1882) for crippled and handicapped children was a pioneer institution in giving the best possible care and training to unfortunate children.

Templeton mills produce textiles, printed matter, paper and allied products, plywood, gypsum and miscellaneous items. Six furniture factories employ six out of ten Templeton workers.

BIRCH HILL WILDLIFE MANAGEMENT AREA has public hunting in Royalston, Winchendon, and Templeton.

TEWKSBURY (Middlesex County, sett. 1637, incorp. 1734, alt. 120, pop. 22,755, area 20.70 sq. mi., town meeting, routes, Mass. 38, 133) was probably named for Tewksbury, England. The original proprietors laid out bridle paths (then called bridal paths) in order to attend church; many of the present roads follow the crooked old lanes.

The *Reverend Sampson Spaulding Homestead* (private) (1735), East St., is a good example of Colonial Georgian architecture, has two-and-a-half stories and stands in attractive surroundings.

TISBURY (Dukes County, alt. 80, pop. 2257, area 17.80 sq. mi., incorp. 1671, town meeting, routes, unnumbered island highways and streets) has a similar history to Edgartown. Both towns were settled the same day. Tisbury was a notable whaling port during the late 18th and early 19th centuries. Fishing was another longtime occupation. Today, summer residents with private homes, together with tourists, provide the town's economic base.

Island Transport Company provides bus service to and from Tisbury to all other Martha's Vineyard villages. Scheduled air service to Boston and New York City is available at Martha's Vineyard Airport in Tisbury. Tisbury and Oak Bluffs are the only two Dukes County towns with planning boards and zoning bylaws.

TOLLAND (Hampden County, sett. *c.* 1750, incorp. 1810, alt. 1520, pop. 172, area 31.93 sq. mi., town meeting, routes, Mass. 8, 57), named for a town in Wales, has always been an agricultural community. Cattle raising and dairying are the chief occupations. An attempt to grow tobacco was not commercially successful.

A foot trail leads by Noyes Pond to Noyes Mountain (alt. 1700), 3.5 mi. From the *Fire Tower* at the summit a striking view is obtained.

About two thirds of Tolland's total acreage is under controlled development as tree farms, timber stands, etc.

TOLLAND OTIS STATE FOREST is located on Otis Reservoir. Facilities: boating, bridle trails, fishing, hunting, fireplaces, picnic tables, campsites (88), swimming, snowmobiling.

TOPSFIELD (Essex County, sett. *c.* 1635, incorp. 1648, alt. 63, pop. 5225, area 12.80 sq. mi., town meeting, routes, US 1, Mass. 26, 97) has a delightful village green. The *Public Library* contains murals by its architect Harold Kellogg. Topsfield was a Colonial era boomtown. By 1648 bog iron mined here was smelted in the Boxford Iron Works. Farming became and remained the town's mainstay until the first half of this century. The town is now a residential community.

The *Parson Capen House* (open May 15–Oct. 15, weekdays except Mon. 10–4:30, Sun. 12–5, also by appointment, small fee), built in 1683, is an outstanding example of the medieval tradition that dominated 17th-century Colonial architecture. This house has the massive central chimney, overhang and lean-to. The second story overhang is in front while the third or attic story overhang is in the rear. The lean-to is somewhat unusual in that it was built as part of the original house. The kitchen has been reproduced in the American Wing of New York's Metropolitan Museum.

Period furnishings include a chair-table, wooden trough, wooden plates and mugs. The brick oven is within a fireplace that is eight feet, six inches wide.

Pine Grove Burying Ground—stones date back to 1663—contains the graves of Vermonter Joseph Smith's (1805–44) ancestors. He founded the Mormon Church.

The annual *Topsfield County Fair,* held each September, features pari-mutuel racing, agricultural, horticultural and animal husbandry displays and exhibits.

BRADLEY W. PALMER STATE PARK (720 acres). The Ipswich River, a fair trout stream, flows through the park. Facilities: 35 miles of bridle trails, 4-mile steeplechase, fishing, hiking, fireplaces, picnic tables.

IPSWICH RIVER WILDLIFE SANCTUARY, Perkins Row off Mass. 97 (2300 acres), is the Massachusetts Audubon Society's largest sanctuary and one of the state's largest arboretums. Noted for wide variety of trees and shrubs. Natural history day camp. The tract was purchased by the society in 1951.

TOWNSEND (Middlesex County, sett. 1676, incorp. 1732, alt. 310, pop. 4281, area 32.66 sq. mi., town meeting, routes, Mass. 13, 119), was named for Charles Townshend, English Secretary of State until 1730 and opponent of the Tories. In 1733 gristmills and sawmills were erected. Cooperage plants utilized local timber.

Near Spaulding Memorial High School, Main St., is an *Octagonal Brick House* (private), a type of architecture conspicuous in homogeneous Massachusetts.

Townsend Harbor (alt. 270) is on the Squannacook River. Right of the center, on the riverbank, is *Spaulding's Gristmill* (open).

Conant House (open July–Oct., Mon., Wed., Fri. 2–4, and by appointment), across the river, was erected about 1744 and later enlarged for a tavern.

WEST TOWNSEND (alt. 330), is a small village. The *Tavern* (open), erected in 1774, was a stagecoach station on the route between Boston and Keene, N.H. The Colonial exterior and the low-beamed rooms remain unchanged.

PEARL HILL STATE PARK. Facilities: swimming, fishing, hiking, picnic tables, campsites (50), hunting, snowmobiling, scenic views.

TRURO (Barnstable County, sett. 1700, incorp. 1709, alt. 22, pop. 1234, area 20.70 sq. mi., town meeting, route, Mid-Cape Highway (US 6)). Truro was settled by Pamet proprietors.

Blackfish schools stranded on sandflats provided early income. Truro men took to boats and, armed with harpoons, helped initiate the whaling industry. Edicts in 1711 and 1713 forbidding the exhaustion of the sparse timber in the process of extracting lime from shell beds left by Indians, restricting the grazing of cattle and requiring the planting of beach grass indicate early concern for the harbors, which began to silt up just at a time when the decline of shore fishing made larger boats necessary. Attempts to save the anchorages were ineffectual. The year 1850 was the peak of expansion with a population of 2051 and a fleet of 111 vessels. Marine disasters, with attendant property loss and business failure, sealed Truro's industrial fate.

The close of the Civil War marked a further decline — Truro had contributed over 200 men. Offshore weirs superseded whalers and codfish boats. Cheaper sources of supply abroad ruined a thriving salt business, and farming without extensive fertilization was unprofitable.

With harbors obliterated and its population dwindled, Truro attracted a colony of artists and writers who have found its quiet simplicity and freedom from crowds a congenial environment for creative work.

No other spot on the Cape is richer in folklore and piquant legend than Truro. Here was the famous Lyars' Bench, utilized for the sole purpose of telling tall stories. There was the old yarn about a sea captain before whose stubborn ire the whole village cowered — all except his daughter, who, apparently a chip off the old block, was determined to have modern improvements in the home. The inspector swears he was called in the night the captain died and found the house in darkness. The explanation is given in a local limerick:

There was an old sea dog named ——
Who stood six foot four in his shoes;
He damned all things modern
Swore they weren't Cape-Coddern
The new-fangled he'd roundly abuse.

He lived with his daughter, Miss ——
Who yearned 'lectric lighting to use;
She won the long fight
But he died the same night,
And his passing soul blew out the fuse!

In Truro, too, they have a refreshing point of view on the "summer people." One anecdote says an affable lady visitor was being carried from the railway station to her destination by the local taxi. She tried without success to make conversation by commenting on the weather, the landscape and the road. Finally she remarked, "What a lot of quaint people one sees around here!"

"Yes, ma'am," said the cabbie, "but most of 'em go home after Labor Day."

Hill of the Churches. In 1826 the Methodists built a chapel on a high hill above the village "to be nearer to God and as a landmark for fishermen." The cupola dome is shaped like a mandarin hat. This church was removed about 1 mi. from its original location and is now an art studio. The next year the Congregationalists chose the top of the same hill for the site of a large church, long to be known as the *Bell Meeting House.* The name is derived from its Paul Revere bell. The church, in good repair, is used for summer services.

NORTH TRURO. At the beach end of Depot Rd. is the *Bayberry Candle*

Place (open), looking like an old sail loft, sheathed with weather-beaten gray shingles. Here bayberry candles are dipped by hand for the summer trade.

SOUTH TRURO has the *Old Methodist Church* (1851). It has not been used in recent years and looks lonely and forlorn on its high, barren dunes. South Truro dunes are fine specimens of drumlins, lenticular mounds of unstratified clay, sand and pebbles deposited by receding masses of ice of the glacial period.

Highland Light (*Cape Cod Light*), 5 mi. north and east of US 6, was formerly one of the most powerful Atlantic coast lights.
Pilgrim Spring is 7 mi. north of Truro and lies east off US 6. The Pilgrims came ashore here to get water for beer making. They spent their second night in the New World here by the spring.

TURNER'S FALLS (see MONTAGUE)

TYNGSBOROUGH (Middlesex County, sett. *c.* 1661, incorp. 1809, alt. 112, pop. 4204, area 16.86 sq. mi., town meeting, routes, US 3, Mass. 113, Mass 3A), is a residential and farming town along the Merrimack River, named for the Tyng family, whose coat of arms became its official seal.
St. Joseph's Novitiate (private) is the house of studies of the Marist Brothers. On the grounds is the *Jonathan Tyng House,* built in 1674, for a time the most northerly house in the colony; it served as an outpost of a nearby garrison erected for protection from the Indians. Handwrought stair rails and paneling ornament the interior. In the attic are slave pens and a slave bell.
South of the center on US 3 is the *Robert Brinley Mansion* (private), built in 1803 for "Sir" Robert and "Lady" Brinley, who succeeded the Tyngs as town leaders; the house was famous for its hospitality. Nearby is the *Nathaniel Brinley Mansion* (private), a stately three-story edifice built before 1779 on a high rise of land. It is surmounted by a tall cupola, and on both sides are spacious, two-story verandas, added later.
Tyng's Island is a 65-acre tract formerly owned by the Merrimack Indians; the 1936 flood uncovered many Indian relics here.
Littlehale Homestead is associated with a Colonial tragedy. Mrs. Littlehale, hunting her two young sons who had failed to return when sent to find the cows, saw Indians and ran for help. When she returned the Indians were gone. She never saw her children again.

TYRINGHAM (Berkshire County, sett. 1735, incorp. 1762, alt. 901, pop. 234, area 18.77 sq. mi., town meeting, route, Mass. Pike), was bought from the Stockbridge Indians, was named Tyringham at the suggestion of Lord

Howe, who owned an estate in Tyringham, England. Maple sugar making was learned here from the Indians. A paper mill was built in 1832, and the manufacture of hand rakes began even earlier.

Samuel Clemens (Mark Twain) lived in Tyringham during the summer of 1903. He presented the *Library* with a complete set of his books.

UNION CHURCH (see MOUNT WASHINGTON)

UPTON (Worcester County, sett. 1728, incorp. *c.* 1735, alt. 301, pop. 3484, area 21.65 sq. mi., town meeting, route, Mass. 140), was named for a village in Worcestershire, England. Small industries were inaugurated here, stimulated by Mill River waterpower. By 1835 shoes were the most important manufactured products, but they were superseded by straw hats and bonnets. Dairying and truck gardening have been replaced by manufactures. Upton farms in the late 1960's had but 77 saddle and work horses, 22 dairy cows and 21 beef cattle and/or oxen.

On the southern slope of Pratt Hill and on the right of Upper Mendon Rd., just beyond Brooks farm, are the *Devils Footprints* (r.), impressions in solid rock over two miles apart; both are about five feet long and two feet wide, and both point southward.

WEST UPTON is the home of the largest factory for ladies' wool and straw hats in the world.

UPTON STATE FOREST'S facilities include fishing, hiking, hunting, snowmobiling, scenic views.

WEST HILL WILDLIFE MANAGEMENT AREA (see MENDON).

UXBRIDGE (Worcester County, sett. 1662, incorp. 1727, alt. 270, pop. 8253, area 29.29 sq. mi., town meeting, routes, Mass. 16, 122, 146), called Wacantuck by the Indians, was another town of the Nipmuck "Praying Indians." Agriculture was the main occupation until abundant waterpower led to the erection of several small industrial plants and later of textile factories. The mills are locally owned.

WEST HILL WILDLIFE MANAGEMENT AREA has public hunting.

VAN DEUSENVILLE (see GREAT BARRINGTON)

VINEYARD HAVEN (see TISBURY)

WAKEFIELD (Middlesex County, sett. 1639, incorp. 1868, alt. 100, pop. 25,402, area 7.36 sq. mi., town meeting, routes, Mass. 128, 129), noted for boots, shoes, electronic products and native son Lucius Beebe (1902–66), noted journalist, nightclub columnist and western railroad and history buff, is a pleasant Boston suburb despite its industrial background.

Wakefield was part of Reading until 1812 when it became South Reading. The name was changed to Wakefield in 1868. Cyrus Wakefield established the world's first reported rattan factory on Water Street. The first shoe plant was established by Capt. Thomas Emerson in 1805. 19th-century industries included an iron foundry (1854), piano factory (1863), steam laundry (1885) and knitting mills (1890).

Beebe Memorial Library (1923) designed by Cram and Ferguson.

Hartshorne House (open), 41 Church St., a restored dwelling (1663), has authentic Colonial furnishings.

On Prospect St., between Cedar St. and Fairmont Ave., is the *Emerson House* (private). Its exterior is plain, but details of the interior are wide board floors, pegged instead of nailed; beautiful paneling; hand-hewn beams pinned with wooden dowels; handwrought thumb latches and H and L hinges; and early kitchen equipment, including a Dutch oven, cranes and a spit.

On Main St. are *Crystal Lake,* a local reservoir, *Lake Quannapowitt* and HART'S HILL RESERVATION, a natural park. Nearby stands a *Fire Tower* from the top of which on a clear day are visible the blue Atlantic, the misty Berkshires and the wooded hills of New Hampshire.

WAKESAW RESERVATION is a 600-acre state park with bridle paths and footpaths.

WALES (Hampden County, sett. *c.* 1726, incorp. 1762, alt. 949, pop. 852, area 16.20 sq. mi., town meeting, route, Mass. 19) is surrounded by woodlands, market gardens and dairy farms. It was part of Brimfield until 1762 when it became South Brimfield. The town was renamed in 1826 for James Lawrence Wales, in acknowledgment of a $2000 legacy. Cloth and sawmills used small streams for waterpower in the early days.

Lake George (Wales Pond) has fishing, hunting and picnicking.

Veineke Pond (inaccessible by car). Legend says on its shores are the *Cellar Holes* of an old Hessian village established by Veineke, one of the Hessian soldiers taken prisoner at the surrender of Burgoyne's army in 1777.

NORCROSS WILDLIFE SANCTUARY (1967) is open by appointment.

WALPOLE (Norfolk County, sett. 1659, incorp. 1724, alt. 166, pop. 18,149, area 20.56 sq. mi., town meeting, routes, US 1A, Mass. 27). Named for Sir Robert Walpole (1676–1745), English statesman, and situated on the Neponset River, it was well supplied with waterpower. Factories made cotton goods, cassimeres, satinets, nails, farming implements

Cambridge: Harvard Yard

Cambridge: The MIT Campus.
Courtesy of the Department of Public Relations, MIT

Sudbury: Wayside Inn

Left, above—Andover: Bulfinch Hall at Phillips Andover Academy

Left, below—Williamstown: College chapel

Dedham: America's oldest frame house

Deerfield: "Indian House"

Concord: The Old Manse

Salem: House of the Seven Gables

GRANT'S GENERAL STORE

Saugus: America's first ironworks

Left, above—Reliving history at Sturbridge Village

Left, below—Springfield: Small Arms Museum

Rowe: America's first power plant

and paper. Today manufactures include building papers, shingles, roofing materials, hospital supplies — cotton and gauze — paper and fences.

Blackburn Memorial Building (pool, 2 tennis courts), on the high school campus, is part of an extensive Memorial Park. *Memorial Park Bridge* (1924) honors Walpole's Revolutionary soldiers, sailors and nurses.

On East St. is the *Castle* (private), built in 1898 by Isaac Newton Lewis, a small stone edifice with a battlemented tower now surrounded by woods and a gladioli farm.

WALTHAM (Middlesex County, sett. 1634, town incorp. 1738, city incorp. 1884, alt. 67, pop. 61,582, area 12.41 sq. mi., mayor-council, routes, US 20, Mass. 60, 117, 128).

Waltham, once renowned as the home of the Waltham Watch, is now noted for its space-age electronic equipment, some of which has already reached the moon and several planets.

This manufacturing city situated near the headwaters of the Charles River lies nine miles west of Boston. Rugged and picturesque hills skirt the north and west. The business section and many homes are built along Charles River flats. The river which divides the city not only contributes natural beauty but has been a substantial factor in developing the city's industry, particularly when water was an important power source.

In 1738 Watertown's west precinct was incorporated as Waltham Town. "Walt" means forest or wood; "Ham" is a dwelling or home. When the town was part of Watertown its growth was slow, but after its independence the town thrived as a farming center until mid-19th century.

In 1813 the Boston Manufacturing Company built the first American factory to process raw cotton into finished cloth under one roof. The project prospered and so did the town. Other mills opened: an iron foundry, crayon factory and a laboratory where early experiments with petroleum and its by-products were carried out.

In 1854 the Waltham Watch Company was founded to make the first machine-made watches in America. This business, more than any other, advanced Waltham's prosperity and took its name throughout the civilized world. After WWII, the company, hampered by cheaper imported watches and by outmoded equipment, failed.

Until about 1840 the population was entirely native English stock, but with the change from a strictly agricultural community to a rapidly expanding industrial town, cheap labor became necessary. French, Irish, Poles, Russians, Jews and Italians came to town, with the ultimate result that of the present population about two-thirds are of foreign origin.

Waltham, since WWII, has become a large electronics manufacturing center. Raytheon played a major role in the improvement and manufacturing of radar equipment. Today the firm is heavily involved in the space and missile program. When *Apollo* carried the first three men to the moon, a 70-pound, onboard Raytheon computer helped get them there and back safely.

Precision machine tools, dresses and furniture are a few of the many city products.

Brandeis University was founded in 1947 on the site of the discredited Middlesex Medical College. With a faculty/student ratio of 1 to 3—equalled only by Harvard—Brandeis has become one of the nation's finest liberal arts colleges. Faculty members are outstanding. The school, with its small student body of 1400, is not interested in getting bigger but better. The college was named after Kentucky-born Louis D. Brandeis (1856–1941) who was appointed to the U.S. Supreme Court from Massachusetts and served 22 years.

Architecturally outstanding on the pleasant 260-acre riverside campus are the three chapels, Jewish, Protestant and Catholic, designed by Max Abramovitz. Guides are available at the information booth for personally-conducted tours from 9–4:45 daily.

Waltham Public Library (open weekdays 9–9) (1915), 735 Main St., is a charming adaptation of the late Georgian style. In the Sears Room is a permanent collection of Woodburyana, the gift of the Misses Sears. Charles H. Woodbury, born in Lynn in 1864, was a noted marine artist.

Governor Christopher Gore Mansion (open Apr. 15–Nov. 15, Tues.–Sat. 10–5, Sun. 2–5, closed Mon. and holidays, guided tours, small fee), US 20—Watertown-Waltham frontier, is behind an old stone wall and set back in a widespread lawn dotted with trees. Rebuilt between 1799 and 1804, it may be the work of Charles Bulfinch. It is among the comparatively few New England houses which exemplify the projecting elliptical salon derived from French influence.

Theodore Lyman House (open May 20–Aug. 28, Thur., Fri., Sat. 2–5, and by appointment, small fee), Lyman and Beaver Sts., screened by tall trees, is attractively situated on the shore of Lyman Pond. This manorial structure, with two-story wings and hip roof, was built in 1798 from designs by Samuel McIntire. Like all his work, it shows strong Adam influence and is one of the few houses designed by McIntire outside of Salem. The severity of its masses is relieved by Ionic pilasters, roof balustrades and much fine detail in the Adam manner. The east wing is an addition, and the house was altered in 1882.

Walter E. Fernald School (1848), also known as the Massachusetts School for the Feeble-Minded, Trapelo Rd., is one of the oldest state institutions of its kind in the country and was named for its first superintendent.

WAQUOIT (see FALMOUTH)

WARE (Hampshire County, sett. *c.* 1717, incorp. 1775, alt. 488, pop. 8187, area 34.85 sq. mi., town meeting, routes, Mass. 9, 32, nine mi. n. of Mass. Pike Interchange #8) was "erected" by legislative act into a district, November 1761, and given full township privileges under an omnibus bill signed August 23, 1775. Ware is a translation of an Indian word, Nenameseck, meaning "fishing weir" (pronounced "ware") and applied to places in streams where weirs were built to catch fish.

Much of the town (or parish) was, in Colonial days, within the estate of John Read. Early settlement developed about Ware Center. Ware Center remains much as it was, and the Meeting House, Gould Tavern and Paige's Tavern are notable reminders of 18th-century living.

Ware spreads along both sides of the Ware River. An industrial village, it is a trading center for a considerable area.

Quabbin ("Many Waters") Reservoir on the western side of Ware is the largest man-made body of water in the world exclusively for drinking purposes. With its construction in the '30's the adjacent towns of Enfield, Greenwich and Prescott ceased to exist. Quabbin, an area of serene and scenic beauty with pleasant drives and picnic facilities, is well known to serious fishermen.

A covered bridge spans the Ware River at Gilbertville, joining Ware in Hampshire County and Gilbertville in Worcester County.

SWIFT RIVER WILDLIFE MANAGEMENT AREA has public hunting in Belchertown and Ware.

WAREHAM (Plymouth County, sett. 1678, incorp. 1739, alt. 24, pop. 11,492, area 36.68 sq. mi., town meeting, routes, US 6, Mass. 28), was engaged in whaling and, after the Revolution, in shipbuilding. It is a cranberry center.

Wareham was attacked during the War of 1812. Some ships were burned, and a cotton factory was partly destroyed.

Benjamin Fearing House (private), Main St., part of it 300 years old, is a weather-beaten two-and-a-half-story dwelling.

Tremont Nail Factory (visited by permission), 25 mi. northwest of the house, more than a century old, is still in operation.

WARREN (Worcester County, sett. 1664, incorp. *c.* 1848, alt. 605, pop. 3633, area 27.50 sq. mi., town meeting, routes, Mass. 19, 67), was called Squabaug (Red-Water Place) by the Indians. This town was incorporated as Western and renamed in 1834 after Gen. Joseph Warren, author of the "Suffolk Resolutions" and Revolutionary hero, killed at Bunker Hill, 1775. An outpost frontier town, it was heavily garrisoned against Indian attacks.

Warren's industrial activity, at its height in the 19th century, has declined. Native Nathan Read is said to have constructed and in 1789 successfully operated a steamboat.

Warren-made steam pumps have been used throughout the world. Warren mills currently produce pumps, punching machines, bias tape and miscellaneous goods.

WARWICK (Franklin County, sett. *c.* 1739, incorp. 1763, alt. 940, pop. 492, town meeting, route, Mass. 78), was granted in 1735 to survivors and descendants of soldiers serving in Canadian campaign of 1690 under Capt. Gardner of Roxbury. First known as Gardner's Canada, the town grew rapidly after the French and Indian Wars. Its rugged, picturesque, mountainous land caused it to be bypassed by modern transportation. With the opening of the West, its population and industries decreased.

Northwest (off Mass. 78) looms *Mt. Grace* (alt. 1628), providing distant views. The state today owns about one third of the town's area.

Warwick achieved fame during its 200th anniversary (1963) when native son Fred Harris, descendant of pioneer settlers, promoted an Old Fashioned Independence Day and a four-day Labor Day weekend celebration which drew more than 15,000 spectators to the Labor Day parade. This was more than 30 times the town's population.

MT. GRACE STATE FOREST lies alongside Mass. 78 between Orange and Winchester, N.H. Facilities: fishing, hunting, fireplaces, picnic tables, ski trails, ski tow, snowmobiling.

WARWICK STATE FOREST'S facilities include fishing, hiking, hunting, snowmobiling, swimming in nearby Moore's Pond.

WASHINGTON (Berkshire County, sett. *c.* 1760, incorp. 1777, alt. 1412, pop. 406, area 38.20 sq. mi., town meeting, route, Mass. 8), is one of the first towns named for George Washington.

Most Washingtonians work in nearby towns. The town's two businesses are a garage and a 57-bed nursing home.

St. Andrew's Chapel, no longer active except on special occasions, is a lovely stone building of Gothic design.

WATERTOWN (Middlesex County, sett. 1630, incorp. 1630, alt. 20, pop. 39,307, route, Mass. 20).

Watertown is a vigorous community squeezed within inadequate boundaries. Original boundaries included the present town, all of Waltham and Weston and parts of Belmont, Cambridge and Lincoln. Disagreement over a meetinghouse location led to the formation of Weston. A schoolhouse argument created Waltham.

In 1630 the flagship *Arbella* arrived with Lady Arbella Johnson and her husband, Sir Richard Saltonstall.

Exhausted and ill, the company rested in Charlestown before splitting into two congregations. One group went to Boston with Pastor Wilson, and one hundred families followed Rev. George Phillips to make the colony's first inland settlement. Colonists sailed up the Charles River to the fertile lands about Gerry's Landing (Cambridge) where they built their first homesteads. Because it was so well watered, they named the region Watertown.

A democratic, liberal spirit determined institutions and conduct. Three men, John Oldham (1600–36), Plymouth Colony exile, Sir Richard Saltonstall (1610–94) and Rev. George Phillips (1593–1644), instituted a continuing democratic pattern. Oldham knew Plymouth's mistakes: lack of democratic spirit, absentee control by English proprietors and the aristocratic pretensions of a few citizens. He was determined these mistakes would not be repeated in Watertown. The first selectmen were elected in 1634. Watertown had the first such board in New England.

Under Rev. Phillips and his successor, the church, as democratic as the town meeting, was constantly under fire. That no Quakers were hung in Watertown was a matter of deep concern to neighboring congregations who regarded themselves as God's appointed representatives.

Pre-Revolutionary Boston was full of Tories. Many Whigs fled to Watertown. Refugee printer Benjamin Edes (1732–1803), publisher of the inflammatory *Boston Gazette and Country Journal,* which sent political news with a strong Whig bias all over the country, printed and distributed his subversive literature here.

A tremendous impetus was given to industrial development in 1816 by the choice of Watertown for the United States Arsenal. During the Civil War Walker and Pratt supplied ammunition and gun carriage castings. By 1875 the population had increased to approximately 6000, but there it hung until the Cambridge subway opened in 1909. A flood of newcomers aided local industries.

Celia Thaxter House (private), 262 Main St., onetime residence of the poet, stands in a small, neat yard.

Abraham Browne House (open May–Oct., Mon.–Fri. 2–5, Nov.–Apr., Tues.–Fri. 2–5, small fee), 562 Main St., behind its green hedge and pines, is largely a restoration, but the original part (1633) and its chimney remain. Its three-part casement windows are claimed to be the only ones extant in New England.

Governor Christopher Gore Estate is bisected by the Watertown-Waltham line (see WALTHAM).

Perkins School for the Blind (open) was founded in 1829, opened in South Boston in 1832 and removed to Watertown in 1912. Its first director was Dr. Samuel Gridley Howe, assisted by his wife, Julia Ward Howe, the abolitionist, best known now as the author of "The Battle-Hymn of the Republic." Helen Keller spent part of a year here. Formerly Perkins Institute and Massachusetts School for the Blind.

Edmund Fowle House (owned by Watertown Historical Society), 28 Marshall St., is where Mrs. George Washington was entertained by Mrs. James Warren, December 1775. A plaque reads "During the British Occupation of Boston, the seat of Government of Massachusetts was in Watertown. In this house met committees of the second and third Provincial Congress from April 22, 1775 to July 19, 1775 and the Executive Council from July 19, 1775 to September 18, 1776."

The Watertown Redevelopment Authority was negotiating for the land and buildings of the former U.S. Arsenal.

WAYLAND (Middlesex County, sett. *c.* 1638, incorp. 1780, alt. 127, pop. 13,461, area 15.28 sq. mi., town meeting, routes, US 20, Mass. 27, 30), was named for Francis Wayland, clergyman and president of Brown University (1827–55). He was instrumental in establishing here in 1848 a *Free Library* said to be the first free library in Massachusetts. Shoemaking and the harvesting of meadow grass were once important in the town; today Wayland is a so-called "bedroom" town of Boston.

Unitarian Church (1815), its design derived from Sir Christopher Wren, is well proportioned and has a charming tower with a Paul Revere bell.

Home of Lydia Child (private), Old Sudbury Rd. Authoress and abolitionist, she gave up her work as editor of the *Juvenile Miscellany,* the first American periodical for children, to follow William Lloyd Garrison in his anti-slavery crusade.

COCHITUATE STATE PARK includes Lake Cochituate (591 acres). Facilities: beach, bathhouse, boating, fishing, fireplaces, picnic tables.

WEBSTER (Worcester County, sett. *c.* 1713, incorp. 1832, alt. 450, pop. 14,917, area 12.53 sq. mi., town meeting, routes, Mass. 12, 16, 193), was named for Daniel Webster. Industrialization began when Samuel Slater in 1811 set up a cotton mill, which proved so successful that four years later five more mills were built. New industries were attracted by the completion of the Norwich and Worcester Railroad in 1840. Today textile and shoe industries are first in importance. Several Webster industries were recently devastated by a large fire which swept their plants. They soon were back in operation after moving to new quarters and securing new equipment and machinery.

George St. *Burying Ground* has graves marked with fieldstones; large ones indicate old men; small ones, young men.

Webster may be best known for its long-name lake. One spelling is *Chargoggagomanchaugagochaubunagungamaug.* This tongue twister is said to mean in Indian, "You fish your side of the lake. I fish my side. Nobody fishes the middle." The word, unfortunately, must be too long for sign painters and cartographers as the lake is now usually called Lake Webster.

WELLESLEY (Norfolk County, sett. 1660, incorp. 1881, alt. 145, pop. 28,051, area 10.50 sq. mi., representative town meeting, routes, Mass. 9, 16, 135) is the seat of Wellesley College. Its proximity to Boston, rural atmosphere, pleasant homes, and beautiful college campus make Wellesley an attractive town. Though not a manufacturing center, there are several industries. Generally, Wellesley comprises farms and residences.

Wellesley is an adaptation of the family name of Harvard man Samuel Welles, who in 1763 established his home here, within the town of Natick. In 1881 Samuel Welles' grandson-in-law, H. Hollis Hunnewell, bought the vast Welles estate from the several heirs and named it Wellesley.

First white settler Andrew Dewing erected a garrison house in 1660. In 1881 a petition was granted whereby the settlement became a separate town. That it was poor compared with other communities is clear from the absence of fine Colonial houses. Farmers depended upon wood, bark, hoop poles and faggot sales to supply them with the necessities they could not raise. About 1850 the town took a new lease on life. In 1883 sidewalks were laid and a fire department was organized. A board of health was established in 1889.

In 1871 a Female Seminary, later *Wellesley College,* was founded. Harvard man Henry Fowle Durant (1822–81) of Hanover, N.H., established the seminary to offer women an education equivalent to that provided for men but also "to establish an institution for the greater glory of God." On August 18, 1871, the first cornerstone was laid by Dr. Durant's wife. On September 8, 1875, Wellesley College opened its doors to students. Two hundred were turned away for lack of room. The main building contained the first laboratories for scientific investigation made available for women in the United States.

Songwriter Katharine Lee Bates (1859–1929) was a Wellesley graduate.

Dana Hall, a girls' preparatory school, opened its door to 30 students four years after the founding of the college. It now has an enrollment of about 420. *Mother Seton High School* (private) has 300 female students. *Ten Acre* (1910) is a school for younger girls, with about 200 pupils.

The town has many names with important historical, scientific and literary associations. Isaac Spoge, illustrator of Grey's "Botany" and a friend and collaborator of Audubon, was a resident of Wellesley. Scotsman Alexander Graham Bell (1847–1922) lived here when he invented the telephone as did Dr. W. T. G. Morton (1819–68), co-discoverer of the use of ether in surgery.

Babson Institute, founded by economist Roger Babson (1875–1967) in 1919, provides a practical training in business fundamentals, business ethics and executive control. From a humble beginning in a single residence, the institute is situated in Babson Park—a tract of 135 acres covering one of the highest points of land in Wellesley.

Coleman Map Building (open daily 2–9, free), Wellesley Ave., the largest building on the Babson Institute campus, is a large relief map of the United States. This map is built on a spherical surface in exact proportion to the actual curvature of the earth. It is 65 feet long (east and west) by 45 feet in width (north and south) and covers an area of 3000 square feet. This map shows in proportional relief the exact topographical elevations of the country. Spectators view the map from a balcony. The map cost $150,000 and took 17 years to complete.

Babson World Globe, outside Coleman Map Building, is 28 feet in diameter and weighs 21.5 tons. The earth looks as it would if the viewer were 5000 miles away in space. The globe rotates to represent night and day.

WELLFLEET (Barnstable County, sett. *c.* 1724, incorp. 1763, alt. 25, pop. 1743, area 20.47 sq. mi., town meeting, route, Mid-Cape Highway (US 6)) was formerly in the Billingsgate section of Eastham. Whaling and oystering were the principal sources of wealth until the British blockade when the community became destitute. Col. Elisha Doane, the town's wealthiest man, reaped a fortune by trafficking with the enemy. In 1967 local historian Miss Judith Stetson stoutly maintained—and possibly she is right—that Col. Doane was a patriot, not a wartime profiteer.

Secretly, Wellfleet traders regained prosperity by barter with England and France, until the Embargo Act of 1807 again interrupted business. In 1850 Wellfleet, with 30 vessels, was second only to Gloucester as a cod and mackerel port. From 1830 to 1870 the town enjoyed a virtual monopoly of oystering in New England. It still derives some income from fishing, but the main source is the tourist trade.

Town Hall, a good example of simple, early 19th-century New England churches, has an open octagonal cupola. The present structure (1962) is a somewhat enlarged but "faithful copy" of the original which burned during the March 1960 blizzard. Town offices are on the first floor and the free public library on the second floor. Directly in front of the hall, on a granite boulder, is the *Pilgrim Memorial Tablet,* commemorating the expedition of a group of Pilgrims who on December 6 and 7, 1620, explored Wellfleet Harbor in the *Mayflower's* shallop before going on to Plymouth.

Also at the center is *Belvernon* (private), the home of Capt. Lorenzo Dow Baker (1840–1908), who engaged in coastwise shipping trade in his 85-ton schooner, the *Telegraph.* While loading bamboo in the West Indies he decided to take a few bananas back to the states. The new fruit caused a sensation. This exploit was the nucleus of the United Fruit Company (est. 1899). Capt. Baker became managing director of the Jamaica division of the firm. "Cap'n Baker" in his palmy days continued to take an interest in the town of his birth. Cap'n Dow, according to historian Stetson, was responsible for bringing the first "summer persons" to the Cape in 1885. He actively promoted tourism, a far more important local economic factor than bananas. The house is owned by Reuben Baker, a descendant of Cap'n Dow. In the summer of 1967 Baker was in Vietnam directing the activities of United Fruit Company vessels which were supplying American troops.

Goodie Hallet was stoned out of early Eastham, having borne an illegitimate child to Black Sam Bellamy, a notorious pirate, and taken possession of a shack on Wellfleet Beach. Goodie, it is said, bartered her soul to the Devil in exchange for her lover's drowned body. The Devil apparently kept his bargain, for in April 1717, Bellamy and his crew were shipwrecked off the Back Shore near Goodie's Hut.

WELLFLEET BAY WILDLIFE SANCTUARY, west side of US 6 (650 acres), is one of the most interesting places to visit on the Cape. The sanctuary, located on the site of the former Austin Ornithological Research Station, includes a sizable salt marsh. Campsites and cottages are available for Massachusetts Audubon Society members and their families. Interesting nature trails. Beach buggy tours to Monomoy Point and Nauset Beach. Summer film programs and beach walks. Natural history day camp.

WENDELL (Franklin County, sett. 1754, incorp. 1781, alt. 1164, pop. 405, area 31.65 sq. mi., town meeting, route, Mass. 2). Wendell was named in honor of Judge Oliver Wendell of Boston. By 1810 the town reached its maximum population of 983. Two stories account for tiny *Mormon Hollow:* (1) settlers were people who left a passing Mormon caravan; (2) settlers embraced Mormonism and left to join a colony of the Latter-Day Saints.

Logging and chicken and dairy farming are the major Wendell industries. Campers in nearby Erving State Forest usually purchase supplies in Wendell.

WENDELL STATE FOREST'S facilities include swimming, fishing, boating, hiking, picnicking, hunting, snowmobiling.

WENHAM (Essex County, sett. 1635, incorp. 1643, alt. 67, pop. 3849, area 7.75 sq. mi., town meeting, routes, Mass. 1A, 22, 97) is a pleasant village that is rapidly gaining favor with commuters. This popularity does not meet with the approval of all the older residents.

The frame *First Church* (1843) has been frequently painted by artists. The interior has been restored. The pulpit is a copy made from the wood of the original. First pastor John Fiske was described by Cotton Mather as ranking "among the most famous preachers in primitive New England."

The second house along the green and past the church is the *Henry Hobbs House* (private). Built in 1747 the house has the typical gambrel roof, panel wainscoting, exposed beams, H and L hinges, eight fireplaces and brick oven. Tory Nathaniel Brown, whom Marbleheaders unsuccessfully tried to tar and feather, lived here.

Clafin-Richards House (open Mon.–Fri., closed Feb. and holidays, contribution expected), almost directly opposite Hobbs House, built in 1664, has rare serpentine braces — reportedly the only ones in New England — and a collection of dolls from various countries.

Wenham Lake was the scene of John G. Whittier's poem "The Witch of Wenham." During the clipper ship era, ice harvested from this lake was shipped to Europe and the tropics.

WEST BARNSTABLE (see BARNSTABLE)

WEST BECKET (see BECKET)

WEST BOYLSTON (Worcester County, sett. 1642, incorp. 1808, alt. 481, pop. 6369, area 12.69 sq. mi., town meeting, routes, Mass. 12, 110, 140), is a Worcester suburb along the banks of the *Wachusett Reservoir* (good fishing). Early settlers were farmers. Waterpower furnished by the Nashube, Quinnepoxet and Stillwater Rivers stimulated industry. Early mills made footwear and textiles. The town lost some of its manufacturing capacity when land was purchased for the creation of *Wachusett Reservoir* in 1905.

Noted natives: Robert Bailey Thomas (1766–1846) originated *The Farmer's Almanac;* Erastus Bigelow (1814–79) invented the power loom for carpet weaving and Thomas Keyes, Jr., invented the orrery, an instrument to illustrate the movement of the solar system, and a machine to warp cloth.

Today about 100 West Boylston workers produce paper, ice cream, hooked rug patterns, sheet metal products and engravings.

WEST BRIDGEWATER (Plymouth County, sett. 1651, incorp. 1822, alt. 50, pop. 7152, area 15.49 sq. mi., town meeting, routes, Mass. 24, 28, 106). The town was deeded to six people in trust for 56 proprietors of Duxbury plantation. In 1645 Massasoit gave up his claims to the land for 30 worth of "knives, hatchets, skins, hoes, coates, and cotton."

A few mills were established along its rivers during the 19th century, but the town is predominantly agricultural, growing smaller garden crops and specializing in dairying and poultry raising. Electronic and wood products and machine braided rugs are made in residential West Bridgewater.

Memorial Park is on the site of an old gristmill. The river has been diverted through the park in a series of waterfalls.

The *Bridgewater Historical Society Museum* (open), 162 Harvard St., has the Massasoit deed given to the purchasers of the Bridgewater settlement.

WEST MEADOWS WILDLIFE MANAGEMENT AREA has public hunting.

WEST BRIMFIELD (see BRIMFIELD)

QUABOAG RIVER WILDLIFE MANAGEMENT AREA has public hunting in Brookfield and West Brookfield.

WEST CUMMINGTON (see CUMMINGTON)

WEST END (see BOSTON)

WEST GRANVILLE (see GRANVILLE)

WEST HARWICH (see HARWICH)

WEST NEW BOSTON (see SANDISFIELD)

WEST BROOKFIELD (Worcester County, sett. 1665, incorp. 1848, alt. 633, pop. 2653, area 20.67 sq. mi., town meeting, routes, Mass. 9, 67), was the first section of the original Brookfield grant to be settled, and prior to 1789 it was the most important section. Several small industries and farming remain the principal local means of livelihood.

In 1798 Isaiah Thomas (1750–1831) edited the first Brookfield newspaper. Ebenezer Merriam & Co. took over the paper (1802). Ebenezer's sons purchased the rights to publish Noah Webster's dictionary.

On Foster Hill Road is a large boulder from which in 1741 famed parson George Whitefield (1714–70) preached to more than 5000 alleged sinners. *Indian Rock,* a natural breastwork, was used by King Philip's warriors in 1675, when they attacked the local fortified house.

West Brookfield in 1956 with her sister towns of Brookfield, East and North Brookfield and Warren celebrated the 300th anniversary of the settlement of Quaboag Plantation of which all the towns were once a part. *Lake Wickaboag* near the town's center has excellent fishing, boating and swimming. The area has many camps and cottages. There is a public beach and a boat club.

Quaboag Park, as the common is known, is one of New England's loveliest village greens.

WEST NEWBURY (Essex County, sett. 1635, incorp. 1819, alt. 100, pop. 2254, area 13.90 sq. mi., town meeting, routes, I–95, US 1, Mass. 113). This residential and agricultural town is spread over a series of high, well-watered hills. Before Newburyport's spectacular growth, which increasingly monopolized foreign commerce, oceangoing vessels ascended the Merrimack to Haverhill, but with the building of the Chain Bridge in the early 19th century the river was closed to ships. West Newbury relapsed into an agricultural calm, and there are no traces today of the comb factory (1770) or of the small shoe manufactories.

Presidents Cornelius Conway Felton of Harvard and Leonard Woods of Bowdoin were born here. Another native was monorail inventor E. Moody Boynton. The first horn combs made in America were manufactured in West Newbury.

The *Training Field,* Main St. (State 125), where Civil War soldiers trained and with its World War Boulder, is surrounded by houses overarched by elms.

Rocks Bridge spans the Merrimack. At this point the river sweeps into a wide course, its broad expanse ruffled by the swift current, between banks on which a few scattered farmhouses and the clustered buildings of tiny Rocks Village at the far side of the bridge create a charming pastoral scene.

CRANE POND WILDLIFE MANAGEMENT AREA (see GEORGETOWN).

WEST OTIS (see OTIS)

WEST ROXBURY (see BOSTON)

WEST SPRINGFIELD (Hampden County, sett. *c.* 1660, incorp. 1774, alt. 204, pop. 28,461, area 16.75 sq. mi., representative town meeting, routes, I–91, US 5, 20, Mass. Pike), a residential suburb of Springfield, has paper product companies and chemical, machine and other factories. The Eastern States Exposition is held here.

The *Common* was the campsite of armies under Generals Amherst, Burgoyne and Riedesel. It was the drill ground of Captain Luke Day's insurgents during Shays' Rebellion.

The *First Congregational Church* (1800) on White Church Hill, Elm Street, now the Masonic Temple, is designed in the manner of Christopher Wren, with less modification than is usual in New England.

The *Day House* (open), north of the common, built in 1754, is an historical museum maintained by the Ramapogue Historical Society. Early period furnishings are in the rooms.

WEST STOCKBRIDGE (Berkshire County, sett. 1766, incorp. 1775, alt. 1140, pop. 1354, area 18.34 sq. mi., town meeting, routes, Mass. 41, 102). This attractive farming village is nestled among valleys and wooded hills. First settler William Bryant came here from Canaan, Conn. Some 40 families followed him. During the early 19th century, West Stockbridge enjoyed prosperity as the eastern terminus of the Hudson and Berkshire Railroad. A paper mill, marble quarries, sawmills and limekilns flourished but petered out. The town is a well-known summer resort.

WEST STOCKBRIDGE CENTER (alt. 915) was a former marble quarrying district.

WEST TOWNSEND (see TOWNSEND)

WEST UPTON (see UPTON)

WEST WORTHINGTON (see WORTHINGTON,

WEST TISBURY (Dukes County, sett. 1669, incorp. 1892, alt. 10, pop. 453), named for the English birthplace of Governor Thomas Mayhew, was first known as *Tackhum-Min-Eyi* or *Takemmy* (Indian, "The Place Where One Goes to Grind Corn").

The town had saltworks on the shore, smokehouses on the hills where fat herring were cured and prepared for market, brickworks and a lumber trade. But it has now placidly settled down to farming, fishing and cultivating summer tourists.

Every wildflower known to eastern Massachusetts has been found in the town. Glacial boulders appear in the midst of freshwater springs and ponds. Many Algonquin names survive. *Manitouwattootan* ("Christian-town") was applied in 1659 to a reservation for the "Praying Indians."

Music Street was named because, after one family acquired a piano, all the others on the street followed suit.

Experience Mayhew House (private), a typical Cape Cod type, is the oldest house in the town. To the south, the Atlantic pounds hard-packed white sands of *South Beach,* rarely patronized by swimmers because of the heavy undertow.

Abel's Hill Cemetery on the main highway contains lichen-covered tombstones bearing odd epitaphs.

WESTBOROUGH (Worcester County, sett. *c.* 1675, incorp. 1717, alt. 300, pop. 12,594, area 21.57 sq. mi., town meeting, routes, I–495, Mass. 9, 30, 135) was granted by the General Court to several proprietors in return for services to the colony. One grant was of 500 acres, made in 1659, to Charles Chauncy (1592–1672), second president of Harvard College, but revoked in 1659 when it was found to be a section of the Marlborough grant of that year. Westborough was called Chauncy until it was separated from Marlborough.

Westborough's agricultural character was changed by the busy Boston-Worcester Turnpike, a stagecoach route after 1810. Its industrial character was established when the Boston and Albany Railroad was run through the village in 1835. Boots and shoes were the principal manufactures, but straw hats, sleighs and tools were also made.

From Westborough Center, west on Main St. to the junction with Ruggles St.; left on this to Eli Whitney St. which is the fifth street on right to the *Site of the Birthplace of Eli Whitney* (1765–1825). The site of the home of the inventor of the cotton gin is marked by a boulder.

On Ruggles St., south of Eli Whitney St., a marker says: "An Indian trail prior to 1630 crossed here. The Old Connecticut Path." On *Jack Straw Hill,* back of the marker, Jack Straw lived. Jack Straw, believed to have been the first Massachusetts Indian converted by the white men, was one of two Indians taken to London by Sir Walter Raleigh and presented to Queen Elizabeth.

Chauncy Lake: fishing, bathing, boating, picnicking.

Hoccomocco Pond, named by the Indians after an evil spirit, was the scene of the activities of one Tom Cook, a highwayman born in Westborough in 1738, who used to rob the well-to-do and give to the poor. The wealthy paid this local Robin Hood large sums annually for immunity from his depradations.

WESTBOROUGH FIELD TRAIL AREA has public hunting.

WESTFIELD (Hampden County, sett. 1600, town incorp. 1669, city incorp. 1920, alt. 144, pop. 31,433, area 46.82 sq. mi., mayor-council, routes, US 20, 202, Mass. Pike, 10). The first road was cut through in 1668, and travel increased so rapidly that four years later Capt. Aaron Cook opened a tavern here.

Westfield Athenaeum (open weekdays 9–9, Sun. 2–6), corner of Elm and Court Sts., overlooking the green, is an attractive brick building with limestone trim, housing the library. On the upper floor is the *Edwin Smith Historical Museum,* which has a well-furnished Colonial kitchen and a typical late-18th-century New England living room. *Jasper Rand Art Museum* exhibits well-known American artists' works.

Westfield State College (1839), Western Ave., is the second oldest state teachers' college in the state. It was the first coeducational state teacher's college in the United States.

Grandmother's Garden, one block off US 20, is a city-owned, old-fashioned flower garden.

Stanley Park and Carillon (open May–Oct., 8 A.M.–sunset, free), Kensington Ave. off US 20, is a 100-acre park with many flower gardens. The 25 English bells and 61 Flemish bells of the 96-foot-high carillon are played for concerts. Summertime concerts are held every Thursday and Saturday evening and on Sunday afternoons. There is a 30 by 32 foot map of the U.S. inlaid with slate. In the pond area there is an authentic covered bridge, an old mill and water wheel, a rustic bridge and a blacksmith shop.

The covered bridge, an exact replica of one still standing in West Arlington, Vermont, was authenticated by the Society for the Preservation of Covered Bridges.

A five-acre arboretum with a 30-foot fountain in the center is illuminated at night with varicolored lights.

Savage Arms Corporation moved here from Chicopee in 1960.

HAMPTON PONDS STATE PARK'S facilities include swimming, boating, fishing, picnic tables.

WESTFORD (Middlesex County, sett. 1653, incorp. 1729, alt. 160, pop. 10,368, area 30.25 sq. mi., town meeting, routes, I–495, Mass. 110, 225).

Col. John Robinson, a Minuteman leader on April 19th, was a native of Westford, once part of Chelmsford. His birthplace (Robinson Rd.) is marked by a large boulder.

The *Arthur J. Hildreth Homestead* (*c.* 1680), Hildreth St., and the *Capt. Pelatiah Fletcher Homestead* (*c.* 1720), Howell Rd., both have witches' stairs in their attics. They are narrow staircases — to facilitate witches' comings and goings — which go up on the side opposite to the regular or human staircase.

Offset printing and granite quarrying are major industries in this small residential town.

WESTHAMPTON (Hampshire County, sett. 1762, incorp. 1778, alt. 618, pop. 793, area 27.07 sq. mi., town meeting, routes, Mass. 60, 66). West Northampton was set off as Westhampton in 1778. In 1765 a lead mine, partly owned by Ethan Allen, was opened. It furnished lead for Revolutionary War bullets. Natural resources led to the establishment of grist and lumber mills, and many of the attempted manufactures were connected with the natural resource of timber: chairs, boxes, potash and firewood. A brass foundry was also in operation at one time. Today dairying, farming and lumbering are the chief occupations.

Sylvester Judd House (1816) is at the Westhampton Village. Sylvester was the first town clerk and onetime publisher of the *Hampshire Gazette.*

South of the village is the *Hale House.* Here lived Rev. Enoch Hale (1753–1837), brother of Nathan Hale, for 57 years minister of the town. He was author of a spelling book, now a literary curiosity, written according to the then advanced ideas of adapting style and content to the understanding of the child.

Pine Island Lake is a popular summer residential area.

WESTMINSTER (Worcester County, sett. 1737, incorp. 1759, alt. 1064, pop. 4273, area 35.64 sq. mi., town meeting, routes, Mass. 2, 2A, 12, 31, 140). This was a part of grants made by the legislature to the veterans of the Narragansett War.

During the 19th century Westminster became an industrial community, but tanning and the manufacture of cotton cloth, bricks and chairs have been replaced by lumbering, dairying and poultry. In the village is a cracker factory that at one time caused Westminster to be called "Cracker Town." A second cracker factory, under the same management as the first, opened recently. Paper and adhesives are major products.

Gen. Nelson "Bearcoat" Miles (1839–1925), the Indian-fighting general who rounded up Geronimo, was born here. The *Town Library* has Miles' memorabilia. Rear Admiral Frank W. Fenno, Jr., famed WWII submariner, was born here.

WESTON (Middlesex County, sett. *c.* 1642, incorp. 1712, alt. 203, pop. 10,870, area 16.8 sq. mi., town meeting, routes, US 20, Mass. 30, 117, 128), formerly a small village, has expanded with the recent suburban movement. The village and environs, however, still have many lovely homes in the middle-class bracket. During the Revolution there was a beacon on Sanderson's Hill. Weston, a farming town, became briefly an industrial community. Industries left in the 1840's.

Noted residents have included Parson Edmund H. Sears (1810–76), who wrote "It Came Upon a Midnight Clear" and attorney Arthur Train, who wrote the Mr. Tutt stories.

Weston College with its justly famed *Seismological Observatory* headed by

Father Daniel Linehan, a Jesuit with a Harvard Ph.D. in geology and an Arctic explorer, prepares men for active religious and intellectual apostolates. This Jesuit college is affiliated with Boston College. Jesuit scholar Linehan is one of the world's leading seismologists.

Regis College (1927) is a Roman Catholic women's college with about 1300 students and 100 faculty members.

The *Weston Public Library,* corner School St. and Boston Post Rd., is an attractive brick building which houses a small collection of fine Japanese ivories.

The *Artemas Ward House* (private), corner of Concord Rd. and the Post Rd., was built in 1785 by twin brothers named Easton and sold about four years later to Artemas Ward, son of Gen. Ward of Revolutionary fame. It is a broad gable house with white clapboards, fine dentil mouldings in the cornice and a shingled roof.

The *Col. Elisha Jones Place* (private) (1751), or Golden Ball Tavern, 662 Boston Post Rd., built by Col. Jones, was Tory headquarters during the Revolution. It is a two-and-a-half-story mansion with two wings. At this house, John Howe, a British spy sent out in 1775 by Gen. Gage to report on rebel ammunition stored on the Worcester Road, was discovered. Though he escaped and reached Worcester, the Weston patriots so aroused the countryside that Howe reported to Gage that any attempt at the movement of troops in that direction would result in certain defeat—with the result that Lexington was chosen for the British line of march.

WESTPORT (Bristol County, sett. 1670, incorp. 1787, alt. 7, pop. 9791, area 53.01 sq. mi., town meeting, routes, US 6, Mass. 177).

WESTPORT MILLS, a small village, is built around a textile plant. The first mill was built in 1812.

CENTRAL VILLAGE. In 1652 the land here, then in Dartmouth, was purchased from the Indians by Myles Standish. The first settlement was made 18 years later; many settlers were Quakers. They established their right to their own religious forms and beliefs, but when the town was devastated during King Philip's War the Plymouth Court declared this was "an evidence of the wrath of the Almighty against the people for their neglect to worship in the Puritan faith."

The *Friends' Meeting House* at the center was moved to its present site in 1840. In the meetinghouse yard stands a granite *Memorial to Captain Paul Cuffee* (1759–1817), son of a freed Negro slave; Capt. Cuffee, a Friend, amassed a fortune at sea and won important civil rights for his race when he successfully refused to pay the personal property tax, basing his refusal on his lack of citizenship rights; he was the first Negro to be granted all privileges enjoyed by white men in Massachusetts. He once attempted to form a colony for previous Negro slaves in Sierra Leone.

Westport River is used for swimming, boating and fishing. Picnic sites are along the bank.

HORSENECK BEACH STATE RESERVATION has scenic sand dunes. Facilities: swimming, bathhouse, picnic sites. The Elizabeth Islands and Gay Head on Martha's Vineyard are visible from the beach.

WESTWOOD (Norfolk County, sett. middle to late 1600's, incorp. 1897, alt. 262 (High Rock 374), pop. 12,750, area 10.56 sq. mi., town meeting, routes, I–95, US 1, Mass. 1A, 109, 135) was established legally in 1736 as the Clapboard Trees (also West, or Third Parish of Dedham). Once a farming town, the only soil turning today is done by retired middle-class residents. Sizable farms have been replaced by real estate subdivision.

Original Clapboard Trees Meeting House, now on the green at the junction of Route 109 and Pond Street, was bought at auction, dismantled, moved here by oxcart and reassembled as the home of the new First Baptist Society. Parish factions were unable to agree on a new building site. The squat steeple has a well proportioned belfry.

"New" (1809) Meeting House of the Clapboard Trees Parish, also of white clapboards and with dark green blinds and doors, but with a high slender steeple, overlooks another triangular green, less than one mile away, at the intersection of Nahatan and Clapboardtree Streets.

Baker Homestead (private) (*c.* 1680), 955 High Street, is the oldest house in town — the home of five generations of Bakers. Betsey Metcalf Baker is credited with starting the straw hat industry in this area. As a child of 12 in Providence, desiring a bonnet like an imported one she admired, she devised a method for splitting and braiding straw and created the first straw bonnet ever made by anyone in this country. She taught her skills to her friends and neighbors. Many women in West Dedham and surrounding towns earned pin money with this home industry. Devout Betsey would not accept money for her bonnets or her teaching, since she considered her talents God-given and not to be capitalized upon.

WEYMOUTH (Norfolk County, sett. 1622, incorp. 1635, alt. 100, pop. 54,610, area 17.5 sq. mi., representative town meeting, routes, Mass. 3, 18, 128) is a half-dozen villages, each a compact industrial center surrounded by its own residential section.

WEYMOUTH LANDING with its ancient wharves retains its seaport air.

SOUTH WEYMOUTH lies near a great pine grove, an oasis of quiet, some two miles square.

Weymouth, Massachusetts, second oldest settlement, for nearly two centuries was a fishing and farming town with fertile farms and first-rate dairies. Mills polluted streams. Commercial fishing was finished. Once this source of fertilizer was no longer available, country farms declined.

The first industry, a tannery, was established in 1697. James Clapp founded the Clapp Shoe Company in 1853 and it lasted four generations. He pioneered the use of French kid and patent kid leathers and replaced steam by electric-powered machinery. A latecomer, the Stetson Shoe Company, also brought Weymouth additional prosperity.

After the discovery of bog iron ore in 1771 small factories including nail manufactories began. Nineteenth-century industries were hammocks, heels and fireworks.

Today Weymouth, though a residential town, manufactures shoes, fertilizers, chemical coatings, electrical switches, photographs and electric power.

WHATELY (Franklin County, sett. 1672, incorp. 1771, alt. 290, pop. 1145, town meeting, routes, I–91, US 5, 10, 91) was named for Thomas Whately of England by Gov. Hutchinson. Machinist tools, brooms, spinning wheels and pottery have been made here. Today's chief products are potatoes, tobacco and onions.

Whately has the original town *Pound* (1771), West Lane, created to impound stray cattle and horses until their owners could be located. The site of the stockade — for protection from Indians — is marked by a large boulder on Main Street.

Whately residents are great readers. In one recent year more than 49,000 books were circulated from *S. White Dickinson Library* (11,000 vols.). This averages nearly 50 books annually by every man, woman, child and babe. The library (1949), erected by the late Dickinson's daughter, contains an unusually fine reference works collection.

WHITE VALLEY (see BARRE)

WHITINSVILLE (see NORTHBRIDGE)

WHITMAN (Plymouth County, sett. *c.* 1670, incorp. 1875, alt. 119, pop. 13,059, area 6.70 sq. mi., town meeting, routes, Mass. 18, 27, 58), is a major shoe manufacturing center. Known as "Little Comfort," or South Abington, Whitman was named for Augustus Whitman when it became a separate town.

Early products were ship timbers and boxwood. White oak timbers for the *Constitution* were cut in nearby forests and were squared in local mills. Agriculture is limited, but Whitman is noted for fine hens.

The *Commonwealth Shoe and Leather Company,* a large shoe manufacturing plant, and the *United Shank and Finding Company,* a subsidiary of the United Shoe Machinery Corporation and one of the largest factories of its kind in the world, are major industries.

WIANNO (see BARNSTABLE)

WILBRAHAM (Hampden County, sett. 1731, incorp. 1763, alt. 937, pop. 11,984, area 25 sq. mi., town meeting, route, US 20). North Wilbraham is the political center of Wilbraham. The first settlement, made by Nathaniel Hitchcock, was farther south in a section called Outward Commons. In 1741 the region was set aside as the Fourth Precinct of Springfield.

The *Public Library* is located on Boston Road.

Wilbraham Academy, founded in 1817 as Wesleyan Academy in Newmarket, N.H., was moved eight years later to Wilbraham and occupies the group of brick buildings on the hill. In 1912 it became a college preparatory school for boys after having been a coeducational institution for 95 years.

STATE GAME FARM (open). This 132-acre farm raises Chinese ring-necked pheasants. In recent years the farm has specialized in the propagation of pheasants for stocking natural coverts throughout the state.

WILLIAMSBURG (Hampshire County, sett. 1735, incorp. 1771, alt. 530, pop. 2342, area 25.57 sq. mi., town meeting, routes, Mass. 9, 143). This town was once in Hatfield. The earliest settler was for 17 years without a close neighbor. By the end of the 18th century many small factories utilizing abundant waterpower were producing leather, cotton and woolen goods, shoes, buttons, pens, penholders, hardware, woodwork and ironware. In 1874 a dam burst, releasing a raging flood that drowned 136 people and washed out the entire industrial section. Many mills were not rebuilt.

Meekins Library is an attractive gray granite building which was given by farmer Stephen Meekins, who made $40,000 raising sheep.

HAYDENVILLE. Cloth-covered buttons are believed to have been first manufactured here by machinery.

Hayden House (private), home of Lt. Gov. Hayden (1863–1966), is a dignified brick dwelling, built about 1800.

WILLIAMSTOWN (Berkshire County, sett. 1749, incorp. 1765, alt. 700, pop. 8454, area 46.73 sq. mi., town meeting, routes, US 7, Mass. 2, 43), lies in a valley among encircling hills. Winding roads threading the wild and lovely hill country come suddenly upon fields of corn, buckwheat and barley on the outskirts of this serene and dignified college town.

Williamstown's chief industries are manufacturing plants of General Cable, Anken Chemical and Hoover Transmission Companies. There are several modern motels and restaurants and the *Williams Inn,* situated on the college campus. Two golf courses, *Taconic* in Williamstown and *Waubeeka Springs* in South Williamstown are open to the public.

For more than a hundred years after the Pilgrims settled Plymouth, little was known of remote northwestern Massachusetts, cut off by the high Hoosac mountain wall. It could be reached only by the old Mohawk warpath through the Taconic hills, along which came Five Tribes — braves to spread terror through the settlements.

Williamstown's destiny was decided in 1755 when, before leaving for the French and Indian War, Col. Ephraim Williams made a will leaving money for the establishment and support of "a Free School forever in the township west of Fort Massachusetts, called West Hoosac, provided it be given the name of Williamstown."

Six weeks later Col. Williams was killed. The free school started in 1790. Three years later it was chartered as Williams College. Dr. Ebenezer Fitch, its first president, had four faculty members. Church and college were closely interbound. Students were required to attend chapel every morning and church on Sundays. There were frequent extra noon and evening prayer meetings. Yet the student body was far from sanctified. Morning chapel often found the Bible nailed to the pulpit, and once it is even rumored to have been burnt. In vain the pious teachers labored with revivals and prayer to dispel the Devil.

Despite Satan's repeated onslaughts, both town and college grew. After the Civil War, land was purchased for use as summer residences. College buildings increased in number and in beauty of architecture. Spring Street was opened and, with its banks, offices, theater, police court and new Colonial type post office, became the center of civic activity.

Williams has an international reputation for high scholastic standards. The mad race among many colleges and universities, notably state-suported institutions, for bigger student bodies and fancy buildings has not infected Williams. The college, for men only, has 1250 students with a 215-member faculty. Many college facilities are available to Williamstown residents.

What to See and Do

College tours can be arranged at Hopkins Hall through the campus guide service. Tours are conducted weekdays 10–12 and 2–4. The average tour lasts about 45 minutes. Visitors can, of course, spend as much time as they like in the various museums.

Notable college buildings (shown on the free guided tour) include *Griffin Hall,* the most beautiful building on the campus. Built in 1828, reconstructed in 1842 and renovated in 1952, Griffin was formerly the chapel but is now used for faculty meetings and classes. *Thompson Memorial Chapel* is a Gothic structure with notable stained-glass windows. Col. Williams was interred here with full military honors shortly after the building was completed in June 1920. The *Hopkins Observatory,* the oldest college observatory in the nation, was named after its founder, astronomy professor Albert Hopkins. *Hopkins Hall,* the college administrative center, was named after Mark Hopkins, Williams president (1836–72). *West College,* built in 1790, was gutted by fire in 1950. Graduate and undergraduate sentiment for its preservation was so strong that college authorities built an entire new dormitory within the shell of the original structure. *Clark Hall,* the geological laboratory, has the Wilder Cabinet of 15,000 minerals and the Black precious stone collection.

Williams College Museum of Art (open Mon.–Sat. 9–12, 2–4, Sun. 2–5, free), formerly the Lawrence Art Museum, is located on Main St. across from the College Chapel. Founded in 1926, the museum occupies Lawrence Hall, of which the original brick octagon, designed by Thomas Tefft of Providence, served as the college's first library (1846–1925). The octagon contains an Ionic rotunda, a fine example of Greek Revival style. A replica of a full-length portrait of donor Amos Lawrence of Boston painted in 1846 is here. The building was extended in 1800 by wings parallel to Main Street. In the 1920's a rear addition provided classrooms and gallery space. Two more galleries were provided in 1938. One contains fine examples of Medieval and Renaissance religious art, notably a life-size seated Madonna, Central Italian, *c.* 1450, carved in wood and retaining most of its original paint and gilding. The other contains Spanish paintings and furniture collections.

Other collections include ancient Egyptian objects, two large reliefs from the 9th-century palace of Assurnasirpal at Nineveh, Greek and Etruscan pottery, Roman glass, British and American portraits, early American furniture and painting and sculpture from the Italian Renaissance to the present, as well as drawings and prints.

The permanent collection is being developed, with the help of endowment funds, to provide a broad representation of world art in original examples without attempting to overlap areas covered by the superb collections of the *Sterling and Francine Clark Art Institute.* Among masters represented are Barye, Bourdelle, Braque, Copley, de Chirico, Delacroix, Demuth, Dürer, Gainsborough, Guardi, Homer, Inness, Léger, Maillol, Panini, Picasso, Prendergast, Raeburn, Rembrandt, Reynolds, Ribera, Rodin, Romney, Rouault, Stanzioni, Stuart, Toulouse-Lautrec, Valdés Leal, Villon and Weenix. Four Italian Gothic paintings were given in 1960 by the Samuel H. Kress Foundation from the Kress Study Collection.

Like other college museums, the Williams College Museum of Art is an important aid to instruction in art history and the practice of art. During the college year there are monthly temporary exhibitions designed to supplement this instruction and occasional ones during the summer season.

Chapin Library (open winter, Mon.–Fri. 9–12, 1–5, summer, Mon.–Fri. 9–12, 1–4), 2nd floor, Stetson Hall, contains manuscripts, rare books incunabula, prints, Americana.

Adams Memorial Theatre is used, during the college terms, by college organizations and for other dramatic presentations. During the summer the Williamstown Theatre Foundation, Inc., presents a series of plays by an equity company and operates an apprentice school.

Sterling and Francine Clark Art Institute (1955), South Street, contains

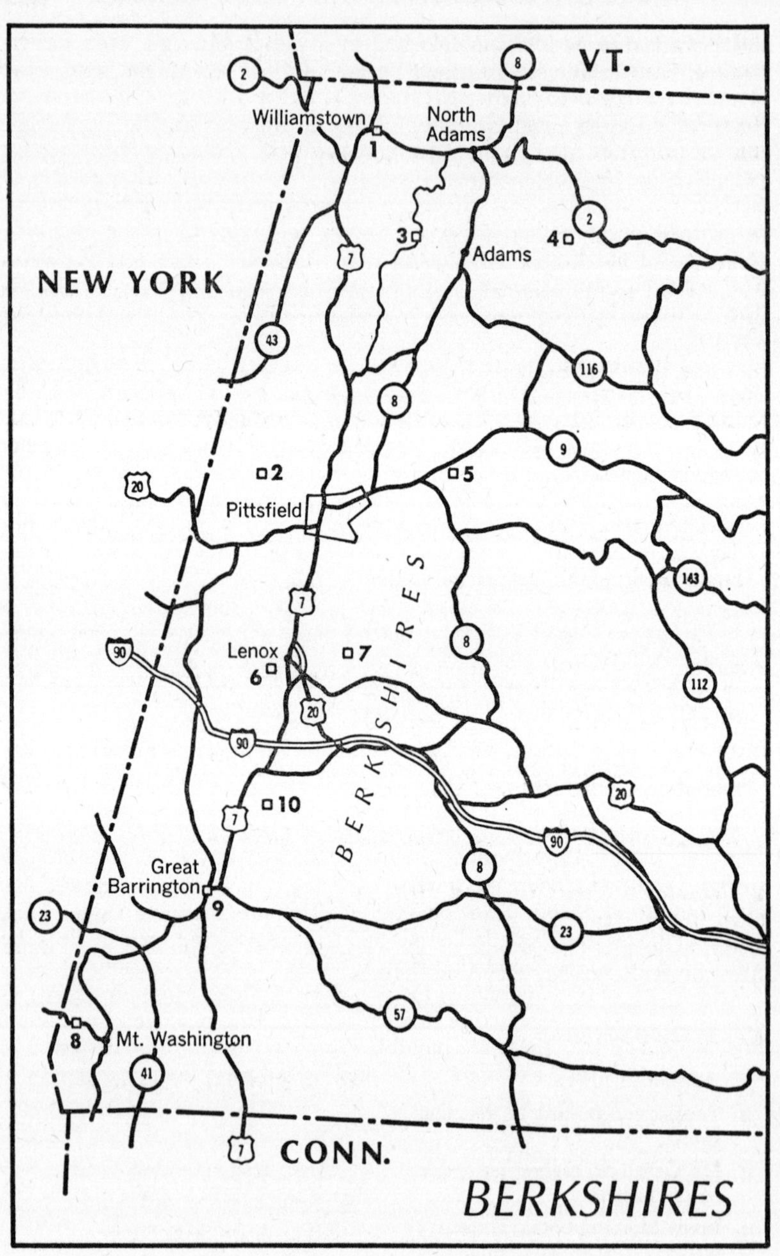

VT.
NEW YORK
Williamstown
North Adams
Adams
Pittsfield
Lenox
BERKSHIRES
Great Barrington
Mt. Washington
CONN.
1
2
3
4
5
6
7
8
9
10
BERKSHIRES

European and American art collected by the late Mr. and Mrs. Robert Sterling Clark. Notable paintings include *Virgin and Child with Four Angels* by Piero della Francesca, *Holy Family* by Rubens, *Crucifixion* by Rembrandt and an extensive group of French Impressionist works including 30 paintings by Renoir. Recent acquisitions include a 14th-century polyptych by Ugolina da Siena, Fragonard's *Warrior* and Monet's *Rouen Cathedral — Full Sunlight.* American art is represented by Stuart, Inness, Sargent, Remington and Winslow Homer. Selections from the extensive collection of old English, continental and American silver are displayed. The prints and drawings may be seen on prior application to the curator. The institute is open daily 10–5, except Mondays and the month of February.

Haystack Monument, Mission Park, marks the birthplace of foreign missions. The result of an 1806 afternoon's talk by five students was the founding of the American Board of Commissioners for Foreign Missions. In 1956 a "Haystack Fellowship" was established to bring foreign students to study at Williams.

GOODELL HOLLOW SKI AREA is a private area for use of Greylock Ski Club members only. 3 rope tows, 20-meter ski jump, ski lodge, 1.5 mi. Stoney Lodge Trail, beginners' classes.

PETERSBURG PASS SKI AREA (just over the York State line) has double chair lift, rope tow, 4 trails for novice, intermediate and expert, instruction, ski shop, ski rentals, meals, snacks, lodge, cocktails, warming hut, ski patrol. Open daily. Phone: Glenview 8-4580.

TACONIC TRAIL STATE PARK'S facilities include hiking, hunting, snowmobiling, scenic views.

WILLIAMSTOWN WILDLIFE MANAGEMENT AREA has public hunting.

Williamstown House of Local History (open during library hours), in town library, Main St., has books, maps, pictures, letters and other local historical items. The records of the Hopkins Post of the G.A.R. (Grand Army of the Republic) may be seen here.

Key to the Berkshires

1. Williams College
2. Tourist and trading center, state forest
3. Mt. Greylock, highest point in Massachusetts
4. Savoy Mountain State Forest
5. Wahconah Falls State Park
6. Tanglewood, Berkshire Music Festival
7. October Mountain State Forest
8. Bash Bish Falls State Forest
9. Summer resort and skiing
10. Bear Town State Forest

Novitiate of the Carmelite Fathers' Chapel, Oblong Rd., was formerly Nobel Prize winner Sinclair Lewis' estate, *Thorwald.* The severe simple chapel is dominated by a life-size, hand-carved crucifix against a glass block. The hand-carved Stations of the Cross were made in Oberammergau and the hand-carved figures of Our Lady of Mount Carmel and St. Joseph's were made in Italy.

WILMINGTON (Middlesex County, sett. 1639, incorp. 1730, alt. 96, pop. 17,102, area 17.08 sq. mi., town meeting, routes, Mass. 38, 62, 129). Wilmington, settled in 1639, was named for Lord Wilmington, a member of the Privy Council. In 1730 the General Court joined pieces of Reading (then called Redding) and Woburn into what is now Wilmington. Until recently Wilmington was a residential and farming community. Cranberries and apples were major crops. Hop making was a local industry. The Baldwin apple, developed here by James Butters, was promoted by Loammi Baldwin.

Local industries hire about 500 workers. The local work force nearly tripled when the Research and Advanced Development Division, Avco Corporation, established a unit here in 1958.

Local products include paint, powdered products, chemicals, electronic equipment, plastic containers, varnish and food machinery. Many Wilmington residents commute to work elsewhere.

Sheldon House (private) was the home of Asa G. Sheldon, author of "Asa G. Sheldon, Wilmington Farmer," who in 1835 cut down Pemberton Hill in Boston and removed the earth by oxcart.

WINCHENDON (Worcester County, sett. 1753, incorp. 1764, alt. 1000, pop. 6635, area 42.53 sq. mi., town meeting, routes, Mass. 12, 140), long known as "Toy Town" from toys produced in local factories, is now a residential manufacturing town with diversified industries.

The town was settled by Ipswich residents. Originally known as the Plantation of Ipswich-Canada, it has been known as Winchendon since its incorporation in 1764. Once an agricultural community, local pines were soon cut and shingles were made in local mills. "Shingletown" was a popular nickname during the 1700's. Cotton fabrics have been made here since 1843; denim is still made. In recent years the town lost considerable business because metal, paper and plastics have replaced many items like butter tubs, formerly made of wood.

Furniture, textiles, freezers and toys are major products.

LAKE DENNISON STATE PARK (US 202). Facilities: swimming, boating, fishing, hiking, picnic sites, campsites (50), hunting, snowmobiling, scenic views.

OTTER RIVER STATE FOREST surrounds Beaman Pond. Facilities: beach, bathhouse, lifeguards, fishing, hunting, fireplaces, picnic tables, campsites (118), snowmobiling.

BIRCH HILL WILDLIFE MANAGEMENT AREA has public hunting in Royalston, Winchendon, and Templeton.

WINCHESTER (Middlesex County, sett. 1640, incorp. 1850, alt. 50, pop. 22,269, area 6.50 sq. mi., representative town meeting, routes, US 3, Mass. 38). Winchester, a residential suburb of Boston, has a few industries employing about 750 workers. The town was called successively Woburn Gates, South Woburn and Black Horse Village. Col. Winchester, a Watertown businessman, presented his municipal namesake with $3000. Edward Converse, the "Father of Winchester," erected a gristmill.

On this mill site was built in 1830 a plant housing various enterprises, among them those of Joel Whitney and Amos Whittemore. Whitney built veneer making machinery; Whittemore introduced shoe pegging machinery, an innovation that forced him to raise his women binders' wages because of the hostility to machine production felt by his competitors, the old-fashioned shoemakers. The plant was bought by the United Shoe Machinery Corporation in 1929.

By 1860 three tanneries were in operation. Leather manufacture was important. The Mackey Metallic Fastener Corporation (1893), absorbed in time by the United Shoe Machinery Corporation, attracted many workers, causing a building boom. Today the town is largely residential, with few factories producing gelatin, watch hands, calibration equipment, paper boxes, knitted goods and assembled homes.

Resident Edwin Ginn founded Ginn, the schoolbook-publishing house, and made a $1,000,000 gift to create the World Peace Foundation. Resident Samuel McCall, editor, was author of biographies of Thaddeus Stevens and Thomas B. Reed and governor of Massachusetts (1916–19). *Winchester Public Library* (1930), Washington St. and Mystic Valley Parkway, recently enlarged, houses a small museum.

MIDDLESEX FELLS RESERVATION RECREATION AREA: 2630 acres of woodland and meadows patrolled by MDC mounted police, zoo, foot and bridle trails, natural and artificial ice skating, picnic sites, freshwater fishing, observation tower, swimming pool. For details see Middlesex Fells Reservation.

Winchester, home of Gov. (1961–63/65–69) John A. Volpe (b. 1908), was also the residence of Gov. Edward Everett (1836–40).

Canal buffs will find interesting material on the Middlesex Canal in the *Winchester Library.*

WINDSOR (Berkshire County, sett. 1767, incorp. 1771, alt. 2031, pop. 468, area 35.13 sq. mi., town meeting, routes, Mass. 8A, 9). Originally called Gageborough for the governor, Gen. Thomas Gage, Windsor changed its name, presumably for patriotic reasons.

In the center is a four-story *Observation Tower* (open). Mt. Greylock can be seen.

EAST WINDSOR (alt. 1320). At the center in the gorge beside Walker Brook is the old *Red Mill* that for many years turned out lollipop sticks and butchers' skewers.

WINTHROP (Suffolk County, sett. 1635, incorp. 1852, alt. 10, pop. 20,335, area 1.55 sq. mi., representative town meeting, route, Mass. 45), was named for Gov. John Winthrop. The region first appears in the records as Pullen Point.

On Shore Drive flood tides in winter and early spring, whipped by northeasters, hurl spray 40 feet or so in the air against the seawall.

POINT SHIRLEY (fishing, deep-sea trips, yacht races) is on Shirley St. A small settlement at Shirley Point, named for the royal governor, came into being in 1753 as a fishing enterprise. This failed, however, and the buildings were used to shelter Boston victims of the smallpox epidemic of 1765 and later yet a party of Acadian refugees.

Winthrop today is a residential suburb of Boston and a popular resort. Forts Banks and Heath, once U.S. military installations, located here for more than a century, are no longer in operation.

WOBURN (Middlesex County, sett. 1640, town incorp. 1642, city incorp. 1888, alt. 107, pop. 37,406, area 12.86 sq. mi., mayor-council, routes, I–93, US 3, Mass. 38, 128).

This Boston suburb and manufacturing city has isolated hills, streams, valleys, ravines and glens. Roman Catholic and Greek Orthodox groups broke down the once Congregational homogeneity — much to the distress of established citizens. Religious differences were eventually compromised. The city's population now includes American-born Irish, Italians, Swedes and Greeks.

In 1636, when Charlestown residents felt the village was becoming crowded, the town fathers selected Woburn as being ideal for larger farms.

Two 18th-century incidents are interesting: Ichabod Richardson, seized by the British and kept prisoner for seven years, returned home to find his wife had married a Josiah Richardson. Mrs. Richardson returned to her first husband. Simon Reed swapped his wife to James Butters of Wilmington for a yoke of oxen. Reed is reported to have had the better bargain.

Woburn was the birthplace of Tory Benjamin Thompson (1753–1814), one of the world's first great scientists and a nobleman of the Holy Roman Empire.

The Middlesex Canal (1803) helped Woburn's development. Between 1800 and 1850 the town rapidly changed to an industrial community. Shoe manufacturing and leather tanning predominated. During the pre-Civil War decade the increased demand for unskilled and semiskilled labor brought in foreign labor. By 1865 there were 21 tanning and currying plants and four factories making patent and enameled leather. Machinery, glue, chemicals and foundry products were added.

Woburn's current products include upper and patent leather, ice cream, chemicals, gears, electronic equipment and gelatin.

What to See and Do

Count Rumford Statue (in front of Winn Memorial Library, Pleasant St.). Benjamin Thompson has a well-deserved international reputation as a scientist, statesman, philanthropist, economist, military leader and world citizen. Tory Thompson, later Count Rumford, was a great American by any standards. The statue reveals a shrewd Yankee face and wiry figure. It is a replica of the Kaspar von Zumbusch statue in the English Gardens in Munich.

Thompson was a boyhood friend of Woburn's other celebrity, engineer Loammi Baldwin (1749–1807). Together they tramped 20 miles daily to attend Harvard College. At 14 Thompson's scientific knowledge enabled him to calculate a solar eclipse within four seconds of accuracy, and during his years of apprenticeship to a Salem storekeeper he made chemical and mechanical experiments. At 18 he moved to Concord, New Hampshire (then called Rumford). At 19 he married Col. Benjamin Rolfe's widow. Her wealth and influence helped his career.

Suspected of Tory sympathies, Thompson migrated (1776) to England and thence to Bavaria, countries which shared the fruits of his versatile genius. In 1791 he was created a count of the Holy Roman Empire. He chose his title after his wife's hometown. He presented London's Royal Society his most important scientific theory, that heat was a form of motion. Late in life he married the widow of the scientist Lavoisier. They later separated.

Count Rumford's Birthplace (open weekdays 9–5, free), 90 Elm St., a modest, buff-colored frame house, with gambrel and lean-to roofs, was erected in 1714 by the count's grandfather. The future count lived here only during babyhood. His family moved to another Woburn residence. On the first floor hangs an oil copy of the Gainsborough portrait of the count (original at Harvard). Rumford was the only Yankee painted by Gainsborough. Compare the avid youthful grace and charm with the severe maturity in the statue before the library.

Upstairs is an original Rumford Roaster. Scientist Rumford was interested in heat. One of the first fireless cookers is a cylindrical iron oven which when heated long retains its heat.

The garden perpetuates the count's fondness for flowers. The cannon in the yard was captured from the British in Portland Harbor in the War of 1812, and its position is a comment, probably unconsciously ironic, on the count's Tory sympathies. Another irony, equally unconscious and far more amazing, was President Adams' invitation to return and command West Point. Wisely, Rumford remained abroad. He died and was buried in France.

The *Winn Memorial (Woburn Public) Library* (*c.* 1877) was the first of H. H. Richardson's libraries.

Horn Pond Mountain (off Woburn Parkway) is ascended by footpath. East from the summit are the charming Mystic lakes and Blue Hills.

Hiker's Monument, a very masculine bronze, is the work of the first wife of sculptor H. H. Kitson. At the left corner, across from this statue, is a *Ventilator Cowl from the United States Ship Maine,* retrieved from Havana Harbor after the 1898 explosion which precipitated the Spanish War. It is a visible embodiment of the slogan "Remember the Maine."

The *Ancient Burying Ground,* junction of Park and Center Sts., contains the graves of ancestors of Presidents Pierce, Garfield, Cleveland and Benjamin Harrison.

WOODS HOLE (see FALMOUTH)

WORCESTER (Worcester County seat, sett. 1673, town incorp. 1722, city incorp. 1848, alt. 400, pop. 176,572, area 37.16 sq. mi., manager-council (Plan E), routes, I–290, US 20, Mass. 9, 12, 110, 122).

Worcester is a major U.S. industrial center. The name is pronounced WOO-ster. Some of our British brethren call it WAR-cester or WAR-chester.

Hills rescue Worcester from monotony. Zoning and city planning increase its variety and beauty. Factories are counterbalanced by municipal parks.

Excellent transport facilities, diversified manufactures and busy streets give the city a vital function in New England's life.

The first impression, one of tremendous commercial and industrial activity, is soon supplemented by a realization that Worcester is a cultural center, interested in arts, higher learning and historical research.

History and Development

Old Worcester was the scene of dramatic, musical and civic events unsurpassed in New England. Here Fanny Kemble, Sarah Bernhardt, Joe Jefferson, Edwin Booth, beautiful Lillie Langtry and Charlotte Cushman were seen in never-to-be-forgotten roles. Daring Lola Montez danced here.

Patti and Jenny Lind sang. Rubinstein played his own compositions. Here appeared many celebrities, Victoria Woodhull, Charles Dickens, P. T. Barnum, Thackeray, Kossuth, the Revolutionary Amazon Deborah Sampson and Abraham Lincoln. In 1854 "The Angel Gabriel" (J. S. Orr) attacked the Papacy. Here Matthew Arnold complained of having been served cold oysters at luncheon. Here was exhibited in 1818 Columbus, the first elephant seen in Ameria, and here the amazing P. T. Barnum gravely produced an ancient colored woman whom he declared was George Washington's nurse — 161 years old!

In Mechanics Hall were held for many years Worcester's famous Musical Festivals, which are still a noteworthy annual event, held now in the Memorial Auditorium.

Worcester is the home of several institutions of learning: Clark University, Holy Cross College, State College at Worcester, Becker Junior College, Worcester Polytechnic Institute, Assumption College, Worcester Junior College, and Quinsigamond Community College.

Worcester names with their major contributions to civilization include: Ichabod Washburn, wiredrawing processes and wire forms; William A. Wheeler, metal machine tools; Thomas E. Daniels, power planing machine; H. H. Bigelow, leather heeling machine; George Crompton, looms. Not to be omitted, also, is the name of Vermont-born J. C. Stoddard, inventor of a steam calliope, which he played in an excursion from Worcester to Fitchburg in 1856, greatly startling the citizens along the way.

At the time of the building of the Blackstone Canal (1828), laborers came over in great numbers from Southern Ireland and were followed in 1845 by many of their countrymen during the Potato Famine in Ireland. French-Canadian workers came to Worcester after the Civil War. Today their descendants number about 17,000. Beginning in 1868, the demand for skilled engineers and craftsmen attracted many Swedish immigrants. Thirty years ago one fifth of the population was of Swedish descent. In the 1890's began an influx of Poles, Jews, Lithuanians, Italians, Greeks, Armenians, Syrians and Albanians, which terminated in 1914. Negroes form a definite group. Such divergent racial strains have brought to the city cultural backgrounds which differ widely, giving Worcester a cosmopolitan stamp, preserved by fraternal organizations, singing societies and athletic associations of the various groups.

By 1970 there were 85,000 persons of foreign stock including Canadians, Irish, Russians and Swedes.

In 1674 Daniel Gookin and John Eliot visited the Nipmuck Indians. Gookin returned in 1682 with a small group of followers. They left during Queen Anne's War in 1702. In 1712 some settlers including Jonas Rice returned to found a permanent settlement. Within five years more than 200 colonists had moved here.

The Revolutionary War was popular with local residents. The town had its Revolutionary Committee. Publisher Isaiah Thomas escaped from the wrath of Boston's Tories and continued publishing his newspaper *The*

Massachusetts Spy here. The broadsides and pamphlets which came from his presses did much to unify anti-British and pro-Revolutionary sentiment throughout New England.

In 1786 the courthouse was besieged by impoverished farmers. This major demonstration of Shays' Rebellion was frustrated by Chief Justice Artemas Ward. In 1791 a Worcester Court decided that the clause in the Bill of Rights stating that "all men are born free and equal" was applicable to Negro slaves.

Textile manufacturing began in 1789 when the Worcester Cotton Manufactory was organized. This attempt was premature because of the primitive state of cotton processing equipment. It was still cheaper to import English-made cotton. Domestic-made paper, however, found a ready market. The advent of steam power started the city on its way to becoming a major American industrial center.

What To See and Do

City Hall (open), erected in 1898 from plans by Richard Howland Hunt, is in a modified Italian Renaissance style. The Florentine campaniles rise 205 feet. Within, on the main stairway given by Worcester, England, hang the helmets and breastplates of two of Cromwell's soldiers who fell at the battle of Worcester. A *Bronze Star* set in the sidewalk marks the spot where Isaiah Thomas stood on July 14, 1776, and read for the first time to a New England audience the Declaration of Independence.

Worcester Common today comprises a scant five acres of the twenty acres set aside in 1669 by the proprietors for use as a training field and to accommodate a meetinghouse and school building. From 1800 a clock made by Abel Stowell of Worcester kept time in the steeple of the meetinghouse, and the equipment was completed in 1802 by the purchase of a bell weighing nearly a ton from the foundry of Revere and Sons, Boston. There was not always a spirit of coordination between the dials of the clock and the clapper of the bell, for the latter periodically went on striking sprees that lasted until the arrival of its official guardian, or, more often, until the mechanism ran down. In 1888 the bell was moved to the *New Old South Church* at the corner of Main and Wellington Sts. The bell was moved again in 1966 when the Old South and Tatnuck Congregational Churches merged as *The First Congregational Church* of Worcester, 1070 Pleasant Street.

A *Hidden Graveyard* lies in the area between Salem Square and the Bigelow shaft. In it are the graves of several hundred citizens buried between 1730 and 1795. In 1854 the headstones were recorded, laid flat on the graves and the whole area covered with earth and seeded.

Worcester County Horticultural Society (1842), corner of Elm and Chestnut Streets. The present building was built in 1929. Free flower shows are held during the summer. There is also a four-day chrysanthemum show (Nov.) and a March show ($1.00). The society has an outstanding 4000-volume library (open to public). In 1955 an experimental orchard of old varieties of apples was started in North Grafton; scions have been shipped all over this country and to Europe.

Worcester Science Museums (open daily 10–5, Sun. 1–5, closed Mon., free), 21 Cedar St. (Daniels House), has live animals and science and natural history exhibits ranging from minerals to space technology.

Municipal War Memorial Auditorium (open) occupies a block between Highland, Salisbury and Harvard Sts. and Institute Rd. It was erected by the city of Worcester in 1933. Built of Indiana limestone with a base of granite, it is of modified classic design and monumental proportion.

War Memorial Murals, the principal decoration of the Memorial Chamber, located directly over the foyer, honor Worcesterites who died in WWI. Leon Kroll, nationally known American artist, spent three years executing this work. The central panel, one of the largest murals in the world, measures 57′ × 30′. Its theme, based upon resurrection or rebirth, implies the renewal of a pledge to defend our way of life. Two smaller murals, each 25′ × 16′, symbolically depict land, air and sea defenses. The World War Memorial Flagstaff, from which the flag, floodlighted at night, is never lowered, rises 90 feet from a base of bronze and granite, directly opposite the auditorium.

Worcester Historical Society (open Tues.–Sat. 2–5, closed Aug., free), 39 Salisbury St., was founded in 1875. Thousands of objects on display: Indian artifacts, utilitarian tools, barn and kitchen exhibits, toys, costumes, glass, china, furniture. Research library. The society will furnish information and directions to other historical highlights in Worcester.

Worcester Art Museum (open Mon.–Sat. 10–5, Sun. and holidays 2–5, Oct.–Apr. special exhibitions are open Tues. evening until 10, free), 55 Salisbury St., founded in 1896 by Stephen Salisbury III, is a much finer museum than is often found in many cities with several times Worcester's population. Twenty galleries trace the history of fine arts from prehistoric times to the present.

Hogarth, Gainsborough, Raeburn, Reynolds and Romney, genre pictures by the Dutch painters and Venetian carnival scenes by Canaletto and Guardi are exhibited in *Gallery XIII.* In the French collection are *The Card Player* by Cézanne and *Girl on a Balcony* and *The Promenade* by Henri Matisse. There are also two paintings by Claude Monet, *Waterloo Bridge* and *Water Lilies,* and works by Derain, Picasso and others. Portraits by Gilbert, Sully, Peal, Copley and Inman, landscapes by the Hudson River Schools and various works by Earl, Eakin, Whistler, Sargent, Homer, Blakelock, Fuller, Hassam, Hunt, Inness, Metcalf and Wyant are on display.

Stained-glass exhibits include two windows from the Chapel of Borsham House (English) about 1400, a 13th-century window from Strasbourg, a fragment from a window in Chartres Cathedral (13th century, French) and the "Peacock Window" by John La Farge. Among the representative pieces of Eastern art is a collection of Japanese prints showing the work of such masters as Hiroshige and Hokusai. The evolution of American furniture is traced through Chippendale, Sheraton and Adam.

American Antiquarian Society (open Mon.–Fri., except holidays, 9–5),

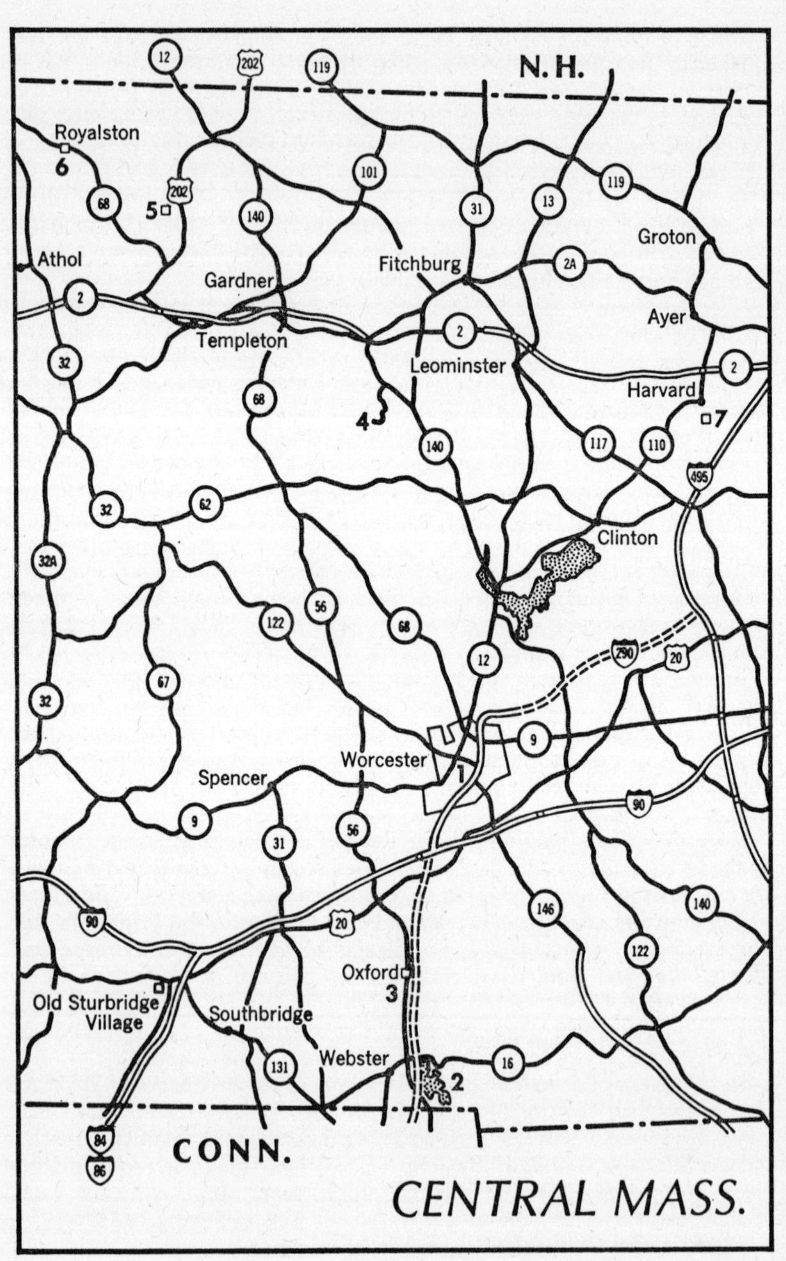
N.H.
Royalston
6
5
Athol
Gardner
Fitchburg
Groton
Ayer
Templeton
Leominster
Harvard
7
4
Clinton
Worcester
1
Spencer
Oxford
3
Old Sturbridge
Village
Southbridge
Webster
2
CONN.
CENTRAL MASS.

corner of Salisbury St. and Park Ave., was founded in 1812 by Isaiah Thomas. Its collections on American history and culture prior to the year 1877 are preeminent. Two thirds of all recorded materials printed in this country by the year 1820 are in its library and the total of printed pieces numbers 750,000. A large manuscript collection is also present in the library which attracts scholars and writers from around the world.

The *Site of the Birthplace of George Bancroft* (1800–91), early American historian and founder of the Naval Academy and Minister Plenipotentiary to Great Britain (1846–49), is indicated, opposite Massachusetts Ave., by a small boulder bearing a bronze tablet (see WRITERS).

Clark University, opposite University Park on Main St., was founded in 1887 by Jonas Gilman Clark (1815–1900). Reversing the patterns at most American colleges and universities, Clark was organized by first president Dr. Granville Stanley Hall as an institution solely concerned with graduate study and research. As such, it became the second titled graduate school in the U.S. and the first in New England. As a result of a special provision in Mr. Clark's will, an undergraduate division for men (Clark College) was established in 1902. Undergraduate women were first admitted in 1941, the same year the Division of Business Administration was founded. The evening college was established in 1953 and today serves over 1500 area adults.

Sigmund Freud gave his only American lectures here in 1909; Clark is the birthplace of modern rocketry, through the pioneering work of Robert H. Goddard, and also was the site of the founding of the American Psychological Association; the first graduate school of geography was established at Clark in 1920 by Dr. Wallace W. Atwood, second president.

Today Clark has enrolled 2800 students, taught by 230 faculty members. It offers 19 undergraduate majors, 15 master's degree programs and 12 doctoral degree programs.

Holy Cross College (1843), on Mount St. James, was founded by Rt. Rev. Benedict Joseph Fenwick, second Bishop of Boston, who requested the Society of Jesus to staff and administer the college. He willed the college to the Jesuits. It was New England's first Catholic college. Today, it is a men's liberal arts college granting bachelor's degrees and a master's degree in chemistry. The college had 2400 students and 175 faculty members.

Key to Central Massachusetts

1. Worcester Polytechnic Institute, Art Museum, Woodman Armory, Clark University, Holy Cross College
2. Lake Chargoggagomanchaugagochaubunagungamaug
3. Clara Barton birthplace
4. Motor road to top of Mt. Wachusett
5. Otter River State Forest
6. Old Houses and falls, Birch Hill dam
7. Federated Womens Clubs State Forest

Worcester Polytechnic Institute (1865), located between Institute Rd., Park Ave. and Salisbury St., offers undergraduate and graduate programs in engineering and science; beginning in 1968, it offered degree programs in business management and the humanities.

Over half of the college's 20 major buildings have been constructed since 1953 to provide additional modern laboratory and classroom facilities, housing and library. "Worcester Tech's" Alden Research Laboratories in nearby Holden are world-renowned for model studies of waterways. Present enrollment is about 1750 full-time students and 235 faculty members.

Worcester State College (1874), 486 Chandler St., is a publicly supported arts, sciences and education college. Until 1921 both men and women students were admitted; from 1921 to 1937 only women were admitted, and in 1937 it again became coeducational.

Principal (1874–1909) E. Harlow Russell made this institution a copioneer with Clark University in child psychology studies. Students come primarily from the Greater Worcester area to this 50-acre commuter campus. There are 1600 students.

Assumption College (100-acre campus in Worcester's Westwood Hills), a Catholic men's liberal arts and sciences college, directed by the Assumptionist Fathers, grants Bachelor of Arts, Master of Arts, Master of Arts in Teaching degrees and a Certificate of Advanced Studies. Originally established (1904) as a secondary school, it expanded into a four-year college. In 1953 the original West Boylston Street campus was almost totally destroyed by a tornado. The present buildings in the new campus location have been built since 1955. Assumption's present enrollment: 1400 students.

Worcester Junior College (1905), privately operated, has 2500 students and 100 faculty members. Accredited by New England Association of Colleges and Secondary Schools, it offers transfer and terminal programs in liberal arts, business and engineering.

Becker Junior College (1887), a junior college of 650 students and 35 faculty members, occupies 20-odd buildings in Worcester's park section. Business oriented Becker also offers a journalism program.

Trumbull Mansion (private), 6 Massachusetts Ave., was originally located at Trumbull Sq. and was the second court house of Worcester. Up its steps marched Judge Artemas Ward through the ranks of Daniel Shays' army. Refused entrance, he opened and adjourned court in the United States Arms Hotel.

Bancroft Tower, a battlemented stone structure, offers a fine observation point within the city. Another fine city view can be seen from *Worcester's Municipal Airport.*

John Woodman Higgins Armory, Inc. (open Mon.–Fri. 8:30–4:30, Sat. 8:30–12 noon, closed Sun. and holidays, free.), 100 Barber Ave. This historical and art museum is devoted to metal craftsmanship and exhibits items from the Stone, Bronze and Early Iron Ages and products from our own Modern Alloys Age. The interior is designed after the halls of the 10th Century Hohenwerfen Castle, Salzburg, Austria. The Ancient Wing exhibits armor and arms of the Medieval and Renaissance periods; over 100 complete armors, including mounted knights in full panoply, are on view; furniture, banners, tapestries, stained glass and paintings (among them Brueghel's famous *Forge of Vulcan*) complete the effect of the bygone era.

Craft Center (1951), 25 Sagamore Rd., a nonprofit, community-supported education institution, provides craft classes, conducted by a full-time craftsmen-instructors staff. Group and individual instruction is offered in eight studio workshops which are fully equipped with hand and power tools and housed in a modern well-planned building.

Exhibitions are scheduled throughout the year. The center is open Mon.–Sat. 9–5; exhibits are also open Wed. 7–9 P.M.

Davis Tower, the gift of a former mayor of the city, offers a fine view of the lake. On the tower a bronze tablet — no longer here — recounted the story of Samuel Lenorson. In 1690 the Lenorsons built their cabin near the present tower. In 1695 Samuel, age 12, the only son, was stolen by Indians. Nothing was heard from him until the spring of 1697, when, after the sack of Haverhill, captives Hannah Dustin and Mary Neff were brought to an island at the junction of the Merrimack and Contoocook Rivers. Here they met young Sam. The three captives killed ten Indians and escaped to Haverhill. The General Court voted that Samuel be paid £12, 10s. for "the just slaughter of so many of the Barbarians."

Timothy Paine Home (private), 140 Lincoln St. "Paine the Tory" was a Mandamus Councilor. In 1774 patriots forced him to resign. John Adams, some 20 years after teaching in Worcester, was a Paine guest when his host offered a toast to "the King." Embarrassed patriots toasted His Majesty and then Adams — so the story runs — offered a toast "to the Devil." Consternation reigned; no one knew what to do, when Mrs. Paine, smiling, remarked to her husband, "My dear, as the gentleman has been so kind as to drink to our king, let us by no means refuse to drink to his." The house, now called the "Oaks," houses the D.A.R.'s Timothy Bigelow Chapter.

Green Hill Park (open), opposite Burncoat Park, is named for Andrew H. Green, a Worcester native, later known as the "Father of Greater New York" through his efforts in making civic and public improvements in that city. Herds of elk and bison are pastured within the park which also has a "barnyard zoo." There is an 18-hole *Municipal Golf Course,* archery butts and provisions for tobogganing and skiing.

QUINSIGAMOND STATE PARK (now in two separate locations, one on Lake Ave. s. of Belmont St. and one on Regatta Point). Facilities: boating, beach, swimming, sailing and instructions, tennis, picnic sites. Lake Quinsigamond is the site of the annual Eastern Intercollegate Rowing Regatta.

WORCESTER COUNTY — the largest in area — (est. 1731, pop. 637,969, area 1511.82 sq. mi., shire town, Worcester), includes the cities of Fitchburg, Gardner, Leominster, Worcester and the 56 towns of Ashburnham, Athol, Auburn, Barre, Berlin, Blackstone, Bolton, Boylston, Brookfield, Charlton, Clinton, Douglas, Dudley, East Brookfield, Grafton, Hardwick, Harvard, Holden, Hopedale, Hubbardston, Lancaster, Leicester, Lunenburg, Mendon, Milford, Millbury, Millville, New Braintree, Northborough, Northbridge, North Brookfield, Oakham, Oxford, Paxton, Petersham, Phillipston, Princeton, Royalston, Rutland, Shrewsbury, Southborough, Southbridge, Spencer, Sterling, Sturbridge, Sutton, Templeton, Upton, Uxbridge, Warren, Webster, Westborough, West Boylston, West Brookfield, Westminster and Winchendon.

WORCESTER METROPOLITAN AREA (pop. 344,320, area 429.47 sq. mi.) includes the city of Worcester and the towns of Auburn, Berlin, Boylston, Brookfield, East Brookfield, Grafton, Holden, Leicester, Millbury, North Brookfield, Northborough, Northbridge, Oxford, Shrewsbury, Spencer, Sutton, Upton, West Boylston, Westborough.

WORONOCO (see RUSSELL)

WORTHINGTON (Hampshire County, sett. 1764, incorp. 1768, alt. 1493, pop. 712, town meeting, routes, Mass. 112, 143).

WORTHINGTON CENTER is a dairy and potato farming center. Maple sugar provides seasonal revenue.

SOUTH WORTHINGTON. *Birthplace of the Rev. Russell H. Conwell* (open), the educator who founded Temple University in Philadelphia. The main building dates back to about *c.* 1800, but the veranda and kitchen are recent additions.

South Worthington Cascade is a gentle but beautiful falls with a 50-foot drop.
West Worthington Falls, River Rd., plunges 75 feet down a tree-bordered gorge. In summer there is only a sparkling rivulet falling over bare rocks into the chasm, but in floodtime there is a roaring torrent.

CANADA HILL WILDLIFE MANAGEMENT AREA (see CHESTER).

WRENTHAM (Norfolk County, sett. 1660, incorp. 1673, alt. 253, pop. 7315, area 22.02 sq. mi., town meeting, routes, I–495, US 1, Mass. 1A, 121, 140), originally part of Dedham, was named after Wrentham, England. During King Philip's War, all hands fled to Dedham after Wrentham was burned. Woolen and cotton mills were established in the early 19th century. Straw hat making was begun in 1798 by Mrs. Naomi Whipple. Jewelry factories were opened. Summer folk aid prosperity. A granite stone in the village center marks the site of the first meetinghouse (1684).

YARMOUTH (Barnstable County, sett. 1639, incorp. 1639, pop. 12,033, town meeting, routes, US 6, US 6A, Mass. 28) includes Yarmouth Port, and South and West Yarmouth.

Yarmouth is known for its elm-shaded streets. Its history is typical of the Cape. After the Revolution it struggled to adapt itself to new conditions. A large share of the ships which New England sent in response to alluring opportunities offered by the Napoleonic Wars were commanded and sailed by Cape Codders with those of Yarmouth in the forefront. The years 1815–1855 saw the zenith of its prosperity, with activity ashore and afloat. Just before the Civil War, however, the glory of the American merchant marine began to fade. Fishing concentrated in Gloucester, Boston and Provincetown. Yarmouth's fleet, like those of the other Cape towns, went out of existence.

Capt. Asa Eldridge of Yarmouth, one of the famous Cape skippers, made a memorable racing voyage across the Atlantic in the clipper *Red Jacket.*

At the center on US 6 the *Thatcher House* (open as antique shop) bears the date 1680 on its large, square chimney.

YARMOUTH VILLAGE lies inland between Yarmouth Port on the north shore and South and West Yarmouth on the south shore overlooking Nantucket Sound. Yarmouth is the center of the Cape's cranberry industry.

SOUTH YARMOUTH, Mass. 28. *Indian Burying Ground,* about 0.5 mi. east of the center off Station Ave., contains a pile of unhewn stones with a chiseled inscription: "On this slope lie buried the last of the native Indians of Yarmouth."

TOWN PARK and BEACH on Nantucket Sound. A large pine grove (picnicking) and a fine beach (bathhouses, small fee) make this a most attractive spot.

YARMOUTH PORT (US 6A) overlooks Barnstable Harbor and Cape Cod Bay. Excellent beaches.

Col. John Thatcher House (open mid-June–Sept., daily except Sun. 10–12 and 2–5, and by appointment, small fee), corner of Thatcher Lane and King's Highway (US 6A). The original part of this house was built in 1680. Exhibits, period furnishings. (SPNEA).

Winslow Crocker House (open mid-June–Sept., daily except Sun. 10–12 and 2–5, small fee), adjacent to Col. Thatcher House. Period furnishings and interesting woodwork. (SPNEA).

ZOAR (see CHARLEMONT)

ZYLONITE (see ADAMS)

What's Happened in Massachusetts

What's Happened in Massachusetts

1000–08 Norsemen from Greenland visit New England.
1524 Giovanni da Verrazano cruises New England coast.
1602 Bartholomew Gosnold reaches Massachusetts Bay.
1603 Martin Pring explores Maine and Massachusetts coasts.
1604–05 De Monts and Champlain explore Maine and Massachusetts coast.
1605 George Weymouth explores Massachusetts coast.
1607–08 George Popham trys to colonize "Northern Virginia" (New England).
1609 Henry Hudson cruises New England coast.
1614 Manhattan's Adriaen Block sails to Nahant Bay. John Smith maps New England coast. Region thereafter known as New England.
1620 *Mayflower* lands at Provincetown and Plymouth with Pilgrims, John Carver elected first Governor. Plymouth Hill fortified.
1621 Pilgrims celebrate Thanksgiving and build their first meeting house.
1623 Myles Standish conducts first organized war against the Indians. Dorchester men establish Cape Ann fishing post.
1630 John Winthrop arrives with 11 ships and 900 settlers; Boston begins.
1631 Massachusetts' maritime history commences when Gov. Winthrop launches the *Blessing of the Bay* on Mystic River.
1634 Anne Hutchinson outrages Boston's clergy.
1635 Boston opens Public Latin School for Boys.
1636 General Court establishes college in Newtowne, (Cambridge).
1638 First printing press in America set up in Cambridge by Stephen Daye. Lynn has a shoe factory.
1639 A fulling mill is in operation in Rowley.
1641 Salem men produce salt by evaporating sea water.
1642 Harvard holds first commencement.
1643 Colonists organize New England Confederation to combat Indians and New Amsterdam Dutch.
1645 Latin school opens in Roxbury.
1646 John Eliot translates Bible into Indian tongue.
1647 Popular education begins. Law requires elementary schools in towns of 50 persons and secondary schools in towns double that size.
1648 Margaret Jones of Charlestown is hanged for being a witch.

1649 General Court passes legislation controlling practice of medicine.

1652 Property ownership and church affiliation is required for voting right. First bookstore opens in Boston.

1657 Halfway Covenant allows converted as well as baptized church members to vote.

1660 Trade and Plantation Council commences its activity in London.

1675 King Philip makes war on colonists.

1677 Massachusetts produces medical treatise on smallpox and measles.

1684 Bible Commonwealth passes with revocation of Massachusetts Charter.

1687 Britain sends Andros to govern Dominion of New England.

1689 Irate colonists overthrow Andros.

1691 New Massachusetts Charter abolishes church membership as prerequisite for voting.

1692 Witches abound in Salem. Hysteria spreads.

1699 Early law to avoid spread of infectious diseases.

1704 *Boston News Letter,* first American newspaper, appears.

1734 Jonathan Edwards preaches hell-fire sermons in Northampton and begins Great Awakening.

1735 John Adams, 2nd U.S. President, is born.

1742 Faneuil Hall becomes Boston's Town Hall and market place.

1745 Gov. William Shirley leads Massachusetts troops to the capture of Louisburg.

1761 Lawyers organize Suffolk County Bar Association.

1763 Pontiac's braves devastate Massachusetts frontier in second serious Indian uprising.

1764 Great Britain commences policy of imperial control. Passes Sugar Act.

1765 Population: 240,433. Stamp Act, designed to increase imperial revenue, follows Sugar Act.

1766 Colonials inaugurate boycott. Great Britain repeals Stamp Act and modifies Sugar Act.

1767 Britain's Townshend Act places duties on paint, glass and tea. Massachusetts in a fever of excitement; Boston merchants alarmed by appearance of customs officials. John Quincy Adams, 6th U.S. President, is born.

1768 Massachusetts develops Circular Letter to provide unity among colonies. Hancock's sloop *Liberty* lands cargo in defiance of authorities. British troops arrive in Boston.

1770 British sentry fires on rioters near Old State House. Sam Adams agitates. Boston resentment runs high. Colonial pressure repeals Townshend Act.

1773 Britain's Tea Act leads to Boston Tea Party; Britain answers with Coercive Measures. Closes port of Boston.

1774 Angry colonists vote to resist British taxation at mass meeting in Faneuil Hall.

1775 Paul Revere, William Dawes and Dr. Samuel Prescott ride to Lexington and Concord. Bunker's Hill is fought. Gage evacuates Boston, George Washington commands Continental Army.

1776 Population: 299,841. Massachusetts unanimously approves Declaration of Independence, publicly proclaimed from Old State House.

1778 Popularly elected constitutional convention meets in Cambridge.

1780 Massachusetts ratifies state constitution containing Bill of Rights. John Hancock elected governor. Judicial interpretation of constitution abolishes slavery. Academy of Arts and Sciences organized in Boston.

1781 Massachusetts Medical Society is founded.

1784 *Empress of China* makes maiden voyage to Orient.

1785 Massachusetts surrenders her western lands to national government.

1786 Bridgewater develops machinery for cotton manufacture. Shays leads rebellion of debt-ridden farmers. Gen. Rufus Putnam and others organize Ohio Land Company starting the New England movement to Ohio.

1788 Massachusetts ratifies federal Constitution and becomes the sixth state to enter Union. Massachusetts suggests amendments to the Constitution from which Bill of Rights develops.

1789 President George Washington visits Boston; Governor John Hancock refuses to call on him, insisting the governor of Massachusetts is a more important personage than the President of the United States. The *Franklin* of Boston is first American ship to reach Japan. The *Atlantic,* of Boston, sails to Bombay and Calcutta. Steam-propelled paddle boat invented by Nathan Reed used on Wenham Pond, begins trips between Danvers and Beverly.

1790 Population: 378,787.

1792 Paul Revere opens Boston bell foundry.

1794 Middlesex Canal, 27 miles long, connecting Merrimack and Mystic Rivers, is 18th-century wonder.

1796 John Adams elected second President of the United States. Boston creates Boston Dispensary to provide medical aid for the poor.

1800 Population: 422,845. Thomas Jefferson elected President. Massachusetts Federalists panic.

1802 Dr. Benjamin Waterhouse employs Jenner vaccination technique at Harvard.

1803 New England States and New York threaten to secede from the Union in protest over Louisiana Purchase. War with Tripoli (1801–05); Massachusetts makes history with Capt. Preble and the *Constitution.*

1810 Population: 472,040. Philharmonic Society founded, first New England orchestra.

1812 Massachusetts House of Representatives condemns federal government for leading country into war with England.

1814 Hartford Convention convenes; conservative Federalist delegates from Massachusetts condemn War of 1812, threaten nullification and secession. Francis C. Lowell's steam power looms hum in Waltham and lead to industrialization of Lawrence, Lowell, Fall River and New Bedford.

1815 *North American Review* and Handel and Haydn Society founded. First peace society in the world organized in Boston.

1818 People discuss building Capc Cod canal, which materializes a hundred years later (1909).

1820 Population: 523,287. Conservative Massachusetts reacts to westward expansion; calls a constitutional convention which incorporates cities, removes religious tests for office holders and discards all qualifications for the franchise excepting a small property tax which Daniel Webster, John Adams and Judge Joseph Story resist because it allows "the poor and the profligate to control the affluent." Maine acquires statehood making Missouri Compromise possible.

1821 Boston has a real public high school.

1822 City Charter granted Boston.

1823 Jonas Chickering manufactures a piano.

1824 John Quincy Adams elected sixth President of the United States.

1825 American Unitarian Association organizes in Boston. First High School for Girls in the United States opens.

1826 Massachusetts boasts its first railroad (horse-drawn), constructed for hauling granite blocks from Quincy to Bunker Hill Monument, Charlestown. Prohibitionists commence activity. John Adams and Thomas Jefferson, both signers of the Declaration of Independence and both Presidents of the United States, die on July 4, exactly 50 years from the signing of the Declaration.

1829 Perkins Institution for the Blind founded.

1830 Population: 610,408.

1831 Garrison commences antislavery crusade. Founds *The Liberator* in Boston.

1832 New England Anti-Slavery Society forms in Boston.

1833 Constitutional amendment separating church and state passes Legislature. Abolition sentiment grows; New England Anti-Slavery Society becomes American Anti-Slavery Society. Boston Academy of Music founded.

1834 Angry mob burns Ursuline Convent, Charlestown, in anti-Catholic outburst.

1835 Horace Mann at work. Founds normal school in Lexington with Samuel Hall.

1837 Mary Lyon establishes Mount Holyoke College, South Hadley, first American women's college. Emerson delivers "America's

Intellectual Declaration of Independence" in his Phi Beta Kappa Address at Harvard.

1838 Lowell Mason introduces Music in Boston public schools. Evening medical courses offered at Tremont Temple.

1840 Population: 737,699.

1846 Anaesthesia successfully used at Massachusetts General Hospital.

1847 Louis Agassiz lectures on embryology at Lowell Institute.

1849 Garrison submits petition for women's suffrage.

1850 Population: 994,514. National Women's Rights Convention meets in Worcester.

1852 Boston Public Library, made possible by public subscription, opens.

1855 Legislature appoints "Nunnery Committee" to investigate secrets of Catholic convents and schools.

1856 Massachusetts gives its electoral vote to John C. Fremont, first Republican candidate for President. He loses.

1860 Population: 1,231,066.

1861 Baltimore mob attacks Sixth Massachusetts Regiment on its way to Washington.

1863 Marie Jakrysewka founds New England Hospital for Women and Children.

1864 State Board of Charities is established.

1865 Law forbids discrimination against any race in public places. Massachusetts Institute of Technology opens. Labor of children under ten in factories is prohibited.

1867 New England Conservatory of Music opens in Boston. Mary Baker Eddy founds Christian Science in Lynn.

1869 First State Board of Health is established. Evening schools established. Last whaler sails from New Bedford.

1870 Population: 1,457,351. Massachusetts Woman's Suffrage Association elects Julia Ward Howe president.

1872 Dr. Susan Dimock has nurse's training school at New England Hospital for Women and Children. Fire sweeps Boston (loss of $70,000,000).

1876 Alexander Graham Bell successfully experiments with telephone.

1880 Population: 1,783,085. Public opens Art Museum at Copley Square, Boston.

1881 Henry Lee Higginson endows Boston Symphony Orchestra.

1882 Henry Wadsworth Longfellow dies in Cambridge; Ralph Waldo Emerson dies in Concord.

1887 Labor Day is declared legal holiday. Legislature passes Employers' Liability Act. Clark University established as second purely graduate school in America.

1889 Cotton spinners organize National Cotton Mule Spinners Union.

1890 Population: 2,238,943.

1891 James Russell Lowell dies.

1892 First Church of Christ, Scientist, Boston. John Greenleaf Whittier dies.
1894 Boston and Maine RR opens North Station.
1897 Boston has first subway in the United States.
1899 South Station opens.
1900 Population: 2,805,346.
1902 President Theodore Roosevelt names Massachusetts Supreme Court Chief Justice O. W. Holmes, Jr., as associate justice, U.S. Supreme Court.
1907 Savings banks permitted to conduct life insurance business.
1908 Ford Hall Forum established in Boston.
1910 Population: 3,366,416.
1911 Workmen's Compensation Act passed.
1912 Minimum wage law passed. Lawrence textile workers and Boston street car operators strike. Department of Labor and Industry established.
1916 President Wilson names Louis D. Brandeis, Kentucky-born Boston lawyer, to U.S. Supreme Court.
1917 John F. Kennedy, 35th U.S. President, born in Brookline.
1918 German submarine near Orleans bombards tug and three coal barges, causing consternation; air forces ordered to Cape.
1919 Boston Police Strike.
1920 Population: 3,852,356.
1923 Massachusetts ex-governor Calvin Coolidge succeeds Warren G. Harding as President of the United States.
1924 Massachusetts women vote. Coolidge elected President.
1926 Beverly shoe machine plant is the largest in world. Drs. Minot and Murphy discover pernicious anemia cure. They receive Nobel Prize.
1927 Anarchists Nicolo Sacco and Bartolomeo Vanzetti, Italian aliens, executed at State Prison seven years after their conviction for their alleged participation in the robbery-murder of a paymaster and guard in 1920 (see HISTORICAL NOTES).
1928 Roger Babson predicts unusually good business year in 1929. Submarine S4 sinks off Provincetown with 40 men.
1929 Earthquake rocks state. Ex-President Calvin Coolidge returns to Northampton law practice. Boston University celebrates 60th anniversary.
1930 Population: 4,249,614. Massachusetts Bay Colony Tercentenary Celebration.
1932 Presidential election: Roosevelt (D) 800,148, Hoover (R) 736,959, Thomas (Socialist) 34,305 and Foster (Communist) 4821 votes.
1933 Convicts fire Charlestown State Prison. Calvin Coolidge dies at 60.
1934 Massachusetts textile workers answer general textile strike call.
1935 Mr. Justice Holmes dies at 93. Boston Public Latin School cele-

brates 300th anniversary. Teachers' Oath Bill, requiring all public school and college teachers to take oath of allegiance to Constitution, becomes law.

1936 Harvard University celebrates 300th anniversary. Election: Roosevelt (D) 942,716, Landon (R) 768,613, Lemke (Union) 118,369, Thomas (Socialist) 5111, Browder (Communist) 2930, votes.

1937 Child labor amendment with significant national implications, again defeated. Teachers' Oath Law repeal passed by legislature, but vetoed by governor. FDR delivers "quarantine" speech, attacking aggressors against international speech.

1939 Harvard Law School professor Felix Frankfurter named to U.S. Supreme Court.

1940 Population: 4,316,721. Election: Roosevelt (D) 1,076,522, Willkie (R) 939,700, Thomas (Socialist) 4091, Browder (Communist) 3806.

1942 Coconut Grove nightclub fire, worst in Boston's history, with 499 dead.

1944 Election: Roosevelt (D) 1,035,296, Dewey (R) 921,350. Harvard produces first digital computer.

1948 Election: Truman (D) 1,151,788, Dewey (R) 909,370, Wallace (Progressive) 38,157.

1950 Population: 4,690,514. Brink's Boston office robbed by masked bandits of $2,775,395.12 ($1,218,211.29 in cash). Robbers eventually caught and convicted.

1952 Election: Eisenhower (R) 1,292,325, Stevenson (D) 1,083,525, Hallinan (Progressive) 4636. Congressman John F. Kennedy defeats incumbent U.S. Sen. Henry Cabot Lodge (R).

1956 Election: Eisenhower (R) 1,393,197, Stevenson (D) 948,190, Hass (Socialist Labor) 5573. U.S. Sen. John F. Kennedy narrowly defeated for vice-presidential nomination by Sen. Estes Kefauver (Tenn.).

1958 John F. Kennedy reelected to U.S. Senate.

1960 Sen. John F. Kennedy narrowly defeats Richard Nixon (Calif.) and becomes first Catholic president. Names brother Robert U.S. Attorney General. Population: 5,148,578. Election: Kennedy (D) 1,487,174, Nixon (R) 976,750.

1961 JFK names Harvard Economics Professor John Kenneth Galbraith as ambassador to India and Pulitzer-Prize-winning Harvard historian Arthur M. Schlesinger, Jr., as special presidential assistant.

1962 Highwaymen hold up U.S. Mail truck in Plymouth and steal $1,551,277—largest cash robbery in U.S. history.

1963 President John F. Kennedy (1917–1963), 35th President, slain, Nov. 22 in Dallas, Texas.

1964 Election: Johnson (D) 1,786,422, Goldwater (R) 549,727.

1968 Election: Nixon (R) 766,844, Humphrey (D) 1,593,082.

Index

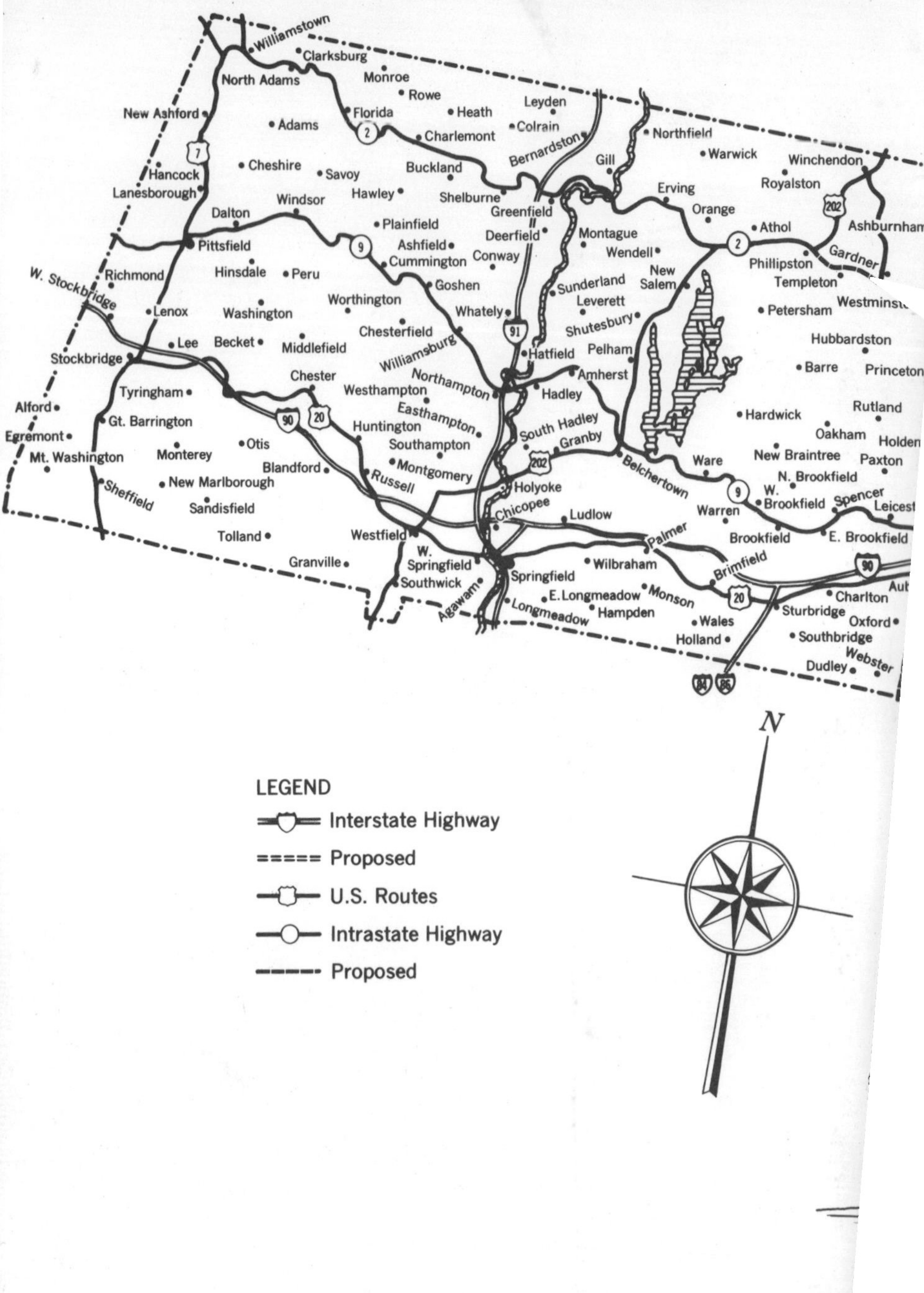

Williamstown
Clarksburg
North Adams
Monroe
Rowe
New Ashford
Adams
Florida
Heath
Leyden
Colrain
Charlemont
Bernardston
Northfield
Warwick
Winchendon
Hancock
Cheshire
Savoy
Buckland
Gill
Royalston
Lanesborough
Windsor
Hawley
Shelburne
Erving
Orange
Dalton
Greenfield
Plainfield
Athol
Ashburnham
Pittsfield
Ashfield
Deerfield
Montague
Wendell
Phillipston
Gardner
Hinsdale
Peru
Cummington
Conway
New Salem
Templeton
Richmond
W. Stockbridge
Goshen
Sunderland
Leverett
Petersham
Lenox
Washington
Worthington
Whately
Shutesbury
Chesterfield
Lee
Becket
Middlefield
Williamsburg
Hatfield
Pelham
Hubbardston
Stockbridge
Chester
Northampton
Amherst
Barre
Princeton
Tyringham
Westhampton
Hadley
Alford
Gt. Barrington
Easthampton
Hardwick
Rutland
Egremont
Huntington
South Hadley
Oakham
Holden
Mt. Washington
Monterey
Otis
Southampton
Granby
Ware
New Braintree
Paxton
Blandford
Montgomery
Belchertown
N. Brookfield
New Marlborough
Russell
Holyoke
W. Brookfield
Spencer
Sheffield
Sandisfield
Chicopee
Ludlow
Warren
Leicester
Tolland
Westfield
Palmer
Brookfield
E. Brookfield
Granville
W. Springfield
Springfield
Wilbraham
Brimfield
Southwick
Agawam
E. Longmeadow
Monson
Charlton
Longmeadow
Hampden
Sturbridge
Oxford
Wales
Southbridge
Holland
Webster
Dudley
7
2
9
202
91
90
20
84
86
N
LEGEND
Interstate Highway
Proposed
U.S. Routes
Intrastate Highway
Proposed